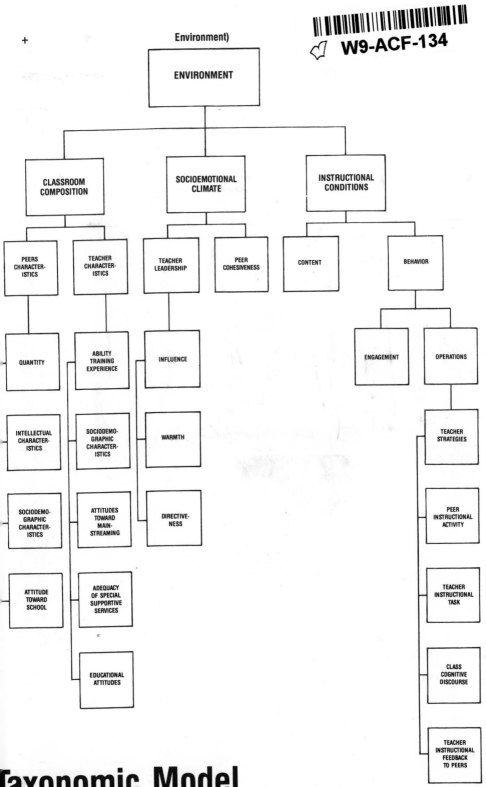

Environment)

ENVIRONMENT

CLASSROOM COMPOSITION

SOCIOEMOTIONAL CLIMATE

INSTRUCTIONAL CONDITIONS

PEERS CHARACTERISTICS

TEACHER CHARACTERISTICS

TEACHER LEADERSHIP

PEER COHESIVENESS

CONTENT

BEHAVIOR

QUANTITY

ABILITY TRAINING EXPERIENCE

INFLUENCE

ENGAGEMENT

OPERATIONS

INTELLECTUAL CHARACTERISTICS

SOCIODEMOGRAPHIC CHARACTERISTICS

WARMTH

TEACHER STRATEGIES

SOCIODEMOGRAPHIC CHARACTERISTICS

ATTITUDES TOWARD MAINSTREAMING

DIRECTIVENESS

PEER INSTRUCTIONAL ACTIVITY

ATTITUDE TOWARD SCHOOL

ADEQUACY OF SPECIAL SUPPORTIVE SERVICES

TEACHER INSTRUCTIONAL TASK

EDUCATIONAL ATTITUDES

CLASS COGNITIVE DISCOURSE

TEACHER INSTRUCTIONAL FEEDBACK TO PEERS

# Taxonomic Model

# MAINSTREAMING
## Learners and Their Environment

Martin Kaufman
Judith A. Agard
Melvyn I. Semmel

BROOKLINE
BOOKS
Cambridge, MA

**Library of Congress Cataloging-in-Publication Data**

Kaufman, Martin, 1941-
 Mainstreaming : learners and their environment.

 Bibliography: p.
 Includes index.
 1. Mentally handicapped children — Education.
1. Mainstreaming in education.  I. Semmel, Melvyn I.
II. Agard, Judith Andrews, 1938-   III.  Title.
LC4661.K29  1986   371.9′046    84-23746
ISBN 0-914797-11-5
ISBN 0-914797-21-2 (pbk.)

Published by
**Brookline Books, Inc.**
**PO Box 1046**
**Cambridge, MA 02238-1046**

Printed in the United States of America.

This book is dedicated to all those who trusted and had confidence that this research effort could contribute to improving educational opportunities for handicapped children in the least restrictive environment.

# Table of Contents

# Acknowledgements

Improved understanding and discovery of relationships based on research findings occur incrementally and often in a disjointed fashion. Today's research encompasses yesterday's, and will provide the grist for shaping tomorrow's inquiry. The conceptual breadth, design considerations, measurement strategies, and analytic techniques reflected in Project PRIME were premised on prior and concurrent research efforts. The authors acknowledge with appreciation the many individuals who shared their theories, methods, and experience.

The magnitude and complexity of Project PRIME required the considerable resolve of Federal and state education agency administrators. The authors acknowledge the support of these administrators. This research is just one example of the professional leadership which characterized the administration of Dr. Edward Martin, Associate Commissioner for the Bureau of Education for the Handicapped, U.S. Office of Education. The professional and personal support of Dr. James Moss, Director of Research, Bureau of Education for the Handicapped, U.S. Office of Education, provided the impetus for initiating this research, and for sustaining it to this conclusion.

The Federal commitment was stimulated by the compelling request of the Texas Education Agency to join in sponsoring this research. The authors recognize the critical importance of the unwavering leadership and support of Dr. Robert Montgomery, Assistant Commissioner for Special Education and Special Schools; Mr. Don Partridge, Director of Special Education; and their staff at the Texas Education Agency. In particular, we acknowledge Dr. Robert Winn, Director of Special Education Program Evaluation, for his initiative in stimulating this Federal/state research partnership. The leadership and commitment of Dr. Jerry Vlasak, Director of Special Education Administration, Texas Education Agency, was responsible for the external and internal administrative coordination necessary to involve the 43 school districts throughout the state in this research.

The authors recognize the invaluable thoughtfulness, direction, and encouragement provided by the Project PRIME Advisory Committee. The committee membership included Drs. Bruce Balow, Marilyn Brewer, Don MacMillan, Garry McDaniels, Dan Ringelheim, Dan Sufflebeam, and was chaired by Sam Ball. Both the continuity in their oversight and their insistence on conceptually integrating the analysis and reporting of the Project PRIME results were invaluable to the authors. Their individual and collective professional experiences and perceptiveness provided significant insights. The authors also acknowledge with appreciation the thoughtful consulting advice provided by Drs. Gary Borich, Tom Cook, Robin Daws, Nathan Gage, Eugene Glass, Paul Lohnes, Richard Snow, and Herbert Walberg.

The authors gratefully acknowledge the critical cooperation and assistance provided by the local education agency administrators. These individuals voluntarily participated in the study, obtained parental permissions, facilitated logistical scheduling and administration of the Project PRIME instrument battery, and were patient in resolving data collection problems. The hundreds of teachers and thousands of children who so openly permitted us to observe them and their classrooms — and who shared their attitudes, feelings, and experiences by completing the various instruments — are deserving of special recognition. Without access to schools, teachers, and students, and their willingness to provide the time and reflection to permit systematic data collection, research of naturally occurring events cannot occur.

The development of the Project PRIME instrument battery — administrative questionnaires, teacher and student instruments, and observation systems — was only possible because of the extraordinary efforts, skill, and cooperation of several groups. The administrative questionnaires were developed by staff at the Bureau of Education for the Handicapped, U.S. Office of Education; staff at the Texas Education Agency; and faculty at the University of Texas at Austin. The authors wish to recognize the significant contribution of Dr. Sandra Harrison to the development and refinement of items for the teacher and student instruments. Dr. Donald Veldman is deserving of particular recognition for his psychometric advice and analytic efforts in developing scales for the teacher and student instruments. The authors acknowledge Dr. Alba Ortiz and Isaura Barrera for their assistance in translating these instruments into Spanish. In addition, our thanks to Jane Burnette, Ann Mabry, and Pam Walters for contributing to the preparation of the technical manuals for the teacher and student instruments.

The staff at the Center for Innovation in Teaching the Handicapped at Indiana University provided the conceptual foundations for developing or modifying cognitive demand, behavior management, pupil participation, and classroom contextual observational systems. These individuals included Drs. Carol Ames, Al Fink, Ted Frick, Ted Hasselbring, Bill Lynch, Dorothy Semmel, and Sivasailam Thiagarajan. These individuals also made significant contributions to the design and development of materials which were essential to training observers, validating the training, and assessing the maintenance of observer reliability.

The authors also express their warm appreciation to Dr. Robert Soar, Ruth Soar, and Marjorie Ragosta at the Institute for Development of Human Resources, University of Florida, for refining the Florida Classroom Climate Schedule, preparing training materials, and helping interpret classroom climate findings.

Efficient processing of the massive quantity of data required the use of machine scoreable response formats. The authors recognize, with gratitude, the assistance of Dr. Robert Panos and Chuck Beauregard of National Computer Systems in the design, production, and shipping of these materials. Their energies and creativity significantly contributed to the success of the Project PRIME data collection and data entry activities. Their thoroughness in data checking minimized the loss of data due to error.

The data collection activities presented complex and difficult logistical problems. The sample size and geographic dispersion, range of measurement techniques, skills and sensitivity required of data collectors, number of data collectors, and continuous need for communication and quality control each presented unique problems. The authors acknowledge the coordinating efforts of Meredith Adler in arranging the training of trainers for each observation system, and in arranging and conducting the regional workshops for training local observers. Jerry Olson and Ted Frick contributed creative and innovative use of telecommunications for validating the effectiveness of the training and the proficiency and reliability of each trained observer.

Betty Corbit, Sandra Harrison, and Ann Mabry provided unwavering logistical support in preparing data collection schedules, problem-solving, supporting the 43 local Project PRIME coordinators, data tracking, and assisting in data checking. The magnitude and complexity of this data collection could not have occurred without the dedication of the 43 local Project PRIME coordinators and the hundreds of trained data collectors.

The data analysis staff of Project PRIME was located at both the University of Texas at Austin and Indiana University. The data analysis group at Indiana University was responsible for the data reduction and analysis of the individual learner background and competence measures. The authors acknowledge the efforts of Ted Frick, Jerry Olson, and Chad Sivasailam for their analytic contributions.

The data analysis unit at the University of Texas at Austin was responsible for organizing and editing the response surface from all instruments. They provided the analytic direction for data reduction and aggregation for generating data analysis tapes as well as assisted in the design and conduction of the data analyses for the classroom environment and learner-by-classroom-environment chapters. This unit was directed by Dr. Donald Veldman. His statistical concern for identifying and selecting straightforward, robust, and interpretable strategies for data reduction and analysis avoided many potential analytic pitfalls. His concern for parsimony provided direction for scaling procedures and decisions related to data aggregation. We also recognize Hugh Poyner, John Sheffield, John Mitchell, and Jim Sherill for their creative problem solving contributions in the massive data checking, data reduction, and data aggregation activities which preceded the data analysis.

To both units, the authors express appreciation for their assistance in managing, analyzing, and interpreting these mammoth and complex data.

Hundreds of individuals gave of their time, experience, and spirit to Project PRIME. For each mentioned, there are tens we have only collectively acknowledged. Even so, we are certain that inadvertently we have overlooked others deserving of recognition and for this we apologize.

The collective professional skills, experience, insights, and perceptiveness of the Project PRIME staff must be mentioned. The final report and this book are not the product of individuals but rather the collective intellectual energies of Drs. Judith Baker, Louise Corman, Jane Faulman, Ted Frick, Jay Gottlieb, Sam Guskin, Linda Morra, Nancy Safer, and Don Veldman. They ensured that the integrity of the Project PRIME conceptual model was sustained during data analysis and their writing. The editorial skills of Barbara Hobbs assured consistency and clarity in the manuscript. To Nancy O'Grady, Kathy Highland, and Ruth Lamothe, our appreciation for the endless drafts and tables they prepared and proofed.

To the loved ones of the authors—we are indebted for your support, encouragement, and patience with work schedules that often obviated personal obligations and priorities, intrusively entered the space and conversation of your homes, and excessively occupied our thought and attention.

To the entire Project PRIME staff—your enthusiasm, commitment, and intellectual visions provided the professionally synergistic environment which permitted this work to be accomplished, individual growth to occur, and personal friendships to develop.

Finally, the authors are indebted to Dr. Milton Budoff, editor of Brookline Books. We deeply appreciate the professional insight and effort Dr. Budoff exerted in providing the impetus and energy to make these research findings and instruments available. His editorial assistance in reducing the length of the manuscript and enhancing the readability of the technical presentations, while maintaining the conceptual and methodological integrity of the research, was critical. Most important, we appreciate the opportunity, encouragement, and support provided in the preparation of this book.

M.J.K.
J.A.A.
M.I.S.

# Preface

With *Mainstreaming: Learners and Their Environment*, BROOKLINE BOOKS is pleased to inaugurate its Special Education Research Monograph Series.

Project PRIME (Programmed Re-entry into Mainstreamed Education) was a ground breaking, almost breathtaking special education research project. Even now, ten years after the widespread mainstreaming of mildly handicapped students, Project PRIME presents the broadest, most comprehensive conception of the complexities involved in maintaining and supporting handicapped students within the mainstream of regular classrooms.

Classical research sought to understand the particular dynamics of special education for students who could not cope within the regular education program by comparing the effectiveness of two administrative arrangements: special and regular classroom placements. The implication was that these placements each constituted a distinct treatment that was more similar within each placement than across placement types. Administrative placements, i.e., regular or special classrooms, were used in the "efficacy studies" in a vacuum of unspecified variables without attention to the actual structure of the placement, nor the content of the instruction.

This situation continued until the landmark study conducted by Goldstein, Moss, and Jordan (1965) in Illinois which sought to control the critical variables of placement and prescribe a program that defined the within-classroom-curriculum elements of a special classroom.

Project PRIME went further. It remains relevant to the debates about mainstreaming, even ten years after its completion.

- The scope and breadth of Project PRIME's conceptualization is unusual in special education research. The designers of Project PRIME engaged in a careful and sophisticated analysis of the issues related to mainstreamed and segregated placements. They identified educational and social goals, examined the applicable theory and literature from non-special education disciplines as well as the usual special education sources, sought to integrate theories related to the complex array of factors involved in the legislative mandate to mainstream, and

xiii

operationalized the identified variables by developing or adapting an instrument base to test the theory. Most important, this research team went into classrooms and described what actually happens educationally and socially *within* each of the three educational settings: regular, resource, and special self-contained. Thus, while examining the usual variable domains of learner background and academic and social competence, they have also argued cogently for and researched the variable domains of how the composition of the classroom peer group and characteristics of the teacher, its socioemotional climate, and the instructional conditions obtained within each classroom setting varied *within* and *among* these settings, and was related to the criterion variables associated with academic and social competence.

- In numbers, no special education research effort has utilized the sample sizes of students, teachers, classrooms, or schools studied. Project PRIME sought samples representative of the population of a major state (Texas).
- The measures produced by Project PRIME are an excellent empirically and statistically constructed set of instruments. They are far more sophisticated, as a group, than any other similar set of instruments available in special education. They remain a major by-product of this research effort.
- Observers were trained in large numbers but with careful attention to quality control factors.
- The level of data analysis was highly sophisticated, as described in Chapter 3. The large number of variables required sophisticated data reduction techniques and means of combining scores into scales for both descriptive and predictive purposes.
- From the beginning, Project PRIME was a Federal-state initiative — two agencies of government undertaking a large-scale cooperative effort to provide data that would help school districts understand the complexity of educating special needs students in the least restrictive environment (i.e., in regular classroom placements) to provide information that might improve practice.

Why then publish this volume now, almost ten years later? The most germane reason is that the conceptualization underlying Project PRIME and the results of the analyses of the most innovative features of that conceptualization remain a major source of empirical descriptions of the characteristics and features of the three major educational settings for mildly handicapped students: the regular, resource, and special self-contained classrooms. As a basic premise, the designers of Project PRIME, the authors of this book, assumed there was variability *within* the two administrative arrangements (regular and special) and the now-common additional arrangement (the resource room) and sought to describe the range of variability both *within* and *among* these settings. The results of these analyses of *what happens within the classroom* provide some support for "What is special about special education?" — a classical question raised repeatedly by special educators uncertain that they are providing more than a more sheltered, some would say overprotected, environment for children with handicapping conditions.

Brookline Books is proud to publish this landmark work because Project PRIME constitutes a milestone in special education research related to the education of the mildly handicapped. Though concerned with mainstreaming educable mentally retarded students (EMR), the conceptualization as much as the findings will present a new theoretical basis on which to consider the effectiveness of special education. Special education placements constitute a set of interventions; and special educators and researchers must consider the processes involved within those interventions, as they relate to both the group within which the intervention occurs *and* the student. Issues raised for discussion should include the individual clinical directions of the training offered special needs students and the juxtaposition of that service orientation with the interpersonal group dynamic of the classroom and peer group.

Clearly, this is not a complete conceptualization but, as a research effort, it represents several new and radical directions for special education research and practice.

*Mainstreaming: Learners and Their Environment* is divided into five parts. The last, consisting of Chapter 11, presents the major findings, summarizes the implications for practice, and indicates directions for considering the research findings. This summary chapter provides a roadmap through the findings of the research, and is an excellent aid for readers interested in specific issues. Other aids are included to help the reader navigate through this complex study: The Project PRIME taxonomic model appears inside the front cover, the test name abbreviations are listed inside the back cover, and the last section of Chapter 1 details the book's organization and indicates the concerns discussed in its four major sections.

Milton Budoff, Ph.D.
January, 1986                                                     Series Editor

# Part I

# 1
# Overview

Tim is an attractive, well coordinated 8½ year old boy who is presently in the third grade in a public school system. He has a history of marginal academic performance dating back to kindergarten, but this year his teacher reports that he is encountering severe academic difficulties as well as displaying disruptive behavior. Tim was referred to the school psychologist by the classroom teacher for a psychological evaluation. The school psychologist observed Tim during his classroom day, and conferred with his classroom teacher. Observation of Tim has confirmed the teacher's report that Tim has few friends in his class, tends to play alone, has difficulty following directions, and becomes distracted and disruptive when working in a large group or working independently. He works best in a small group or one-to-one arrangement. His standardized test scores reflect a Full Scale IQ score of 70 on the Wechsler Intelligence Scale for Children, with a Verbal IQ of 65, Performance IQ of 75, and a little subtest scatter. As measured by the Wide Range Achievement Test, Tim is functioning at 1.5 grade level in reading and spelling and 1.8 grade level in arithmetic. Relative to his classmates, Tim's academic performance is very poor. His inability to read with comprehension results in both his lack of classroom participation and inappropriate or incorrect answers to the teacher's questions.

Tim also displays poor social development. Based upon conversations with Tim, the school psychologist reported that Tim has a negative attitude

3

toward school and his teacher, a low self-concept, and feelings of isolation from and rejection by his peers. Consultation with Tim's parents indicated they were concerned about Tim's school difficulties this year, but noted no particular problems at home except for an increasing reluctance on Tim's part to go to school. Both parents felt that Tim has always been slower in his development than his older brother and sister, who are at present average students in the fourth and sixth grade. They noted that Tim tends to play with younger children in the neighborhood, although children his own age are available.

Although Tim is fictitious, it is estimated there are one million children with similar characteristics for whom school personnel and parents must make placement and programming decisions. To make effective placement decisions and to provide appropriate services for these students, educators need information describing the available educational environments and knowledge concerning the relationships among child characteristics, educational environments, and academic and social competencies. When there is little empirically-based information available, educators and parents are forced to make decisions based on assumptions, hopes, or speculations about the nature of instructional opportunities available in a classroom and their effects on increasing competencies.

This book derives from Project PRIME (Programmed Re-Entry into Mainstreamed Education), a large-scale descriptive-correlational study conducted in Texas in the early 1970s, which was designed to provide information for:

- describing the teachers and peers, social climate, and instructional practices available to educable mentally retarded learners in regular, resource, and special self-contained classes, and
- understanding the relationships among variations in learner competence, learner background, and classroom environment.

The Project PRIME study presented in this book was designed to provide a comprehensive conceptual and practical framework for examining naturally-occurring variations in these three alternative instructional settings (regular, resource, special self-contained classes), recognizing that variation within type of setting may be as great as across settings. To examine the effects of these variations, a taxonomic model was developed to classify and compare classroom environments. Since programming and placement decisions require information related to both learners and classroom environments, the model included variables associated with the student, the peers, the teacher, and the environment. The model was developed from theory, empirical evidence, and educational issues.

# Alternative Classroom Environments
# for Mentally Retarded Children

Two major positions have governed the provision of services to educable mentally retarded (EMR) children: programming separate from or integrated with regular classmates.

The segregational approach developed from premises such as:

- Social and vocational skills are functionally more significant than cognitive skills for assuring independent and productive adult functioning.
- EMR students need to be protected from the achievement orientation of regular classes and the social rejection of normal peers.
- Regular education teachers do not have sufficient time or training to provide appropriate instruction for EMR students.
- Nonhandicapped students are distracted and delayed in their learning activities when EMR students are integrated into regular classes.

Professionals and parents accepting these beliefs view a special education self-contained classroom and a social/vocational curriculum orientation as the most appropriate instructional setting for EMR students.

In contrast, the integrational approach is based on such beliefs as:

- EMR students need to be encouraged to acquire higher levels of academic proficiency to adjust to an increasingly complex society.
- The social acceptance and emotional support available in a self-contained classroom is artificial and placement in one creates the stigma it was designed to prevent.
- Appropriate materials and consultation assistance enables regular teachers to provide appropriate instruction to EMR students.
- Procedures and materials for individualizing instruction have been developed that are effective in permitting both the nonhandicapped and EMR students in a regular classroom to proceed at a pace commensurate with their abilities.

Professionals and parents with these views recommend that the primary placement and programming for EMR learners be in the regular classroom, with supplemental support (special education resource class, consultation, aid, etc.) provided as necessary.

These two approaches do not necessarily imply different goals but rather different means. While presented as a dichotomy, in practice they overlap. EMR students in special self-contained classes are often integrated with nonhandicapped students for limited portions of the school day, e.g., for nonacademic periods such as art, music, physical education, lunch, study hall, etc. Similarly, many mainstreamed EMR children receive most of their academic instruction in a special resource class with other handicapped students. For each approach, the amount of time an EMR learner spends with nonhandicapped peers may not differ considerably.

While the two approaches probably provide different classroom environment experiences at the elementary school level, there is also marked overlap between them. For example, like the resource teacher, the teacher of a special education self-contained class will stress acquisition of basic skills. Less typically, the resource class teacher may use materials having a social/vocational orientation, that being more of a focus in special self-contained classes.

These two alternative approaches, the special self-contained class and the regular/resource class combination, share the common goals of maximizing the functioning of the child to attain an adult life as independent and productive as possible. Traditionally, segregational approaches have assumed a retarded level of functioning in adulthood, and prepared the student for this outcome. Historically, integrational approaches have employed strategies to remediate or compensate for intellectual, academic, and/or behavioral deficits so the child can meet the demands of a regular education environment. The following section reviews the historical evolution of the two approaches.

## The Segregational Approach

Early attempts to educate mentally retarded children were conducted so they might function as normal productive citizens in the mainstream of society. When Itard, in 1798, took charge of Victor, "The Wild Boy of Aveyron," it was with the conviction that Victor was mentally arrested because of social and educational neglect and could be cured. Influenced by the philosophies of Locke and Rousseau, Itard believed that all persons were conceived in perfection, but that their final condition resulted from their interaction with an imperfect world (Lane, 1976). Even though Itard acknowledged he had not achieved his goal after five years of working with Victor, he had made the first recorded attempt to educate a mentally retarded child. He identified many environmental conditions used in the education of seriously retarded children for many years, including an intensive treatment approach and a developmental curriculum based on sensory stimulation techniques.

While Itard is credited with the idea and practice of training individual mentally retarded children, Gugenbuhl is credited with the idea and practice of institutional care and training of groups of mentally retarded children (Lazerson, 1974). Gugenbuhl's work, begun in 1839, was founded on the belief that through a segregated setting and established instructional techniques, it would be possible to create a therapeutic environment to train mentally retarded children to be useful and productive citizens who could be returned to the mainstream of society.

Whereas cure, normalcy, or at least amelioration was the intent of early institutions for mentally retarded children, by 1885 the intent had changed and the institutions were being transformed from residential schools to custodial asylums (Lazerson, 1974). This transformation was complete by 1918. Three major reasons for this shift in emphasis have been presented (e.g., Davies & Ecob, 1959; Kanner, 1964; Lazerson, 1974):

1. A tremendous increase in admissions to institutions.
2. The hereditarian theory of the nature of intelligence, formulated around 1880, which posited that intelligence was genetically determined and therefore a limiting factor in personal development. If intelligence were fixed, then educational training would be a wasted effort. Thus, only custodial care was warranted.
3. Pedigree studies of families such as the Jukes (Dugdale, 1877), the Zeroes (Jörger, 1905), and the Kallikaks (Goddard, 1912) led to the idea that society needed to be protected from the harm done by the presence of retarded persons in the community.

These opinions gave rise to the public demand for the segregation of all mentally defective persons "with the aim of purifying society, of erecting a solid wall between it and its contaminators" (Kanner, 1964, p. 85).

From 1885 through the first two decades of this century, the approach to the cure and treatment of retarded individuals was dominated by hereditarian views of the nature of intelligence. Segregation was no longer considered a short-term intervention, but rather a long-term placement.

These decades also saw the emergence of the public school as the major site for the care and education of EMR children (Lazerson, 1974). Large numbers of EMR children were being identified due to compulsory school attendance laws, the immigrations from non-English speaking countries, and the development and use of IQ tests. Institutions simply could not accommodate them. Goddard (1910), who established an educational classification system for mentally retarded children based on his translation of the Binet intelligence test, was very influential in shaping attitudes and opinions concerning the value of intelligence testing for diagnosing mental retardation and the possibility of educating mentally retarded children. His recommendation for this group of children was widely heard:

...[this] special group of children...requires very special attention....Our
public school systems are full of them, and yet superintendents and boards of
education are struggling to make normal people out of them. One of the most
helpful things that we can do would be to distinctly mark out the limits of this
class and help the general public to understand that they are a special group
and require special treatment, in institutions when possible, in special classes
in public schools, when institutions are out of reach (Goddard, 1910, p. 364).

Goddard did not consider normalcy an appropriate goal for even the mildly
retarded child. The "feeble-minded" were best removed from the regular
environment and trained to whatever extent possible in vocational and
survival skills.

By 1922, 23,000 retarded pupils were enrolled in special day schools or
classes. The special self-contained class became the standard classroom
environment for decades to come. Typically, the special self-contained class
consisted of a small group of children with a similar degree of retardation, as
defined by an IQ score range, who were taught by a specially trained teacher,
using methods and materials different than those used in regular classes.
Return to the regular class was not a goal of these classes and, from 1930
onward, their curricula stressed social and vocational competence (Erdman &
Olson, 1966). Hungerford, DeProspo, and Rosenzweig (1948), for example,
developed a program of occupational education for retarded students in New
York City schools which emphasized occupational information and social
placement. In the Illinois Curriculum, Goldstein and Seigle (1958) stressed
life situations with which the retarded student would need to cope — learning
to live safely, to keep healthy, to earn a living, and to manage money.

In summary, the segregated special self-contained class has a long
historical tradition as a special education instructional setting for EMR
children, providing a long-term placement with focus on social and
vocational preparation and the environmental conditions necessary to help
these children attain these competencies. These environmental conditions
have included special teaching techniques; individual and/or small-group
instruction or tutoring; teacher warmth, support, and directiveness; and relief
from the competition and social alienation of the regular class.

## The Integrational or Mainstreaming Approach

As early as 1875, an occasional voice questioned the value of segregation for
the mentally retarded child. Wynter (1875), for example, argued for the
benefits of mixing "imbeciles" with "sane" members of society. Through the
power of imitation, she argued, the imbeciles learn from those of greater
intelligence. The segregated setting was viewed as intensifying idiocy.

However, such voices were largely drowned out by those extolling the advantages of the segregated environment.

It is within the last two decades that legal, social, and educational forces have come to challenge the special self-contained class as the predominant instructional setting for the education of EMR children. The increasing concern about the adequacy of special self-contained classes also reflected growing support for the influence of the environment on the development of intelligence — the idea that manipulation of the environment can increase or decrease intellectual performance.

Studies conducted during the late 1950s and the 1960s investigated the effectiveness of special class placement as compared with regular class placement of mentally retarded children (Bacher, 1965; Baldwin, 1958; Blatt, 1958; Carroll, 1967; Cassidy & Stanton, 1959; Diggs, 1964; Goldstein, Moss, & Jordan, 1965; Kern & Pfaeffle, 1962; Kirk, 1964; Mayer, 1966). These studies, the so-called "efficacy studies," compared special and regular instructional pi ograms assuming homogeneity of treatment within each educational setting. They also defined pupil outcome narrowly, usually emphasizing academic achievement. The findings of these studies were equivocal: They did not support regular or special classes as the most appropriate placement for retarded children. Educators such as Johnson (1962), however, used the efficacy studies to question why mentally retarded children did not clearly achieve more academically in special classes than in regular classes when the former had fewer pupils, supposedly better trained teachers, and more financial resources available on a per capita basis.

The criticism of special classes resulting from the efficacy studies reflected a growing dissatisfaction with the assumptions governing education in special self-contained classes. These classes stressed social and vocational training rather than academics, with reading and math teaching directed at the acquisition of "survival skills." Consequently, these students barely attained literacy and remained in this terminal placement. The critics argued that these children could benefit from more challenging educational opportunities.

There was increasing concern over the disproportionate number of minority group children placed in special classes for the mentally retarded. This was due, it was claimed, in part as a result of the use of culturally-biased IQ tests which were administered in English to non-English speaking or ESL children (e.g., Mercer, 1974). Special classes were seen as denying these children the opportunity of an equal education, serving instead as "dumping grounds" for those whom the system could not readily accommodate or tolerate (Lazerson, 1974). These children were segregated from their normal peers under the guise of receiving "special" educational services (*Hobson* v. *Hansen*, 1967; *Larry P.* v. *Riles*, 1972).

Placement in special classes created stigmas, according to some. Dunn (1968), for example, stated that "removing a child from the regular grades for special education probably contributes significantly to his feelings of inferiority and problems of acceptance" (p. 9). Studies investigated social acceptance and rejection (Baldwin, 1958; Johnson, 1950; Johnson & Kirk, 1959), social adjustment (Ainsworth, 1959; Cassidy & Stanton, 1959; Goldstein et al., 1965; Kern & Pfaeffle, 1962; Thurstone, 1960), and self-concept (Mayer, 1966; Meyerowitz, 1962) of handicapped children in both regular and special classes. In court cases, the detrimental effects of the "mentally retarded" label were cited as fact. The research data, however, were not conclusive. MacMillan, Jones, and Aloia (1974) reviewed the studies concerning the effect of the mentally retarded label and concluded "While many accept as fact that labeling children mentally retarded has detrimental effects, conclusive empirical evidence of these effects was not found" (p. 257).

Methodological problems plague studies of this effect. Such problems include the lack of control for possible devaluations of the self which occurred prior to being labelled, the appropriateness of the instruments used with mentally retarded subjects, and the comparability of responses given by mentally retarded and nonmentally retarded subjects to personality measures. Despite this, studies such as Meyerowitz's (1962) continue to be cited as evidence that special class placement has a debilitating effect on the child's self-image.

## Judicial Affirmation of the Integrational Approach

The trend toward integration was supported by court decisions which applied the doctrine of the least restrictive environment to the education of handicapped children. Judicial concern for the educational programming and placement of EMR children was evident in such cases as *Pennsylvania Association for Retarded Children (PARC)* v. *Commonwealth of Pennsylvania* (1971). The court stated:

> It is the Commonwealth's obligation to place each mentally retarded child in a free, public program of education and training appropriate to the child's capacity, within the context of presumption that, among the alternative programs of education and training required by statute to be available, placement in a regular public school class is preferable to placement in special public school class and placement in special public school classes is preferable to placement in any other type of program of education and training.

According to this court, the least restrictive alternative referred to the degree of discrepancy between an EMR child's placement in a regular educational program. As discussed by Burgdorf (1975), the court held that "there is a presumption that children should be in regular classes and there have to be good reasons why not" (p. 14). The court did not require that every child needing special education services receive them in a regular classroom environment: The court did require that a child be integrated whenever he could profit by such integration. "The law has never stated that equal treatment means identical treatment for different types of persons" (Burgdorf, p. 11).

In response to these concerns and, subsequently, the requirements of P.L. 94-142, school systems developed a continuum of educational settings to assure that handicapped children are educated in the least restrictive environment. These settings differ in degree of integration into regular classes. The least restrictive alternative is the regular class with no special services and the most restrictive is the special day or residential school with no access to normal peers. In between are various degrees of integration — usually based on the amount of time spent in the regular class, although educators do not always agree on the basis for defining these intermediate positions. Massachusetts primarily classifies its special education students by proportion of time spent outside regular education. In addition, variables such as directness, intensity, type, and duration of instruction or services offered (e.g., Bruininks & Rynders, 1971; Kaufman et al., 1975) have been considered.

Instructional supports and supplementary services are provided to the mainstreamed child and/or regular class teacher, usually through a resource class (Baarstad, 1965; Barkdale & Atkinson, 1971; Beery, 1972; Bruininks & Rynders, 1971; Ebert, Dain, & Phillips, 1970; Gardner, 1971; Hammill & Weiderholt, 1972; Hartman & Rockhold, 1973; Prouty & Prillaman, 1970; Reger, 1973). The resource class is an instructional setting in which the child receives instruction on a regularly scheduled basis, spending the rest of the day in the regular class or with instructional or related service specialists. The objective of resource class instruction is to remediate or compensate for identified deficits in language, reading, arithmetic, and/or social behaviors so that the child can perform more effectively in the regular classroom. A specially trained teacher provides the child with educational and/or behavioral assessment to identify special needs. Special materials/activities or individualized instruction in problem areas are used to strengthen skills or alleviate problems.

The resource teacher must at the same time work to remediate or help the student compensate for his deficit and increase his rate of learning so the discrepancy in achievement with nonhandicapped peers is diminished, ultimately permitting him to function adequately in the regular classroom. The resource teacher's goal is twofold: Helping the remedial student function in the regular class, while working to remediate the student's deficit. Concurrently, the regular education teacher must adapt curriculum materials to allow the student to perform while in the regular program.

In applying the doctrine of least restrictive alternative to the education of handicapped children, the courts and the legislatures recognized that the regular class may not be the most appropriate placement for all EMR learners. Educators were left the task of applying the principle, but little definitive research or tested practice exists to assist the educator or parent in determining the appropriateness of particular educational environments for an EMR learner. The extensive body of research that investigated the relative benefits of special and regular classes yielded inconclusive findings for the most part, and there have been few studies of the resource class as a support system. Descriptive information about the unique characteristics of the instructional settings and predictive information concerning the relationships of learner and classroom environmental characteristics to learner competencies are necessary if placement and programming decisions for EMR children are to reflect sound educational judgment based on research rather than social trendiness. These goals are addressed by the study described in this book.

## The Rationale for a Taxonomy of Learners and Classroom Environments

Theory provided a starting point for determining the major areas or domains to be considered in the PRIME taxonomy as well as the variables that defined each domain.

To make appropriate programming and placement decisions for EMR children, it is necessary to show how classroom environmental conditions affect learner competencies, and, hence the interaction of the student and his environment. Social scientists have long been involved in attempts to predict such learner competencies. Several general conceptual models have been used for such purposes.

For example, the personological model asserts there are pervasive personality dispositions or traits which influence an individual's behavior across situations and lead to consistency in behavior. Traits have been viewed as relatively stable, highly consistent attributes of a person which must be identified as a prerequisite to understanding behavior. Allport (1958) states, for example:

> Man's nature, like all of nature, seems to be composed of relatively stable structures. The success of psychological science, therefore, as of any science, depends in large part upon its ability to identify the major structures, substructures, and microstructures (elements) of which its assigned portion of the cosmos is composed (p. 250).

According to the model, a person has a characteristic level of a trait such as aggressiveness which, if identified, would predict aggressive behavior for that individual across situations. A modification of this personological model holds that although situations have some effect on behavior, given two or more people with differing levels of aggressiveness, the amount of aggression displayed by each individual remains constant from situation to situation (Argyle & Little, 1972). Thus, aggressiveness is present regardless of the situation, although situations may inhibit or exacerbate exhibitions of aggressive behavior. To change the behavior, it is not enough to manipulate the situations to which the aggressive person is exposed: The individual and internal dynamics underlying the trait must be altered.

From the perspective of the school, this model restricted to only personality characteristics has limited utility. In considering the students' success in school, background characteristics (such as age, sex, socioecnomic status, ethnic group, and previous educational experiences) must be considered. Coleman et al. (1966) provided evidence for the importance of personological factors in education, reporting that differences between school (which may be considered educational differences) had little relation to the verbal achievement of students compared to the relation between verbal achievement and personological factors such as the child's background and attitudes. Thus, while personological factors must be included in a model designed to predict academic and social competence, it must be broader conceptually.

Working from a different perspective, experimental psychologists and sociologists developed an environmental model. Experimental psychologists characterized behavior as either respondent or operant but in either case as environmentally determined. Social role theory also points to behavior varying with situations. In role theory, roles are viewed as sets of norms and these norms are prescriptions for behavior (Brown, 1965). Settings or situations vary in the degree to which they prescribe and limit the range of expected and acceptable behaviors for persons in particular roles. As Barker (1968) has found, in some settings the rules for enacting specific role behaviors impose narrow limits on the range of possible behaviors (e.g., church, school, or theater), whereas in others the range of possible behaviors is broad.

The environmental model posits that because certain response patterns are appropriate to particular settings while others are not, different settings become the occasion for eliciting particular behaviors in different degrees (Mischel, 1968). Consistent with this conceptual approach, psychologists and educators have studied the susceptibility of learner competencies to restricted (Dennis & Dennis, 1935; Dennis & Najarian, 1957) and stimulated environmental experiences (Garber, Heber, Hoffman, & Harrington, 1974; Rynders & Horrobin, 1975).

Direct intervention studies related to the environmental influence on schooling of mentally retarded children are illustrated by infant and preschool programs such as the Milwaukee Project (Garber, 1974). By providing experiences potentially lacking in the natural environment of high-risk infants, the Milwaukee Project demonstrated that the experimental group consistently performed 20 IQ points above the control group.

The PRIME taxonomic model serves two functions. First, it depicts the dimensions of the learners and their educational environments, and the major constructs defining each variable domain. Descriptive information for the variable domains allows the examination of commonly-held assumptions regarding the characteristics of the three classroom environments available to EMR students and indicates the variations within each type of educational setting.

The second function of the taxonomic model is to provide a framework for considering the relationships between learners and their classroom environments; that is, to investigate the relationships among the variable domains.

In the taxonomic model, competence is viewed as a function of the learner performing a specific role within an environment defined by a specific setting. Mathematically, this model is depicted by the equation:

$$C = (L_r, E_s),$$

where:

$C$ = competence
$L$ = learner
$E$ = environment
$r$ = role
$s$ = setting

In the present study, the learner is an EMR or nonhandicapped child who is functioning in the role of student in a specific environmental setting — regular, resource, or special self-contained class. In a larger context, the class is a subsystem of the school, school district, and community. However, given that the focus of the study is on programming and placement decisions for EMR children, classes were considered to be the most critical and proximal unit of study. At a global level, then, the individual child enters the class, which provides an educational environment designed to promote certain learner competencies. It is within the class that the child assumes the role of learner; a role specific to the class setting which defines and limits the range of possible behaviors (Barker, 1968).

## The Major Variable Domains

Five major variable domains were identified for study in this research. These were the learners' backgrounds and competencies, both academic and social; the composition of the classroom; and the instructional conditions within the classroom. (See Project PRIME taxonomic model inside the front cover.)

### Learner Background

By the time the child enters the social system of a class and assumes the role of learner, he is also actively involved in many other systems — the community, school, family, etc. In short, the child comes to school with a personal history based on personal characteristics and prior experiences. As stated by Dunkin and Biddle (1974): "...pupils will differ depending on whether they come from lower- or middle-class homes, have experienced socialization as a boy or girl, have suffered the loss of a parent, or come from a stimulus-rich or stimulus-deprived environment" (p. 41). Differences in such background characteristics and experiences are likely to affect the individual's interpretation of the role of learner and performance of that role in the class. Prior research on the relationship of learner background and educational outcomes suggested that three constructs are of major importance: individual, family, and school background.

### Learner Competence

A major goal of education is to promote learning and socialization. The criteria of academic and social competence define successful school functioning in terms of the child's ability to meet the demands made by the school environment. Competence subsumes not only academic and social status but also academic and social behavior, and attitudes toward self, school, and peers.

### The Classroom Environment

There are as yet few theoretical approaches that fully conceptualize a broad range of classroom environmental variables and systematically relate these to learner competencies. As stated by Hunt and Sullivan (1974): "So much depends on educational environments, yet so little is known about how to describe them that any discussion is likely to be disappointing" (p. 88). Several models have been developed to characterize the educational environment (Moos, 1973; Hoffman & Lippitt, 1960; Hunt & Sullivan, 1974), but these models suffer from overlapping domains and an exclusive focus on the teacher. Because of the limitations of other models, this study developed a general model of the class as a social system. The model conceptualizes the educational environment as a contextual force contributing to the learner's academic and social competence.

The first requirement of a social system is that there be participants. In the class social system, the participants are the teacher and the peer group, of which the learner is a part. Social systems theory posits two critical functions: maintenance and production functions (Katz & Kahn, 1966). In the class social system, maintenance functions are those related to establishing the class as a social unit. Production functions are those related to implementing instructional objectives. These functions are similar to those described by group dynamics theorists (Bales, 1958; Bales & Slater, 1955; Parsons & Bales, 1955). Groups expend energy to maintain a positive atmosphere and harmonious social relationships, and to perform work efficiently and productively. The classroom environment results from and contributes to the group's efforts toward these goals.

Drawing on social systems and group dynamics theory, the educational environment can be construed as consisting of *participants* engaged in two major classroom system functions which will realize the desired outcomes of the system — maintaining a *socioemotional climate* and maintaining *instructional conditions*. The taxonomic model provides the learner with a class environment that consists of three sets of dimensions — classroom composition, socioemotional climate, and instructional conditions.

**Classroom Composition**: The backgrounds and attitudes of both the teacher and the peer group are important factors in determining the social acceptance and instructional integration of a mainstreamed mentally retarded student.

**Socioemotional Climate**: A positive climate and harmonious relationships are thought to contribute to a student's educational achievement. While the importance of the classroom's social climate to a child's development has long been recognized, this concept has rarely been clearly defined. According to Schmuck and Schmuck (1975), "...the concept of climate summarizes the group processes that are worked out by a teacher in interaction with students and between the students in the classroom." Thus, both the teacher's leadership style and the peer group's cohesiveness contribute to the socioemotional climate of the classroom as it affects a particular learner.

**Instructional Conditions**: Whereas the socioemotional climate of the class i concerned with its affective tone and the nature of the social relationships that exist, instructional conditions are concerned with teacher and student academic tasks. Instructional conditions consist of two major constructs — a physical milieu (or "instructional context") and activities (or "instructional behavior").

## Approach to the Problem

In sum, the PRIME taxonomic model posed the following study questions related to each domain to guide the research process.

### Learner Background

1. With whom were the mainstreamed EMR learners in this study placed? What were the age characteristics of their peers?
2. What were the integration patterns of the EMR learners in this study? What was the amount of time they were integrated and what was the content of the activities for which they were integrated?
3. What were the characteristics of the EMR learners associated with the extent and nature of their integration into regular classrooms?

### Learner Competence

1. What were the academic and social competencies of the nonhandicapped, mainstreamed, and special self-contained EMR learners?
2. To what extent do the academic and social competencies of the mainstreamed EMR and nonhandicapped learners overlap?

### Classroom Composition

1. Can regular class teachers be provided with appropriate training and support materials and services which will enable them effectively to instruct EMR learners?
2. Do regular class peers provide more appropriate role models for EMR learners than do other EMR learners?
3. Are regular class teachers likely to provide the warm, supportive, structured environment that has been thought important for EMR learners?
4. Do regular teachers have or develop negative attitudes toward the mainstreaming of EMR learners?
5. Do nonhandicapped students develop negative attitudes toward school when EMR learners are placed in their classrooms?

## Socioemotional Climate

1. Can the regular class and the regular class teacher provide the warm, supportive, accepting environment supposedly needed by EMR learners?
2. Can the regular class teacher provide the structured environment needed by EMR learners?
3. Do disruptiveness and friction occur in the regular classroom when EMR learners are mainstreamed?
4. Does the regular class teacher need to devote excessive amounts of time to managing behavior when EMR learners are mainstreamed?

## Instructional Conditions

1. Within the regular, resource, and special self-contained classrooms, what are the instructional contexts (physical quality, special instructional services, academic content, and teacher-made materials) and operations (teacher strategies, peer instructional activities, teacher instructional tasks, class cognitive discourse, teacher instructional feedback) that result in maximum instructional engagement?
2. Within each of the three settings, what are the instructional contexts and operations which create an instructional atmosphere which provides for individual differentiation and an appropriate level of academic emphasis?

## Academic Competence

1. What are the learner background and classroom environmental factors associated with the academic competence of the nonhandicapped and EMR learners in the three educational settings?
2. Are the environmental factors associated with the academic competence of the nonhandicapped learners similar in magnitude and pattern to those associated with the academic competence of the EMR learners?
3. Are similar environmental factors associated with the development of the three different competency areas (academic status, behaviors, and attitudes)?

## Social Competence

1. What dimensions of the three different classroom settings promote or inhibit social competence among EMR learners?
2. What are the relationships between the regular classroom environment and the social competence of nonhandicapped students?

# The Organization of this Book

This book consists of four parts. Part I describes the context for the study and presents an issues-oriented historical perspective of programming for EMR learners. Chapter 1 discusses the Project PRIME taxonomic model. Chapter 2 describes the design, sampling, instrumentation, and data collection procedures used. Chapter 3 provides a rationale for the various data reduction, transformation, and analysis strategies employed.

Parts II and III are organized according to the five variable domains composing the taxonomic model. Part II is concerned with the learner components. Chapter 4 describes the learners' individual, family, and educational background characteristics and discusses the interrelationships among these background measures for the three samples of learners: nonhandicapped, mainstreamed, and special class EMR learners. Chapter 5 presents data concerning learners' academic and social status, behaviors, and attitudes toward school.

Part III, which is concerned with the environmental elements of the model, provides a description of three classroom settings — regular, resource, and special self-contained classes. Each chapter considers one domain of the classroom environment — teacher and peer participants composing the classroom, its socioemotional climate, instructional conditions — providing a theoretical and empirical justification for the specific constructs included in each domain and discussing the relationships among the domain's variables. Chapter 6 presents information on the teachers and peers composing each regular, resource, and special self-contained class. Chapter 7 describes the socioemotional climate: teacher leadership styles and degree of peer cohesiveness in each classroom environment. Chapter 8 concerns the instructional conditions which characterize the programming available in each setting.

Part IV is concerned with the relationships of the learner and environmental elements of the model. Chapter 9 presents the relationships between learner academic competencies and learner background and the three environmental domains. Chapter 10 examines the same relationships in terms of social competencies. Chapters 9 and 10 not only present relationships between learners and their classroom environments but also explore which relationships are consistent across settings and learners.

In Part V, Chapter 11 seeks to integrate the results of this complex study. It first presents the general conclusions of the study, reviews the findings relevant to each study question, and suggests implications of the study for practice in schools and for the particular roles that special education might play.

For the reader's convenience, the Project PRIME taxonomic model is shown on the inside front cover and a list of test acronyms is provided inside the back cover.

Four appendices are also included, providing further information on sampling procedures, test instruments, data collection procedures, and learner profiles.

# 2
# Methodology

This chapter presents Project PRIME's methodology:

1. the rationale for the project design,
2. the procedures used to select the sample,
3. the instrumentation used in the study, and
4. the data collection procedures used.

Data reduction and analysis procedures are presented in Chapter 3. A complete description of the study's purposes and procedures, including all supporting documents, is available in Kaufman, Semmel, and Agard (1973).

Project PRIME was designed to describe and examine the relationships between learners and their classroom environments to determine the extent to which mainstreaming is a viable educational alternative. To meet this goal, the study was large-scale to assure adequate representativeness of school districts, students, and practices. Three groups of students were contrasted: mainstreamed students and their classroom environment; nonmainstreamed or segregated EMR learners, to provide a description of this traditional placement for retarded students; and nonhandicapped contrast learners, to provide a basis for determining the extent to which regular teachers changed or needed to change the regular classroom environment to accommodate an EMR learner.

A clear definition of what constitutes a distinctly different educational setting was required since extensive variability is present within special education programming. Our criteria included:

- The setting must exist as an organizationally discernable unit.
- The setting must represent distinct placement alternatives for EMR learners.
- The setting must allow for philosophical, conceptual, and operational variations.

The alternative classroom settings selected for the Project PRIME study were regular, resource, and special self-contained classes. A descriptive-correlational design was employed.

# Design

## Selecting a Research Paradigm

Historically, studies in special education have been concerned with comparing the efficacy of one alternative educational setting with another. One often-cited limitation of the research designs of earlier efficacy studies is that students were not randomly placed in alternative classroom settings. Another was that the classroom environmental conditions available in the alternative settings were not adequately described. The common assumption was that, within each setting, classes were environmentally similar. The application of experimental and quasi-experimental designs to research comparing the efficacy of various instructional settings is based on the premise that the instructional practices available within any one type of educational setting are relatively uniform while those across the different types of settings vary extensively. Kirk (1964), in cautioning against uniformity of practices in self-contained classes, stated:

> ...there has not been a clear-cut definition of a special class, the curriculum, or the qualifications of special teacher. Special classes vary widely in organization and curriculum and teaching methods. Qualifications of teachers vary from well-trained teachers to those subjected to short-term summer courses taught largely by instructors who have little training or experience with special classes. The administrative labeling of a group of retarded children as a special class for the purpose of receiving state subsidy does not assure its being a special class for experimental purposes (pp. 62-63).

Similar statements may be made concerning the environmental variation across classrooms in regular and resource class settings.

These unclear classroom environmental variations within each program type made use of comparative experimental paradigms premature. The Project PRIME design recognized the strong likelihood of such variability and chose a design that examined a broad array of program characteristics. Although this strategy made descriptions of the variations within a given program type possible, it required large samples of classrooms.

The descriptive/correlational paradigm selected permitted descriptions within each of the alternative settings — each setting constituting an independent sample — and eliminated the need to define in advance the components of the educational program available in each classroom type. The variations within a type are described by examining the practices in a classroom — alleviating the need for randomizing student assignments, a procedure alien to real-world special education practice. The paradigm focussed on the collection of practical information on within-setting descriptions and relationships. The use of this paradigm required the use of a large sample of naturally-occurring variations within each alternative educational setting and the measurement of large numbers of variables representing the multiple dimensions on which the settings might differ. This approach should be distinguished from more experimentally-controlled laboratory interventions which are designed to assure the fidelity of implementation of a fixed treatment.

## Considerations of the Unit of Analysis

The concerns related to the selection of an appropriate unit of analysis have been discussed extensively in the literature (Brophy, 1975; Cooley & Lohnes, 1976; Glass, 1967). This problem was a particularly vexing one in the design of Project PRIME. Each of the two purposes of the project — describing alternative classroom environments and examining relationships between individual learners and their classroom environments — required a different unit of analysis.

For the descriptive analyses, there is no question regarding the appropriate unit of analysis: The learner is the unit of analysis for the description of learner background and competence (Part II), and the setting (regular, resource, and special self-contained classes) is the unit of analysis for the description of the variations in classroom composition, socioemotional climate, and instructional conditions that constitute the environment (Part III).

When the analysis shifts from these descriptions to an examination of the relationships between competence and environment (Part IV), it is less clear what the unit of analysis should be. Although many important educational questions can be addressed by examining the relationships between the classroom environment and the accomplishments of the class as a whole, questions concerning the appropriateness of placement and programming decisions for EMR learners need to be addressed by examining the relationships between classroom environmental variations and the competencies of a unique EMR learner. Brophy (1975) argues that, even for nonhandicapped students, examining the relationships between the individual student and the environment is critical for understanding effective classroom practices:

> Students in the same classroom, no matter how homogenous, show great individual differences in their personal characteristics and in the kinds of interactions that they have with the teacher. Consequently, research which is designed to better understand classroom processes and/or to link up classroom processes with student outcomes must begin to take into account these student individual differences and use the student as the unit of statistical analysis if significant improvements over the existing knowledge base are to be achieved (p. 14).

In selecting the appropriate unit of analysis, we had to consider the independence of the replications. In the descriptive analyses, independence was not a problem since each learner or class was represented only once. However, in the relationships' analyses the learner and the classroom environment are considered to be an interrelated dyad, both conceptually and statistically. Ideally, the relationships' analyses should be based on independent replications of unique learner/classroom environment dyads.

Independent replications require that each teacher/class unit be assigned to one and only one learner. However, in Project PRIME, more than one learner may have been assigned to a single teacher/class unit; thus, the study's representation of a unique learner will not necessarily represent a unique environment. Two requirements of the project prohibited unique assignment of learners to environments: the need to obtain a large sample at a reasonable cost and the need to take into account the potential attrition of students.

Obtaining a large sample of learners and environments was difficult due to the relatively low incidence of EMR learners in the elementary schools — and an even lower incidence of mainstreamed EMR learners. In addition, the number of special resource and self-contained classes is obviously much smaller than the number of EMR learners. The need to obtain a large sample of learners and class environments necessitated taking more than one learner from each class.

This oversampling within classrooms helped control for possible attrition. Since the design required the use of individual rather than class aggregates, the loss of a single learner per class with no available substitute would have resulted in the loss of the environmental unit from the study.

Virtually every mainstreamed EMR learner in the participating districts was included in the sample without regard to the uniqueness of the regular or resource classroom assignment. In sampling nonmainstreamed students, at least two and often three students were selected from each special self-contained class. These sampling procedures resulted in approximately one unique regular classroom environment for every one-and-one-half nonhandicapped or mainstreamed EMR learner. The problem of independence of replications for special self-contained classroom environments was more acute, as indicated by the ratio of only one unique classroom environment for every two nonmainstreamed EMR learners.

The problem of achieving independent units of analysis was most complex for dyads consisting of a mainstreamed EMR learner and the resource class. Since most school buildings had only one or two special education resource class teachers, a design requiring independent resource class units would have limited sampling to only one or two students from any particular building. By permitting a single resource environment to serve several learner/resource class dyads, it was possible to use all the mainstreamed EMR learners sampled. This lack of independence was a notable problem with each resource class assigned to an average of three EMR learners.

Elementary schools were selected as the focus for studying the alternative classroom environments available to EMR learners. Because special education programming is most often provided for EMR children from 6-12 years of age, the elementary school level provided the maximum opportunity to capture a full range of learners in a variety of classroom environments (Kaufman, Agard, & Vlasak, 1973b). The majority of elementary school EMR learners receiving special education services are typically in grades 3-6. Children identified as EMR learners in grades 1 and 2 are often more seriously and more visibly handicapped than those typically identified in grades 3-5. Sixth-grade EMR learners in an elementary school at the time of the study were often of junior high school age or older and were retained because a program for older students was not available. To assure typical EMR learners, the sample of EMR children was restricted to grades 3-5 age range.

In sum, a descriptive/correlational study of mainstreamed and nonmainstreamed elementary-aged EMR learners who experienced naturally occurring environmental variations in regular, resource, and special education self-contained environments in grades 3, 4, and 5 was selected.

## Research Site Considerations

Sites were needed where special education programming varied and state and local education agencies were likely to cooperate. The passage of SB 230 (Comprehensive Special Education Program for Exceptional Children) by the 61st Texas State Legislature in 1969 and the subsequent regulations and guidelines (Texas Education Agency, 1971) made Texas a suitable site for this large-scale study. The legislation had two major objectives: to make special education services available to all handicapped children and to require that each child's program be appropriate. The provision of comprehensive special education services was defined in the legislation to mean services to handicapped children from 3-21 years, including children with all handicapping conditions living in Texas. The provision of appropriate special education services was defined in the legislation to include provision of:

- adequate appraisal services,
- a variety of available instructional arrangements,
- appropriate instructional media and materials, and
- supporting professional and paraprofessional personnel.[1]

The objective of the Texas special education legislation was to encourage local education agency efforts in establishing and providing comprehensive special education programs that were consistent with local school district needs and resources.

To achieve this objective, Plan A, an alternative to allocating state funds on a unit-weighted system, was developed. Plan A provided for special education resources to be directed to local districts on the basis of the total number of students in average daily attendance. Funding was no longer contingent upon prior identification of a special number of similarly labelled handicapped children or restricted only to funds for special self-contained class teachers. Instead, districts could design programs — including support personnel, teachers, and administrators — to be consistent with local needs and beliefs. Districts that did not implement Plan A were reimbursed on a unit-weighted system (Plan B). Under Plan B, a school district diagnosed and classified a minimum of eight chidlren as mentally retarded in order to form a special education class unit. The state paid the salary of the teacher for each special education class unit but no funds were provided for support personnel. Plan B was considered restrictive by many local education agencies.

The appropriation of state funds for special education for the school year 1970-71, when the Comprehensive Special Education Program was initially implemented, reflected a nearly 100% increase in state expenditures for the education of EMR learners. The marked increase in appropriation of funds for special education services created a need to evaluate the state's effort to provide comprehensive and appropriate special education programs to justify the increased expenditures.

The State of Texas provided a unique field test site for studying the provision of comprehensive special education services for EMR learners. First, the objective of the Texas special education legislation was to encourage local education agency efforts in providing and establishing comprehensive special education programs that were consistent with local school district needs and resources. Second, the state provided financial incentives to local education agencies to encourage the integration of EMR learners into the regular education program through reimbursing the local districts twice for those students who were integrated for more than half the school day. That is, the state education agency allowed integrated students to be counted in the regular education average daily attendance count in addition to providing funds for special education services.

Third, the state education agency was perceived as philosophically encouraging the instruction of EMR learners in the regular classroom whenever the children could profit from such instruction and stressing the importance of providing a continuum of services so that each child's individual educational needs could be met.

Fourth, Plan A was designed to allow more flexible use of the state's special education financial allocation by encouraging local education agencies to select and use personnel and resources according to their particular needs.

Finally, the state was committed to gathering information related to its implementation of comprehensive special education services for EMR learners. A cooperative research effort was undertaken by the Federal government and the State of Texas to investigate the issues related to mainstreaming, since Texas' Plan A approach represented a probable direction for special education practice nationally.

## Sampling

The principal objective of the sampling design was to obtain the broadest representation of variations in educational placement and programming for EMR learners. To assure maximum variation in classroom environments as well as sufficient replications of each environmental setting necessary for a multivariate descriptive/correlational study, a large sample of school districts, school buildings, and classes was required. In addition to reasons discussed earlier, this need was further dictated by the fact that potentially useful stratification measures were not known, requiring oversampling to assure the inclusion of significant program variations.

Sampling procedures were designed to assure the maximum number of unique learner/classroom environment dyads, particularly dyads of mainstreamed EMR/nonhandicapped learners. Because of certain aspects of the sampling process and the naturalistic design of the study, caution is needed when interpreting the findings.

## Sample Description

The final sample was composed of 43 school districts or cooperatives (several small districts) with the mean percentage of the student population in each ethnic group as follows: 63.71% Anglo ($SD = 25.76$), 12.97% Black ($SD = 12.04$), and 22.75% Spanish surnamed ($SD = 25.71$). The ranges within districts for the three ethnic distributions were 4-98% Anglo, 0-40% Black, and 0-92% Spanish surnamed. The wide disparity and large standard deviations attest to the fact that many districts comprised predominantly Anglo or Spanish-surnamed students while none were predominantly Black.

From these 43 districts, 141 school buildings were selected, each having four or more regular or special classes. Each regular class contained at least one mainstreamed EMR learner. From each special self-contained class, at least one nonmainstreamed EMR learner was selected. Within these school buildings, 262 regular education, 132 special education resource, and 127 special self-contained teachers constituted the teacher sample. In most cases, the designated regular educator saw the EMR learner either for 50% of the school day or the longest period of time.

The sample of students contained 356 mainstreamed and 273 nonmainstreamed EMR learners, and 356 nonhandicapped students as a contrast sample. The mainstreamed EMR learners were roughly evenly distributed over grades 3, 4, and 5 (107 in grade 3, 129 in grade 4, 120 in grade 5).

The decision rules that guided the 6-stage sample selection process and the cautions to be considered in interpreting the results are presented in Appendix A.

## Instrumentation

The dilemma of what to measure and at what level of specificity was the most vexing measurement problem encountered in the study. Glass (1969) summarizes this problem clearly when he argues that researchers:

...are advised to heed a vast assortment of data. They are warned that anything that feeds into a program (antecedents), happens during it (transitions), and results from it (outcomes) may prove to be critical to the success of the program. They are also told that it is vital to consider not only what happened (observations) but what should have happened (intents). (p. 39)

The Project PRIME descriptive/correlational design required detailed measurement of each of the learner and environment domains described in the taxonomic model. Specification of the precise subdomains and variables resulted from conceptual and empirical reduction of the data from these instruments. Instrumentation was developed to provide information on the multiple facets encompassed within these domains (see Appendix B). This section presents the measurement objectives of Project PRIME, describes the instrument development procedures, and provides an overview of the instruments administered. See Kaufman, Semmel, and Agard (1973) for a more extensive documentation of the instrumentation, including a discussion of the methodological issues involved in the Project PRIME instrument development.

## Measurement Objectives

In addition to the extensive information needs dictated by a descriptive/correlational design, criticism of existing large-scale evaluation has suggested other measurement considerations (Bowles & Levin, 1968; Michelson, 1970). Michelson, for example, has argued that multiple measures of student competence are needed. The development of academic skills, while important, is not the only objective of the school. Other objectives, including the ability to function in social groups, positive feelings toward oneself and others, and enjoyment of school, should all be considered legitimate outcomes of schooling. Furthermore, there is a growing awareness that behavior such as attention to task and appropriate verbal and social participation are important school objectives. They are significant in their own right as well as mediators of the development of more distal competencies such as academic achievement and social competence (Jackson, 1968; Stallings, 1975).

The PRIME taxonomic model includes both academic and social competence domains. Within these domains, the model includes proximal measures of behavior and attitudes as well as the distal measures of academic achievement and social status.

Several concerns governed the choice of measurement procedures. One concern was the degree of inference required. High-inference ratings of broadly-defined attributes and low-inference ratings of the frequency of specific behaviors can both provide usable information on such characteristics as learner cooperation and teacher warmth. The Project PRIME instrumentation included both high- and low-inference techniques.

A second concern was the source of the information. Both individual attributes and environmental characteristics depend on the perspective of the reporting individuals. Perceptions of individual learner behaviors (such as friendliness) or environmental characteristics (such as degree of harmony) may differ depending on whether the learner, the teacher, or the peer group is the source of information. A complete description of learner and environment characteristics requires measurement from multiple perspectives. The Project PRIME instrumentation was developed to obtain information from different sources to assess the same or similar constructs.

In sum, the Project PRIME instrumentation was designed to measure learner and environmental characteristics from multiple perspectives using both high- and low-inference techniques. Whenever agreement among sources and type of measurement was high as evidenced by high scale intercorrelations or loadings on a common factor, these measures were combined to form a single construct with greater validity.


## Instrument Development and Description

The instrumentation for Project PRIME consisted of four major types: (a) standardized achievement tests, (b) sociometric instruments and rating scales, (c) teacher questionnaires, and (d) observation systems. In Table 2-1, the teacher and student (learner and peer) instruments are described in terms of the persons involved, the method of administration, the number and response mode of the items, and the psychological content and reliability of each empirically derived scale. The observation systems are described in terms of the persons observed, the type of observation, and the content. Extensive documentation of the developmental history and psychometric properties is available in the form of published test manuals prepared by Agard and various colleagues for those instruments which were judged to have utility beyond the scope of the present study.[2]


### Achievement Tests
The Metropolitan Achievement Test (MAT) served as the principal measure of student achievement. The MAT was selected because it was widely used and respected in Texas public schools, and had recently been revised. Only the mathematics and reading subtests were administered. Student MAT scores were computed for total reading and total mathematics using the scoring procedures developed by the MAT authors.

Table 2-1
Project PRIME Instruments

I. LEARNER INSTRUMENTS

1. METROPOLITAN ACHIEVEMENT TEST (MAT)

**Levels: Primary I, Primary II, Elementary, Intermediate.**

**Persons involved:** Selected handicapped and nonhandicapped learners. Each EMR learner received both the Primary I and the Primary II level; each nonhandicapped learner received the level appropriate to his grade.

**Method of administration:** Administered in three (or four depending on the level) small-group sessions organized by test level.

**Content:** Subtests include word knowledge, word analysis (Primary I and Primary II only), reading, total reading, mathematics computation (Primary II, Elementary, and Intermediate only), mathematics concepts (Primary II, Elementary, and Intermediate only), mathematics problem solving (Primary II, Elementary, and Intermediate only), and total mathematics.

2. CHILDREN'S QUESTIONNAIRE (CQ)

**Persons involved:** Selected handicapped and nonhandicapped learners

**Method of administration:** Administered verbally to each learner individually in a single session.

**Number and response mode of items:** Contains 38 questions requiring short verbal responses, usually yes or no. Test administrator recorded learner responses on an answer sheet.

**Content:** Contains questions on the social, economic, and educational background of the learner and his feelings about school. Scaling analysis yielded four internally consistent, meaningful scales:

Academic Ambition (alpha = .53)
Family Size (alpha = .90)
Comparative Attitude toward School This Year/Last
Year (alpha= .62)
Cognitive Affluence of Home (alpha = .68)

3. ABOUT YOU AND YOUR FRIENDS (AYYF)*

**Persons involved:** Selected handicapped and nonhandicapped learners

**Method of administration:** Administered verbally in four separate small-group sessions.

**Number and response mode of items:** Contains 96 forced-choice binary questions; learners wrote yes or no on an answer sheet.

Table 2-1, continued

Content: Scaling analysis yielded four internally consistent, meaningful scales:

Isolation/Anxiety (alpha = .80)
School Enthusiasm (alpha = .74)
Academic Self-Concept (alpha = .73)
Misbehavior (alpha = .78)

4.  HOW DO YOU FEEL--Part I (HDYF-I)

Persons involved: Selected handicapped and nonhandi-capped learners

Method of administration: Administered verbally in two separate small-group sessions.

Number and response mode of items: Contains 41 state-ments requiring the learner to show how he feels about each statement by filling in a smiling, plain, or sad face.

Content: Scaling analysis yielded one internally consistent, meaningful scale:

Attitude toward School Activities (alpha = .85)

5.  HOW DO YOU FEEL--PART II (HDYF-II)

Persons involved: Selected handicapped and nonhandi-capped learners

Method of administration: Administered verbally in one small-group session.

Number and response mode of items: Contains 33 state-ments requiring the learner to show how he about each statement by filling in a smiling, plain, or sad face.

Content: Designed to measure retrospective change in attitude toward school from fall to spring. Scaling analysis yielded five internally consistent, meaning-ful scales:

Attitude toward Reading (alpha = .68)
Attitude toward Mathematics (alpha = .74)
Feelings about Peers (alpha = .70)
Current Attitude toward Teacher/School (alpha = .74)
Retrospective Attitude toward Teacher/School Last Year (alpha = .71)

II.  TEACHER INSTRUMENTS

A.  Instruments related to target learners

**Table 2-1, continued**

1. TEACHER RATING SCALE (TRS)*

    **Persons involved:** All teachers who instructed the selected learners

    **Method of administration:** Teachers completed the questionnaire during time released by other Project PRIME classroom testing.

    **Number and response mode of items:** Contains 85 descriptions of behavior; teacher rated each learner using 5-point frequency of occurrence rating scale.

    **Content:** Scaling yielded four internally consistent, meaningful scales:

    > Academic Effort/Success (alpha = .98)
    > Antisocial Behavior (alpha = .90)
    > Outgoing/Expressive Behavior (alpha = .90)
    > Anxiousness (alpha = .75)

2. SELECTED CHILDREN'S BACKGROUND QUESTIONNAIRE (SCBQ)

    **Persons involved:** Selected teacher for each selected learner

    **Method of administration:** Teachers completed the questionnaire during out-of-school hours and received financial reimbursement.

    **Number and response mode of items:** Contains 27 items which require checking the appropriate response.

    **Content:** Contains questions on the demographic (age, sex, SES, ethnic group) and educational background of the selected learners; for handicapped learners, contains questions on the time integrated, age first received special education services, and previous special education placement.

3. SELECTED CHILDREN'S EDUCATIONAL EXPERIENCE QUESTIONNAIRE (SCEEQ)

    **Persons involved:** Selected regular and special self-contained teachers and principal resource teachers of selected mainstreamed learners

    **Method of administration:** Teachers completed questionnaire during out-of-school hours and received financial reimbursement.

    **Number and response mode of items:** Contains 27 items---19 questions requiring checking the appropriate response and 8 two-dimensional charts.

    **Content:** Contains questions on the learner's academic ability, and school experiences, instructional techniques employed with the learner, and the availability of special education services for that learner.

**Table 2-1, continued**

B.　Instruments related to teacher of class

1.　TEACHER ADMINISTRATIVE QUESTIONNAIRE (TAQ)

**Persons involved:** Selected regular and special self-contained teachers and principal resource teachers of selected mainstreamed learners

**Method of administration:** Two questionnaire versions were developed; one for regular and one for special teachers. Teachers completed questionnaires during out-of-school hours and received financial reimbursement.

**Number and response mode of items:** Contains 136 items (103 questions and 33 two-dimensional charts) for regular teachers; 123 items (92 questions and 31 charts) for special teachers.

**Content:** Contains questions concerning the personal and professional background of the teacher, educational attitudes, inservice training, demographic information on the students instructed, ability level of the students instructed, instructional materials and services, educational plans, teaching techniques, instructional arrangements and grouping procedures, involvement and teacher attitudes toward various features of the special education program. Also included was the EEOS Verbal Facility Scale (Coleman et al., 1966).
　　　Scaling analysis yielded two internally consistent, meaningful scales:

　　　Importance of an Open, Warm Environment
　　　　　(alpha = .84)
　　　Importance of a Structured, Controlled Environment (alpha = .79)

2.　CLASSROOM INTEGRATION QUESTIONNAIRE (CIQ)

**Persons involved:** Selected regular and special self-contained teachers and principal resource teachers of selected mainstreamed learners

**Method of administration:** Questionnaire items were included as a separate part of the Teacher Administrative Questionnaire.

**Number and response mode of items:** Contains 25 student behavior descriptions that require the teacher to indicate preferred placement along a continuum of special education placement alternatives.

**Content:** Scaling analysis yielded two internally consistent, meaningful scales:

　　　Attitude toward the Integration of Students with
　　　　　Problems　(alpha = .79)
　　　Attitude toward the Integration of Students with
　　　　　Social Problems (alpha = .86)

**Table 2-1, continued**

3.  TEACHER CLASSROOM CLIMATE QUESTIONNAIRE (TCCQ)*

    **Persons involved:** Selected teachers

    **Method of administration:** Teacher completed the questionnaire during out-of-school hours and received financial reimbursement.

    **Number and response mode of items:** Contains 67 items describing the classroom climate to be rated on a 5-point frequency-of-occurrence scale.

    **Content:** Scaling analysis yielded six internally consistent, meaningful scales:

    > Cooperation/Diversification (alpha = .83)
    > Friction (alpha = .81)
    > Rigidity/Control (alpha = .65)
    > Individualization (alpha = .79)
    > Difficulty (alpha = .77)
    > Competition (alpha = .73)

4.  TEACHER EDUCATIONAL ATTITUDE QUESTIONNAIRE (TEAQ)

    **Persons involved:** Selected teachers

    **Method of administration:** Teachers completed the questionnaire during out-of-school hours and received financial reimbursement.

    **Number and response mode of items:** Contains 53 items to be rated on a 4-point scale indicating extent of agreement.

    **Content:** Scaling analysis yielded four internally consistent, meaningful scales:

    > Traditional Authority (alpha = .83)
    > Professional Satisfaction (alpha = .76)
    > Teacher Cohesiveness (alpha = .85)

## III. PEER INSTRUMENTS

1.  GUESS WHO (GW)*

    **Persons involved:** All students (peers) in the selected learner's classroom

    **Method of administration:** Administered in two separate classroom sessions.

    **Number and response mode of items:** Contains 28 descriptions requiring one peer nomination for each. Students wrote name of each child nominated on a pupil answer sheet.

    **Content:** Scaling analysis yielded four internally consistent, meaningful scales:

    > Brightness (alpha = .77)
    > Dullness (alpha = .70)
    > Disruptive Behavior (alpha = .83)
    > Quiet/Good Behavior (alpha = .61)

Table 2-1, continued

2.   HOW I FEEL TOWARD OTHERS (HIFTO)*

**Persons involved:** All students (peers) in the selected learner's classroom

**Method and administration:** Administered in one classroom session.

**Number and response mode of items:** Each student rated every other student as a friend by marking a smiling, plain, or sad face or a question mark in a circle.

**Content:** Yielded percentage distribution measures of

      Sociometric Status
           Acceptance (interjudge consistency
                coefficient for nonhandicapped
                students = .75)
           Rejection (interjudge consistency
                coefficient for nonhandicapped students
                = .74)
      Attitude toward Peers
           Peers Liked (interjudge consistency
                coefficient for nonhandicapped students
                = .81)
           Peers Disliked (interjudge consistency
                coefficient for nonhandicapped students
                = .81)
      Class Social Cohesiveness

3.   YOUR SCHOOL DAYS (YSD)*

**Persons involved:** All students (peers) in the selected learner's classroom

**Method of administration:** Administered in two separate classroom sessions.

**Number and response mode of items:** Contains 65 forced-choice binary questions to which each student wrote the words yes or no on an answer sheet.

**Content:** Scaling analysis of aggregated class item means yielded four internally consistent, meaningful scales:

      Harmony (alpha = .86)
      Discordance (alpha = .76)
      Cognitive Emphasis (alpha = .78)
      Flexibility (alpha = .57)

**Table 2-1, continued**

IV. **OBSERVATION INSTRUMENTS**

1. FLORIDA CLIMATE AND CONTROL SYSTEM (FLACCS)

   **Persons observed:** Selected learner, classmates, and involved teachers

   **Method of observation:** Selected learner and peers were observed in all instructional situations for two complete school days.

   **Type of observations:** A sign system was used to quantifying classroom climate and control behaviors and five high-inference rating scales. Observation time segments were two minutes, with eight-minute intervals between segments.

   **Content:** Contains 34 teacher and 40 learner verbal and nonverbal positive and negative affective behaviors; 43 teacher verbal and nonverbal control behaviors, and 34 learner task-oriented or deviant behaviors. Individual rating items on the FLACCS include student differentiation, peer freedom, teacher directiveness, teacher central focus, peer interest and attention, and learner socialization. Behavior item scores are expressed as percentage of two-minute time elements in which behavior was observed at least once. Rating scales were expressed as average ratings: the sum of the ratings divided by the total number of time elements. Factor scales are expressed as the average number of behaviors of that type that were observed in a two-minute time element.
   Scaling analysis yielded two internally consistent, meaningful scales related to the social behavior of the learner.

   > Positive Social Behavior (alpha = .72)
   > Negative Social Behavior (alpha = .74)

   and five scales related to the classroom climate

   > Warm Teacher Behavior (alpha = .84)
   > Harsh, Coercive Teacher Behavior (alpha = .88)
   > Disruptive Peer Behavior (alpha = .86)
   > Peer Friendliness (alpha = .80)
   > Pupils Happy/Climate Positive (alpha = .84)

2. INDIANA BEHAVIOR MANAGEMENT SYSTEM II (IBMS-II)

   **Persons observed:** Selected learner and involved teachers

   **Method of observation:** Selected learner was observed in all instructional situations for two complete school days.

**Table 2-1, continued**

**Content:** Contains a teacher and a student on-task behavior category as well as 8 student off-task behavior categories (self-involvement, noise, verbal and physical aggression, verbal and physical resistance) and 12 teacher control categories (e.g., direct verbal demands, conditioned stimulus signals, criticism, punishment, empathy, redirection). Scores are expressed as percentages of ten-second time elements in which behavior occurred one or more times.

3. INDIANA COGNITIVE DEMAND SCHEDULE (ICDS)

   **Persons observed:** Selected learner, classmates, and involved teachers

   **Method of observation:** Selected learner and peers were observed in all instructional situations for two complete school days.

   **Type of observation:** Used low-inference category system of teacher's demands, learner or class responses, and teacher feedback. Frequency and type of demand, response, and feedback recorded sequentially in real time. Observation time segments were four minutes, with one-minute intervals between segments.

   **Content:** Contains 11 categories representing a continuum of low to high cognitive demands and student responses, two procedural categories, and 4 feedback categories--none, positive, negative, and information. Scores are expressed as rates per unit of time.

4. INDIANA PUPIL PARTICIPATION SCHEDULE (IPPS)

   **Persons observed:** Selected learner and classmates

   **Method of observation:** Selected learner and peers were observed in all instructional situations for two complete mornings.

   **Type of observation:** Used low-inference category system of frequency and type of participatory behavior. Participatory interchanges engaged in by selected learner and class recorded in real time. Observation time segments were ten minutes, with no more than five-minute intervals between segments.

   **Content:** Categories include student hand raises, teacher responses to student hand raises, teacher elicitation of student responses when student did not raise hand, student responses to teacher, (a) when student raised hand, and (b) when student did not raise hand, and student queries. Scores are expressed as rates per unit of time. Composite measures include:

   Number of observed initiations per pupil per hour
   Number of observed responses per pupil per hour
   Number of observed verbalizations (initiations plus responses) per pupil hour
   Number (per pupil hour) of verbalizations that were questions.

**Table 2-1, continued**

5. CLASSROOM STATUS DATA (CSD)

**Object of observation:** The physical features of the classroom and activities of the selected learner, teacher, and peers

**Method of observation:** The CSD was an integral but separate section of each of the above observation systems. Each time an observer entered a classroom, descriptive physical information was recorded. Information on instructional context was recorded at the regular intervals called for by the observation system in use, i.e., every four minutes on the IBMS and ICDS and every ten minutes on the IPPS and FLACCS. Rating scales evaluating teacher performance were completed every forty minutes on the ICDS and IBMS and every fifty minutes on the FLACCS and IPPS, or whenever the coder left the classroom.

**Type of observation:** A sign system was used to describe the physical and instructional context of the setting. High-inference rating scales were used to rate teacher performance.

**Content:** Contains descriptive physical information, including class size, type of class, classroom physical quality and orderliness, personnel in class, and displays in classroom; instructional context information, including academic content, learner-teacher observer position in class, student seating arrangement, structure for classroom activities, teacher task, and pupil task; and evaluation of teacher and class on such things as organization, flexibility, stimulation, structure, relevance, and happiness.

Contextual information scores are expressed as percentages of observed time in which the particular contextual factors were observed. Rating scales are expressed as weighted average ratings: the weighted (by time) sum of ratings divided by the time observed.

---

\* These instruments are part of the published Project PRIME Instrument Battery; Agard and colleagues, 1978.)

## Sociometric Instruments and Rating Scales

The PRIME instrument battery included:

1. Four learner ratings scales to measure learner self-concept and attitudes—Children's Questionnaire (CQ), How Do You Feel Part I and Part II (HDYF-I, HDYF-II), and About You and Your Friends (AYYF)
2. A teacher rating scale to measure the learners' academic and social behavior—Teacher Rating Scale (TRS)
3. Three teacher rating scales to measure teacher educational attitudes and classroom climate—Classroom Integration Questionnaire (CIQ), Teacher Educational Attitudes Questionnaire (TEAQ), and Teacher Classroom Climate Questionnaire (TCCQ)
4. Two sociometric instruments, one which measured peer responses to the learners' academic and social behavior—Guess Who (GW)—and another which measured learners' sociometric status and attitude toward peers—How I Feel Toward Others (HIFTO)
5. A peer rating scale to measure the classroom climate—Your School Days (YSD)

Three preliminary steps were required before the development of the sociometric instruments and the rating scales:

1. determining the psychological content to be measured,
2. delineating the characteristics of potential respondents, and
3. assessing the appropriateness of existing instruments.

The psychological content of the instruments was based on the constructs of the learner and classroom environment taxonomy and the theoretical or conceptual structures related to each construct. Instrument content, response format, item syntax, and vocabulary had to be appropriate for use with students of various sociocultural backgrounds, previous school experience, levels of reading skill, language facility, test motivation, and task attentiveness. Instruments for teachers needed to take into account the differences in educational programs, goals, and practices associated with regular, resource, and self-contained class settings.

Existing instrumentation was reviewed to determine whether the content was relevant for measuring the constructs in the taxonomic model and whether the instrument was psychometrically appropriate for anticipated respondents. No existing sociometric or attitudinal rating scales were judged appropriate for Project PRIME use. Therefore, these measurement needs were met through the development of new instrumentation.

The construction stage of instrument development included: generating an item pool, determining response formats, developing administrative procedures, and conducting pilot tests of the instrument. For each instrument, a pool of items related to the constructs of interest was compiled from existing instruments. The items most appropriate in terms of clarity, content relevance, and suitability to respondents were selected from the pool and rewritten to be consistent with an instrument format.

Consideration of the students' response characteristics resulted in certain critical design decisions affecting response formats and administrative procedures. The academic ability of the EMR learners required administrative procedures that would minimize reliance on student reading and writing skills. Thus, instructions and items were read to the students to facilitate comprehension. Response formats were restricted to simple written responses such as yes/no or darkening a circle containing one of several faces. Further, given the short attention span and previous school failures of EMR learners, instruments were administered individually or in small groups, and the length of any particular testing session was limited to a maximum of 20-30 minutes. Finally, low English-proficient Spanish-speaking students required procedures to assure valid measurement: Local education agencies were encouraged to use bilingual test administrators and provide Spanish versions of the instruments based on the Spanish language patterns of Mexican-Americans residing in Texas. A separate Spanish language test development process was completed to assure consistency with the English language forms.

A limited vocabulary was used for the student rating scale items. An interrogative rather than declarative sentence was used to draw maximum attention to the fact that a response was expected. A forced-choice, binary (yes/no), or 3-point (happy, plain, or sad face) response mode was used whenever possible to further clarify and simplify the students' task. The decision to reduce the cognitive demands of the student instruments by using the simple response alternatives sacrificed reliability to an unknown extent. However, reliability considerations had to be balanced with the even greater concern for measurement validity. In an effort to counter the decrease in reliability due to use of binary scales, more stimulus items were included (Cronbach, 1971). Appendix B includes samples of each instrument.

The design and implementation of the sociometric instruments was also based on consideration of student characteristics. The sociometric status instrument, *How I Feel Toward Others* (HIFTO), required each student to rate his attraction toward every other student by marking one of four faces (smile, plain, frown, and question mark). Students had to be able to read the first names of their classmates; those who could not were tested individually. The peer nomination instrument, *Guess Who* (GW), required each student to copy from a list on the chalkboard the name of the classmate he selected as the best fit to each verbal description read aloud by the test administrator. Students who were unable to copy their classmates' names were tested individually.

For the teacher instruments, items were rewritten to assure they possessed clear behavioral referents, would be applicable to both regular and special class settings, and could use a 4- or 5-point response continuum based on either frequency of occurrence or extent of agreement. The teacher response forms were designed to be self-explanatory and easy-to-use.

After the initial construction activities were completed, the student and teacher instruments were critically reviewed by professionals in special education, psycholinguistics, and psychometrics, as well as school administrators and teachers. The instruments were then pilot-tested on small samples of teachers and students. Revisions were then made: Sentence structure and/or vocabulary was changed, ambiguous items were clarified, and items deemed inappropriate for specific sample subgroups were modified or deleted.

Both student and teacher rating instruments were then subjected to scale development procedures to provide a parsimonious and reliable set of learner and environment descriptors. Scaling was accomplished through a factor-analysis procedure, with the derived factor scales serving to define the constructs measured by the instrument. This scaling process is discussed in the following chapter.

Data collected from *How I Feel Toward Others* (HIFTO) were scored by dividing the number of smiles and frowns a learner received from peers (sociometric status) and the number of smiles and frowns a learner gave peers (feelings about peers) by the total number of classmates completing the instrument. Measures of class social cohesiveness were obtained by computing the class means and standard deviations for smiles and frowns given/received.

For *Guess Who* (GW), the items were factor analyzed and the scores for the resulting scales were computed using binary scaling. Binary scaling was selected because it yielded the highest external validities and resulted in the least class size distortion. Each item on the scale was scored "1" if a learner was nominated by one or more peers for that item and "0" if not nominated for that item. Thus, the scale score has a range from 0 to the number of items on the scale for which the learner could have been nominated at least once.

## Teacher Questionnaires

There were three teacher questionnaires:

1. The Teacher Administrative Questionnaire (TAQ), used to obtain information on the teacher's background, training, and experience; educational attitudes and practices; attitudes toward mainstreaming; and use and value of special educational resources.

2. The Selected Children's Background Questionnaire (SCBQ), used to inquire about the personal background of the learner.
3. The Selected Children's Educational Experience Questionnaire (SCEEQ), used to inquire about the school history of the learner.

In developing the questionnaires:
- The broad content of areas was defined and within these areas specific information needs were identified.
- Questions were developed to obtain the identified information.
- The response format and specific response alternatives were developed for each question.

The questionnaires used a variety of question/answer formats:
- yes/no questions
- checklist information questions
- time estimation questions
- exact numerical questions
- exact numerical charts (e.g., how many of the students in your class in each handicapping condition are members of each ethnic group)
- attitudinal questions
- attitudinal charts (e.g., rate each of the following characteristics of the intellectual atmosphere and social climate of elementary school classes in terms of its importance to you)
- personnel assignment questions (e.g., which of the following personnel assist you in the implementation of the handicapped students' educational plans)
- personnel assignment charts (e.g., for each person listed, indicate whether he participated actively, was consulted, or did not participate in determining which handicapped children would be integrated into regular classes)
- rank-order evaluation questions (e.g., rank order the five most important behaviors you consider when evaluating children that need to be referred for special education services)
- program evaluation charts (e.g., how would you evaluate the following aspects of the special education instructional materials you receive)

In addition to basic demographic, attitudinal, and process questions, the TAQ included the verbal facility scale from Coleman et al. (1966) and the *Classroom Integration Questionnaire* (CIQ). Because the regular and special education teachers were expected to differ in their experience with the special education planning and programming process, the questions asked of the two types of teachers differed slightly, requiring two versions of the TAQ (regular and special education).

The teacher questionnaires were reviewed by professional educators and administrators of special education, including (a) Texas Education Agency professional staff, (b) the Advisory Committee of the University of Texas Southwest Regional Special Education Instructional Materials Center, and (c) a panel of University of Texas at Austin special education faculty. These special educators reviewed the questions for clarity and relevance, revised the question wording and/or format, provided additional response alternatives, and suggested additional questions.

The questionnaires were pretested by regular and special education teachers in five school districts widely different in geographic location, district size, ethnic composition, and special education programming. After the pretest, respondents commented on the clarity and appropriateness of the questions and response alternatives. Finally, the questionnaires were reviewed and approved by the Texas Education Agency Reports Management System and the Texas Chief State School Officer, Dr. J.W. Edgar.

The general conclusion of the professional reviewers and pretest respondents was that the questions were clear and appropriate and allowed for a wide variety of responses.

## Observation System

Within the PRIME taxonomic model, certain classroom-environment and learner-behavior characteristics were thought to be best measured through observational techniques. Characteristics such as participation, cognitive discourse, behavior management, attention, teacher warmth and directiveness, and instructional context were to be measured through observation.

The observation instruments were developed through a process similar to that of the sociometric and rating scale instruments. The demands placed on an observer had to be taken into consideration. For example, the number of categories requiring observer discrimination and differentiation had to be manageable and the format for coding observations had to facilitate rapid recording.

Observation systems vary in their method of classification of behavior and in their methods of quantification. Behavior may be classified by a category or a sign system. In a category system, one aspect of classroom behavior is segmented into a set of mutually exclusive categories, permitting finer-grained behavior to be recorded. Sign systems do not permit sequencing or calculation of behaviors per unit of time, but they do permit empirical or logical clustering of items into broad descriptive composite measures.

Methods of quantification vary depending on whether behavior is recorded in continuous real time or through a time-sampling procedure. Real-time recording permits measurement of the actual rate per unit of time of the occurrence of a behavior. Time sampling does not allow calculation of rates but rather permits calculation of the proportion of time segments in which behavior occurs. Typically, categorical systems record a few behavioral elements either continuously or over quickly reoccurring time samples while sign systems record many behavioral elements over larger samples of time. The selection of a particular method of classification and quantification depends on the objectives of the observation system. The Project PRIME taxonomic model sought to capture detailed frequency information, such as the level and rate of the class cognitive discourse, and estimates of such broad-gauged variables as teacher warmth and peer harmony.

A review of classroom observation systems identified three systems which met the criteria for selection: the *Indiana Behavior Management System* (IBMS; Fink & Semmel, 1971), the *Indiana Cognitive Demand Schedule* (ICDS, Lynch & Ames, 1971), and the *Florida Climate and Control System* (FLACCS; Soar, Soar, & Ragosta, 1971). No extant instrumentation was considered satisfactory for assessing pupil participation and instructional context. Two new observation systems were developed: the *Indiana Pupil Participation Schedule* (IPPS; Semmel & Meyers, 1971) and the *Classroom Status Data* (CSD; Semmel & Hasselbring, 1971).

Each classification system, whether category or sign, was reviewed to ensure discriminable and operationally-defined coding categories. Machine-scorable recording forms to permit rapid and accurate coding of information were also developed. Multi-media training materials were developed for each system to permit a decentralized training model.

Since the Project PRIME research design focussed on both the learner and class as units of analysis, the observation systems had to be designed to capture both individual learner and teacher/peer behavior. This was accomplished by indicating coding notations for both the target learner and class on all the recording booklets except the IBMS (the IBMS being designed to capture the behavior of only one student). Thus, for each observation item, parallel responses were obtained for the individual learner and the class as a whole.

Separate coding booklets were developed for the *Indiana Pupil Participation Schedule* (IPPS), *Indiana Cognitive Demand Schedule* (ICDS), *Indiana Behavior Management System* (IBMS), and the *Florida Climate and Control System* (FLACCS). The *Classroom Status Data* (CSD) system was included in the coding booklet for each of these four systems, providing descriptive information related to the physical and instructional context and academic content within which the observation system was being used. Also included in each observation booklet was a high-inference rating scale evaluating teacher performance, based on the teacher characteristics Rosenshine and Furst (1971) found predictive of academic achievement in previous research. This scale was later discarded because it possessed a strong unidimensional "halo" component.

Data generated from the observation systems were reduced first by aggregating across time segments to form aggregated sums of individual learner or teacher/class behaviors. These sums were either divided by real time (in category systems) to obtain rate measures or by time segments (in sign systems) for percentage-of-time-segment measures. In the categorical systems, in certain instances, individual categories were summed to form broader categories. Decisions to form these combinations were based on coder-agreement scores and patterns of coder errors. For high-inference rating scales, average rating scores were computed by dividing the sum of the ratings received by real time or by the number of time segments in which the ratings were obtained.

After individual sign system items were aggregated to obtain measures of the percentage of time segments in which this behavior occurred, the individual item measures were factor analyzed and unit-weighted to form factor scales. Since each learner could have a score ranging from 0.00-1.00 for each item (the percentage of time segments in which that behavior was observed), the minimum score for each factor scale was 0 and the maximum (if each behavior was exhibited at least once during each time segment) was the number of items on the scale. A score of 2.00 on the scale suggests that an average of two behaviors representing the scale construct (i.e., warm teacher behavior) occurred per time segment; a score of 0.5 suggests that, on average, one behavior representing the scale construct occurred in half the time segments (i.e., warm behavior was exhibited in half the time segments).

In summary, the PRIME instrumentation was based on particular measurement considerations that led to the development of sociometric instruments, rating scales, questionnaires, and observation systems designed, constructed, and scaled to provide a reliable and parsimonious set of measures that describe the domains of the taxonomic model. In the next section, we describe the data collection procedures used to administer these instruments.

# Data Collection Procedures

Data collection procedures were needed that would insure the punctual collection of reliable information in a structured, standardized form from 43 school districts in a region covering approximately 270,000 square miles. The procedures employed to ensure this goal are summarized in this section to acquaint the reader with the basic data collection activities of the study. A detailed description is available in *Project PRIME: Interim Report I 1971-1972 — Purpose and Procedures* (Kaufman, Semmel, & Agard, 1973).

## Project PRIME Staff Selection and Development

Decentralized data collection procedures were developed using a network of local district coordinators, test administrators, and observers. In many districts, the local special education director served as the district Project PRIME coordinator; in other districts, a consultant or other special education staff member served as coordinator. In some districts, particularly the larger Project PRIME districts, a new staff person was employed to be coordinator with responsibility to the local special education director or their designee. Although it caused some administrative difficulties, this individualized approach encouraged each district to use its own staff capabilities as much as possible.

Local manpower needs for test administrators and observers were usually met by employing substitute school teachers from each school district. The use of substitute teachers had several advantages. First, these individuals were known by the school principals, teachers, and children; and therefore were minimally disruptive to regular classroom activities. Second, the substitute teachers were legally able to cover classrooms if specific instrumentation necessitated that the regular teacher leave the room. Third, the use of local personnel overcame the geographic problems inherent in a state-wide study involving a large number of school districts. In addition, the use of local community resources resulted in a test/observer staff with cultural backgrounds similar to those of the students. This was particularly important in districts with diverse ethnic student populations.

The local test administrators were responsible to the local district Project PRIME coordinators, who in turn received instructions, supervision, and support from the state Project PRIME coordinator and staff.

Two workshops were conducted to provide information and direction to the local Project PRIME coordinators. The first workshop, held in October, 1971, had five principal objectives:

1. an orientation to the goals and objectives of Project PRIME;
2. a discussion of the local school district's responsibilities and duties;
3. a discussion of the sample selection procedure;
4. a discussion of selection of test administrators; and
5. a discussion of achievement test procedures and schedules.

The second Project PRIME workshop was held in December, 1971. The objectives for the second workshop were:

1. a discussion about the activities necessary to build a master file for all students and teachers involved in Project PRIME;
2. a discussion of the form, content, and purpose of the attitudinal and social adjustment instruments;
3. instructions concerning general administrative procedures for these instruments;
4. a discussion of concerns centered on testing minority group children; and
5. the introduction of the form, content, and purpose of the classroom observation systems.

During the workshop, the Project PRIME instruments to be administered were presented, the process of instrument development was outlined, and the rationale behind each instrument was discussed. Comments and questions from the Project PRIME coordinators were aired and answers provided or solutions developed. One entire session was spent in a panel discussion of the problems to be anticipated when testing minority group children. The panel discussed specific test items and general areas of sensitivity, the appropriate way to use the Spanish versions of the instruments, and the need for sensitive and responsive test administrators. During the discussion, every effort was made to sensitize local coordinators to cultural issues. Coordinators were asked to select test administrators who would be sensitive to individual children's reactions and who would not pressure, antagonize, or humiliate any child for the purpose of obtaining Project PRIME data.

## Data Collection Time Sequence

Data collection occurred at four different times during the school year (Table 2-2). The following section outlines the procedures used during these four data collection periods.

### Training of the Observers

The large number of observers needed  $(N = 528)$ , the wide geographic distribution of school districts, and the number of classroom observation systems used required comprehensive and innovative training procedures. First, multi-media self-instructional training packages were developed which included a programmed instruction manual, videotapes, audiotapes, and a training workbook which accompanied the audiovisual materials. The

**Table 2-2**

**Timeline of Project PRIME Instrument Administration**

| October, 1971 | January, 1972 | February March, April, 1972 | May, 1972 |
|---|---|---|---|
| Metropolitan Achievement Test | How Do You Feel (Part I) | Indiana Pupil Participation Schedule | Children's Questionnaire |
| | About You and Your Friends | Individual Cognitive Demand Schedule | How Do You Feel? (Part II) |
| | Teacher Rating Scale | Indiana Behavior Management Schedule | Selected Children's Background Questionnaire |
| | How I Feel Toward Others | Florida Climate and Control Schedule | Selected Children's Educational Experience Questionnaire |
| | Guess Who | Classroom Status Data | Teacher Administrative Questionnaire |
| | Your School Days | | Classroom Integration Questionnaire |
| | | | Teacher Educational Attitudes Questionnaire |
| | | | Teacher Classroom Climate Questionnaire |
| | | | Metropolitan Achievement Test |

materials for IBMS, ICDS, and IPPS were developed by the Center for Innovation in Teaching the Handicapped (CITH), Indiana University, Bloomington, Indiana. The FLACCS materials were developed by the Institute for Development of Human Resource (IDHR), University of Florida, Gainesville, Florida.

The actual training of observers was conducted by a training team consisting of 19 University of Texas at Austin graduate students. The developers of the observation systems at CITH and IDHR instructed this training team in the content of the observation systems and the techniques to be used in training observers. Following this, the training team conducted workshops at 17 regional Educational Services Centers throughout the state. During these five-day workshops, each observer was trained to use the IPPS and one of the other three observation systems. Training included field observation as well as classroom use of programmed material and videotapes.

A centralized quality control check of the observer trainees was instituted. Data from criterion tests administered to observer trainees was transmitted to CITH at Indiana University. Reliability data with individual diagnostic comments on the strengths and weaknesses of each trainee was transmitted back to the training team member conducting the session. Trainers received this information within 12 hours of test administration, enabling them to analyze the progress of their trainees and provide appropriate guidance. At the end of each workshop, the names of trainees who failed to achieve satisfactory coding skills were sent to the state coordinating office, which transmitted them to the local school district for appropriate action. Roughly 15% of the trainees on each observation system were recommended to be dropped because of their low coding test scores. (See Appendix C for further information.)

At the completion of the week's workshop, the newly trained observers reported to their local district Project PRIME coordinator to receive specific instructions and to obtain their observation schedules.

## Collecting the Data

The development of the observation schedules was based on several considerations. First, the necessity of observing the mainstreamed EMR learner in both regular and resource classes. Second, the desirability of observing EMR learners in a variety of subject matter areas. Because behavior may vary with many situational factors (time of day, type of class, number of students present), it was necessary to obtain learner observations in multiple situations to increase the stability of the observation measures. In order to obtain a variety of settings, subject matter areas, and situations, observers followed a particular learner throughout the day (minus time out for observer breaks and lunch), coding the student, teacher, and peers on a specific observation system. Because observation data collection is expensive and potentially disruptive to the school program, the time spent in observing each learner was restricted to the minimum time sufficient for acquiring stable and representative estimates of observed behavior. Informed opinion suggested that two days of observation for each system would be adequate, especially if separated in time by at least two weeks.

Each learner, then, was observed for two complete days on each of the observation systems (IBMS, ICDS, and FLACCS) and for two mornings on IPPS, with the observation periods at least two weeks apart. This observation schedule resulted in the equivalent of seven days of observation per learner. Since the CSD was built into each of the other four systems, CSD observation covers the equivalent of seven days. Observation schedules were developed for each learner and translated into schedules for observers. These learner schedules employed a design counterbalanced across days of the week, observation systems, and observeers.

Although the learners were observed during the entire day, only observations from selected regular, resource, and special self-contained class teachers were used to describe a learner's behavior. Even with this restriction, an average of 75% of the available observation data on each learner was used.

Teacher and peer observation data were generated by aggregating across the observation booklets of all learners with the same teacher and peers. Since the sampling procedures assured that each teacher had at least two target learners in class, teacher and peer observation data were based on a minimum of 14 days of observation spread across at least three weeks and encompassing four different observation systems. This extensive observation database assured the stability of the teacher and peer observation measures.

The use of these observation scheduling procedures resulted in the collection of almost 5,000 days of observation data, describing 7 days of school activities for each target learner and 14 days of activities for each learner's teacher and peers.

## October Data Collection

The first data collection period was in October, 1971, with the administration of the MAT. Only the reading and the mathematics subtests were administered. The MATs were administered in small-group sessions. All learners in the school who received the same test level were tested together. As suggested by the MAT authors, the subtests were administered in separate testing sessions. All achievement testing was spread out over a four-day period. Whenever possible, the MAT test administrators were school staff or other persons experienced in the administration of standardized tests.

The nonhandicapped learners were tested at the level appropriate for their grade level. The EMR learners were tested at two levels, Primary I and Primary II, in that order. There were two reasons for using two levels of the test for the

EMR learners. The first was to allow for a wider range of achievement scores in the various subtests. This wider range was needed because the mathematics computation achievement of EMR learners is frequently several grades above their level of reading and/or mathematics problem-solving achievement. Second, the use of two levels of the achievement test prevented the basal and ceiling problems often encountered when obtaining measures of achievement from a population sample that has much within-group variance. Administering the lower level Primary I test first provided the EMR learner with an early success experience prior to taking the more difficult Primary II test. For analytical purposes, the form in which the EMR learner obtained a score closest to 50% correct was selected.

## January Data Collection

The second test administration period was during January, 1972. By this time, students' attitudes and behaviors were expected to have stabilized with the passing of almost a semester of the school year. During this period, two learner attitude instruments (AYYF and HDYF-I), two peer sociometric instruments (HIFTO and GW), the peer classroom climate rating scale (YSD), and the teacher rating scale of learner competence (TRS) were administered.

Local Project PRIME coordinators selected and trained the test administrators for this testing. The sociometric and attitudinal test administrators included testers from the fall achievement testing, substitute teachers, teachers' aides, and university students taking courses in educational psychology or tests and measurements. Each test administrator received a packet of materials to assist in the administration of the sociometric and attitudinal instruments.

In addition to the material provided the test administrator, the local Project PRIME coordinators were given materials in October and January to facilitate public relations activities with parents, teachers, and principals. These materials consisted of an overview of Project PRIME and letters of support from the state education department. The Project PRIME staff and Texas Education Agency consultants were also available to address interested groups at the school district's request.

## February-April Data Collection

The third and most complex data collection period was during February, March, and April, 1972, when procedures were instituted to collect classroom observation data. The intensity of the training provided, the rigor of the quality control measures instituted, and the magnitude of the data collected were unique to educational research. The observation training materials and procedures are briefly summarized in Appendix C. A complete description is available in Kaufman, Semmel, and Agard (1973).

**May Data Collection**

The fourth data collection period occurred in May of 1972. During this period, MAT posttests were administered using the same procedures that were employed during the October pretesting. In addition, two learner (HDYF-II, CQ) and three teacher (TCCQ, TEAQ, CIQ) attitude instruments were administered and teachers were asked to complete the two questionnaires requesting information on the learners' demographic and educational background (SCBQ, SCEEQ). Teachers also completed the administrative questionnaire (TAQ) providing information on their own background; the demography of their class; their instructional techniques, materials, and services; and their evaluation of the special education program. The time demands placed on teachers to complete this number of instruments during May required that Project PRIME provide payment for the instruments completed.

## Summary

This chapter has provided an overview of the design, sampling, instrumentation, and data collection procedures used in Project PRIME. The methodological considerations discussed and procedures described provide a foundation for understanding what data were obtained, how they were obtained, the conditions under which they were obtained, and from whom they were obtained. This description, coupled with the data analysis strategies discussed in Chapter 3, provides a basis for understanding and interpreting Project PRIME's findings.

## Technical Notes

1. These provisions parallel those later embodied in P.L. 94-142, the Federal Education for All Handicapped Children Act.

2. For information concerning the availability of these instruments, contact Brookline Books.

# 3
# Data Reduction and Analysis

This chapter presents the framework for the data reduction and analysis activities. The first section describes the process of delineating the constructs and their operational definitions encompassed by the Project PRIME taxonomic model. The second section outlines three levels of variables and the statistical methods used to analyze them. Successively, then, the factor analytic scaling methods used to reduce the questionnaire data are described, the problem of missing data is considered, and the methods of analyzing relationships among variables are outlined. Also included is a discussion of the various cautions the reader must exercise when interpreting and generalizing beyond the findings from these particular Project PRIME data.

## Analytic Framework

The data obtained in Project PRIME were conceptualized as representing five descriptive domains. Two domains depict the individual learner; the other three characterize the classroom environments encountered by these learners.

*Learner background* includes measures such as age, sex, ethnicity, family socioeconomic status, and previous school experience.

55

*Learner competence* includes measures of both academic and social performance, and serves as the basic criterion domain to which the other domains are ultimately to be related.

*Classroom composition* consists of measures describing the teacher and students demographically and attitudinally.

*Socioemotional climate* contains measures that register peer and teacher affect and class management.

*Instructional conditions* include measures that describe the context, activities, and structure that typify the various classes which were observed.

The variables in each domain may be conceptualized at three levels of aggregation:

1. specific item responses or observational descriptors;
2. scale scores and other composites such as rates and ratios compiled over time units; and
3. composites of these second-level measures, referred to here as "constructs."

Beyond this level are the higher-order subdomain and domain levels which are not variables per se, but rather conceptual clusters of variables.

Data were collected for the three learner groups as follows: (a) the *nonhandicapped* learners only in the regular classes that corresponded one-to-one to those of the mainstreamed EMR learners; (b) the *mainstreamed EMR* learners in regular and in resource classes; and (c) the *nonmainstreamed EMR* learners in special self-contained classes, though many did spend some time (less than 50% of the school day) in regular classes.

This framework — five variable domains and three learner groups in three instructional settings — was used as the basis for the data analyses. First, the data was reduced to form the scales and constructs representing each of the five domains. Next, the three learner groups and their settings were described using these measures. The relationships among variables, both within and across domains, were then examined in an effort to link the three environment and learner background domains to each of the 12 constructs (see the Taxonomic Model inside the front cover) which comprise the learner competence domain. Finally, the database was viewed from a rather different perspective: to identify empirically the major types or profiles of learners and environments that existed in the samples and examine the degree of association that exists between types of learners and types of environments (see Appendix D).

## Data Reduction

The multiple-source, multiple-method instrument battery yielded a vast amount of information about the learners and their environment. The raw data from the instrument battery comprised 28 magnetic computer tapes, or 12.7 miles of information. The reduction of this mass of minutely specific detail to manageable and analyzable form required far more time and effort than did the analyses that followed.

The location and correction of identification and data errors, along with the decoding of the questionnaire and observation data into manageable form, was a laborious process — but one which was essential to maintain the integrity of the database. Despite efforts to salvage the maximum amount of usable data, missing values still presented formidable problems. These are discussed below.

Three types of data reduction were carried out: across respondent units, across variables, and across time points. For the observation data, all three types of reduction were necessary in many cases. Some variables, such as certain teacher characteristics, required no reduction at all.

## Reduction Across Respondents

Reduction across respondents is essentially a matter of aggregating to various *units of analysis* (i.e., learner or teacher/class). For instance, peer harmony is a construct that is logically defined at the classroom level — one score for each classroom in the sample. One source of data for this construct is the sample of class peers who completed the *Your School Days* questionnaire. Even before the 65 items in this instrument could be reduced to factor scales, it was necessary to reduce the 13,258 peer protocols to 607 class records containing item means.

In most cases, reduction of this type required careful consideration of the number of original respondents available and the assurance of stable composites or scales. Most classroom composites of peer data were restricted to classes of 10 or more peers.

Data from the sociometric instruments, which yielded separate protocols for every child in each class containing a Project PRIME learner, were reduced to records that contained sociometric data for each Project PRIME learner. For the *How I Feel Toward Others* instrument, composites were computed to reflect the peers' collective attitude toward the learner and also the learner's response to the peer group. Composites were computed for each class, reflecting the degree of social attraction among the peers in the class.

Generally, aggregation over respondents preceded aggregation over variables (e.g., *Your School Days*), and aggregation over time for the observation methods preceded other types of aggregation.

## Reduction Across Time Points

Data from the observation systems were routinely aggregated to four levels of analysis:

1. teacher by learner by activity type by instruction type;
2. teacher by learner;
3. learner; and
4. teacher.

This kind of aggregation could not be done in a simple hierarchical fashion, since the time observed varied greatly from one unit to another at each particular level.

If an observation system required the coding of teacher and/or learner behavior every two minutes, each two-minute time segment could be viewed as an "item" from a "questionnaire." From this perspective, reduction across time resembles reduction across variables. The primary difference is that the time observed varies from learner to learner and from teacher to teacher.

For observation systems using continuous real-time coding, time observed is taken into account by computing two types of composite scores: rates and ratios. A *rate* measure is obtained by dividing the frequency of the behavior by the total time observed (e.g., number of cognitive demands made by the teacher divided by the number of hours observed). A *ratio* measure is obtained by dividing the frequency of a subcategory by the frequency of all categories in a logically-coherent set (e.g., the proportion of all demands made by the teacher which were cognitive level demands). Scores of zero on rate measures are meaningful; but for ratio measures where the denominator (all relevant categories) is zero, the measure must be treated as missing data at the aggregate level.

Ratio measures were developed for the observation systems that used time sampling (IBMS and FLACCS). For these systems, counts were made of the number of time segments in which a specific behavior occurred and the total number of time segments. Ratio scores for each level of aggregation were obtained by dividing the time segments in which the behavior was observed by all time segments. If the time segments are brief, these ratio measures will approximate the rate measures from real-time observation.

Average ratings were obtained for certain observation systems (FLACCS and CSD). In these systems, observers provided high-inference ratings of specific class events using a time-sampling procedure. At each level of aggregation, ratings were summed and divided by number of time segments to produce an average rating.

In order to account for varying amounts of time observed, ratings, frequencies, time counts, and time-segment counts must be carried through each level in an aggregation hierarchy. For example, a teacher-level rate must be computed from total frequency and total time observed rather than as an average of rate scores computed at the teacher-by-learner level.

## Reduction Across Variables

Every item on every questionnaire obtained from learners, peers, and teachers could be viewed as a separate variable to be carried into the data analysis process. There are two major reasons for reducing the massive number of individual items to a relatively small number of composite measures prior to analysis: parsimony and reliability.

The developers of the Project PRIME instrument battery deliberately built into each instrument multidimensional and redundant measures of the constructs included. Composite variables could have been formed based on the underlying dimensions considered by the developers in the design of the instruments, but there would be no certainty that the respondents had actually responded to the item content as the developers intended. Furthermore, use of the underlying dimensions as a basis for forming composites would not serve the goal of parsimony: The instruments were too rich in the number of dimensions included.

Thus, it seemed preferable to form composites by isolating homogeneous clusters using an empirical analysis of item response patterns. The resulting scales reflect the constructs of the respondents, which often differed in number and substance from those intended by the developers of the instruments. The empirically-defined scales also possess, by definition, the maximum internal consistency possible. Factor analysis was the procedure chosen for this purpose.

Reliability is the second major reason for reducing item data to composite scales. Even if analysis of individual items or conceptual clusters of items was feasible, each of these measures alone is quite unstable. Each item can be construed as yielding three kinds of variance: (a) *common* — that shared with one or more other items, (b) *unique* — due to the idiosyncratic properties of the item, and (c) *error* — random measurement error. Only the first of these components is of interest, and the factor analytic procedure ensures that the composites formed from the items will contain as much common variance as possible.

To avoid artifacts due to metric and item format, at the initial state of data reduction, composite scales were derived from factor analyses using only item sets from single instruments. In a few instances the data were received in an already reduced, composite form — notably the Metropolitan Achievement Test scores. In some cases, differences in metrics among items or highly negatively related relationships within a set of items precluded meaningful use of factor analysis. Thus, some second-level composites were constructed on a logical basis, particularly in the case of observation measures.

Even after this initial reduction of items to scales, the total number of variables available was unmanageably large and further selection and compositing was carried out, guided by the PRIME taxonomic model, and confirmed whenever possible by empirical analysis. In most cases, a single composite could be defined to represent a construct in the model. Other constructs defied such representation and were treated as variable subdomains (sets), rather than a single dimension. At the highest level of the model, each construct (e.g., learner background) was necessarily a domain.

## Psychometric Considerations

Wherever possible, the reliabilities of the second-level composite variables were assessed, most often by computing an alpha coefficient of internal consistency. External validities of the composite — their ability to differentiate groups or relate to other variables in expected ways — were also computed. This information was used in selecting the second-level variables to carry into the third or construct stage of the reduction process.

Another aspect of the measures was also carefully considered in selecting and modifying many of the scales; namely, their distribution properties, particularly skewness and truncation. A moderately skewed variable is of little concern since the data analysis methods to be used are quite robust against such departures from their assumptions. A severely truncated distribution, however, (e.g., one with 50% zero scores) with a long tail can cause considerable distortion of correlational statistics. In some cases, the metric of a measure was redefined to obtain a more symmetric distribution of scores.

The within-domain analyses reported in Parts II and III required the use of variables scaled in such a way that the original item metric could be recovered to facilitate communication with the reader. In Part IV, where the learner competencies were the criteria for cross-domain analyses, the original scaling was irrelevant. In order to maximize the fit between the data and the assumptions of the statistical methods to be used, all variables at the third level (domain constructs) were subjected to a normalizing transform ($T$ scaling). To avoid problems of missing data at this level, means ($X = 50$) were also substituted. This normalization/standardization was carried out separately within each sample/setting data set.

The final result of the data reduction process was a set of composite measures representing the five domains of the taxonomic model, scaled both in raw-score form and in normalized form suitable for cross-domain analysis. Except for certain descriptive analyses, the same variable list was defined for each sample/setting data set (nonmainstreamed EMR/special self-contained class, mainstreamed EMR/regular class, mainstreamed EMR/resource class, and nonhandicapped/regular class).

# Factor Analytic Techniques

Factor analysis was the principal method of reduction employed to reduce the item level to composites (or scales) and the composite level to constructs. The particular factor-analytic techniques used, namely, image analysis, are discussed because factor-analytic procedures played such an important role in defining the Project PRIME set of variables.

Factor analysis is a technique which clusters items into homogenous subsets that reflect the underlying structure of the items. Composite scores are computed for those subsets, resulting in a new data set consisting of scores on a vastly reduced number of more reliable and more general composite variables.

The factor-analytic procedure used to reduce the Project PRIME instruments and composites was image analysis. In contrast to principal components analysis, which considers both shared and unique variance (variance specific to only one item), image analysis considers only shared variance (variance that two or more items have in common). In image analysis, the principal concern is with replicability of measurement across items; unique item variance is of no interest.

Image analysis (Guttman, 1953; Kaiser, 1963; Veldman, 1967) involves three analytic procedures: (a) the unique variances subtracted from the correlation matrix yield the in-common variance-covariance matrix, (b) the in-common matrix is subjected to a principal components analysis to extract the maximum variance in a set of factors, and (c) a varimax rotation is conducted to redefine sets of variables, maximizing their simple structure.

The final product of the image analysis is a defined factor structure containing an optimal number of uncorrelated factors (item sets). Each factor is comprised of those items from the original item pool that loaded on the factor. The factors form the basis for defining the scales that measure the hypothetical constructs represented by the instrument.

Scales are formed from the factor structure by assigning each item to the factor scale on which it loads most highly; thus, each item is assigned to only one scale. This assignment of items to scales is the basis for computing the scale scores using a unit-weighted scaling procedure.

Unit-weighted scaling, rather than factor-weighted scaling, is used for both theoretical and practical reasons. Theoretically, the image analysis procedure locates sets of items that cluster together; therefore, it is conceptually consistent to consider all items on a scale as equal contributors rather than weighting items based on factor loadings. Practically, unit-weighted scores (a) are easier to compute and adjust for missing data, (b) are less subject to over-fitting effects, (c) provide a closer approximation to an oblique rotation (which permits correlated factors and, hence, is more reflective of real-world relationships), and (d) have been demonstrated empirically to have equally high or higher validity than factor-weighted scores (Dagenais & Marascuillo, 1973; Goldberg, 1972; Veldman & Parker, 1970).

After scale scores have been computed, each unit-weighted factor scale is subjected to a stepwise internal consistency analysis to determine the number of items from the original factor scale to include in the final scale. The first step is the computation of an alpha coefficient of internal consistency for the two items on the scale with the highest factor loadings. A second alpha coefficient is computed based on these two items plus the item with the third highest factor loading. Successive alpha coefficients are computed, each time adding the item with the next highest factor loading, until all the items that loaded on that scale are included. Items are dropped from a scale if they are added to the scale after the peak in the trend of alpha values has occurred. The factor scales are rescored, using the reduced item content as determined by the alpha analysis procedure.

# Problems Related to Missing Data

After the reduction process was complete but before relationship analyses could begin, the vexing problem of missing data had to be considered.

## Reduction Process

One of the major advantages of reducing item data to scale scores is that a value can be estimated even for subjects who fail to answer all items of a particular scale. Provided the subject responded to half the items on the scale, the mean of the items answered by the individual can be substituted for the missing item scores.

## Redefinition of the Sample

Roughly twice as many nonhandicapped learners as EMR mainstreamed learners were tested. Every available protocol was utilized in the construction of scales. For the learner within-domain analyses and the cross-domain analyses, one nonhandicapped learner was selected in each class to correspond to each mainstreamed EMR learner. The subject included had the most complete data record.

## Pairwise Deletion of Cases

Some within-domain analyses were carried out with correlation matrices in which each coefficient was based on those subjects who had valid scores for the pair of variables concerned. The difficulty with this method is that when some of the variable pairs have a very low $N$, the pattern of relationships can become badly distorted and logically inconsistent. Application of some multivariate methods to such matrices was impossible, and other procedures had to be employed to deal with the incomplete data.

## Row-Wise Deletion of Cases

Some analyses, especially those involving relatively few variables, were carried out using only subjects who had valid scores for all variables. The danger with this method is that when the sample size is greatly reduced, not only is the stability of results seriously weakened but also the sample used may not be representative of the original group.

## Priority-Ordered Substitution

Priority-ordered substitution was used for only a few variables deemed to be of crucial importance for which there were appropriate substitution variables. For instance, father's education was chosen as the focal variable for estimating a learner's socioeconomic class. Teachers did provide a direct estimate of family SES, but this turned out to be a 3-point scale at best; father's education was measured by an 11-point scale.

Five other variables, the first four obtained from teacher reports and the fifth from a learner questionnaire, had substantial relationships with father's education:

| Order | Variable | Correlation with Father's Education | Scale Points |
|-------|----------|-------------------------------------|--------------|
| 1 | Mother's education | .85 | 11 |
| 2 | Father's occupation | .69 | 11 |
| 3 | Socioeconomic status | .69 | 3 |
| 4 | Mother's occupation | .56 | 11 |
| 5 | Cognitive affluence of home | .53 | 9 |

The mean of father's education value was computed for each scale point on each of these variables from the available data. The relationships with the two occupation variables were not monotonic, confirming the inadvisability of using them to form a linear composite.

For each learner whose father's education score was missing, the record was scanned in the order indicated until a valid estimator was located. The mean value for the scale-point on that variable was then used as the father's education score. In the total sample, 33% of the cases did not have a father's education score. Application of the substitution procedure reduced this to 9%.

## Substitution of Sample Means

In the cross-domain analyses, the problem of missing data was eliminated by substituting sample means for all missing scores after application of a normalizing transform to all valid data on all variables. Comparison of correlations before and after this substitution revealed very minor changes (never more than 0.05) due to moderate reduction of the variance of some variables.

# Data Analysis

A variety of statistical techniques was applied to explore relationships among variables in each domain and finally across domains, focusing on the 12 learner competencies as criteria.

In the analysis of simple relationships, some of the variables were nominal (categorical) in nature and were studied through the use of bivariate cross-tabulations, using the Pearson product-moment correlation coefficient. Other techniques used were multiple correlation analysis, and analysis of covariance.

## Multiple Correlation Analysis

The basic equation for the general linear model, fundamental to all the multivariate methods used to study relationships among the variables, is:

$$Y = a_0U + a_1X_1 + ''' \ a_kX_k + E$$

Where, $Y$ is the criterion variable to be predicted

$X$ is a predictor variable

$a$ is a weight for the predictor

$U$ is the unit vector[1]

$E$ is an error variable

When the weights have been defined by a mathematical procedure, a predicted $Y$ value may be obtained for each subject in the sample:

$$\hat{Y} = Y - E$$

The weights are so defined as to make the sum of squares of $E$ (over all subjects) as small as possible. The success of this fitting of the weights, the prediction of the criterion by the "X" variables, is expressed as a multiple correlation coefficient which varies between limits of zero and one. The square of this value ($R^2$) may be interpreted directly as the proportion of criterion variance "explained" by, or associated with, the set of predictors. (Readers unfamiliar with the statistical term variance are referred to Mosteller and Moynihan, 1972, pp. 16-19.)

## Analysis of Covariance and Independent Contributions

Two regression equations using the same criterion, in which the predictors in one equation are a subset of those in the other, may be compared for the difference in $R^2$ they produce. This difference is the variance associated uniquely with the variable(s) omitted in the smaller equation. For example, consider these two equations in abbreviated notation:

$$P \leqslant A + S$$
$$P \leqslant A$$

Where, $P$ is a performance value
$A$ is an ability value
$S$ is a value representing the sex of the person

The $R^2$ for the first equation must equal or exceed that of the second, since it contains more potentially predictive information. The difference between the two $R^2$ values is sometimes called the "independent contribution" or the "unique contribution" of the variable(s) omitted in the smaller equation. When the omitted variable(s) represent group membership, the term "analysis of covariance," in its usual meaning, is appropriate. In the example above, the $R^2$ difference represents sex differences in performance with ability "held constant" — statistically controlled.

## Commonality Analysis[2]

This technique extends the comparison of regression models beyond the calculation of the independent contribution of each predictor variable. Almost invariably, the sum of the independent contributions of all predictors is less than the $R^2$ obtained from all. When the predictors are substantially intercorrelated, the amount of non-unique variance may be greater than any or even all of the unique variances together. The diagram in Figure 3-1 exemplifies this phenomenon.

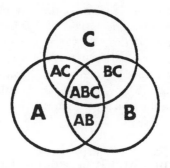

**Figure 3–1**

This is the simplest possible example of a commonality analysis. Diagrams of this sort lead to language suggesting that the predictor variances can be "mapped" onto the variance of the criterion to identify the largest unique and overlapping "areas."

Circle C represents the total variance of the criterion, while Circles A and B represent the total variances of the two predictor variables. The fact that the circles overlap — share variance — indicates that they are correlated, with the amount of overlap reflecting the degree of correlation. The areas labelled with single letters represent unshared variance; e.g., area "C" is criterion variance unpredictable from "A" and "B." The $R$ for A and B against C is reflected by the relative sizes of C and (AC + BC + ABC). Areas AC and BC represent the independent contributions of the two predictors. Area ABC is called a "joint contribution" of the predictors; it is variance shared by the predictors which is also related to the criterion.

Commonality analysis identifies the proportion of criterion variance associated with every unique *and* joint source. Interpretation of the joint contributions remains a challenge to the investigator's ingenuity (or imagination) but at least all the effects are made explicit in an unambiguous metric.

**Computational Process**

Proportions of variance for the unique and joint effects are computed from the $R^2$ values obtained from a series of multiple regression equations. Consider the following three-predictor example, in which $U$ represents a unique contribution and $J$ represents a joint contribution, with subscripts to indicate the sources.

$$U_A = R^2_{ABC} - R^2_{BC}$$

$$U_B = R^2_{ABC} - R^2_{AC}$$

$$U_C = R^2_{ABC} - R^2_{AB}$$

$$J_{AB} = R^2_{ABC} - R^2_C - U_A - U_B$$

$$J_{AC} = R^2_{ABC} - R^2_B - U_A - U_C$$

$$J_{BC} = R^2_{ABC} - R^2_A - U_B - U_C$$

$$J_{ABC} = R^2_{ABC} - J_{AB} - J_{AC} - J_{BC} - U_A - U_B - U_C$$

The unique contributions can be tested for statistical significance, but the joint contributions cannot.

## Sets of Variables as Sources

The logic of commonality analysis does not restrict its applications to the use of single variables as sources of the effects. A source may be defined by inclusion or exclusion of a *set* of predictors in the regression equations. This permits nominal variables such as ethnic group to be studied along with other nominal and/or continuous variables. Each of the categories of a nominal variable is represented in the equation by a separate binary variable, and the entire set is either kept or omitted together. By this method, domains of predictors may be treated as multivariate sources.

**Negative Joint Contributions:** Inconsistencies among the correlations of predictors with each other and with the criterion can lead to computation of negative shared (joint) variance. When this occurs, the unique $R^2$ of a predictor will be larger than its total $R^2$. This indicates that a suppressor effect is operating and that the unique $R^2$ may be overestimated. In simple equations, the causes of such phenomena can sometimes be determined by examining the pattern of the intercorrelations of the variables; in multivariate data sets, identification of suppressor effects is much more difficult and was not attempted.

**Differential Inflation of $R^2$:** Any multiple correlation coefficient is inflated to some extent, compared to the "true" or population value being estimated from a finite sample. The smaller the sample and the larger the number of predictors, the greater the inflation of $R^2$.

When comparing equations using the same model but based on different sample sizes, the $R^2$s may not be comparable because of the differences in sample size. This is a particular concern when the ratio of subjects to variables is low.

When sets of variables representing different domains are used in a commonality analysis and the numbers of variables per domain are grossly unequal, the "larger" domains will yield more inflated estimates of their contributions to prediction of the criterion than will the "smaller" ones. The severity of this problem was alleviated by generating random variates and adding them to the small domains to make all domains equal in size. This process notably increases the $R^2$ of the sets containing the random variates.

Two methods of correcting for this differential inflation were used with the Project PRIME data to guard against misinterpretation of the results of the final cross-domain commonality analysis. The first method involved the reduction of larger domains by the application of principal-components analysis and the computation of factor scores as "variance-carrying vehicles." A second method was to apply a shrinkage formula (Kerlinger & Pedhazur, 1973; Nunnally, 1967) to each of the $R^2$s.

## Application to Project Prime Data

Commonality analysis was the major analytic technique used to assess the relationships within the Project PRIME database. Use of this method was predicated on two beliefs: First, that the predictive variables within and between domains would be substantially intercorrelated and hence would potentially share predictive variance and, second, that identification of that shared variance was preferable to ascribing it to one or the other of the predictors through an ordered regression procedure.

In presenting data from the commonality analyses, the total $R^2$ for the full model is provided. This total $R^2$ represents the amount of variance in a dependent measure that was accounted for by all its predictor sets together. Next shown is the total $R^2$ and unique $R^2$ for each predictor set. The unique $R^2$ represents the amount of variance accounted for by a predictor set after the effects of all other predictor sets have been subtracted. The total $R^2$ of a predictor set represents the unique $R^2$ of a predictor set plus all joint contributions made by that set and any other set. The total $R^2$ of a multivariate predictor set is equal to the square of its multiple correlation with the dependent measure; for single-variable predictor sets, the total $R^2$ is equal to the squared bivariate correlation between the predictor and the dependent variable. The algebraic sum of all unique and shared $R^2$s is equal to the total

$R^2$ for the full model. The sum of the total $R^2$s of the predictor sets is not a meaningful number.

As a guard against examining chance relationships, interpretation of the commonality analysis results was sequential. First, only equations in which the full model $R^2$ was significant were examined further. Second, from those significant equations only predictor sets with significant total or unique $R^2$s were examined further. Third, only subsets of the significant predictor sets were examined further. Finally, for those significant predictor sets or subsets, bivariate correlations between variables within the set or subset and the criterion were examined. Thus, in order for a bivariate correlation to be examined, the subset and/or set to which it belonged had to be a significant predictor. This filtering process reduced the number of bivariate correlations examined and hopefully avoided consideration of chance relationships.

## Cluster (Profile) Analysis

Cluster (profile) analysis of the Project PRIME data addresses questions of a different nature. The scores of each learner in a particular domain, such as learner competence, may be viewed as a descriptive profile. Learner profiles will be more or less similar to each other. This leads directly to the notion of types of learners — groups whose profiles are most homogeneous within groups and heterogeneous between groups.

The particular clustering algorithm used with the Project PRIME data is called "hierarchical grouping" (Veldman, 1967). It begins with $N$ one-person "groups," and in a stepwise fashion combines them a pair at a time, at each step choosing the combination which results in the smallest possible increase in within-group variance. There is no way of defining the "right" number of groups, but the increases in within-group variance at each step can be examined to locate a combination that consists of particularly dissimilar profiles.

Once a decision has been made regarding the most interesting number of profiles, the mean of each group on each of the variables in the profile can be determined, and these profiles of group means can be used to describe the types of learners that have been identified. Means may also be computed using variables *not* included in the profile, and analysis of variance can be used to test the significance of group differences.

The logic of profile typing permits identification of both environmental and learner types. Using simple bivariate cross-tabulations, we can determine the extent to which particular types of learners are found in particular types of environments.

## Cautions Regarding Inference

The purposes and limitations of the design of the study must be clearly understood if the reader is to avoid unjustified inferences from, or criticism of, the results to be reported in this book.

Project PRIME was a descriptive/correlational study of mainstreaming as it was implemented in the State of Texas in 1971-72. Strictly speaking, inferences beyond that year and that locale to other times, places, and manners of implementation are questionable to an unknown degree. Undoubtedly, many, if not most, of the major findings could be replicated elsewhere, but we can only speculate about which of them have such generality. In general, the interpretations have been guided by the following considerations: the size of a relationship and/or the order of magnitude of a difference; the extent to which a finding is supported by other findings within the Project PRIME database (internal consistency) and by previous research or educational theory (external validity); the extent to which several findings form a logical, consistent pattern (nomological network strength); and the absence of strong alternative interpretations (e.g., methodological artifacts) that "explain away" a finding. However, there are many sources of error of potential importance that must be considered; some are identified here.

### Tests of Statistical Significance

Tests of significance for correlations and mean differences involve a variety of rather stringent assumptions. Some of them can be violated with only minor consequences, while others are critical. Statistical tests were used in the data analysis primarily as guides to select the most vivid effects rather than as a basis for justifying inferences.

In addition, many, many analyses were computed; five percent of them will be statistically significant by chance. Which five percent? Degrees of freedom are inflated in most analyses for subtle reasons such as substitution of means for missing data, the use of higher-order aggregates, and the lack of independence in the unit of analysis. The reader is encouraged to suspend the kind of critical attitude which would be appropriate regarding an analysis of experimental data. Project PRIME was not an experiment; it was a descriptive/correlational study of mainstreaming during one year in one large, geographically diverse state.

## Interpretation of Relationships

Drawing sound conclusions about the relative importance of a series of relationships is much more difficult than it appears at first glance. Generally, there is more faith in the argument for the presence of a relationship if the coefficient is strong than in the argument for a lack of relationship if the coefficient is weak. There are more reasons why a strong relationship might be masked (e.g., low variable reliability, sample restriction) than a weak relationship inflated. Hence, the inclination is to believe that only some of the weak relationships presented represent valid findings. All kinds of distortion are possible; and for every pairing of variables, the direction and degree of bias may be different.

Even if one assumes a true relationship exists, interpretation of such a relationship is far from straightforward. Two variables may be related because: (a) one causes the other, (b) both are caused by another variable, measured or not, (c) random sampling error exists, or (d) the sample was not randomly selected. It is this last possibility which is particularly troublesome in a descriptive survey study such as Project PRIME. Students are not randomly assigned to public schools or even classrooms within schools. Pupils and environmental characteristics may be associated only because of selective assignment.

## Comparability of Relationships

Comparability of relationships is another interpretation concern. We have already discussed how different numbers of variables in predictor sets can affect the comparability of the predictive power of the sets. Differences in the adequacy with which constructs are represented by the variables chosen and the psychometric properties of the variables, especially the variance, also make comparisons of relationships difficult. Differences in the numbers of learners or classes in what are otherwise comparable equations can create artifactual comparative findings.

## Nonrandom Sampling

This is the most crucial feature of the Project PRIME database with regard to reaching firm conclusions. It is probable that the sample studied may not be typical of school children generally, particularly in terms of ethnic group, social class, or school district characteristics. More important is the fact that EMR learners were almost certainly not randomly assigned to teachers or the varieties of mainstreaming practices. Such assortative mating of the children with environments makes causal inference virtually impossible.

Statistical control of variables artificially tied together by the vagaries of real-world nonrandomness is possible to a limited degree only. Identification of a large joint contribution in a commonality analysis tells us nothing about what the picture might have been using sampling methods that prevent such tied variance. However, it does locate the problem and suggest a fruitful target for further research.

## Change Over Time

No variable in the final set chosen for analysis was measured more than once. Inferences about *change* in these children are completely unwarranted. What happened to these children during the course of the year cannot be determined any more than what happened the year before or the year after data collection. Project PRIME took *one* very detailed look at nonhandicapped and EMR learners, their background, competence, and educational environment. The relationships among these aspects of their educational process is what is presented in this book.

## Technical Notes

1. $a_0U$ serves to equate the mean of Y and $\hat{Y}$.

2. Commonality analysis was used basically as a heuristic device to present the common and unique elements in the variance for each domain and to relate these elements to other variable sets. No claim is made as to causal relationships from this analytic strategy. The segregation of variance into common and unique elements is a worthy goal, but the commonality analysis procedures used may not achieve the orthogonality of the elements of the variance required to achieve that goal.

# Part II

# 4
# Learner Background Characteristics

Chapter 1 emphasized that competence is a function of learners and their environments. This chapter describes the background characteristics of the elementary school-age learners in the three samples: mainstreamed and nonmainstreamed educable mentally retarded (EMR) learners and nonhandicapped learner classmates of the mainstreamed EMR learners. Background characteristics and the representativeness of the three learner samples are important for the generalizability of the Project PRIME results.

In addition, three issues related to mainstreaming practices are considered. The first of these concerns the chronological age of EMR learners in relation to their peers. A placement consideration is whether EMR learners should be placed with chronological agemates or younger students whose cognitive development is presumably more equivalent to that of the EMR learner. Iano (1972) discussed problems with either placement and suggested ungraded or cross-grade classes as a third alternative. The other two issues address temporal integration; that is, the amount of time EMR learners spend in regular classes. Temporal integration is the primary distinction between the two groups of EMR learners. MacMillan and Semmel (1977) suggest that temporal integration serves as a necessary criterion in identifying mainstreaming programs. Within "mainstreaming" or "nonmainstreaming" programs, however, learners can spend varying amounts of time

75

in regular classes and be integrated for various academic and nonacademic subjects. The second and third issues examine the extent and nature of the actual integration experienced by the learners in this study and explore factors related to temporal integration.

Questions:
1. With whom were the mainstreamed EMR learners in this study placed? What were the age characteristics of their peers?
2. What were the integration patterns of the EMR learners in this study? What was the amount of time they were integrated and what was the content of the activities for which they were integrated?
3. What were the characteristics of the EMR learners associated with the extent and nature of their integration into regular classrooms?

## The Learner Background Model

The model used to organize the learner background characteristics included three learner background domains: individual, family/home, and school (Figure 4-1). Extensive previous research indicates a strong relationship between children's school functioning and individual and family/home characteristics. The meaning of such relationships, however, is not always apparent. One possibility is that individuals are socially stratified on the basis of their background characteristics and, as a result, tend to have different life experiences. These potential differences in experiences would undoubtedly account for much of the variation in school functioning attributed to individual and family/home variables.

The third domain, school experience, was included because the previous school experiences of children labelled EMR and the special education services provided by their school systems are important in describing the sample. School background measures reflected the EMR learner's current school experiences in terms of integration and past school experiences, especially past placement decisions.

## Description of Learner Background

### Individual Background Characteristics: Age, IQ, Sex

Chronological age provides an index of the learner's level of cognitive and social development as well as the accrual of learning experiences. IQ provides

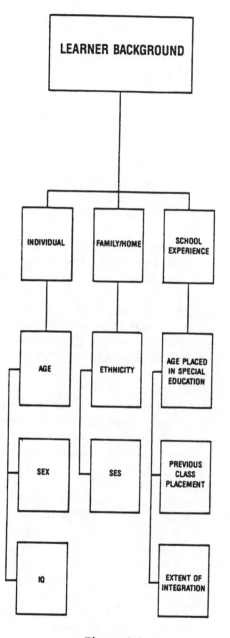

Figure 4–1
Learner Background
(Project PRIME Taxonomic Model)

an estimate of cognitive development and, for EMR learners, the severity of cognitive impairment.

Sex differences related to schooling suggest that males and females often have quite different social experiences in the classroom. Musgrove (1971) examined variations in Stanford Achievement Test scores for second graders and reported that females outperformed males on all subtests. Teachers have been found to have well-defined sex-role expectations of their students and to be biased in favor of behaviors traditionally associated with the female role (Fagot & Patterson, 1969; Feshbach, 1969). Jackson and Lahaderne (1967) found that over 80% of teachers' prohibitory responses were directed toward males. Good and Brophy (1972) reported that teachers tend to be more positive and reinforcing to low-achieving females than low-achieving males. Gender appears to be associated with different social experiences in a classroom.

Information was obtained for the three individual background variables for each learner group from the *Selected Children's Background Questionnaire* (SCBQ), completed by the teachers who participated in the study.[1] Because IQ data were furnished by the schools participating in the study, the learners were tested at different times and with different instruments. Two-thirds or more of the learners in each group, however, were tested during the study year or within the prior 18 months. About 96% of the self-contained special class learners and 73% of the mainstreamed EMR learners were tested with one of three individual intelligence tests: the WISC, the WPPSI, or the Stanford-Binet. Correlations between scores on these individual intelligence tests approximate $r = 0.80$ (Nunnally, 1959, p. 191). California Mental Maturity Scale group intelligence test scores were available for approximately 56% of the nonhandicapped learners. Other group tests commonly administered to the nonhandicapped learners were the Otis/Lennon and the Primary Mental Abilities instruments.[2]

## Age

Table 4-1 presents the mean ages for the three learner groups. The learners ranged in age from 8-15 years. Figure 4-2 presents a summary of the age distributions for the three learner groups in the study. The age means for the mainstreamed EMR and the nonmainstreamed EMR learners were comparable with the mean age for the nonhandicapped learners, approximately one year lower. The difference between mean ages for the EMR and nonhandicapped groups is largely attributable to the relatively greater number of EMR learners who were 11 years old or older. As can be seen in Table 4-1, the age distribution for the nonhandicapped learner group increased from age 8 to a mode at age 10 and then declined in frequency in the 11- and 12-year-old categories. By contrast, the distribution for both EMR groups was markedly skewed, with increasing frequencies from age 8-12+ years.

## Table 4-1
### Background Characteristics: Age, Gender, and IQ by Type of Setting

| Individual Background Characteristics | Type of Learner | | | | | | | | | | | |
|---|---|---|---|---|---|---|---|---|---|---|---|---|
| | Nonhandicapped | | | | Mainstreamed EMR | | | | Nonmainstreamed EMR | | | |
| | X | SD | % | N | X | SD | % | N | X | SD | % | N |
| Age | 9.7 | 1.1 | | 325 | 10.8 | 1.3 | | 330 | 10.9 | 1.3 | | 232 |
| 8 | | | 15 | | | | 2 | | | | 4 | |
| 9 | | | 26 | | | | 16 | | | | 10 | |
| 10 | | | 32 | | | | 23 | | | | 20 | |
| 11 | | | 22 | | | | 29 | | | | 30 | |
| 12+ | | | 5 | | | | 31 | | | | 35 | |
| IQ | 94.7 | 14.5 | | 165 | 68.2 | 10.4 | | 258 | 66.2 | 8.5 | | 223 |
| Sex Male | | | 53 | 356 | | | 60 | 356 | | | 65 | 273 |

79

Table 4-2 presents the mean ages of the nonhandicapped and mainstreamed EMR learners at each grade level. The one-year difference found between the mainstreamed and nonhandicapped learners was maintained at each of the three grade levels.

## IQ

The mean IQ scores for the three groups are presented in Table 4-1. The mean IQ score for the mainstreamed EMR learners (68.2) was not substantially different from that for the nonmainstreamed EMR learners (66.2). In both instances the mean IQ scores are only slightly less than two standard deviations below normal — the upper bounds of the EMR classification according to the Texas definition.

The mean IQ score for the nonhandicapped learners was 94.7. Further analyses showed that the average IQ of the nonhandicapped learners declined somewhat with age. The mean IQ of the nonhandicapped learners less than 8.5 years of age was 102, whereas the mean IQ of those older than 10.5 was 90. A second placement trend may have been operative in the schools in this study — that of placing older EMR students with lower-ability nonhandicapped peers, though these peers would be considered average in terms of IQ.

Both EMR learner groups in this study represented relatively higher-functioning EMR learners. This suggests that some caution should be used in generalizing the findings of the PRIME study to other EMR populations.

Table 4-2
Mean Chronological Ages of Nonhandicapped and
Mainstreamed EMR Learners by Grade Level

| Grade | Type of Learner | |
| | Nonhandicapped (N = 325) | Mainstreamed EMR (N = 330) |
| --- | --- | --- |
| Third grade | | |
| X̄ | 8.6 | 9.7 |
| SD | 0.7 | 1.0 |
| Fourth grade | | |
| X̄ | 9.7 | 11.0 |
| SD | 0.7 | 1.1 |
| Fifth grade | | |
| X̄ | 10.6 | 11.7 |
| SD | 0.6 | 0.8 |

## Sex

As shown in Table 4-1, 60% of the mainstreamed EMR learners, 65% of the nonmainstreamed EMR learners, and 53% of the nonhandicapped learners were males. Hence, the distribution of males in the EMR groups was from 7-12% greater than in the nonhandicapped learner group. These results are consistent with demographic data on sex distributions reported previously in the mental retardation literature (MacMillan, 1977). Robinson and Robinson (1976) reported that almost all studies dealing with abnormalities among children reveal a higher incidence in males than females.

## Family/Home Background Characteristics

Ethnicity and socioeconomic status (SES) defined family/home background characteristics.[3]

## Ethnicity

Table 4-3 presents the distribution of ethnicity for each of the three learner groups. All three groups showed a higher proportion of Spanish-surnamed and Black learners than would be predicted from national or state estimates of the prevalence of these "minority" groups in the school-age population. A review of census data from the State of Texas (Office of the Governor, 1972), based on a 20% sample of the state, indicated that the ethnic group distribution for elementary school children in 1970, the year prior to the study, was about 61% Anglo, 24% Spanish surnamed, and 15% Black. In this study, 41% of the nonhandicapped learners were Spanish surnamed, 19% were Black, and 40% were Anglo. There were slightly more Spanish surnamed, more Black, and many less Anglo learners in the mainstreamed group than in the nonhandicapped group: 48% Spanish surnamed, 30% Black, and 22% Anglo.

The proportion of Spanish-surnamed learners increased as a function of increasing age in both the mainstreamed EMR and nonhandicapped groups. Spanish-surnamed learners were in the majority among the older learners of these groups. The proportion of Black learners decreased within the mainstreamed EMR group as a function of increasing age. Close to half the younger (8-10 years of age) mainstreamed EMR learners were Black, but less than a fourth of the older mainstreamed learners were Black. By contrast, Black learners were represented in approximately equal proportions (17-21%) at all age levels within the nonhandicapped learner group. The proportion of Anglo nonhandicapped learners declined from a majority at ages 8 and 9 to only 21% at the highest age level.

The nonmainstreamed EMR learners were divided almost equally among the three ethnic groups; with 36% Anglo, 34% Spanish surnamed, and 31% Black learners. This reflects the ethnic stratification procedure used to select the nonmainstreamed EMR learner sample (see Appendix A). Thus, the nonmainstreamed EMR learner group contained a greater proportion of Anglo learners and a smaller proportion of Spanish-surnamed learners than did the mainstreamed EMR learner group. No particular relationship was found between ethnicity and age within the nonmainstreamed EMR groups.

Table 4–3
Family/Home Background Characteristics

| Family/Home Background Characteristics | Type of Learner | | | | | |
| --- | --- | --- | --- | --- | --- | --- |
| | Nonhandicapped | | Mainstreamed EMR | | Nonmainstreamed EMR | |
| | % | N | % | N | % | N |
| Ethnicity | | 338 | | 349 | | 269 |
| Anglo | 40.0 | | 22.0 | | 36.0 | |
| Black | 19.0 | | 30.0 | | 31.0 | |
| Spanish-surnamed | 41.0 | | 48.0 | | 34.0 | |
| SES: Father's education | | 348 | | 348 | | 267 |
| Level 1: Some grade school to completed grade school | 24.1 | | 42.5 | | 36.7 | |
| Level 2: Some junior high to completed junior high | 14.9 | | 22.6 | | 20.3 | |
| Level 3: Some high school to completed high school | 43.5 | | 27.6 | | 32.2 | |
| Level 4: Some higher education | 17.5 | | 7.3 | | 10.8 | |
| SES: Family intactness | | 330 | | 320 | | 241 |
| Intact home | 79.7 | | 66.6 | | 68.0 | |
| Nonintact home | 20.3 | | 33.4 | | 32.0 | |

## Socioeconomic Status

**Father's Education:** Information about learners' family/home background characteristics was provided by teachers on the SCBQ instrument. Parents' educational level has been found to be a relevant predictor of children's school functioning (Coleman et al., 1966). Armor's (1972) reanalysis of the Coleman data led him to conclude that parents' education was one of the strongest predictors of achievement across various groups.

For descriptive purposes, the father's education was stratified into four levels (Level 1 representing the lowest level of education).[4] Table 4-3 indicates that fathers of the nonhandicapped learners tended to be more highly educated than fathers of the learners in either of the EMR groups.

The mainstreamed EMR learners' fathers tended to be somewhat less educated than the fathers of the nonmainstreamed EMR learners — approximately 35% of the fathers of the mainstreamed EMR learners achieved levels of education including at least some high school whereas 43% of the fathers of nonmainstreamed EMR learners had achieved comparable levels. Further analyses of the data suggested that the differences in father's education between nonhandicapped and EMR learners stemmed primarily from the lower educational levels attained by the fathers of the Anglo and Black learners in the EMR groups. Only slight differences were found among the fathers of the Spanish-surnamed learners in the three groups.

Even the fathers of the nonhandicapped learners were not quite as well educated as 1970 Texas Census data (Office of the Governor, 1972) suggest was typical of the Texas population. The census data revealed that 70% of Texas adults were at one of the two higher education levels. Whereas among the Project PRIME nonhandicapped learners, 61% of the learners' fathers had attained one of these levels. The data are not strictly comparable, however, since the census data were based on a 20% sample of males and females over 25 years old, whereas the PRIME sample consisted only of males who were parents of third-, fourth-, or fifth-grade children. The census data probably underestimates the average educational level of males in the state since it include females as well as males, and higher education has not traditionally been considered as essential for females as for males.

The relatively high proportions of minority group members in the Project PRIME samples may partially explain the somewhat lower than average educational attainment of the learners' fathers, since minority group members have traditionally completed fewer numbers of years of formal education. Across all three groups, greater proportions of fathers of Anglo learners had achieved higher educational levels than fathers of Black learners who, in turn, had relatively higher reported levels of education than the fathers of Spanish-surnamed learners.

Not surprisingly, nonhandicapped learners with fathers with higher educational status had higher IQ scores. A smaller proportion of the older nonhandicapped learners had fathers who had attended secondary school or beyond; a corollary, no doubt, of the larger proportion of the older nonhandicapped learners who were Spanish surnamed.

**Family Intactness:** Family intactness was a second index of the social and economic climate of the home. Family breakdown tends to have a dysfunctional effect upon a child's performance in school (McCord, McCord, & Thurber, 1962). Mayeske et al. (1972) reported that children who benefitted most from schooling have both parents in the home.

The learners in each of the two EMR groups were more likely to come from single-parent homes than were the nonhandicapped learners (Table 4-3). Thirty-two percent of the nonmainstreamed EMR learners and 33% of the mainstreamed EMR learners were living with one parent, usually the mother. In contrast, only 20% of the nonhandicapped learners were living with a single parent. A higher proportion of Black learners came from single-parent homes than Anglo or Spanish-surnamed learners. However, more EMR learners than nonhandicapped learners came from single-parent homes in all ethnic groups.

## Discussion

To the degree that father's education and family intactness measure socioeconomic status, a higher proportion of the EMR learners than nonhandicapped learners in this study came from a low socioeconomic background. This finding is hardly surprising since the cultural-familial link between low socioeconomic status and mild mental retardation is well established (Robinson & Robinson, 1976).

The high proportion of minority group learners in this study compared with state and national averages raises some questions concerning the generalizability of the results. Particularly troublesome is the confounding of age and ethnic background for the nonhandicapped and mainstreamed EMR learner groups, as indicated by the high proportion of Spanish-surnamed learners in the older age groups. This is further complicated by the fact that, among nonhandicapped learners, the proportion of older Spanish-surnamed learners increased while the proportion of older Anglo learners decreased. Among the mainstreamed EMR learners, a similar increase of older Spanish-surnamed learners with age was accompanied by a decrease in the proportion of older Black learners. Also, nonhandicapped learners' age and IQ were confounded with father's education. Thus, the age, IQ, ethnic groups and father education interactions require care when making comparisons between learner groups and when attributing predictive effects to either the age or ethnic group variables.

Because the nonhandicapped learners were randomly selected from the classes of the mainstreamed EMR learners, the ethnic distributions for the two groups could be expected to be similar. Thus it is somewhat surprising to observe a higher proportion of Blacks and a slightly higher proportion of Spanish-surnamed learners among the mainstreamed EMR group. The reader is reminded that one impetus toward mainstreaming was to rectify the charge that minority group children were disproportionately labelled EMR learners and placed in special education classes. These data suggest that the mainstreamed EMR learner group may indeed have had a disproportionate number of minority group children. This, however, does not necessarily imply that some of the minority group learners were erroneously classified. Both socioeconomic measures used in this study showed more minority group learners to come from lower socioeconomic backgrounds. Thus, in this study, ethnic background factors are inextricably linked with lower socioeconomic factors, the latter being classically associated with cultural-familial retardation (Robinson & Robinson, 1976).

## School Experience

Three aspects of the school experiences of the EMR learners were considered for school background: the age the learner was first placed in special education; the classroom placement of the learner in the previous year, whether in regular or special education; and the extent to which the learner was integrated in the regular class in terms of size and subject matter.[5]

### Age Placed in Special Education

Age placed in special education indicates how early in schooling an EMR learner's special needs were identified and special services provided. Earlier placement may indicate several things. For some learners, earlier placement may indicate a more generalized or more severe impairment in level of functioning, resulting in earlier diagnosis and placement. Early placement may also indicate a level of activism on the part of the parents in seeking services for their child.

As can be seen in Table 4-4, 32% of the mainstreamed and 36% of the nonmainstreamed EMR learners were identified at ages 6-7. The majority of the mainstreamed (64%) and nonmainstreamed EMR learners (60%) received special education services no later than their eighth year (approximately third

Table 4-4

School Experience of Each Learner Group

| School Experience Measure | Nonhandicapped | | | | Type of Learner Mainstreamed EMR | | | | Nonmainstreamed EMR | | | |
|---|---|---|---|---|---|---|---|---|---|---|---|---|
| | X | SD | % | N | X | SD | % | N | X | SD | % | |
| Age placed in special education | | | | | | | | 290 | | | | |
| 6-7 | | | | | | | 32.1 | | | | 36.2 | |
| 8 | | | | | | | 31.7 | | | | 23.8 | |
| 9 | | | | | | | 20.0 | | | | 21.7 | |
| 10 | | | | | | | 16.2 | | | | 18.3 | |
| Previous class placement | | | | | | | | 306 | | | | |
| Special education all day | | | | | | | 37.6 | | | | 73.2 | |
| Special education and nonacademic regular | | | | | | | 2.9 | | | | 10.9 | |
| Special education and academic regular | | | | | | | 15.7 | | | | 11.3 | |
| Regular and some special education | | | | | | | 41.5 | | | | 2.1 | |
| Regular education all day | | | | | | | 2.3 | | | | 2.5 | |
| Extent of integration | | | | | | | | | | | | |
| Percentage of time integrated | | | | | 72.1 | 17.5 | | 318 | 31.7 | 28.3 | | |
| Percentage of time integrated for academics | | | | | 61.1 | 24.0 | | 321 | 25.9 | 18.3 | | |
| Percentage of learners integrated for content areas | | | | | | | | 321 | | | | |
| Reading | | | | | | | 54.0 | | | | | |
| Math | | | | | | | 60.0 | | | | | |
| Language arts and spelling | | | | | | | 75.0 | | | | | |
| Science and social studies | | | | | | | 91.0 | | | | | |

Percentage of content
area time spent in
regular class

| | Mean | SD | | | | N |
|---|---|---|---|---|---|---|
| Reading | 72.9 | 25.6 | | | | 168 |
| Math | 79.8 | 24.2 | | | | 192 |
| Language arts and spelling | 77.5 | 23.3 | | | | 227 |
| Science of social studies | 95.7 | 11.1 | | | | 259 |
| | | | | | | 356 |

Percentage of time
in content areas[a]

| | Mean | SD | Mean | Mean | SD | |
|---|---|---|---|---|---|---|
| Reading | 14.2 | 13.0 | 15.2 | 19.2 | 14.9 | |
| Math | 19.1 | 16.4 | 17.5 | 15.4 | 12.6 | |
| Language arts and spelling | 27.4 | 16.2 | 26.1 | 23.9 | 14.9 | |
| Science or social studies | 20.9 | 20.3 | 17.3 | 7.4 | 13.8 | |
| Other | 18.4 | 12.2 | 25.1 | 34.1 | 18.2 | |
| | 356 | | 356 | 273 | | |

[a] Mean scores for mainstreamed EMR learners were computed from observation data obtained in the regular class and in the resource class. The weight aggregation computation procedures did not permit computation of standard deviations scores for this group.

grade). There were no indications the nonmainstreamed EMR learners had been identified and placed any earlier than the mainstreamed EMR learners. There is evidence, however, that Anglo EMR learners in both groups tended to be identified and placed earlier than Black or Spanish-surnamed EMR learners. As can be seen in Table 4-5, among the mainstreamed EMR learner group, 78% of the Anglo learners were placed in special education between the ages of 6 and 8 years, while only 65% of the Black learners and 53% of the Spanish-surnamed learners were placed at these ages. Within the nonmainstreamed EMR learner group, 71% of the Anglo learners, 43% of the Black learners, and 65% of the Spanish-surnamed learners began receiving services between the ages of 6 and 8.

Nonmainstreamed EMR learners from higher SES backgrounds, as indicated by father's education, tended to be identified and placed at an earlier age.

## Previous Class Placement

School placement history of the EMR learners in regular or special education is of interest. Critics of special classes have charged that labelling and placement in special classes may well be perceived by children as rejection and failure in the school environment (Dunn, 1968). Earlier identification and placement, then, might indicate a longer history of feelings of rejection and early-and-serious school failure. MacMillan, Jones, and Aloia (1974), however, point out that the effects of labelling and placement on the self-concepts of handicapped children have not been empirically demonstrated and are simply the subject of speculation.

Information on these variables was provided by teachers' responses to the Selected Children's Background Questionnaire. The EMR learners' previous class placement ranged from:

1. assigned to special education class all day,
2. assigned to special education class and attended nonacademic regular class,
3. assigned to special education class and attended some academic and nonacademic regular classes,
4. assigned to regular class and attended special education class (i.e., resource room), or
5. assigned to regular class all day.

Only 38% of the mainstreamed EMR learners were in full-time special education programs during the year prior to this study (Table 4-4), whereas 73% of the nonmainstreamed EMR learners were in full-time special education programs. Mainstreamed EMR learners (42%) tended to be in regular programs during the previous year, receiving some special education services. An additional 16% of this group were placed in special education classes but attended regular classes for some academic instruction. The mainstreamed EMR learners in this study had tended to interact with nonhandicapped learners in the year prior to the study.

## Extent of Integration

Prior to the emphasis on mainstreaming, EMR learners in special self-contained classes were occasionally placed with nonhandicapped students for nonacademic activities such as music, art, or physical education. EMR learners who were generally well behaved and had reasonable academic skills were placed in regular classes for particular science or social studies projects only when the regular and special education teachers both agreed that the EMR learner would benefit and other students would not be distracted or delayed.

In mainstreaming programs, however, EMR learners are expected not only to receive instruction with nonhandicapped students for considerably longer periods of time but also in varied subject areas. The focus shifts from spending most of the school day in a special class with occasional participation in the regular program to being instructed most of the day in the regular class while receiving remedial or supplemental instruction in a special education resource class setting.

Time spent in regular grades or temporal integration has been identified as a critical element of mainstreaming programs (Kaufman et al., 1975; MacMillan & Semmel, 1977). The amount of time EMR learners spend in regular classes and the subject or content areas for which they are integrated can vary considerably. Frequently, these decisions are made on the basis of

**Table 4-5**
**Percentage of Mainstreamed and Nonmainstreamed EMR Learners
of Each Ethnic Group Placed in Special Education at Various Ages**

| Age placed in special education | Type of Learner | | | | | |
| | Mainstreamed EMR | | | Nonmainstreamed EMR | | |
| | Anglo (N=60) | Black (N=91) | Spanish-surnamed (N=139) | Anglo (N=88) | Black (N=72) | Spanish-surnamed (N=74) |
|---|---|---|---|---|---|---|
| 6-7 | 36 | 36 | 24 | 49 | 22 | 35 |
| 8 | 42 | 29 | 29 | 22 | 21 | 30 |
| 9 | 8 | 24 | 22 | 17 | 25 | 23 |
| 10 or older | 12 | 11 | 22 | 12 | 32 | 12 |

subject matter or instructional content: The student might be assigned to the resource class for reading and/or mathematics instruction but receive instruction in all other subjects in the regular class.

*Percentage of total integration* indicates the proportion of the school day the EMR learner typically spent in regular classes for academic as well as nonacademic activities. *Percentage of academic integration,* on the other hand, reflects the EMR learner's degree of academic involvement in regular classes. This score was created by dividing the number of hours integrated for academic activities by the number of hours spent in academic activities in all settings. These data were obtained from observer reports in the *Classroom Status Data* (CSD) system.

The mainstreamed EMR learners by definition spent more time in regular classes than did the nonmainstreamed EMR learners. The mean percentage of integrated time was 72.1% for the mainstreamed EMR group and 31.7% for the nonmainstreamed EMR group. The relatively large standard deviations suggest a great deal of variance in the amount of time individual EMR learners spent in the regular class. Some mainstreamed learners spent only half the day in the regular class, while others spent nearly the whole day. Similarly, some nonmainstreamed EMR learners spent close to half the day in the regular class. The mainstreamed EMR learners were integrated an average of 61.1% of the time that they spent in regular classes for academic activities. Of the nonmainstreamed EMR learners who were integrated for some academic activities, the mean was 25.9%, considerably lower than the mean percentage for the mainstreamed EMR learners.

The percentage of instructional time the EMR learners in this study spent in various content areas was examined. The variables included: (a) the percentage of time the EMR learners were integrated for academics (reading, math, language arts, spelling, science, or social studies), (b) the subject or content areas for which the EMR learners were integrated, (c) the percentages of instructional time in various subject areas which the EMR learners received in regular classrooms, and (d) whether or not the overall proportion of time EMR learners spent in various subject areas appears to have changed as a function of being mainstreamed.

Examination of the subject matter instructional pattern for mainstreamed EMR learners (Table 4-4) suggests that slightly more than half the learners (54%) were reported to be integrated for reading and 60% integrated for mathematics, although 75% were reported integrated for language arts/spelling and 91% for science or social studies.

For those learners who were integrated, the mean percentage of the specific subject matter time they spent in the regular class was relatively high for reading, language arts/spelling, and mathematics (between 70% and 80%); and almost all (95.7%) science and social studies instruction was reported to occur in the regular class.

Although the mainstreamed EMR learners received academic instruction in both regular and special education settings, the allocation of time for instructional content was relatively similar to that for the nonhandicapped learners (Table 4-4). Nonhandicapped learners spent 14% of the time in reading, 19% in mathematics, 27% in language arts/spelling, and 21% in science and social studies. The mainstreamed EMR learners spent a slightly smaller proportion of their time in all of these activities except reading and a somewhat greater proportion of their time (25%) in other activities such as art, music, physical education, psychomotor and/or perceptual training, social or vocational training, classroom management and organization, transitional activities, and free time.

Overall, the instructional pattern for the mainstreamed EMR learners was more similar to that of the nonhandicapped learners than the nonmainstreamed EMR learners. Nonmainstreamed EMR learners spent slighty more time in reading (19%), about the same time in math (15%) and language arts/spelling (24%), much less time in science and social studies (7%), and considerably more time in other activities (34%) than either nonhandicapped or mainstreamed EMR learners.

All learners, regardless of classroom placement, appear to have received approximately similar amounts of instructional time in the basic academic skill content areas (reading, math, language arts/spelling). However, the nonmainstreamed EMR learners, and to a lesser extent the mainstreamed EMR learners, spent larger portions of the school day engaged in nonacademic "other" activities than did the nonhandicapped learners.

## Discussion

Most of the EMR learners in this study were labelled and placed in special education relatively early in their school careers — most often by the end of the third grade. Anglo learners and those from more educated families (higher SES) tended to be placed earliest. One explanation for this finding might be that these parents are more active, and perhaps less intimidated, in planning with school personnel and demanding services for their children. A second explanation might be the hesitancy of school districts to place minority children in EMR classes as quickly as nonminority children. This hesitancy reflects a considerable sensitivity to potential erroneous classification.

The largest number of mainstreamed EMR learners had previous experience in regular classes, either as members of a regular class or attending regular classes for some academic instruction. For many learners and school districts in the study, mainstreaming was not a new practice but had been ongoing at some level for at least a year. It suggests that a sizeable number of mainstreamed learners had time to "settle in" to the regular education experience, and that some of the school districts had time to overcome start-up problems. The experiences, if any, of many mainstreamed EMR learners with special self-contained classes had been at least two years prior to the study. Any negative effects of special class placement on the self-concepts of these learners can be presumed to have been diminished.

The average mainstreamed EMR learner spent nearly three-fourths of the day in regular classes, and even the nonmainstreamed EMR learners spent, on the average, nearly a third of their day in regular classes. The percentage of academic integration and the subject matter revealed some interesting mainstreaming patterns.

First, it was found that a sizeable group of mainstreamed EMR learners were not integrated for reading and math. For those learners, the resource class offered a total instructional program; reading and math programs in these circumstances were developmental rather than remedial.

The most common pattern was to mainstream EMR learners for science and social studies. This finding is consistent with previous research but is somewhat puzzling. Typically, science and social studies texts are written at grade level and fewer individualized materials are available in the areas of science and social studies than in reading and math; hence, individualized instruction or content at an appropriate cognitive level is less likely. Equally of interest was the relative absence of social studies and science from the curricula in special self-contained classes. The need for effective instruction in these areas is no less important than the *three Rs* and would appear to require attention.

All three learner groups spent approximately the same amount of time in reading, math, language arts, and spelling. At these grades, the special self-contained classes are as academically oriented as regular education classes.

There were no indications that lack of coordination between regular and special education caused the mainstreamed EMR learners to miss any of the critical academic content areas. However, Chapter 10 provides some indications of concerns that may arise from the lack of coordination between regular and special education evidenced in the strength of the predictive model for explaining variations in learner academic achievement.

While the mainstreamed EMR learners spent more time in "other" activities than the nonhandicapped learners, they spent considerably less time in these activities than did the nonmainstreamed EMR learners. Since the "other" activities category includes social, vocational, and perceptual/motor training activities, questions are raised as to whether the program received by the mainstreamed EMR learners actually met all their educational needs. It must be remembered, however, that the "other" category is extremely robust because it includes art, music, and traditional activities. Therefore, conclusions as to whether programs received by mainstreamed EMR learners are appropriately balanced in terms of content must await the results of other studies.

# Background Characteristics of Learners by Setting

Having presented the individual, family/home, and school background characteristics, this section provides a profile description for each learner's group.

## Mainstreamed EMR Learners

The mainstreamed EMR learners ranged in age from 8-12 or more years, with an average age of about 10.5 years. Sixty percent of the mainstreamed EMR learners were males, and the average IQ score for this group was approximately 68. Nearly half (48%) of the mainstreamed EMR learners were Spanish surnamed, and almost a third (30%) were Black. Thus, more than three-fourths of the mainstreamed EMR learners were members of minority groups. A higher proportion of the younger mainstreamed learners were Black, while the proportion of Spanish-surnamed learners increased with age.

Nearly two-thirds of the mainstreamed EMR learners came from lower social status backgrounds as indicated by their fathers' lower level of education (graduation from junior high school or lower). A third of the learners in the mainstreamed group came from single parent homes, primarily living with their mothers.

The majority of mainstreamed EMR learners had been identified and placed in special education no later than their eighth year. Forty-two percent of the mainstreamed learners had been placed in regular classes the previous year with some special education services, while another 16% attended regular classes for some academic subjects. Thus, most of these learners had prior experiences with mainstreaming. The average mainstreamed EMR learners spent approximately three-fourths of the total day in the regular class and received about two-thirds of their academic instruction in that setting. Only about half the mainstreamed learners were integrated for reading, a slightly higher percentage for math, and nearly all for language arts/spelling, science, and social studies. The proportion of time spent by mainstreamed learners in various subject areas was very similar to that of nonhandicapped learners, although they did spend a slightly higher percentage of their time in "other" activities.

## Nonmainstreamed EMR Learners

The nonmainstreamed EMR learners were very similar to the mainstreamed EMR learners in their age, IQ, and sex distributions, and in family intactness. In ethnicity, the nonmainstreamed EMR learners were almost equally divided among the three ethnic groups. Judging by the fathers' educational level, 57% of the nonmainstreamed learners came from lower SES backgrounds.

The nonmainstreamed EMR learners were similar to the mainstreamed EMR learners in the age placed in special education, but 73% of the nonmainstreamed EMR learners had been placed in full-time special education programs during the previous year. During the year of the study, the average nonmainstreamed EMR learner spent almost a third of the day in regular classes. The proportion of time nonmainstreamed learners spent in various content areas was similar to that of nonhandicapped and mainstreamed EMR learners for reading, math, and language arts/spelling. However, much less time was spent in science and social studies, and considerably more in "other" activities.

## Nonhandicapped Learners

The nonhandicapped learners differed from the mainstreamed and nonmainstreamed EMR learners on most dimensions. The mean age for the nonhandicapped learners was about 9.5 years, approximately one year lower than that of the EMR learners. Fifty-three percent of the nonhandicapped learners were male. The average IQ of the nonhandicapped group was 94.7. Approximately 40% of the nonhandicapped learners were Anglo, and a similar proportion were Spanish surnamed, while only 19% were Black. These proportions represent a higher percentage of minority group students than found across the state of Texas or the nation. A higher proportion of the younger nonhandicapped learners were Anglo, with an increasing proportion of Spanish-surnamed learners at the older ages.

Though the nonhandicapped learners tended to come from higher social status backgrounds than the EMR learners (only 39% of their fathers had not attained a secondary education), there was still a higher proportion of learners from low social status backgrounds than would have been found in the state population as a whole. The nonhandicapped learners were more likely to come from intact homes than the EMR learners, with only 20% coming from single parent homes.

In summary, the mainstreamed and nonmainstreamed EMR learners were comparable on most background characteristics examined. They differed, however, in ethnicity, the extent of participation in regular classes (both in the year prior to and the year during the study), and the proportion of time spent daily in various academic areas. The nonhandicapped learners differed from the learners in both EMR groups on every individual and family/home characteristic included in the model. They did not differ greatly from the mainstreamed learners, however, in the proportion of their school day spent in various academic areas.

# Relationships Among Learner Background Variables

Federal and state legislation requires placement teams and administrators to consider carefully the characteristics and needs of each handicapped learner in making placements in regular or special education settings. It seems reasonable, then, to assume that certain learner characteristics (e.g., IQ) would be related to the amount of total time and the amount of academic instructional time the EMR learners spent in regular classes. Table 4-6 presents the bivariate correlations between the learner background measures and the two integration measures. As can be seen, all of these correlations were quite low.

Two commonality analyses were performed using learner characteristics to predict percentage of total integration and percentage of academic integration. Because the bivariate correlations between the learner background characteristics and the integration measures were so low, learner academic and social competencies were included as two additional predictor sets in the commonality analyses. It was thought that factors such as academic achievement, social acceptance, or social behavior might be related to the integration measures, thus increasing the variance.

**Table 4-6**
**Correlations Between Learner Background Characteristics**
**and Percentage of Time Integrated for Mainstreamed EMR Learners**

| Learner Background Characteristics | Percent Total Integration | Percent Academic Integration |
|---|---|---|
| Age | .13 | .17 |
| IQ | -.08 | -.08 |
| Sex | -.02 | -.02 |
| Ethnicity | | |
|   Anglo | -.05 | -.03 |
|   Black | -.03 | -.04 |
|   Spanish-surnamed | .08 | .06 |
| SES: | | |
|   Father's education | -.08 | -.09 |
|   Home intactness | .02 | .02 |
| Age placed in special education | .05 | .11 |
| Previous class placement | .10 | .08 |

The commonality analyses showed neither percentage of total integration nor percentage of academic integration to be significantly predicted by the learner background and competency characteristics [$R^2$ total integration = 0.07 (ns); $R^2$ academic integration = 0.09 (ns)].

These results are surprising. From these analyses it would appear that decisions concerning the percentage of time an EMR learner was mainstreamed were based not on learner characteristics such as IQ, achievement, or behavior, but on other factors. One possibility is that mainstreaming decisions were made at the school building level, with the amount of time EMR learners were integrated depending on the tolerances and preferences of the regular education teachers involved and the time the resource classroom teacher had available.

Another possibility is that informal or formal district policies regarding the mainstreaming of EMR learners determined the amount of time learners were integrated. Thus, in some districts all mainstreamed EMR learners may have been routinely integrated for approximately the same amount of time and for the same subjects. In other districts formal or informal "maximum" integration policies may have been operating. In this case, two districts might have used learner characteristics to guide integration decisions: In one district the brightest, most competent EMR learners might have been integrated only up to the district's formal or informal maximum of 66% of the day, whereas in the other district the higher-ability EMR learners might have been integrated up to 95% of the day.

In any case, it seems likely that the passage of P.L. 94-142 regarding the placement of handicapped learners will necessitate changes in the way integration decisions are made.

## Summary

This chapter addresses the three issues related to mainstreaming. There was a consistent trend across all grades to place mainstreamed EMR learners in classes with nonhandicapped learners who were a year younger. Placement in multi-grade classes or with students a year younger might effect a reasonable compromise between the mainstreamed EMR learner's social and cognitive level and interests and his cognitive and achievement level. It is not known how EMR learners perceive being placed with younger nonhandicapped learners. It may be negatively perceived. This topic seems an important one for future research.

The second issue concerned the patterns of integration found in the proportion of time integrated and subjects for which EMR learners were mainstreamed. The average mainstreamed EMR learner was integrated for almost three-fourths of the day; the segregated EMR learner for nearly one third of the day. A sizeable proportion of the mainstreamed EMR learners, however, were not integrated for reading instruction or for math. Thus, it seems likely that even in mainstreaming programs many EMR students receive their total reading and math programs in special education classes. Given this practice, resource teachers need to offer developmental reading and math programs rather than remedial and supplemental work, or work with regular class teachers to support these students in their reading and math classes.

Almost all the mainstreamed learners were integrated for science and social studies despite the fact that these are content areas for which few individualized materials are available, using instead texts which require reading skills at grade level. This practice indicates a need for the development of individualized science and social studies curricula as well as for high interest/low vocabulary science and social studies texts.

Mainstreamed EMR learners spent much less time in "other" activities than nonmainstreamed EMR learners. This finding indicates mainstreamed EMR learners were not spending time in perceptual/motor, social, or vocational training activities — curricula areas which have traditionally been associated with EMR learners. These findings reinforce the cautions of researchers (MacMillan & Semmel, 1977; Kaufman et al., 1975) that mainstreaming cannot be considered a unitary treatment, but must be defined in terms of factors such as temporal, instructional, and social opportunities.

Finally, with regard to the third question raised, no relationships were found between learner characteristics and the amount of time EMR learners were integrated into regular classes, whether total time or academic time. Apparently, integration decisions were made on other bases than learner characteristics — e.g., the school had no special class and only provided a resource room option, or vice versa. Changes in Federal and state requirements for the placement of handicapped children will require refocusing decision-making in the placement process on learner needs and characteristics.

# Technical Notes

1. Several criteria guided the selection of individual, family/home, and school background variables from those available in the Project PRIME database. Variables were evaluated with respect to their (a) importance in describing the groups, (b) likelihood of being significantly related to learner school competencies, (c) amount of missing data, (d) reliability of the data available, and (e) the degree of correlation among available background variables.

2. Since the distribution of intelligence tests administered to each sample varied, it appears tenuous to make comparisons across samples. Although comparisons among subgroups within samples are less hazardous, resulting differences must also be interpreted with caution. It is possible, for example, that a systematic bias existed in the selection of tests administered to different ethnic or socioeconomic subgroups. Thus, the differences found between subgroups might be attributable to the tests taken. Because of these problems and those of missing data, IQ was not used in the analyses in subsequent chapters of the book.

3. Father's educational level and family intactness were selected from several potential SES measures available. Not chosen were teacher's estimate of family SES, father's occupational level, mother's occupational level, mother's educational level, and learner's report of cognitive affluence in the home. The psychometric and statistical properties of the parent education level measures were important considerations in selecting an SES measure. Although the available occupational indexes had as much variability as the educational indexes, there was reason to question the linearity of the occupational levels. Of the two available parent education measures, father's education was selected because it was thought to have a greater impact on a family's social and economic style of life than mother's educational level. Priority-ordered substitution, a statistical procedure described by Veldman (1974), provided the means for estimating the level of father's education for most of the learners missing this information. (See Chapter 3.)

4. In the predictive models, father's education was represented by an 11-point scale.

5. Age placed in special education, previous class placement, and extent of integration were only relevant for the EMR learner groups, and thus this information is presented only for mainstreamed and nonmainstreamed EMR learners. To keep the analyses equivalent for the nonhandicapped and EMR learner groups, school background measures are not used in subsequent chapters.

# 5
# Learner Competence in School

This chapter focusses on the school-related competence of the three learner groups. Included are:

- Descriptions of the learner competence model, its conceptual rationale, and methods of empirical verification;
- Descriptions of the academic and social competencies of the nonhandicapped, mainstreamed EMR, and nonmainstreamed EMR learners;
- An examination of the extent to which the academic and social competencies of the mainstreamed EMR learners overlapped with those of the nonhandicapped learners; and
- An examination of the interrelationships among competencies within the respective learner groups.

Learner competence represents the principal outcome of the educational programming process. The development of the learner competence model was guided by the concern that the specific competency dimensions be important and meaningful to educators. Thus, the description of learner competence based upon the model is expected to provide relevant information to those making planning and programming decisions. Furthermore, if the

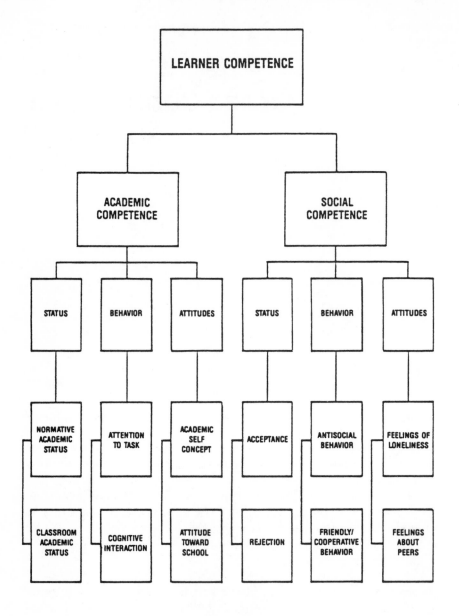

Figure 5-1
Learner Competence
(Project PRIME Taxonomic Model)

competence dimensions between nonhandicapped and EMR learners overlap, there can be important implications for the placement of EMR students in regular classes.

The chapter is divided into three major sections. In the first section the model of learner competence is presented and the stages in its development and empirical verification briefly recounted. In the second, the conceptual rationale for the model is elaborated and the competencies of the three learner groups are described. In the third, the degree of overlap in the competencies of the mainstreamed EMR and nonhandicapped learners is examined and the interrelationships among the multiple competency dimensions are explored.

## Model of Learner Competencies

The goals of public education are derived from the values of the supporting society and community. Although American education is relatively decentralized, there is generally common agreement that educational goals are multiple in nature, with each community weighing its priorities somewhat differently.

Historically, special education has placed greater emphasis on social/affective goals than on academic goals. This has been reflected in the emphasis on warm, supportive teaching environments and methods, and socially- and vocationally-oriented curricula. The current integrational approach has redirected attention toward academic competencies while still recognizing the importance of social competence. Regular education recognizes both academic and socio-affective objectives, emphasizing the former without denying the importance of the latter. Although determining educational objectives may sometimes be difficult, there is general agreement that objectives in both the academic and social domains are important for all students.

The model of learner competence presented here (see Figure 5-1) reflects this dual emphasis: the belief that the educational objectives for handicapped students are essentially the same as those for nonhandicapped students.

The model was constructed in stages. Learner competence was defined in terms of two broad domains: academic and social competence. The measures selected from the Project PRIME learner database assessed learner achievement (status), behavior, and attitudes within each of these two domains. Whenever possible, the measures represented different sources of information; that is, teacher, peers, or direct observation. These measures formed the basis for the factor analysis process of the second stage.

**Table 5-1**
**Learner Academic Competence Image Analysis**
**Primary Loadings After Varimax Rotation**

| Scale | Instrument | Factor Loading |
|---|---|---|
| Factor I: Normative Academic Status (eigenvalue = 5.07) | | |
| Reading posttest | MAT | .81 |
| Math posttest | MAT | .81 |
| Teacher's estimate of learners' end-of-the-year reading level | SCEEQ | .81 |
| Teacher's estimate of learners' end-of-the-year math level | SCEEQ | .76 |
| Factor II: Classroom Academic Status (eigenvalue = 1.53) | | |
| Academic effort/success | TRS | .75 |
| Outgoing/expressive behavior | TRS | .69 |
| Brightness | GW | .51 |
| Dullness | GW | -.47 |
| Factor III: Attitude Toward School (eigenvalue = 1.32) | | |
| Attitude toward reading | HYDF II | .58 |
| Attitude toward teacher/school | HYDF II | .55 |
| Attitude toward math | HYDF II | .54 |
| Attitude toward school | HYDF I | .42 |
| School enthusiasm | AYYF | .36 |
| Academic ambition | CQ | .25 |
| Factor IV: Cognitive Interaction with the Teacher (eigenvalue = .37) | | |
| Total active participation | IPPS | -.41 |
| Low-level discourse | ICDS | -.36 |
| High-level discourse | ICDS | -.30 |
| Factor V: Academic Self-Concept (eigenvalue = .29) | | |
| Academic self-concept | AYYF | .38 |
| Factor VI: Attention to Academic Tasks (eigenvalue = .14) | | |
| On-task behavior | IBMS | .20 |

Note. 43.9% of the total variance is common among the 19 scales.
The six factors account for 90.1% of that common variance. Abbreviations:
MAT = Metropolitan Achievement Test, SCEEQ = Selected Children's Educational
Experiences Questionnaire, TRS = Teacher Rating Scale, GW = Guess Who, HYDF
= How Do You Feel, AYYF = About You and Your Friends, CQ = Children's
Questionnaire, IPPS = Indiana Pupil Participation Schedule, ICDS = Indiana
Cognitive Demand Schedule, IBMS = Indiana Behavior Management System.

Factor analyses (image analysis with varimax rotation) were conducted for each domain separately.[1] The resulting factor structure for the academic competence domain is presented in Table 5-1 and that for the social competence domain in Table 5-2. In the model construction, factor analysis was viewed as a confirming technique to verify the conceptual structure rather than as an exploratory technique.

The results of the factor analysis led to formulation of the learner competence model which consists of five levels:

*Level 1* is comprised of the academic and social competence domains.

**Table 5—2**
**Learner Social Competence Image Analysis**
**Primary Loadings After Varimax Rotation**

| Scale | Instrument | Factor Loading |
|---|---|---|
| Factor I: Social Status (eigenvalue = 2.01) | | |
| Acceptance | HIFTO | .63 |
| Rejection | HIFTO | -.63 |
| Factor II: Friendly/Cooperative Behavior (eigenvalue = .85) | | |
| Socialization | FLACCS | .49 |
| Positive social behavior | FLACCS | .43 |
| Factor III: Feelings About Peers (eigenvalue = .23) | | |
| Peers liked | HIFTO | .49 |
| Peers disliked | HIFTO | -.48 |
| Factor IV: Antisocial Behavior (eigenvalue = .23) | | |
| Antisocial behavior | TRS | .53 |
| Disruptive behavior | GW | .49 |
| Negative social behavior | FLACCS | .33 |
| Aggression/resistance | IBMS | .30 |
| Factor V: Feelings of Loneliness (eigenvalue = .13) | | |
| Misbehavior | AYYF | .38 |
| Isolation/anxiety | AYYF | .33 |

**Note.** 33.4% of the total variance is common among the 12 scales. The five factors account for 84.2% of that common variance. Abbreviations: HIFTO = How I Feel Toward Others, FLACCS = Florida Climate and Control System, TRS = Teacher Rating Scale, GW = Guess Who, IBMS = Indiana Behavior Management System, AYYF = About You and Your Friends.

*Level 2* subdivides both domains into the three subdomains of status, behavior, and attitudes. Academic competence consists of academic status, academic behavior, and academic attitudes; social competence consists of social status, social behavior, and social attitudes.

*Level 3* further subdivides the subdomains into competency constructs: six academic and six social. This level of the model reflects the structure obtained through the factor analysis, except that the factor analysis resulted in a five- rather than a six-factor solution for social competence. For conceptual reasons, the social acceptance and social rejection measures which both loaded on Factor I (social status) were split to form two social status constructs: acceptance and rejection.

*Level 4* is comprised of the scales used to measure the competency constructs.

*Level 5* contains the items within the instruments used to construct the scales.

Many of the 12 competency constructs consisted of measures drawn from several scales. These measures were combined to form the competency construct. The scores were converted to standardized $T$ scores ($X = 50$, $SD = 10$) for the entire learner sample permitting direct comparison of competency construct scores.[2] The mean standardized scores for each competency construct are presented in Table 5-3.

# Description of Learner Competence

Academic and social competence are used as indicators of successful school functioning: the ability of children to meet the demands of the school and community. Academic competence is used to mean more than achievement: It also denotes a repertoire of personally espoused attitudes and overt behaviors. Children's feelings about school and themselves as learners, the way they interact cognitively with their teachers, and the extent to which they attend to instructional tasks are all viewed as indicative of their level of competence in meeting the academic requirements of the school.

Similarly, children's social competence is reflected in their attitudes and behaviors as well as their social status among their peer group. Specifically, acceptance or rejection by peers, feelings about classmates, loneliness, and positive and negative social behaviors manifested in school are viewed as portraying level of competence in meeting the social demands of the school environment.

## Table 5-3
### Standardized Scores for Learner Competence Variables

| Variable | Regular Class Nonhandicapped Learners | | | Regular Class Mainstreamed EMR Learners | | | Resource Class Mainstreamed EMR Learners | | | Special Self-Contained Class Nonmainstreamed EMR Learners | | |
|---|---|---|---|---|---|---|---|---|---|---|---|---|
| | X | SD | n | X | SD | n | X | SD | n | X | SD | n |
| Normative academic status ($\alpha$=.95) | 58.75 | 7.65 | 348 | 45.00 | 6.99 | 345 | | | | 44.98 | 7.75 | 265 |
| Classroom academic status ($\alpha$=.82) | 55.14 | 9.27 | 355 | 42.50 | 6.71 | 354 | | | | 53.06 | 8.54 | 271 |
| Attention to academic tasks | 52.87 | 7.99 | 305 | 46.46 | 10.81 | 319 | 56.55 | 6.96 | 278 | 51.31 | 8.66 | 250 |
| Cognitive interaction with the teacher | 47.79 | 4.95 | 301 | 46.28 | 6.85 | 320 | 60.40 | 12.23 | 277 | 56.69 | 10.20 | 242 |
| Academic self-concept ($\alpha$=.82) | 50.49 | 10.34 | 349 | 48.04 | 9.52 | 349 | | | | 51.98 | 9.68 | 260 |
| Attitude toward school ($r$=.74)a | 50.78 | 10.58 | 356 | 49.27 | 9.40 | 353 | | | | 49.99 | 9.69 | 273 |
| Acceptance ($r$=.75)b | 51.41 | 8.41 | 344 | 44.64 | 8.22 | 340 | | | | 55.28 | 10.71 | 253 |
| Rejection ($r$=.74)b | 47.91 | 7.98 | 344 | 52.99 | 10.06 | 340 | | | | 48.70 | 11.01 | 253 |
| Friendly/cooperative behavior ($\alpha$=.66) | 49.61 | 9.50 | 302 | 47.79 | 8.48 | 320 | 51.49 | 11.58 | 272 | 53.17 | 10.74 | 240 |
| Antisocial behavior ($r$=.54)a | 47.59 | 7.42 | 351 | 49.79 | 8.10 | 349 | 51.44 | 10.53 | 336 | 52.35 | 10.30 | 272 |
| Feelings of loneliness ($\alpha$=.80) | 46.85 | 9.96 | 349 | 52.27 | 9.69 | 347 | | | | 51.20 | 9.40 | 257 |
| Feelings about peers ($\alpha$=.53) | 48.35 | 9.13 | 344 | 50.72 | 9.26 | 341 | | | | 51.28 | 11.57 | 256 |

a$r$ = average item intercorrelation corrected by the Spearman-Brown prophecy formula.

b$r$ = split class interjudge agreement coefficients corrected by the Spearman-Brown prophecy formula.

## Academic Competence

While inadequate academic achievement, particularly in reading, is the pre...mptive reason for a special education referral (Kaufman, Agard, & Vlasak, 1973a), the teacher making the referral may be concerned about other problems manifested by the student: short attention span or unwillingness to participate in class discussions, activities, or assignments; discouragement about school work; growing dislike of school; poor behavior; etc. Academic status, behaviors, and attitudes are the subdomains comprising academic competence. Each of these subdomains is considered in the following section.

### Academic Status

An individual's academic status refers to a state or condition as well as to a position in relation to others. Two frames of reference were used to depict academic status: the student's normative academic status (performance as it relates to that of a standard reference group, e.g., all nine-year-olds), and classroom academic status (performance as it relates to the other students in the classroom). The two types of status provide complementary information and were expected to convey a more complete and accurate picture of the learner's academic progress than the use of just one (Sax, 1974).

Normative academic status is based on student achievement in relation to national norms. Since mildly retarded students were presumably referred for diagnosis and placement because of poor achievement, it is not surprising their achievement scores on standardized tests are lower than those of non-EMR students (Guskin & Spicker, 1968).

Standardized achievement tests provide evidence of reliability and validity, and permit comparisons of data across studies in which the same achievement measures were used. Standardized tests, however, often have weaknesses when used with EMR learners. There may be a lack of agreement between the test content, which presumably reflects the traditional regular class, and the instructional coverage of the special class. Cultural biases may be reflected in the item content and selection of the standardization sample, which could lead to lower scores among the minority children who are disproportionately represented among EMR learners (Holtzman, 1971; Jensen, 1970). Finally, unclear test instructions and/or confusing formats are particularly devastating to low-achieving or poorly-motivated students (Klein, 1971). Since the scores of EMR learners on standardized achievement measures may reflect any or all of these difficulties, Project PRIME used teacher estimates of the learner's achievement relative to grade-level norms as a supplementary indicator of normative academic status.

Classroom academic status was based on teacher and peer perceptions of a student's academic performance in relation to that of others in the same class. These perceptions were acquired from informal and subjective observations of the learner's performance in class discussions and on group projects, written assignments, and teacher-prepared tests. They have the advantage of reflecting the learner's performance as it relates to the actual process and content of classroom instruction.

Research evidence suggests that a student's classroom academic status is related to class placement. Towne and Joiner (1966), for example, found that EMR learners' Self-Concept-of-Ability scores increased when they changed from regular to special class placement. Lawrence and Winschel (1973) posited that the improved scores may have resulted from the change in the peer reference group since their academic status relative to their peers was quite different.

Like measures of normative academic status, measures of classroom status have shortcomings. Teachers' ratings of students' academic achievement may not be highly correlated with standardized achievement test scores or even with achievement ratings from other teachers (Averch et al., 1972). Teacher and peer ratings of achievement can be influenced by non-cognitive factors such as social class or school behavior. Also, student scores on classroom-referenced achievement measures are difficult to compare across classrooms precisely because they do not reflect a common frame of reference. Thus, a nonmainstreamed student's academic status is judged by his special class teacher — whose frame of reference is her students' relatively low academic performance — and by EMR peers who are ranking performance in relation to their special classmates. By contrast, the mainstreamed EMR learner's status is judged by nonhandicapped peers and a regular class teacher, both of whom use higher-level academic standards based on normative grade curricula and peers as the basis for judgment. The following section presents the indices used to measure normative and classroom academic status and describes the three learner groups. A summary of the results of normative and classroom academic status for the three learner groups is provided in Table 5-4.

**Normative Academic Status:** The Metropolitan Achievement Test (MAT) total math and reading pre- and posttest scores were used as the primary indicator of learner normative academic status. The learners' total math and total reading raw scores were converted to standard scores according to criteria set forth by Durost et al. (1971). Two items on the *Selected Children's Educational Experiences Questionnaire* (SCEEQ), which asked the teachers to estimate the learners' beginning- and end-of-the-year reading and math grade

Table 5-4

Academic Status: Descriptive Statistics

| Measure | Nonhandicapped Learners | | | Mainstreamed EMR Learners | | | Nonmainstreamed EMR Learners | | |
|---|---|---|---|---|---|---|---|---|---|
| | X | SD | N | X | SD | N | X | SD | N |
| Normative Academic Status | | | | | | | | | |
| MAT reading achievement | | | | | | | | | |
| Pretest | 57.21 | 12.60 | 308 | 39.44 | 9.89 | 333 | 37.38 | 10.67 | 243 |
| Posttest * | 61.84 | 12.49 | 341 | 41.43 | 10.26 | 329 | 41.15 | 11.16 | 233 |
| Gaina | 4.19 | 6.01 | 268 | 2.16 | 6.80 | 310 | 3.05 | 5.34 | 212 |
| MAT math achievement | | | | | | | | | |
| Pretest | 67.48 | 12.97 | 320 | 44.24 | 11.77 | 345 | 41.76 | 13.37 | 252 |
| Posttest * | 2.31 | 14.21 | 335 | 46.25 | 13.95 | 323 | 45.89 | 14.65 | 233 |
| Gaina | 4.33 | 6.20 | 273 | 1.94 | 8.87 | 314 | 3.50 | 6.50 | 220 |
| SCEEQ reading grade level | | | | | | | | | |
| Beginning of the year | 3.29 | 1.18 | 294 | 1.80 | .79 | 347 | 1.80 | 1.13 | 231 |
| End of the year * | 4.20 | 1.30 | 294 | 2.41 | .98 | 348 | 2.43 | 1.32 | 231 |
| Gaina | .91 | .44 | 294 | .61 | .37 | 347 | .61 | .43 | 231 |
| SCEEQ math grade level | | | | | | | | | |
| Beginning of the year | 3.31 | 1.09 | 291 | 2.07 | .88 | 346 | 2.09 | 1.21 | 231 |
| End of the year * | 4.22 | 1.17 | 291 | 2.77 | 1.03 | 347 | 2.78 | 1.44 | 231 |
| Gaina | .91 | .42 | 291 | .69 | .42 | 346 | .69 | .49 | 231 |

Classroom Academic Status

| | | | | | | | | | |
|---|---|---|---|---|---|---|---|---|---|
| Academic effort/success | 132.55 | 31.57 | 340 | 90.18 | 25.45 | 335 | 122.42 | 29.50 | 265 |
| Outgoing/expressive behavior | 20.16 | 5.10 | 340 | 13.79 | 4.38 | 335 | 19.20 | 5.18 | 265 |
| Brightness | 1.59 | 1.71 | 346 | .49 | .92 | 344 | 2.00 | 1.71 | 259 |
| Dullness | 1.45 | 1.43 | 346 | 2.97 | 1.70 | 344 | 2.16 | 1.54 | 259 |

**Note.** Only starred normative academic status variables were used in the composite; all four classroom status variables were uses in that composite. Abbreviations: MAT = Metropolitan Achievement Test, SCEEQ = Selected Children's Educational Experiences Questionnaire.

[a]Not residualized.

levels, were used as secondary indicators. The internal consistency (alpha) coefficient for this four-variable composite is 0.95.

*Gain Scores:* From both the pre- and posttest scores on the MAT and the teachers' beginning- and end-of-the-year estimates on the SCEEQ, it was possible to compute gain scores in math and reading. However, the correlations between the MAT pre- and posttest scores and those between the teacher's beginning- and end-of-the-year estimates were so high there was little reliable variance remaining in the gain scores. Because of this high correlation and restricted variance, these gain scores did not correlate strongly (i.e., $r < .05$) with any of the other competency variables nor did they load on the normative academic status factor. Therefore, only the MAT math and reading posttest scores and the teachers' end-of-the-year estimates of the learners' math and reading grade levels were included in the composite scales for normative academic status.

*MAT Posttest Math and Reading Scores:* The MAT was administered to the selected learners at the end of the school year. The nonhandicapped learners were given the form appropriate for their grade level: Third graders were given the Primary II form; fourth graders, the Elementary form; and fifth graders, the Intermediate form. The EMR learners were given both the Primary I and II forms, and then the form most appropriate to their ability level (the form on which they obtained the closest to 50% correct) was selected.

In general, the nonhandicapped learners obtained MAT total math and reading scores that placed them in the lower third of the percentile ranks when compared with the national norm group (see Table 5-5). Only the nonhandicapped third graders approached the average percentile rank in total reading score. The fourth- and fifth-grade nonhandicapped learners obtained slightly better standings in math than in reading.

The mainstreamed EMR learners on average obtained MAT total math and reading scores which placed them in the lowest percentile ranks when compared to national norms (see Table 5-5). No large difference was evident between their reading and math performance as measured by the MAT.

Because the age distribution of the nonmainstreamed EMR learners was identical to that of the mainstreamed EMR learners, and the average mainstreamed EMR learner was in the fourth grade the year of the study, the average end-of-the-year MAT standard reading and math scores of the nonmainstreamed EMR learners (see Table 5-4) were transformed to percentile ranks using end-of-the-fourth-grade national norms. Both standardized scores were equivalent to the first (lowest) percentile rank.

Table 5-5
Metropolitan Achievement Test Total
Mathematics and Reading Posttest Scores by Grade

| Learner grade | Nonhandicapped Learners | | | | | | Mainstreamed EMR Learners | | | | | |
|---|---|---|---|---|---|---|---|---|---|---|---|---|
| | Mathematics Percentile | | | Reading Percentile | | | Mathematics Percentile | | | Reading Percentile | | |
| | X | rank | N | X | rank | N | X | rank | N | X | rank | N |
| 3 | 62.15 | 23 | 100 | 58.29 | 40 | 104 | 40.66 | 1 | 92 | 37.89 | 2 | 101 |
| 4 | 72.37 | 24 | 124 | 58.28 | 18 | 124 | 45.65 | 1 | 118 | 42.82 | 1 | 116 |
| 5 | 81.40 | 28 | 111 | 69.02 | 23 | 113 | 51.33 | 1 | 112 | 43.13 | 1 | 111 |

Table 5-6
Teacher's Mean Estimates of End-of-the-Year
Mathematics and Reading Grade Level Equivalent by Groups

| Learner grade | Nonhandicapped Learners | | | | | | Mainstreamed EMR Learners | | | | | |
|---|---|---|---|---|---|---|---|---|---|---|---|---|
| | Mathematics | | | Reading | | | Mathematics | | | Reading | | |
| | X | SD | N | X | SD | N | X | SD | N | X | SD | N |
| 3 | 3.56 | 1.10 | 41 | 3.49 | 1.08 | 41 | 2.00 | .77 | 47 | 1.85 | .79 | 47 |
| 4 | 4.35 | 1.05 | 64 | 4.28 | 1.29 | 64 | 3.13 | 1.20 | 62 | 2.78 | 1.18 | 63 |
| 5 | 4.88 | 1.25 | 62 | 4.97 | 1.21 | 65 | 3.02 | 1.03 | 60 | 2.57 | 1.07 | 61 |

*Teacher Estimates of Learner Math and Reading Levels at the End of the School Year*: The SCEEQ was administered to the learners' teachers at the end of the school year. Table 5-6 presents teachers' mean estimates of the end-of-the-year math and reading levels of third-, fourth-, and fifth-grade nonhandicapped and mainstreamed EMR learners. The nonhandicapped learners were estimated to be somewhat below their actual grade level in achievement. At the end of grade 5, for example, the estimated math and reading levels of the nonhandicapped learners were approximately at a beginning fifth-grade level.

Teachers' mean estimates of the math and reading levels of the mainstreamed EMR learners were consistently lower than their estimates of the math and reading levels of the nonhandicapped learners — by over one standard deviation regardless of grade level. The gap was largest for the fifth-grade mainstreamed learners, who were estimated to be close to two years behind their nonhandicapped peers in math level and over two years behind in reading level.

Because of the identical age distribution of the nonmainstreamed and the mainstreamed EMR learners, the average grade level of the mainstreamed EMR learners (4.7) was assigned to the nonmainstreamed EMR learners. The estimated end-of-the-year math and reading levels of the nonmainstreamed EMR learners were both about two years below this grade level.

*Normative Academic Status Composite Scores:* The scores on the four measures of normative academic status were summed and standardized ($\bar{X} = 50, SD = 10$) to form the normative academic status composite scores (see Table 5-3). As would be expected from the scores for the individual measures, there was a substantial difference between the normative academic status score of the nonhandicapped learners and that of the mainstreamed EMR learners. The nonhandicapped group score was approximately 1.4 standard deviations above that of the mainstreamed EMR group. The score of the nonmainstreamed EMR group was similar to that of the mainstreamed group.

**Classroom Academic Status**: Four scales were used to indicate the learners' classroom academic status. The first two, the academic effort/success scale and the outgoing/expressive behavior scale, were measures of teacher perceptions derived from the *Teacher Rating Scale* (TRS). The second two, the brightness scale and the dullness scale, were measures of peer perceptions derived from *Guess Who* (GW). Descriptive statistics for the classroom academic status variables are given in Table 5-4.

*Academic Effort/Success*: This scale, derived from the TRS, consists of 40 items, such as "Finishes work on time," "Can concentrate on tasks for long periods," and "Works at difficult assignments until he/she gets them done." The teacher rated the learner "never" (= 1), "rarely" (= 2), "sometimes" (= 3), "usually" (= 4), or "always" (= 5) on each of the 40 items. The minimum score on the scale is 40; the maximum, 200. Internal consistency of the scale is 0.98.

The nonhandicapped and the mainstreamed EMR learners were rated by regular teachers. The nonhandicapped learners obtained a mean academic effort/success score of 132.55, indicating that on the average teachers rated the nonhandicapped learner as "sometimes" displaying academic effort and success as measured by the scale items. The mean score for the mainstreamed EMR learners was 90.18, which can be interpreted as a rating of "rarely" displays academic effort and success. The scores for the nonmainstreamed EMR learners, based on ratings from special teachers, indicated a mean score of 122.42, an average rating of "sometimes" displays academic effort and success.

*Outgoing/Expressive Behavior*: The outgoing/expressive behavior scale, also derived from the TRS, consists of six items such as "Is spontaneous in contributing ideas" and "Contributes to class discussions." The teacher rated the learners on a 5-point scale, where "never" was scored as 1 and "always" as 5. The minimum score possible is 6 and the maximum is 30; the internal consistency of the scale is 0.90.

Regular teachers rated the nonhandicapped and the mainstreamed EMR learners on this scale. Teachers assigned a mean rating of 20.16 to the nonhandicapped learners (Table 5-4). On average, the nonhandicapped learners were viewed by their teachers as "sometimes" outgoing or expressive. The mean score for the mainstreamed EMR learners was 13.78, which approximates a rating of "rarely" displays outgoing/expressive behavior. Nonmainstreamed EMR learners' mean score of 19.20 indicated a teacher rating of "sometimes" displays outgoing/expressive behavior as measured by the scale items.

*Brightness*: The brightness scale, derived from *Guess Who*, a peer nomination rating scale, consists of five items such as "Who is the smartest in the class?" and "Who always knows the answers to the teacher's questions?" The minimum score on the scale is 0; the maximum, 5. A score of 3 indicates that the target learner was nominated by one or more classmates for three of the five items. The internal consistency of the scale is 0.77.

Nonhandicapped learners obtained a mean score of 1.59, indicating that the nonhandicapped learner was, on average, nominated by at least one classmate for one or two of the brightness items. The mainstreamed EMR learners were seldom nominated by their nonhandicapped peers for the brightness items (a mean score of 0.49). Nonmainstreamed EMR learners obtained a mean score of 2.00 on the brightness scale, indicating that these learners were likely to be nominated for two of the five brightness items by their EMR classmates.

*Dullness*: This scale, also derived from the *Guess Who* instrument, consists of five items. Representative of these items are "Who is the worst in math (arithmetic)?" and "Who never knows the answers in class?" On this scale, higher scores indicate lower classroom academic status. The internal consistency of the scale is 0.70.

Nonhandicapped learners obtained a mean score of 1.45, indicating that, on the average, they were nominated by peers for one or two of the five dullness items (Table 5-4). The mainstreamed EMR learners obtained a mean score of 2.97, indicating they were likely to be nominated by nonhandicapped peers for almost three of the five dullness items, somewhat more than were their nonhandicapped classmates. The nonmainstreamed EMR learners' mean score of 2.16 indicated these learners were nominated for two of the five items by their EMR classmates.

*Classroom Academic Status Composite Scores*: The classroom academic status composite score for each of the three learner samples was obtained by summing and standardizing the scores on the academic effort/success, the outgoing/expressive behavior, the brightness, and the dullness scales (see Table 5-4). Before the composite scale was formed, a constant of 5 was subtracted from the dullness scale to invert the directionality of the scale. An internal consistency coefficient of 0.79 was obtained for the multiple-item construct.

The classroom academic status of the mainstreamed EMR learners in regular classes was substantially lower than that of the nonhandicapped learners. Their mean standardized score was approximately 1.3 standard deviations below that of the nonhandicapped learners. This result is particularly striking since the mainstreamed EMR learners were placed in classes with chronologically younger nonhandicapped learners who were relatively low in academic achievement.

While the nonmainstreamed EMR learners' classroom academic status score was similar to that of the nonhandicapped learners, they were judged by their EMR peers and the special class teacher, whereas the nonhandicapped learners were judged by their nonhandicapped peers and the regular class teacher.

**Discussion:** There is little question that both the mainstreamed and nonmainstreamed EMR learners in the Project PRIME study were seriously deficient in reading and math when compared with the national norms and to the nonhandicapped learners. Both groups had been identified and designated as eligible for special education services because of their poor academic functioning. Both groups had similar math and reading scores on the Metropolitan Achievement Test. There was no evidence that the most seriously academically deficient EMR learners were placed in special self-contained classes. Supporting findings, which are presented in Chapter 4, show no relationship between EMR learner normative academic competence and the amount of time spent with nonhandicapped learners in the regular classroom.

Although the nonhandicapped learners scored higher than the EMR learners, they were still low in achievement: They scored in the lowest third of percentile ranks except for third graders' reading. Teacher estimates of nonhandicapped learners' end-of-the-year reading and math grade levels were consistent with the MAT scores. Since the nonhandicapped learners were randomly selected from the peers in the mainstreamed EMR learners' regular classes, the relatively low normative academic status of the nonhandicapped learners suggests that the mainstreamed EMR learners were often placed in regular classes with low-achieving peers who were also about a year younger. This placement should have reduced the potential discrepancy between the achievement level of the mainstreamed EMR learners and that of their nonhandicapped classmates. The normative academic status data, however, suggest the discrepancy was still substantial. The mainstreamed EMR learners' standardized achievement test scores usually fell in the lowest percentiles and their teachers generally estimated their achievement level to be two or more years behind their grade-level placement.

Although the mainstreamed EMR learners did not appear to differ substantially from the nonmainstreamed EMR learners in normative academic status, they did differ considerably in classroom academic status. This difference was considered to be largely due to the difference between the reference groups used as the basis for the ratings. The ratings for nonmainstreamed EMR learners were made by their special class teachers and their EMR peers, and were higher than those given the mainstreamed EMR learners by their regular teachers and nonhandicapped classmates. Subsequent analyses showed that ratings given to the mainstreamed EMR learners by their resource teachers were higher than those given by their regular teachers although lower than those given to the nonmainstreamed learners by their special self-contained class teachers. While this could be due to actual differences in either learner academic effort with different teachers or teacher ratings, with the special education teachers giving more favorable ratings, it seems more likely a result of the referent groups.

## Academic Behavior

Educational theory and research have focused on learner behavior as an important contributor to achievement. In Carroll's (1963) model, academic behavior is considered a mediator of academic learning: The degree of learner achievement is thought to be partly dependent upon the time spent on learning, which to some extent reflects the learners' perseverance. Wiley (1973), Cooley and Lohnes (1976), and Wiley and Harnischfeger (1974) have presented models that incorporate learners' characteristics and their behavior with external factors to predict academic achievement. Empirical evidence that learners' academic behavior predicts achievement test scores has been provided by Stallings and Kaskowitz (1974) and McKinney et al. (1975).

Appropriate academic behavior provides the teacher with immediately observable information on the learner's current level of interest and skill acquisition. These observations serve to guide the teacher's instructional support (Nuthall, 1968). "Outstanding" elementary teachers indicated that a student's expression of interest, enthusiasm, and willingness to participate are more reliable evidence of learning and successful teaching than achievement scores (Jackson & Belford, 1965; Lortie, 1975).

Project PRIME examined two specific aspects of pupils' academic behavior which research suggests may be relevant to achievement: attention to academic tasks and cognitive interaction with the teacher. A student's attention to academic tasks is typically indicated by the orientation of his head and eyes toward the lesson instruction. Silberman (1970) concluded that (a) most of the time pupils appear to be paying attention, (b) some apparent attention is faked, and (c) the degree of attention in a classroom seems to be related to the teacher's effectiveness and the achievement level of the class. Attention to task has been shown to be positively related to achievement in the first (Samuels & Turnure, 1974), fourth (Cobb, 1972), and sixth (Lahaderne, 1968) grades.

Among EMR learners, inability to pay attention, short attention span, lack of concentration, and distractibility have long been recognized as related to serious learning problems (Denny, 1964; Dunn, 1973; Kirk, 1972; Robinson & Robinson, 1976; Zeaman & House, 1963). Dunn (1973) concluded that one way to foster learning among EMR learners is to find devices which draw their attention to the task and reduce distractions. A student's inability to pay attention is often thought to result from inappropriate, dull, or difficult materials and methods used in regular class instruction (Kirk, 1972; Robinson & Robinson, 1976). Thus, attention is presumed to increase in special and

## Table 5-7
## Academic Behavior: Descriptive Statistics

| Measure | Nonhandicapped Learners | | | Mainstreamed EMR Learners | | | | | | Nonmainstreamed EMR Learners | | |
| --- | --- | --- | --- | --- | --- | --- | --- | --- | --- | --- | --- | --- |
| | | | | Regular Class | | | Special Resource Class | | | | | |
| | X | SD | N | X | SD | N | X | SD | N | X | SD | N |
| Attention to academic task | | | | | | | | | | | | |
| Attention to task a | .83 | .11 | 305 | .72 | .18 | 319 | .89 | .11 | 278 | .80 | .14 | 250 |
| Cognitive interaction with teacher | | | | | | | | | | | | |
| Total cognitive interaction with teacher b | 9.76 | 6.59 | 301 | 8.14 | 12.02 | 320 | 29.05 | 22.08 | 277 | 22.37 | 15.88 | 242 |

a Proportion of 10-second time segments learner was on task.
b Average number of responses per hour.

resource classes, where a more appropriate match between student capability and instruction may be achieved in a lower student-teacher ratio.

In addition to attending to task, educational theorists from Dewey (1925) to Piaget (Flavell, 1963) have emphasized the need for students to become actively involved in the learning process. Although students may appear to pay attention, it is primarily through cognitive verbal interactions with teachers that they convey active involvement in learning.

Past research on verbal interaction in the classroom has focused on specific participatory behaviors of nonhandicapped students. Evidence on the relationships of these behaviors to achievement is inconsistent. Dunkin and Biddle (1974) reported five studies that found no relationships between amount of pupils' talk and achievement. However, Brophy and Evertson (1975) found that the frequency of pupil-initiated questions was positively related to gains in pupils' learning. Pupil-initiated comments were found to be positively related to learning gains when the pupil had the teacher's permission to speak, but were negatively related when the pupil did not have permission.

In this study, learner attention to academic task and cognitive interaction with the teacher were examined through the use of systematic classroom observation. Behavioral measures for the mainstreamed EMR learners were available in both the regular and resource classes. The descriptive results for the three learner groups on academic behavior are summarized in Table 5-7.

**Attention to Academic Task**: To measure the academic-attention-to-task component of the model, the attention-to-task category on the Indiana Behavior Management System (IBMS) was used. Learner on-task behavior (attention to task) was defined as:

> Pupils' head and eyes are oriented towards persons or objects related to the lesson or lesson instructions. "Lesson" is defined by the teacher (Fink & Semmel, 1971, p. 141).

At 10-second intervals, the observer coded the learner's current behavior as either on-task or as one of eight mutually-exclusive and exhaustive categories of off-task behavior. (Observer reliability for IBMS categories is discussed in Appendix C.) Learner attention was scored as a proportion of all 10-second segments in which on-task behavior was coded; that is, as the number of on-task codes divided by the number of on-task plus off-task codes.

The on-task behavior of the nonhandicapped learners with their regular teachers was on average somewhat greater than that of the mainstreamed EMR learners. Nonhandicapped learners obtained a mean score of 0.83, indicating they were on task for 83% of the time segments in which they were observed (Table 5-7). Mainstreamed EMR learners were on task for 72% of the time segments observed in the regular classroom and for 89% of the time segments observed with their principal resource teachers. The nonmainstreamed EMR learners were similar in on-task behaviors to the nonhandicapped learners, being on task for 80% of the time segments. Their mean on-task score was about midway between the means for the mainstreamed EMR learners in regular and resource classrooms. The attention- to-academic-task standardized scores are given in Table 5-3.

**Cognitive Interaction with the Teacher**: The Individual Cognitive Demand Schedule (ICDS) was used to measure students' total cognitive interaction with the teacher.[3] The total cognitive interaction with the teacher scale consists of 11 categories of cognitive discourse divided into high- and low-level response categories. Observers coded both the number and the type of cognitive responses the learner made to teacher demands. From this information, the frequency of cognitive interactions per hour of observation was calculated. Observer reliability on the ICDS categories is discussed in Appendix C.

The nonhandicapped learners and the mainstreamed EMR learners had about the same number of cognitive interactions with the regular classroom teacher (Table 5-7)—on average, 10 and 8 responses per hour, respectively. Considerably more cognitive interaction is evident for the mainstreamed EMR learners with their special resource teachers, an average of 29 cognitive responses per hour. The cognitive interaction responses per hour observed for the nonmainstreamed EMR learners in special self-contained classes averaged about 22 responses.[4] (See Table 5-3 for the standardized scores.)

**Discussion**: The learners, regardless of group, were found to be attending to task a majority of the time they were observed. There was a sizable difference, however, between the proportion of time the mainstreamed EMR learners were on task in the regular class (72%) and in the resource class (89%). The average percentage of observed time on task for both the nonhandicapped and the mainstreamed EMR learners was about midway between the two values for the mainstreamed EMR learners.

It seems likely that the greater degree of cognitive interaction in the resource and special classes may be due to the lower pupil/teacher ratio and the more individualized focus of the teacher in special education settings. In classes with fewer students, the teacher can spend more time with individual students, monitoring their behavior and engaging them in cognitive interaction. A smaller class probably has fewer distractions than a larger class, making it easier for EMR learners to stay on task. No matter what the explanation, a mainstreamed student apparently experiences more instructionally related interactions with the resource teacher than with the regular teacher. The instructional situation available in all three settings is discussed in Chapter 8.

## Academic Attitudes

Attitudes are relatively enduring systems of cognitive and affective evaluation reflecting beliefs which the individual has formulated about objects of social concern (Shaw & Wright, 1967). Academic attitudes refer to attitudes toward school learning and the learning process. A student's academic attitudes are assumed to play an important role in learning. If schools are to promote a healthy learning environment, they must foster positive academic attitudes (Blair, Jones, & Simpson, 1968).

We examined two kinds of academic attitudes generally considered to be important to learners: academic self-concept and attitudes toward school. Academic self-concept refers to students' perceptions of their scholastic abilities, as well as their feelings about those abilities. Attitude toward school refers to students' affective reactions toward their experiences with the teacher, subject matter, and available activities.

It seems reasonable to assume that students' academic self-concepts develop largely from their experiences in school, particularly those that shape their perceptions of how others evaluate their scholastic abilities. Self-concept theory suggests that students with negative academic self-concepts who anticipate failure in academic settings may behave in ways which bring about their failure. In addition, students with negative academic self-concepts may avoid academic situations, or at least view them negatively and keep their participation to a minimum.

Academic self-concept not only influences behavior but also has been shown to be related to achievement. Students with poor academic self-concepts have been found to perform less well academically than students with positive self-concepts (Brookover, Paterson, & Thomas, 1962; Dennell, 1971; Ruckhaber, 1966), a finding also reported for EMR learners (Snyder, 1966).

Since EMR learners have often met with failure in school situations, it is not surprising they have been found to have lower academic self-concepts than their nonhandicapped peers (Snyder, 1966). Studies that have compared the self-concepts of mainstreamed and nonmainstreamed EMR learners have been inconsistent. Of three studies on this topic, one found that mainstreamed students have a higher self-concept (Carroll, 1967), one found that nonmainstreamed students have a higher self-concept (Towne & Joiner, 1966), and one found no differences (Walker, 1972).

Although the promotion of a positive attitude toward school is considered a goal of the school, only a moderate amount of research has been conducted on this subject. Most studies have found that the vast majority of students say they like school, even when their questionnaire responses are given anonymously (Jackson, 1968; Tenenbaum, 1940; Sister Josephina, 1959). Students with low ability have been found to like school as much as students of higher ability (Berk, Rose, & Stewart, 1970; Tenenbaum, 1944). In addition, low-SES children are reported to like school as much as or more than their middle-class peers (Berk, Rose & Stewart, 1970; Ehrlich, 1968; Neale & Proshek, 1967) and Black and Spanish-surnamed students have been found to like school as much as Anglo students (LaBelle, 1971).

Several investigators have reported low relationships between attitudes toward school and achievement (Brodie, 1964; Dusewicz, 1972; Rosen, 1956), although others have failed to find a relationship (LaBelle, 1971) or have reported differences only when students with very positive or very negative attitudes comprised the sample (Jackson, 1968).

A few studies have compared mainstreamed and nonmainstreamed EMR students' attitudes toward school. Budoff and Gottlieb (1976) found that mainstreamed students have more positive attitudes toward school than do nonmainstreamed students. Findings of other studies point in a similar direction. Schurr (1967) reported that special class students revealed increasing dissatisfaction with their placement over time, and Iano (1972) indicated that reintegrated students tend to like their current regular class placement more than their previous self-contained class placement.

The scales used to measure academic self-concept and attitude toward school in this study as well as descriptions of the three learner groups are provided in the following sections. It should be noted that the measures of academic attitudes reflect the learners' general attitudes concerning their academic abilities and their school. Academic attitudes were less tied to a specific class setting than were academic status and behavior. The descriptive statistics on academic attitudes for the three learner groups are summarized in Table 5-8.

**Academic Self-Concept:** The academic self-concept scale derived from *About You and Your Friends* (AYYF) was used as an indicator of the students' academic self-concepts. It consisted of 21 items such as "Are you smart?" and "Do you think you know as much as the other children in your class?" Each learner responded to these questions by writing "yes" (scored as 2) or "no" (scored as 1) on an answer sheet. The minimum possible score is 21; the maximum, 42. The internal consistency of the scale is 0.82.

All three groups of learners, on average, reported moderately positive academic self-concepts. The scores presented in Table 5-8 indicate the average number of positive responses given by nonhandicapped learners, mainstreamed and nonmainstreamed EMR learners were 14, 13, and 15, respectively. The three groups reported feeling much the same about their academic abilities.

**Attitudes Toward School:**Five scales were used to measure the learners' attitudes toward school.[5] The first three—attitudes toward reading, mathematics, and teacher/school — were derived from *How Do You Feel, Part II* (HDYF-II); the fourth—attitude toward school activities—was derived from *How Do You Feel, Part I* (HYDF-I); and the fifth — school enthusiasm — was derived from *About You and Your Friends* (AYYF.)

**Attitude Toward Reading**: This scale consisted of six HDYF-II items such as "Think about the books you use for your reading now. How do you feel?" and "Do you remember the reading books you used at the beginning of the year?"

Each item was suffixed by "How do you feel?", "Which is your face?", or a comparable question. As each item was read aloud, the learner responded by

**Table 5–8**
**Academic Attitudes: Descriptive Statistics**

| Measure | Nonhandicapped Learners | | | Mainstreamed EMR Learners | | | Nonmainstreamed EMR Learners | | |
|---|---|---|---|---|---|---|---|---|---|
| | X | SD | N | X | SD | N | X | SD | N |
| Academic self-concept | | | | | | | | | |
| Academic self-concept | 34.95 | 4.49 | 349 | 33.88 | 4.15 | 349 | 35.59 | 4.21 | 260 |
| Attitude toward school | | | | | | | | | |
| Attitude toward reading | 14.79 | 2.63 | 337 | 14.62 | 2.82 | 330 | 14.50 | 2.90 | 236 |
| Attitude toward mathematics | 14.18 | 3.26 | 337 | 13.70 | 3.33 | 330 | 14.14 | 3.03 | 236 |
| Current attitude toward teacher/school | 15.27 | 2.90 | 337 | 14.98 | 2.87 | 330 | 14.86 | 2.73 | 236 |
| Attitude toward school activities | 52.85 | 8.13 | 344 | 53.18 | 7.27 | 347 | 54.07 | 7.80 | 263 |
| School enthusiasm | 54.19 | 5.15 | 349 | 52.88 | 4.81 | 349 | 53.43 | 4.99 | 259 |

marking one of three faces which best represented his feelings: a smiling face (= 3), a neutral or indifferent face (= 2), or a frowning face (= 1). For the attitude-toward-reading scale, the minimum possible score was 6 and the maximum possible score was 18; the internal consistency was 0.68. As indicated in Table 5-8, the nonhandicapped, mainstreamed EMR, and nonmainstreamed EMR learners all had relatively positive attitudes toward reading. In each of the samples, the average reponse per item fell almost midway between the neutral and the positive options.

**Attitude Toward Math:** The attitude toward math scale consisted of six HDYF-II items. Representative of them are "Think about how you did in math when you started school in the fall. How do you feel?" and "Show how you feel when you think about working math problems now...." These items were administered and scored in the same manner as the attitude toward reading items. The maximum possible score was 18; the internal consistency was 0.74. All three groups had relatively positive attitude-toward-math scores (see Table 5-8).

**Current Attitude Toward Teacher/School:** This scale was also derived from the HDYF-II, was administered and scored in the same manner as the other HDYF-II scales, and consisted of six items such as "Think about the teacher you have now. How do you feel?" and "Think about what school is like now...." The minimum score on this scale was 6, the maximum score was 18, and the alpha coefficient was 0.74. The scores on this scale, like the scores on the other two HDYF-II scales, were relatively positive for all three groups (see Table 5-8).

**Attitude Toward School Activities:** This scale was derived from HDYF-I. The item format and response modes were identical to those of HDYF-II. The attitude-toward-school- activities scale consisted of 22 items. Representative of them are "It is time to do a page of math (arithmetic) problems. How do you feel?" and "You are visiting your aunt and uncle. They ask you if you like your school...." The minimum score on the attitude toward school activities scale was 22 and the maximum was 66; internal consistency was 0.85. Regardless of group, the learners were quite positive in their attitudes toward school activities (see Table 5-8), and did not differ from each other.

**School Enthusiasm:** The fifth indicator was the school enthusiasm scale which was derived from AYYF. It consisted of 30 items such as "Do you like school?" and "Do you like to be with other children?" As an item was read to a small group of target learners, each responded by writing "no" (= 1) or "yes" (= 2) on the answer sheet. A minimum score was 30; the maximum score was

60; internal consistency was 0.84. All three group means on this scale exceeded the neutral score of 45, indicating, on average, the learners felt equally enthusiastic toward school (see Table 5-8).

**Attitude Toward School Composite Score:** Scores on the five scales were summed and standardized. The standardized mean score was remarkably similar for the three learner groups (see Table 5-3).

**Discussion:** The academic self-concept and the attitude toward school scores were relatively positive for all three groups. It is sometimes suggested that students suffer from a failure set (MacMillan, 1971). If this is so, it was not evident in the self-reports of the EMR learners of this study.

## Social Competence

The learners' social competence was also defined by their social status, behaviors, and attitudes. We have taken the approach that the reactions of others and their observable behavior, as well as individuals' feelings about themselves and their peers, define the individuals' competence to meet the social demands of their environments. Children are said to be socially competent within the context of their educational environments (in this case, their classes) to the extent that they are well accepted by their classmates, have favorable attitudes toward themselves and their classmates, and generally engage in prosocial behaviors.

Mead (1934) proposed that social competence is a product of the interaction of the individual with others' attitudes toward the individual rather than stemming from the individual alone. Interpersonal competence is postulated to be an important determinant of successful adjustment. Mead (1934) and Sullivan (1953) agreed that individuals who are perceived favorably by others tend to perceive others favorably and to behave in ways that reinforce acceptance by others. Conversely, individuals who are perceived negatively by others tend to perceive others negatively and to act in ways that increase others' negative perceptions. Social theorists such as Mead (1934) and Sullivan (1953) suggest that the elements of social competence are interdependent. Each of these conditions of social competence has been seen as an important goal in the education of EMR learners. In particular, special classes have tended to stress the importance of the development of interpersonal behavior skills. In the following sections, previous research and the present findings related to social status, behavior, and attitudes are discussed.

## Social Status

It has long been believed, and research has confirmed, that mentally retarded children generally are not well liked by their nonhandicapped peers (Johnson, 1950). This belief that mentally retarded children need to be sheltered from these negative attitudes was in part responsible for their placement in special classes. Research findings have supported this idea. For example, Thurstone (1960) found that EMR children received higher social acceptance scores from their EMR peers in self-contained classes than from their nonhandicapped peers in the regular classes. Ironically, placement in special classes has recently been proposed as a major reason for the rejection of EMR children by nonhandicapped children (Dunn, 1968). Dunn argued that placement in special classes isolates EMR children from the mainstream of school activity, exaggerates their differences in the eyes of nonhandicapped children, and results in their having to bear the stigma of the placement and the handicap label. But there is little evidence that the special class placement per se is a major reason for the poor social status EMR children have with their nonhandicapped peers. Goodman, Gottlieb, and Harrison (1972) found little difference between the ratings that nonhandicapped schoolmates gave to EMR students in regular classes as opposed to special classes.

One reason suggested for EMR children's low social status is perceived or actual misbehavior (Johnson, 1950). It is presently unknown whether EMR children actually exhibit extensive misbehavior or whether other children perceive the behavior differently from similar behavior exhibited by them. The latter possibility was suggested by Gardner (1966) and has been supported in a laboratory study (Gottlieb, 1975a). Also, physical appearance, neatness, and appropriate use of verbal and nonverbal information may affect the EMR child's social status (Gottlieb, 1976): Deviation from an accepted standard in appearance and/or behavior is likely to negatively impact social status. The extent of the impact remains to be determined.

Social status is often considered as a continuum with acceptance at one end and rejection at the other. An important psychometric issue in research on social status is the meaning of scores derived from different types of sociometric instruments. The traditional sociometric measure asks students to select one or more classmates as a friend, as someone to help with school work, as a playmate, etc. The acceptance score is then determined by the number of times each student is chosen. Other instruments ask each student to rate all the other students in the class, making it possible to score the number of acceptances each student receives as well as the number of rejections. Evidence suggests that acceptance and rejection may not constitute a single continuum and therefore should be scored separately (Bryan, 1974; Trent, 1957).

In this study, social acceptance and rejection were used as two indices of social status. Preliminary analysis of these data indicated that acceptance and rejection loaded on the same factor but were not correlated with the same variables (Gottlieb, 1975b). Social acceptance was related to teachers' and peers' perceptions of academic performance, whereas rejection was related to teachers' and peers' perceptions of misbehavior. Conceptual biases and these results led to the maintenance of separate acceptance and rejection constructs.

**Acceptance:** Acceptance was measured by one scale, which was derived from *How I Feel Toward Others* (HIFTO). The HIFTO required each child to rate his attraction for every other child in the class by marking one of four faces: a smiling face for friends, a frowning face for classmates whom the student did not want to have as friends at that time, a neutral face for classmates whom the student did not particularly like or dislike, or a question mark for classmates the student did not know (don't know). The social acceptance variable consisted of the number of smiles the target learner received from peers divided by the total number of ratings received other than "don't know."

On the average, the nonhandicapped learners received smiles from 52.86% while the average for the mainstreamed EMR learners was 37.75%. This is consistent with previous findings which suggest that nonhandicapped students do not accept EMR students as readily as they accept other nonhandicapped students. However, most of the mainstreamed EMR learners were not without friends. Nearly all of the mainstreamed EMR learners (about 94%) were accepted by at least three of their regular class peers (see Table 5-9).

The nonmainstreamed EMR learners were rated as friends by an average of 61.49% of their classmates. This indicates high peer acceptance within the special self-contained classrooms. The standardized scores for this measure are presented in Table 5-3.

**Rejection:** Social rejection was measured by the same instrument as acceptance, the HIFTO. The extent of rejection of a learner was computed as the percentage of frowns given by classmates (see Table 5-9).

On the average, the nonhandicapped learners received frowns from 17.92% of their classmates while the mainstreamed EMR learners' average was 26.67%. Although considerable variance is evident in the scores, the nonhandicapped learners, on the average, appear to have been less socially rejected than the mainstreamed EMR learners. One cannot say that the mainstreamed EMR learners were totally rejected. Only 13% of the mainstreamed learners were rejected by as much as half of their regular class peers.

The nonmainstreamed EMR learners were given frowns by an average of 19.34% of their classmates, differing little from the nonhandicapped learners' scores (see Table 5-9).

**Discussion:** The patterns of acceptance and rejection scores differ markedly for the different groups of learners. The mainstreamed EMR learners were rejected by a greater proportion of their nonhandicapped peers than were the nonhandicapped learners. Their standardized mean acceptance score was approximately 0.70 standard deviations lower than that of the nonhandicapped group and their standardized mean rejection score was 0.50 standard deviations higher. The nonhandicapped and the mainstreamed groups, however, also received 29.22% and 35.58% neutral or "don't know" scores, respectively; computed as total nominations received minus smiles plus frowns. Thus, on average, 73.32% of the regular class peers did not reject the mainstreamed EMR learners in their classrooms. Furthermore, nearly all of the mainstreamed EMR learners had at least three friends in their regular class.

The nonmainstreamed EMR learners were rejected by less than 20% and accepted by more than 60% of their classmates. The nonmainstreamed EMR learners received ratings from their EMR peers which were somewhat similar in pattern to the ratings received by the nonhandicapped learners from their nonhandicapped peers.

These results suggest that EMR students are likely to experience relatively more acceptance and less rejection if placed in special self-contained classes with EMR peers than if placed in regular classes with younger, low-achieving nonhandicapped peers. If a high level of social acceptance is thought to be critical to the well-being of a particular EMR student, a special self-contained class would seem to be the best placement. But few of the mainstreamed EMR learners were without friends in the regular classes, and it is likely that being highly accepted is not critical to either type of students: Even a few friends are sufficient to feel part of the regular class.

Table 5–9
Social Status: Descriptive Statistics

| Measure | Nonhandicapped Learners | | | Mainstreamed EMR Learners | | | Nonmainstreamed EMR Learners | | |
|---|---|---|---|---|---|---|---|---|---|
| | X | SD | N | X | SD | N | X | SD | N |
| Acceptance Percentage of smiles received | 52.86 | 18.77 | 344 | 37.75 | 18.34 | 340 | 61.49 | 23.90 | 253 |
| Rejection Percentage of frowns received | 17.92 | 16.60 | 344 | 26.67 | 17.42 | 340 | 19.34 | 18.98 | 253 |

## Social Behavior

Learner social behavior has been of interest to researchers largely in terms of its relationship to social acceptance and rejection by peers. Research with nonhandicapped children has indicated that sociometrically-accepted children exhibit considerably different patterns of behavior from those displayed by sociometrically-rejected children (Binney & Powell, 1953). Sociometrically-low nonhandicapped children exhibit nonconforming behaviors, bodily self-contact, solitary activities such as walking around or throwing objects, and the tendency not to smile.

Given the frequent finding that EMR children tend to have lower social status than their nonhandicapped peers (Baldwin, 1958; Gottlieb, 1975a; Johnson, 1950), one would expect differences in the observable behaviors of EMR and nonhandicapped students, with EMR students exhibiting prosocial behaviors less frequently and disruptive or aggressive behaviors more frequently than other students.

However, observation studies have failed to confirm differences in the actual frequency of misbehavior exhibited by EMR and non-EMR children. Gampel, Gottlieb, and Harrison (1974), for example, compared the classroom behaviors of four groups of students: nonhandicapped students, students with low IQs who had never been identified for special class placement, mainstreamed EMR students from special classes, and EMR students in a special self-contained class. Four months after the EMR students were placed in regular classes, the behaviors of the mainstreamed, nonmainstreamed, and nonlabelled low-IQ students did not differ from the behavior of their average IQ nonhandicapped peers. Mainstreamed EMR students' behavior did differ from the behavior of the nonmainstreamed students: They displayed significantly less restless behavior, gave fewer negative verbal responses, and received fewer negative verbal responses than the nonmainstreamed students. A subsequent study confirmed the finding: At the end of the first school year, the mainstreamed students displayed significantly more prosocial behavior than did the nonmainstreamed students (Gottlieb, Gampel, & Budoff, 1975).

Project PRIME examined the friendly/cooperative and antisocial behaviors of the nonhandicapped, mainstreamed EMR, and nonmainstreamed EMR learners. Behavioral measures were available for the mainstreamed EMR learners in both their regular and resource classes.

**Friendly/Cooperative Behavior:** Two scales were used as indicators of friendly/cooperative behavior: socialization (a measure of the frequency of social contact) and positive social behavior. Both of these scales were derived from the Florida Climate and Control System (FLACCS) observation instrument.

*Socialization:* This measure was derived from observer ratings of the frequency of the learner's verbal and nonverbal interaction with peers. The observer watched the classroom for 2 of every 10 minutes and rated the learner as either "almost never" (= 1), "occasionally" (= 2), or "frequently" (= 3) interacting with peers. An average rating was subsequently determined by dividing the sum of the socialization scores by the number of two-minute intervals observed. It should be noted that this is not a rate (frequency per unit of time) but an average rating.

The average socialization score for a target learner could range from 1-3. Overt socialization behaviors were infrequent for all three groups of learners. Each of the average ratings presented in Table 5-10 represents a rating about midway between "almost never" and "occasionally."

*Positive Social Behavior:* The positive social behavior scale was derived from the factor analysis of the FLACCS and consisted of 15 learner descriptors such as "Smiles, laughs with another" and "Is enthusiastic." The positive social behavior scale had an alpha value of 0.65. At the end of each series of two-minute observation periods, the observer marked those descriptors that applied to the target learner. Coding of the positive social behavior scale was binary. That is, a descriptor (item) was scored "1" if there were one or more occurrences of the behavior during a two-minute observation interval, and "0" if not. A total score was obtained for each two-minute interval, and subsequently averaged to form an average rating of positive social behavior for the learner. The average ratings could range from 0-15. To obtain an estimate of the minimum number of positive behaviors typically occurring per hour, the average ratings for the two-minute intervals were multiplied by 30. This is a minimum value: If one type of behavior occurred more than once per observation it was recorded only once.

In general, few items received a coding of "1" during the observed two-minute intervals (see Table 5-10). The nonhandicapped learners obtained a mean rating of 0.50, equivalent to displaying a minimum of 15 positive behaviors per hour. The mainstreamed EMR learners obtained a mean rating of 0.42 when observed in regular classes (a minimum rate of 13 positive behaviors per hour) and 0.62 when these learners were observed in resource classes (a minimum rate of 19 positive behaviors per hour). The mainstreamed EMR learners seemed to show more friendly/cooperative behavior in resource classes than did either group in regular classes. The mean rating of the nonmainstreamed EMR learners was almost identical to that of the mainstreamed EMR learners in resource classes. All ratings were accompanied by relatively large standard deviations, which indicates learners received substantially different ratings. The mean scores should be interpreted with caution.

*Friendly/Cooperative Behavior Composite Scores*: The scores on the socialization and the positive social behavior scales were summed and standardized to form the friendly/cooperative behavior composite score (see Table 5-3). There were only slight differences among the means of the three groups on this measure.

**Antisocial Behavior**: Both teacher ratings and observation instruments were used to determine the frequency of the antisocial behavior of the three learner groups. Ratings from regular class teachers as well as resource teachers were available for the mainstreamed EMR learners.

There were three indicators of antisocial behavior: The TRS antisocial behavior scale, the FLACCS negative social behavior scale, and the IBMS II aggression/resistance scale.[6]

*TRS Antisocial Behavior*: This scale was derived from the Teacher Rating Scale (TRS), and consisted of 33 items. Two representative items are "Attempts to dominate or bully other children" and "Is aggressive in underhanded ways." The teacher(s) of each target learner rated them on each item, using a 5-point scale ("never" = 1, "rarely" = 2, "sometimes" = 3, "usually" = 4, or "always" = 5). The minimum score on this scale was 33, the maximum 165. The alpha value of internal consistency was 0.98, based on average teacher ratings.

The mean score for the nonhandicapped learners was 66.32, equivalent to an average rating per item of 2.0, or "rarely" displaying antisocial behavior (Table 5-10).

The mean scores for the mainstreamed EMR learners in regular classes (73.06) and in their resource classes (74.84) were nearly identical and similar to the mean score for the nonmainstreamed EMR learners (74.68). On the antisocial behavior scale, then, the average rating per item for the EMR learners, regardless of learner type or teacher type, was about 2.3, corresponding to a response only slightly above "rarely" displays antisocial behavior. The EMR learners were not rated very differently from the nonhandicapped learners in antisocial behavior.

*Negative Social Behavior*: The negative social behavior scale was derived from the factor analysis of the FLACCS. There were 20 descriptors on the scale. Representative of them are "Uncooperative, resistant" and "Makes disparaging remarks." The scale was developed in the same manner as the FLACCS positive social behavior scale. The potential score range was from 0-20 with an alpha coefficient of 0.74.

Negative social behavior occurred occasionally among all groups of learners (Table 5-10). The nonhandicapped learners received an average

Table 5-10

Social Behavior: Descriptive Statistics

| Measure | Nonhandicapped Learners | | | Mainstreamed EMR Learners | | | | | | Nonmainstreamed EMR Learners | | |
|---|---|---|---|---|---|---|---|---|---|---|---|---|
| | | | | Regular Class | | | Special Resource Class | | | | | |
| | X | SD | N | X | SD | N | X | SD | N | X | SD | N |
| Friendly/cooperative behavior | | | | | | | | | | | | |
| Socialization | 1.48 | .37 | 301 | 1.42 | .39 | 315 | 1.54 | .49 | 265 | 1.63 | .44 | 238 |
| Positive social behavior | .50 | .53 | 302 | .42 | .43 | 320 | .62 | .73 | 272 | .64 | .62 | 240 |
| Antisocial behavior | | | | | | | | | | | | |
| Antisocial behavior | 66.32 | 23.61 | 340 | 73.06 | 25.11 | 334 | 74.84 | 23.21 | 310 | 74.68 | 25.47 | 265 |
| Negative social behavior | .06 | .18 | 302 | .09 | .21 | 320 | .13 | .32 | 272 | .14 | .25 | 240 |
| Aggression/resistance | .00 | .00 | 305 | .00 | .00 | 319 | .00 | .01 | 278 | .00 | .01 | 250 |

rating of 0.06 and the mainstreamed EMR learners received an average rating of 0.09 in the regular class. These values translate to minimum hourly rates of two to three negative behaviors on average. The average rating of negative social behavior of mainstreamed EMR learners in the resource room was 0.13, or a minimum of four negative behaviors per hour on average, differing little from the regular classroom rating. The nonmainstreamed EMR learners received an average negative social behavior rating of 0.14, nearly identical to that received by the mainstreamed EMR learners in the resource class. These average ratings must be used with caution because the standard deviations are relatively large, indicating that different individuals received substantially different ratings.

*Aggression/Resistance*: The final indicator, the aggression/resistance scale of the IBMS, was also an observation scale. This scale was composed of four learner aggression or resistant off-task categories: verbal aggression, physical aggression, verbal resistance, and physical resistance. An observer recorded the target learner's behavior during 10-second time segments as either on task or as one of eight mutually exclusive and exhaustive off-task behaviors, four of which represented aggressive or resistant behavior. The aggression/resistance score was calculated by dividing the sum of the time segments in which any one of the four aggressive/resistant behaviors occurred by the total number of time segments. This score represents the proportion of all 10-second behavior segments in which the target learner was either aggressive or resistant.

Aggressive/resistant behavior was rarely observed in any learner group (Table 5-10). The mean proportion of observed time segments in which aggression/resistance was coded was negligible for all learner groups and settings.

*Antisocial Behavior Composite Score*: The mean score for the three antisocial behavior scales was summed and standardized to obtain the antisocial behavior composite score (see Table 5-3). The scores on this composite were similar for all three groups.

**Discussion**: To the extent that the Project PRIME learners were representive of their classmates, the results for social behavior suggest that relatively little peer-to-peer social interaction was observed in the regular or special classes. It seems probable that teachers do not tolerate extensive socializing among students. For all learners, regardless of setting, the data did suggest that friendly/cooperative behaviors occurred more frequently than antisocial behaviors.

Substantial differences between the groups in friendly/cooperative or antisocial behaviors were not evident. The mainstreamed EMR learners were observed to display less friendly/cooperative behavior and slightly more antisocial behavior in the regular classes than did nonhandicapped learners but the differences were too small (not exceeding 0.20 standard deviations) to have educational significance.

## Social Attitudes

Social attitudes are largely comprised of social self-concepts and attitudes toward peers. An individual's social self-concept can be thought of as his view of his social abilities; that is, his sense of belonging, acceptance, and adequacy in social situations. Children's social self-concepts develop from experiences in social situations (Sullivan, 1953). Children with poor social self-concepts may try to avoid social situations (McCandless, 1973). Thus, while children may be physically present in school, they may rarely participate in classroom interactions and may withdraw during social periods such as free time or lunch.

EMR children tend to rely somewhat more on others' evaluations of them to shape their self-perceptions than do nonhandicapped children (Ellis, 1963). EMR children are also likely to be rejected by relatively more of their nonhandicapped peers (Johnson, 1950). If these children perceive themselves as rejected, this perception could negatively affect their social self-concepts. Evidence suggests that these children do in fact perceive that they are viewed negatively by nonhandicapped children, ascribe more positive traits to children in nonhandicapped schools than to children in their own special schools (vonBracken, 1967), and have somewhat poorer self-concepts than their nonhandicapped peers (Snyder, 1966).

In fact, very little research has been conducted on attitudes of EMR children toward their nonhandicapped peers. Theories of interpersonal attraction suggest several determinants of positive and negative attitudes toward others which have implications for predicting the attitudes of EMR children. Thibaut and Kelley (1959) and Homans (1961) believed that people tend to like those persons who provide them with rewards, chief among which is social acceptance or approval. Thus, in reciprocal reward theory, people are thought to like those persons who like them in return. Homans (1961) further suggested that an individual's reaction to acceptance or approval is mediated by his self-esteem: People react unfavorably and reject persons or situations that give them more approval or acceptance than they feel they deserve.

Other interpersonal attraction theorists have posited that similarity of observable valued characteristics influences attraction between people. Festinger (1954) suggested that people evaluate themselves by comparing themselves with others and that the most satisfying comparisons are with similar others. In his view, people accept and wish to associate with similar others. Similarity in race, SES, and ability have all been found to be related to interpersonal attraction (Bonney, 1946, 1949; Byrne, Clore, Worchel, 1966). Studies with elementary school children have found that children also tend to like others of the same sex (Baker, 1976; Gronlund, 1953).

In the current study, two constructs were used to depict a learner's social attitude: feelings of loneliness and feelings about peers. A summary of the descriptive results for social attitudes is provided in Table 5-11.

**Feelings of Loneliness**: Feelings of loneliness — the isolation/anxiety scale from AYYF — contains 19 items such as "Is it hard for you to make friends?" and "Do you feel left out of things in your class?" Each child responded to the items as they were read aloud by writing "yes" (= 2) or "no" (= 1) on the answer sheet. The minimum score on this scale was 19, the maximum 38, and alpha value of internal consistency 0.76.[7]

The three learner groups did not differ substantially in mean scores (Table 5-11) — all were close to the absolute midpoint (28.5). The mean score for each of the EMR groups corresponded to about 10 affirmations of the isolation/anxiety items while the mean score for the nonhandicapped learners was about 9 affirmative items. The standardized scores for this measure are reported in Table 5-3.

**Feelings About Peers**: Feelings about peers were measured by two scales, using HIFTO: peers liked, indicated by the percentage of classmates given smiles by the learner (i.e., those classmates the learner desired to have as friends); and peers disliked, indicated by the percentage of frowning faces marked (classmates not desired as friends). These scales were somewhat ipsative, yielding a correlation of -0.52. This correlation is affected by the existence of two other choices: a neutral face and a question mark. Because of the ipsative nature of the scales, the "peers disliked" score was subtracted from the "peers liked" score for "the feelings about peers" composite. Split-class correlation coefficients were 0.68 and 0.69 for "peers liked" and "peers disliked" respectively.

All three groups reported liking a higher percentage of learners in their respective classes than they disliked (see Table 5-11). The nonhandicapped learners liked relatively fewer of their classmates than did either the mainstreamed or nonmainstreamed EMR learners. The mainstreamed EMR learners liked relatively more of their regular classmates than did the nonhandicapped learners, supporting vonBracken's (1967) suggestion that EMR children may ascribe positive traits to nonhandicapped children even though they may perceive themselves as viewed negatively by them. The three groups differed little in the percentage of classmates that they reported disliking. See Table 5-3 for the standardized scores for this measure.

Table 5-11
Social Attitudes: Descriptive Statistics

| Measure | Nonhandicapped Learners | | | Mainstreamed EMR Learners | | | Nonmainstreamed EMR Learners | | |
|---|---|---|---|---|---|---|---|---|---|
| | X | SD | N | X | SD | N | X | SD | N |
| Feelings of loneliness | | | | | | | | | |
| Isolation/anxiety | 27.75 | 3.76 | 349 | 29.30 | 3.66 | 347 | 28.90 | 3.55 | 257 |
| Feelings about peers | | | | | | | | | |
| Peers liked (% smiles given) | 49.56 | 21.05 | 344 | 56.02 | 23.69 | 341 | 61.02 | 26.45 | 256 |
| Peers disliked (% frowns given) | 20.16 | 17.61 | 344 | 17.50 | 16.41 | 341 | 19.43 | 20.69 | 256 |

**Discussion**: EMR learners were no more negative in social attitudes than were the nonhandicapped learners. Self-reported feelings of loneliness did not indicate that the lack of acceptance of mainstreamed EMR learners in regular classes had a harmful effect on their self-concepts. To the extent that the self-report scores accurately reflect the feelings of the EMR learners, neither EMR group seemed to feel any less socially adequate than the nonhandicapped learners. Both groups of EMR learners tended to be more accepting of their classmates than were the nonhandicapped learners. Thus, in spite of not being highly accepted in regular classes, the mainstreamed EMR learners still thought of many of their nonhandicapped peers as friends and did not report feeling extremely lonely.

# Profiles of the Learners

To integrate the findings for each learner group, the following profiles of an average nonhandicapped learner, mainstreamed EMR learner, and nonmainstreamed EMR learner were constructed based on mean scores on the academic and social competence measures. It should be remembered, however, that there was considerable variance on some of the competency measures — some members of the learner groups deviate markedly from these profiles.

## Nonhandicapped Learner

Both MAT math and reading scores as well as teacher estimates of math and reading level indicated that the average nonhandicapped learner was a low achiever, and was likely to be in the lowest third of percentile ranks according to national norms. Corroborative evidence came from the nonhandicapped learner's teachers, who felt that these learners were achieving somewhat below grade level. The teachers, however, characterized the nonhandicapped learner as sometimes displaying academic effort and success as well as outgoing and expressive behavior in class. On the brightness and dullness scales of the peer nomination instument, regular class peers tended to nominate the nonhandicapped learner for about as many brightness as dullness items — about one or two out of a possible five.

The nonhandicapped learner was observed attending to academic tasks about 83% of the time, was on task much of the time, and had approximately 10 cognitive interactions per hour with the teacher.

The nonhandicapped learner tended to be moderately positive in academic attitude, both in attitude toward self and school. Specifically, the nonhandicapped learner:

- responded to two-thirds of the items on the scale measuring academic self-concept in the positive direction;
- reported positive reactions toward experiences with the teacher, subject matter, and available activities in school;
- ranged from neutral to positive in average response to items on each of the attitude-toward-school indicators;
- was accepted by about 53% of regular class peers and rejected by about 18%; reported liking 50% of the regular class peers and disliking only 20%;
- was likely to engage in somewhat more friendly/cooperative than antisocial behaviors;
- socialized in class infrequently;
- displayed about 15 or more positive behaviors in an hour;
- displayed few negative social behaviors; rarely displayed antisocial behavior; and
- did not report feelings of lonelineess.

## Mainstreamed EMR Learner

The average mainstreamed EMR learner was very low in academic achievement, with MAT math and reading scores in the lowest percentile according to national norms. The regular teachers estimated the mainstreamed EMR learner's math and reading achievement to be two or more years below grade level. They reported the mainstreamed EMR learner rarely displayed academic effort and success and was rarely outgoing and expressive in class. The peers in the regular class thought the mainstreamed EMR learner was characterized by three out of five items describing dullness but by one or no items describing brightness.

Mainstreamed EMR learners were observed to be on task about 72% of the time in the regular class; about 8% less time than was found for the nonhandicapped learner. They were more attentive to task in the resource class, attending to task 89% of the time observed. The mainstreamed EMR learner had about eight cognitive interactions per hour with the regular class teacher and more than three times as many interactions with the resource teacher.

The mainstreamed EMR learner

- was moderately positive in academic attitudes, not substantially different from the nonhandicapped learner in either academic self-concept or attitude toward school;
- was accepted by relatively fewer regular class peers (38%) and rejected by relatively more regular class peers (27%) than was the average nonhandicapped learner;
- differed little from the nonhandicapped learner in social behaviors in the regular class;
- displayed more friendly/cooperative behaviors than antisocial behaviors and slightly more friendly/cooperative behaviors in the resource class than in the regular class, although all prosocial behaviors were observed infrequently;
- rarely displayed antisocial behaviors;
- did not report feeling more lonely than the nonhandicapped learner, even though less accepted and more rejected than the nonhandicapped learner; and
- reported liking 56% of their regular class peers (a slightly higher percentage than reported by the nonhandicapped learner) and disliking about 18% (slightly lower than their nonhandicapped classmates).

## Nonmainstreamed EMR Learner

Like the mainstreamed EMR learners, the nonmainstreamed EMR learners were low in academic achievement. The special class teachers estimated their end-of-the-year reading and math levels to be equivalent to a grade score of 1.50-1.75. These teachers felt their students sometimes displayed academic effort and success as well as being outgoing and expressive. On these measures the nonmainstreamed EMR learner was given the same rating by the special teacher as the nonhandicapped learner was given by the regular teacher. In addition, the special class peers nominated the nonmainstreamed EMR learner for as many brightness items as dullness items, about two out of a possible five.

The nonmainstreamed EMR learner was observed to be attending to academic task 80% of the time and generally made about 22 cognitive responses to special teacher demands per hour and, like the nonhandicapped and mainstreamed EMR learner, reported moderately positive academic attitudes in affective reactions to experiences with school, their teachers, and the available activities.

Greater social acceptance seemed to occur in the special self-contained class than in the regular class. The nonmainstreamed EMR learner was accepted by 61% of his classmates — a slightly greater level of acceptance than was accorded the nonhandicapped learners by regular class peers and considerably more than was accorded the mainstreamed EMR learners by regular class peers — and was rejected by 19% of special class peers.

While peer-to-peer social interactions occur less frequently in special classes, like the other learners, the nonmainstreamed EMR learner was:

- more likely to engage in friendly/cooperative than antisocial behaviors;
- rarely displayed antisocial behaviors;
- reported having positive feelings toward many of his special class peers; and
- did not report feeling more lonely than did the other two types of learners.

# Relationships

This section examines the relationships among the learner academic and social competence measures by examining:

- the pattern of competence overlap between nonhandicapped and mainstreamed EMR learners; and
- the extent to which the competency areas are interrelated.

## Convergence of Competency Scores of the Mainstreamed EMR Learners with Those of the Nonhandicapped Learners

Students labelled retarded are commonly assumed to differ from students who are not so labelled. Regular teachers are apprehensive about mainstreaming EMR students into their classes because of these differences. For example, they report they do not feel confident in their ability to teach mentally retarded students (Deno, 1973). If the competencies of EMR students overlap those of nonhandicapped students in school-related functioning, teachers may be reassured and more willing to accommodate their classrooms to the needs of the EMR student.

Differences were reported between the mainstreamed EMR and nonhandicapped learners in current academic achievement levels and in the various social status measures. The magnitude of the differences, however, was sometimes quite small, suggesting sizeable overlap in the distributions on these characteristics.

The descriptive data on the academic and social competency composites based on the factor scores were standardized over the three learner groups. To assess the amount of overlap between the mainstreamed EMR and nonhandicapped learners in scores on the competency measures, however, the data for only these two groups were pooled and frequency distributions for each composite were calculated for this combined group. These distributions were then divided into quartiles. The percentage of mainstreamed EMR learners in each quartile was calculated. Since there were 356 mainstreamed EMR learners and 356 nonhandicapped contrast learners in these analyses, each quartile contained 178 learners. If the mainstreamed EMR learners were similar in distribution to the nonhandicapped learners, the percentage of mainstreamed EMR learners per quartile would be close to 50.

As expected, the smallest overlap occurred between the mainstreamed EMR and nonhandicapped learners' scores on measures of academic status. For normative academic status, 3% of the highest quartile and 94% of the lowest quartile consisted of mainstreamed EMR learners. The fact that any mainstreamed EMR learners were in the highest quartile in normative academic status is surprising and suggests that some of the EMR learners may have been mislabelled. About a third of the second highest quartile consisted of mainstreamed EMR learners while about a third of the third quartile consisted of nonhandicapped learners, indicating overlap between these two groups in the middle range of the distribution. It should be recalled that many of the nonhandicapped learners were below average in academic achievement and were about a year younger than the mainstreamed EMR learners. The data suggest that placing EMR learners in low-achieving classes a grade below their chronological age results in overlap with some proportion of their peers in achievement. EMR learners can be grouped with class peers for instruction rather than requiring a separate lesson, facilitating the teacher's instructional programming and making the mainstreaming of instruction realistic rather than cosmetic. The pattern for classroom academic status was basically similar to that for normative academic status—the overlap of scores was slightly larger.

Mainstreamed EMR learners made up about one-fourth of the top quartile of social acceptance and about three-fourths of the bottom quartile. For social rejection, mainstreamed learners constituted about two-thirds of the highest quartile and one-third of the lowest quartile. But the middle two quartiles of both social acceptance and rejection had a nearly equal representation of mainstreamed EMR and nonhandicapped learners.

Mainstreamed EMR learners made up approximately three-fourths of the lowest quartile on cognitive interaction and on attention to task and two-thirds of the highest quartile on feelings of loneliness. But, again, there were many mainstreamed EMR learners with scores similar to those of nonhandicapped learners, particularly in the middle of the range of scores.

Of the several areas of competence in which considerable score overlap occurred, the most surprising was social behavior, since many have argued that poor social behavior is almost as important a reason for referral as poor academic performance and that poor social behavior is responsible for EMR children's low social status. Yet 45% of the highest quartile on friendly/cooperative behavior and 40% of the lowest quartile on antisocial behavior consisted of mainstreamed EMR learners. There were slightly more mainstreamed EMR (60%) than nonhandicapped learners (40%) in the highest quartile of antisocial behavior. There was sufficient overlap to question the contention that students labelled as EMR typically are highly disruptive.

The distributions for three of the attitude composites — academic self-concept, attitude toward school, and feelings about peers — also showed considerable overlap of scores.

In summary, the areas in which the scores for the mainstreamed EMR learners were most divergent from those for the nonhandicapped learners were academic status, academic behavior, social status, and feelings of loneliness. Even in these areas, however, there was some overlap in the distribution. There was considerable overlap for the two groups' scores on the composites measuring social behaviors, academic attitudes, and feelings about peers. It should be noted, however, that these score overlaps occurred across districts and do not indicate how similar any individual EMR learner was to the nonhandicapped learner from the same regular class.

Clearly, then, the scores of some EMR children are likely to be similar to the scores of nonhandicapped children in some competencies. For these EMR children, mainstreaming is likely to be a viable educational alternative. Regular class placement is likely to promote their academic and social growth and to cause few problems for their regular class teachers. EMR children who differ extremely from nonhandicapped children in the various competencies may find regular class placement less beneficial, and may pose more problems for the teacher. The overlaps among the distributions in competencies highlights the need for individualized educational programming. District-wide criteria for placement and programming decisions for EMR students based on too few behaviors and competencies will result in inappropriate educational programs for many students.

## Interrelationships of Learner Competencies

Placement and programming decisions often reflect assumptions about the relationships among learner competencies. For example, when a child is well

below classmates in achievement, misbehaves, is rejected by his peers, has a
negative self-concept, and has a poor attitude toward school, an assumption is
generally made that these factors are related, even causally related. That is, it
might be assumed that the child's poor achievement is causing him to
misbehave, be rejected by the peer group, feel negatively about himself, and
dislike school. Providing the child with an educational program that
alleviates the academic problems will result, *ipso facto*, in better behavior,
social acceptance, a more positive self-concept, and an improved attitude
toward school. However, the validity of such an assumption must be
examined.

Table 5-12
Percentage of Variance in Each Competency Construct
Accounted for by the Eleven Remaining Competency Constructs

| Construct | Nonhandicapped Learners (N = 275) | Mainstreamed EMR Learners (N = 286) | Nonmainstreamed EMR Learners (N = 198) |
|---|---|---|---|
| Normative academic status | 26 | 26 | 23 |
| Classroom academic status | 41 | 30 | 31 |
| Attention to academic task | 19 | 21 | 17 |
| Cognitive interaction with the teacher | 4 | 5 | 10 |
| Academic self-concept | 28 | 15 | 22 |
| Attitude toward school | 27 | 14 | 24 |
| Acceptance | 61 | 55 | 66 |
| Rejection | 60 | 54 | 63 |
| Friendly/cooperative behavior | 5 | 11 | 13 |
| Antisocial behavior | 38 | 22 | 21 |
| Feelings of loneliness | 23 | 4 | 10 |
| Feelings about peers | 16 | 9 | 20 |

An approach to examining this assumption was to analyze the degree of association among the competency constructs. Regression analyses were computed, predicting each of the 12 competencies from the remaining 11. Only the measures reflecting behavior in the regular class for each mainstreamed EMR learner in the regression analyses were used. The analyses were computed separately for each learner group and included only those learners with scores on all 12 competencies. Table 5-12 lists the total percentage of variance in each competency that was accounted for by the other 11.

The data presented in Table 5-12 suggest that certain competencies are predicted relatively well by the other 12. It should be noted that the actual amount of variance accounted for in a particular competency cannot be compared across learner groups since the groups differed in size. In each of the three groups, however, the two social status competencies — acceptance and rejection — and one academic status competency — classroom academic status — have more variance explained by the remaining 11 competencies than did the other competencies. On the other hand, very little variance in cognitive interaction and friendly/cooperative behavior was explained by the other competency measures in any of these learner groups. These competencies may be determined primarily by environmental rather than personological learner-related variations. Teachers have considerable influence over their students' levels of cognitive interaction and friendly/cooperative behavior. For example, students whose teachers lecture but do not ask questions would be unlikely to have frequent cognitive interactions with their teachers. Similarly, teachers who do not allow peer-to- peer interactions would be unlikely to foster high levels of friendly/cooperative behavior among their students.

Bivariate correlations between the competencies were also computed. In these analyses, all 16 measures were employed for the mainstreamed EMR learners (regular and resource behavioral competencies). Again, the analyses were executed for only those learners with scores on all competencies. The results are reported in Table 5-13 for the correlation coefficients equal to or greater than 0.20.

In general, the bivariate correlation coefficients among the academic and social competence constructs were not large. The majority were smaller than 0.20, and a few exceeded 0.40. The nature of the relationships was often similar across the three groups. In each of the three groups, normative academic status was positively related to classroom academic status ($r = 0.43, 0.35$, and $0.43$ for the nonhandicapped, mainstreamed, and nonmainstreamed learners, respectively). Thus, learners with high normative status tended to have high classroom status. Classroom academic status but not normative academic status, was positively related to social acceptance ($r = 0.43, 0.34, 0.30$,

Table 5-13
Bivariate Correlations Equal to or Greater than .20
among the Learner Competencies

| Competence Composite | Nonhandicapped Learners (N=275) | | | | | | | | | | |
|---|---|---|---|---|---|---|---|---|---|---|---|
| | 2 | 3 | 4 | 5 | 6 | 7 | 8 | 9 | 10 | 11 | 12 |
| 1. Normative academic status | 43 | | | | | | | -26 | | -25 | |
| 2. Classroom academic status | | | | 28 | | 43 | -32 | -41 | | -23 | |
| 3. Attention to task | | | | | | | | | | | |
| 4. Cognitive interaction | | | | | | | | -39 | | | |
| 5. Academic self-concept | | | | | 38 | | | | | -33 | |
| 6. Attitude toward school | | | | | | | | | | -30 | 30 |
| 7. Acceptance | | | | | | | -74 | -41 | | | |
| 8. Rejection | | | | | | | | 42 | | 22 | |
| 9. Antisocial behavior | | | | | | | | | | | |
| 10. Friendly/cooperative behavior | | | | | | | | | | | |
| 11. Feelings of loneliness | | | | | | | | | | | |
| 12. Feelings about peers | | | | | | | | | | | |

| Competence Composite | Mainstreamed EMR Learners (N=223) | | | | | | | | | | | Nonmainstreamed EMR Learners (N=198) | | | | | | | | | |
|---|---|---|---|---|---|---|---|---|---|---|---|---|---|---|---|---|---|---|---|---|---|
| | 2 | 3 | 4 | 5 | 6 | 7 | 8 | 9 | 10 | 11 | 12 | 2 | 3 | 4 | 5 | 6 | 7 | 8 | 9 | 10 | 11 |
| 1. | 35 | 30 | | | | | | | | | | 43 | | | | | | | | | |
| 2. | | | | | | 34 | -24 | | | | | | | | | | 30 | -25 | -21 | | |
| 3. | | | | | | | | -32 | | | | | | | | | | | -32 | | |
| 4. | | | | | | | | | | | | | | | | | | | | | |
| 5. | | | | | 26 | | | | | | | | | | | 34 | | | | | |
| 6. | | | | | | | | | | | | | | | | | | | | | |
| 7. | | | | | | | -66 | | | | 23 | | | | | | | -78 | | | |
| 8. | | | | | | | | 28 | | | -20 | | | | | | | | | | |
| 9. | | | | | | | | | 25 | | | | | | | | | | | | |
| 10. | | | | | | | | | | | | | | | | | | | | | |
| 11. | | | | | | | | | | | | | | | | | | | | | |
| 12. | | | | | | | | | | | | | | | | | | | | | |

Note. Decimal points have been omitted.

respectively) and negatively related to social rejection ($r = $ -0.32, -0.24, -0.25, respectively). Children's academic status with their peers seemed to be determined more from their academic ability relative to their peers than from their performance on normative academic achievement tests.

Learners who were characterized by high levels of antisocial behavior tended to be less attentive to task ($r = $ -0.39, -0.32, -0.32). Those learners with positive academic self-concepts also tended to be positive in their attitudes toward school (0.38, 0.26, 0.34). Social acceptance of learners was negatively related to their social rejection by peers (-0.74, -0.66, -0.78) and positively related to their classroom academic status. The correlation coefficients between acceptance and rejection were the largest for each group. Since both acceptance and rejection were derived from the same sociometric instrument and were mutually exclusive choices, the high correlations may in part be a measurement artifact. As two other rating options were also available on the HIFTO, scores on acceptance and rejection were not, however, totally dependent on each other.

Other relationships of interest were found for two of the three groups. Nonhandicapped and nonmainstreamed EMR learners who were low in classroom academic status tended to engage more frequently in antisocial behavior (-0.41, -0.21, respectively), providing support for the common assumption that poor academic performance is related to misbehavior in the classroom. This relationship was not found among the mainstreamed EMR learners, possibly because there was less variance in the classroom academic status scores for this group. Regular class learners, both nonhandicapped and mainstreamed EMR, who engaged in high levels of antisocial behavior were more often socially rejected by their peers (0.42, 0.28, respectively).

A significant relationship was not found among the nonmainstreamed EMR learners. Not finding a significant relationship, of course, does not prove that no relationship existed. It may be, however, that norms for acceptable behavior are more rigid or more clearly articulated and enforced in the regular class, resulting in the rejection of students deviating from those norms. In the special class, on the other hand, a wider range of behaviors may be accepted by both the teacher and the peer group. These possibilities need to be examined in future research.

Social acceptance was positively related and social rejection negatively related to the learners' feelings about peers in both EMR groups (0.23, -0.31 for mainstreamed and nonmainstreamed, respectively), but not among the nonhandicapped learners. These findings are consistent with other research which has reported that people tend to like those they perceive as liking them (Jones, 1974). For nonhandicapped and nonmainstreamed EMR learners, positive feelings about peers were associated with positive feelings about school in general (0.30, 0.26).

Several relationships existed for the nonhandicapped learners but not for the EMR learners. The nonhandicapped learners with high normative academic status were less apt to display antisocial behavior (-0.26). Learners high in classroom academic status tended to have positive academic self-concepts (0.25); those who reported feeling lonely were likely to be low in normative (-0.25) and classroom academic status (-0.23), to have negative academic self-concepts (-0.33) and attitudes toward school (-0.30), and to be socially rejected by their peers (-0.22). These relationships indicated that for nonhandicapped children, achievement in academic areas was associated with their attitudes toward themselves and school, their feelings of not fitting in with others in the school situation, and their levels of misbehavior as well as their rejection by others.

For the mainstreamed EMR learners, normative academic status was positively related to attention to task in the regular class (0.30). Mainstreamed EMR learners high in normative academic status tended to be more often on task in their regular classes than mainstreamed EMR learners who were low in normative status. It is, of course, impossible to tell the direction of this relationship (whether higher-achieving EMR learners can follow more of what is transpiring in the class and thus stay on task or whether their greater on-task behavior results in greater learning and higher achievement). Still, regular class teachers may wish to become more cognizant of whether or not the EMR child is actually on task at various times.

The correlations among the behavioral competencies for mainstreamed EMR learners suggest some consistency of behavior across regular and resource settings. Attention to task in the resource class was positively related to attention in the regular class (0.22) and negatively related to antisocial behavior in the regular class (-0.21). Similarly, antisocial behavior tended to occur in both settings (0.37), and was negatively related to attention to task in those settings (-0.36). Friendly/cooperative behavior was positively associated in both settings (0.25) but was also associated with antisocial behavior in the resource class (0.26). It almost appears as if certain EMR learners are simply more socially active than others, consistently engaging in social interactions that are sometimes positive and sometimes negative in nature. There were no additional relationships among competencies for the nonmainstreamed EMR learners.

To review, this chapter discussed the interrelationships of competencies which have bivariate correlation coefficients equal to or greater than 0.20. Few of these exceeded 0.40, but several relationships occurred consistently across the three groups. The initial regression analyses suggested that the social status measures, as well as the classroom academic status measures, were predicted relatively well by the 11 remaining composites for all three groups. The bivariate correlational analyses revealed these competencies were interrelated. The reason the social status measures were predicted so well by the other competency measures is their high correlation with each other. This correlation may be an artifact resulting from their coming from the same instrument and being partially dependent on each other.

The results of the bivariate analyses suggested that, regardless of group, children's academic ability and performance level relative to that of their class peers is associated with their social status with those peers, that children with positive self-concepts concerning their academic competence also tend to have positive attitudes toward school, and that children's off-task behavior is associated with their displaying antisocial behavior. Other relationships were found within one or two of the groups. With only one exception, the learners' academic behaviors were not associated with their academic status. In fact, cognitive interaction with the teacher was not related to any of the other competencies. Mainstreamed EMR learners' attention to task and their social behavior competencies in the regular class were positively related to the parallel measures in the resource class, suggesting some consistency in behaviors across settings.

The number of relationships among the competencies was relatively small and most relationships were of low magnitude. It is possible that this is in part due to a design artifact.[11] It is also possible, however, that there may be less "spill-over" effect from one competency to another than is commonly assumed.

## Summary

While group means for the mainstreamed EMR learners diverged most from the nonhandicapped learners for measures of academic status, academic behavior, and social status, there was considerable overlap in these scores as well as in social behaviors, academic attitudes, and feelings about peers when the nonhandicapped learner was low-achieving and younger than the mainstreamed EMR learner. Given these circumstances, mainstreaming can be a viable educational option. Teachers can integrate the mainstreamed learners into the instructional program of their regular classmates, especially when the nonhandicapped learners are somewhat younger and low-average in functioning.

The considerable overlap on the social behavior composites suggests that EMR students may cause fewer behavior problems in regular classes than has often been indicated and that social behavior problems probably are not a principal reason for their low social status in regular classes, at least as indicated by the measures employed in this study.

For the EMR children whose performance diverges from their nonhandicapped classmates, regular class placement may be less beneficial and pose more instructional and, perhaps, management problems for the teacher. The decision must be made on an individual basis, considering the student's current level of performance, the performance levels of his classmates, and the ability of the teacher to accommodate to the child's special needs. Any attempts to make district-wide administrative decisions governing mainstreaming placement and programming may well result in many inappropriate educational programs for EMR students.

# Technical Notes

1. The total Project PRIME learner sample ($N = 1852$) was used in each analysis. Originally, there were 33 measures of academic competence and 15 of social competence. However, during the factor analytic process several competence measures were dropped. A measure was dropped if it was a subscale that was part of a total scale score, if its correlation with another indicator was so high ($r = 0.90$ or higher) that the correlation matrix could not be inverted, or if its correlation with the other indicators was so low ($r = 0.10$ or lower) and had so little intrinsic variance that it did not load on any factor.

Results of the listwise image analyses ($N = 482$) for academic and social competence are presented in Tables 5-1 and 5-2 respectively. The pairwise results were almost identical. Reported in these tables are the rotated loadings obtained when the factors were forced to the number which empirically described the simple structure of the two domains.

As shown in Table 5-1, a six-factor solution was considered the most satisfactory for academic competence, with the first three factors accounting for most of the common variance. Table 5-2 presents the five-factor solution obtained for social competence. The scales and respective items comprising these academic and social factors are defined operationally in a subsequent section of the text.

2. For each of the scales, $z$ scores were calculated, based on all available data (all learners combined, maximum $N = 953$). For each learner, the $z$ scores for the scales comprising each construct were averaged. The average $z$ scores were then restandardized to $T$ scores. When only one indicator for a given construct was available, the raw score was converted directly to $T$ scores. This compositing procedure minimized problems of missing data.

3. The cognitive interaction with the teacher factor described in Table 5-1 lacked empirical support. The three scales defining the factor had a relatively low reliability coefficient (alpha $= 0.55$). In addition, the loadings and the bivariate correlations were relatively low. Further examination revealed that the total active participation scale was an inappropriate measure of cognitive interaction with the teacher since it included nonverbal participation (hand raising) which was not highly correlated with the verbal components of participation. Further, the low- and the high-level discourse scales were found to have several aberrant distributional properties. For these reasons,

the total active participation scale was omitted from the "cognitive interaction with the teacher" composite, and the high- and low-level discourse scales were combined and renamed the "total cognitive interaction with the teacher" scale and was used to operationally define this construct.

4. The number of responses made by the target learners appears high when compared with the average number of demands per student made by the teacher (reported in Chapter 8). This discrepancy suggests the target learners had more cognitive responses than the typical peers, and may reflect an artifact of the observation process. Teachers were aware of who the target learners were and may have called on them more often than their peers while the observer was present.

5. Although the academic ambition scale loaded on this factor (see Table 5-1), it was not included in the composite because it had relatively low reliability (alpha = 0.55); item analysis revealed several problems in interpreting the meaning of the scale; and it had the lowest factor loading.

6. The disruptive behavior scale also loaded on the antisocial behavior factor (see Table 5-2), but because the *Guess Who* instrument from which the scale was derived was not administered in the resource classes, scores for this scale were not available for that environment. For this reason, and because the alpha coefficient was only minimally reduced when the internal consistency of the factor was computed without the scale, the disruptive behavior variable was not included in the final composite.

7. Two scales, the misbehavior scale and the isolation/anxiety scale, loaded on the feelings of loneliness factor (see Table 5-2). For the final analysis, however, it was decided to define the feelings-of-loneliness construct by the isolation/anxiety scale alone, rather than forming a composite of the two variables. The isolation/anxiety scale had an internal consistency of 0.76, whereas the alpha value of the composite factor was only 0.52. It was selected in preference to the misbehavior scale, since isolation/anxiety was thought to sample information more relevant to the feelings-of-loneliness construct.

8. The competency constructs were the product of within-domain factor analysis. Since the factor analysis procedure used was designed to generate orthogonal factors, the lack of many relationships of large magnitude among the competencies may be in part the result of a design artifact. However, the use of unit-weighted composite scoring reduces the orthogonality of the factor scales somewhat.

# Part III

# 6

# Teacher and Peer
# Characteristics

Decisions about the placement of EMR learners have traditionally been guided by concern for the educational setting: the effects of both teacher and peer characteristics on the EMR learner(s). Special self-contained classes for EMR learners were originally established because it was thought that the academic or behavioral needs of these children could best be met in separate small classes for children similar in achievement and IQ. In these special classes, students would benefit from the use of special materials and services and be taught by specially trained teachers who would provide a warm, supportive environment and be protective against the potential negative attitudes and behaviors of regular class teachers and peers.

Adherents of mainstreaming claim these advantages of special self-contained classes have not been clearly achieved, and that EMR learners do benefit by placement in regular classes where they have nonhandicapped peers as role models. They point out that regular teachers are dealing with substantial differences among their regular students and suggest that, with in-service training and support, regular teachers can provide a suitable learning environment for EMR students. Special materials and services can be delivered to the regular teacher as easily as to the special teacher (Dunn, 1968). With the passage of P.L. 94-142, placement in the least restrictive environment

153

is expected, and Congress, by this posture, has taken a position that placement in the most normalized setting is most desirable.

Proponents for both settings seem to agree that EMR children:

- do best in certain types of classroom environments;
- the peer group is a critical part of the environment;
- certain teacher skills and attitudes are important in creating an appropriate learning environment; and
- teachers of EMR students need the support of special materials and services.

Issues related to the regular class/special class placement decision, then, seem to be:

- Whether regular class teachers can be provided with appropriate training and support and with appropriate student support services which will enable them to instruct EMR learners?
- Whether regular class peers provide more appropriate academic role models for EMR students than do other EMR learners?
- Whether the regular class teacher is inclined or likely to provide the warm, supportive, structured environment thought to be important for EMR learners?

In the development of individualized educational programs, the important question of how much time should be spent in special education or regular class placements must be considered for each student. Students may benefit from a special education class setting while establishing minimal skills and confidence in a given subject area. Having accomplished these objectives, they can increasingly participate in and benefit from regular class placement. Placement in regular classes of EMR learners is often accompanied by expressed concerns on such issues as the effects of the EMR learner on the regular class teachers and on nonhandicapped students. Some fear the presence of EMR learners adversely affects the intellectual climate of the class—that these students will dominate the teacher's time, and consequently nonhandicapped students will be bored and neglected. Thus, two additional issues related to mainstreaming are:

- Whether or not regular class teachers have or develop negative attitudes toward the mainstreaming of EMR students?
- Whether or not nonhandicapped peers develop negative attitudes toward school when EMR learners are placed in their classrooms?

This chapter examines the significance of these characteristics of the classroom environment for EMR children, indicating why particular teacher and peer characteristics were included in the Project PRIME model; presents descriptive information related to the teacher and peer characteristics of the three types of classroom settings; and considers the above issues related to the placement of EMR students in regular or special education classrooms.

# Rationale for Examining Teacher and Peer Characteristics

Certain theoretical orientations, such as social learning and social comparison theory, support the idea that teacher and peer characteristics are important in the placement and education of EMR children. Social learning theory (Bandura, 1969) contends that modelling of others is a fundamental process through which the individual acquires new behaviors or modifies existing ones. A sizeable body of research has found that modelling procedures result in a considerable amount of learning and that children are responsive to peer models (Bandura, Grusec, & Menlove, 1967; Hartup & Coates, 1967). Modelling procedures have been found to influence learning in both nonhandicapped (Bandura & Walters, 1963) and institutionalized children (Bandura, Blanchard, & Ritter, 1968). Children who are highly dependent and have low self-esteem, feelings of incompetence, and low intelligence are especially responsive to modelling influences (Bandura, 1971). Since EMR children often exhibit these characteristics (Drotar, 1972; Turnure & Zigler, 1964), they seem especially sensitive to the influence of peer models and may respond positively to the more demanding academic learning environment of regular classes if they can find support for their efforts.

The Coleman et al. (1966) report on equality of educational opportunity concluded that the social composition of the student body was more highly related to achievement than any other school factor. Mayeske and his associates (1973b), in further analyses of the same data, concluded that the most influential school factors on individual achievement were the achievement and motivation levels of the student body.

Social comparison theorists have emphasized the importance of similarity between individuals and their peer groups. Rosenkrantz (1967) found that similarity promotes modelling. Festinger (1954) proposed that the similarity of an individual's ability, attitude, and opinions to those of the peer group affects one's self-evaluation, the degree to which one strives to be more competent, and one's attitudes toward and acceptance by the group. According to Festinger, individuals have a basic drive toward self-evaluation of abilities, opinions, and attitudes that are shaped through comparisons with others. Persons viewing themselves as different from others tend to change their self-evaluations and their behaviors or attitudes to be more like their comparison group.

Thus, social comparison theory posits that mainstreamed students will be positively affected by peer group characteristics such as higher levels of competence, positive attitudes toward school, and the composition of the group members. For example, academically more competent peers may motivate mainstreamed students to strive academically. However, competent peers may also adversely affect the self-concepts of mainstreamed students, especially their academic self-concepts. Towne and Joiner (1966) reported that EMR learners' self-concepts of ability improved after they were placed in special classes. But their reference group also changed; in the latter situation, EMR learners probably compared themselves to their special, not their regular, classmates.

Festinger suggests that individuals tend to stop making comparisons with those whom they view as too different from themselves, i.e., "noncomparable." If EMR learners and their peer groups are too academically different, they may come to be viewed as different and perhaps be isolated by nonhandicapped students.

Social comparison and social learning theory suggest that the intellectual and sociodemographic characteristics of the classroom and peer group as well as the group's values and attitudes can affect the EMR learner's academic and social functioning. For these reasons, peer intellectual, sociodemographic, and attitudinal characteristics were included in the Project PRIME taxonomic model (Figure 6-1).

The rationale and descriptive information for the specific variables selected to represent these characteristics in the Project PRIME model are presented in the next section. The settings considered are regular ($N = 262$), special self-contained ($N = 127$), and special resource ($N = 132$) classes.

## Peer Characteristics and Attitudes

Although the effect of regular class size on handicapped students had not been investigated, a number of studies had explored the relationship between class size and nonhandicapped students' achievement. These studies generally fail to indicate that class size greatly influences the learning of nonhandicapped

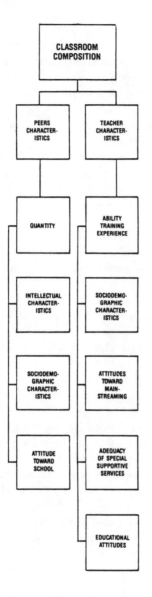

Figure 6-1
Teacher and Peer Characteristics
(Project PRIME Taxonomic Model)

children, but Moody, Bauswell, and Jenkins (1973) point out flaws in the previous research which argue against accepting this evidence as final. In their own investigation, they found that with fourth-grade subjects, reduction in class size affected the learning of selected mathematical content when testing was done immediately after learning. Children taught individually or in groups of 2-3 made significantly larger gains than children taught in a group of 23. Their findings suggest that the academic accomplishments of EMR children may be affected by the number of students in the class.

The number of handicapped students integrated into a regular class may also have important consequences. Although there is little previous research, it seems probable that introducing EMR learners into a regular class alters the regular class academic and social environment — adding to the number should increase these effects.

The number of students in the class and the number of handicapped students in the class were used as measures of quantity in the regular classes. Only class size was used for the special self-contained and special education resource classes.

Regular and special self-contained class teachers provided class size information on the TAQ items. The number of students present in the resource classroom came from the observation systems, and was the number of students present at the time the class was observed, not actual enrollment. The descriptive data for these variables in the regular and special self-contained classrooms are summarized in Table 6-1.

The average regular class had about 29 students enrolled, and the average special self-contained class had about 12 students enrolled. The average resource class was observed to have 7.20 students present at any one time ($SD = 3.13$, $N = 90$), and a mean of 20.20 students in a day ($SD = 8.54$, $N = 114$).

Table 6-2 shows the percentage of regular classes that contained from one to six or more handicapped students. Although the mean number of handicapped students per class was four, 29% of the classrooms had five or more handicapped students. Clearly, the EMR learners in the Project PRIME study often were not the only handicapped students in their regular classes.

The number of handicapped students reported in the regular classes was surprisingly large. Underlying most conceptions of mainstreaming is the assumption that regular teachers will have to contend with one, or at most, two handicapped children. The Project PRIME data suggest this was not the case, at least for some districts in Texas. Almost two-thirds of the regular class teachers reported they were teaching three or more handicapped children, and almost a third reported they were teaching five or more handicapped children. A sizeable number of regular class teachers may have felt that, as they feared, mainstreaming meant they would have to teach large numbers of

## Table 6-1
### Peer Characteristics and Attitudes by Variable Sets for Regular and Special Self-Contained Classes

| | Instructional Setting | | | | | | | |
| | Regular | | | | Special Self-contained | | | |
| Peer Variable | X | SD | % | N | X | SD | % | N |
|---|---|---|---|---|---|---|---|---|
| **Quantity** | | | | | | | | |
| Number of students in class | 29.23 | 4.54 | | 251 | 11.92 | 2.95 | | 112 |
| Number of handicapped students in class | 3.67 | 3.05 | | 250 | | | | |
| **Peer Intellectual Characteristics** | | | | | | | | |
| Percentage of classes at each level | | | | 262 | | | | |
| Third grade | | | 31 | | | | | |
| Fourth grade | | | 37 | | | | | |
| Fifth grade | | | 32 | | | | | |
| Percentage of peers who were one or more years behind in reading | 47.16 | 25.13 | | 245 | | | | |
| Third grade | 41.21 | 25.97 | | 77 | | | | |
| Fourth grade | 45.53 | 24.16 | | 89 | | | | |
| Fifth grade | 55.30 | 23.45 | | 78 | | | | |
| **Peer Sociodemographic Characteristics** | | | | | | | | |
| Percentage of peers of each ethnic group | | | | 206 | | | | 113 |
| Anglo | 37.37 | 35.74 | | | 29.98 | 31.92 | | |
| Black | 15.99 | 24.69 | | | 32.48 | 35.48 | | |
| Spanish surnamed | 46.63 | 39.93 | | | 37.54 | 35.42 | | |
| Percentage of low-SES residents in school area | 33.10 | 31.33 | | 238 | 33.31 | 34.36 | | 212 |
| Percentage of classes in each geographic location | | | | 238 | | | | 116 |
| Urban | | | 43 | | | | 48 | |
| Suburban | | | 40 | | | | 41 | |
| Rural | | | 17 | | | | 11 | |
| **Peer Attitude Toward School** | | | | | | | | |
| Harmony | 34.80 | 2.15 | | 246 | 36.14 | 1.76 | | 118 |

handicapped children. On the other hand, having so many handicapped learners in the same class may allow teachers to group handicapped learners with similar educational needs and levels for instructional purposes.

## Peer Intellectual Characteristics

Two variables were used to represent the intellectual characteristics of the regular class peers of the selected learners — class grade level and percentage of class members one or more grades behind in reading achievement. Regular teachers' TAQ responses were the source of this information. Table 6-1 provides descriptive information on these variabes.

Of the 262 regular classes in the Project PRIME sample, 81 (31%) were third-grade classes, 98 (37%) were fourth-grade classes, and 83 (32%) were fifth-grade classes.

The academic achievement level was measured by the percentage of class members who were one or more grades behind in reading. This percentage was often quite high and increased with grade level. The mean percentages were 41% for third grade, 46% for fourth grade, and 55% for fifth grade. At least 40% of the class members were a year or more behind in reading in 25% of the third-grade classes, 57% of the fourth-grade classes, and 76% of the fifth-grade classes.

Two tactics useful for minimizing the potential distance from nonhandicapped peers were placing EMR students in classes with a large number of students both younger and relatively low-in-academic-ability (Budoff, 1972). Chapter 5 noted that many of the nonhandicapped learners in

Table 6-2
Percentages of Regular Classrooms Containing from One to Six
or More Handicapped Students

| Number of Handicapped Students | Percentage of Classes |
|---|---|
| 1 | 28 |
| 2 | 17 |
| 3 | 16 |
| 4 | 10 |
| 5 | 10 |
| 6 | 19 |

this study were low in achievement. The mean end-of-the-year MAT total reading scores for the nonhandicapped learners at each grade level were below the 40th percentile and for the fourth- and fifth-grade level nonhandicapped learners were in the lowest quartile. Since the nonhandicapped learners were randomly selected from among the mainstreamed EMR learners' regular class peers, it seems clear the mainstreamed EMR learners had been placed in classes with many low-achieving peers. This placement may have been made deliberately and systematically or may result from a school district policy of placing low-achieving students from low-SES homes in their neighborhood schools, where low achievement is prevalent. Placement with higher-achieving peers would not have been possible unless the school drew from a mix of neighborhoods varying in socioeconomic level. These findings do raise questions about a key argument for mainstreaming: that it provides EMR learners with more appropriate academic role models. Since many low-achieving nonhandicapped students display undesirable academic behavior, they may not be more appropriate as role models than EMR classmates in special self-contained classes.

But if the difference in achievement level between the mainstreamed EMR learners and their regular classmates is too great, the EMR learners will not compare their behavior with that of their regular class peers, and nonhandicapped peers will probably not serve as role models. Thus, while one probably should consider the level of peer achievement that may optimize modelling behavior by EMR learners in making a mainstreamed placement, research data are not available to suggest what this optimal achievement gap might be.

## Peer Sociodemographic Characteristics

Peer sociodemographic characteristics which were examined were: (a) ethnic composition of class, (b) socioeconomic level of the community, and (c) locale (urban, suburban, or rural) in which the students live.

Most studies of the effects of the ethnic composition of student groups on the self-concepts of group members have examined the relationship between the degree of integration of Black students and their self-concepts. The assumption, derived from Clark and Clark's (1939) classical studies, was that segregated students would have low school-related self-concepts. Findings from this line of research have been equivocal. Some studies have found that segregated Black students have higher self-concepts than desegregated Black students (Coleman, 1966; Harootunian, 1968); other studies find no difference (Bienvenu, 1968; Williams & Byars, 1968); whereas others report higher school-related self-concepts for desegregated Black students (Caplin, 1969). In a review of these studies, Zerkel (1971) proposes that the lack of consistency in findings is likely to be due to differences in definition, instruments, and research designs.

Since ethnic composition tends to be highly related to socioeconomic composition, it is important that effects actually due to socioeconomic conditions not be attributed to ethnic composition. Although Mayeske et al. (1973b) found that peer ethnic-sociodemographic composition was not as important as peer achievement-motivational composition for individual achievement, they also found considerable correlation between the two. They hypothesized that concentrating large numbers of poor children in the same school has an "aggregate effect," impeding the progress that could otherwise be expected from any individual student. Social learning theory would suggest that such an aggregate effect could be due to a lack of models displaying academically-relevant behaviors and attitudes. Lower-class students express lower need-achievement than middle-class students (Rosen, 1956, 1959) and are more likely to have lower occupational and educational aspirations (Sewell, 1961; Sewell, Haller, & Strauss, 1957). In addition, the socioeconomic level of the community from which students come seems likely to be related to other factors such as the condition of the school facility, the quality of academic materials available, and the experience and expertise of the teaching staff. These factors, in turn, could influence the degree to which individual students are stimulated to utilize their potential.

Whether children live in urban, suburban, or rural settings has been related to school functioning. For example, Rugoff (1961) found that regardless of family status, children in suburban settings had the highest scholastic scores (IQs) and more of them planned to go to college. Rural pupils showed poorer educational achievement. For example, Randhawa and Fu (1973) hypothesized that rural and urban children are exposed to different adult values concerning achievement and education. Furthermore, the daily life experiences and probable future life experiences of rural children may make much school-related work seem irrelevant.

In this study, three variables — ethnic group, socioeconomic level, and geographic location — were the measures of the sociodemographic characteristics of the learners' peer group. These variables were examined for the peers in the regular and special self-contained classes but not for those in the resource classes. Ethnic composition of the class was obtained from the teachers (a TAQ item) and three variables were created — percentages of students in the class who were Anglo, Black, and Spanish surnamed. The Principal's Administrative Questionnaire (PAQ) provided the remaining information. The percentage of residents in the area of the school who were lower social class was derived from PAQ information and was used as the measure of peer SES. The principals also indicated whether their schools were in a rural, suburban, or urban location. The descriptive results for peer sociodemographic characteristics are summarized in Table 6-1.

In regular classes, the mean percentages were: Anglo students 37%, Black students 16%, and Spanish-surnamed students, 47%. Twenty-nine percent of the regular classes had no Anglo students, and 38% had no Black students. Only 17% of the classes had no Spanish-surnamed students. In approximately 37% of the regular classes, the majority of students were Anglo; and in 41%, the majority were Spanish-surnamed. Blacks were in the majority in only 7% of the regular classes.

One third (33%) of the schools in which EMR learners were mainstreamed were in areas in which more than 40% of the residents were from lower-SES homes. Approximately, 40% were in suburban areas, 43% in urban areas, and 17% in rural areas.

At least half the students were Anglo, Black, or Spanish-surnamed in 21%, 29%, and 37% of the special self-contained classes, respectively. The mean percentages were: 30% Anglo students, 32% Black students, and 38% Spanish-surnamed students. Twenty-six percent of the self-contained classes had no Anglo students, 36% had no Black students, and 30% had no Spanish-surnamed students. Almost a third (31%) of the schools which contained self-contained classes were in areas in which more than 40% of the residents were lower class. Only 11% of the schools with special self-contained clases were in rural settings, whereas 41% were in suburban settings, and 48% were in urban settings.

The pattern of ethnic group membership in both regular and special self-contained classes indicated both settings contained sizeable proportions of Spanish-surnamed students. It was more likely for an Anglo or a Spanish-surnamed than for a Black EMR learner to be placed in a regular or special class where there were many children of the same ethnic group.

A sizeable number of students in this sample were found in schools in low socioeconomic areas. Mayeske's (1973b) work suggests that this may have a debilitating effect on individual achievement, and may in part explain why such a large number of seemingly lower achieving regular classes are included in this study. A later chapter will consider the relationship between class socioeconomic status and learner competencies.

## Peer Attitudes Toward School

A frequently expressed concern is that the positive feeling toward school of nonhandicapped students might change as more handicapped children are mainstreamed. Anderson and Walberg (1968) found that peer attitude toward school was related to the affective learning of individual students; that is, the individual student's attitude toward school work was more positive when his classmates found the school experience satisfying and enjoyable. Findings concerning the relationship between individual attitude and achievement have been somewhat equivocal. Several investigators (Brodie, 1964; Dusewicz, 1972; Rosen, 1956) have found a small relationship between school attitudes and achievement while other studies have failed to find any relationship (LaBelle, 1971) or have reported differences only when students with very positive or very negative attitudes comprised the sample (Jackson, 1968).

Although it seems reasonable that the attitude toward school prevalent in a class is related to the intellectual and sociodemographic characteristics of the class, the relationship between satisfaction with the school experience and classroom composition in terms of such factors as ability, socioeconomic level, and ethnic group is largely unexplored. The few studies available indicate that low-ability students like school as much as higher-ability students (Berk, Rose, & Stewart, 1970; Tenenbaum, 1944), low-SES children as much (Berk, Rose, & Stewart, 1970; Neale & Proshek, 1967) or more (Ehrlich, 1968) than their middle-class peers, and Black and Spanish-surnamed students as much as Anglo students (LaBelle, 1971).

*Your School Days* (YSD), measuring the degree to which class members view their classroom and school experience as enjoyable and rewarding (the harmony scale, alpha = 0.86), was used to estimate the regular and special self-contained classroom peers' attitudes toward school. The scale consisted of 21 items requiring a yes or no response. Descriptive results for this measure are presented in Table 6-1.

The mainstreamed and segregated EMR students both reported their school experience was enjoyable (mean scores on the scale were 34.80 and 36.14 respectively, indicating that in the average class, EMR students typically gave positive responses to two-thirds of the items).

Although the potentially-negative effects of mainstreaming on nonhandicapped students within the class has been a concern, these data show no evidence of negative class attitudes toward school in regular classes. The premainstreaming or comparative data were not available.

The mean of the attitude-toward-school scores differs little for students in special self-contained classes and students in regular classes. Proponents of mainstreaming have sometimes pictured EMR children in special self-contained classes as an unhappy group, dissatisfied with their classes and their school experience. Regular class/special self-contained class comparisons cannot legitimately be made because the regular and special classes in the Project PRIME sample differ in several respects. However, it would seem that students in the special self-contained classes are no more dissatisfied with their school experience than students in regular classes.

# Teacher Characteristics and Attitudes

The fact that teacher characteristics influence pupil functioning is seldom questioned. Teachers create the learning environment in which desired learner competencies can be attained and determine the instructional content level, methods, and aids which are employed at any given time.

The prominent position of the teacher has led to the search for specific teacher characteristics and behaviors that impact on learner behaviors and skill attainment. Among the teacher characteristics identified are attitudes and beliefs, and background characteristics such as ability, training, experience, and sociodemographic characteristics. These characteristics can be expected to directly or indirectly influence learner competencies. For example, Dunkin and Biddle (1974) suggest that demographic characteristics, such as age or race, may cause pupils to respond differently to teachers and influence their achievement and attitude toward school. They write that:

> Much of teaching is presumably *coping* behavior on the part of the teacher and is thus subject to beliefs held by the teacher concerning the curriculum, the nature and objectives of the teaching task, expectations for pupils, and norms concerning appropriate classroom behavior. Thus, a reasonably good prediction of the classroom behavior of the teacher can presumably be obtained by finding out what the teacher thinks she prefers to, ought to, and will do in the classroom (p. 412).

Teacher attitudes and beliefs, then, along with teacher background characteristics such as ability, training, experience, and social demographic characteristics, are thought to affect the academic and social functioning of the EMR child and were included in the Project PRIME model to describe teacher characteristics in the three classroom settings (see Figure 6-1).

## Teacher Training, Ability, and Experience

Traditionally, teachers' salaries have been governed by the teacher's level of training and years of teaching experience. Presumably, salary levels are so structured because training and experience are expected to be related to learner outcomes. Several recent studies have examined this assumption, with conflicting results. Shim (1965) and Hanushek (1971) found that the degree held by the teacher and the number of years of teaching experience were unrelated to student achievement; Bargen and Walberg (1974), on the other hand, found teacher training and experience were significantly related to student achievement, particularly in the early grades. Coleman et al. (1966) found that number of years of teaching experience had little impact on student outcomes, but that the teacher's educational level did influence achievement of Black students in the third grade. Coleman et al. (1966) reported that teacher verbal ability had an increasing effect on Black student achievement between grades 3-6. Hanushek (1971) found teacher verbal ability to be an important predictor of the achievement of Anglo students as well, but not of Spanish-surnamed students.

Four variables were used to describe the training, ability, and experience of the teachers in the Project PRIME model. Teacher responses to three TAQ questions provided information on their educational degree status, number of years of teaching experience, and number of hours of special education in-service training. The information on hours of in-service training is presented later in this section with information on support services.

The fourth variable was teachers' scores on the verbal facility scale (alpha = 0.84). The measure included in the TAQ was similar to the Coleman et al. (1966) measure. Twenty-eight sentences, each with a word missing, were presented and the teachers were asked to select one of five words which best completed the sentence. The possible range of the verbal facility measure was from 1 to 28. Descriptive results for the teacher ability, training, and experience variables are summarized in Table 6-3.

Of the regular class teachers ($N = 253$), the highest degree attained by 37% of the teachers was a bachelor's degree. Approximately 21% had a master's degree or a master's plus additional hours. The remaining 21% had a bachelor's degree plus additional hours. The mean number of years of teaching experience for regular class teachers was 10.73 years; 30% of the teachers had taught 5 years or less. The mean verbal facility score for regular class teachers was 22.97.

Of the teachers of special self-contained classes ($N = 112$), the highest degree attained by 24% was a bachelor's degree; 34% held a master's degree or more. The mean number of years of teaching experience for this group was 10.54 years; 42% were in their first 5 years of teaching. The mean verbal facility score for the teachers of self-contained special classes was 22.42.

Twenty-seven percent ($N = 117$) of the resource teachers held master's degrees or master's plus additional hours; 19% had only a bachelor's degree. The average resource teacher had taught 10.17 years; 44% had taught 5 years or less. The mean verbal facility score for resource teachers was 22.29.

Since the three teacher groups differed in some.respects, such as ethnicity, comparisons among them are somewhat questionable. The most evident difference was that the special education teachers in this sample, whether special class or resource room, were more likely than regular classroom

## Table 6-3
### Background Characteristics of Regular, Special Self-Contained, and Special Resource Teachers

| | Teacher Type | | | | | | | | | | | |
|---|---|---|---|---|---|---|---|---|---|---|---|---|
| | Regular | | | | Special Self-contained | | | | Special Resource | | | |
| Background Characteristics | X | SD | % | N | X | SD | % | N | X | SD | % | N |
| **Teacher Ability, Training, and Experience** | | | | | | | | | | | | |
| Educational degree status | | | | 253 | | | | 112 | | | | 117 |
| B.A. | | | 37.15 | | | | 24.11 | | | | 18.80 | |
| B.A. + additional hours | | | 41.11 | | | | 41.96 | | | | 53.85 | |
| M.A. or more | | | 21.74 | | | | 33.93 | | | | 27.35 | |
| Hours of special education in-service training | 3.56 | 4.95 | | 229 | 34.40 | 38.10 | | 100 | 65.61 | 65.52 | | 110 |
| Years of teaching experience | 10.73 | 9.35 | | 254 | 10.54 | 9.80 | | 114 | 10.17 | 9.70 | | 119 |
| Verbal facility | 22.97 | 3.86 | | 248 | 22.42 | 4.54 | | 110 | 22.29 | 4.46 | | 118 |
| **Teacher Sociodemographic Characteristics** | | | | | | | | | | | | |
| SES of family | | | | 253 | | | | 114 | | | | 117 |
| Lower class | | | 4.89 | | | | 3.51 | | | | 5.13 | |
| Lower middle class or above | | | 91.27 | | | | 96.49 | | | | 94.87 | |
| Ethnic group | | | | 250 | | | | 113 | | | | 117 |
| Anglo | | | 78.80 | | | | 62.83 | | | | 70.09 | |
| Black | | | 12.00 | | | | 28.22 | | | | 22.22 | |
| Spanish surnamed | | | 9.20 | | | | 8.85 | | | | 7.89 | |

teachers to have taken college courses beyond the bachelor's degree or to hold a master's degree. The EMR learners in this study were, for the most part, served by trained special education teachers.

## Teacher Sociodemographic Characteristics

The effects of teacher sociodemographic characteristics, especially teacher ethnicity and socioeconomic status, became an important issue in the 1960s. The inferior academic performance and supposedly poor attitudes toward school of disadvantaged minority group children were partly attributed to poorly trained, hostile, uncaring teachers who could not understand or relate to culturally different children (Herndon, 1968; Kozol, 1968). These studies recommended that it would be best if such children were instructed by teachers from the same ethnic group who had also experienced economic disadvantage (Tenenbaum, 1972). On the other hand, Clark (1965) cautioned that minority group members who have risen from lower-class status to the middle-class status of the teaching profession often react negatively to lower-class students in an attempt to escape the painful memory of their own previous status.

Although much was written about the effects of teacher ethnicity and socioeconomic status (SES), many accounts were first-person experience-based reports rather than controlled studies. The importance of these variables must be assumed from popular literature or from theoretical positions such as social learning theory (Bandura, 1971), which suggest that the ethnicity and SES of a model teacher are important characteristics to be considered.

Two variables, SES of family while growing up and ethnic group, were used as measures of teacher sociodemographic characteristics in this study. Teacher responses to two TAQ items were the source of this information. Descriptive results for these variables are provided in Table 6-3.[1]

Of the regular teachers in this sample, 91% reported middle-class backgrounds and only 5% lower-class backgrounds. Most of the teachers were Anglo (79%); only 12% were Black, and 9% Spanish-surnamed.

Of the teachers of special self-contained classes, only 4% reported coming from lower-class backgrounds; 96% came from middle-class backgrounds. Sixty-three percent of the teachers in this group were Anglo, 28% were Black, and 9% were Spanish-surnamed.

Of the special education resource teachers, 5% claimed lower-class backgrounds and 95% middle-class backgrounds. Anglo teachers comprised 70% of the resource teacher groups; Blacks, 22%; and Spanish-surnamed, 8%.

Thus, almost all of the teachers in all three teacher groups reported coming from middle-class backgrounds, and most were Anglo. Most students in the sample were from lower-class backgrounds. Thus, it would have been virtually impossible for most of the students in this study to have been taught by teachers from a similar socioeconomic background. Further, it was unlikely that Spanish-surnamed or Black students were taught by a teacher of the same ethnic group.

## Teacher Attitudes Toward Mainstreaming

Teacher attitudes toward mainstreaming have been assumed to be critical in determining the success of mainstreaming efforts (Gickling & Theobald, 1975). Studies have shown that regular education teachers do not possess particularly positive attitudes toward EMR students (Combs & Harper, 1967). Since EMR learners in special classes have generally been placed there because a regular class teacher and the placement team believed they were failing to achieve in the regular class, there is little reason to assume they would be welcome in the regular class. A survey in Tennessee found that 49% of 230 regular education teachers felt helping special education students was an imposition, and 61% felt special classes to be the most effective placement for mildly handicapped children (Gickling & Theobald, 1975). Shotel, Iano, and McGettigan (1972) reported the attitudes of regular education teachers toward the mainstreaming of EMR students were less positive following a year's experience with mainstreaming.

Four measures were used to assess teacher attitudes toward mainstreaming. Three measures were administered to regular, self-contained, and resource teachers. The first and second measures, the attitude toward integration of students with cognitive problems scale (alpha = 0.79) and the attitude toward integration of students with social problems scale (alpha = 0.86), were based on a factor analysis of 24 items, each describing a child with specific school-related problems. These items were drawn from the *Classroom Integration Questionnaire*, administered as part of the TAQ. Teachers were asked to choose the most appropriate placement for each child from the following options: (a) in the regular classroom, (b) in the regular classroom all day with supplemental materials and advice, (c) in the regular classroom plus the resource room, (d) in the special self-contained classroom, and (e) exclusion from public education. (The maximum score possible for each scale is 60.)

The third measure available for all three groups of teachers, appropriateness of mainstreaming, was assessed by responses to a single question on the TAQ. The question asked whether the teacher considered serving mildly handicapped children in the regular classroom a good idea for most, some, a few, or no handicapped children.

A fourth measure administered only to regular and resource teachers concerned the number and seriousness of problems in their classrooms that were a result of mainstreaming. Problems in the regular classroom were assessed from the regular teachers' responses to 13 items, which comprised one question on the TAQ (regular teachers version). Problems in the resource room were assessed from the resource teachers' responses to 14 items, which comprised one question on the TAQ (special teachers version). Teachers who attributed many serious problems to mainstreaming received high scores on this measure: A high score indicated a negative attitude toward mainstreaming. Table 6-4 presents means and standard deviations for the three groups of teachers on these four measures.

Table 6-5 presents a breakdown of the problems resulting from mainstreaming cited by the regular class teachers. Table 6-6 presents their suggestions for solving the problems resulting from mainstreaming.

The regular teachers' mean response to the items concerning the appropriate placement of handicapped children with cognitive problems fell midway between "regular class with supplemental materials" and "regular class with resource room." Their mean response to the items concerning students with social problems corresponded to "regular class with resource room." Their mean response indicated they thought it was "a good idea for some handicapped children" to be mainstreamed and that, in general, problems resulting from mainstreaming were minor.

Approximately half the regular class teachers found the lack of time to work individually with as many students, the lack of appropriate materials, and the EMR learner's inability to participate in group projects to be problems. Slightly less than half the regular class teachers reported having problems because the handicapped child disrupted the class activities. Relatively few teachers reported problems with declining morale among the class, additional time spent in meetings, or scapegoating of the EMR learner (see Table 6-5).

When asked how to alleviate these problems, more than two-thirds of the regular class teachers suggested reducing class size and providing an aide. More than half reported needing more preparation time and more materials. Interestingly, less than one-third of the teachers felt they needed assistance in managing behavior (see Table 6-6).

The mean ratings of teachers of special self-contained classes and the special resource teachers on their attitude toward integration of students with cognitive and social problems indicated they thought the appropriate placement for such students was in the "regular class with resource room" (see Table 6-4). They also felt mainstreaming was "a good idea for some handicapped children." When questioned about problems in the resource room, teachers indicated only "minor problem."

These results, particularly those related to regular class teacher attitudes, present a relatively optimistic picture. Regular class teachers have frequently

## Table 6-4
### Teachers' Mean Scores on Measures of Attitude

| Attitude Measure | Regular | | | Special Self-Contained | | | Resource | | |
|---|---|---|---|---|---|---|---|---|---|
| | X | SD | N | X | SD | N | X | SD | N |
| Teacher attitudes toward maintreaming | | | | | | | | | |
| Attitude toward Integration of Students with Cognitive Problems scale | 42.06 | 7.50 | 239 | 36.78 | 7.64 | 113 | 39.09 | 7.0 | 114 |
| Attitude toward Integration of Students with Social Problems scale | 37.38 | 4.85 | 239 | 33.65 | 3.69 | 113 | 36.27 | 4.1 | 114 |
| Appropriateness of mainstreaming | 2.76 | .87 | 247 | 2.91 | .76 | 110 | 3.00 | .8 | 118 |
| Problems in regular class or resource room | 15.12 | 9.23 | 245 | —— NA —— | | | 13.84 | 8.7 | 115 |
| Teacher report of adequacy of special support services | 2.06 | .81 | 232 | 2.97 | .67 | 114 | 3.10 | .57 | 119 |
| Teacher educational attitudes | | | | | | | | | |
| Importance of an open, warm environment | 34.26 | 4.91 | 227 | 33.99 | 5.17 | 108 | 33.95 | 4.75 | 117 |
| Importance of a structured, controlled environment | 25.88 | 6.38 | 237 | 24.53 | 7.90 | 109 | 22.58 | 7.67 | 115 |
| Belief in traditional authority | 35.81 | 7.43 | 251 | 34.40 | 6.98 | 101 | —— NA —— | | |

been assumed to have basically negative attitudes toward the mainstreaming of handicapped students, raising considerable concern about their reactions to mainstreaming. Project PRIME determined that most regular class teachers expressed somewhat favorable attitudes. After at least one year of experience, they felt that mainstreaming was appropriate for some handicapped children, many cognitive and social problems could be handled in the regular classroom with resource help, and only minor problems resulted from mainstreaming.

The regular teachers expressed slightly more confidence in their ability to handle academic problems than behavior problems. The data presented in

Table 6–5
**Mainstreaming Problems Reported by Regular Teachers**

| Problems | Percentage of Teachers Citing Problem |
|---|---|
| Lack of time to work with as many children individually | 54.6 |
| Lack of appropriate materials for handicapped child | 53.5 |
| Handicapped child could not participate in group projects | 47.4 |
| Handicapped child disrupted class activity | 44.1 |
| Took longer for preparation | 38.5 |
| Bright children bored | 32.1 |
| Discipline problems among regular children increased | 29.2 |
| Personal feelings of frustration, pressure, tension, and depression | 28.5 |
| Academic progress of rest of class slowed down | 20.5 |
| Disruptions because handicapped children leave and return to room | 20.2 |
| Classroom social cohesion reduced | 17.6 |
| Children's morale fell | 11.7 |
| Time spent in committee meetings | 11.2 |
| Handicapped child used as scapegoat | 7.9 |

Note.  N = 262

Chapter 5 indicated that the mainstreamed EMR learners did not differ greatly from the nonhandicapped learners in social behavior. Thus, it seems unlikely that the social behavior of the mainstreamed EMR learners would have been a major problem for the regular class teachers. However, nearly half the regular class teachers felt the handicapped child disrupted class activities. The mainstreamed EMR learners were found to be off task somewhat more frequently than the nonhandicapped learners. It is possible that the mainstreamed EMR learners' inattention to task was disruptive to their regular class peers.

## Adequacy of Special Support Services

One common explanation for the regular education teachers' presumed negative attitudes toward the integration of EMR learners has been their lack of confidence in their ability to teach EMR students successfully (Deno, 1973). The Tennessee survey (Gickling & Theobald, 1975) found that only 15% of 230 regular education teachers felt they had the skills to help special education students. This supports the findings of Shotel, Iano, and McGettigan (1972): only 11-16% of their regular education teachers felt elementary education teachers had the training and competency to teach EMR learners.

Table 6-6
Suggestions of Regular Teachers for Alleviating Problems

| Ways to Alleviate Problems | Percentage of Teachers Citing Solution |
|---|---|
| Smaller class size | 76.9 |
| Teacher aide | 67.5 |
| More teacher preparation time | 59.0 |
| More or different curriculum materials | 58.1 |
| Clearly defined educational objectives | 47.7 |
| Financial assistance for classroom | 46.3 |
| In-service training | 37.3 |
| Assistance in behavior management | 29.5 |

Note. N = 262

To help teachers cope more effectively, the regular class teacher is offered support services, e.g., aides, instructional materials, in-service training, educational plans, and consultative assistance (Deno, 1973; Dunn, 1968). Gickling and Theobald (1975) reported that 81% of 230 regular teachers stated they would feel more comfortable if special education personnel assisted in providing services in the regular class, and 95% stated they would take advantage of the opportunity to work with special education personnel. In the Shotel et al. (1972) study, 32-38% of the regular teachers felt elementary teachers had the competency to teach EMR learners when given support services. Regular class teachers' feelings about mainstreaming may be influenced by the effectiveness of the support services they are receiving.

To measure the Project PRIME teachers' feelings about the adequacy of special education support services, a single composite measure was created from several TAQ items which asked about availability of special education materials, education plans, consultation, and in-service training; and the value of each service. For the purpose of creating the composite measure, not receiving a particular form of assistance was considered the lowest level of effectiveness for that service. The ratings given to the services were summed and a mean score was computed for those teachers who provided information on at least two of the four kinds of assistance (see Table 6-4). Table 6-7 presents information regarding the percentage of teachers in the three educational settings who reported receiving various support services. Table 6-8 provides an indication of the value given to each service by those teachers who received the service. Value was rated in terms of effectiveness (5 = very, 4 = somewhat, 3 = slightly, 2 = not effective) for the services other than in-service training. For in-service training, the values were 4 = very, 3 = somewhat,

Table 6-7
Percentage of Teachers Receiving Various Support Services

|  | Teacher Type | | |
|---|---|---|---|
|  | Regular (N=262) | Special Self-Contained (N=127) | Special Resource (N=132) |
| Special education in-service training | 43.9 | 78.7 | 78.0 |
| Teacher aide | 6.9 | 68.5 | 59.0 |
| Consultative help | 66.4 | 85.8 | 86.8 |
| Educational plan | 32.4 | 62.2 | 82.6 |
| Special education materials | 38.2 | 87.4 | 87.1 |

and 2 = slightly. Thus, a "somewhat effective" rating represents the second highest possible score.

Between 30% and 40% of the regular teachers reported receiving an educational plan or special educational materials, 44% received in-service training (mean number of hours was 3.56, $SD$ = 4.95, $N$ = 229), and 66% received consultative help. Almost no regular teachers had an aide. Those regular teachers who received support services generally rated them close to "somewhat effective."

Most teachers of special self-contained and resource classes received all the different types of support services, although less than two-thirds of the resource class teachers had aides, and 62% of the teachers of special self-contained classes received educational plans. The average special self-contained teacher received 34.40 hours of special education in-service training ($SD$ = 38.10, $N$ = 100), and the average resource teacher received 65.61 hours ($SD$ = 62.52, $N$ = 110). The mean rating of support services for both groups was "somewhat effective."

The data indicate the regular class teachers did not receive the support services they needed to successfully teach EMR learners. The relatively poor record of service delivery makes findings regarding the positive attitude of regular class teachers toward mainstreaming even more surprising. It should

**Table 6–8**
**Teacher Ratings of Effectiveness of Selected Support Service That They Received**

| Special Support Service | Teacher Type | | | | | | | | |
|---|---|---|---|---|---|---|---|---|---|
| | Regular | | | Special Self–Contained | | | Resource | | |
| | X | SD | N | X | SD | N | X | SD | N |
| Special education in-service training | 2.74 | .50 | 180 | 2.86 | .49 | 99 | 2.97 | .46 | 108 |
| Consultative help | 4.04 | .76 | 174 | 4.40 | .60 | 109 | 4.38 | .59 | 114 |
| Educational plan | 3.86 | .70 | 85 | 4.05 | .74 | 79 | 4.15 | .62 | 109 |
| Special educational materials | 3.68 | .71 | 100 | 4.04 | .56 | 111 | 4.11 | .54 | 115 |

**Note.** For special education in-service training, the range is 2–4 (4 = very effective, 3 = somewhat effective, 2 = slightly effective). For the other three services, the range is 2–5 (5 = very effective, 4 = somewhat effective, 3 = slightly effective, 2 = not effective).

be remembered, however, that EMR students taught by these teachers were in the resource room rather than the classroom for varying amounts of time. Regular class teachers may have viewed services provided by the resource room teachers as sufficient for maintaining the EMR child in the regular class. However, the less restrictive placement would be the regular classroom with needed support — which typically was not available.

## Teacher Educational Attitudes

Some research evidence indicates that the educational beliefs or attitudes of teachers relate to their teaching behavior (Dobson, Goldenberg, & Elsom, 1972; Rexford, Willower, & Lynch, 1972). Three such attitudes seem to be particularly important considerations in the mainstreaming of EMR students — belief in the importance of an open, warm environment; belief in the importance of a structured, controlled environment; and belief in traditional authority.

Special education lore emphasizes the importance for EMR children of a warm, supportive climate which is structured, with carefully followed routines (Connor & Talbot, 1970; Kolburne, 1965). Mainstreaming, as an innovative administrative and instructional practice, requires changes or accommodations in instructional practices within the regular classroom environment to meet EMR students' educational needs. It seems reasonable to assume that the stronger the teacher's belief in traditional educational authority and practices, the less willing the teacher is to accept mainstreaming practices. Lipton (1968) has shown that teachers whose attitudes indicated high resistance to change were less successful at teaching EMR readers. Traditional or custodial educational attitudes have been related to teacher unwillingness to accept innovative educational practices (Hoy & Blankenship, 1972; Nussel & Johnson, 1969).

Although educational attitudes have generally been considered as opposite ends of a single continuum, Kerlinger (1967) provides evidence that the dimensions of progressivism and traditionalism are relatively orthogonal and that the same individual can be high or low on both.

Little research has related teacher educational attitudes to learner outcomes. Most studies have tried to assess the extent to which different educational attitudes are held, examine the relationship of other teacher characteristics to teacher attitudes, or examine the relationship between teacher attitudes and teaching behavior. Rural teachers are reported to have more progressive attitudes than urban teachers, teachers rated highly by principals to have more traditional attitudes than those not rated highly, and males to have slightly more progressive attitudes than females (Harrison &

Scriven, 1970). Studies comparing younger teachers with older, more experienced teachers have produced somewhat mixed results. Harrison and Scriven (1970) found younger teachers to be more traditional, and suggested this was because they felt insecure in their new roles. Gorton (1971), on the other hand, suggests that older, more experienced teachers place much more emphasis on discipline, control, and formality than do younger teachers.

In the current study, three complementary measures of teacher educational attitudes were used. Two scales, the importance of an open, warm environment (alpha = 0.84) and the importance of a structured, controlled environment (alpha = 0.79), were the products of the factor analysis of 21 items comprising two TAQ questions and were available for all three types of teachers. The two TAQ questions presented 21 descriptions of characteristics of the climate and intellectual atmosphere in elementary school classes and asked the teachers to rate the characteristics in terms of importance (1 = very important, 2 = moderately important, 3 = slightly important, and 4 = not important). The scores on each of these two scales were determined by computing average rating across items and multiplying that number by 10. The third measure, traditional authority (alpha = 0.83), a scale that resulted from factor analysis of the *Teacher Educational Attitudes Questionniare* (TEAQ), was available for regular and special self-contained class teachers and was composed of 17 statements such as "The old days were probably the best," "We need a revival of respect for the teacher," "Too often today discipline is sacrificed for freedom." Teachers were asked whether they agreed, probably agreed, probably disagreed, or disagreed with the statements.

Table 6-4 presents the means and standard deviations for the three groups of teachers on the educational attitudes measures. The score distributions were quite similar across the three teacher types. For all three, the mean item response on importance of an open, warm environment corresponded to the response category "moderately important." For both the regular and special self-contained class teachers, the mean item response on importance of a structured, controlled environment fell midway between "moderately important" and "slightly important"; for the special resource teachers, the mean was "slightly important."

On the traditional authority scale, the mean item response for both the regular and special self-contained class teachers corresponded to "probably disagree." The resource teachers did not complete the TEAQ and thus had no score on the traditional authority scale.

All three groups of teachers put a moderate emphasis on an open, warm classroom climate and slightly less emphasis on structure and control. The orientation of the regular and special self-contained teachers was they probably disagreed with the use of traditional authority as a primary controlling orientation.

It was surprising to find no hint that special education teachers emphasize a warm, open environment or a structured setting more than regular class teachers. Though regular and special education teachers do not differ in the amount of stress they report placing on these climate dimensions, they might still vary in the actual classroom climate they create. Also, the terms "warm" and "structured," although frequently used, do not specify critical levels of warmth and structure. Thus, finding that both groups of teachers only moderately stress warmth and structure does not imply the EMR learners in this study were not in climates that met their needs: No conception exists as to what is "warm enough" or "structured enough."

The fact that the regular class teachers were inclined to disagree with the statements describing traditional positions in education may explain, in part, their favorable attitudes toward mainstreaming.

## Teacher and Peer Characteristics by Setting

The regular classes in which EMR learners were placed contained a greater number of students than did the special self-contained classes, almost a three-to-one ratio, and often contained a relatively high proportion of low-achieving peers and several handicapped students. These classes were generally located in urban or suburban areas and frequently in low-SES areas. Many of the regular classes contained a high proportion of Spanish-surnamed peers but few classes were predominantly Black. Generally, the regular class peers of the mainstreamed EMR learners found their school experience enjoyable and satisfying.

The regular class teachers of the mainstreamed learners were predominantly Anglo and middle class and had been teaching about 10 years. They felt relatively positive about mainstreaming despite the fact that they received few support services other than those provided in a resource class setting. The regular class teachers thought an open, warm classroom environment "moderately important"; a structured, controlled environment "slightly important"; and expressed moderate disagreement with statements positing the use of traditional authority as the basis for controlling the class.

The special self-contained classes had fewer students than did the regular classes; and in almost one-third of the classes, a majority of the students were Black. These classes were often located in urban or suburban areas and often in low-SES areas. The class members generally had a positive attitude toward school.

Table 6-9
Participant Composition Predictor Sets and Variables

| Predictor Sets | Variables |
|---|---|
| 1. Quantity | Number of students in the class<br>Number of handicapped students in the class[a][b] |
| 2. Peer intellectual characteristics[a] | Grade[b]<br>Percentage of peers one or more grades behind in reading |
| 3. Peer sociodemographic characteristics | Percentage of students who are Anglo<br>Percentage of students who are Black<br>Percentage of students who are Spanish-surnamed<br>Percentage of students who are of lower SES<br>Urban/not urban location<br>Rural/not rural location |
| 4. Peer attitude toward school | Attitude toward school |
| 5. Teacher ability, training, and experience | Educational degree status<br>Hours of special education in-service training<br>Years of teaching experience<br>Verbal facility |
| 6. Teacher sociodemographic characteristics | SES<br>Black/not Black<br>Spanish-surnamed/not Spanish-surnamed |
| 7. Teacher educational attitudes | Importance of an open, warm environment<br>Importance of a structured, controlled environment<br>Belief in traditional authority |
| 8. Teacher report of the adequacy of special support services | Teacher report of adequacy of special support services |
| 9. Teacher attitude toward mainstreaming | Attitude toward the Integration of Students with Cognitive Problems scale<br>Attitude toward the Integration of Students with Social Problems scale<br>Appropriateness of mainstreaming<br>Problems in regular class[a] |

[a] Available only for regular classes.

[b] Not used in Part IV analyses.

Like the regular classes, the special self-contained classes generally had middle-class, Anglo teachers with approximately 10 years teaching experience. However, the special self-contained class teachers were more likely than the regular class teachers to be Black and have college coursework beyond the bachelor's level.

Most of the teachers of the special self-contained classes received support services and felt that an open, warm classroom environment was moderately important, and a structured environment slightly less important. Like the regular class teachers, they were mildly disapproving of traditional educational positions.

There were still fewer students in the resource classes at any given period than in the special self-contained classes. The resource class teachers of the mainstreamed EMR learners were more likely than the regular teachers to be Black and to have college course work beyond the bachelor's level. The resource class teachers generally received support services and their attitudes toward the open, warm and structured, controlled-classroom dimensions were similar to those held by the regular class teachers.

## Relationships Among the Variables

The prior section presented descriptive information related to teacher and peer variables in the Project PRIME model. This section investigates the relationship between these variables. An unsuccessful attempt was made to reduce the variable set to a more manageable number of variables by factor analyzing the variables. Instead, the variables were logically grouped and considered in sets in all subsequent analyses for this chapter. Table 6-9 presents these variable sets.

### Teacher Attitudes Toward Mainstreaming

To determine aspects of the classroom which might be related to regular class teacher attitudes toward mainstreaming, Predictor Sets 1-8 from Table 6-9 were used to predict each of the four attitudes toward mainstreaming measures of Set 9. If a predictor set explained a significant proportion of the variance in a particular attitude measure, with or without variance from other sets partialled out, the bivariate correlations between the variables in that set and the attitude measure were then examined.

Table 6-10 presents the results of the commonality analyses in which the total $R^2$ of the full equations reached a level of statistical significance. In

## Table 6-10

### Results of Commonality Analyses for Attitudes Toward Mainstreaming Total R2 and Unique R2 for Dependent Variables

| Source | Attitude Toward Integration of Students with Cognitive Problems Scale | | Attitude Toward Integration of Students with Social Problems Scale | | Appropriateness of Mainstreaming | | Problems in Regular Class | |
|---|---|---|---|---|---|---|---|---|
| | Total R2 | Unique R2 | Total R2 | Unique R2 | Total R2 | Unique R2 | Total R2 | Unique R2 |
| Full equation with all predictor sets Quantity | .23 | | .25 | | .21 | | .36 | |
| Peer intellectual characteristics | .04 | .03 | .03 | | | .03 | | |
| Peer socio-demographic characteristics | .05 | | | | | | | |
| Peer attitude toward school | | | | | | .02 | | |
| Teacher ability, training, and experience | .07 | .03 | .06 | .05 | | | | |
| Teacher socio-demographic characteristics | .07 | .03 | .05 | .03 | | | | |
| Teacher educational attitudes | .07 | .03 | .12 | .08 | | | | |
| Teacher report of the adequacy of special support services | | | | | .11 | .09 | .31 | .25 |

Note. Only those R2s which were significant at the .05 level are reported.

Table 6-11

**Bivariate Correlations Between Dependent Variables of Significant Predictor Sets in Mainstreaming Attitudes Commonality Analysis**

| | Dependent Variables | | | |
|---|---|---|---|---|
| | Attitude Toward Integration with Students with Cognitive Problems Scale | Attitude Toward Integration with Students with Social Authority | Appropriateness of Mainstreaming | Problems in Regular Class |
| **Quantity** | | | | |
| Number of students in the class | | | .15 | |
| Number of handicapped students in the class | | | .04 | |
| **Peer intellectual characteristics** | | | | |
| Grade | .06 | .01 | | |
| Percentage of peers one or more grades behind in reading | .15 | .15 | | |
| **Peer sociodemographic characteristics** | | | | |
| Percentage Anglo | .15 | | | |
| Percentage Black | -.08 | | | |
| Percentage Spanish-surnamed | -.08 | | | |
| Percentage lower-SES | -.10 | | | |
| Urban-not urban location | -.03 | | | |
| Rural-not rural location | .17 | | | |

| | | | | |
|---|---|---|---|---|
| Peer attitude toward school | | | .08 | |
| **Teacher ability, training, and experience** | | | | |
| Educational degree status | -.11 | -.20 | | |
| Hours of special education in-service training | .12 | .09 | | |
| Years of teaching experience | -.17 | -.18 | | |
| Verbal facility | .18 | .02 | | |
| **Teacher demographic characteristics** | | | | |
| SES | -.09 | -.13 | | |
| Black-not Black | -.23 | -.12 | | |
| Spanish surnamed-not Spanish-surnamed | .04 | .17 | | |
| **Teacher educational attitudes** | | | | |
| Importance of an open, warm environment | -.03 | .07 | .12 | |
| Importance of a structured, controlled environment | -.19 | -.31 | -.23 | .55 |
| Traditional authority | -.20 | -.19 | -.26 | .10 |

addition, Table 6-10 presents the total $R^2$ and unique $R^2$ for each significant variable set. Table 6-11 presents bivariate correlations between the attitude measures from Table 6-10 and the variables of their significant predictor sets.

The four attitude measures in Table 6-10 represent regular teachers' attitudes toward mainstreaming. The commonality analyses showed that the eight teacher and peer predictor sets accounted for approximately 23% of the variance in the teachers' attitude toward integration of students with cognitive problems, 25% of the variance in teachers' attitude toward integration of students with social problems, 21% of the variance in the teachers' estimates of appropriateness of mainstreaming, and 36% of the variance in teachers' reported problems in the regular class.

The teacher educational attitudes set accounted for significant proportions of the variance in all four mainstreaming attitude measures. In fact, this set accounted for more variance than any other set in the attitude toward integration of students with social problems, the attitude toward mainstreaming, and the problems-in-the-regular-class measures. Examination of the bivariate correlations (Table 6-11) between the variables of this significant predictor set and the attitude measures shows that the teachers' ratings on the importance of a structured, controlled environment scale were negatively related to the attitude toward integration of students with cognitive and social problems and the appropriateness of mainstreaming, but positively related to problems in the regular class. Thus, teachers who rated a structured, controlled environment important tended to be negative toward the integration of EMR children and reported more problems related to mainstreaming. Similarly, teachers who believed most strongly in traditional authority tended to oppose the integration of EMR children. This is shown by the negative correlations of attitude toward integration and appropriateness of mainstreaming.

The total $R^2$ and/or unique $R^2$ of three other predictor sets—peer intellectual characteristics; teacher ability, training, and experience; and teacher sociodemographic characteristics—significantly predicted both of the attitudes toward integration measures. Inspection of the relationship between individual variables of the three predictor sets and the attitude toward integration measures showed most of these relationships to be quite small—less than 0.20 (Table 6-11). The percentage of the class behind in reading and years of teaching experience were negatively related to attitudes toward integration of both students with cognitive problems and students with social problems. Other variables from these sets were more important for one attitude-toward-integration measure than the other. "Teacher verbal facility" was positively related and "teacher being Black" negatively related to the attitude toward integration of students with cognitive problems. "Teacher educational degree status" was negatively and "teacher being Spanish-surnamed" positively related to attitude toward integration of students with social problems. The cognitive-problems measure was also signficantly predicted by the peer sociodemographic characteristics set. From Table 6-11 it can be seen that both rural location and the percentage of students who were Anglo had positive correlations with the attitude toward integration of students with cognitive problems. Appropriateness of mainstreaming was the only mainstreaming attitude measure to be significantly predicted by the class-size set. Surprisingly, the number of students in the class had a small, positive relationship with appropriateness of mainstreaming. The bivariate correlations between the attitude measures and all other predictor variables were smaller than $\pm 0.15$.

Because teacher educational attitudes were significantly related to all four teacher attitudes toward mainstreaming measures, further commonality analyses were performed to determine what aspects of the classroom might be related to teacher educational attitudes. Sets 1-6 in Table 6-9 were used to predict each of the three teacher educational attitudes of Set 7. The results of these analyses are presented in Table 6-12.

The three peer and two teacher predictor sets did not significantly predict the regular teacher's belief in the importance of an open, warm environment. The five predictor sets accounted for 12% of the variance in the importance of a structured, controlled environment and 14% in traditional authority.

The teacher ability, training, and experience set accounted for a significant amount of variance in both measures. The bivariate correlations in Table 6-13 showed a small positive relation between number of years of teaching experience and both educational attitudes. Thus, teachers with more years of experience rated a structured, controlled environment more important and believed more strongly in traditional authority. A negative correlation between teacher verbal facility and traditional authority suggests that teachers high in verbal ability believed less in traditional authority.

The fact that peer intellectual characteristics and peer attitude toward school had higher (and significant) $R^2$ when predicting the importance of a structured, controlled environment only after the effects of other sets had been partialled out suggests that a suppressor effect may have been operating. No sizeable bivariate correlations between this dependent measure and the variables of the three sets can be found in Table 6-13.

The total $R^2$ of the quantity set and of the peer sociodemographic set each accounted for significant proportions of the variance in traditional authority. From the data in Table 6-13, it can be seen that the number of EMR students and the percentage of Anglo students in the class was negatively related and the percentage of Spanish-surnamed students was positively related to this belief. Thus, the teachers who believed less in traditional authority tended to be the teachers who had fewer integrated EMR students, greater proportions of Anglo students, or smaller proportions of Spanish-surnamed students in class.

The initial commonality analyses found the teacher's belief in traditional authority and in the importance of structure and control in the classroom to be negatively related to positive attitudes toward mainstreaming. Since mainstreaming can be considered an educational innovation, these results are consistent with the results of studies by Hoy and Blankenship (1972) and Nussel and Johnson (1969) which showed teacher belief in traditional order to be negatively related to adoption of innovative practices. Particularly interesting was the sizeable correlation between the problems regular teachers reported and the importance they placed on structure and control. It may be that the cognitive or behavioral problems of EMR children become more salient in an extremely orderly, controlled classroom where teaching proceeds in more of a "lockstep" fashion.

Number of years of teaching experience was found to relate positively to the importance of structure and control in the classroom and to belief in traditional authority. This finding supports the previous research of Gorton (1971) which also showed older, more experienced teachers more likely to rate discipline and control as important.

The finding of a negative relationship between the percentage of the class behind in reading and the teacher's belief that cognitive or social problems could be handled in the regular class also seems important. It suggests that teachers who have lower-ability classes and who already may be teaching at several grade levels do not feel they can adequately handle the additional problems that become their responsibility when EMR students are mainstreamed. Since placement in classes with many lower-achieving peers seems to be frequently selected for mainstreamed EMR students, this finding creates a paradox of sorts.

Also interesting are those variables not found to be related to teacher attitudes toward mainstreaming. Although support service factors, the number of integrated EMR learners, peer sociodemographic characteristics, and class size had been thought to be potentially important, for the most part they were not found to be related to teacher attitudes toward mainstreaming.

## Peer Attitudes Toward School

To determine which aspects of the classroom might be related to peer attitudes toward school in the regular classes, Variable Sets 1-3 and 5-9 from Table 6-9 were used to predict peer attitudes toward school.

The results for the commonality analyses for peer attitude toward school are reported in Table 6-12. The three peer and the five teacher predictor sets

## Table 6-12

### Results of commonality Analyses for Teacher Educational Attitudes and Peer Attitude Toward School

#### Total R2 and Unique R2 for Dependent Variables

| | Dependent Variables | | | | | |
| | Importance of a Structured, Controlled Environment | | Traditional Authority | | Peer Attitude Toward School | |
|---|---|---|---|---|---|---|
| | Total R2 | Unique R2 | Total R2 | Unique R2 | Total R2 | Unique R2 |
| Full equation with all predictor sets | .12 | | .14 | | .41 | |
| Quantity | | | .03 | | | |
| Peer intellectual characteristics | | .03 | | | .11 | .08 |
| Peer sociodemographic characteristics | | | .05 | | .24 | .20 |
| Peer attitude toward school | | .02 | | | | — |
| Teacher ability, training, and experience | | | .07 | .05 | | |
| Teacher sociodemographic characteristics | | .04 | | | .04 | .03 |
| Teacher educational attitudes | | | — | | | |
| Teacher report of the adequacy of special support services | | | — | | .02 | |
| Teacher attitude toward mainstreaming | | | — | | | |

**Note.** Only those R2s which were significant at the .05 level are reported.

together accounted for almost 41% of the variance. Three sets — peer intellectual characteristics, peer sociodemographic characteristics, and teacher sociodemographic characteristics — accounted for significant proportions of the variance both before and after the effects of other sets had been partialled out. Teacher report of the adequacy of special supportive services was significant only when the contribution it made with other sets was included.

The bivariate correlations presented in Table 6-13 show that peer attitude toward school in the regular classes was negatively related to grade, percentage of students who were Anglo, and teacher report of the adequacy of special support services. The correlations indicate positive relationships to percentage of students in the class who were Spanish-surnamed, percentage of students of lower SES, urban location, and the teacher being Black. These correlations suggest that peer attitude toward school was most positive among younger children from poor, urban neighborhoods who were in classes that had low proportions of Anglo students or high proportions of Spanish-surnamed students, and were taught by Black or Spanish-surnamed teachers. The negative correlation between teacher reports of the adequacy of special support services and peer attitude toward school may have occurred because of the likely negative relationship between adequacy of special support services and the characteristics described above. It should be remembered that the contribution of this variable was significant only when the effects of the other sets were not partialled out.

The results for regular classes showed grade and ethnic composition to have substantial correlations with peer attitudes. The fact that third-grade classes were more enthusiastic about school than fifth-grade classes confirms previous findings that younger students enjoy school more than older students (Jackson, 1968). It is unclear why the percentage of students who were Spanish-surnamed was positively related to attitude toward school and the percentage of students who were Anglo was negatively related. The homes of the Spanish-surnamed students may be somewhat more traditionally structured, placing greater value on authority, for instance, than Anglo homes. Were this so, Spanish-surnamed students might be more accepting of the school situation than Anglo students. Another possibility is that Spanish-surnamed students are more reluctant than Anglo students to express negative feelings publicly.

It is somewhat heartening to note that the number of EMR students in the class was not found to be related to the attitude of the class toward school. Instead, factors not inherent to mainstreaming practices were found to be important. The following section relates these findings to the mainstreaming issues raised in the beginning of this chapter.

Table 6-13
Bivariate Correlations Between Dependent Variables
and Variables of Significant Predictor Sets in Teacher
Educational Attitudes and Peer Attitudes Commonality Analyses

| | Dependent Variables | | |
|---|---|---|---|
| | Importance of a Structured, Controlled Environment | Traditional Authority | Peer Attitude Toward School |
| **Quantity** | | | |
| Number of students in the class | | −.01 | |
| Number of EMR learners in the class | | −.16 | |
| **Peer reading deficiencies** | | | |
| Grade | −.05 | | −.27 |
| Percentage of peers one or more grades behind in reading | .11 | | .12 |
| **Peer sociodemographic characteristics** | | | |
| Percentage Anglo | | −.18 | −.45 |
| Percentage Black | | −.08 | .01 |
| Percentage Spanish-surnamed | | .21 | .40 |
| Percentage lower SES | | .04 | .19 |
| Urban/not urban | | .02 | .18 |
| Rural/not rural | | −.03 | −.01 |
| **Peer attitude toward school** | −.09 | | |
| **Ability, training, and experience** | | | |
| Educational degree status | .01 | −.07 | |
| Hours of special education in-service training | .03 | .01 | |
| Years of teaching experience | .21 | .15 | |
| Verbal facility | −.04 | −.17 | |
| **Teacher sociodemographic characteristics** | | | |
| SES | | | .15 |
| Black/not Black | | | .11 |
| Spanish-surnamed/not Spanish-surnamed | | | |
| **Teacher educational attitudes** | | | |
| Importance of an open, warm environment | | | |
| Importance of a structured, controlled environment | | | |
| Traditional authority | | | |
| **Teacher report of the adequacy of special support services** | | | −.15 |

## Summary

Several issues related to mainstreaming EMR learners were raised at the beginning of this chapter. The findings presented in this chapter related to each issue will be summarized and their implications discussed.

One issue was whether regular class teachers can be provided with appropriate training and support materials and services. While this study found that teachers who received support services felt they were somewhat effective, less than half the regular teachers received special training and few received support services and materials. These findings raised questions as to how the training and support needs of regular class teachers can be met. More than half the regular teachers cited lack of appropriate materials as a relatively serious problem they had encountered in implementing mainstreaming. Since most of the regular classes were in schools that were beyond their first year of mainstreaming, this lack of materials seems to be more than a "start up" problem.

In mainstreaming, EMR learners receive instruction in two settings, which requires materials in the resource room and the regular classroom. A practical solution might be for resource teachers to allow materials to flow with the student back to the regular classroom. This represents an extension of the communication between teachers about a student's current work and objectives.

Teachers cited a lack of time to work individually with children as a serious problem. The regular teachers, on the average, were responsible for the instruction of 29 students, four of whom were reportedly EMR learners. Only 7% reported having the support of a teacher's aide. Many felt an aide would have eased some of their mainstreaming problems and allowed them time to individualize instruction for many students, especially the EMR learners. Very little individualized instruction or even small-group instruction was observed in the regular classes (see Chapter 8). There is a reluctance to assign special education aides to regular classes where some of their time may be spent working with nonhandicapped students. If EMR learners are to be mainstreamed, however, it seems imperative that regular class teachers as well as special class teachers have access to the special education support services provided by teachers' aides.

A second issue is whether low-achieving regular class peers are more appropriate academic role models for EMR learners than are other EMR learners. Such placements, common in Texas at the time of this study and also reported in California schools (Meyers, MacMillan, & Yoshida, 1975), may provide less appropriate academic role models than those found in the special class. But the relative similarity in ability between mainstreamed EMR learners and their low- achieving regular class peers eases the regular class teacher's burden, may stimulate more appropriate behaviors, and may minimize pejorative self-labelling in the mainstreamed EMR learners.

A third issue was whether the regular class teacher was inclined to provide the warm, structured environment often thought necessary for EMR learners. Regular and special education teachers felt an open, warm classroom climate was moderately important. A structured environment was rated as less important, though regular teachers who had been teaching longer placed more emphasis on it.

Regular class teachers expressed somewhat positive attitudes toward mainstreaming despite the fact they had not been provided effective support services for the EMR learners in the classes. Teachers who placed importance on a structured, controlled environment or who supported more traditional education practices tended to be least enthusiastic about mainstreaming. These educational attitudes were positively related to the number of years the teacher had taught. It would seem that the regular teachers best suited for mainstreaming are probably those who are relatively new to teaching, even though they do not have sufficient experience to adapt curricula and materials to students' individual needs. To have regular teachers who are both relatively positive toward mainstreaming and somewhat experienced, it may be best to select teachers who have had at least a few years of teaching experience.

Finally, concerns were raised as to whether regular class peers develop negative attitudes toward school when EMR learners are placed in their classrooms. There were no such indications expressed by students in regular classes with an EMR learner, and few teachers reported declining class morale as a problem associated with mainstreaming.

One cautionary note: If special materials and services are considered essential for an EMR learner's education, it is unlikely they will be delivered in the regular class setting unless strong support and administrative attention is given to the problem. The management of special education support services so that they flow with the child during the school day rather than being restricted to a special classroom setting is one of the greatest challenges encountered in implementing mainstreaming practices.

## Technical Notes

1. Because of a lack of variability in sex and the high correlation between age and years of teaching experience, these two variables were not included.

# 7
# The Socioemotional Climate

All learning, including learning in school, is embedded in a social context. The school context we refer to as the socioemotional climate of the classroom. Climate may be thought of as the group dynamics operating in the classroom. According to Schmuck and Schmuck (1975),"...the concept of climate summarizes the group processes that are worked out by a teacher in interaction with students and between the students in the classroom" (p. 24). Aspects of the socioemotional climate have often been considered important in the placement and education of EMR learners. Special educators have stressed the need for a warm, accepting, supportive environment to minimize experiences of failure; with highly controlled, structured environments and daily routines to help EMR learners focus their attention on the learning task and reduce fragmented behavior and misbehavior (Kirk & Johnson, 1950; Kolburne, 1965).

The introduction of mainstreaming raises questions regarding the socioemotional climate in regular classes and the impact EMR learners might have on the socioemotional climate of the regular classroom.Deservedly or not, EMR learners have often been described as misbehaving (Johnson, 1950) and as deviating from the academic, behavioral, and social norms of their regular class peers — behaviors which often precipitate the referral to special education. Concerns have been expressed that EMR learners might change the environment of regular classes, forcing the teacher to devote considerable time to managing behavior.

This chapter examines such issues as:

- the extent to which the regular class provides a warm, supportive, accepting climate and a structured environment;
- whether disruptiveness and friction occur in regular classrooms when EMR students are mainstreamed; and
- the extent to which the regular class teacher devotes time to managing behavior when EMR learners are mainstreamed.

This chapter explains the relevance of the socioemotional climate for nonhandicapped and EMR learners and presents the rationale for selecting specific dimensions of the socioemotional climate included in the Project PRIME model (see Figure 7-1). This chapter also presents descriptive information related to the variables included in the model, determine the most parsimonious way of describing the dimensions of the socioemotional climate, and examine the relationships among these dimensions. Finally, issues regarding the nature of the socioemotional climate available to EMR learners in regular and special education classroom settings are examined.

## The Influence of Teacher Leadership

The most significant actor in the classroom is the teacher. The teacher stands and talks to the class 68% of the time, and can promote pupil-to-pupil interactions, reduce interpupil conflict, increase pupil self-esteem, and affect pupil social status (Adams, 1968; Withall, 1951; Mitzel & Rabinowitz, 1953). The impact of teacher leadership on children occurs through the many functions the teacher performs: planning, establishing goals, directing the group toward attainment of goals, regulating the quality of interaction among group members, providing encouragement, demonstrating positive regard to group members, and maintaining group morale (Schmuck & Schmuck, 1975). The leadership role provides the teacher with a basis of power, which includes control over assignment of grades and honors, punishment, course content and assignments, and classroom environment (including seating).

Leadership can be considered in terms of "acts which help the group achieve its preferred outcomes" (Cartwright & Zander, 1968). Leadership acts increase the group's ability to function because they facilitate the setting of

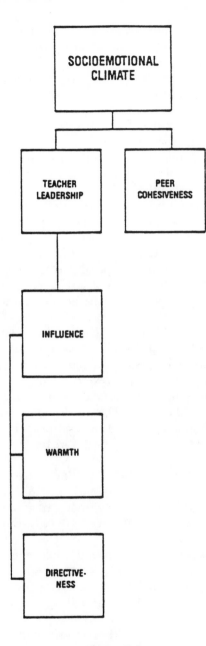

Figure 7-1
Socioemotional Climate
(Project PRIME Taxonomic Model)

group goals, move the group toward its goals, improve the quality of interactions among the members, and build the cohesiveness of the group. Within the classroom, certain dimensions of teacher leadership style determine whether or not the teacher functions effectively as a leader. These dimensions include methods of influence used by the teacher and the teacher's warmth and directiveness.

Teachers' methods to influence students vary, and these variations may have implications for the socioemotional climate of the class. French and Raven (1959) identified five types of influence used by leaders. *Reward influence* stems from the teacher's ability to distribute material and personal rewards. *Coercion* is based on the teacher's ability to distribute punishments such as poor grades, disapproval, dislike, rejection, corporal punishment, or expulsion. *Legitimacy-based influence* stems from the assigned rights and obligations of the teacher's role, exemplified by the statement: "You must do as I say because I am the teacher." *Referent influence* stems from a process of identification, the student being attracted to the teacher and expressing attitudes or behavior similar to those displayed or admired by the influencing agent. *Expert influence* derives from the acknowledged expertise of the influencing agent.

An additional type of influence is an indirect one, *environmental influence*, and is derived from the beliefs, values, attitudes, and behaviors of individuals in the immediate physical and social environment. Agents using environmental influence must be able to exercise control over crucial elements of the person's environment, and can take actions which will modify that person's environment so the desired behavior changes occur (Cartwright & Zander, 1968). One example of environmental influence is a teacher arranging class seating to separate pairs of children who are likely to whisper or behave disruptively.

Most research conducted on methods of influence has sought to determine the effectiveness of various types of influence. Berrio (1972) experimentally manipulated bases of influence with kindergarten and nursery school children. Legitimate and referent influence produced greater compliance over time than reward and coercion. Zander and Curtis (1962) reported that motivation to achieve was found to be stronger under referent influence while feelings of failure when not achieving were more intense under coercive influence. Millet (1973) suggested that the effectiveness of different types of influence vary with race and social class as well as the interaction of teachers' and students' race.

It seems reasonable to expect that the methods of influence employed by the teacher are related to pupil attitudes toward school, self-concepts, cohesiveness, off-task behavior, and other measures of group and individual functioning. There is evidence these relationships exist. Raven (1973) found the use of coercive influence negatively correlated with attitudes toward school, teachers, and learning. However, little research has been conducted on the relationship of teacher influence to learner outcomes.

## Teacher Influence Styles

Information obtained from classroom observations was used to examine the amount of time teachers spent influencing or managing student off-task behavior and the types of influence used in managing this behavior. In addition, teachers were asked to report the types of influence they used in their classes.

Observers reported teachers' responses to student off-task behavior on the Indiana Behavior Management System (IBMS). A majority of teachers (61-72%, depending on teacher type) attempted to influence or manage student off-task behavior in only 3% or fewer of the observation segments, a rate which equals about a minute and a half per hour spent in managing students' behavior (Table 7-1).

Using a series of 10-second time samples, the observers also recorded on the IBMS which of several types of responses the teacher made to student off-task behavior. These responses were categorized by type of teacher influence:

1. coercive influence included criticism and threat or actual use of physical or nonphysical punishment;
2. reward influence included the promise of incentives;
3. legitimate influence included direct verbal commands such as "stop," the use of quick short signals such as a snap of the fingers, refocusing attention, or reminding children of classroom rules;
4. referent influence included sympathetically interpreting the child's behavior (e.g., "You did that because you're tired today"), asking for a reason for a behavior, or empathizing with the child;
5. environmental manipulation included making work assignments exciting, presenting material in a dramatic manner, or providing successful experiences every day.

In addition to the IBMS, coercive influence was also rated using the Florida Climate and Control System (FLACCS) harsh/coercive teacher behavior scale. Observers noted whether any of the 15 behaviors on this scale occurred in each 2-minute observation segment. The percentage of teachers who used the different types of influence for varying amounts of time are presented in Table 7-1.

A large majority of teachers (78-88%, depending on teacher type) were observed using legitimate influence during at least 1% of the observation segments. (A 1% rate equals about ½ minute of legitimate influence exercised per hour if each segment is exactly 10 seconds.) Approximately three-quarters of the teachers were never observed using referent or coerceive influence, and virtually no teacher was observed using reward influence. A similar pattern, with lower percentages, was evident on the FLACCS: 63% of the regular class teachers, 77% of the special resource teachers, and 56% of the special self-contained teachers never displayed the behaviors included on the harsh/coercive teacher behavior scale during the observations. The apparent discrepancy between the IBMS and FLACCS measures may have resulted from the inclusion on the FLACCS harsh/coercive scale neutral behaviors such as "orders/commands" and "uses firm tone."

Teacher report information was obtained from two *Teacher Administrative Questionnaire* (TAQ) questions that asked teachers to note the frequency with which they used different motivation and behavior management techniques to influence student behavior. Options were never (= 10), rarely (= 20), sometimes (= 30), usually (= 40), and always (= 50). The range for each scale is 10-50. Teachers seldom responded at the extremes of the scale (never or usually) so these scale points were collapsed for Table 7-1. Teachers' reports were generally consistent with observers' information. For example, 86-93% of the teachers, depending on teacher type, said they used legitimate influence, at least sometimes. Seventy-two percent of the regular class teachers, 90% of the special resource teachers, and 82% of the special self-contained teachers reported rarely or never using coercive influence. In contrast to observers' reports, most teachers (82-93%) reported using rewards at least sometimes. Almost all teachers (96-100%) reported they managed students' behavior indirectly through certain types of enviornmental effects, such as presenting material in an entertaining way.

On the whole, Project PRIME teachers spent relatively little time managing students' off-task behavior. This finding is encouraging, suggesting that regular class teachers do not devote an excessive amount of time to managing behavior when retarded students are mainstreamed. When teachers did attempt to manage behavior, they were much more likely to use legitimate influence than other types of influence. This finding was reported by teachers and confirmed by observers. The predominant use of legitimate influence is not hard to understand. The teacher who is presenting a lesson to the class and observes the off-task behavior of a child must make a difficult decision. Is it better to manage the behavior of one child and risk losing the attention of the rest of the class, or ignore the child's behavior and risk its escalation? One resolution is to influence the child's behavior using an authority-based technique — a snap of the fingers, a one-word command, or speaking the child's name.

According to teachers' reports, positive influence techniques such as reward or environmental manipulation were used by teachers much of the time. However, this was not confirmed by observers. In fact, teachers were rarely observed offering rewards. This apparent discrepancy between teacher and observer reports may have resulted from the fact that teacher influence behavior was observed as it related to the teachers' attempts to influence (or manage) student off-task behavior. It seems likely that reward influence and environmental manipulation would be used by teachers as before-the-fact strategies to keep the class on task and prevent off-task behavior. According to Kounin (1970), techniques of group management such as these far outweigh disciplinary techniques in their power to influence the behavior of children. Teachers may have been referring to such strategies in reporting their influence techniques.

Coercive techniques were seldom reported by teachers or observed. More than three-fourths of the teachers were never observed using coercive influence, and others rarely. The observed and reported frequencies of coercive influence may underestimate its actual influence in the classroom: The observer's presence may have inhibited the use of these techniques by teachers and teachers may tend to underreport their use.

## Teacher Warmth

Teacher warmth is viewed as an important variable, particularly in special education. Furthermore, teacher warmth is considered an important variable in the execution of teacher leadership functions. The research to date has failed to demonstrate conclusively any causal relationships between teacher warmth and student outcomes, though individual studies have found significant relationships. In reviewing the research, Dunkin and Biddle (1974) concluded that any significant relationships that could be cited from a particular study were almost certain to be denied or reversed by other studies. This conclusion is substantiated by two literature reviews. Rosenshine and Furst (1971) and Heath and Nielson (1974) reported the same pattern of conflicting findings of acceptance of student ideas and criticism.

Most explanations cite methodological weaknesses. Heath and Nielson (1974) complained that the research designs of most studies were fundamentally weak and that the operational definitions of the behavior examined in many instances lacked even face validity. Rosenshine and Furst (1971) reported that most of the studies they considered employed very general, vaguely-defined categories of teaching behavior rather than specific, observable, and operationally-defined variables.

The conceptual clarity of particular variables used in previous research has also been questioned. For example, Dunkin and Biddle (1974) expressed

Table 7-1

Teacher Leadership by Instructional Setting

| Teacher Leadership Variable | Regular | | | | Special Resource | | | | Special Self-contained | | | |
|---|---|---|---|---|---|---|---|---|---|---|---|---|
| | X | SD | % | N | X | SD | % | N | X | SD | % | N |
| **Off-Task Behavior** | | | | | | | | | | | | |
| Percentage of IBMS observation segments teachers were observed to be off task | 2.76 | 2.45 | | 253 | 2.52 | 2.15 | | 125 | 3.32 | 2.41 | | 124 |
| 0 | | | 9 | | | | 16 | | | | 6 | |
| 1 | | | 28 | | | | 25 | | | | 23 | |
| 2 | | | 19 | | | | 18 | | | | 18 | |
| 3 | | | 15 | | | | 13 | | | | 13 | |
| 4+ | | | 28 | | | | 28 | | | | 39 | |
| **Influence** | | | | | | | | | | | | |
| **Coercive** | | | | | | | | | | | | |
| Percentage of IBMS observation segments teachers were observed using coercive influence | .34 | .60 | | 253 | .23 | .28 | | 125 | .39 | .48 | | 124 |
| 0 | | | 82 | | | | 83 | | | | 75 | |
| 1 | | | 15 | | | | 17 | | | | 21 | |
| 2 | | | 1 | | | | 0 | | | | 4 | |
| 3+ | | | 2 | | | | 0 | | | | 0 | |
| Number of harsh/coercive teacher behaviors observed per 2-minute observation segments on the FLACCS | .52 | .52 | | 250 | .35 | .39 | | 121 | .52 | .48 | | 123 |
| 0 | | | 63 | | | | 77 | | | | 56 | |
| 1 | | | 31 | | | | 21 | | | | 41 | |
| 2 | | | 5 | | | | 2 | | | | 3 | |
| 3+ | | | 1 | | | | 0 | | | | 0 | |

| Variable | M | SD | N | M | SD | N | M | SD | N |
|---|---|---|---|---|---|---|---|---|---|
| Teacher report on TAQ of frequency she used coercive influence | 20.50 | 5.44 | 253 | 17.06 | 4.83 | 119 | 18.87 | 5.37 | 114 |
|   Never | 13 | | | 28 | | | 22 | | |
|   Rarely | 59 | | | 62 | | | 60 | | |
|   Sometimes | 28 | | | 10 | | | 17 | | |
|   Usually/always | 0 | | | 0 | | | 0 | | |
| **Reward** | | | | | | | | | |
| Percentage of IBMS observation segments teachers were observed using reward influence | .00 | | 253 | .03 | .06 | 125 | .05 | .13 | 124 |
|   0 | 100 | | | 99 | | | 98 | | |
|   1 | 0 | | | 1 | | | 2 | | |
|   2 | 0 | | | 0 | | | 0 | | |
|   3+ | 0 | | | 0 | | | 0 | | |
| Teacher report on TAQ of frequency she used reward influence | 29.21 | 6.90 | 252 | 32.31 | 6.35 | 117 | 31.62 | 6.54 | 111 |
|   Never/rarely | 38 | | | 8 | | | 7 | | |
|   Sometimes | 56 | | | 42 | | | 50 | | |
|   Usually/always | 26 | | | 50 | | | 43 | | |
| **Referent** | | | | | | | | | |
| Percentage of IBMS observation segments teachers were observed using referent influence | .30 | .28 | 253 | .30 | .39 | 125 | .38 | .36 | 124 |
|   0 | 82 | | | 78 | | | 77 | | |
|   1 | 18 | | | 20 | | | 21 | | |
|   2 | 0 | | | 1 | | | 2 | | |
|   3+ | 0 | | | 0 | | | 0 | | |

(Continued on next page)

Table 7-1  (continued)

|  | Instructional Setting | | | | | | | | |
|  | Regular | | | Special Resource | | | Special Self-contained | | |
| Teacher Leadership Variable | X | SD | N | X | SD | N | X | SD | N |
|---|---|---|---|---|---|---|---|---|---|
| Influence (continued) | | | | | | | | | |
| Legitimate | | | | | | | | | |
| Percentage of IBMS observation segments teachers were observed using legitimate influence | 2.07 | 1.84 | 253 | 1.93 | 1.78 | 125 | 2.47 | 1.83 | 124 |
| 0 | | 12 | | | 22 | | | 13 | |
| 1 | | 37 | | | 28 | | | 23 | |
| 2 | | 23 | | | 22 | | | 25 | |
| 3 | | 11 | | | 10 | | | 15 | |
| 4+ | | 17 | | | 16 | | | 25 | |
| Teacher report on TAQ of frequency she used legitimate influence | 31.70 | 4.70 | 253 | 29.62 | 5.64 | 119 | 30.22 | 5.28 | 112 |
| Never/rarely | | 7 | | | 14 | | | 13 | |
| Sometimes | | 61 | | | 63 | | | 65 | |
| Usually/always | | 32 | | | 23 | | | 22 | |
| Environmental manipulation | | | | | | | | | |
| Teacher report on TAQ of frequency she used environmental manipulation | 34.12 | 4.38 | 252 | 35.84 | 4.49 | 119 | 35.99 | 3.92 | 114 |
| Never/rarely | | 2 | | | 4 | | | 0 | |
| Sometimes | | 57 | | | 35 | | | 38 | |
| Usually/always | | 41 | | | 61 | | | 62 | |

## Warmth

| | M | SD | % | n | M | SD | % | n | M | SD | % | n |
|---|---|---|---|---|---|---|---|---|---|---|---|---|
| Number of warm teacher behaviors observed per 2-minute observation segments on the FLACCS | .98 | .73 | | 250 | 1.69 | 1.18 | | 121 | 1.21 | .87 | | 123 |
| 0 | | | 27 | | | | 15 | | | | 22 | |
| 1 | | | 50 | | | | 35 | | | | 46 | |
| 2 | | | 20 | | | | 29 | | | | 27 | |
| 3+ | | | 2 | | | | 21 | | | | 5 | |

## Directiveness

| | M | SD | % | n | M | SD | % | n | M | SD | % | n |
|---|---|---|---|---|---|---|---|---|---|---|---|---|
| Observer ratings of degree of pupils' freedom on the FLACCS | 2.82 | .74 | | 250 | 3.13 | .81 | | 120 | 2.92 | .84 | | 123 |
| 1 (rarely free) | | | 5 | | | | 5 | | | | 4 | |
| 2 | | | 23 | | | | 17 | | | | 24 | |
| 3 (occasionally free) | | | 57 | | | | 42 | | | | 47 | |
| 4 | | | 13 | | | | 35 | | | | 20 | |
| 5 (usually free) | | | 2 | | | | 2 | | | | 4 | |
| Teachers' reports on TCCQ of degree to which rigidity/control is used in own classes | 23.06 | 4.07 | | 251 | | | | | 22.69 | 4.66 | | 101 |
| Never/rarely | | | 16 | | | | | | | | 26 | |
| Sometimes | | | 69 | | | | | | | | 55 | |
| Usually/always | | | 15 | | | | | | | | 17 | |

Note. IBMS = Indiana Behavior Management System; FLACCS = Florida Climate and Control System; TCCQ = Teacher Classroom Climate Questionnaire.

concern that certain variables unite the constructs of teacher warmth and directiveness, constructs which they believed to be very different. They argued that investigations of warmth and directiveness should be pursued independently, allowing for possible combinations of high-teacher directiveness and high-teacher warmth.

In this study, the "warm teacher" behavior scale from the FLACCS observation system was used to measure teacher warmth. This scale includes 12 items such as "is warm," "listens carefully," "supports child," and "praises child." The observers noted whether the behaviors occurred in each two-minute observation segment. Seventy-three percent of the regular class teachers, 85% of the special resource teachers, and 78% of the special self-contained teachers exhibited one or more kinds of warm behavior in an average 2-minute observation segment (Table 7-1).

Most teachers, regardless of whom they taught, exhibited one or more types of warm behavior during a 2-minute observation segment. There were no indications the regular class teachers provided a warm classroom environment less frequently than the special education teachers.[1] Twenty-seven percent of the regular, 22% of the special self-contained, and 15% of the resource class teachers were never observed displaying warm behavior. Clearly, one must consider the characteristics of the individual teacher rather than the setting when placing an EMR learner in a warm, supportive classroom environment.

## Teacher Directiveness

A classroom system has a number of specific functions to be regulated, including physical movement, verbal interaction, content or goals, work processes, timing of work, division of labor, control of deviancy, and evaluation of both work products and soundness of ideas. These functions are delegated to the teacher. "Teacher directiveness" refers to the degree to which the teacher shares this power and responsibility with the members of the class as a group (democratic system) or on an individual basis with particular students (laissez-faire system). The directive teacher has been described as one who sets the classroom goals, directs the students to the precise tasks to which they will give attention, directs specific processes of working, and regulates who will perform which tasks (Hughes, 1968).

Teacher directiveness has been of interest to educators for at least 50 years. A primary concern of the progressive educational movement, for example, was whether teachers should direct children's learning. Lewin, Lippitt, and White's classic study (1939) revealed that groups of boys with autocratic leaders were characterized by hostility, competitiveness, and strong dependency but were quantitatively productive. Boys with laissez-faire leaders were disorganized, frustrated, and produced little work. Groups with democratic leaders were qualitatively superior in performance and displayed openness, friendly communication, and independence.

This and other studies have been cited by different educational writers as supporting either a directive or nondirective style of teaching. The fact that the same studies have been cited by authors espousing opposing viewpoints indicates that research findings regarding teacher directiveness are ambiguous and inconsistent (Anderson, 1959). Soar (1972) reviewed this research and concluded that it provided support for nondirective teaching behavior. On the other hand, Anderson's 1959 review concluded that directiveness is positively related to morale (satisfaction and attitudes) and possibly to productivity (learning).

In Project PRIME, teacher directiveness was examined using observers' ratings on the FLACCS pupil-freedom scale and teachers' reports on the *Teachers' Classroom Climate Questionnaire* (TCCQ) rigidity/control scale. On the FLACCS, observers rated pupil freedom on a 5-point scale where 1 = "rarely free," 3 = "occasionally free," and 5 = "generally free." On the TCCQ, teachers indicated whether eight items such as "pupils not allowed to talk while working," "students not supposed to move around," "children only allowed to use materials as instructed," "asking permission for things like sharpening pencils required," and "teacher planning of all activities" (1 = never, 2 = rarely, 3 = sometimes, 4 = usually, 5 = always) occurred in their classes. Possible scores on this scale ranged from 8 to 40.

The regular class observed mean rating on the pupil-freedom scale was 2.8, the special resource class mean was 3.1, and the special self-contained class mean was 2.9 (Table 7-1). Thus, in all classrooms the average pupil freedom rating was equivalent to "occasionally free." These ratings were generally consistent with teachers' reports on the TCCQ of the degree to which they controlled the activities in their classes. As indicated in Table 7-1, the majority of regular and special self-contained teachers reported they were sometimes directive. (This scale was not administered to resource teachers.)

On the whole, these results suggest that most classrooms were neither highly directive, authoritarian nor loosely-structured open classrooms. Rather, teachers seem to have combined moderate structure and directiveness with occasional opportunity for pupils' choice and freedom. Despite the fact that special education has stressed the need for a high degree of structure and carefully adhered to routines in classes (Kirk & Johnson, 1950), only about one-sixth of the regular and special self-contained classes in this sample were found to be highly structured. Chapters 9 and 10 examine whether the less structured and moderate directiveness of Project PRIME classrooms adversely affected the academic and social competencies of the educable mentally retarded learners.

## The Classroom Peer Group:   Peer Cohesiveness

In many ways a group of classroom peers is similar to other kinds of social groups. Both social and classroom groups can be expected to evolve interaction patterns among members, develop norms about matters relevant to the group's purpose(s), and exert varying degrees of influence on individual members. The extensive group dynamics literature contributes to understanding the group processes that exist among classroom peers. The classroom peer group differs from social groups in at least two important respects: membership in the classroom group is involuntary and the official leader (teacher) is a powerful authority who is not appointed by the members (students). Research directly concerned with child peer group processes is relatively recent, and the findings about social groups remains to be tested in the classroom.

In its broadest meaning, the term "group" refers to people whose relationships with each other are significantly interdependent. Although the nature of the members' interdependence may vary in different kinds of groups, it is this feature of interlocking relationships which distinguishes a group from a random collection of individuals. Theorists of group dynamics have emphasized particular forms of interdependence they believe to be most crucial to characterize a group.

Given these interdependent relationships, it follows that members experience consequences of belonging or not belonging to a particular group. The forces that cause people to remain in a group rather than leave have been referred to as "group cohesiveness." Argyle (1969) describes the importance of cohesiveness:

> A group can hardly be regarded as a group, as opposed to a collection of individuals, unless there is some minimal degree of attraction to the group. The overall level of attraction towards the group, "cohesiveness," is one of the most important dimensions of social groups, and can be equated with "loyalty" (p. 220).

Empirical studies have documented three major consequences of cohesiveness relevant to the study of classroom groups: the power of the group to influence its members and bring about conformity to group norms, high participation and loyalty of members reflected in frequent communication and low absenteeism, and increased self-esteem accompanied by reduced anxiety among members (Cartwright & Zander, 1968).

Although cohesiveness has been a central concept in discussions of small-group theory, it has not played a major role in discussions of classroom groups. However, some theorists have incorporated the construct of cohesiveness in their theory of education in a fundamental way (e.g., Schmuck & Schmuck, 1975). Even educational theorists not using the term "cohesiveness" in their writings are in fact concerned with it.

For example, Walberg and Anderson conducted a series of studies based largely on a conceptual model of Getzels and Thelen to determine the impact of classroom climate on various indices of educational attainment (Anderson & Walberg, 1968; Walberg, 1970; Walberg & Anderson, 1968). A major conclusion was that factors such as personal relations among class members and tendencies for class members to be treated equally were good predictors of learning on a physics project. The concepts employed by Walberg and Anderson are similar, if not the same, as those typically employed to define cohesiveness.

Classroom cohesiveness was also indirectly studied in a series of investigations conducted by Bovard (1951, 1956a, 1956b) to determine the effects of different styles of teachers' leadership on classroom behavior. Group-centered classes, as opposed to leader-centered ones, resulted in greater attraction to both the group as a whole and individual members. A major criterion in judging the effects of different teaching styles in those studies was attraction to group, a critical element of cohesiveness.

Classroom-related research and theory, then, suggest that cohesiveness has a great deal of utility as a construct for predicting a variety of classroom phenomena, even though it has been most frequently employed in the study of small groups. Cohesiveness as it relates to the socioemotional climate of the classroom was defined by Project PRIME as happiness or satisfaction among members, cooperation and minimal competition, a lack of friction or disruptiveness, and a social structure in which friendship choices are distributed fairly evenly across all members of the group rather than confined to a few members.

In this study, cohesiveness in the regular and special self-contained classes was defined operationally by pupil happiness, a facilitating classroom climate, the amount of friction in the class, and the sociometric structure of the class.

*Pupil happiness* was measured by the FLACCS pupils happy/climate positive scale and also by student reports on a YSD scale measuring unhappiness (the YSD discordance scale). The FLACCS scale consisted of two items, which were rated from 1 (low) to 5 (high) by observers. Thus, the range on this scale was 2-10. The YSD scale comprised 13 items such as "Are most of the children unhappy in your class?" and "Are the children in your class always fighting with each other?" The range on this scale was 13-26.

The average of observers' ratings on the FLACCS pupils happy/climate positive scale indicated that most pupils appeared happy much of the time and most of the time the climate was positive (Table 7-2). On the other hand, pupil self-reports indicated that students thought about half the happiness items were appropriate descriptions of their classes (Table 7-2).

*A facilitating climate* was measured by teacher ratings of 19 items on the TCCQ (cooperation diversification scale) as either never (= 1), rarely (= 2), sometimes (= 3), usually (= 4), or always (= 5) true of their classes. Some items included on the scale were "The children enjoy the class activities," "Within the classroom, there is a wide enough diversity of books to meet each child's needs and interests," and "Children try to help each other with their work." The scores on this scale ranged from 19-95. As shown in Table 7-2, 54% of the regular and 58% of the special self-contained teachers reported the classroom climate was usually or always facilitating.

*Disruptiveness and friction among pupils* was measured both by observation and by teacher report. The observation measure, the FLACCS disruptive peer behavior scale, contained 20 items such as "is uncooperative-resistant," "makes disparaging remark," "commands," "teases," "tattles," "resists, disobeys directions," and "demands attention." The observers noted the occurrence of these behaviors in each 2-minute observation segment. Teacher reports of friction in the classroom came from the TCCQ friction scale, a scale with 13 items, including "Some children don't like the other children in the room," "Certain students impose their wishes on the whole class," and "There is constant bickering and fighting." The teacher indicated whether or not each statement was never (= 1), rarely (= 2), sometimes (= 3), usually (= 4), or always (= 5) true of the class.

Observers reported that no disruptive behavior occurred in 73% of the regular classes (Table 7-2), in 76% of the resource classes, or in 64% of the special self-contained classes. In the remaining classrooms where disruptive behavior was observed, one to two kinds of disruptive behavior per 2-minute observation segment were reported by observers. It is not clear from these figures whether this rate represented a continuing low incidence of disruptiveness in these classrooms (e.g., one student engaged in some out-of-bounds behavior) or a few occasions when the entire class was out of control.

The teacher reports on the TCCQ were generally consistent with the observation data. Ninety-eight percent of the regular and special self-contained teachers reported there was at least some friction in the classroom. However, 54% of the regular teachers and 60% of the special self-contained teachers reported that friction was rare (Table 7-2). The remaining teachers generally reported there was sometimes friction but did not report it as a usual occurrence.

Indicators of the *sociometric structure* of the regular and self-contained classes were derived from the HIFTO instrument (Table 7-2). On the HIFTO, each student in a class rated whether he liked (smiling face), disliked (frowning face), was neutral toward, or did not know each of the other students in the class. A class mean score was obtained by summing these individual ratings and dividing the sum by the total number of students who received ratings.

In almost all regular (86%) and special self-contained classes (90%) more than 41% of the total responses given by class members were smiles, and in no class were frowns more than 40% of the total. The mean percentage of students receiving one or more frowns was 20.50 in regular classes and 19.34 in special self-contained classes. There were no regular or special classes in which more than 40% of the class members received one or more frowns.

In general, the observer reports on peer cohesiveness indicated that most pupils were happy much of the time and there was generally a positive climate. These observations were confirmed by reports of the majority of teachers, who described the classroom climate as facilitating. Students, on the other hand, revealed greater variability in self-reports of general level of happiness, as indicated by the number of negative responses to items on the YSD scale.

The discrepancy between observer ratings and pupil reports of happiness could have been due to two factors. First, the observation measure (FLACCS pupils happy/climate positive scale) is a rather gross two-item rating which reflects observer general impressions of pupil happiness and it is possible it does not tap more subtle signs of pupils' discontent. Second, it may be that elementary-aged students were unable to generalize their classroom experience, responding instead in terms of single events. Specifically, the YSD instrument presents certain descriptors of classrooms (e.g., children fighting) and requires the students to indicate whether each descriptor characterizes their classroom. Young children may give an affirmative response if the described event happened only once or recently, rather than as a typical occurrence.

Observer and teacher reports agreed that friction and disruptive behavior rarely occurred in classrooms in this study. In fact, disruptive behavior was never observed in 73% of the regular classes, 76% of the resource classes, and 64% of the special self-contained classes. Thus, it is clear that the majority of regular classes did not experience disruptiveness and friction as a result of mainstreaming EMR learners. In about one-fourth of the regular classes some disruptive behavior was observed, and a higher percentage, though not a majority, of regular class teachers reported there was occasional friction. Without premainstreaming information, or comparison classes where

Table 7-2

Peer Cohesiveness by Instructional Setting.

| | Instructional Setting | | | | | | | | | | | |
|---|---|---|---|---|---|---|---|---|---|---|---|---|
| | Regular | | | | Special Resource | | | | Special Self-Contained | | | |
| Peer Cohesiveness Variable | X | SD | % | N | X | SD | % | N | X | SD | % | N |
| **Pupil happiness** | | | | | | | | | | | | |
| Observer ratings on FIACCS pupils happy/climate positive scale | 7.5 | 1.0 | | 250 | 7.7 | 1.0 | | 120 | 7.4 | 1.0 | | 123 |
| Pupils' self-reports of happiness on YSD discordance scale | 18.2 | 1.4 | | 253 | | | | | 19.5 | 1.2 | | 119 |
| **Facilitating climate** | | | | | | | | | | | | |
| Teacher report on TCCQ of degree to which a facilitating climate exists in own class | 66.68 | 7.45 | | 251 | | | | | 66.54 | 7.82 | | 101 |
| Never/rarely | | | 0 | | | | | | | | 2 | |
| Sometimes | | | 46 | | | | | | | | 39 | |
| Usually/always | | | 54 | | | | | | | | 58 | |
| **Disruptiveness and friction** | | | | | | | | | | | | |
| Number of disruptive pupil behaviors observed per 2-minute observation segments on the FIACCS | .42 | .54 | | 250 | .33 | .40 | | 121 | .53 | .54 | | 123 |
| 0 | | | 73 | | | | 76 | | | | 64 | |
| 1 | | | 23 | | | | 23 | | | | 28 | |
| 2 | | | 3 | | | | 0 | | | | 8 | |
| 3+ | | | 1 | | | | 0 | | | | 0 | |

| | Mean | SD | | n | Mean | SD | | n |
|---|---|---|---|---|---|---|---|---|
| Teacher report on TCCQ frequency of friction in own class | 30.88 | 5.94 | | 251 | 29.65 | 6.16 | | 101 |
| Never/rarely | | | 54 | | | | 60 | |
| Sometimes | | | 43 | | | | 38 | |
| Usually/always | | | 2 | | | | 1 | |
| Sociometric structure |  |  |  |  |  |  |  |  |
| Percentage of smiles given on HIFTO | 49.61 | 8.84 | | 256 | 61.22 | 13.31 | | 122 |
| 0-20 | | | 0 | | | | 0 | |
| 21-40 | | | 13 | | | | 8 | |
| 41-60 | | | 75 | | | | 40 | |
| 61+ | | | 11 | | | | 0 | |
| Percentage of frowns given on HIFTO | 20.50 | 7.21 | | 256 | 19.34 | 9.78 | | 122 |
| 0-20 | | | 54 | | | | 55 | |
| 21-40 | | | 44 | | | | 43 | |
| 41-60 | | | 0 | | | | 0 | |
| 61+ | | | 0 | | | | 0 | |

Note. FLACCS = Florida Climate and Control System; YSD = Your School Days; TCCQ = Teacher Classroom Climate Questionnaire; HIFTO = How I Feel Toward Others.

mainstreaming was not occurring, it is not possible to know if this disruptiveness and friction resulted from the addition of EMR learners to the class. Approximately one-third of the regular classes were located in areas that were predominantly lower socioeconomic areas. Such classes have often been characterized as more disruptive than classes in middle or upper socioeconomic areas. Thus, it seems highly likely that the disruptiveness and friction observed in some of the regular classes were related to factors other than mainstreaming.

The distributions of liking and disliking responses depict the sociometric structure of the class as a whole and were obtained with the classroom as the unit. These descriptive statistics are unlike most reports of sociometric data in prior studies, which typically focus on the social status of individual students and the extent to which observed distributions of status are similar to chance distributions (Gronlund, 1959). The Project PRIME sociometric score distributions indicated that the degree of acceptance among classmates (smiles) far exceeded that of rejection (frowns) in the majority of regular and special self-contained classes.

# Summary of Teacher Leadership and Peer Cohesiveness Variables

In sum, teachers of EMR learners in both regular and self-contained classes spent a minimum amount of time managing off-task behavior and predominantly used influence methods based on the legitimacy of their role when they did manage behavior. Most teachers also reported using reward influence and careful arrangement of the environment to manage behavior. Most EMR learners were in classes where the teacher exhibited warm behaviors fairly steadily, although about one fourth of the regular and special self-contained teachers were never observed to exhibit warm behaviors, and more than one third of each group were observed to exhibit some harsh, coercive behaviors. A somewhat higher percentage of resource teachers than regular teachers were observed using warm behaviors, and somewhat fewer were observed using harsh, coercive behaviors.

Most of the EMR learners were in classes that combined moderate structure and directiveness with some opportunity for pupil choice and freedom. Although observers generally reported a positive climate in the regular and self-contained classes and teachers reported a classroom environment that was usually facilitating, there were some signs of pupil discontent. However, friction and disruptiveness were relatively rare. In most classes the degree of acceptance of other students in the class far exceeded the degree of rejection.

Regular and special self-contained classes often came from different school buildings — buildings that may have varied widely on any number of characteristics. As a result, comparisons cannot legitimately be made between the two classroom environments or the two groups of teachers. Still, through the years so much stress has been placed on the socioemotional environment of the special class that the socioemotional climate of a special class might be expected to be very different from that of almost any regular class. It is surprising to note how similar the environments seem in terms of teacher influence styles, warmth, and directiveness, and pupil happiness, disruptiveness, and friction. Certainly these data on the socioemotional characteristics of classrooms do not support placing an EMR learner in one environment over another.

# Relationships Among Socioemotional Climate Variables

In considering factors influencing the socioemotional climate of the classroom for EMR learners, the role of teacher and peer group were considered independently. However, they interact to form the socioemotional climate of the class (Schmuck & Schmuck, 1975). This section presents a more parsimonious way of describing the dimensions of the socioemotional climate of the classroom, taking into account the relationships among measures representing a single dimension. The results of factor analyses will be incorporated into this description.

Also considered are the relationships among the dimensions of the socioemotional climate using correlational techniques. Lastly, commonality analysis is used to explore the specific effect of teacher leadership on peer cohesiveness.

## Underlying Structure of Socioemotional Climate

To determine the underlying structure of the socioemotional climate, factor analyses were performed for those dimensions of the socioemotional climate (teacher influence and peer cohesiveness) that were initially defined by multiple measures. Teacher warmth was defined by only one measure (the FLACCS warm teacher behavior scale) and teacher directiveness was defined by only two measures (one observer measure, the FLACCS pupil freedom scale; and one teacher report measure, the TCCQ rigidity/control scale). There was no need for a factor analysis of these dimensions.

## Teacher Influence

The scales used to define teacher influence (the TAQ influence scales, the IBMS influence scales, and the FLACCS harsh/coercive influence scale) were submitted to an image analysis followed by varimax rotation. Subjects in the factor analyses were 561 teachers of regular and special self-contained classes.

Three factors emerged, two of which were considered meaningful dimensions of teachers' influence: teacher coercive-legitimate influence and teacher positive influence, having alpha reliability coefficients of 0.71 and 0.62, respectively. The teacher coercive-legitimate influence factor was comprised of the coercive and the legitimate influence scales from the TAQ. The teacher positive influence factor consisted of the TAQ reward influence and environmental manipulation scales.

The teacher positive influence factor is easily interpretable in that it is comprised of teacher use of reward influence and environmental manipulation — the arrangement of certain aspects of the classroom environment to promote positive behavior among children. The teacher coercive-legitimate factor is less readily interpretable. The fact that use of coercive and legitimate influence clustered on the same factor indicates that these types of influence may represent points on a continuum of one type of influence rather than separate influence methods. That is, the use of legitimate influence, such as a snap of the fingers or a quick one-word command, may be similar to, but less forceful than, coercive influence as a means of managing student behavior.

## Peer Cohesiveness

The measures used to define peer cohesiveness (YSD, TCCQ, and FLACCS scales and the means and standard deviations of the HIFTO categories) were submitted to an image analysis followed by varimax rotation. The unit of analysis was the classroom. Mean scores were computed for the students in the 561 regular and special self-contained classes.

A three-factor solution was obtained which included two factors which could be interpreted as meaningful dimensions of peer cohesiveness: peer dislike (alpha = 0.87) and peer harmony (alpha = 0.56). The peer dislike factor was comprised of the mean percentage of pupils receiving one or more frowns, the mean percentage of frowns given, the mean percentage of smiles given (negative loading), and the standard deviation of frowns given. The peer harmony factor was comprised of the YSD discordance scale, the FLACCS disruptive peer behavior scale, and the TCCQ friction scale (all of which had negative loadings) and the FLACCS pupils happy/climate positive scale and TCCQ cooperation/diversification scale (which had positive loadings).

The peer dislike factor was comprised of constructs basic to group dynamics theory such as the internal attractiveness, or lack of it, among group members as reflected in the sociometric scores. Peer harmony pertains to rewards, such as happiness and lack of friction, obtained by accepting the group's values. These two factors are similar to the cohesiveness factors obtained by Hagstrom and Selvin (1965): sociometric cohesion and social satisfaction. Taken together, the results of both studies indicate that cohesiveness is not a unidimensional construct, as suggested by some (e.g., Lott & Lott, 1965). Theories which equate cohesiveness with attraction appear to be inaccurate; rather, attraction seems to be one facet of cohesiveness.

## Relationships Among the Dimensions of the Socioemotional Climate

To explore the relationships among the dimensions of the socioemotional climate, correlation coefficients (presented in Table 7-3) among the five teacher leadership variables (teacher positive influence, teacher coercive-legitimate influence, teacher warmth, teacher control, pupil freedom) and two peer cohesiveness measures (peer dislike and peer harmony) were examined. The following are significant relationships ($p < .01$) which were found for the regular classes.

1. The use of positive influence by regular class teachers was positively associated with their use of coercive-legitimate influence.
2. The more frequently regular class teachers were observed displaying warmth, the less likely they were to be controlling, and the greater the pupil freedom in their classes.
3. Regular class teachers who were controlling tended to use more coercive-legitimate influence and allowed less pupil freedom than teachers who were less controlling.
4. Regular classes with a high degree of peer harmony were more likely than classes with less harmony to have a low level of peer dislike, and teachers who displayed warmth were not often controlling and infrequently used coercive-legitimate influence.

Correlation coefficients among these measures for the special self-contained classes revealed a similar pattern of relationships ($p < .01$) (see Table 7-3).

1. Special self-contained classes with high levels of pupil freedom tended to have teachers who displayed more frequent warmth and used less coercive-legitimate influence than classes characterized by less pupil freedom.

2. Special self-contained classes with a high degree of peer harmony were more likely to have a low level of peer dislike and teachers who infrequently used coercive-legitimate influence than classes with less harmony.

All other correlation coefficients for the two class settings were nonsignificant.

Correlations among measures of teacher leadership and peer cohesiveness, then, revealed a general pattern of predictable relationships. For example, the negative relationship was significant between peer harmony and teacher use of coercive-legitimate influence and directiveness. However, peer harmony was positively related to teacher warmth. Also, a significant negative correlation was obtained between teachers' warmth and use of directiveness.

Only one coefficient in the intercorrelation matrix was somewhat surprising. There was a significant positive relationship between regular class teacher use of positive influence and use of coercive-legitimate influence, although a negative relationship between these types of influence could have been anticipated. Closer inspection indicated that the positive sign of this correlation may have resulted from the fact that both types of influence were actually inversely related to a third variable, years of teaching experience. Analyses of variance revealed that teachers with the fewest years of teaching

Table 7-3
Intercorrelation Matrix of Teacher
Leadership and Peer Measures

| | Measure | 1 | 2 | 3 | 4 | 5 | 6 | 7 |
|---|---|---|---|---|---|---|---|---|
| 1. | Teacher positive influence | — | 30* | 00 | -09 | 13 | 06 | 07 |
| 2. | Teacher coercive-legitimate influence | 15 | — | -12 | 24* | 04 | 11 | -35 |
| 3. | Teacher warmth | -09 | -22 | — | -16* | 25* | -11 | 27* |
| 4. | Teacher directiveness | 01 | 23 | -10 | — | -18* | 06 | -21* |
| 5. | Pupil freedom | 02 | -25* | 32* | -14 | — | -01 | -11 |
| 6. | Peer dislike | 04 | 02 | -06 | -24 | -06 | — | -16* |
| 7. | Classroom harmony | 01 | -32* | 12 | -02 | 09 | -28* | — |

Note. Numbers above the diagonal are based on regular classes (N = 262). Below the diagonal are for special self-contained classes (N = 127). Decimal points have been omitted.

*p <.01.

experience (0-3 years) employed more positive influence and also more coercive-legitimate influence than teachers with greater experience ($p < .01$). It is possible that relatively inexperienced teachers have not developed a stable set of strategies for managing off-task behavior. Teacher training programs often stress positive influence techniques for managing classroom behavior. Experienced teachers, however, may pressure new teachers in the same school to use strong or even harsh measures to maintain discipline in the classroom (Gorton, 1971). As a result, inexperienced teachers may first attempt to manage off-task behavior with positive influence techniques, and if those methods fail, resort to coercive-legitimate techniques to restore immediate order.

## Prediction of Peer Cohesiveness by Teacher Leadership

Commonality analyses were used to examine the relationships among measures of teacher leadership and peer cohesiveness. For purposes of analysis, a unidirectional relationship is posited: Teacher leadership style affects peer cohesiveness in the classroom. However, it can also be expected that aspects of peer cohesiveness can affect teacher leadership style. For example, in a class that is highly disruptive with much friction among peers, a teacher may be more prone to use harsh, coercive influence methods and be less warm and more directive than in a well-behaved, cohesive class.

To determine which dimensions of teacher leadership affect the specific peer cohesiveness measures of peer dislike and peer harmony, commonality analyses were performed on each of these dependent measures with the classroom as the unit of analysis. Predictors in each equation were (1) teacher warmth, (2) a teacher directiveness set (the TCCQ rigidity/control scale and the FLACCS pupil freedom scale), (3) teacher coercive-legitimate influence, and (4) teacher positive influence. These two commonality analyses were performed separately for 238 regular and 94 special self-contained classes.[2] Table 7-4 presents the results.

The commonality analyses in which peer dislike was the dependent measure yielded a total $R^2$ of only 0.03 for regular and 0.04 for special self-contained classes. This equation was not significant for either sample.

The four predictors accounted for significant percentages of variance in peer harmony in both regular and self-contained classes. In regular classes, all four predictors explained 23.2% of the variance in harmony ($p < .0001$). In this equation, significant portions of variance in harmony were uniquely accounted for by teacher use of coercive-legitimate influence, warmth, directiveness, and positive influence. Teacher warmth was positively associated with classroom harmony, while directiveness and the use of coercive-legitimate influence were negatively related to harmony. The joint contribution of teacher directiveness and use of coercive-legitimate influence accounted for 2.8% of the variance in harmony in regular classes. That is, that aspect of directiveness which covaries with coercive-legitimate influence contributed to reduction in harmony among students in mainstreamed classes.

Teacher coercive-legitimate influence, which was significantly correlated with positive influence, functioned as a suppressor variable in this equation. Supplemental regression analyses indicated that classrooms with the most harmony were those in which teachers frequently used positive influence but seldom used coercive-legitimate influence; classrooms in which teachers frequently used coercive-legitimate influence but rarely used positive influence were the least harmonious.

In the special self-contained classes, the four predictors explained 12.2% of the variance in harmony ($p < .05$). A significant portion of variance was uniquely accounted for by teachers' use of coercive-legitimate influence, which was negatively related to harmony. The unique contributions of the other predictors were nonsignificant, and no sizeable joint commonalities were obtained among any combination of predictors in this equation.

The commonality analyses revealed that the teacher leadership predictors were significantly related to peer harmony in both regular and special self-contained class settings. Each of the four measures of teacher leadership contributed significantly to the variance in peer harmony in regular classes, but only teacher coercive-legitimate influence significantly predicted peer harmony in special self-contained classes. The significant contribution of teacher warmth and teacher directiveness to peer harmony in regular classes indicates that these two dimensions are important aspects of teacher behavior, despite the fact that their relationships to pupil academic achievement have not been conclusively demonstrated (Rosenshine & Furst, 1971). It is unclear why warmth and directiveness were not significant predictors of harmony in special self-contained classes, where warm and structured environments are considered preferable for teachers of EMR learners (Kirk & Johnson, 1950). Perhaps warmth and directiveness result in beneficial consequences for nonmainstreamed EMR learners when outcomes other than cohesiveness are examined.

The four measures of teacher leadership failed to account for significant amounts of variance in peer dislike in either regular or special self-contained classes. This finding is somewhat surprising in view of the fact that some special educators have suggested that teachers play a critical role in influencing the extent to which EMR children are socially accepted or unaccepted by their peers (e.g., Lapp, 1957). The fact that teacher styles of leadership did not significantly affect sociometric attraction patterns is understandable, however, when one considers that several factors other than those included here have been found to affect pupil sociometric status. Sex

Table 7-4

Total and Unique Percentage of Variance as Explained in Selected Instructional Differentiation Variables

| Predictor | Peer Dislike | | | | Harmony | | | |
|---|---|---|---|---|---|---|---|---|
| | Regular Class | | Special Self-Contained Class | | Regular Class | | Special Self-Contained Class | |
| | Total $R^2$ | Unique $R^2$ | Total $R^2$ | Unique $R^2$ | Total $R^2$ | Unique $R^2$ | Total $R^2$ | Unique $R^2$ |
| Full model | 3 | | 4 | | 23** | | 12** | |
| Warmth | | | | | 8** | 7** | 3 | 2 |
| Directiveness set | | | | | 6* | 4* | 1 | 1 |
| Coercive/legitimate influence | | | | | 10* | 8* | 10** | 9** |
| Positive influence | | | | | 1 | 3* | 1 | 0 |

Note. $\underline{N}$ = 232 for regular classes, and 90 for special self-contained classes.

*$\underline{p}$ < .01.
**$\underline{p}$ < .05.

(Gronlund, 1959), intelligence (Dentler & Mackler, 1962), physical appearance (Cavior & Dokecki, 1973), social behavior (Lippit & Gold, 1959), and general mental health (Schmuck & Schmuck, 1975) of the pupils have all been shown to be related to sociometric status, although most studies have not examined sociometric patterns at the classroom level. It is likely that teacher leadership has substantially less impact on dislike among classroom peers than certain peer characteristics or behaviors.

In sum, teacher leadership styles were found to be related to peer harmony among the students in both regular and special self-contained classrooms but were shown to be unrelated to general dislike among classroom peers. Chapters 9 and 10 examine the effects of these aspects of socioemotional climate on the learner social and academic competence.

# Summary:
# Implications for the Placement of EMR Learners

At the beginning of this chapter, several issues related to the placement of EMR learners were raised. This section reviews those issues, summarizes the findings related to each, and discusses their implications.

One issue raised was whether the regular teacher could provide the warm, supportive, accepting environment allegedly needed by EMR learners. A related issue was whether the regular class could provide the necessary structured environment. About three-fourths of the regular class teachers in this study exhibited warm behaviors; the remaining quarter of the sample were never observed displaying warm teacher behaviors. A higher percentage of resource class teachers (85%) were observed exhibiting warm teacher behaviors. Thus, even if the regular class teacher was not warm, it was likely the mainstreamed EMR learner would experience a warm, supportive environment in the resource class.

For the most part, the regular class teachers in this study combined a moderate amount of structure and directiveness with some opportunities for pupil freedom. Only about one-sixth of the regular class teachers were highly directive, and resource room teachers did not provide a more structured environment than did the regular class teacher. Thus, if it is true, as commonly assumed, that EMR learners require a highly structured classroom environment, most regular classrooms may fail to provide an appropriate environment. It should be pointed out, however, that there was no evidence from this study that special self-contained classes provide either more directive or more supportive classroom environments than regular classes.

A third issue was whether disruptiveness and friction increase in regular classrooms when EMR learners are mainstreamed. Related to this was a fourth issue — whether the regular class teacher must devote excessive amounts of time to behavior management when EMR learners are placed in the class. It was found that most regular class teachers spent relatively little time managing behavior in the classroom: three-fourths of the teachers spent an average of 1½ minutes per hour or less managing behavior. Similarly, disruptive behavior was never observed in three-quarters of the regular classes, and most teachers reported friction to be rare. Thus, the data did not show increased disruptiveness and friction nor any evidence that regular class teachers spend much time managing behavior as a result of mainstreaming EMR learners into their classrooms. Most regular class teachers spent surprisingly little time managing off-task behavior in their classrooms.

When making placement decisions for EMR learners, the special self-contained class is often proposed because it is assumed to provide a warm, supportive, highly structured climate. Although special self-contained teachers in this study were found to exhibit warm behavior, there was no evidence that regular class teachers were any less warm. A highly structured, directive environment did not predominate in either setting.

## Technical Notes

1. The measure of warmth from the FLACCS employs a sign observation system. In a sign system, each type of behavior which occurs in a given time segment is recorded only once, regardless of how many times it occurs in that segment. Therefore, a teacher with a mean of 3 may have displayed each of 3 different kinds of behavior 1 time during the average two-minute segment, while a teacher with a mean of 1 may have displayed only 1 type of behavior as often as 10 times. Frequencies obtained on teacher warmth, then, are difficult to interpret because there is no way of knowing whether one teacher is actually warmer or simply more variable than another.

2. Missing data resulted in the exclusion of 24 regular and 33 special self-contained classes.

# 8

# The Instructional Conditions

The instructional conditions of the classroom impact the level of academic and social skills students attain, as well as the behaviors and attitudes they express. The background and attitudes of the teacher and peers as well as the warmth, structure, and harmony of the socioemotional climate establish the framework within which the instructional process is implemented. This chapter discusses the theoretical foundation for an instructional conditions model (Figure 8-1), considers the importance of these conditions for EMR learners, and presents descriptive information regarding the instructional conditions in the three educational settings under study.

The rationale for the self-contained classes for EMR learners was that specially trained teachers using particular instructional techniques with fewer students would provide the most appropriate instructional conditions. Mainstreaming advocates have suggested that advances in instructional materials, techniques, and classroom organization patterns make it possible for EMR learners to be accommodated within regular education, providing they also receive special support services such as instruction in a resource class. Yet little is known about how differences in class size, teacher skill, and educational technology advances affect the instructional conditions available to EMR learners (other than being able to establish differences among instructional settings in the number of students and the training of teachers).

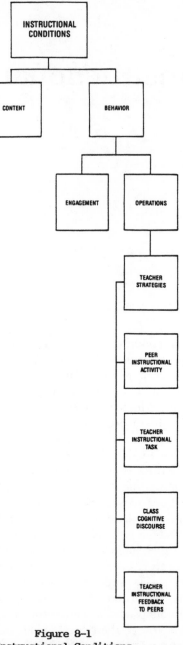

Figure 8-1
Instructional Conditions
(Project PRIME Taxonomic Model)

In order to develop an individual education plan (IEP) for an EMR learner, educators need to know the instructional conditions generally found in the settings in which the students may be placed. To make sound placement decisions for EMR learners, educators need to consider the three issues which comprise the focus of this chapter.

- What are the differences in the instructional conditions present in the three educational settings available to EMR learners — namely, regular, resource, and special self-contained classes?
- Within each setting, what are the instructional contexts and operations that result in maximum instructional engagement?
- Within each setting, what are the instructional contexts and operations that create an instructional atmosphere which provides for individualized instruction and an appropriate level of academic emphasis?

# Instructional Conditions Model

The instructional conditions model conceptualizes the class as (a) an environmental unit in which its participants (b) function as a social system (c) whose primary focus is information processing.

An *environmental unit* is a physically bounded, internally differentiated organization described by its physical milieu, activity patterns, and the relationship existing between the milieu and the activity patterns. A class may be considered an environmental unit (Barker, 1968; Gump, 1971). It is bounded by space and time (a particular room at a specified time of day) within a physical milieu (furniture, equipment, media) and described by regular patterns of activity (curricula, instructional activities). The milieu both supports and constrains the nature of the activity and constitutes the instructional context. The activity patterns constitute the instructional behaviors.

A *social system* is an entity that consists of interrelated and interdependent elements organized to exchange material, energy, and information with the environment to attain some objective or produce some effect or product (Kelly, 1974; Ryans, 1968). The objective of an educational social system is the attainment of academic and social competence.

Two participant subsystems exist within the class social system: a peer subsystem and a teacher subsystem. The peer subsystem consists of the individual learners. The teacher subsystem consists of the teacher and other adults such as aides and parent volunteers performing an instructional function. The teacher subsystem occupies a central position in the class system, exercising almost complete control over the instructional program (Hall, 1973).

Certain characteristics of social systems are relevant to a description of the instructional conditions of a class (Immegart & Pilecki, 1973). First, a system tends toward entropy — a state of randomness, disorder, and, eventually, dissolution. Within a class, if there is insufficient structure and/or direction, the participants will move in the direction of apathy, confusion, and disengagement. An important function of the teacher is to maintain the internal instructional engagement of the system through a series of behavior-controlling instructional operations. Second, a social system is future-oriented and evolutionary in nature, which suggests that a second important function of the teacher is to develop instructional program strategies that will produce the learner competencies desired. Third, a system functions by incorporating energy, material, and/or information from the environment and tranforming that input to produce an output. In the classroom, the process of input, incorporation, and transformation is represented by the interactive sequence of teacher and learner instructional activities, tasks, and cognitive discourse, which furthers academic and social competence. Finally, a system is self-regulating through the use of a feedback process to assess its own activity and output and to order and control the internal forces that affect it. Within the classroom, the teacher provides feedback to students to assure that system engagement is maintained and to indicate the progress of the learner in obtaining the desired system outcomes. A teacher is attuned to the feedback generated by the students and regulates the instructional operations on the basis of that feedback.

*Information processing,* defined as the provision and processing of instructional information, is the principal function of the class social system (Ryans, 1968). The information-processing aspect of the class functions as a mediator between system inputs (the student's current educational status) and system outputs (educational competencies). The information processed by the class includes skills, behaviors, and attitudes in the academic and social domain.

These mediated information-processing activities are performed through a series of instructional behaviors that determine the extent to which the class system is actively engaged and the nature of the operations controlling that engagement. Thus, engagement describes the level of instructional activity, and operations describe the nature of that activity.

Ryans (1960) has described teacher operations as:

- sensing, identifying, and classifying the environmental inputs, including learner characteristics and available educational resources;

- evaluating potential information-processing activities, given the availability of resources, perceived learner needs, and the content to be communicated;
- selecting appropriate information content, media and materials, grouping patterns, and teacher and learner tasks to facilitate information processing;
- planning, ordering, and implementing the intended information-processing activities;
- evaluating the learner's acquisition of information and integration of that information into the cognitive structure and behavioral repertoire; and
- storing the information obtained from the evaluation, either internally through a mental awareness of student success or externally in the form of cumulative student records.

The operations defined in the instructional conditions model are those strategies, activities, tasks, interactions, and feedback patterns that are used by teachers to perform the operations that Ryans defined.

The instructional conditions model contains seven major clusters of variables organized in two major dimensions: *instructional context* and *instructional behavior*. The *instructional context* describes the relatively stable, externally-controlled aspects of the classroom environment and establishes the conditions within which instructional behaviors occur. There are two aspects of *instructional behavior: instructional engagement*, the degree to which instructional activity is occurring, and *instructional operations*, the characteristics of the activities that induce and maintain an engaged system.

The model includes five *instructional operations*, which are organized hierarchically: *teacher strategies* are the most global operation; *peer instructional activity* and *teacher instructional tasks* are more specific operations; and *class cognitive discourse* and *teacher instructional feedback to peers* are at the most detailed level of instructional operations. These five operations, plus instructional context and instructional engagement, are the seven variable clusters that describe the instructional conditions of a class.

The complete list of variables included in the instructional conditions model is presented in Table 8-1. Although the model was developed from theoretical and conceptual insights derived from ecological psychology, social systems, and information processing, the model has empirical support.[1]

In summary, the instructional conditions model is a conceptualization of a class as an information-processing system that consists of an environmental unit and a set of participants who process information in order to develop learner academic and social competencies. An effective classroom is viewed as an information-processing environment that is concerned with (a) arranging an appropriate instructional context, (b) encouraging active student engagement, (c) selecting and implementing appropriate instructional strategies, (d) providing relevant student activities, (e) utilizing effective instructional tasks, (f) engaging in appropriate cognitive discourse, and (g) generating adequate learner feedback, all under the direction of the teacher.

## Description of Instructional Conditions

What are the differences in the instructional conditions in the three alternative settings? Although educators may be able to provide verbal descriptions of typical regular, resource, and self-contained special education classes, there is little quantitative evidence regarding the nature of the instructional conditions existing in these administratively defined settings. Yet, because of the inherent differences among the settings in the number of students present, the level of intellectual demand, and the amount of time students are present for instruction, considerable variation might be expected. The descriptive findings presented in this section define the unique instructional characteristics of regular, resource, and special education self-contained classes considering the seven variable clusters of the instructional conditions model.

### Instructional Context

The *instructional context* for class behavior consists of physical quality, special instructional services, academic content, and teacher-made materials (Table 8-2). Teachers exercise varying degrees of control over these four dimensions. The physical quality of the classroom and the provision of special instructional services are stipulated by factors external to the classroom. Instructional decisions concerning the teaching of academic content and the development of teacher-made materials are part of the pre-instructional planning process and are subject to teacher control.

#### Physical Quality
The physical quality of a classroom may affect both the degree of engagement and the type of instructional operations that occur within the class as well as a specific learner's ability to pay attention and remain engaged. Research on various components of physical quality suggests that these components, when considered in isolation, do not have much effect on nonhandicapped or

**Table 8-1**

**Definition of Instructional Conditions Constructs**

| Component | Complete Variable Title | Source | Variable Definition | Scoring | Use |
|---|---|---|---|---|---|
| | | | *Instructional Context* | | |
| **Physical quality** | | | | | |
| Physical Climate | Index of observed physical climate | CSD | The average of observer ratings for the following five items was calculated—<br>Extent to which classroom—<br>  Is clean<br>  Is adequately lit<br>  Has appropriate temperature<br>  Is spacious<br>  Is attractive<br>  Is modern | 5-point scale (1 = not, 5 = very) | D |
| Orderliness/quiet | Index of observed orderliness/quiet | CSD | The average of observer ratings for the following two items was calculated—<br>Extent to which classroom—<br>  Is orderly<br>  Is quiet | 5-point scale (1 = not, 5 = very) | D |
| Abundance of materials | Percentage of observed time abundance of materials was available | CSD | Observers answered—<br>  Is abundance of materials available? | | D |
| | Physical quality observation index (α = .72) | | A composite was made of the above three measures, each standardized before summing | | D, WDR, PLC |
| Special instructional services | | | | | |

(Continued on next page.)

Table 8-1 (continued)

| Component | Complete Variable Title | Source | Variable Definition | Scoring | Use |
|---|---|---|---|---|---|
| | | | Instructional Context (continued) | | |
| Special instructional materials | Percentage of teachers who received special instructional materials | TAQ | Teachers answered—If you have a handicapped child who needs instructional materials not available in your classroom, how soon after a request has been made do you receive materials? (Teachers checked 1 of 6 possible items or checked "never received materials") | not received = 0 received = 1 | D |
| Educational plans | Percentage of teachers who received special instructional materials | TAQ | Teachers answered—When do you usually receive the educational plans for the handicapped child you instruct? (Teachers checked one of 6 possible items or checked "do not usually receive a plan") | not received = 0 received = 1 | D |
| Special instructional services | Number of special instructional services received (materials, plans) | | Constructed from above two items | number of services = 0, 1, or 2 | D, WDR, |
| Value of materials | Index of value of special instructional materials | TAQ | The sum of teacher ratings on the following was calculated: Are the materials— Useful Adequate Promptly delivered | 3-point scale (1 = low, 3 = high) Index range = 3-9 | D |
| Value of plans | Index of value of educational plans | TAQ | The sum of teacher ratings on the following was calculated: Are the materials— | 3-point scale (1 = low, 3 = high) | D |

|  |  |  |  |  |
|---|---|---|---|---|
|  |  | Useful<br>Adequate<br>Promptly delivered |  | D |
| Academic content | CSD | Percentage of observed class time spent in each of the following content areas:<br>Reading<br>Language arts<br>Spelling<br>Mathematics<br>Science<br>Social studies<br>Perceptual training<br>Art<br>Music<br>Transitional activity<br>Other | At the end of each time segment, the observer checked the content area that was being studied (time segments were 2, 4, or 10 minutes in duration depending on the observation system) |  |
| Teacher-made materials | TAQ | Percentage of instructional materials made by the teacher | Teachers answered—<br>What proportion of the materials you use with your students do you make yourself? (For regular and self-containd special techers, the average of responses for reading, mathematics, spelling/language arts, and science/social studies was calculated; for resource teachers, the average of responses for reading, mathematics, and spelling/language arts was calculated.) | D<br>WDR,<br>PLC |

(Continued on next page.)

Table 8-1 (continued)

| Component | Complete Variable Title | Source | Variable Definition | Scoring | Use |
|---|---|---|---|---|---|
| | | Instructional Engagement | | | |
| Teacher attention to instruction | Percentage of observed time elements the teacher was on task | IBMS | Every 10 seconds, the observer checked 1 out of 13 choices indicating whether the teacher was on task or which of 12 types of responses he or she made to students' off-task behavior | | D |
| Peer interest and attention | Index of observed peer interest and attention | FLACCS | The average of observer ratings obtained once every 10 minutes was calculated | 5-point scale (1 = pupils generally apathetic and uninterested, 5 = interest general and high | D, WDR, PLC |
| Peer verbal participation | | | | | |
| Peer initiations | Number of observed initiations per pupil per hour | IPPS | Observers counted | | D |
| Peer responses | Number of observed responses peer pupil per hour | IPPS | Observers counted | | D |
| Peer verbal- ization | Number of observed verbalizations (initi- ations plus responses) per pupil per hour | | The sum of the above two measures was calculated | | D, WDR, PLC |

| Variable | Measure | Instrument | Description | Scale | |
|---|---|---|---|---|---|
| Peer questions | Number (per pupil per hour) of verbalizations that were questions | IPPS | Observers counted | | D |

### Teacher Strategies

**Instructional differentiation**

| Variable | Measure | Instrument | Description | Scale | |
|---|---|---|---|---|---|
| Individualization | Teacher perception of individualization scale ($\alpha$ = .79) | TCCQ | Teachers rated 12 items such as— I often spend extra time with children who have individual learning problems; I make classroom assignments based on each child's individual needs | 5-point scale (1 = always, 5 = never) Range = 12-60 | D |
| Cooperation/ diversification | Teacher perception of cooperation/diversification scale ($\alpha$ = .83) | TCCQ | Teachers rated 19 items such as— Within the classroom, there is a wide enough diversity of books to meet each child's needs and interests; students are encouraged to explore new activities independently | 5-point scale (1 = always, 5 = never) Range = 19–95 | D |
| Student differentiation | Observed student differentiation index | FLACCS | At the end of each observation period (about an hour), the observer rated the amount of differentiation | 5-point scale (1= pupils almost always work at same activity, 5 = pupils usually work at different activities) Range = 1-5 | D |
| Teacher central focus | Percentage of observed time segments the teacher is the central focus | FLACCS | Once every 10 minutes, the observer checked appropriate circle if the teacher was the central focus | | D |

(Continued on next page.)

Table 8-1 (continued)

| Component | Complete Variable Title | Source | Variable Definition | Scoring | Use |
|---|---|---|---|---|---|
| | | | **Teacher Strategies (continued)** | | |
| Flexibility | Peers' perception of instructional flexibility ($\alpha = .57$) | YSD | Peers answered 8 questions such as— Is everyone in your class given the same assignment? Does the teacher give you special assignments if you finish your work before the others? | For items loading positively on the scale, no = 1, yes = 2; for items loading negatively, yes = 1, no = 2. Range = 8-16 | D |
| **Peer instructional activity** | | | | | |
| Peer instructional activity (type of instruction X group structure) | Percentage of observed time peers were engaged in each type of instruction and group structure— Student self-directed, individual instruction Student self-diected, small-group instruction Student self-directed, large-group instruction Teacher-directed, individual instruction Teacher-directed, small-group instruction Teacher-directed, large-group instruction | CSD | At the end of each time segment, the observer checked which types of instruction and group structures the students were engaged in | | D, WDR, PLC |
| Special education instruction group size | Average number of students the teacher worked with at a time | TAQ | Teachers responded to— How many children on the average do you work with at a time? | | D |

| Variable | Code | Description | | |
|---|---|---|---|---|
| Maximum size of instructional group | TAQ | Teachers responded to—What is the maximum-sized group you work with? | | D |
| Average number of students the teacher worked with individually every day | TAQ | Teachers responded to—How many children do you work with individually every day? | | D |

## Teacher Instructional Task

| Variable | Code | Description | | |
|---|---|---|---|---|
| Teacher instructional task | CSD | Percentage of observed time the teacher performed each of the following tasks: Introducing or motivating, Explaining, Questioning or drilling, Directing, Supervising, Summarizing or reviewing, Testing | At the end of each time segment, the observer checked which tasks the teacher was performing | D, WDR, PLC |

## Class Cognitive Discourse

Amount of cognitive discourse

| Variable | Code | Description | | |
|---|---|---|---|---|
| Teacher cognitive demands | ICDS | Number of observed teacher cognitive demands per hour | During 4 out of every 5 minutes, the observer checked which of 13 different types of demands the teacher was making | D |
| Peer cognitive responses | ICDS | Number of observed peer cognitive responses per hour | During 4 out of every 5 minutes, the observer checked which of 13 different types of responses the student was making | D |

Table 8-1 (continued)

| Component | Complete Variable Title | Source | Variable Definition | Scoring | Use |
|---|---|---|---|---|---|
| Total cognitive discourse | Total number of observed teacher cognitive demands and peer responses per hour | | The sum of the above two items was caculated | | D, WDR |
| Demand rate | Demand rate per pupil per hour | | Calculated from the total number of teacher cognitive demands and the number of students present in the class | | D, WDR |
| Type of cognitive discourse | | | | | |
| Type of demands | Percentage of total teacher cognitive demands at each of the following levels:<br>Very low<br>Moderately low<br>Moderately high<br>Very high | | Calculated from the type of teacher cognitive demands and the total number of demands | | D |
| Variety of demands | Average number of different types of demands made by the teacher during a 4-minute segment | | The observer counted the number of different types (maximum is 13) of demands made by the teacher during 4 out of every 5 minutes | | WDR |
| Index of cognitive discourse | Index of cognitive discourse occurring at each of the following levels:<br>Very low ($\alpha$ = .94)<br>Moderately low ($\alpha$ = .95)<br>Moderately high ($\alpha$ = .96)<br>Very high ($\alpha$ = .95) | | At each level, a sum of the following 4 standardized a/ items was calculated:<br>Average number of demands per hour<br>Proportion of demands at that level to total number of demands<br>Average number of responses per hour<br>Proportion of responses at that level to total number of responses | | WDR, PLC, |

Teacher Instructional Feedback to Peers

## Amount of instructional feedback

| | | | |
|---|---|---|---|
| Total feedback remarks | Total number per hour of observed teacher feedback remarks to peer cognitive responses | ICDS | For 4 out of every 5 minutes, the observer checked which type of feedback the teacher gave to peers' cognitive responses | D, WDR |

## Type of instructional feedback

| Type of feedback remarks | Percentage of the total feedback remarks of each of the following types: Positive Negative Information | | Calculated from the type and the total frequency of feedback remarks | D |
|---|---|---|---|---|
| Index of feedback remarks | Index of teacher feedback remarks of each of the following types: Positive ($\alpha = .80$) Negative ($\alpha = .88$) Information ($\alpha = .92$) | | For each type of feedback remark, a sum of the following 4 standardized a/ items was calculated: Average number of feedback remarks of that type per hour Proportion of feedback remarks of that type to total number of feedback remarks Average number per hour of low demands followed by feedback remarks of that type Average number per hour of high demands followed by feedback remaks of that type | WDR, PLC |

Note. Source instruments and scales are described in Chapter 2. Abbreviations: CSD = classroom status data obtained for 1 minute of every observation period on each observation instrument, TAQ = Teacher Administrative Questionnaire, IBMS = Indiana Behavior Management System, FLACCS = Florida Climate and Control System, IPPS = Indiana Pupil Participation Schedule, TCCQ = Teacher Classroom Climate Questionnaire, YSD = Your School Days, ICDS = Individual Cognitive Demand Schedule, D = descriptive findings, WDR = within-domain relationships, PLC = prediction of learner competence.

a Standardization was to $\overline{X}$ = 50, SD = 10.

b In regular settings, specified learners are nonhandicapped learners; in resource and self-contained settings, specified learners are EMR learners.

EMR learner outcomes, but when the various components are combined, they may be more significant. As Dunkin and Biddle (1974) suggest, "one needs only to enter a crowded, poorly lighted, poorly equipped ghetto classroom to begin to understand why teaching is less effective in such an environment" (p. 43).

In this study, physical quality was determined by observer ratings on the CSD, which was included as part of each of the observation instruments. The observers rated the adequacy of the physical climate (lighting, temperature, spaciousness, modernness, and cleanliness), the extent of order and quiet, and the percentage of time the class had an abundance of materials available. Each time observers entered a classroom they rated the physical climate and orderliness/quiet on a scale from 1 (not adequate) to 5 (very adequate), with a midpoint of 3 (moderately adequate), and noted whether or not an abundance of materials was available.

The average class, regardless of setting, was observed to be slightly better than adequate in physical climate and orderliness/quiet (see Table 8-2). The low standard deviations reveal that classes did not vary much in their observed ratings. The average observer ratings indicate an abundance of materials was available about 60% of the time in the regular classes and almost 70% of the time in the resource and special self-contained classes. The index of physical quality — a composite formed by summing the standardized scores ($X = 50$, $SD = 10$) from the physical climate, orderliness/quiet, and abundance of materials measures — showed very little difference among the three settings.

## Special Instructional Services

Special instructional services are those support services provided by the special education program to assist teachers in the instruction of EMR learners. These services are particularly important components of a mainstreaming program, providing students with the support needed to function in the regular class, and regular class teachers with the information and materials needed to provide individualized instruction for the mainstreamed students (Birch, 1974; Kirk, 1972). Information about special instructional services was obtained with the TAQ which asked teachers if they had received special instructional materials and/or an individual educational plan (IEP) for the EMR learners (see Table 8-2).

Regular class teachers were more likely to receive instructional materials than educational plans for their mainstreamed EMR learners. Nearly half the teachers received instructional materials, but only one-fourth received educational plans. Less than one-fifth (18%) received both materials and plans, and nearly half (47%) received neither.[2]

Virtually all resource class teachers received some special instructional services. In fact, 77% received both materials and educational plans for their students. All teachers in special self-contained classes received at least one of the two special instructional services: Special instructional materials were received by 5%, and educational plans by 37%. The majority (59%) received both.

Teachers were asked to evaluate special materials and educational plans according to dimensions of usefulness, adequacy, and promptness of delivery along a 3-point (low, moderate, high) scale. Ratings were summed across the three dimensions, producing possible evaluation scores of 3 (low on each dimension) to 9 (high on each dimension). The average ratings for both services in all settings were close to or slightly above 6, a rating that indicated that the teachers perceived the services as having moderate overall value (see Table 8-2). However, the standard deviations reveal that the teachers were not in close agreement in their evaluations.

## Academic Content

The amount of time allocated to each academic subject area, although usually specified by state and local regulations, is at least partially subject to individual teacher variation (Wiley & Harnischfeger, 1974).

Historically, the academic content offered by special education classes has differed from that of regular classes. Educators of EMR learners have often favored a developmental program based on student needs rather than a modified version of the regular program and have usually emphasized social and vocational competence rather than academic competence (Stevens, 1971; Wrightstone et al., 1971). The advent of mainstreaming has changed the instructional content offered to EMR learners. Mainstreaming programs at the elementary level appear to have accepted the academic and social goals of the regular curriculum, providing supportive instruction in those areas needed for appropriate functioning in the regular class.

Project PRIME examined the percentage of time teachers in each of the three settings spent in the following areas: reading, spelling, language arts, mathematics, science, social studies, art, music, perceptual training, foreign language, transitional (changing from one subject to another), and other (e.g., free time) activities. The percentages were determined from observations made on the CSD. An observer followed a target learner all day, recording the amount of time spent by that learner with each teacher in each content area. As the learner moved from one class to another, a different teacher was observed. The percentage of time spent by each teacher in each content area was obtained by aggregating across the observations made with all target learners.[3]

There were some systematic differences among settings in the percentages of time observed in different subject areas. Reading instruction occurred 15% of the observed time in regular classes, 28% in resource classes, and 20% in special self-contained classes (see Table 8-2). There was little difference

## Table 8-2
### Instructional Context by Instructional Setting

| Dimensions of Instructional Context | Instructional Setting | | | | | | | | | | | |
|---|---|---|---|---|---|---|---|---|---|---|---|---|
| | Regular | | | | Special Resource | | | | Special Self-Contained | | | |
| | X | SD | % | N | X | SD | % | N | X | SD | % | N |
| **Physical quality** | | | | | | | | | | | | |
| Index of observed physical climate | 3.44 | .47 | | 254 | 3.61 | .53 | | 127 | 3.59 | .52 | | 127 |
| Index of observed orderliness/quiet | 3.54 | .41 | | 254 | 3.71 | .42 | | 127 | 3.66 | .50 | | 127 |
| Percentage observed time abundance of materials was available | 57.93 | 23.79 | | 254 | 67.83 | 23.77 | | 127 | 68.15 | 28.23 | | 127 |
| Physical quality observation index (composite of above three measures) | 48.12 | 6.61 | | 254 | 51.40 | 6.73 | | 127 | 50.98 | 7.49 | | 127 |
| **Special instructional services** | | | | | | | | | | | | |
| Teachers who received each type of service | | | | 243 | | | | 117 | | | | 109 |
| Received both special instructional materials and ed. plan for handicapped students | | | 18.52 | | | | 76.92 | | | | 58.72 | |
| Received materials, not plans | | | 28.40 | | | | 18.80 | | | | 36.70 | |
| Received plans, not materials | | | 5.76 | | | | 3.42 | | | | 4.59 | |
| Received neither materials nor plans | | | 47.33 | | | | .85 | | | | 0.00 | |
| Index of value of special instructional materials | 6.19 | 1.78 | | 115 | 6.53 | 1.77 | | 114 | 6.72 | 1.61 | | 107 |
| Index of value of educational plans | 6.03 | 1.42 | | 59 | 6.45 | 1.63 | | 94 | 6.41 | 1.74 | | 69 |

Academic content

Percentage of observed class
time spent in each content area

| | Mean | SD | N | Mean | SD | N | Mean | SD | N |
|---|---|---|---|---|---|---|---|---|---|
| Reading | 15.34 | 12.09 | 254 | 27.60 | 19.43 | 127 | 20.43 | 13.76 | 127 |
| Language Arts | 14.52 | 10.54 | 254 | 15.15 | 13.99 | 127 | 14.83 | 8.51 | 127 |
| Spelling | 12.62 | 9.43 | 254 | 10.13 | 14.46 | 127 | 8.19 | 9.72 | 127 |
| Mathematics | 19.41 | 17.65 | 254 | 20.73 | 18.83 | 127 | 16.50 | 13.19 | 127 |
| Science | 8.37 | 12.66 | 254 | .91 | 2.77 | 127 | 3.27 | 8.43 | 127 |
| Social studies | 11.66 | 12.04 | 254 | 1.37 | 3.57 | 127 | 3.04 | 5.25 | 127 |
| Perceptual training | .35 | 1.10 | 254 | 7.88 | 10.59 | 127 | 4.48 | 6.08 | 127 |
| Art | 2.51 | 3.24 | 254 | 3.19 | 5.25 | 127 | 6.09 | 5.26 | 127 |
| Music | .66 | 2.34 | 254 | .46 | 1.97 | 127 | 1.42 | 2.79 | 127 |
| Transition and other | 14.56 | 8.92 | 254 | 12.59 | 9.82 | 127 | 21.76 | 11.95 | 127 |

Teacher-made materials

| | Mean | SD | N | Mean | SD | N | Mean | SD | N |
|---|---|---|---|---|---|---|---|---|---|
| Percentage of instructional materials made by the teacher[a] | 32.17 | 22.63 | 246 | 36.25 | 20.95 | 116 | 35.21 | 20.11 | 111 |

[a] For teachers in regular and special classes, the percentage is the average of responses in the following subject areas: reading, arithmetic, language arts, spelling, science, and social studies. For teachers in resource classes, the average includes only reading, arithmetic, language arts, and spelling.

among the three settings in the amount of time spent in mathematics, spelling, and language arts. Mathematics was observed about 19% of the time; language arts, 15%; and spelling, about 10%. Instruction in science and social studies was observed more frequently in regular than in special classes. In regular classes, 8% of the observed time was spent in science and 12% in social studies. In resource rooms, only 1% of the observed time was spent in each of these areas, and in special self-contained classes, 3%. Perceptual training was almost never observed in regular classes; in resource classes it occurred 8% of the observed time; in special self-contained classes, 4%. Art instruction was observed about 3% of the time in regular and resource classes and 6% in special self-contained classes. Music activities occurred the least frequently (about 1% of the time) of the content areas observed. Transitional and other activities (classroom management involved in changing tasks, etc.) were observed 15% of the time in regular classes, 13% in resource classes, and 22% in special self-contained classes. These results for regular and special self-contained classes support the academic time data reported for nonhandicapped and nonmainstreamed EMR learners in Chapter 4.

## Teacher-Made Materials

The availability of self-made instructional materials is an aspect of the instructional context almost completely determined by teacher planning activities. Teachers may develop their own instructional materials for several reasons: (a) the school system does not provide enough materials; (b) the materials available do not provide enough variety or practice in the skill areas needed, (c) do not cover the ability ranges within the class, and/or (d) are not attractive or motivating and do not appeal to particular student interests. Generating materials should permit greater flexibility and individualization and, if done with concern toward student motivation, induce greater student interest and attention.

The availability of teacher-made materials was determined from a TAQ question which asked teachers what proportion of the materials used in various subject areas they made themselves. These proportions were averaged across the subject areas. For teachers in regular and special self-contained classes, the subject areas were reading, arithmetic, language arts, spelling, science, and social studies. Because resource class teachers typically spent little time in science or social studies instruction, the percentage of materials they made in these two areas was not included in their average.

The proportion of teacher-made materials was similar across the three settings, with teachers making an average of about one-third of what they used in academic subjects (see Table 8-2). However, there was considerable variability around this average.

## Discussion

The instructional context present in regular, resource, and special self-contained classes was similar in some respects and different in others. The physical quality of the classroom and its orderliness/quiet were rated by observers as about average across all settings. An abundance of materials was noted in more than half the observations, although there was a slight tendency for the special education classes to have more materials present more frequently than the regular classes. Thus, the belief that special classes have a greater array of instructional resources may have some empirical support. However, the majority of regular class observations suggests materials were available to accommodate the individual needs of the EMR learners.

The availability of special instructional services varied with the type of service and setting. About half the regular teachers received special materials and one fourth received educational plans, at a time prior to the passage of P.L. 94-142. Among the special teachers, almost all received special materials. Sixty percent of the special self-contained and 80% of the resource teachers received educational plans.

The failure to deliver special instructional services to the regular teachers suggests the mainstreaming process, newly instituted in many schools, may have been beset with start-up difficulties. The support mechanisms required for mainstreaming programs were not implemented. Many regular teachers had to go it alone. Regardless of the delivery problems, those teachers who did receive materials and educational plans judged them to be of moderate value.

The pattern of academic content varied across settings. Reading instruction was observed more frequently in the special self-contained classes, particularly in the resource classes, than in the regular classes, but science and social studies were observed more frequently in the regular classes. Transitional activities and art were more frequently observed in the special self-contained classes than in either the resource or regular classes. There was little systematic difference among the settings in mathematics, spelling, and language arts.

These findings for academic content offer only limited support for the belief that special self-contained classes at the elementary level provide less emphasis on academic content. Less time was spent in these classes than in regular classes on science and social studies and more time was spent on art, music, transitional, and other activities. More time was also spent on reading and about the same amount of time on language arts and mathematics. The academic content of resource classes reflects their emphasis on providing supplemental instruction in the basic tool subjects. The low proportion of time spent in transitional activities in the resource class probably reflects the fact that most transition occurred between classes (students coming and going to the resource class) rather than in the class itself.

## Instructional Behavior

Instructional behaviors occur in a classroom within the supports and constraints defined by the instructional context. Two components of instructional behavior are considered in the instructional conditions model: instructional engagement and instructional operations.[4]

### Instructional Engagement

Instructional engagement is defined as the extent to which the teacher and students are interested and attentive and participate verbally in the instructional process. Both teacher and student behaviors contribute to the level of engagement that occurs in a class, although it is usually the teacher's instructional decisions that determine the holding power of a particular instructional activity. Thus, the teacher specifies and arranges the academic activities and student self-monitoring determines the extent students are engaged in specific task assignments (Wiley & Harnischfeger, 1975).

Carroll (1963), Wiley and Harnischfeger (1974), and Cooley and Lohnes (1976) have developed models of instruction in which the amount of active time spent learning is a critical determinant of academic achievement. In a reanalysis of the Coleman et al. (1966) data, Wiley and Harnischfeger (1974, 1975; Wiley, 1975) found great variability in the amount of time students spent actively learning, and that total amount of active learning time was the most important determinant of achievement. Rosenshine and Furst (1971) concluded that student opportunity to learn instructional materials is one of the most important factors contributing to student achievement.

Rosenshine (1977) defined engaged time as an interaction between opportunity to learn and attention to task, with opportunity to learn as the provision of appropriate content. In this study, teacher attention to instruction served as a measure of opportunity to learn; and peer interest, attention, and verbal participation as measures of attention to task.

**Teacher Attention to Instruction**: Through the provision of instructional opportunities to students, the teacher hopes to engage students in learning activities. As Dreeben (1973) stated:

> The teacher's primary task is to design and engage pupils in learning activities sufficiently engrossing that pupils find these activities substantially more attractive than prescribed alternatives. Under these circumstances, maintaining the student's absorption in the task at hand and getting his attention are tasks of great immediacy and importance for instructional reasons (p. 466).

Teacher attention to instruction was measured by observer ratings on the IBMS. From these ratings, the percentage of observed time segments when the teachers were not managing student off-task behavior was calculated. Teachers, regardless of setting, were observed attending to instruction an average of 97% of the time (see Table 8-3). The low standard deviations reveal that teachers did not vary much in the frequency of their observed on-task behavior.[5]

**Peer Interest and Attention**: At a minimum, students should pay attention to the instructional events occurring. Jackson (1968) has expressed the student's role in an information-processing system:

> Face-to-face confrontation of students and teacher, though necessary, is obviously not enough to ensure the attainment of educational goals. In addition to merely being there, the participants must attend in a more profound fashion. They must look at and listen to the objects of their lessons. They must selectively perceive the world of the classroom, shutting out some sources of stimulation and concentrating on others.... In short, they must become involved in their school work (p. 85).

Research studies using observation methods have indicated that most of the time most students seem to be attending to the content of the lesson or task at hand (Forness & Esveldt, 1975; Jackson, 1968, Kowatrakul, 1959). However, some students' attention is faked (Jackson, 1968); therefore, attention alone is not a sufficient indicator of students' instructional engagement.

The FLACCS was used to measure peer interest and attention. Observers rated student behavior during a 2-minute time segment on a 5-point scale, where 1 = "pupils generally apathetic," 2 = "a few pupils interested," 3 = "about half interested much of the time," 4 = "most pupils interested much of the time," and 5 = "interest general and high." The ratings, obtained every 10 minutes, were averaged across observations.

The mean value of the index of class interest and attention was between 3 and 4 in each setting, suggesting that more than half the students were interested in what was happening much of the time during the observed time segments (Table 8-3). The mean ratings did not vary much within each instructional setting.

**Peer Verbal Participation**: Student attention is a necessary prerequisite for the operation of the instructional information-processing system, but it is not enough to ensure that the student understands what is being presented. Furthermore, some attention may be faked (Jackson, 1968). Therefore, a more active condition of participation seems to be the critical determinant. The idea that students need to be visibly active in the learning process was posited by John Dewey (1925). Contemporary theorists such as Piaget (Flavell, 1963), Bruner (1966), and Gagne (1968) have reemphasized the importance of active participation for cognitive growth. Although most students may appear interested and attentive, active verbal participation may be rare. For example, Forness and Esveldt (1975) reported that their sample of first- and second-grade boys was observed to be attending (defined as eye or head orientation toward the instructional task or teacher) more than half the time, but they were engaged in active participation (a verbal or physical response) only 10% or less of the time.

Peer verbal participation was measured by the IPPS as the *number of initiations* (verbalizations without first being called on by the teacher) and *responses* (verbalizations in response to being called on by the teacher) made by the students in the class. Responses could be either by one student alone or a chorus of students responding to general questions. Each participatory behavior was further categorized according to whether it was a statement or question.

In regular class settings, the average observed verbalization rate per student was 5.4 per hour (Table 8-3). This rate translates into each student speaking about every 11 minutes. Since teachers tend to alternate class discussion with seat work, the verbalization rate is probably higher for the discussion time. Students in the regular classes initiated slightly more than they responded. These students only occasionally asked questions in class; their individual rate was less than one question (0.6) per hour.

There are notable differences between regular and resource classes. Students in resource classes had an average rate of 23.4 verbalizations per hour; each student speaking, on average, every 2-3 minutes. About 60% of these student verbalizations were responses to a teacher question or recognition of a hand-raise. Resource class students asked an average of three questions per hour.

Students in self-contained classes had a verbal participation rate of 13.2 verbalizations per hour; slightly more than half being responses. Hence, in the special education self-contained classes, each student spoke, on average, every 4-5 minutes. The average rate of student questioning was 1.8 questions per hour.

Regardless of the participation rate, students tended to ask few questions. In regular classes, 11% of student verbalizations were questions; in resource classes, 13%; and in special self-contained classes, 14%. The rate of student questioning, as well as the other rates, had large standard deviations, suggesting that classes were quite varied in their verbal participation.

Table 8-3

Instructional Engagement Within the Class by Instructional Setting

| Dimensions of Instructional Engagement | Instructional Setting | | | | | | | | |
|---|---|---|---|---|---|---|---|---|---|
| | Regular | | | Special Resource | | | Special Self-Contained | | |
| | X | SD | N | X | SD | N | X | SD | N |
| Teacher attention to instruction | | | | | | | | | |
| Percentage of observed time elements the teacher was on task | 97.24 | 2.44 | 253 | 97.48 | 2.14 | 125 | 96.68 | 2.40 | 124 |
| Peer interest and attention | | | | | | | | | |
| Index of observed peer interest and attention | 3.53 | .56 | 250 | 3.73 | .55 | 121 | 3.58 | .49 | 123 |
| Peer verbal participation | | | | | | | | | |
| Number of observed initiations per pupil per hour | 3.00 | 4.80 | 250 | 9.60 | 8.40 | 116 | 6.00 | 5.40 | 126 |
| Number of observed responses per pupil per hour | 2.40 | 2.40 | 250 | 13.80 | 13.20 | 116 | 7.20 | 5.40 | 126 |
| Number of observed verbalizations (initiations plus responses) per pupil per hour | 5.40 | 6.00 | 250 | 23.40 | 18.60 | 116 | 13.20 | 9.00 | 126 |
| Number (per pupil per hour) of observed verbalizations that were questions | .60 | 1.20 | 250 | 3.00 | 3.00 | 116 | 1.80 | 1.20 | 126 |

**Discussion**: Teacher attention to instruction was extremely high in all instructional settings, with teachers being off task in only 3% of the time elements they were observed. Peer interest and attention was moderately high and similar across settings. Verbal participation was the lowest in the regular classes (5.4 verbalizations per hour), more than twice as high in the special self-contained classes (13.2 verbalizations per hour), and four times as high in the resource classes (23.4 verbalizations per hour).

All three settings provided a similar and high degree of teacher engagement. Peer interest and attention was also similar in all three settings. Only verbal participation differentiated the three settings, with the students in special education classes experiencing considerably more intensive interactions with their teacher than the students in regular classes. This intensity of teacher/peer interaction appeared to be a distinguishing feature of the special education settings.

## Instructional Operations

Instructional operations are those functions that induce and maintain an engaged system. Within the instructional conditions model, certain operations are related to teacher instructional directive functions, and others to student productive or learning functions. These are considered together because there is an interactive relationship between teacher and student operations. The teacher establishes the organization, direction, and duration of the instructional operations and, to a considerable extent, determines the level of student interaction. In the instructional operations dimension of the model, the focus is on the teacher.

Research literature is replete with attempts to categorize instructional operations. Gump (1967) classified teachers according to their role in an instructional segment, such as watcher-helper, action director, recitation leader, reader, or tester. Wright and Nuthall (1970), following earlier work by Bellack (1966), studied teacher moves in the instructional situation and categorized teacher behavior as structuring, soliciting, reacting, or monologue moves. Perkins (1964, 1965) listed teacher role categories as leader-director, resource person, supervisor, specialization agent, and evaluator. Lundgren (1972) used the categories motivating, planning, informing, leading discussion, disciplining, counseling, and evaluating. In reviewing these classification systems, Dunkin and Biddle (1974) conclude that the underlying dimensions along which instructional operations might be organized are not clear; the lists appear to be *ad hoc*.

Miller, Galanter, and Pribram (1967) provide a theoretical rationale for the study of instructional operations, based on their concept of a plan, defined as "any hierarchical process in the organism that can control the order in which a sequence of operations is to be performed" (p. 252). In an information-processing system, the plan, which may be implicit, is derived from the teacher's perceptions and values related to the class instructional system. It is subject to modification and refinement as the instructional activity progresses.

It serves to organize and direct the instructional operations at several levels of specificity. The molar units of the plan are *teacher strategies* — a general approach to instruction, or teaching style. At a more specific level are *peer instructional activities* — including the size of the group and whether the student task is teacher or student (self-) directed — and *teacher instructional tasks* — including such roles as questioning, explaining, directing, or supervising. At the most specific level are the *class cognitive discourse* — the teacher's cognitive demands and student responses — and *teacher instructional feedback* — the teacher's verbal reactions to a student's verbal cognitive response.

**Teacher Strategies**: Teacher instructional strategies refer to a general teaching style of approach to instruction that reflects personal values and experience. Dunkin and Biddle (1974, p. 323) define a strategy as "the extended and substantive properties of the exchanges between teacher and pupils." An instructional strategy serves as a general guide specifying the instructional operations that constitute the class instructional program. This study was concerned with two strategies particularly relevant to the instruction of EMR learners: instructional differentiation and cognitive emphasis.

*Instructional Differentiation*: Instructional differentiation is a teacher strategy that provides individualized instruction appropriate to individual needs, using a variety of instructional techniques, alternative instructional activities, and teacher movement about the room to respond to individual requests for assistance. Instructional differentiation has always been a major tenet in the design of instructional programs for EMR learners in special self-contained classes.

Research suggests that instructional differentation may be more widely advocated than practiced, and when advocated, the research is limited. Bosco (1971) found that most regular class teachers highly favored establishing individual goals for students, but only about one-fourth reported actually developing them. Teachers spent most of their time in the front of the room, rather than circulating and attending to individual needs (Adams, 1971). Wolfson (1968) and Goodlad and Klein (1970) have identified grouping practices as an instructional operation that relates to instructional differentiation, and special education literature has generally assumed that providing instruction in small groups enhances individual differentiation (Krienberg & Chow, 1973). Wolfson (1968) found that teachers who said they individually differentiated instruction were observed to engage in small-group instruction and individual conferences. Cronbach (1967) and Morine (1975) have shown that individual differentiation can be described when the class is one large group. Heathers (1972) suggests that individual differentiation will be reflected in teachers' instructional tasks. Even in special self-contained classes, Goodlad and Klein (1970) found an absence of intraclass grouping, suggesting that individualization through small-group instruction was minimal.

Six measures of instructional differentiation were used to examine the type and amount of instructional differentiation available in the Project PRIME regular, resource, and special self-contained classes. Two measures, derived from the TCCQ, reflect teachers' perceptions of the individualization and diversification in their classes. They were obtained from regular and self-contained teachers but not from resource teachers. The *individualization scale* included 12 items and covered such topics as the frequency with which classroom assignments are based on each child's needs and the extent to which teachers work with individual children. The *cooperation/diversification scale* included 19 items concerned with topics such as the frequency with which students are encouraged to explore new activities independently and use library books and reference materials in addition to textbooks. Teachers rated each item on a 5-point frequency-of-occurrence scale: 1 = never, 2 = rarely, 3 = sometimes, 4 = usually, 5 = always. Table 8-4 presents the means and standard deviations of teachers' total scores on the two scales. The means can be divided by the number of items in the scale to obtain the average item frequency-of-occurrence rating.

Regular class teachers claimed they sometimes or usually implemented behaviors considered to reflect individualization ($\overline{X} = 3.6$), while teachers in special self-contained classrooms reported a higher average frequency of individualization behaviors ($\overline{X} = 4.1$).

The average rating for cooperation/diversification (3.5) was the same for regular and special self-contained class teachers. Teachers in both settings felt that behaviors designed to provide opportunities for cooperation and diversification sometimes or usually occurred in their classes.

The third measure of instructional differentiation, the *student differentiation index*, obtained from the FLACCS, was based on an observer 5-point rating scale recorded about once an hour. It was averaged across observations. Limited differentiation was observed in all three settings. Regular classes were given an average differentiation rating of between 1 (almost all students work at same activity) and 2 (most students work at same activity most of the time); resource and special self-contained classes received average ratings between 2 and 3 (most students work at same activity about half the time).

The fourth measure was also taken from the FLACCS. Observation data were collected on whether the teacher was the central focus of the activity. Regular class teachers, on average, were observed as the central focus, directing a lesson either to the whole class or a subgroup, about two-thirds of the time. Resource class teachers were observed as the central focus 62% of the time. The special self-contained class teachers were observed as the central focus only slightly more than half the time. Within each setting, teachers evidenced rather large variability in the amount of time they were the central focus of class activity.

The fifth measure was *peer perception of teacher flexibility*, a scale derived from YSD. Class members were asked whether certain behaviors representing teacher flexibility occurred in their class — whether students worked on different projects, were able to move about the room without asking permission, or worked on different assignments. Scale scores were obtained by summing the mean responses (1 = no, 2 = yes for items loading positively, the reverse for items loading negatively) given by all students in the class to each of the eight items on the scale. In both the regular and special self-contained classes, the typical mean item response was about 1.5, indicating students felt about half the instructional flexibility items were appropriate descriptors. YSD was not administered in the resource class.

As a sixth measure, teachers reported on the TAQ whether they used any of seven individualizing techniques (programmed instruction, educational games, audio-visual materials, behavior modification, individual work contracts, peer teaching, and learning centers) in their classes. The number of different techniques used was computed, yielding a score that ranged from 0-7. Teachers in all settings reported using an average of four or five individualizing techniques, although the type of technique reported varied depending on the educational setting. For example, 43% of the regular teachers, 71% of the resource teachers, and 60% of the special class teachers reported using programmed instruction.

Using the above six measures, a composite differentiation was developed for the regular and special self-contained settings by standardizing each measure ($\bar{X} = 50$, $SD = 10$) and summing the standardized scores. On this index, self-contained special classes were slightly more than one standard deviation higher than regular classes (Table 8-4). A composite score was not developed for the resource setting because data were not obtained on all six measures for that setting.

In addition to the individual differentiation index based on teacher, peer, and observer ratings, a more precise behavioral index of instructional differentiation was derived from the CSD — the average percentage of

## Table 8-4
## Teacher Strategies by Instructional Setting

| Dimensions of Teacher Strategies | Regular | | | | Special Resource | | | | Special Self-Contained | | | |
|---|---|---|---|---|---|---|---|---|---|---|---|---|
| | X | SD | % | N | X | SD | % | N | X | SD | % | N |
| **Individual differentiation** | | | | | | | | | | | | |
| Teacher perception of individualization scale | 43.60 | 5.61 | | 251 | | | | | 49.12 | 4.43 | | 101 |
| Teacher perception of coopera-tion/diversification scale | 66.68 | 7.44 | | 251 | | | | | 66.54 | 7.78 | | 101 |
| Observed student differentiation index | 1.84 | .59 | | 250 | 2.35 | .84 | | 121 | 2.49 | .68 | | 123 |
| Percentage of observed time segments the teacher is the central focus | 66.63 | 20.18 | | 250 | 62.08 | 24.94 | | 121 | 55.23 | 22.00 | | 123 |
| Peers' peception of instruc-tional flexibility scale | 12.00 | .83 | | 253 | | | | | 12.68 | .85 | | 119 |
| Number of individualizing techniques teachers reported using | 4.48 | 1.62 | | 262 | 4.64 | 1.97 | | 132 | 4.39 | 1.99 | | 126 |
| Individual differentiation index (composite of above six measures) | 32.74 | 4.65 | | 235 | | | | | 37.74 | 4.40 | | 91 |

| | Mean | SD | N | Mean | SD | N | Mean | SD | N |
|---|---|---|---|---|---|---|---|---|---|
| Percentage of observed time the academic content or instructional activity of the specified learner is different from that of his or her peers | 6.92 | 8.38 | 237 | 1.74 | 5.62 | 132 | 17.18 | 14.01 | 126 |
| Percentage of teachers reporting use of each of the following techniques: | | | 255 | | | 119 | | | 114 |
| Programmed instruction | 43.14 | | | 71.43 | | | 59.65 | | |
| Educational games | 92.16 | | | 100.00 | | | 96.49 | | |
| Audio-visual materials | 85.10 | | | 93.28 | | | 92.11 | | |
| Behavior modification | 71.37 | | | 86.55 | | | 83.33 | | |
| Individual work contracts | 38.43 | | | 34.45 | | | 20.18 | | |
| Peer teaching | 79.61 | | | 68.91 | | | 69.30 | | |
| Learning centers | 50.59 | | | 60.50 | | | 67.54 | | |

Cognitive emphasis

| | Mean | SD | N | Mean | SD | N |
|---|---|---|---|---|---|---|
| Peers' perception of cognitive emphasis scale | 34.71 | .91 | 253 | 33.39 | 1.52 | 119 |

observed time the academic content and/or instructional activities assigned to target learners in each setting, nonhandicapped or EMR, was different from that assigned to the majority of the class.

In regular class observations, teachers, on average, differentiated between a specified nonhandicapped learner and the rest of the class 7% of the time. In resource classes, this differentiation was 2% and in special self-contained classes, 17% for select EMR learners. The striking difference between the average differentiation observed in the special education resource and self-contained classes appears to reflect their different formats. Typically, small groups of students with similar problems attend a resource class together, obviating need for the teacher to individualize instruction, i.e., the groupings of students result in homogeneous small-group activity. In contrast, a special self-contained class may contain students with diverse needs at different skill levels. Teachers assign materials appropriate to needs or skill levels.

*Cognitive Emphasis*: The second teacher strategy, cognitive emphasis, was defined as the students' perceptions of the importance of cognitively-challenging and academically-demanding activities in the classroom. Teachers vary in the degree to which they emphasize the need for students to expand an answer, generate several acceptable answers rather than only one, evaluate multiple problem-solving alternatives, develop and test hypotheses, and make critical judgments. They also vary in the degree to which they encourage students to work quickly, do their best work, and try to get good grades.

Compared with nonhandicapped students, EMR students learn more slowly, are less able to generalize, acquire less information through incidental learning, have difficulty ignoring distractions and attending to task, and have a history and expectancy of failure (Kirk, 1972; MacMillan, 1971). Recommendations for facilitating the learning of EMR students have included using concrete and familiar materials, providing for practice to be spaced over time, limiting the amount of information presented in any one period, reducing distractions and/or extraneous information, highlighting important concepts, presenting tasks in the same order each time, providing for longer exposure and/or repetition of the concepts to be learned, and presenting materials in systematic, short, and simple steps (Dunn, 1968; Kirk, 1972; Kolstoe, 1970). Though not explictly stated by these authors, it is likely that EMR learners are offered concepts which are less challenging and have lowered cognitive emphasis than those tasks offered nonhandicapped students.

The YSD was used to obtain student perceptions of cognitive emphasis. Class members were asked whether certain behaviors (e.g., giving reasons for their answers, telling what books say in their own words) or characteristics (e.g., importance of grades, competition) that reflect an cognitive-processing emphasis were descriptive of their class. Cognitive-emphasis scores were obtained by summing the mean response (1 = no and 2 = yes for items loading positively, the reverse for items loading negatively) given by all students in the class to the 19 scale items. For the regular classes, the mean item response was 1.83. On average, the peers within these classes thought 83% of the items accurately described their class. Students in special self-contained classes perceived less cognitive emphasis, considering 76% of the items to be accurate descriptors (item mean = 1.76). The cognitive emphasis scale mean for regular classes was one standard deviation above the scale for the special self-contained classes. Resource class students did not complete the YSD.

**Discussion**: In the regular classes (a) observers viewed almost all students working at the same activity all or most of the time; (b) teachers felt that behaviors characterizing individualization and diversification usually or sometimes occurred in their classes; (c) about half the class peers viewed behaviors characterizing flexibility as descriptive of their class; and (d) most of the time the teacher was observed to be the central focus of activity.

In the special self-contained classes both teacher and observation measures reflected greater individualization and flexibility than occurred in the regular classes. However, there was no difference in the teachers' perception of cooperation/diversification. The specific individualizing techniques used by the regular and special teachers differed, but the number of techniques used did not. Overall, on the composite index of instructional differentiation, the special self-contained teachers were a standard deviation higher than the regular teachers. They individualized instruction more frequently. Resource teachers homogenously grouped their students for instruction. Hence, they rarely individualized instruction. The regular teachers were observed differentiating academic content or activity assignments about 7% of the time, whereas the self-contained special teachers were observed differentiating 17% of the time; in neither case was the degree of differentiation particularly high (see Table 8-4).

The observation findings on instructional differentiation revealed that relatively little differentiation occurred in the regular classes, although the teachers and peers perceived individualization and flexibility as occurring more frequently than the observation findings would suggest. The changes in instructional materials, technology, and organizational patterns thought to facilitate the use of instructional differentiation strategies in regular classes were not as widely used as one might have expected (e.g., Dunn, 1968).

Most peers agreed there was an emphasis on cognitive processes in these classes, although the EMR special self-contained class members perceived less cognitive emphasis than did the nonhandicapped regular class students. This provides further support for the commonly held view that regular classes have a stronger academic focus than do special classes. This focus is perceived by the class members themselves.

**Peer Instructional Activity:** Two interrelated classification systems were used to describe peer instructional activity in the Project PRIME instructional conditions model. In these systems, instructional activity is defined by either communication acts (Lewis, et al., 1968) or roles (Gump, 1967). In both systems, activity is considered independent of group size. Because group size or structure have been related to student tasks (Torrance, 1970), a system which combines group structure with group task was used for classifying student activities. Group structure was defined as individual, small-group, or large-group; group task as either student- (self-) directed activity (working on material) or teacher-directed activity (listening to or interacting with the teacher). Large-group was defined as most of the class. In special classes, large-group instruction need not involve large numbers of students. These two aspects of instruction considered together formed six instructional activities, which reflected certain common elementary school instructional patterns:

| INSTRUCTIONAL PROBLEM | EXAMPLE |
|---|---|
| student self-directed individual instruction | individualized seatwork (perhaps while the teacher works with other students individually or in small groups) |
| student self-directed small-group instruction | small group projects (2-5 students) |
| student self-directed large-group instruction | common written assignments (perhaps with the teacher circulating about the room) |
| teacher-directed individual instruction | teacher tutorials |
| teacher-directed small-group instruction | reading or other instructional groups |
| teacher-directed large-group instruction | class lecture/discussions |

Research on the nature of student tasks suggested that regular elementary classrooms are characterized primarily by two types of instructional activities: seatwork, which consisted of students working individually on their own materials without direct teacher instruction, and whole-class activity directed by the teacher. Seldom are students observed in small-group, self-directed activity. For example, Gump (1967), Adams and Biddle (1970), and Goodlad and Klein (1970) reported that the regular elementary class is characterized by whole-group, teacher-directed instruction for about 65-75% of the time. Although the predominance of large-group, teacher-directed instruction has been frequently criticized, Westbury (1973) states it is used and will probably continue to be used because it offers an effective teaching strategy. According to Westbury, it

> serves some task attention, gives some measure of control over the activity of students, facilitates coverage of content and offers a drill and practice session that leads to some mastery of the facts which are regarded as symbols of school learning (p. 103).

Furthermore, Westbury maintains that more instructional resources will have to be provided before teacher-directed individualization is a real option.

In this study, the patterns of peer instructional activity were determined through classroom observation. Each time observers were in a classroom (regardless of the information system employed), they recorded two types of information: the *type of student task*—working on print or nonprint materials, listening, interacting with the teacher or aide, or interacting with peers—and the *group structure*—individual, small groups, or large group. Working on print and nonprint materials was considered a student self-directed task; listening or interacting with the teacher or aide was considered a teacher-directed task. The two instructional tasks in conjunction with the three group structure combinations formed the six peer instructional activities. The peer instructional activity measures were scored as percentages of time classes were observed in each student task/group structure combination.[6]

Peers in regular classes spent about three-fourths of the observed time in large-group instruction, which was fairly evenly divided between student self-directed and teacher-directed activities (Table 8-5). Small-group and individual instruction occurred about 10% of the time. Small-group instruction was fairly evenly divided between teacher- and student-directed activities, but individual instruction was almost entirely student directed. Teachers in regular classes were almost never observed in teacher-directed, individual instruction. Summing across group structure, regular class peers were observed spending 52% of their time in self-instruction, 42% in teacher-directed instruction, and 6% in noninstructional activities.

The patterns of instructional activity in the resource rooms and special self-contained classes were noticeably different from those found in the regular classes as well as being different from each other. Regardless of the type of task, resource class students were observed 50% of the time in small groups, 25% in a large group, and 22% individually. None of the other five instructional activities occurred more than 15% of the time. About twice as much resource class instruction was teacher-directed (65%) as was self-directed (32%).

In the special self-contained classes, students were observed slightly more often in teacher-directed instruction than in self-instruction (49% vs. 44%, respectively). Instruction also occurred more often in a group (44% in large groups, 30% in small groups) than individually (20%). The three most frequent patterns of instructional activity were self-instruction in a large group, teacher instruction in a small group, and teacher instruction in a large group: Each was observed 22% of the time.

The standard deviations of the observed activity patterns are generally large, suggesting the classes were quite variable in the percentage of time students spent in the six activity patterns.

In the special education settings, additional information was obtained on the group structure. Special education teachers were asked on the TAQ about the size of their instructional groups (see Table 8-5). Resource and special self-contained teachers reported the average size of their instructional group was 6-7 students, with a maximum of 8-9 students. Group size tended to be more variable in self-contained than resource classes. The special education teachers reported they typically worked individually with about nine students each day.

In sum, the pattern of student activity varied with the type of instructional setting. Regular class instruction was predominantly large-group instruction, about equally divided between teacher-directed and self-directed tasks. Small-group instruction (either teacher- or self-directed) occurred infrequently. Individual teacher-directed instruction almost never occurred. In the special self-contained classes, large- (whole-) group instruction was also predominant, but this pattern occurred far less frequently than in the regular classes. Teacher-directed instruction with small groups or individuals occurred for substantially greater proportions of time in the special education classes than in the regular classes. In the resource classes, the predominant method of instruction was teacher-directed small groups. Teacher-directed instruction, regardless of group size, occurred, on the average, about 45% of the time in the regular and special self-contained classes and about 65% of the time in the resource classes.

These findings indicate that real differences existed in the pattern of instructional activity used in the three settings. The regular classes alternated between lecture/discussion and whole-class seatwork; the special self-contained classes used several instructional patterns, and the resource classes concentrated on small instructional groups. The pattern of peer instructional activity appears to be a discriminating feature of the three settings.

Table 8-5

Peer Instructional Activity by Instructional Setting

| Dimensions of Peer Instructional Activity | Instructional Setting | | | | | | | | |
| | Regular | | | Special Resource | | | Special Self-Contained | | |
| | X | SD | N | X | SD | N | X | SD | N |
|---|---|---|---|---|---|---|---|---|---|
| **Peer instructional activity** | | | | | | | | | |
| Percentage of observed time peers were engaged in each type of instruction and group structure | | | | | | | | | |
| Student self-directed, individual instruction | 10.36 | 10.06 | 254 | 14.70 | 15.17 | 127 | 13.76 | 10.90 | 127 |
| Student self-directed, small-group instruction | 4.13 | 5.00 | 254 | 5.16 | 5.14 | 127 | 8.09 | 5.85 | 127 |
| Student self-directed, large-group instruction | 38.00 | 14.62 | 254 | 12.02 | 11.24 | 127 | 21.81 | 13.85 | 127 |
| Teacher-directed, individual instruction | 1.12 | 2.19 | 254 | 6.97 | 8.61 | 127 | 5.81 | 7.56 | 127 |
| Teacher-directed, small-group instruction | 6.03 | 7.49 | 254 | 45.24 | 24.25 | 127 | 21.55 | 17.40 | 127 |
| Teacher-directed, large-group instruction | 35.12 | 12.96 | 254 | 12.84 | 13.96 | 127 | 21.99 | 11.69 | 127 |
| **Special education instruction group size** | | | | | | | | | |
| Teacher report of the average number of students worked with at a time | | | | 5.90 | 2.54 | 117 | 6.60 | 4.20 | 101 |
| Teacher report of the maximum size of intructional group | | | | 8.37 | 3.54 | 115 | 9.63 | 5.01 | 104 |
| Teacher report of the average number of students worked with individually every day | | | | 8.75 | 8.34 | 111 | 9.02 | 7.76 | 98 |

**Teacher Instructional Tasks**: Seven tasks are included in the teacher instructional tasks or activities of the instructional conditions model: Introducing or motivating, explaining, questioning or drilling, directing, supervising, summarizing or reviewing, and testing. In any given lesson, most of these tasks are employed, but depending on a teacher's instructional goals and strategies, certain tasks may be emphasized more than others. For example, teachers wishing an interchange of student ideas emphasize questioning, whereas teachers wishing students to be continuously apprised of their progress might emphasize testing. Dunkin and Biddle (1974) reported that teacher lecturing or explaining occupies 16-24% of classroom interaction time, teacher questioning characterizes 10-16%, and teacher directing, 10% or less.

In this study, observers determined the teacher instructional tasks for each observed time segment by recording which of the seven tasks the teacher was performing. These task measures were scored as percentages of time the teacher engaged in each task. Since there was an "other" category (used primarily when the teacher was out of the room), the sum of the mean percentages of time observed in each task is not 100%. The sum of the seven tasks represents the total percentage of time the teacher performed instructional functions.

In each instructional setting, the teachers spent about 33% of the observed time supervising (Table 8-6). During this time students worked by themselves while the teacher monitored them from a desk or by walking around the room. Teachers gave instructions on how to do specific work about 20% of the time. Teacher questioning or drilling occurred about 13-17% of the observed time, depending on the setting. The remaining tasks were observed less than 10% of the time. Teachers were quite variable in their apportionment of time to the seven tasks. These findings are in agreement with the findings of other studies.

**Class Cognitive Discourse**: Class cognitive discourse focussed on the information-processing capability of the students. The tasks students are expected to perform include: selectively encoding information from the environment; organizing information into conceptual systems; and solving problems through inference, generalization, and application of information (Taba, 1966). To this end, teachers are responsible for transmitting stable bodies of knowledge in a manner that enables the learner to internalize the knowledge into his cognitive structure (Ausubel, 1967). Several schemes have been developed to describe and categorize the range of cognitive behaviors that occur in the classroom (Bloom et al., 1956; Guilford, 1967; Smith & Meux, 1962; Taba, 1966). These models are hierarchical: Performance of a cognitive behavior at one level requires the ability to perform the behaviors at the preceding levels.

Table 8-6
Teacher Instructional Task by Instructional Setting

| Dimensions of Teacher Instructional Task | Instructional Setting | | | | | | | | |
|---|---|---|---|---|---|---|---|---|---|
| | Regular | | | Special Resource | | | Special Self-Contained | | |
| | X | SD | N | X | SD | N | X | SD | N |
| Teacher instructional task | | | | | | | | | |
| Percentage of observed time teacher peformed each of the following tasks: | | | | | | | | | |
| Introducing or motivating | 4.88 | 3.85 | 254 | 6.38 | 6.45 | 127 | 4.42 | 3.72 | 127 |
| Explaining | 8.22 | 4.70 | 254 | 7.49 | 5.61 | 127 | 7.90 | 6.79 | 127 |
| Questioning or drilling | 13.48 | 8.12 | 254 | 17.50 | 12.50 | 127 | 16.05 | 8.30 | 127 |
| Directing | 19.38 | 10.13 | 254 | 23.77 | 14.82 | 127 | 20.73 | 10.61 | 127 |
| Supervising | 33.56 | 13.84 | 254 | 31.33 | 15.43 | 127 | 35.11 | 13.66 | 127 |
| Summarizing or reviewing | 4.45 | 3.09 | 254 | 2.88 | 3.46 | 127 | 2.79 | 2.89 | 127 |
| Testing | 6.32 | 4.48 | 254 | 5.11 | 6.74 | 127 | 3.60 | 3.97 | 127 |

The close relationship between the level of teacher demand and the level of student responses (Arnold, Atwood, & Rogers, 1973; Dunkin & Biddle, 1974; Minskoff, 1967; Wilson, 1973) suggests that teachers shape and control the level of cognitive interaction engaged in by their students.

Two aspects of cognitive discourse were examined in the Project PRIME classes: amount and cognitive level (very low, moderately low, moderately high, and very high). Observers coded the number and cognitive level of teacher demands and the number and cognitive level of individual student responses to teacher demands on the ICDS (see Table 8- 7).[7]

In regular classes, cognitive discourse — either a teacher cognitive demand directed toward a specific student or an individual cognitive response — occurred at an average rate of 118.8 per hour of observation, or nearly two per minute. Peers made nearly as many cognitive responses per hour as teachers made cognitive demands (57.6 vs. 61.2, respectively). The regular class teacher demand rate per student was 2.4 per hour: Each student, on average, received a cognitive demand every 25 minutes.

In the resource classes, cognitive remarks were made at an average rate slightly above two per minute, or 122.4 per hour. Teachers exceeded students in the number of cognitive remarks made per hour; 58% (70.8) were teacher demands and 42% (51.6) were peer responses. Resource class teachers made 13.2 cognitive demands per student per hour in their classes, about one cognitive demand every 4 minutes.

Special self-contained class teachers had an average class demand rate similar to that of resource class teachers (70 cognitive demands per hour). However, the students in special self-contained classes were more responsive than those in resource classes, so the total number of demands and responses made per hour averaged 131.4. Close to half the cognitive remarks were in the form of student responses (47%, 61.2). The demand rate per pupil per hour in special self-contained classes was 9.0; about one cognitive demand for each student every 6-7 minutes. The standard deviations are relatively large for these observations in all three settings.

Teacher cognitive demands were classified into four levels representing different aspects of cognitive processing, from simple/concrete to complex/ abstract. *Very low-level demands* included (a) repeating or recognizing operations that require simple, habitual, almost automatic responses which may require noticing, identifying, or describing items actually present and involve no memory or transformation process and (b) chaining operations that require already-learned responses that form a natural sequence, or chain, such that each specific segment of the response suggests the next segment automatically. *Moderately low-level demands* included recalling operations which required direct remembering of previously-learned or acquired information. *Moderately high-level demands* included conceptualizing

Table 8-7

Class Cognitive Discourse by Instructional Setting

| Dimensions of Class Cognitive Discourse | Instructional Setting | | | | | | | | |
|---|---|---|---|---|---|---|---|---|---|
| | Regular | | | Special Resource | | | Special Self-Contained | | |
| | X | SD | N | X | SD | N | X | SD | N |
| **Amount of cognitive discourse** | | | | | | | | | |
| Number of observed teacher cognitive demands per hour | 61.20 | 30.00 | 251 | 70.80 | 36.60 | 125 | 70.20 | 34.80 | 122 |
| Number of observed peer cognitive responses per hour | 57.60 | 28.20 | 251 | 51.60 | 30.60 | 125 | 61.20 | 28.20 | 122 |
| Total number of observed teacher cognitive demands and peer cognitive responses per hour | 118.80 | 58.20 | 251 | 122.40 | 66.00 | 125 | 131.40 | 63.00 | 122 |
| Demand rate per pupil per hour | 2.40 | 1.20 | 251 | 13.20 | 11.40 | 125 | 9.00 | 7.80 | 122 |
| **Type of cognitive discourse** | | | | | | | | | |
| Percentage of total teacher cognitive demands at each of the following levels: | | | | | | | | | |
| Very low | 34.28 | 17.16 | 251 | 46.73 | 19.82 | 125 | 47.41 | 17.14 | 122 |
| Moderately low | 15.73 | 14.52 | 251 | 15.16 | 16.03 | 125 | 17.28 | 12.29 | 122 |
| Moderately high | 18.63 | 13.07 | 251 | 13.66 | 11.41 | 125 | 12.98 | 8.71 | 122 |
| Very high | 22.43 | 15.77 | 251 | 19.28 | 15.34 | 125 | 16.94 | 10.84 | 122 |

operations which required demonstration of the understanding of concepts, including supplying the correct meaning of a term, giving the correct label for a set of examples, comparing and/or contrasting concepts, and formulating generalizations. *Very high-level demands* included problem-solving operations which establish relationships between available information in the form of concepts, rules, or strategies. These include understanding causes of an event; deriving conclusions, deductions, hypotheses, or interpretations; free associating and/or elaborating on an idea; judging the value of an idea by making comparisons with a standard; and/or solving problems. Demands concerning procedures were observed and included in the total frequency scores but not in the categorization; therefore, the sum of the average percentages in each of the four categories was less than 100%.

In all three settings, teacher cognitive demands were at the very low level more frequently than any other level. In regular classes, slightly more than one-third were low-level and slightly more than one-fifth were high-level demands. In resource and special self-contained classes, nearly half the demands were low-level (47% in each) and less than one-fifth were high-level demands.

These findings, summarized in Table 8-7, are consistent with other studies which report the majority of cognitive demands made by teachers require students to rely on memory only (Arnold, Atwood, & Rogers, 1973; Bane, 1969; Davis, Morse, Rogers, & Tinsley, 1969; Dunkin & Biddle, 1974; Gallagher, 1965; Minskoff, 1967; Mueller, 1972; Susskind, 1969). Most investigators have criticized the overuse of memory-level cognitive demands. Sanders (1966) suggests that at least one-third of the class time be spent at cognitive-processing levels higher than simple cognitive recall.

In sum, regular class teachers made about one cognitive demand per minute and special class teachers had a slightly higher rate. On a student basis, cognitive demands were made much more often in special self-contained and resource classes than in regular classes. Students typically made fewer responses than teachers made demands. The proportion of teacher cognitive demands at a low level of discourse was about one-third in regular classes and nearly one-half in the special resource and self-contained classes.

Although the special class teachers made somewhat more cognitive demands per hour than the regular class teachers, the real difference was not in the rate of demands per se but in the demands made per student. The smaller class size of the special classes resulted in considerably more demands per student even though the total number of demands differed little from that in the regular class. The teacher cognitive demand behavior was similar in the three settings, though there was greater cognitive demand intensity in the special class settings. However, the cognitive level of the demands made in the special classes was lower than it was in the regular classes.

**Teacher Instructional Feedback to Peers**: Teacher instructional feedback to peers should provide students with information regarding the appropriateness of their performance and should provide teachers with information regarding the appropriateness of the instructional program for students' interests and abilities.

Ladas and Osti (1973) conclude that feedback can be one of a teacher's most effective tools for maintaining student attention and participation. Even when addressed to an individual learner, public feedback may have an indirect "ripple" effect on the other students who have been internally attending and generating their own responses (Solomon & Rosenberg, 1964).

Both positive and negative feedback are required by students: negative feedback to indicate that students are not performing in an appropriate manner; positive feedback as a reward, reinforcing the emitted behavior. Too much negative feedback may have a depressing effect on learning activity. A balance of positive and negative reinforcement is necessary.

Feedback also provides the student with the reason for the adequacy or inadequacy of the response (Brophy & Evertson, 1974) and may be more useful if accompanied by additional information.

Zahorik (1970) suggests that teachers should make greater use of negative feedback than they typically do. In his study, third- and sixth-grade students generally thought the more frequently used positive feedback evoked positive feelings and conveyed information about correctness, but did not usually explain or provide direction; negative feedback often provided such information.

Feedback is a particularly critical element in the education of EMR learners. Referring to Herbert Goldstein's model of inductive teaching, Minskoff (1967) and Mischio (1975) reported that feedback is one of the four crucial aspects to consider when applying the inductive teaching method with EMR learners. Immediate positive feedback should follow a correct response. If the response is incorrect, the teacher should not provide the correct answer; instead, the teacher should ask the student to evaluate the incorrect response and respond again. Such a procedure is aimed at encouraging EMR learners to rely less on the teacher as the only source of instructional stimulation, and more on other sources of information, particularly their own ability to reason.

In Project PRIME, information on the frequency and type of feedback was obtained through classroom observation. Using the ICDS, observers recorded the frequency and type of feedback the teacher provided to each peer cognitive response.[8] Because feedback and cognitive discourse information were collected simultaneously, there is an artifactually close relationship between the two.

Teachers in regular and special self-contained classes averaged 49 feedback remarks per hour; teachers in resource classes had a slightly lower rate, 44 remarks per hour (see Table 8-8). Although there was little variation across settings in the number of feedback remarks teachers made per hour, the variation in class size led to variation in the average number of remarks each student received per hour. In regular classes, the feedback rate was 1.93 remarks per student per hour. In resource classes, the rate was 8.17; in special self-contained classes, 6.31.

In addition to determining whether or not the teachers provided feedback, the Project PRIME observers also determined the type of feedback provided. Information feedback included three types of feedback comments: information only, positive feedback and information, and negative feedback and information. These three types were not mutually exclusive. Comments could be both positive and informational or negative and informational. The comments that were categorized as positive feedback provided positive reinforcement or both positive reinforcement and information. Similarly, comments that were negative only and those that were both negative and informational were categorized as negative. The average percentages sum to more than 100% due to the overlap in categories. In the following discussion, the terms "positive," "negative," and "information" are used without reference to the overlap inherent among them.

Most teacher feedback was positive regardless of the setting (88% of all feedback remarks were positive). About 10% of the feedback remarks were negative, and about 20% provided information, either alone (as with evaluation) or in conjunction with positive or negative reinforcement. Although the average proportion of the various types of feedback was the same in all settings, it is interesting that resource class teachers were more variable than special self-contained class teachers in their use of various types of feedback. (See Table 8-8.)

Comparison between the rates of cognitive discourse and teacher soliciting-responding-reacting moves (Bellack, et al., 1966) was not perfect since students did not always respond cognitively to teacher demands, and teachers did not always provide feedback to student responses. In the regular classes, students responded to 94% of the teacher cognitive demands and teachers provided feedback to 85% of the student responses. Resource class students responded to only 73% of the teacher demands and teachers gave feedback to 85% of the student responses. In special self-contained classes, students responded to 87% of the teacher cognitive demands, and 80% of the student responses received feedback. (See Table 8-7.)

In sum, teachers, regardless of setting, provided almost 50 feedback remarks per hour, most of which were positive. When frequency of feedback is adjusted for number of students in the class, the feedback rates per student in the special classes were 3-4 times as great as in the regular classes. Again teacher behavior per se did not differ in these settings; rather, it was the concentration of this behavior on relatively few students that differed.

Table 8-8

Teacher Instructional Feedback to Peers by Instructional Setting

| Dimensions of Teacher Instructional Feedback to Peers | Instructional Setting | | | | | | | | |
|---|---|---|---|---|---|---|---|---|---|
| | Regular | | | Special Resource | | | Special Self-Contained | | |
| | X | SD | N | X | SD | N | X | SD | N |
| Amount of instructional feedback | | | | | | | | | |
| Total number per hour of observed teacher feedback remarks to peer cognitive responses | 49.20 | 22.20 | 251 | 43.80 | 25.80 | 125 | 49.20 | 25.20 | 122 |
| Type of instructional feedback | | | | | | | | | |
| Percentage of total feedback remarks of each of the following types: | | | | | | | | | |
| Positive | 88.49 | 10.39 | 251 | 87.81 | 14.30 | 125 | 87.76 | 7.15 | 122 |
| Negative | 9.81 | 6.42 | 251 | 10.01 | 8.84 | 125 | 11.22 | 7.08 | 122 |
| Information | 19.96 | 14.27 | 251 | 16.77 | 15.04 | 125 | 17.88 | 12.78 | 122 |

# Discussion of Descriptive Findings

The descriptive results presented in this section address the first issue raised in this chapter — the instructional conditions present in the three educational settings typically available to EMR learners. The instructional conditions present in each setting were related to the setting's basic design and orientation. Regular classes are designed to provide instruction to larger groups of students (> 20 students) with varying levels of ability who are usually present for the whole day. Teachers are expected to follow an "official" school curriculum for that grade level and are provided with appropriate grade level materials. Resource classes consist of about 7-10 students, present for an hour or two a day, who come from a regular class for remedial, support, or supplemental instruction. Teachers of these classes are expected to provide individual or small-group instruction for particular, diagnosed skill deficits. Special self-contained classes consist of about 12-15 students who are usually present for the whole day. Teachers of these classes are expected to implement a curriculum, including special instructional materials, appropriate for the functioning level of the students in the class. The underlying design of each setting has implications for the instructional conditions found within it.

## Regular Classes

Regular classes were engaged in traditional academic content most of the time. Teachers were on-task 97% of the time they were observed and the students were moderately attentive. Although there was some attempt at providing instructional differentiation, it was only moderately successful. The students perceived a cognitive academic emphasis. The principal instructional modes were teacher-directed or student self-directed or large-group activity with teachers either supervising, directing, or questioning. The frequency of cognitive demands per student was low, with most demands requiring a low level of cognitive processing; the feedback rate per student was also low, although generally positive.

## Special Self-Contained Classes

The Project PRIME special self-contained classes were less oriented toward academic subject matter, particularly science and social studies, than were the regular classes. More time was spent in art, training in basic cognitive processes, and transitional and other activities. Although there was little difference between special self-contained and regular classes in the extent of observed teacher attention or student interest and attention, the student participation rate in the special self-contained classes was more than twice that in the regular classes, with greater instructional differentiation but less perceived cognitive academic emphasis than the regular classes. Large- (whole-) group instruction occurred about half as often as it did in regular classes, and the use of individual and small-group instruction was more than doubled. Slightly more instruction was teacher-directed than in the regular classes, but the specific teacher instructional tasks were similar to those of the regular class teachers. The cognitive demand rate per student was higher, and the cognitive level of the demands was lower. The type of feedback was similar to but the feedback rate per student was higher than in the regular classes. Special self-contained class teachers had special instructional materials available and most had received an individual educational plan for their students.

## Resource Classes

The academic content of the Project PRIME resource classes was heavily oriented toward reading and mathematics; science and social studies were rarely taught. Teacher attention and student interest and attention were similar to the other settings. Individual student verbal participation rate was nearly twice the rate that occurred in the special self-contained classes and more than four times as high as the regular class rate. Compared to the special self-contained class, teacher-directed activity was usually in small groups. The cognitive demand rate per student per hour was higher, with a similarly high proportion that were low level; there was a slightly higher and mainly positive feedback rate per student, with more easily available special education services.

The three settings, then, differed on those instructional conditions for which they were designed to differ. There is indeed something special about special education. Many of the differences between special and regular education settings were due to the presence of fewer students. This allowed more focussed academic work; more small-group and individual instruction; and higher per pupil rates of verbal participation, cognitive demands, and instructional feedback. The primary negative instructional feature of special self-contained classes was that they were less academically demanding as evidenced by relatively low levels of cognitive demands. Though, it is worth remembering that in the regular classes more than one-third of the cognitive demands were coded as low level.

The instructional program was structured differently for the three settings. Regular classes were academically oriented toward the whole class, with little individualization or opportunity for individual students to actively

## Table 8-9
### Bivariate Correlations of Peer Engagement with Instructional Context and Operations

| Variable | Peer Interest and Attention | | | Peer Verbalization | | |
|---|---|---|---|---|---|---|
| | Regular Class | Special Resource Class | Special Self-Contained Class | Regular Class | Special Resource Class | Special Self-Contained Class |
| **Peer engagement** | | | | | | |
| Peer interest and attention | 100 | 100 | 100 | 03 | 23 | -03 |
| Peer verbalization | 03 | 23 | -03 | 100 | 100 | 100 |
| **Instructional context** | | | | | | |
| Physical quality | 32 | 23 | 34 | -06 | 11 | -02 |
| Special instructional services | -16 | 06 | -04 | 05 | -20 | 19 |
| Teacher-made materials | 13 | 04 | 04 | -05 | 28 | -08 |
| **Peer instructional activity** | | | | | | |
| Student self-directed, individual | -17 | -26 | -19 | 00 | -23 | -07 |
| Student self-directed, small groups | -05 | -25 | -02 | -06 | -26 | -04 |
| Student self-directed, large group | 17 | 06 | 12 | 00 | -25 | -11 |
| Teacher directed, individual | -13 | -24 | -16 | 01 | -05 | 14 |
| Teacher directed, small groups | 02 | 25 | 16 | -04 | 44 | 24 |
| Teacher directed, large group | -10 | 03 | 04 | 06 | -15 | -18 |

## Teacher instructional task

| | | | | | |
|---|---|---|---|---|---|
| Introducing or motivating | -07 | 19 | 00 | 00 | 23 | 09 |
| Explaining | 00 | 03 | -02 | -02 | 02 | 00 |
| Questioning or drilling | -06 | 07 | 09 | -01 | 30 | 11 |
| Directing | 07 | -09 | -16 | 10 | 00 | 13 |
| Supervising | -04 | -04 | -03 | -04 | -30 | -09 |
| Summarizing or reviewing | 00 | 07 | 15 | 02 | 06 | -03 |
| Testing | 10 | -09 | 12 | -07 | 05 | -18 |

## Class cognitive discourse

| | | | | | |
|---|---|---|---|---|---|
| Very low cognitive discourse index | -04 | -15 | -07 | -12 | -07 | 20 |
| Moderately low cognitive discourse index | -08 | 25 | 12 | 01 | 26 | 12 |
| Moderately high cognitive discourse index | -10 | 04 | 13 | 13 | 10 | -04 |
| Very high cognitive discourse index | 04 | -01 | -03 | -05 | -02 | 03 |
| Total number of demands and responses | -02 | 15 | 06 | -02 | 20 | 28 |
| Demand rate | -02 | 30 | 01 | 04 | 45 | 41 |
| Variety of demands | -01 | 13 | 06 | -06 | 02 | 23 |

## Teacher instructional feedback to peers

| | | | | | |
|---|---|---|---|---|---|
| Total number of feedback remarks | -02 | 10 | -01 | -02 | 08 | 30 |
| Positive feedback index | -01 | 15 | 04 | -01 | 14 | 36 |
| Negative feedback index | -12 | -06 | -13 | -01 | -07 | -21 |
| Information feedback index | -04 | 16 | 06 | 00 | 13 | -05 |

Note. N = 262 for regular classes, 132 for resource classes, and 127 for self-contained special classes. Values above .14 are significant for the regular class; values above .17 are significant for the special resource and self-contained special classes. Decimal points have been omitted.

participate. The special self-contained classes were less academically demanding, used more individualization and provided more opportunities for individual participation and feedback. While the resource classes had less individualization, the students present were grouped for need and level of performance. Interestingly, physical quality, teacher attentiveness, student interest and attention, the pattern of teacher tasks, and the type of feedback were not affected by the level of student cognitive skills or class size, and were similar across settings.

## Relationships Among Elements of the Instructional Conditions Model

The next two sections examine the relationships between two aspects of the class information-processing system — engagement and instructional differentiation — and the instructional context and operations available in the class.

### Relationships Between Peer Instructional Engagement and Instructional Operations

Information relating the two levels of peer engagement — peer interest and attention (an index of observed interest and attention) and peer verbalization (the number of observed verbalizations per student per hour) — with both each other and the other instructional conditions was derived from an intercorrelation matrix (Table 8-9) and a set of commonality analyses (Tables 8-10 and 8-11). All analyses used the class as the level of aggregation and unit of analysis. Criterion measures were the two levels of peer engagement, maintaining attention and active verbal participation. The predictors were 27 of the instructional conditions variables clustered into five sets, representing instructional context, peer instructional activity, teacher instructional task, class cognitive discourse, and teacher instructional feedback to peers.[9]

Examination of Table 8-9 reveals that the two measures of peer engagement were not related. In the regular and special self-contained classes, the correlation between the peer engagement measures is near 0; in the resource class the correlation is 0.23. Thus, those classes that maintained a high level of peer interest and attention were not necessarily the same ones that obtained high levels of peer verbalization. Each measure was examined separately to determine the instructional conditions associated with it due to low correlations between the engagement measures.

**Peer Interest and Attention:** The results of the commonality analyses of peer interest and attention are presented in Table 8-11. For the regular classes, the

Table 8-10
Variables Employed in Commonality Analyses
as Peer Measures of Instructional Engagement

| Component | Variables |
|---|---|
| Criterion Measures | |
| Peer engagement | Peer interest and attention<br>Number of observed verbalizations per pupil per hour |
| Predictor Measures | |
| Instructional context | Physical quality observation index<br>Percentage of instructionaal material made by teacher<br>Number of special instructional services received |
| Peer instructional activity | Student self-directed, individual instruction<br>Student self-directed, small-group instruction<br>Student self-directed, large-group instruction<br>Teacher-directed, individual instruction<br>Teacher-directed, small-group instruction<br>Teacher-directed, large-group instruction |
| Teacher instructional task | Introducing or motivating<br>Explaining<br>Questioning or drilling<br>Directing<br>Supervising<br>Summarizing or reviewing<br>Testing |
| Class cognitive discourse | Very low cognitive discoursse index<br>Moderately low cognitive discourse index<br>Moderately high cognitive discourse index<br>Very high cognitive discoursse index<br>Total number of demands and responses per hour<br>Demand rate per pupil per hour<br>Variety of demands |
| Teacher instructional feedback to peers | Total number of feedback remarks per hour<br>Positive feedback index<br>Negative feedback index<br>Information feedback index |

five predictor sets explained 26% of the variance in peer interest and attention. Instructional context and peer instructional activity were the two predictor sets with significant total and unique $R^2$s. Among the bivariate correlations between peer interest and attention and the instructional context measures, the physical quality of the class had the highest correlation. The correlations with the peer instructional activity variables revealed (a) a negative relationship between peer interest and attention and the percentage of time spent in student self-directed, individual instruction and (b) a positive relationship between peer interest and attention and the percentage of time spent in student self-directed large-group instruction (Table 8-9).

In the resource classes, the total $R^2$ between peer interest and attention and the five predictor sets was 0.42. Two sets had significant total and unique $R^2$s: peer instructional activity and cognitive discourse. The bivariate correlations for the peer instructional activities set present a mixed picture. Percentage of time spent in individual instruction was negatively related to peer interest and attention, whether teacher-directed or self-directed. The percentage of time in small-group instruction was positively correlated with peer interest and attention when teacher-directed but negatively correlated when self-directed. The percentage of time in large-group instruction, regardless of mode of instruction, was unrelated to peer interest and attention. The correlations with the class cognitive discourse set revealed that peer interest and attention were positively related to the index of moderately low cognitive discourse and the total demand rate per student.

In the special self-contained classes, the total $R^2$ between peer interest and attention and the five predictor sets was 0.41. Only instructional context and peer instructional activity had significant total and unique $R^2$s. The fact that other sets had a higher unique than total variance results from uninterpretable suppressor effects among these sets. The bivariate correlations within the instructional context set show peer interest and attention to be positively related to the physical quality of the classroom. Within the peer instructional activity set, peer interest and attention was negatively related to percentage of time in self-directed individual instruction.

The commonality analysis results suggest that peer interest and attention are more closely related to those aspects of instructional conditions defined by the Project PRIME model in the special self-contained and resource classes than in the regular classes. In all three settings, peer interest and attention were related to the physical quality of the class.[10] While it is possible that the additional materials, orderliness and quiet, and physical climate which comprise the physical quality index have a direct impact on peer attention, it is also possible that students in communities with the financial resources to support schools of high physical quality also have children who are reared to pay attention.

Peer instructional activity was the only other predictor set consistently related to peer interest and attention, although the particular type of activity related to attention varied with the instructional setting. In all three settings, student self-directed individual instruction was negatively related to peer interest and attention. In the regular classes, the percentage of time spent in self-instruction in large groups was positively related to peer interest and

Table 8-11

Total and Unique Percentage of Variance Explained in Peer Interest and Attention

| | | | Instructional Setting | | | |
|---|---|---|---|---|---|---|
| | Regular | | Special Resource | | Special Self-Contained | |
| Predictor | Total R2 | Unique R2 | Total R2 | Unique R2 | Total R2 | Unique R2 |
| Full model | 26* | | 42* | | 41* | |
| Instructional context | 15* | 13* | 5 | 4 | 12* | 12* |
| Peer instructional activity | 7* | 5* | 15* | 14* | 10* | 9* |
| Teacher instructional task | 2 | 2 | 5 | 8 | 5 | 10* |
| Class cognitive discourse | 2 | 1 | 14* | 10* | 4 | 12* |
| Teacher instructional feedback to peers | 2 | 2 | 4 | 3 | 6 | 9* |

Note. N = 262 for regular classes, 132 for resource classes, and 127 for special self-contained classes.

*p < .05.

attention. In the resource classes, the percentage of time in teacher-directed small-group instruction was positively related to peer interest and attention. In these resource classes, and to a lesser extent in the regular and special self-contained classes, teacher-directed individual instruction and student-directed small-group instruction were also negatively related to peer interest and attention. The finding that the proportion of time spent in self-directed individual instruction was negatively related to peer attention suggests that individual seatwork is not an operation that maintains engagement. The finding that teacher-directed individual instruction was negatively related to peer attention suggests that while the teacher may improve the attention of one student by working directly with him, the attention of the other students is reduced.

**Peer Verbalization**: The commonality analyses predicting peer verbalization (Table 8-12) produced little information which was uniquely interesting.[11] The results of the analyses revealed that only in the special education settings was peer verbalization related to the instructional conditions defined by the Project PRIME model. Class cognitive discourse was the only set that explained a significant proportion of variance in verbal participation in the resource and special self-contained classes. In both settings, not surprisingly, the demand rate per student and the total frequency of demands and responses were positively related to peer verbalization.

**Discussion**: Inducing and maintaining an engaged system is an important instructional consideration. The two levels of peer engagement — interest and attention, and verbalization — function quite differently. The level of interest and attention shown by peers was moderate and similar across settings. Its strong relationship to the physical quality of the classroom suggests that class interest and attention may be in part a socioeconomic status phenomenon. However, student interest and attention were also related to instructional activity and may be affected by teacher manipulation of certain instructional conditions.

Peer verbalization was unrelated to peer interest and attention and was low (on a per student basis) in regular classes but high in special education classes. Peer verbalization was not related to any instructional condition measures within the regular class. In both the special self-contained and resource classes, peer verbalization was related to the demand rate per student and the total frequency of demands and responses, which leads to the obvious conclusion that arranging for more cognitive discourse may lead to greater verbalization. Attention and verbalization as elements of the instructional system are influenced through different mechanisms: attention, through the nature of the instructional activity, and verbalization, through the extent of cognitive discourse and probably class size.

Table 8-12

Total and Unique Percentage of Variance Explained in Peer Verbalization

| | Instructional Setting | | | | | |
| | Regular | | Special Resource | | Special Self-Contained | |
| Predictor | Total R2 | Unique R2 | Total R2 | Unique R2 | Total R2 | Unique R2 |
|---|---|---|---|---|---|---|
| Full model | 10 | | 51* | | 35* | |
| Instructional context | | | 13* | 4* | 4 | 2 |
| Peer instructional activity | | | 23* | 4 | 9 | 1 |
| Teacher instructional task | | | 17* | 4 | 7 | 7 |
| Class cognitive discourse | | | 26* | 10* | 19* | 9 |
| Teacher instructional feedback to peers | | | 4 | 4 | 16* | 3 |

Note. N = 262 for regular classes, 132 for resource classes, and 127 for special self-contained classes.

*p <.05.

277

Table 8-13

Bivariate Correlations of Teacher Strategies with Context, Activities, Tasks, Discourse, and Feedback

| | Teacher Strategies | | | | | | |
| | Individual Differentiation Index | | Learner-Peer Content/Activity Difference | | | Cognitive Emphasis | |
| Variable | Regular Class | Special Self-Contained Class | Regular Class | Special Resource Class | Special Self-Contained Class | Regular Class | Special Self-Contained Class |
|---|---|---|---|---|---|---|---|
| **Teacher Strategies** | | | | | | | |
| Individual differentiation index | 100 | 100 | 10 | — | 28 | -05 | -03 |
| Learner-peer content/activity difference | 10 | 28 | 100 | 100 | 100 | -13 | 06 |
| Cognitive emphasis | -05 | -03 | -13 | — | 06 | 100 | 100 |
| **Instructional context** | | | | | | | |
| Physical quality | 16 | 30 | -03 | 07 | -09 | -01 | -09 |
| Special instructional services | 15 | -04 | 03 | -06 | -09 | -03 | 00 |
| Teacher-made materials | 19 | 15 | 11 | 03 | -05 | -02 | -26 |
| **Peer instructional activity** | | | | | | | |
| Student self-directed, individual | 16 | 22 | -01 | 59 | 41 | -03 | -11 |
| Student self-directed, small groups | 37 | 24 | 19 | 31 | 21 | -18 | -04 |
| Student self-directed, large group | -09 | -12 | -27 | -23 | -31 | 04 | 11 |
| Teacher-directed, individual | 12 | 23 | -06 | 57 | 52 | 03 | 12 |
| Teacher-directed, small groups | 13 | -14 | 67 | -34 | -04 | -14 | -04 |
| Teacher-directed, large group | -30 | -14 | -12 | -32 | -37 | 15 | 01 |

## Teacher instructional task

| | | | | | | |
|---|---|---|---|---|---|---|
| Introducing or motivating | 00 | 16 | 16 | -01 | -09 | 02 | 03 |
| Explaining | -04 | 03 | -11 | 10 | -11 | 07 | 05 |
| Questioning or drilling | -11 | 05 | 18 | -15 | 19 | -06 | 03 |
| Directing | -13 | 05 | 26 | -10 | 22 | 04 | 10 |
| Supervising | 31 | 04 | -20 | 24 | -12 | -03 | -16 |
| Summarizing or reviewing | -22 | -39 | -03 | -05 | -12 | 17 | 15 |
| Testing | -01 | -20 | -10 | -11 | 01 | 04 | 04 |

## Class cognitive discourse

| | | | | | | |
|---|---|---|---|---|---|---|
| Very low cognitive discourse index | -15 | -22 | 30 | -04 | 15 | 07 | 13 |
| Moderately low cognitive discourse index | 11 | 07 | 00 | -19 | -11 | -07 | -10 |
| Moderately high cognitive discourse index | 08 | -07 | -04 | -11 | -02 | -14 | 04 |
| Very high cognitive discourse index | -06 | 10 | -19 | 11 | -09 | 06 | -10 |
| Total number of demands and responses | 05 | -29 | 03 | -25 | -03 | -07 | 07 |
| Demand rate | 08 | -10 | 03 | -20 | 13 | -12 | 12 |
| Variety of demands | 05 | -19 | 05 | -19 | 07 | 00 | 02 |

## Teacher instructional feedback to peers

| | | | | | | |
|---|---|---|---|---|---|---|
| Total number of feedback remarks | 03 | -25 | 02 | -24 | -06 | -07 | 10 |
| Positive feedback index | 01 | -15 | 02 | -23 | -03 | -07 | 08 |
| Negative feedback index | -15 | -23 | 04 | -07 | -06 | 02 | 05 |
| Information feedback index | -14 | 11 | -11 | -19 | -06 | 08 | 12 |

Note. N = 262 for regular classes, 132 for resource classes, and 127 for special self-contained classes. Values above .14 are significant for the regular class; values above .17 are significant for the special resource and self-contained classes. Decimal points have been omitted.

### Relationships Between Teacher Instructional Strategies and Other Instructional Operations

Two instructional strategies of particular concern to EMR learners are instructional differentiation and cognitive emphasis. The commonality analysis equations for cognitive emphasis did not produce any enlightening results. The results for cognitive emphasis are included in the tables (see Tables 8-13 and 8-16), however.[12]

Information relating the instructional strategies with each other and with other instructional conditions was derived from an intercorrelation matrix (Table 8-13) and a set of commonality analyses.

Criterion measures for the commonality analyses were two measures of instructional differentiation — the individual differentiation index[13] (a high-inference composite of teacher attention to individual needs, flexibility of movement about the room, and use of a variety of materials and equipment) and the learner-peer content/activity difference (a low-inference measure of the percentage of time a teacher had specific learners working on academic content or instructional activities different from the majority of the class). Predictors included 27 of the instructional condition variables clustered into five sets representing instructional context, peer instructional activity, teacher instructional task, class cognitive discourse, and teacher instructional feedback to peers (Table 8-14).

In the regular classes, the two measures of instructional differentiation were not highly correlated ($r = 0.10$), suggesting that individual differentiation represented a different facet of instructional differentiation than did learner-peer content/activity difference. The restricted variance in the regular class teachers' scores on the learner-peer content/activity difference measure may account for the low correlation. In the special self-contained classes, the correlation was higher ($r = 0.28$), suggesting a limited congruence of the two measures in that setting.

**Individual Differentiation Index:** The results of the commonality analyses for the individual differentiation index are presented in Table 8-15. The full equation explained 40% of the variance in regular classes, with the predictor sets of instructional context, peer activity, and teacher task each explaining a significant proportion of the variance, independently, both with and without the effects of the other predictors partialled out (unique $R^2$ and total $R^2$). The peer instructional activity and teacher instructional task sets jointly predicted 40% of the variance in addition to the unique variance predicted by each set separately.

Examining the bivariate correlations between each predictor variable and the criterion suggests that the individual differentiation index in the regular classes was positively related to all of the instructional context measures, the percentage of time teachers used student-directed individual or small-group instruction, and the percentage of time spent supervising; and was negatively related to the percentage of time the teachers used teacher-directed large-group instruction and the percentage of time spent summarizing and reviewing. The strong relationship between the percentage of time the teachers supervised

Table 8-14
Variables Employed in Commonality
Analyses of Teacher Instructional Strategies

| Component | Variables |
|---|---|
| **Criterion Measures** | |
| Teacher strategies | Individual differentiation index |
| | Learner-peer content activity difference |
| | Cognitive emphasis |
| **Predictor Measures** | |
| Instructional context | Physical quality observation index |
| | Percentage of instructional material made by teacher |
| | Number of special instructional services received |
| Peer instructional activity | Student self-directed, individual instruction |
| | Student self-directed, small-group instruction |
| | Student self-directed, large-group instruction |
| | Teacher-directed, individual instruction |
| | Teacher-directed, small-group instruction |
| | Teacher-directed, large-group instruction |
| Teacher instructional task | Introducing or motivating |
| | Explaining |
| | Questioning or drilling |
| | Directing |
| | Supervising |
| | Summarizing or reviewing |
| | Testing |
| Class cognitive discourse | Very low cognitive discourse index |
| | Moderately low cognitive discourse index |
| | Moderately high cognitive discourse index |
| | Very high cognitive discourse index |
| | Total number of demands and responses per hour |
| | Demand rate per pupil per hour |
| | Variety of demands |
| Teacher instructional feedback to peers | Total number of feedback remarks per hour |
| | Positive feedback index |
| | Negative feedback index |
| | Information feedback index |

and the percentage of time they used student-directed individual or small-group and teacher-directed large-group instruction ($r = 0.25$ and $-0.52$, respectively) was responsible for the variance shared by the teacher-task and peer-activity sets.

For the special self-contained classes, the full equation explained almost 80% of the variance in the individual differentiation index. Every predictor set made a significant total and unique contribution to the variance in the individual differentiation index, although the class cognitive discourse set explained a larger proportion of the variance than did the other sets. In addition to the variance explained by peer activity and cognitive discourse uniquely, these two sets jointly explained 7% of the criterion variance.

Examining the bivariate correlations (Table 8-13) between the various instructional conditions variables and the individual differentiation index for the special self-contained classes reveals that individual differentiation was positively related to the physical quality of the classrooms and the percentage of time the teachers used student self-directed individual, small-group instruction or teacher-directed individual instruction. It was negatively related to the percentage of time the teachers were summarizing and reviewing or testing, the very low cognitive discourse index, the total number of demands and responses, the variety of demands, the total amount of feedback, and the negative feedback index. The relatively strong relationships existing between the use of teacher-directed small-group instruction and the number of teacher demands ($r = 0.49$), the number of peer responses ($r = 0.42$), and the very low discourse index ($r = 0.30$) are responsible for the proportion of variance accounted for jointly by the peer activity and the class cognitive discourse sets.

**Learner-Peer Content/Activity Difference**: The results of the commonality analyses for learner-peer content/activity difference are reported in Table 8-15. The full equation explained over 50% of the variance in the measure for the regular class setting. Peer instructional activity was the most important predictor set, uniquely accounting for half the total explained variance. The teacher task and class cognitive discourse sets also accounted for significant proportions of the variance. The student-activity/teacher-task combination jointly explained 8% of the criterion variance.

The bivariate correlations for the regular classes suggest the learner-peer content/activity difference was positively related to the percentage of time teachers used small-group, particularly teacher-directed, instruction; the percentage of time the teachers were introducing, motivating, questioning, drilling, or directing; and the very low cognitive discourse index. Learner-peer content/activity difference was negatively related to the percentage of

Table 8-15

Total and Unique Percentage of Variance Explained in Selected Instructional Differentiation Variables

| Predictor | Individual Differentiation Index | | | | Learner-Peer Content/Activity Difference | | | | | |
|---|---|---|---|---|---|---|---|---|---|---|
| | Regular Class | | Special Self-Contained Class | | Regular Class | | Special Resource Class | | Special Self-Contained Class | |
| | Total $R^2$ | Unique $R^2$ | Total $R^2$ | Unique $R^2$ | Total $R^2$ | Unique $R^2$ | Total $R^2$ | Unique $R^2$ | Total $R^2$ | Unique $R^2$ |
| Full model | 40* | | 79* | | 54* | | 65* | | 66* | |
| Instructional context | 9* | 5* | 11* | 6* | 2 | 0 | 1 | 0 | 2 | 2 |
| Peer instructional activity | 19* | 11* | 16* | 14* | 46* | 27* | 56* | 42* | 43* | 29* |
| Teacher instructional task | 14* | 8* | 20* | 16* | 16* | 4* | 7 | 4 | 14* | 16* |
| Class cognitive discourse | 5 | 3 | 40* | 22* | 12* | 3* | 10 | 2 | 17* | 4 |
| Teacher instructional feedback to peers | 6* | 0 | 17* | 7* | 2 | 1 | 9* | 1 | 2 | 3 |
| Activity/task[a] | | 4 | | 7 | | 8 | | | | |
| Activity/discourse[a] | | | | | | | | 6 | 11 | |
| Activity/feedback[a] | | | | | | | | 6 | | |

Note. N = 262 for regular classes, 132 for special resource classes, and 127 for special self-contained classes

[a] The probability level for the precentage of unique variance explained jointly by two or more sets was not available.

*p <.05.

time teachers used student-directed large-group instruction, the percentage of time the teachers supervised, and the very high cognitive discourse index. The interrelationships between teacher supervising and the various peer activities discussed with regard to the individual differentiation index were responsible for the joint variance accounted for in this measure of instructional differentiation.

In the resource setting, the full model explained 65% of the variance in the learner-peer content/activity difference. Peer instructional activity was the most important predictor for this setting, uniquely explaining almost two-thirds of the predicted variance. Teacher feedback to peers was the only other set with a significant total $R^2$; however, most of the predictive power of this set was shared with peer activity.

In the resource classes, the learner-peer content/activity difference score was positively related to teacher use of teacher- or student-directed individual instruction and student-directed small-group instruction. The learner-peer content/activity difference score was negatively related to teacher use of teacher-directed small-or large-group instruction; student-directed large-group instructions; and the total number of feedback remarks, the positive feedback index, and the information feedback index.

In the special self-contained classes, the full model explained 66% of the variance in learner-peer content/activity difference. Similar to the regular classes, the peer instructional activity set uniquely accounted for almost half of the predictable variance, but teacher task and class cognitive discourse were also signficant sets. The peer activity-cognitive discourse combination jointly accounted for 11% of the variance.

For the special self-contained classes, the learner-peer content/activity difference score was positively related to the percentage of time the teachers used teacher- or student-directed individual instruction and student-directed small-group instruction and the percentage of time the teachers were questioning or directing; and was negatively related to the teachers' use of teacher- or student-directed large-group instruction. The interrelationships existing between teacher-directed small-group instruction and the level of cognitive discourse discussed with regard to individual differentiation were also responsible for the shared variance observed here.

**Discussion**: Individualizing instruction is a critical strategy for EMR learners. Teachers must consider the instructional objectives, the instructional activities, and their context (e.g., the size of the group), and the teacher instructional tasks. The results suggest it is possible to determine the specific instructional contexts and operations employed by teachers to implement instructional strategies.

# Implications of Instructional Conditions for Educational Planning

The portrayal of the class as an information-processing system has been used in this chapter as a framework for addressing three issues pertaining to the education of EMR learners: (a) describing the instructional conditions within the settings in which EMR learners are placed, (b) investigating the instructional context and operations that are associated with the development and maintenance of instructional engagement, and (c) determining the instructional context and operations involved in the implementation of instructional strategies. The first issue was addressed in the descriptive section of the chapter. The second and third issues were addressed in the previous section which examined the relationships among aspects of the instructional conditions model.

The differing aspects of the alternative educational settings available to EMR learners have been described. The regular class settings had greater academic emphasis but less peer verbal participation and individualization than the two special education settings. The most important operational aspect of the class is the type of peer instructional activity. The settings differed in the types of activities which predominate: in regular classes, it was

Table 8-16
Total and Unique Percentage of Variance Explained in Cognitive Emphasis

| Predictor | Instructional Setting | | | |
| --- | --- | --- | --- | --- |
| | Regular Class | | Special Self-Contained Class | |
| | Total R2 | Unique R2 | Total R2 | Unique R2 |
| Full model | 13 | | 34* | |
| Instructional context | | | 11* | 10* |
| Peer instructional activity | | | 5 | 6 |
| Teacher instructional task | | | 5 | 8 |
| Class cognitive discourse | | | 4 | 8 |
| Teacher instructional feedback to peers | | | 4 | 8* |

Note. N = 262 for regular classes and 127 for special self-contained classes.
*p <.05.

large-group instruction; in resource classes, it was teacher-directed small-group instruction; and in self-contained classes, it was mixed.

The instructional conditions model identified two instructional programming subdomains. Instructional engagement was defined as reflecting peer interest and attention and peer verbal participation. Instructional differentiation and cognitive emphasis represented different teacher instructional strategies. Each of these is assumed to be an important instructional consideration when planning educational programs for EMR learners. The implications of the associations among instructional conditions variables in predicting engagement and teacher instructional strategies are considered below.

## Maintaining Instructional Engagement

Engagement represents the degree to which an instructional system can prevent the tendency toward entropy or apathy, disorder, confusion, and chaos. At a minimum, the participants in an engaged system are attentive to the productive task; beyond that they may be actively involved through extended verbal participation.

In all three settings, teachers were attentive to the instructional process and students appeared to be interested in what was happening most of the time. In addition, peer interest and attention were related to the physical quality of the classroom. Although a pleasant, well-supplied classroom may directly influence attention, a competing hypothesis is that communities which finance good classroom facilities also encourage children to behave attentively.

Peer interest and attention were also related to instructional activity. In all three settings, individual instruction, whether teacher or student directed, was negatively related to peer attention. In regular classes, attention was postively related to self-directed instruction in large groups; in the special resource and self-contained classes, attention was positively related to teacher-directed small-group instruction. The finding in the regular classes that attention was positively related to student self-directed large-group instruction but not student self-directed individual instruction suggests that involvement in seatwork per se is not the principal factor in predicting attention. Attention seems to be enhanced when seatwork activities are common to a group rather than individually assigned. It may be that the management of such individualization, including both individually-assigned seatwork and teacher-student tutorial sessions, detracts from the general supervisory function that must occur if attention is to be maintained. In the special education setting, the smaller, more homogeneous classes permit more frequent use of teacher-directed small-group instruction, with a concomitant increase in class attention.

Individual verbal participation differed in the three instructional settings. In the regular classes, individual students had an average opportunity to speak about once every 11 minutes. In the special self-contained classes, each student averaged a verbalization once every 4-5 minutes. A student had an opportunity for verbal exchange once every 2-3 minutes in the resource classes. Although the proportion of time spent in teacher questioning or drilling and the total frequency of teacher cognitive demands did not vary dramatically among the settings, the smaller size of the special classes allowed greater opportunity for each student to participate actively.

In the regular classes, peer verbalization, partly because of its low variance, was not predictable from the context and operations defined in the instructional conditions model. Not surprisingly, in the special resource and self-contained classes verbalization was related to the frequency of cognitive discourse and other factors (use of teacher-directed small-group instruction, teacher questioning, and the frequency of feedback remarks) that are associated with class discussion.

This study assumes (and provides some supportive evidence) that engagement is an important quality of the environment. Individual students should pay attention, interact more frequently, enjoy school, and achieve more in classes where their peers are attentive and participate verbally. The findings in this chapter suggest that while all three settings were similar in the level of teacher and peer attention, the mechanisms for maintaining this attention differed across settings. In the regular classes, peer attention was maintained through the use of whole-class seatwork instruction. In the special education settings, attention was maintained through the use of teacher-directed, verbally interactive small groups. In all three settings, the use of individual instruction (either seatwork or tutorial sessions) operated against maintaining attention. Special education classes with fewer students offered greater opportunities for verbal participation resulting from the more intense student-teacher interaction allowed by smaller class size.

## Implementing Teacher Instructional Strategies

The educational programming of EMR learners focussed particularly on two concerns: instructional differentiation and cognitive emphasis. It is thought that EMR learners function best and learn more in an environment where instruction is geared to individual needs and the academic demands are matched to the current level of functioning. In mainstreaming programs, these two instructional concerns become paramount because mainstreamed EMR learners are quite different from typical nonhandicapped learners in areas of achievement, self-concept, and social acceptability.

## Instructional Differentiation

There are four aspects of instructional differentiation.

- individualization — the extent to which planning and instruction is directed toward individual students.
- diversity — the extent to which there is variety in instructional materials and activities.
- differentiation — the extent to which students are provided different instructional programs.
- mobility — the extent to which teachers move about the class.

The factor analysis of the set of instructional conditions variables provided evidence for considering these aspects as dimensions of individual differentiation strategies. The use of these strategies may be inferred behaviorally by considering the percentage of time a specified learner is provided academic content or an instructional activity different from his peers.

There are clear indications that instructional differentiation was not widely practiced in the regular classes. The regular teachers reported that individualization practices sometimes or usually occurred and that they typically used 4-5 of the seven possible individualizing techniques mentioned. However, observer ratings suggested that most students worked at the same activity most of the time, and students perceived that only about half the statements describing instructional flexibility were appropriate descriptions of their class. Regular class teachers were the central focus of instruction about two-thirds of the time; seldom providing students with instructional content or activity different from their peers and almost never using either student self-directed or teacher-directed individual or small-group instruction. In regular classes, the demand and feedback rates per student were also relatively low, a function of the larger group size. Although instructional materials were generally available, special instructional materials, programmed instruction, and learning centers were used by only about half the teachers.

In the special self-contained classes, instructional differentiation was a more prevalent strategy. These teachers reported that individualizing activities occurred more frequently, and peers and observers perceived greater flexibility and differentiation in these classes. The special self-contained class teachers moved about the room and varied the instructional materials provided each child. On a per student basis, the students in the special self-contained classes were afforded greater opportunities to participate verbally in discussions, were asked more cognitive questions, and received more feedback than the students in the regular classes. Programmed instruction, learning centers, and special instructional materials were used more often in the special self-contained classes as well.

The resource class teachers used instructional differentiation strategies to some extent, although less often than the special self-contained classes. While the resource classes were smaller than the special self-contained classes (an average of 7 compared with 12 students), the students were scheduled for instruction as much as possible with those with similar educational needs. The instructional differentiation was structured; incorporated into the design of the instructional groupings. The resource teachers, for example, were almost never observed with specific learners doing something different from the rest of the class, although about half their instruction was conducted in small groups. Due to the small group size, opportunities for students to participate verbally, respond to teacher cognitive demands, and receive feedback were extensive.

In sum, instructional differentiation was more prevalent in the special resource and self-contained classes than in the regular classes.

## Cognitive Emphasis

The second teacher instructional concern, cognitive emphasis, relates to the academic orientation of the class. It is generally acknowledged that special self-contained classes were instituted in part to provide an instructional situation where social and vocational skills received a more prominent focus and the academic environment was appropriately tailored to the educational abilities of EMR learners. Yet, in recent years, special self-contained classes have been criticized for performing this function too well. It is argued that students in these classes are not demonstrating adequate achievement gains and are too isolated from the intellectual stimulation provided by and for nonhandicapped peers: that these students are being undereducated.

It is clear the regular classes had a stronger academic focus than the special self-contained classes. In regular classes, a larger proportion of time was spent on academic subject instruction; teacher and peer instructional activities and tasks; and teacher explaining, summarizing, reviewing, and testing. A higher level of cognitive processing was demanded, and a larger proportion of feedback remarks contained additional information. The students in the regular classes perceived a greater cognitive emphasis than did the students in the special self-contained classes. Finally, the nonhandicapped students in the regular classes, even though they had certain reading deficiencies, were well above their mainstreamed counterparts in academic status. The resource class by its very design had a heavy academic orientation: Instruction in reading, writing, and arithmetic comprised almost three-fourths of the observed instructional time.

While one-third of the teacher cognitive demands in regular classes were rated as very low in cognitive emphasis, almost half the teacher demands in both special education settings were very low in cognitive emphasis. A higher proportion of regular class teacher demands were rated as moderately high or very high in cognitive emphasis (40%), whereas the teachers in special self-contained and resource room classes made fewer high-level demands (30% and 33%, respectively) (see Table 8-7). Though there was a modest difference in the proportion of higher-level demands between the special education settings and the regular classes, the most distinctive differences were in the larger proportion of low-level cognitive demands in the special education settings.

These cognitive emphasis findings were not found to be associated with any of the teacher instructional behaviors. This may reflect the set of expectations teachers have about the level of cognitive emphasis appropriate to their classroom in light of how they perceive their students' abilities.

Regardless, what is disturbing is the large proportion of low level cognitive demands made by teachers in all the educational settings, including regular classes. In general, there was a greater academic emphasis in the regular classes than in the special education settings. Whether this academic emphasis provided appropriate intellectual stimulation and cognitive challenge for the EMR learners or generated frustration and withdrawal can only be inferred from the findings presented in Chapter 5.

## Conclusion

Consistently, the predictive models accounted for more variance in the level of engagement and instructional differentiation in the special classes than in the regular classes. This suggests that the contextual forces and teacher instructional management techniques used in special education classes have a greater impact on learner engagement and individualizing strategy implementation. The speculation is that smaller class size and greater homogeneity of students permits establishment of a more intense instructional program in the special educational settings than is possible in the regular class where teacher efforts become diffused among large numbers of dissimilar students.[14]

Regardless of the setting, the most important dimension of the classroom environment for predicting both learner engagement and instructional differentiation is peer instructional activity. The principal decisions involved in classroom instructional planning are those related to the size of the group instructed and the mode of instruction, i.e., teacher lecture-discussion versus student self-directed seatwork. While these decisions regarding the peer instructional activity are important in all settings, the use of one or another type of activity may be quite different. What appears to be an effective instructional activity in special classes appears inappropriate for instructional management in regular classes.

Even within the same setting, what may be an effective activity for one instructional objective may not be appropriate for another. For example, examination of the bivariate correlations reveals that the regular class use of teacher-directed and student self-directed individual instruction was positively related to individual differentiation but negatively related to peer interest and attention. Student self-directed large-group instruction, on the other hand, was positively related to peer interest and attention but negatively related to leaner-peer instructional differentiation.

In the special self-contained classes, there was less incompatibility among these instructional objectives and their relationships to peer instructional activity.

- Use of teacher-directed individual instruction was positively related to both verbal participation and instructional differentiation.
- Use of teacher-directed small-group instruction was positively related to the two engagement measures.
- Use of teacher-directed large-group instruction was negatively related to both verbal participation and learner/peer instructional differences.

Only student self-directed individual instruction presents difficulties similar to those found in regular classes since it was positively related to instructional differentiation but negatively related to interest and attention.

In the resource class, use of teacher-directed small-group instruction was positively related both to peer interest and attention and verbal participation while student self-directed individual and small-group instruction was negatively related to both engagement measures.

In general, it appears that teachers, especially regular teachers, may face a dilemma when making instructional management decisions. An inconsistency appears when instructional objectives are juxtaposed against the instructional mechanisms used to operationalize them. The teacher can affect the amount of instructional differentiation and engagement in the classroom by manipulating peer-instructional activity. Yet the use of a particular activity operates differently for different instructional management objectives. An activity that appears to foster one particular objective may actively inhibit another. One might argue that the small class size and unique instructional program available in a special class reduces the scope of this dilemma by creating fewer contradictions between the instructional management objectives and the appropriate peer instructional activity.

## Technical Notes

1. The following empirical procedures were used to verify the structure of the model and to establish the definition of each component in terms of a parsimonious set of specific variables. Over 200 intuitively interpretable variables selected to represent various components of an information-processing system were originally included in the model, in order to provide a rich description of the instructional conditions present in different instructional settings. The original variables included individual items; factor scales; and composites from student and teacher rating scales, questionnaires, and classroom observation instruments. When a variable had more than one score per class (e.g., observation instruments), these scores were aggregated to form a single class score. These variables were classified on logical grounds into the seven major conceptual areas presented in the instructional conditions model — instructional context, instructional engagement, and five instructional operations — teacher strategies, peer activities, teacher tasks, class cognitive discourse, and teacher feedback to peers.

Second, the instructional conditions variables were subjected to an image analysis followed by varimax rotation. The image analysis procedure was conducted at various levels of the model. At the most global level, variables which had been assigned to instructional context and to instructional behavior were factored separately. In additional analyses, variables assigned to instructional engagement were factored separately from those assigned to instructional operations, and finally, variables assigned to each of the instructional operations were factored separately.

Data from regular and special teachers were combined in the data reduction analyses. Data were available on about 1,000 teachers from the observation systems. When nonobservation measures were analyzed, the number of teachers with available data was about 600. The results of reduction analyses produced some clearly interpretable variable clusters that were always present regardless of the level of specificity of the analysis or the level of aggregation. Other variable clusters became more clearly defined as the level of specificity within the model increased. Some variables did not cluster empirically, either with other variables within the conceptual component to which they had been logically assigned or with variables from other conceptual components. In addition, certain variables existed within an ipsative set, limiting the relationship these variables could have among themselves and with other variables. The variables that did not form empirical clusters were dropped if there were other variable clusters available to represent the conceptual component; if no other variable cluster was available, the variables were retained, either as individual items or in combination with other variables on logical grounds. Specific clusters of variables, whether formed empirically or logically, were transformed into indexes by standardizing each variable within the composite and then summing the unit-weighted standardized scores. Other variables were retained in their original form.

Empirical support for the instructional conditions model may be inferred from the fact that many variables tended to cluster with other variables within their assigned conceptual component, and variables that did not cluster within the assigned component also failed to cluster with variables from other components.

2. The publisher reminds the reader that these findings preceded P.L. 94-142 by three years and should be interpreted in that context.

3. The observation procedures used for calculating the percentages of time spent in each content area may have resulted in figures not representative of the manner in which teachers actually apportioned their time. For example, if all of the target students associated with a particular teacher attended that teacher's class only for reading instruction, then that teacher would have been observed to be teaching reading for 100% of the time. Conversely, some teachers may have never been observed teaching a particular subject, because their target learners always attended another class for instruction in that area. The fact that the time estimates in each content area were garnered across several days of observation and several students no doubt mitigates some of the bias. Because of the difficulty of interpreting the measures of academic content and the possibility of extremely skewed distributions, these measures were omitted from the predictive analyses later in this chapter and in Part IV.

4. A third component, feedback — the mechanism that exists within the system for providing self-monitoring information to system participants — is traditionally considered as a principal element of an information-processing system. However, due to the circumscribed nature of the feedback data available, feedback is included in the instructional conditions model as one aspect of instructional operations rather than as a major system component.

5. Because of the low variability in teacher attention to task, it was not used in the predictive analyses of learner competencies described in Part IV nor as a criterion measure for determining instructional operations related to measures of engagement described in the next section of this chapter.

6. Interacting with peers was not included as a category in the peer instructional activity dimension because observers were not able to distinguish whether peer interactions were academic or social in content. Thus the sum of the mean percentages of time for the six categories included will be less than 100%.

7. The factor analysis of the instructional conditions variables revealed that the 16 items related to cognitive discourse (the frequency and proportion of teacher demands and peer responses at each cognitive level) represented four factors — one factor for each cognitive level. Based on the factor analysis, indices of cognitive interaction at each level were constructed from the teacher and peer frequency and proportion scores for that level. These composite measures represent the frequency that cognitive discourse at a particular level was observed and the proportion of discourse at that level. Although not discussed here, these four indices are used in the predictive analyses discussed later in the chapter and in Part IV.

8. Factor analysis of the instructional conditions variables revealed three strong factors, representing the teacher feedback to peers component — one factor for each type of feedback, each containing four scores. The four scores represent both the frequency and proportion of a particular type of feedback and the proportion of high and low cognitive demands followed by that type of feedback. For the predictive analyses in this and subsequent chapters, the three composite feedback indices formed on the basis of the factor structure were used.

9. Teacher strategies were not included in the analyses because resource teachers lacked these measures and it was thought important to keep the analyses parallel.

10. In the resource class, the instructional context set was not significantly related to peer interest and attention but the physical quality variable was.

11. The equation predicting peer verbalization in the regular classes was not significant. The peer verbalization measure had relatively little variance and this lack of variance limited the potential multiple correlations with the variables in the equation. In the resource classes, however, about half the variance in peer verbalization was explained by the five predictor sets. All predictor sets except teacher feedback to peers had significant total $R^2$s. The relatively small and, in certain instances, insignificant unique $R^2$s are due to the fact that peer instructional activity shared in predicting criterion variance with teacher instructional task and class cognitive discourse.

The bivariate correlations reveal that peer verbalization was positively related to the availability of teacher-made materials; the percentage of time spent in teacher-directed instruction in small groups; the percentage of time teachers were introducing, motivating, questioning, or drilling; the index of moderately low cognitive demands; the total number of demands and responses; and the demand rate per student. Peer verbalization was negatively related to the teachers' receiving special instructional services, the percentage of time students spent in self-directed activity regardless of the group size, and the percentage of time the teacher supervised.

In the special self-contained classes, the full model explained 35% of the variance in peer verbalization. Class cognitive discourse and teacher instructional feedback to peers were the only predictor sets with significant total $R^2$s. The low and insignificant unique $R^2$s for these sets resulted from the explained variance that both sets shared with each other and with the other predictor sets. The bivariate correlations indicate that, within the class cognitive discourse set, peer verbalization was related to the very low cognitive discourse index, the demand rate per student, the total number of demands and responses, and the variety of discourse. Within the teacher instructional feedback to peers set, verbalization was positively related to total feedback and the positive feedback index, and negatively related to the negative feedback index.

12. The equation predicting cognitive emphasis was not significant for regular classes, suggesting that in regular classes, student perceptions of cognitive emphasis were not related to the particular instructional operations described in the instructional conditions model (Table 8-16). Peer perceptions of cognitive emphasis did not vary much among the regular classes, leaving little variance to be explained by other instructional conditions sets.

For special self-contained settings the total variance explained by the full model was significant. The instructional context explained a significant proportion of the variance both before and after the effects of the other variables were partialled out. The fact that teacher instructional feedback to peers explained a significant proportion of the variance only after the effects of the other sets had been partialled out suggests that a suppressor effect was operating. However, precise specification of the suppressing variable(s) is extremely difficult whenever multivariate data sets are used. Examination of the bivariate correlations (Table 8-13) reveals only one significant relationship: the negative correlation between cognitive emphasis and the availability of teacher-made materials. Cognitive emphasis was not measured in the resource class.

13. The individual differentiation index was not calculated for resource class settings.

14. Other factors such as differences in the variances of the measures and in the degrees of freedom could also result in this effect.

# Part IV

# INTRODUCTION TO
# PART IV

The Project **PRIME** Taxonomic Model (inside the front cover) considers *learner competence* as a function of *learner background* and the *environment*. The domains represented in this model include two learner domains (*learner background* and *learner competence*) and three environment domains (*classroom composition, socioemotional climate,* and *instructional conditions* in the classroom). Earlier chapters have provided a rationale for the variables in each domain, described each variable, and examined the interrelationships among the variables in each domain. The next two chapters examine the relationship of these domains to learner competence: academic competence in Chapter 9 and social competence in Chapter 10.

The educational questions addressed in each chapter are similar:

- What aspects of learner background and environment are related to learner competence?
- Are the relationships between these areas similar for nonhandicapped, mainstreamed EMR learners in regular and resource classes, and nonmainstreamed EMR learners?

Answers to the first question should suggest aspects of the classroom composition, socioemotional climate, and instructional conditions domains to consider when making educational programming decisions for EMR learners. Answers to the second question should suggest the degree to which EMR learners require a substantially different environment from that required by nonhandicapped learners. If similar aspects of the environment are related to academic and social competence, then mainstreamed EMR learners may be more easily assimilated into the regular class environment.

# Analytic Approach

This introductory section to Part IV outlines the general analysis approach used in these chapters and describes the inherent limitations. The approach used to investigate the relationships between learner background and the environment to learner competence involved a sequence of analytic procedures: commonality analysis (see Chapter 3) followed by multiple and bivariate correlational analysis. The variables used in the analysis were those described in prior chapters.

However, some variables were not included. Four criteria accounted for most of the deletions. Variables were not included if:

- they were not available in both regular and special class settings;
- a large number of learners had missing information on that variable (e.g., IQ);
- if the variable was not available for both EMR and nonhandicapped learners (e.g., certain previous special education background variables); or
- if the variable had a strong correlation with another variable that was retained (e.g., grade level was not included because it was strongly related to learner's age).

There were, however, two exceptions to the first criterion: peer reading deficit and number of handicapped students in the class were retained even though these variables were included only in analyses involving the regular class environment. Since the reading deficit in special self-contained classes was 100% and the number of handicapped students was the same as class size, these two variables were not represented in the special self-contained class analyses.

The analytic approach was the same for each of the learner competency measures. Separate analyses were conducted for each learner competency measure and for each type of learner — nonhandicapped, mainstreamed EMR, and self-contained EMR learners. For nonhandicapped and mainstreamed learners, the regular class environment was used as the primary environment; for the nonmainstreamed EMR learners, the self-contained special class environment was used. Since the mainstreamed EMR learners usually received most of their academic instruction in resource classes, each of the academic competence measures was also analyzed, using information about the resource class environment.

In sum, for each of the six social competence measures, Project PRIME conducted three sequential analyses (18 analyses) using the five domains, subdomains and variables described in the earlier chapters by learner type and setting. For each of the six academic competencies, four sequential analyses (24 analyses) were conducted for these learner types by setting, including the resource classes for the mainstreamed EMR learners.

The sequential analytic procedures comprised four stages. The first two stages involved commonality analysis — Stage 1 using a two-set model and Stage 2 using a four-set model. In the two-set model, a specific learner competency was related to the set of learner background variables and the set of environment variables. The two-set model served two purposes: to determine whether the entire set of learner background and environment variables was significantly related to the specific learner competency and, if so, to determine if the environment domains contributed significantly.

If the two sets of learner background and environment domains taken together did not explain a significant proportion of the variance in the learner competence measure, no further analysis of that competency area was undertaken for that group of learners. If the total equation was significant, then the learner background and environment domain sets were examined separately to determine which domain(s) explained a significant proportion of the variance in the learner competency measure.

In the four-set model (Stage 2), the environment variables were divided into three sets representing the three environment domains: classroom composition, socioemotional climate, and instructional conditions.

The Stage 3 analytic procedure involved calculating the multiple correlations between the variables in each subdomain and the specific learner competence of the domains with a significant relationship to the learner competence variable. These $R^2$s were calculated without considering the other variables in the same or other domains. For this reason there is no way of knowing the extent to which the explanatory power of the subdomains (represented by the subdomain $R^2$) may be confounded with other subdomains or variables.

The subdomains that had a significant total $R^2$ were analyzed further in Stage 4 by examining the bivariate (zero-order) correlations between the variables in the subdomain and the specific learner competency measure. To be consistent with the prior procedures, the bivariate correlations were squared, making them total $r^2$s (with the attendant limitations discussed for subdomain $R^2$s). An $r^2$ of .02 was chosen as a relevant minimum contribution to variance. (The actual cutoff point was a bivariate correlation of .125). In the Part IV tables, variables which have a negative correlation with the competency are noted by a negative sign following their $r^2$.


## Presentation of Results


The results of the sequential commonality and correlational analyses are presented in Chapters 9 and 10. The order and format in which the analytic findings are presented are the same for each learner competency measure. Information is provided first for nonhandicapped learners in regular classes; followed by EMR learners in regular classes, EMR learners in resource classes, when appropriate, and EMR learners in special self-contained classes. The analytic results for all types of learners for each competency measure are summarized in two tables — Table 9-1 presents the commonality analysis results and Table 9-2 presents the results of the multiple and bivariate correlations.

Table 9-1 combines the results of the two-and four-set models. It includes the total $R^2$ of the full model, the total and unique $R^2$ for the learner background domain, the total and unique $R^2$ for the environment domain considered as one set, and the total and unique $R^2$ for each of the environment domains (classroom composition, socioemotional climate, and instructional conditions) considered as separate sets.

The findings from the commonality analyses concentrate on two statistics — the total and unique variance explained by each domain or predictor set. The total $R^2$ for a domain is a measure of the maximum predictive power of the domain — the total variance that the domain has in common with the competency measure, including the variance shared with other domains. The unique $R^2$ for a domain represents the pure predictive power of the domain — the variance that domain has in common with the competency measure uncontaminated with the variance shared with other domains.

The variance that only one domain shares with one or more other domains is not presented in these tables, although it can be calculated by subtracting the unique $R^2$ of the domain from the total $R^2$ of the domain. In the four-set model, the variance of one domain may be shared with any of the other domains singularly and/or in combination. For this reason, shared variance is usually difficult to interpret. In the two-set model, the shared variance represents the extent to which the variance which learner background and the environment have in common is also shared with the particular learner competency measure.

Since the variables used in the two- and four-set models are identical, the total $R^2$ for the full model and the total and unique $R^2$ for learner background are identical for the two- and four-set models and these statistics are presented only once in Table 9-1.

Table 9-2 summarizes the results of the multiple and bivariate correlations between the domains, subdomains, and specific variables and the competency in question. These values are squared multiple or bivariate correlations. For the domains, the squared multiple correlations are the same as the total $R^2$ produced by the commonality analyses. As indicated earlier, subdomain (and variable) $R^2$s were not calculated unless the domain (or subdomain) had a significant total $R^2$.

## Limitations of the Analytic Procedures

The analytic procedures have certain limitations. First, it is evident that a large number of variables were employed in these analyses and that the intercorrelation of so many variables might result in some statistically significant relationships occurring by chance alone. A hierarchical analysis procedure was followed in an attempt to prevent the reporting of chance relationships: The degree of relationships between two variables was not investigated unless the higher order constructs which subsumed them were significantly related. In spite of this precaution, some of the relationships reported probably did occur by chance.

Second, the uneven distribution of variables into domains creates a problem for comparability. The larger the number of variables contributing to a predictive equation, the greater the total $R^2$ likely for that equation. Similarly, in commonality analysis, the more variables included in a predictive set, the more powerful that predictive set will be. Since the set of environment variables is much larger than the set of learner background variables (58 versus 6), the relative predictive power of the two sets cannot be compared. Similar problems occur when comparing the predictive power of the three environment domains. To overcome this limitation, a shrinkage formula (Kerlinger & Pedhazur, 1973; Nunnally, 1967) was applied to the $R^2$s for the total equations and to the total and unique $R^2$s for each domain. The shrunken $R^2$s provide an indication of how comparable the domains are in their predictive power. Although the shrunken $R^2$s were not reported, they were considered when making comparative remarks about the findings.

A third caution results from the fact that not all potentially important learner and environment characteristics were included in the predictive analytic model. Omission of important measures may seriously diminish the potential relationship between the domain in which they belong and the competency measures. In addition, the absence of an important measure from a domain may result in other measures which are highly related to the omitted measure serving as a proxy for it. In such a case, the importance of the variables that are included in the model would be speciously inflated. This could be highly misleading, particularly if the proxy was not from the same domain as the variable it represented. Project PRIME expected the power of learner background to explain variance in academic competence might be subject to these limitations. The potentially limiting factors are discussed in detail in Chapter 9.

A fourth limitation is the noncomparability of the $R^2$s for regular and special class equations. The number of students in the two settings is different, resulting in different degrees of freedom for the regular and self-contained class analyses. Therefore, an equation or a domain cannot be said to have more (or less) explanatory power in one setting than in the other. Equation and domain $R^2$s can, however, be compared between the two groups of learners, nonhandicapped and mainstreamed EMR, who are in regular classes.

A fifth limitation results from the calculation of multiple and bivariate correlations in isolation from other variables in the same or other domains. There is no way to know the extent to which the explanatory power of a subdomain (or variable) as measured by its total $R^2$ may be confounded with other variables. The reason for calculating the subdomain $R^2$s in a simple regression model rather than in a commonality model was the excessive computer cost in calculating the latter. Moreover, the number of sets included in the model can result in an unwieldy number of joint contributions to interpret (Cooley & Lohnes, 1976; Kerlinger & Pedhazur, 1973). Preliminary analysis revealed there was limited confounding across the environment domains and, hence, by subdomains in different domains. However, as discovered in Part III, the subdomains within the same domain are related and certain variables in the environment domains are associated with certain learner background measures.

In addition to the procedural limitations, there are certain other limitations when considering the results in Chapter 9. First, as noted earlier, normative academic status is heavily age and grade dependent, and certain environment features are also age and grade dependent. This makes associations between normative academic status and environment difficult to interpret.

Second, normative academic status is a status measure. Although the particular scores used to compute it were end-of-the-year measures, these measures were highly correlated with the beginning-of-the-year measures. Thus, associations between the classroom environment and the normative academic status may reflect a "placement" or "assortative mating" phenomenon. That is, learners with low normative academic status were systematically placed or located in schools with peers having similar backgrounds. Even assuming an observed relationship is real, rather than an artifact of placement, the causal direction of that relationship is ambiguous. For certain findings, such as those concerning negative feedback, it is almost more meaningful to talk of the low normative academic status of the learner and his peers as causing certain teacher behaviors rather than the reverse.

Third, although normative academic status was based on reading and math competence, the classroom environment measures were obtained across all content areas. Certain important relationships may be obscured by this lack of precision in the definition of environment.

Fourth, the pattern of relationships between normative academic status for nonhandicapped learners and the instructional conditions suggests certain complex academic status/instructional conditions/grade relationships. It appears as if lower-achieving nonhandicapped learners were instructed in classes where there was a high proportion of time spent in reading activities at the expense of science and social studies activities. Higher-achieving learners, in contrast, received more science and social studies and less reading instruction. This is directly evidenced in the bivariate correlations between normative academic status and the proportion of time spent in reading and in science and social studies. It is also reflected indirectly in the correlations between normative academic status and those instructional conditions measures related to reading and/or science and social studies instruction.

These relationships between normative academic status and reading-related instructional conditions are further complicated by the fact that less time is spent in reading in higher grade-level classes with older learners ($r = -0.24$) and more time in science and/or social studies ($r = 0.30$). The relationships between the instructional dimensions of the class and normative academic status may reflect the use of certain instructional techniques in classes with younger students who have lower achievement test scores. The extent to which this complex grade/instruction/academic status confounding affects these findings is unknown.

# 9

# Academic Competence

Although schools have multiple objectives, there can be no question that the development of academic competence is the primary objective of the schooling process. Academic achievement and, to a lesser extent, appropriate academic behavior and positive academic attitudes have served as the primary criteria in almost all educational program evaluations. Most program development efforts have been directed toward improving one or the other of these competencies. The research studies designed to delineate the educational factors that affect these competencies number in the thousands.

This chapter addresses issues of academic competence: the learner's level of accomplishment in meeting specified academic goals established by the school. Academic competence is composed of three facets: academic status (or normative and classroom achievement), appropriate academic behaviors, and attitudes (Figure 9-1). The rationale for these competency measures and a description of the specific constructs that constitute each are presented in Chapter 5.

Three major educational programming questions related to academic competence are explored:

- What are the learner background and classroom environmental factors associated with the academic competence of nonhandicapped and EMR learners in the three educational settings?

307

● Are the environmental factors associated with the academic competence of nonhandicapped learners similar in magnitude and pattern to those of EMR learners? (This data should provide insight into the degree to which EMR learners require an environment that is different from that provided for nonhandicapped learners and whether providing these conditions in the regular classroom impedes the progress of the nonhandicapped learners.)

● Are similar environmental factors associated with the development of the three different competency areas (academic status, behaviors, and attitudes)?

## Academic Status

Academic status has been defined as performance on standardized tests, using other grade-equivalent estimations (normative status) and performance ratings given by teachers and peers (classroom status).

Table 9-1 presents the results of the commonality analyses predicting both academic status measures using the general two-set model (learner background, environment) and the specific four-set model (learner background, classroom composition, socioemotional climate, and instructional conditions). Each model was investigated for each learner/setting designation: nonhandicapped learners in regular classrooms, mainstreamed EMR learners in regular classrooms, mainstreamed EMR learners in resource classrooms, and nonmainstreamed EMR learners in special self-contained classrooms. Table 9-2 provides the total variance explained in each academic status measure by each significant domain, subdomain, and individual variable.[1] (Tables 9-3 through 9-9 provide the results of specific supplementary investigations.)

### Regular Setting—Nonhandicapped Learners

#### Normative Academic Status
The learner background and classroom environment together explained 55% of the variance in the normative academic status of the nonhandicapped learners. Background explained 33% of the variance, of which 23% was shared with environment and 10% was unique. Although the unique variances indicate that the environment was a considerably stronger predictor of normative academic status than learner background, application of a shrinkage formula revealed this to be an artifact created by the larger number of variables in the environment domains. The variance jointly explained by

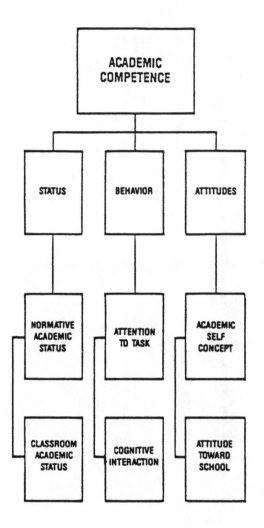

Figure 9-1
Academic Competence
(Project PRIME Taxonomic Model)

## Table 9-1
### Total and Unique Percentage of Variance Explained in Academic Status by Domain

| Predictor | Normative Academic Status | | | | Classroom Academic Status | | |
|---|---|---|---|---|---|---|---|
| | Regular Class | | Special Resource Class | Special Self-Contained Class | Regular Class | | Special Self-Contained Class |
| | Nonhandicapped Learners | Mainstreamed EMR Learners | Mainstreamed EMR Learners | Nonmainstreamed EMR Learners | Nonhandicapped Learners | Mainstreamed EMR Learners | Nonmainstreamed EMR Learners |
| **Full model (M1 or M2)** | | | | | | | |
| Total R2 | 55 | 34 | 36 | 54 | 28 | 31 | 26(ns) |
| **Learner background** | | | | | | | |
| Total R2 | 33 | 13 | 13 | 22 | 12 | 2(ns) | |
| Unique R2 | 10 | 7 | 9 | 6 | 6 | 2(ns) | |
| **Environment** | | | | | | | |
| Total R2 | 45 | 27 | 27 | 48 | 22 | 29 | |
| Unique R2 | 22 | 21 | 23 | 32 | 16(ns) | 29 | |
| **Classroom composition** | | | | | | | |
| Total R2 | 24 | 12 | 11 | 24 | 7(ns) | 15 | |
| Unique R2 | 7 | 9 | 6(ns) | 10 | 3(ns) | 14 | |

| | | | | | | |
|---|---|---|---|---|---|---|
| Socioemotional climate | | | | | | |
| Total R2 | 11 | 3(ns) | 2(ns) | 4(ns) | 5 | 3(ns) |
| UniqueR2 | 3 | 4 | 1(ns) | 2(ns) | 4 | 3(ns) |
| Instructional conditions | | | | | | |
| Total R2 | 25 | 13 | 19 | 32 | 15 | 10(ns) |
| Unique R2 | 9 | 8(ns) | 12 | 16 | 8(ns) | 10 |

Note. Two commonality models were employed. In Model 1 (M1), two sets of variables—one representing learner background and another representing all the environment domains—were used to explain variance in learner competecne. Model 2(M2), a four-set model, used the identical variables as Model 1 but divided the environment variables into three sets, representing the three environment domains—participant composition, socioemotional climate, and instructional conditions.

Table 9-2

Total Percentage of Variance Explained in Academic Status by Domain, Subdomain, and Variable

| Predictor | Normative Academic Status | | | | Classroom Academic Status | | |
|---|---|---|---|---|---|---|---|
| | Regular Class | | Special Resource Class | Special Self-Contained Class | Regular Class | | Special Self Contained Class |
| | Nonhandicapped Learners | Mainstreamed EMR Learners | Mainstreamed EMR Learners | Nonmainstreamed EMR Learners | Nonhandicapped Learners | Mainstreamed EMR Learners | Nonmainstreamed EMR Learners |
| Full model | 55 | 34 | 36 | 54 | 28 | 31 | |
| Learner background | 33 | 13 | 13 | 22 | 12 | | |
| Sex | 3 | | | | 3 | | |
| Age | 15 | | | | 2- | | |
| Ethnic group | 15 | 8 | 8 | 20 | 4 | | |
| Anglo | 15 | | | | 2 | | |
| Black | 5- | | | | 3- | | |
| Spanish-surnamed | 4- | | | | | | |
| Socioeconomic status | 16 | | | 2 | 4 | | |
| Father's education | 17 | | | 2 | 2 | | |
| Family intactness | | | | | | | |
| Environment | 45 | 27 | 27 | 48 | 22 | 29 | |
| Classroom composition | 24 | 12 | 11 | 24 | | 15 | |
| Peer quantity | 2 | | | | | | |
| Number of students in class | 2 | | | | | | |
| Peer reading deficiency | 5- | | | | | | |
| Peer sociodemographic characteristics | 12 | 8 | 6 | 9 | | | |
| Percentage Anglo | 10 | | | | | | |

| Variable | | | | | |
|---|---|---|---|---|---|
| Percentage Spanish-surnamed | 4- | 2- | | 2- | |
| Percentage lower class | 3- | | | 8 | |
| Rural location | | | | | |
| Suburban location | | 4- | 4- | | |
| Urban location | 3- | 4- | 4- | | |
| Peer attitude toward school | 10- | 2 | | | |
| Teacher ability, training, and experience | | | | | |
| Verbal facility | | | | 9- | |
| Hours of special education in-service training | | | | 3- | |
| Years of teaching experience | | | | 4- | |
| Educational status | | | | 2 | 2 |
| Teacher sociodemographic characteristics | | | | | |
| Anglo | | 5- | | 5- | 5- |
| Black | | 4- | | 3- | 4- |
| Teacher attitudes toward mainstreaming | 2 | 4 | | 5 | 4 |
| Attitude toward integration of students with cognitive problems | 2 | 5 | | 4 | 5 |
| Attitude toward integration of students with social problems | | | | 4- | |
| Appropriateness of mainstreaming | 3 | 3 | | | 3 |
| Teacher report of adequacy of special support services | | | 2 | 3 | |

Table 9-2 (continued)

| Predictor | Normative Academic Status | | | | Classroom Academic Status | | |
|---|---|---|---|---|---|---|---|
| | Regular Class | | Special Resource Class | Special Self-Contained Class | Regular Class | | Special Self Contained Class |
| | Nonhandicapped Learners | Mainstreamed EMR Learners | Mainstreamed EMR Learners | Nonmainstreamed EMR Learners | Nonhandicapped Learners | Mainstreamed EMR Learners | Nonmainstreamed EMR Learners |
| Socioemotional climate | 11 | | | | 5 | | |
| Teacher directiveness | | | | | 4 | | |
| Teacher control | | | | | 3 | | |
| Peer cohesiveness | 7 | | | | | | |
| Peer harmony | 6 | | | | | | |
| Peer dislike | 2- | | | | | | |
| Instructional conditions | 25 | 13 | 19 | 32 | 15 | | |
| Instructional context | 4 | | | | | | |
| Teacher-made materials | 3- | | | | | | |
| Instructional engagement | 2 | 2 | 2 | 6 | 4 | | |
| Peer interest and attention | 2 | | | 3 | 3 | | |
| Peer verbalization | | | | 2- | | | |
| Teacher strategies | 4 | 2 | | 7 | 4 | | |
| Individual differentiation | | | | 4- | | | |
| Learner-peer content/activity difference | 4- | | | | | | |
| Peer perception of cognitive emphasis | | | | | | 4- | |
| Peer instructional activity | 10 | 5 | 6 | 4 | | | |

| | | | | |
|---|---|---|---|---|
| Teacher-directed, small group | 8– | 4– | 2– | |
| Teacher-directed, large group | | 2 | 3 | 3– |
| Teacher instructional task | 11 | 4 | 17 | |
| Introducing or motivating | | | 2– | |
| Questioning or drilling | | | 3– | |
| Directing | 2– | 2– | | |
| Supervising | 4– | | | |
| Summarizing or reviewing | 6 | | 3 | |
| Testing | | | 10 | |
| Class cognitive discourse | 9 | 5 | | |
| Very low index | 6– | | | |
| Moderately low index | 2 | | | |
| Very high index | 3 | 3 | | |
| Frequency of discourse | | 5 | | |
| Teacher instructional feedback to peers | 3 | 6 | | 3 |
| Positive index | | 5 | | |
| Negative index | 2– | | | 3– |
| Frequency of feedback | | 5 | | |

Note. All figures are squared correlation coefficients and are statistically significant ($p < .05$). Bivariate correlations were performed with individual predictor variables and multiple correlations were performed with sets of predictor variables. For learner background, statistically significant variables are presented only if the contribution of learner background is significant in the total equation. Similarly, for the environmental domains (participant composition, socio-emotional climate, and instructional conditions), statistically significant subdomains are presented only if the contribution of the domain is significant in the total equation, and significant variables are presented only if the contribution of the subdomain is significant. A minus sign follows the number if the correlation was negative.

background and environment reflects the confounding that exists between certain aspects of learner background and environment.

All the background variables except sex and family intactness were related to normative academic status. Particularly large proportions of variance were accounted for by ethnic group and father's education. Older students, Anglo students, and those students whose fathers had attained a higher level of education had higher normative academic status.

The low amount of variance (3%) accounted for by age was surprising, considering the high correlations between age and grade ($r = 0.79$) and between grade and normative academic status ($r = 0.44$). Additional analyses were conducted using both grade and age and the product of the two to predict normative academic status. This age, grade, and age-by-grade model predicted 28% of the variance in normative academic status. An examination of the mean achievement scores for each age-grade combination revealed a negative relationship between age and normative academic status within each grade level, but a slight positive relationship between age and normative academic status across all grades. This normative within-grade age/normative academic status relationship probably reflects the fact that, within a grade, older students are those who have had to repeat a grade while younger students are those who were permitted to start school early or skip a grade. Across several grades, however, age reflects increased schooling and maturation.

Each of the environment domains predicted a significant proportion of the variance in normative academic status, although classroom composition and instructional conditions were more influential than socioemotional climate even after adjusting for the number of variables in each set.

Among the classroom composition subdomains, peer quantity, peer reading deficiency, peer sociodemographic characteristics, peer attitudes toward school, and teacher attitudes toward mainstreaming were significant. Nonhandicapped learners in classrooms with fewer students behind in reading, with a higher proportion of Anglo students, and with poorer peer attitudes toward school had a higher normative academic status.

In the socioemotional climate domain, only the peer cohesiveness subdomain was significant. Nonhandicapped learners in classrooms with greater harmony had higher normative academic status.

All of the instructional condition subdomains — context, engagement, teacher strategies, peer instructional activity, teacher instructional task, class cognitive discourse, and teacher feedback to peers — predicted a significant proportion of the variance in normative academic status. Nonhandicapped learners had higher academic status in classrooms where there was less use of teacher-made materials, more time when the learner and the other students in the classroom were involved in the same academic content area of instructional activity, less use of teacher-directed small groups, less questioning or directing but more supervising, and a very-high rather than very-low cognitive discourse level.

The shared variance between background and environment may be attributable to confounding relationships existing between learner background and classroom composition ($r = 0.09$) and between learner background and instructional conditions ($r = 0.06$). There were several relationships between learner background and classroom composition. Learners were likely to be in classroom environments in which a large proportion of their peers were of the same ethnic group (correlations between the ethnicity of the learner and the percentage of peers in the classroom who were of the same ethnicity were 0.51 for Anglo learners, 0.42 for Black learners, and 0.60 for Spanish-surnamed learners). Furthermore, Anglo learners were not likely to be in classrooms where there was a high proportion of peers with reading deficiencies ($r = -0.25$) or a high proportion of peers from a lower social class ($r = -0.36$). Learners whose fathers had a high educational status were more likely to be in environments with a high percentage of peers who were Anglo ($r = 0.39$), a low percentage of peers who were Spanish-surnamed ($r = -0.33$), and a low percentage of peers who were from a lower social class ($r = -0.25$). Thus, there appears to be a general learner/peer sociocultural relationship between learner background and classroom composition that is reflected in the high learner background/classroom composition shared variance.

Some of the learner background/instructional conditions shared variance was also the result of a sociocultural phenomenon but the relationships were not as strong. Anglo learners were more likely to be in classrooms where there was greater use of individual differentiation ($r = 0.15$), greater interest and attention ($r = 0.15$), and less very-low ($r = -0.21$) but more very-high ($r = 0.17$) cognitive discourse. Black learners were more likely to be in classrooms of poor physical quality ($r = -0.15$) where there was less interest and attention ($r = -0.19$). Spanish-surnamed learners were more likely to be in classrooms with less individual differentiation ($r = -0.22$), less verbal participation ($r = -0.15$), more very-low cognitive discourse ($r = 0.19$), and more positive feedback ($r = 0.17$).

However, the major learner background/instructional conditions confounding occurs with age. Older learners were in classrooms where there was less time when a specific learner was involved with activities or instruction which differed from those of the other students in the classroom ($r = -0.27$), more cognitive emphasis ($r = 0.19$), less time spent in teacher-directed small groups ($r = -0.30$), and less time spent with the teacher directing ($r = -0.19$).

**Classroom Academic Status**

As expected, the predictive model explained much less of the variance in classroom academic status than it explained in normative academic status. Learner background and environment explained 28% of the variance in the classroom academic status of the nonhandicapped students. Background alone explained 12% of the variance; 6% was shared with environment, and 6% was unique. The environment explained 22% of the variance, 16% uniquely. Although the total portion of variance explained by the environment was significant, the unique portion was not.

All of the variables within the learner background set were significantly related to classroom academic status. Nonhandicapped students were rated higher in academic performance by their teachers and peers if they were female, Anglo rather than Black, and had fathers with high educational status.

Among the classroom environment domains, socioemotional climate and instructional conditions significantly predicted classroom academic status. Teacher directiveness was the only significant predictor in the socioemotional climate subdomain, with learners having higher ratings of academic competence when the teacher was more directive.

Significant instructional condition subdomains were instructional engagement, teacher strategies, and teacher feedback to peers. Nonhandicapped learners were rated higher in classroom academic status in classes with more peer interest and attention, less cognitive emphasis perceived by peers, and less negative feedback to peers.

## Regular Setting — Mainstreamed EMR Learners

**Normative Academic Status**

For the mainstreamed EMR learners, background and regular classroom environment together predicted 34% of the variance in normative academic status. Background alone predicted 13% of the variance even though 6% of that variance was shared with environment, leaving 7% predicted by background uniquely. The regular classroom environment alone predicted 27%, with 21% explained by environment uniquely and 6% shared with background. After the shrinkage formula was applied, learner background and environment appeared about equally predictive.

Among the learner background measures, only age was significant. The age, grade, and age-by-grade model predicted 11% of the variance, much less than was obtained for nonhandicapped learners. Classroom composition and instructional conditions were the only significant classroom environment domains, although the socioemotional climate domain explained a significant unique but not total proportion of the variance. Peer and teacher sociodemographic characteristics, peer attitudes toward school, and teacher attitudes toward mainstreaming were the significant classroom composition subdomains. Mainstreamed EMR learners had higher normative academic status when their regular classroom environment was in a suburban rather than urban location, their teacher was Black rather than Anglo, and their teacher believed mainstreaming to be appropriate.

Among the instructional conditions subdomains, teacher strategies, instructional tasks, and peer instructional activities were significant. Mainstreamed EMR learners had higher normative academic status in classes where there was a lower proportion of time spent in teacher-directed small groups and a higher proportion of time spent in teacher-directed large groups.

The proportion of variance accounted for jointly by background and environment is attributable to a confounding of learner background with classroom composition and instructional conditions.

The joint variance in normative academic status is best explained by examining the correlations between age (the only significant background variable) and the classroom composition and instructional condition variables related to normative academic status.

Older mainstreamed EMR learners were more likely to be in classrooms with a higher proportion of peers who were behind in reading ($r = 0.15$); were Spanish-surnamed ($r = 0.29$) rather than Anglo ($r = -0.21$) or Black ($r = -0.18$); where peer attitudes toward school were lower ($r = -0.17$); and the teacher was Spanish-surnamed ($r = 0.22$) or came from a low-SES family ($r = -0.19$).

The instructional conditions were also confounded with age, with older learners in classrooms where there was less verbalization ($r = -0.17$), less differentiation in content or activity ($r = -0.17$), less use of teacher-directed small groups ($r = -0.15$) but more summarizing ($r = 0.18$), less moderately-high cognitive discourse ($r = -0.15$), and less positive feedback ($r = -0.16$). These relationships between the age of the mainstreamed learner and aspects of the regular classroom environment account for the moderate proportion of variance in normative academic status shared by learner background and environment.

## Classroom Academic Status

Together, learner background and classroom environment explained almost as much of the variance in classroom academic status as they did in normative academic status ($R^2 = 0.31$) for the mainstreamed EMR learners. Background alone was not a significant predictor. Among the environment domains, classroom composition was the only significant predictor. Peer attitude toward school and teacher sociodemographic characteristics and attitudes toward mainstreaming were the significant subdomains. EMR learners were rated more positively in academic performance by their regular classroom teachers and peers when the teacher was Black rather than Anglo and had positive attitudes toward mainstreaming.

## Resource Setting — Mainstreamed EMR Learners

### Normative Academic Status

Learner background and the resource classroom environment explained 36% of the variance in normative academic status. Learner background explained 13% of the variance (as it did in the regular classroom model) but only 4% was shared with environment, leaving 9% unique. The resource classroom environment explained 27% of the variance, the same proportion that was explained by the regular classroom environment even though the resource classroom environment model contained considerably fewer variables. Of the total variance accounted for by the environment, 4% was shared with background and 23% was unique.

Classroom composition and instructional conditions were the significant environment domains. Within the classroom composition domain, the peer sociodemographic characteristics and teacher feelings about support services were significant subdomains. Learners had higher normative academic status in suburban rather than urban areas and in classrooms where teachers felt they received effective support services.

Within the instructional condition domain, engagement, peer instructional activity, cognitive discourse, and feedback were the subdomains with significant total $R^2$s. Mainstreamed EMR learners had higher normative academic status in resource classrooms where there was a greater frequency of cognitive discourse, particularly at a very high level, a greater frequency of feedback, particularly positive feedback, and greater use of teacher-directed large-group rather than small-group instruction.

### Classroom Academic Status

The classroom academic status of the mainstreamed EMR learners was not available for the resource settings.

## Regular and Resource Setting — Mainstreamed EMR Learners

### Normative Academic Status

The full educational program of a mainstreamed student consists of experiences in both the regular and resource classroom settings. One explanation of the comparatively low proportion of variance explained by the two predictive models in the normative academic status of the mainstreamed EMR learners was that neither the regular nor the resource classroom represented a complete view of the learner's instructional experiences and, therefore, neither alone could predict the full amount of explainable variance.

Support for this explanation required developing a predictive model consisting of both the regular and resource classroom environments. In order to include both environments experienced by the mainstreamed learner in the same equation, it was necessary to reduce the total number of predictor variables to a number that would permit statistical manipulation. A reduced number of environmental variables was selected for this combined model by eliminating all variables that had bivariate correlations of less than 0.05 with normative academic status in both the regular and resource environments. The reduced model consisted of 6 learner-background, 41 regular-classroom environment, and 28 resource-classroom environmental variables.[2]

Table 9–3
Total and Unique Percentage of Variance in Normative Academic Status Explained by Learner Background and by the Restricted Definition of the Regular and Resource Environments for the Mainstreamed EMR Learners

| Predictor | Total $R^2$ | Unique $R^2$ |
|---|---|---|
| Full model | 41 | |
| Learner background | 13 | 4 |
| Environment (regular and resource) | 37 | 28 |
| Learner background/environment (joint) | | 9 |
| Regular environment | 23 | 10 |
| Resource environment | 21 | 11 |
| Regular/resource environment (joint) | | 7 |
| Learner background/regular environment (joint) | | 6 |
| Learner background resource environment (joint) | | 3 |

Note. $N = 356$

The three-set predictor model including learner background and the restricted regular and resource classroom environments (the reduced set of measures) explained 41% of the variance in normative academic status (Table 9-3). Learner background explained 13% of the variance, of which 9% was shared with environment and 4% was unique. The regular and resource classroom environments together predicted 37% of the variance, 28% uniquely. The combined regular and resource classroom environments explained more variance both totally and uniquely than did either environment alone. The contribution of the two environments was split about evenly, with the regular and resource settings each explaining about 10% of the variance uniquely and 7% jointly.

In sum, consideration of the full instructional program did improve the prediction of normative academic status for the mainstreamed EMR learners. Furthermore, the resource classroom appears to have an independent effect on normative academic status about equal to the effect of the regular classroom.

## Self-Contained Setting — Nonmainstreamed EMR Learners

### Normative Academic Status

Learner background and classroom environment together accounted for 54% of the variance in the normative academic status of the nonmainstreamed EMR learners. Background alone accounted for 22% of the variance, of which 16% was shared with environment and 6% was unique. Environment alone accounted for 48% of the variance; 16% shared and 32% unique. The environment remained a more important predictor of normative academic status for the nonmainstreamed EMR learners, even after correction for shrinkage. The environment/background confounding occurred within the classroom composition and instructional condition domains.

Within the learner background domain, only learner age and father's education level were significant. Older nonmainstreamed EMR learners and learners whose fathers had a higher level of education had higher normative academic status. Within the environment, classroom composition and instructional conditions were significantly related to normative academic status.

Within the classroom composition domain, the significant subdomains were peer and teacher sociodemographic characteristics: teacher ability, training, and experience; teacher attitudes toward mainstreaming; and teacher feelings about special support services. The nonmainstreamed EMR learners had higher normative academic status in classrooms in rural areas or with teachers who were Black, had lower verbal facility, believed that students with social problems should not be mainstreamed, or felt students received adequate special education support.

Instructional engagement, teacher strategies, peer instructional activity, and teacher instructional task were the instructional condition subdomains related to normative academic status. The nonmainstreamed EMR learners had higher normative academic status when there was greater peer interest and attention and less verbal participation; less individual differentiation; less teacher-directed large-group instruction; and more teacher summarizing, reviewing, and testing, rather than introducing and questioning.

The variance in normative academic status that was jointly accounted for by learner background and environment could be explained by examining the correlations between learner age and father's education and those variables within the classroom composition and instructional condition domains that were related to normative academic status. Older learners were more likely to be in classrooms in which the teacher was Black ($r = 0.27$), had taught for several years ($r = 0.16$), or had lower verbal facility ($r = -0.30$). In addition to the learner age/teacher type confounding, there was also a sociocultural confounding — learners whose fathers had a low level of education were found in classrooms with a high percentage of Spanish-surnamed peers ($r = -0.23$). With regard to the confounding of learner background and instructional conditions, older learners were in classrooms with less verbal participation ($r = -0.30$), proportionately less time spent in teacher-directed large-group instruction ($r = -0.11$), less teacher questioning ($r = -0.17$), and more testing ($r = 0.30$). Learners with fathers having higher levels of education were in classrooms where the students spent less time in teacher-directed small groups ($r = -0.21$) and the teachers spent less time introducing ($r = -0.14$).

**Classroom Academic Status**
The full model predicting classroom academic status was not significant, suggesting that the particular learner background and environmental variables selected for the model do not have a strong relationship with this academic status measure for the nonmainstreamed EMR learners.

# All Settings and Learners — Supplemental Analysis

Previous research provided the basis for examining specific hypotheses beyond the prediction of normative academic status presented above. These supplemental analyses are discussed below.

First, based on findings from previous work by Soar (1977), three socioemotional climate measures — teacher warmth, peer freedom, and teacher directiveness — were investigated for curvilinear effects. No significant curvilinear effects were obtained for any setting/learner combination.

Second, interactive effects between teacher warmth and directiveness and normative academic status were investigated. Classes were split at the median into high and low teacher warmth and high and low peer freedom. Two-way analyses of variance were computed predicting normative academic status using high and low teacher warmth and high and low peer freedom as predictor groups. No significant main effects or interactions were obtained for any setting/learner combination.

Third, the coercive/legitimate measure of teacher influence was separated to assess the effects of coercive and legitimate influence independently. One of the two legitimate influence variables (teacher gives constant reminders to finish or do correct work) was associated with normative academic status ($R^2 = 0.02$) for the nonmainstreamed EMR learners. All other correlations between the component variables of coercive-legitimate influence and normative academic status for other learners were small and insignificant.

Fourth, an important instructional context measure, opportunity to learn, was not included in the predictive model due to measurement problems (see Chapter 8), but it has been established as an important predictor of achievement in other research (Rosenshine & Furst, 1971; Stallings & Kaskowitz, 1974). The instructional conditions variables that come closest to measuring opportunity to learn were the percentages of time the teachers spent in each academic content area. Correlations between these measures and normative academic status are provided in Table 9-4.

The findings for the nonhandicapped and the mainstreamed EMR learners in regular classrooms suggest that regular teachers spend proportionately more time teaching social studies and science rather than the tool subjects. This finding is further supported by the high correlations between peer ethnic composition and academic content. Regular teachers with a high proportion of Anglo students spent more time teaching science and social studies ($r = 0.23$) and less time teaching spelling and language arts ($r = -0.21$). Teachers with a high proportion of Spanish-surnamed students spent more time teaching reading ($r = 0.19$) and language arts and spelling ($r = 0.20$) but less time teaching science and social studies ($r = -0.14$). These findings suggest that teachers may make decisions about the amount of time to spend in different instructional areas based in part on student capabilities and needs.

In the special self-contained classrooms, the amount of time spent in instruction had a positive effect, particularly when considered cumulatively: 15% of the variance in normative academic status could be attributed to the percentage of time spent in academic instruction. Interestingly, instructional time was negatively related to the percentage of Anglo students in the classroom ($r = -0.19$) and positively related to the teacher being Black ($r = 0.16$) or located in a rural area ($r = 0.22$).

Finally, previous research has suggested that the environment may have a different impact on learners from different SES levels. To investigate this

Table 9-4

Bivariate Correlations Between Learner Normative Academic Status
and the Percentage of Time the Learner's Teacher
Was Observed in Each Academic Content Area

| Content area | Correlations with Normative Academic Status | | |
| --- | --- | --- | --- |
| | Nonhandicapped Learners | Mainstreamed EMR Learners[a] | Nonmainstreamed EMR Learners |
| Reading | -20 | -10 | 09 |
| Language arts, spelling | -01 | 01 | 12 |
| Mathematics | -12 | 00 | 18 |
| Science, social studies | 30 | 10 | 07 |
| Total academic instruction | 00 | 09 | 39 |

Note. The percentage of time spent in each content area is based on all teacher observations; it is not limited to the observation period with the specified learner. Decimal points have been omitted.

a refers to regular class teachers only.

## Table 9-5
### Total and Unique Percentage of Variance Explained in Normative Academic Status by Domain for High- and Low-SES Learners

| Predictor | Regular Class | | | | Special Self-Contained Class | |
|---|---|---|---|---|---|---|
| | Nonhandicapped Learners | | Mainstreamed EMR Learners | | Nonmainstreamed EMR Learners | |
| | High SES (n=212) | Low SES (n=136) | High SES (n=121) | Low SES (n=227) | High SES (n=115) | Low SES (n=152) |
| **Full model** | | | | | | |
| Total R2 | 52 | 74 | 67 | 38 | 69 | 70 |
| **Learner background** | | | | | | |
| Total R2 | 34 | 21 | 21 | 10 | 25 | 20 |
| Unique R2 | 7 | 9 | 10 | 2(ns) | 3(ns) | 4(ns) |
| **Environment** | | | | | | |
| Total R2 | 45 | 66 | 57 | 36 | 66 | 66 |
| Unique R2 | 19 | 54 | 45 | 28 | 44 | 50 |
| **Classroom composition** | | | | | | |
| Total R2 | 26 | 33 | 19(ns) | 17 | 34 | 33 |
| Unique R2 | 9(ns) | 18 | 14(ns) | 17 | 15(ns) | 9(ns) |

| | | | | | | |
|---|---|---|---|---|---|---|
| Socioemotional climate | | | | | | |
| Total R2 | 4(ns) | 22 | 7(ns) | 4(ns) | 9(ns) | 9 |
| UniqueR2 | 2(ns) | 3(ns) | 6(ns) | 4(ns) | 1(ns) | 3(ns) |
| Instructional conditions | | | | | | |
| Total R2 | 21 | 36 | 32 | 12(ns) | 42 | 48 |
| Unique R2 | 9 | 17 | 21(ns) | 10(ns) | 22(ns) | 23 |

Note. Two commanality models were employed. In Model 1 (M1), two sets of variables—one representing learner background and another representing all the environment domains—were used to explain variance in learner competecne. Model 2(M2), a four-set model, used the identical variables as Model 1 but divided the environment variables into three sets, representing the three environment domains—participant composition, socioemotional climate, and instructional conditions.

prediction, when each subgroup was considered separately, the learners were split into those whose fathers had completed high school and those whose fathers had not (Table 9-5). For nonhandicapped learners, there were clear differences between those from low- and high-SES backgrounds. The environment was more important, and learner background less important, in predicting normative academic status for low-SES than for high-SES nonhandicapped learners. Within the environment domain, the patterns of squared bivariate correlations were different. Peer ethnicity was an important predictor for high-SES learners while teacher instructional practices (use of student-directed individual or large-group instruction rather than teacher-directed small-group instruction, teacher supervising rather than questioning or directing) were important for low-SES learners.

There appeared to be very little difference for the high- and low-SES nonmainstreamed EMR learners; the results for both groups resembled those obtained for the low-SES nonhandicapped learners.

The models for the low- and high-SES mainstreamed EMR learners were clearly different, however. The total and unique contributions of environment were higher for the high-SES than for the low-SES learners, and the unique contributions of background was significant for the high-SES learners but not the low-SES learners. The model for the high-SES mainstreamed EMR learners resembled that of the low-SES nonhandicapped learners.

## Discussion

There are several striking findings related to the prediction of academic status. First, it is clear there are real differences in the two measures of academic status. The Project PRIME predictive model accounts for more variance in normative academic status than in classroom academic status, and the pattern of variables that predict each academic status measure is different. Normative academic status is predicted by learner background and classroom environmental factors that could be said to influence academic learning. Classroom academic status is predicted by factors that influence academic recognition or peer tolerance. For this reason, the following discussion considers each competency separately.

### Normative Academic Status
The results obtained for normative academic status support earlier findings by Mayeske et al. (1973a) and Stallings and Kaskowitz (1974) that the school environment, when carefully defined, makes a significant and important contribution to the prediction of academic achievement. Part of that

contribution is shared with learner background but there remains a sizeable portion that may be attributed to the classroom environment uniquely.

The models predicting normative academic status were differentially powerful for the three learner groups. The original model explained about the same proportion of variance for the nonhandicapped (55%) and the nonmainstreamed EMR learners (54%), but the model for the mainstreamed EMR learners incorporating the regular and resource classroom environments explained only 41% of the variance. The comparative analyses using high- and low-SES mainstreamed EMR learners suggested poorer predictive power for the low-SES than the high-SES learners. It appears as if the integrated regular and resource class educational program has greater impact for achievement for high-SES EMR learners than it has for low-SES EMR learners, while the segregated self-contained program has an equal impact on both high- and low-SES EMR learners.

Learner background was a more important predictor of normative academic status for the nonhandicapped learners than for the EMR learners. Age, grade, ethnic group, and father's education level each made important contributions to the prediction of normative academic status for the nonhandicapped learners; only age was important for the EMR learners. In addition, learner background was differentially effective in predicting normative academic status for nonhandicapped learners of different SES levels, with background measures more important for high- than for low-SES learners.

The environment domains were more important predictors of normative academic status for nonmainstreamed EMR learners than for either the mainstreamed EMR or the high-SES nonhandicapped learners, even after the application of the shrinkage formula. In addition, these environment domains were even more important predictors for low-SES than high-SES nonhandicapped learners.

This differential effect of classroom environment for low-SES mainstreamed and nonmainstreamed EMR learners suggests that the conceptualization of the regular and resource classrooms as additive elements in the instruction of EMR learners, in practice, operates differentially by SES. The child from a higher-SES home has more assets to bring to the school setting. The combination of regular and resource classrooms for these children seems to work as expected—that is, the resource room is a strengthening supplemental treatment. For the child from a low-SES home who has experienced considerable difficulty learning in school, the pull-out program to the resource room appears to diminish the overall educational impact of his classroom rather than enhance his normative academic status. The implications of this finding for school administrators is that greater effort needs to be made when integrating EMR learners into regular classrooms.

The regular and special educational elements must be better coordinated into a coherent educational program having integrity and focus for the EMR learner, whose background makes him a greater educational risk.

The variance shared by learner background and environment is complex. For all learner groups, learner background was confounded with classroom composition and instructional conditions. For nonhandicapped learners, the learner background/classroom composition shared variance represented the sociocultural similarity between individual students and their school peers discussed by Mayeske et al. (1973a). The learner background/instructional conditions shared variance represented, in part, different instructional patterns used in classrooms differing in sociocultural composition and, in part, different instructional patterns used with different ages. The background/environment shared variance for the mainstreamed and the nonmainstreamed EMR learners was predominantly age related, with older learners in classrooms characterized by certain classroom composition and instructional features.

Because the normative academic status measure was created to be age dependent (i.e., the older a student, the greater his achievement score), the confounding of environment with learner age in the prediction of normative academic status is particularly troublesome. It is unclear whether the bivariate variances between the environmental variables and normative academic status are due to the age or achievement component of the normative academic status measure.

Of the three environment domains, it is obvious that the socioemotional climate made only a minor and, in most cases, insignificant contribution to the prediction of normative academic status. Even among the nonhandicapped learners, most of the variance accounted for by the socioemotional climate was shared with other domains, probably reflecting the overlap between the classroom sociocultural composition and peer harmony.

Within the classroom composition domain, the peer sociodemographic characteristics subdomain was an important predictor of normative academic status for each learner group. For the nonhandicapped learners, the ethnic composition of the peer group was the important variable in the subdomain; while for EMR learners, the urban or rural location of the school was an important variable. The teacher demographic characteristics and attitudes toward mainstreaming subdomains were important predictors for both the mainstreamed and nonmainstreamed EMR learners. The teacher ability, training, and experience subdomain was important for the nonmainstreamed EMR learners. Thus, within the classroom composition domain, peer composition measures appear to be more important for nonhandicapped learners, and teacher measures appear to be more important for EMR learners.

Within the instructional conditions domain, instructional engagement, particularly peer interest and attention, was associated with greater normative academic status for the nonhandicapped and nonmainstreamed EMR learners. Teacher strategies and tasks and peer instructional activities were associated with greater normative academic status for all three learners groups, but the specific strategies, activities, and tasks that were related to normative academic status and the direction of the relationship were different for different groups.

These findings provide two sources of evidence for a differential sensitivity hypothesis for EMR learners (Smith, 1972). First, the overall relative importance of background and environment indicate the environment was a stronger predictor of normative academic status for the nonmainstreamed EMR learners than for the nonhandicapped learners. Second, within the classroom composition domain, teacher characteristics and attitudes were more important and peer characteristics less important predictors of normative status for the EMR learners than for the nonhandicapped learners.

One might speculate that the important elements of the educational program for normative academic achievement for EMR learners is the training of the teacher and the teacher's instructional operations rather than the characteristics or social structure of the peer group. This suggests that EMR learners must be taught to learn — that their learning is not incidental, but must be carefully planned, supported, and reinforced by the teacher.

The next few paragraphs summarize Project PRIME's findings for individual variables as they pertain to expectations based on previous research concerning the relationship of various environmental characteristics to normative academic status.

As expected, for the classroom composition measures, normative academic status was related to peer demographic characteristics and this relationship was stronger for nonhandicapped than for EMR learners. Teacher sociodemographic characteristics were important for the EMR learners but not the nonhandicapped learners. Interestingly, both the mainstreamed and the nonmainstreamed EMR learners had higher normative academic status in classrooms with Black teachers, and the nonmainstreamed EMR learners had higher normative academic status with more experienced teachers who had more professional (not in-service) training.

It was surprising to note that peer attitudes toward school were negatively related to nonhandicapped learners' normative academic status, possibly because Anglo peers have more negative attitudes toward school.

Learners in regular classrooms (both nonhandicapped and EMR) had higher normative academic status when their regular teachers had positive attitudes toward mainstreaming while learners in special self-contained classrooms had higher normative academic status when their special teachers had negative attitudes toward the mainstreaming of students with social problems. These findings suggest that regular teachers' positive attitudes toward mainstreaming may reflect their acceptance of handicapped students and higher expectations for their academic success. For special education teachers, negative attitudes toward mainstreaming may reflect these teachers' commitment to these students' needs for structured learning.

Special education support services were related to normative academic status in special but not regular classrooms. It is possible the lack of variance in this measure for regular classrooms contributed to the lack of a relationship. It is also possible that special services are less critical when resources from the regular program are available.

Teacher educational attitudes were not directly related to normative academic status for any group, although teacher attitudes were related to certain behaviors (i.e., use of small-group instruction) that were related to normative status.

It was disconcerting to find no evidence of the effect of teacher warmth, directiveness, positive influence, or criticism on normative academic status for any learner group. This lack of relationship persisted even when curvilinearity and interaction effects were examined, and when the learner groups were split into high- and low-SES levels. This outcome may be attributable to the lack of variance in these measures, particularly those obtained from direct observation.

Peer cohesiveness, particularly harmony, was an important predictor of normative academic status for the nonhandicapped learners, suggesting that well-managed, harmonious classrooms, which happened to be predominantly middle-class and Anglo, are associated with the academic achievement level of nonhandicapped students. Harmony was also related to normative academic status for the mainstreamed EMR learners. The implication of this finding is consistent with Evertsen's description of the two primary tasks of the teacher: deciding what to teach and developing a harmonious environment where the students cooperate with the teacher as well as among themselves in learning. The teacher's skill in establishing a harmonious socioemotional climate enhances the mainstreamed EMR learners' normative academic status.

Within the instructional conditions domain, predictions regarding the instructional context were partially confirmed. Classroom environments that included extensive teacher-made materials were associated with poor normative academic status for nonhandicapped learners, particularly for the low-SES nonhandicapped learners ($R^2 = 0.06$ for the low-SES nonhandicapped learners), perhaps because lower-SES nonhandicapped learners require well-designed, structured materials to stimulate their interests and meet their instructional needs. Teacher-made materials may not be adequate substitutes for carefully prepared instructional materials.

Instructional engagement, particularly peer interest and attention, was related to the nonhandicapped and the nonmainstreamed EMR learners' academic status. Although peer interest and attention did not affect the mainstreamed EMR learner's normative academic status, his own attentive behavior did (see Chapter 5). Verbalizaton was not related to normative academic status except for the low negative relationship obtained for the nonmainstreamed EMR learners. The content of class discussions observed in this study, involving predominantly low-ability students, may not have been cognitively stimulating or relevant enough to affect normative academic status.

Teacher instructional differentiation strategies were related to normative academic status. This relationship was negative and was more pronounced for the low-SES than for the high-SES nonhandicapped and nonmainstreamed EMR learners. It may be that these learners need a more structured, individualized program or the academic stimulation and learning opportunities provided by teacher-directed large-group instruction.

With regard to the teacher and the peer instructional tasks and activities, teacher-directed small-group instruction was negatively related to normative academic status for the nonhandicapped and mainstreamed EMR learners while teacher-directed large-group instruction was positively related to the mainstreamed EMR learners' academic status. The positive relationship found for lecture/discussion activities for mainstreamed EMR learners may be due to the increased structure and/or intellectual stimulation available to EMR students as part of a large-group teacher-directed activity in comparison to working without active teacher direction.

A negative relationship was found between teacher questioning/drilling and normative academic status. This finding is in agreement with prior research. Although student-directed large-group instruction (seatwork) was unrelated to normative academic status, teacher supervising, which normally occurs during seatwork activities, was positively related to normative academic status for the nonhandicapped learners, particularly the low-SES nonhandicapped learners ($R^2 = 0.11$). Thus, there is indirect evidence of a relationship between teacher-supervised seatwork activities and normative academic status for the low-SES nonhandicapped learners. This evidence supports previous research. These indirect findings suggest that seatwork per se is not effective but seatwork accompanied by the behavior control, structure, and feedback provided through teacher supervision is effective.

The educational implications of these findings, taken together, indicate the importance of (1) teacher-directed instructions, (2) carefully sequenced instruction and materials, and (3) placing the EMR learner in a classroom or grouping where he can be integrated in the instructional process with other students with similar needs rather than being accommodated in a separate, isolated, and unsupervised activity. Thus, to improve the normative academic status of EMR learners, the challenge to the teacher is to design educational lessons in a manner which permits appropriate grouping within the classroom such that either teacher- or peer-supervised cooperative learning activities can occur. This not only requires skilled and experienced teachers but increased consideration by those responsible for placement and scheduling decisions to assure that the EMR learner can be appropriately assimilated into the instructional grouping within a classroom.

In sum, classroom environment does have a critical role to play in predicting normative academic status.

## Classroom Academic Status

Classroom academic status reflects teacher and peer perceptions of learner academic performance. As expected, the nonhandicapped learner's background was an important determinant of his rating. Younger, female, Anglo, high-SES learners received higher ratings by their teachers and peers than did other learners. Although the socioemotional climate and instructional conditions appear to have affected the ratings given to typical nonhandicapped learners by teachers and peers, it is difficult to interpret these findings.

The classroom academic status of the mainstreamed EMR learners is an important dimension of their competence: It reflects how well these learners have been accepted into the academic program of the regular classroom. It is extremely interesting to note that the background of the mainstreamed EMR learner appears to have had little influence on his academic ratings. The classroom environment, however, was very important. Mainstreamed learners received higher classroom academic status ratings from Black than Anglo teachers, and from teachers who believed that mainstreaming was appropriate rather than those who believed it was not.

It is interesting to note that both mainstreamed and nonmainstreamed EMR learners who had Black teachers scored higher on normative academic status measures, and that mainstreamed EMR learners with Black teachers scored higher on classroom academic status measures as well. It would appear that certain values and instructional beliefs demonstrated by Black teachers in this study are effective in generating academic competence in EMR learners. Exactly what these attitudes and practices are is unclear. There were too few Black regular classroom teachers in the study to establish meaningful relationships between teacher ethnic group and the other environmental dimensions. Among the special self-contained classroom teachers, however, Black teachers had a stronger belief in traditional authority ($r = 0.28$), were more directive ($r = 0.49$), were not as warm ($r = -0.15$), used more coercive-legitimate influence ($r = 0.18$), conducted class with less verbalization

($r = 0.18$), used less individual differentiation ($r = -0.26$), did more testing ($r = 0.35$), and used more student self-directed individual activities ($r = 0.20$). These relationships suggest a class in which there is high control, less flexibility, and a strong work orientation.

Taken together, these findings suggest the environment is important. However, examining specific aspects of the environment adds only limited additional clarity. For the nonhandicapped learners, the findings are relatively ambiguous, being tied up with age and sociocultural confounding, and are not completely consistent with previous research. For the mainstreamed EMR learners, it appears as if the diffusion of instruction between the regular and resource classrooms might reduce the impact of the total educational program, although the resource class program makes an important unique contribution.

For both the mainstreamed and the nonmainstreamed EMR learners, teacher background, training, experience, and attitude toward mainstreaming were important. The socioemotional climate did not make a significant contribution. Although the instructional conditions were important, the specific instructional operations that were effective depended on the setting, making specific recommendations difficult.

As discussed above, there is evidence that EMR learners, whether mainstreamed or not, were more strongly influenced by their environment, particularly their teachers and the instructional practices employed, than were nonhandicapped students. The findings for predicting classroom academic status provide further support for the interpretations and implications presented for normative academic status.

## Academic Behavior

Academic behavior consists of students' overt responses to the ongoing academic opportunities present in the classroom. The two aspects comprising academic behavior — attention to task and cognitive interaction — will be discussed separately. Learner background and the three classroom environment domains are expected to be significantly related to attention to task and cognitive interaction with the teacher.

The results of the commonality analyses predicting academic behavior for the nonhandicapped and EMR learners in regular, resource, and self-contained classrooms are presented in Table 9-6. Findings for individual subdomains and variables are presented in Table 9-7. Each setting and type of learner is discussed separately.

Table 9-6

Total and Unique Percentage of Variance Explained
in Academic Behavior Domain

| Predictor | Attention to Task | | | | Cognitive Interaction | | | |
|---|---|---|---|---|---|---|---|---|
| | Regular Class | | Special Resource Class | Special Self-Contained Class | Regular Class | | Special Resource Class | Special Self-Contained Class |
| | Nonhandicapped Learners | Mainstreamed EMR Learners | Mainstreamed EMR Learners | Nonmainstreamed EMR Learners | Nonhandicapped Learners | Mainstreamed EMR Learners | Mainstreamed EMR Learners | Nonmainstreamed EMR Learners |
| Full model (M1 or M2) | | | | | | | | |
| Total $R^2$ | 34 | 22(ns) | 35 | 46 | 36 | 37 | 36 | 53 |
| Learner background | | | | | | | | |
| Total $R^2$ | 2(ns) | | 4 | 2(ns) | 4 | 3(ns) | 2(ns) | 1(ns) |
| Unique $R^2$ | 1(ns) | | 3 | 1(ns) | 3 | 2(ns) | 1(ns) | 3 |
| Environment | | | | | | | | |
| Total $R^2$ | 33 | | 32 | 45 | 33 | 35 | 35 | 50 |
| Unique $R^2$ | 32 | | 31 | 44 | 32 | 34 | 34 | 52 |
| Classroom composition | | | | | | | | |
| Total $R^2$ | 19 | | 7(ns) | 17 | 6(ns) | 15 | 9 | 18 |
| Unique $R^2$ | 14 | | 9 | 16 | 5(ns) | 13 | 7 | 8 |

| | | | | | | | |
|---|---|---|---|---|---|---|---|
| Socioemotional climate | | | | | | | |
| Total R2 | 7 | 13 | 11 | 3(ns) | 1(ns) | 4 | 9 |
| UniqueR2 | 3(ns) | 6 | 6 | 4 | 2(ns) | 1(ns) | 1 |
| Instructional conditions | | | | | | | |
| Total R2 | 15 | 18 | 23 | 25 | 21 | 29 | 40 |
| Unique R2 | 9(ns) | 10 | 13 | 23 | 19 | 21 | 29 |

Note. Two commonality models were employed. In Model 1 (M1), two sets of variables—one representing learner background and another representing all the environment domains—were used to explain variance in learner competecne. Model 2(M2), a four-set model, used the identical variables as Model 1 but divided the environment variables into three sets, representing the three environment domains—participant composition, socioemotional climate, and instructional conditions.

## Table 9-7
### Total Percentage of Variance in Academic Behavior by Domain, Subdomain, and Variable

| Predictor | Attention to Task | | | | Cognitive Interaction | | | |
|---|---|---|---|---|---|---|---|---|
| | Regular Class | | Special Resource Class | Special Self-Contained Class | Regular Class | | Special Resource Class | Special Self-Contained Class |
| | Nonhandicapped Learners | Mainstreamed EMR Learners | Mainstreamed EMR Learners | Nonmainstreamed EMR Learners | Nonhandicapped Learners | Mainstreamed EMR Learners | Mainstreamed EMR Learners | Nonmainstreamed EMR Learners |
| Full model | 34 | | 35 | 46 | 36 | 37 | 36 | 53 |
| Learner background | | | 4 | | 4 | | | |
| Sex | | | 3 | | 3- | | | |
| Environment | 33 | | 32 | 45 | 33 | 35 | 35 | 50 |
| Classroom composition | 19 | | | 17 | | 15 | 9 | 18 |
| Peer quantity | 2- | | | | | | | |
| Peer sociodemographic characteristics | 11 | | | 5 | | 5 | 3 | 7 |
| Percentage Anglo | 7 | | | | | | | |
| Percentage lower class | | | | 2- | | | | |
| Rural location | | | | 2- | | | | 3 |
| Peer attitude toward school | 2- | | | | | | | 2 |
| Teacher ability, training, and experience | | | | | | 5 | | |
| Hours of special education in-service training | | | | | | 4 | | |

| | | | | | | |
|---|---|---|---|---|---|---|
| Teacher sociodemographic characteristics | | | | | | |
|   Anglo | | | | | | 4 |
|   Black | | | | | | 2 |
| Socioeconomic status of family | | | | | | 3 |
| Teacher educational attitudes | 2 | | | | | 3 |
| Socioemotional climate | 7 | 13 | 11 | 25 | | 8 |
|   Teacher warmth | 3 | 4 | | | | |
|   Teacher directiveness | | 4 | 5 | | | 5 |
|   Peer freedom | | 4– | 5– | | | 3– |
|   Teacher influence | | 2 | 4 | | | |
|   Coercive-legitimate | | 2– | 3 | | | |
|   Peer cohesiveness | 4 | | | | | |
|   Peer harmony | 4 | | | | | |
| Instructional conditions | 15 | 18 | 23 | 21 | 29 | 40 |
|   Instructional context | 8 | 3 | 2 | | 2 | 2 |
|   Physical quality | 8 | 2 | | | | |
|   Teacher-made materials | | | | | | 2– |
|   Instructional engagement | 2 | 2 | | | 10 | 11 |
|   Peer verbalization | 2 | 2 | | | 10 | 11 |
|   Teacher strategies | 3 | 3 | | | | 6 |
|   Learner-peer content/activity difference | 3– | 3– | | | | |
| Peer instructional activity | 7 | 6 | | 4 | 8 | 3 |
|   Teacher-directed, individual | | | | | 3 | 14 |
|   Teacher-directed, small group | 4 | | | | | 5 |

Table 9-7    (continued)

| Predictor | Attention to Task | | | | Cognitive Interaction | | | |
|---|---|---|---|---|---|---|---|---|
| | Regular Class | | Special Resource Class | Special Self-Contained Class | Regular Class | | Special Resource Class | Special Self-Contained Class |
| | Nonhandicapped Learners | Mainstreamed EMR Learners | Mainstreamed EMR Learners | Nonmainstreamed EMR Learners | Nonhandicapped Learners | Mainstreamed EMR Learners | Mainstreamed EMR Learners | Nonmainstreamed EMR Learners |
| Student self-directed, individual | | | | 3 | | | | |
| Student self-directed, small group | | | 2- | | | | 2- | 6- |
| Student self-directed, large group | | | 2- | | 2- | | 4- | 2- |
| Percentage of time spent in instructional activity | | | | | | | | 3 |
| Teacher instructional task | | | 8 | | | 6 | 12 | 8 |
| Introducing or motivating | | | 4 | | | 2 | | |
| Questioning or drilling | | | | | | 2 | 11 | 3 |
| Directing | | | | | | | 2- | |
| Supervising | | | 2- | | | 2- | 5- | 3- |
| Summarizing or reviewing | | | | | | 3 | | |
| Testing | | | 3 | | | | | |
| Percentage of time teacher instructing | | | | | | | | 3 |
| Class cognitive discourse | | | | | | | | |
| Very low index | | | | 4 | 9 | 7 | 6 | 21 |
| Moderately low index | | | | | 4 | 6 | 2 | 6 |

| | | | | | |
|---|---|---|---|---|---|
| Moderately high index | | | | | 2 |
| Very high index | | | | 8 | 2 |
| Frequency of discourse | | 14 | 8 | 14 | 26 |
| Teacher instructional feedback to peers | 3 | 19 | 6 | 8 | 20 |
| Positive index | 2 | 13 | 4 | 5 | 17 |
| Negative index | | | 2 | | 3 |
| Information index | | 10 | 2 | 5 | |
| Frequency of feedback | 2 | 14 | 5 | 6 | 20 |

Note. All figures are squared correlation coefficients and are statistically significant ($p < .05$). Bivariate correlations were performed with individual predictor variables and multiple correlations were performed with sets of predictor variables. For learner background, statistically significant variables are presented only if the contribution of learner background is significant in the total equation. Similarly, for the environmental domains (participant composition, socioemotional climate, and instructional conditions), statistically significant subdomains are presented only if the contribution of the domain is significant in the total equation, and significant variables are presented only if the contribution of the subdomain is significant. A minus sign follows the number if the correlation was negative.

## Regular Setting — Nonhandicapped Learners

### Attention to Task

Learner background and environment explained 34% of the variance in learner attention to task. Of the total variance, 2% could be attributed to learner background and 33% to environment. Learner background and environment shared only 1% of the explained variance, leaving the unique contribution of learner background at 1% and the unique contribution of environment at 32%.

The percentage of variance explained by learner background was not statistically significant; thus the variables within the background domain were not studied further.

All three environment sets explained significant proportions of the variance in learner attention. Classroom composition made a total contribution of 19% and a unique contribution of 14%. Within this domain, the subdomain quantity of peers explained a significant proportion of the variance in learner attention. Nonhandicapped students' attention diminished as the number of students in the classroom increased. The sociodemographic characteristics of the classroom peers accounted for the greatest proportion of variance in a learner's attention. Specifically, attention increased as the proportion of Anglo peers increased. Peer attitudes toward school also explained a significant, though small, proportion of the variance, reflecting a negative relationship between learner attention and peers' enjoyment of school. The teacher educational attitudes subdomain explained a small, but significant, proportion of the variance. However, no one attitude explained a significant proportion of the variance independently.

The socioemotional climate accounted for 7% of the variance in nonhandicapped learners' attention. Teacher warmth and classroom harmony were positively correlated with attention.

The instructional conditions domain explained 15% of the variance in learner attention. Instructional context was the only subdomain which explained a sizeable proportion of the variance in attention among nonhandicapped learners; the only salient relationship within this domain was a positive correlation between attention and the index of physical quality.

In summary, all three environment domains contributed significantly to the prediction of the nonhandicapped learners' attention to task. The frequency of attention was positively related to the percentage of Anglo peers, teacher warmth, classroom harmony, and the physical quality of the classroom; attention was slightly negatively related to the number of students in the classroom and peer enjoyment of school. The negative relationship between peer enjoyment and learner attention may be an artifact resulting from the negative correlation between peer enjoyment and percentage of Anglo peers.

## Cognitive Interaction

Learner background and environment together explained 36% of the variance in nonhandicapped learners' cognitive interaction. The total $R^2$ with learner background was 0.04, and the total $R^2$ with environment was 0.33. The shared variance between the two sets was 0.01, reducing only minimally the unique contribution of each.

Within the learner background domain, the learner's sex contributed significantly to the variance in cognitive interaction, with males interacting somewhat more than females.

Neither classroom composition nor socioemotional climate contributed significantly to the variation in cognitive interaction. In contrast, the total contribution of instructional conditions was 25%, with a unique contribution of 23%. The peer instructional activity subdomain made a significant contribution to the prediction of cognitive interaction. Within this subdomain, there was a negative correlation between interaction and the proportion of time spent in student-directed instruction in a large group (individual seatwork). As predicted, the subdomains of classroom cognitive discourse and teacher feedback to peers accounted for relatively large proportions of the variance. For both the classroom discourse and feedback subdomains, the frequency of discourse and feedback was the most significant predictor, reflecting their common measurement with cognitive interaction. The very low demand and the positive- and information-feedback indices were also positively related to cognitive interaction.

In summary, the cognitive interaction of nonhandicapped learners was predicted only by learner background and instructional conditions. Cognitive interaction tended to be higher among males in classrooms where instructional activity was not in student-directed large groups and where the frequency of cognitive interaction and feedback was high.

# Regular Setting — Mainstreamed EMR Learners

## Attention to Task

The learner background and environmental variables explained 22% of the variance in learner attention to task in the regular classroom. This figure was not statistically significant; therefore, no further study of this variable was undertaken.

## Cognitive Interaction

The Project PRIME predictive model did explain a significant percentage of the variance in the regular classroom cognitive interaction of the mainstreamed EMR learners. Learner background did not make a significant total or unique contribution. The environment explained 35% of the variance., virtually all unique.

Classroom composition had significant total and unique relationships with the mainstreamed EMR learners' regular classroom cognitive interaction. The subdomain of teacher ability, training, and experience was related to cognitive interaction. Within this subdomain, there was a positive correlation between the number of hours of special education in-service training provided to the regular classroom teachers and the rate of cognitive interaction. In-service training does have an effect. Teachers who were sensitized to the needs of the EMR learners involved them in the verbal exchanges in classroom, resulting in increased cognitive interactions. The socioemotional climate did not account for a significant proportion of the variance in these learner regular classroom cognitive interactions.

Instructional conditions made a total contribution of 21% and a unique contribution of 19% to the variance in the mainstreamed EMR learner regular classroom cognitive interaction. The subdomain of teacher instructional task was significant. Specifically, there were positive correlations between learners' cognitive interaction and teachers' introducing, questioning, and summarizing; and a negative correlation between cognitive interaction and teachers' supervising. Classroom cognitive discourse and teacher feedback to peers were both significant predictors. Within these two subdomains, the frequency of classroom cognitive discourse and teacher feedback had the highest squared bivariate correlations. However, very low and very high types of demands and all three types of feedback were also related to cognitive interaction.

## Resource Setting — Mainstreamed EMR Learners

### Attention to Task

In the resource classroom, the mainstreamed EMR learners' attention to task was significantly predicted by learner background and the resource classroom environment. Learner background made a significant total contribution of 4%, of which 1% was shared with environment. Environment made a significant total contribution of 32%. Sex was the only learner background measure related to attention in the resource classroom, with females being more attentive than males.

Among the resource classroom environment domains, classroom composition did not explain a significant proportion of the variance in attention to task. Socioemotional climate and instructional conditions were both significant predictors. They shared 8% of the variance in resource classroom attention, making the unique contribution of each domain lower (6% and 10%, respectively).

All the socioemotional climate teacher dimensions measured in the resource classrooms were significantly related to learner attentiveness. Attention to task was higher with teachers who displayed warmth, restricted peer freedom, and did not use coercive-legitimate influence.

Four of the instructional conditions subdomains were related to attention in the resource classroom. Learner attention was higher with greater peer verbalization and lower with a greater proportion of time in which learner content or activity was different from that of the other students in the classroom. Furthermore, attention was positively related to the percentage of time spent in teacher-directed small-group instruction, and was negatively related to the percentage of time spent in student, self-directed small- or large-group instruction (seatwork) and teacher supervising.

The high shared variance between socioemotional climate and instructional conditions may be explained by the positive and negative relationships obtained. The positive relationships were among teacher warmth and peer interest and attention, and the use of teacher-directed small-group instruction. The negative relationships were obtained between teacher warmth and the use of learner self-directed small-group instruction.

In summary, attention to task of the mainstreamed EMR learners in resource settings was related to learner background (sex) and the socioemotional climate and instructional conditions of the classroom. Resource classroom attention was positively related to teacher warmth, peer verbal participation, the use of teacher-directed small-group activities, and teacher introducing. Attention was negatively related to pupil freedom, the use of student-directed small- or large-group activities (seatwork), and teacher supervising.

Although classroom environmental factors were not significantly related to mainstreamed EMR learner attention to task in the regular classrooms, these factors were associated with attention to task in the resource classrooms. As shown in Chapter 5, mainstreamed EMR learners' attention to task was higher in resource classrooms than in regular classrooms.

## Cognitive Interaction

Together, learner background and environment explained 36% of the variance in the mainstreamed EMR learners' cognitive interaction in resource classrooms. The learner background domain explained an insignificant proportion of the variance; environment explained 35% of the variance, of which 34% was unique.

All three of the resource classroom environment domains contributed significantly to the prediction of cognitive interaction. Classroom composition explained 9% of the variance (7% uniquely), with peer sociodemographic characteristics being the only significant subdomain. Within this subdomain, no one measure was significant independently.

Socioemotional climate explained 4% (1% uniquely) of the variance in resource classroom cognitive interaction. No socioemotional climate subdomain was significant.

The instructional conditions domain was the most powerful predictor of mainstreamed EMR learner resource classroom cognitive interaction. The instructional engagement, peer instructional activity, teacher instructional task, classroom cognitive discourse, and teacher feedback subdomains all explained a significant proportion of the variance in resource classroom cognitive interaction. Cognitive interaction in the resource classroom was higher when there was more peer participation, greater use of teacher-directed individual instruction, more teacher questioning, and a higher frequency of cognitive discourse and feedback. Cognitive interaction was lower when there was greater use of student- (self-) directed small- or large-group instruction or when the teacher engaged in a higher proportion of directing or supervising.

In summary, only the instructional conditions present in the resource classroom made a major contribution to the learner's resource classroom cognitive interaction, with learner cognitive interaction being more frequent in classrooms with more teacher-directed individual instruction, more teacher questioning, greater peer participation, and more classroom cognitive discourse and feedback.

## Self-Contained Setting — EMR Learners

### Attention to Task

In the special self-contained classrooms, learner background and environment together accounted for 46% of the variance in learner attention to task. Learner background made an insignificant total contribution, while classroom environment made a total contribution of 45%, of which 1% was shared with background.

All three environment domains contributed significantly to the prediction of learner attention. Among the classroom composition subdomains, both peer and teacher characteristics were important. In the peer sociodemographic subdomain, there was a slight tendency for attention to be higher in classrooms with fewer lower-class peers and in schools not in a rural area. In the teacher sociodemographic subdomain, attention was higher in classrooms with a Black teacher.

Socioemotional climate made a total contribution of 11% (6% unique) to the variance in the learners' attention to task. Two subdomains were significant: teacher directiveness (with peer freedom negatively related to attention) and teacher influence (with teacher use of coercive or legitimate influence positively related to attention). These findings suggest that a structured classroom and control of student behavior are important factors in maintaining student attention.

Instructional conditions accounted for 23% of the variance in attention, although its unique proportion was 13%. Instructional conditions and socioemotional climate shared 8% of the variance in attention. Within the instructional context, a small positive correlation was obtained between attention and the index of physical quality. Within the peer instructional activity subdomain, learner attention was higher in classrooms with higher percentages of student-directed, individual instruction. Attention had a small positive correlation with the index of very high-level discourse in the classroom cognitive discourse subdomain. Feedback was important to attention, with a slight positive correlation between attention and both the index of positive feedback and the frequency of feedback.

The high shared variance between socioemotional climate and instructional conditions may be the result of the relatively high correlation between teacher use of coercive-legitimate influence and student-directed individual instruction ($r = 0.16$), both of which are related to attention.

To summarize, attention to task for the nonmainstreamed EMR learners was related to all three environment domains but not learner background. The nonmainstreamed EMR learners displayed more attention to task in classrooms of high physical quality with teachers who were Black, used coercive or legitimate influence, maintained a high level of cognitive discourse, gave positive feedback, and used student-directed individual instruction. Attention was lower in classrooms that had a higher percentage of lower-class peers, were located in rural areas, or had a high degree of peer freedom.

## Cognitive Interaction

The nonmainstreamed EMR learners' background and special classroom environment accounted for 53% of the variance in cognitive interaction, nearly all due to environment. Background made an insignificant contribution.

All of the environment domains made significant contributions. Classroom composition contributed 18%. Within the peer sociodemographic subdomain, learner cognitive interaction was higher in rural-area schools or classrooms where peers enjoyed school. Within the teacher sociodemographic subdomain, more interaction occurred in classrooms where the teacher was Anglo or came from a family of higher socioeconomic status.

Socioemotional climate accounted for 8% of the variance in cognitive interaction. Within the teacher directiveness subdomain, interaction was higher in classrooms characterized by less peer freedom.

The instructional conditions domain explained 40% of the total variance with a unique $R^2$ of 0.29. All seven subdomains contributed significantly. The instructional context subdomain accounted for a minimal proportion of the variance, with a small negative correlation between the presence of teacher-made materials and cognitive interaction. The subdomain of instructional engagement made a relatively large contribution, with a positive correlation obtained between the amount of cognitive interaction engaged in by the learner and the amount of verbal participation engaged in by the peers. Teacher strategies were also related to learner cognitive interaction. Cognitive interaction was higher in classrooms where the instructional content or activity was different for specific learners than for the rest of the students. Within the peer activity subdomain, learner cognitive interaction had positive correlations with teacher-directed individual or small-group activities and negative correlations with student-directed small- or large-group activities. Findings for the teacher instructional task subdomain revealed that cognitive interaction was higher when teachers spent more time questioning and less time supervising. Within the classroom cognitive discourse and feedback subdomains, the frequency of discourse and feedback and the positive feedback index were highly correlated with cognitive interaction.

In summary, the nonmainstreamed EMR learners' cognitive interaction was predicted by all three special classroom environment domains. Cognitive interaction was enhanced under the following circumstances: the school was in a rural setting; the learner's peers enjoyed school; the teacher was Anglo or from a higher-SES family; there was low peer freedom and few teacher-made materials; there was a high frequency of peer verbalization; specific learners were differentiated from the rest of the students by instructional content or activities; the peer instructional activity was teacher-directed rather than student-directed; the teacher engaged in questioning rather than supervising activities; there was a high frequency of classroom cognitive discourse, particularly very low discourse; and there was positive feedback.

## Discussion

The Project PRIME predictive model, namely, learner background and environment together did explain significant proportions of variance in learner attention to task and cognitive interaction except for the mainstreamed EMR learners' attention to task in the regular classrooms. Academic behavior was only minimally associated with learner background. Sex was the only significant variable: Nonhandicapped males were less attentive than nonhandicapped females, and in the resource classroom mainstreamed EMR males had more cognitive interactions than mainstreamed EMR females.

The classroom environment domains were more predictive, though the specific aspects of the environment predicted the two behaviors differently. Three different patterns emerged when predicting attention to task. For the nonhandicapped learners, attention was associated with the percentage of peers who were Anglo, the physical quality of the classroom, teacher warmth, and peer harmony. For the EMR learners in resource classrooms, learner attention was enhanced in a warm, yet structured classroom, where there was a high level of peer participation, use of teacher-directed small-group instruction, and a high degree of teacher introducing or motivating. For the EMR learners in self-contained classrooms, attention was enhanced in structured classrooms where the teacher used student-directed individual instruction and coercive or legitimate influence.

These differences in patterns reflect the basic differences in the nature of the three settings. In regular classrooms containing large numbers of students, it was not the type of instruction but the sociocultural background of the student body and whatever techniques teachers used to convey a sense of warmth and maintain harmony. In the resource and special self-contained classrooms, however, the type of instruction, particulary the degree of structure and the type of student and teacher activity, was a determining factor. Structure was important in both the resource and special self-contained classrooms. However, the setting controlled the type of activity that effectively elicited attention. In the special self- contained classrooms, teachers who maintained attention made greater use of supervised, individualized seatwork. In the resource classrooms, where students were homogeneously grouped for short periods of intensive instruction, teachers who used small-group lecture or discussion activities were more effective in maintaining learner attention.

Not surprisingly, the instructional conditions domain had the greatest impact on cognitive interaction, with greater learner cognitive interaction occurring in classrooms with more frequent classroom cognitive discourse and concomitant instructional feedback. In the resource and special self-contained classrooms, cognitive interaction was also related to the amount of peer verbal participation and type of instructional activity. In general, learner cognitive interaction for all types of learners and in all three settings was heavily dependent on the specific instructional conditions within the classroom.

## Implications

The development of attention and cognitive interactive behaviors is an important goal of the educational process. Behaviors such as task persistence, receptive listening, and articulate verbalization are important dimensions of a student's academic competence that need to be developed.

What might teachers do to facilitate learner academic behavior? With regard to attention, in the regular classroom, teachers should provide a warm and harmonious environment. In the resource classroom, teachers should provide a warm yet controlled social climate, encourage peer verbalization, and use teacher-directed rather than student-directed small-group instruction. In special self-contained classrooms, teachers should also provide a structured climate, but the most effective mode of instruction is student-directed individual instruction with frequent positive feedback.

To facilitate learner cognitive interaction, in-service training appears to be beneficial for regular teachers of mainstreamed EMR students. However, the most important strategy for all students and settings appears to be obvious — providing frequent opportunities for cognitive discourse within the classroom.

In considering what teachers might do to facilitate positive academic behavior, it may be interesting to compare the findings predicting learner attention and cognitive interaction to those findings presented in Chapter 8 predicting peer interest and attention and verbalization.[3]

A high level of peer participation did not insure a high level of learner cognitive interaction except in special classrooms, and learner attentiveness was not related to the level of attention of the learner's peers. Furthermore, although there were some similarities in the peer and teacher instructional activities related to the academic behaviors of individual learners and classroom peers, there were also important differences. In certain instances, the instructional techniques that were effective in maintaining high engagement had only a minimal effect on an individual learner's behavior and, conversely, activities that permitted greater learner involvement (i.e., teacher-directed individual instruction) may be counterproductive for the classroom as a whole.

Although academic behavior is an important, independent aspect of academic competence, it is also expected to be an important predictor of academic status. A learner who is attentive to the instructional task and actively participating in verbal interactions is expected to achieve greater academic success. Yet, as noted in Chapter 5, with one exception the relationships between learner attention to task and cognitive interaction to normative and classroom academic status were extremely weak. Ironically, the only strong relationship between academic status and behavior among all three learner subgroups was between regular classroom attention to task and normative academic status for the mainstreamed EMR learners. Yet the predictive model for attention to task for the mainstreamed EMR learners in the regular classroom is the only academic behavior model that failed to reach significance. So, although attention in the regular classroom is associated with a mainstreamed EMR learner's achievement, the particular background or environment factors that could be contributing to that attention are not clear.

These findings suggest a differential sensitivity hypothesis. The EMR learners, unlike the nonhandicapped learners, did not attend to task merely because they were in a warm, harmonious environment. EMR learners appear to require a smaller number of pupils and the intensive focussed instruction available through the more active small-group participation of the resource classroom or the teacher-supervised individual self-directed instruction of the self-contained classroom to remain attentive. It is just this relationship that has been the rationale for the need to provide pull-out and self-contained classrooms for delivering special education services rather than sole reliance on the regular classroom environment.

# Academic Attitudes

The academic attitudes of students, particularly their academic self-concept and attitudes toward school, are considered important not only in and of themselves but also because of their presumed relationship to academic behaviors and achievement.

Academic self-concept is described as that facet of a learner's self-concept which encompasses his perceptions of his scholastic abilities and his feelings about those abilities. Self-concept theory suggests that a student's academic self-concept develops from experiences in school, including perceptions of others' evaluations of his abilities.

Attitude toward school is defined as the learner's affective reaction toward his experiences with the teacher, subject matter, and school activities.

## Regular Setting — Nonhandicapped Learners

### Academic Self-Concept
Learner background and environment together failed to account for a significant amount of variance in academic self-concept.

### Attitude Toward School
Background and environment together explained 35% of the variance in attitude toward school. As can be seen in Table 9-8, learner background explained 11% of the variance (10% uniquely and 1% jointly with environment), while environment alone explained 25% (24% uniquely and 1% jointly with background).

Table 9-8

Total and Unique Percentage of Variance Explained in Academic Attitudes by Domain

| | Academic Self-Concept | | | | Attitude Toward School | | | |
|---|---|---|---|---|---|---|---|---|
| | Regular Class | | Special Resource Class | Special Self-Contained Class | Regular Class | | Special Resource Class | Special Self-Contained Class |
| Predictor | Nonhandicapped Learners | Mainstreamed EMR Learners | Mainstreamed EMR Learners | Nonmainstreamed EMR Learners | Nonhandicapped Learners | Mainstreamed EMR Learners | Mainstreamed EMR Learners | Nonmainstreamed EMR Learners |
| Full model (M1 or M2) | | | | | | | | |
| Total R2 | 20(ns) | 21(ns) | 21 | 30 | 35 | 28 | 23 | 27(ns) |
| Learner background | | | | | | | | |
| Total R2 | | | 5 | 4(ns) | 11 | 7 | 7 | |
| Unique R2 | | | 1(ns) | 3(ns) | 10 | 3 | 4 | |
| Environment | | | | | | | | |
| Total R2 | | | 20 | 27 | 25 | 25 | 19 | |
| Unique R2 | | | 16(ns) | 26 | 24 | 21 | 16 | |
| Classroom composition | | | | | | | | |
| Total R2 | | | 10 | 14 | 14 | 14 | 11(ns) | |
| Unique R2 | | | 8(ns) | 15 | 12 | 13 | 7(ns) | |

| Socioemotional climate | | | | | |
|---|---|---|---|---|---|
| Total R2 | 1(ns) | 4(ns) | 2 | 3(ns) | 0(ns) |
| UniqueR2 | 1(ns) | 3(ns) | 1(ns) | 1(ns) | 1(ns) |
| Instructional conditions | | | | | |
| Total R2 | 10(ns) | 8(ns) | 11 | 9(ns) | 10(ns) |
| Unique R2 | 9(ns) | 11(ns) | 10 | 7(ns) | 5(ns) |

Note. Two commonality models were employed. In Model 1 (M1), two sets of variables—one representing learner background and another representing all the environment domains—were used to explain variance in learner competence. Model 2(M2), a four-set model, used the identical variables as Model 1 but divided the environment variables into three sets, representing the three environment domains—participant composition, socioemotional climate, and instructional conditions.

Table 9-9

Total Percentage of Variance Explained in Academic Attitudes
by Domain, Subdomain, and Variable

| Predictor | Academic Self-Concept | | | | Attitude Toward School | | | |
| --- | --- | --- | --- | --- | --- | --- | --- | --- |
| | Regular Class | | Special Resource Class | Special Self-Contained Class | Regular Class | | Special Resource Class | Special Self-Contained Class |
| | Nonhandicapped Learners | Mainstreamed EMR Learners | Mainstreamed EMR Learners | Nonmainstreamed EMR Learners | Nonhandicapped Learners | Mainstreamed EMR Learners | Mainstreamed EMR Learners | Nonmainstreamed EMR Learners |
| Full model | 20(ns) | 21(ns) | 21 | 30 | 35 | 28 | 23 | 27(ns) |
| Learner background | | | 5 | | 11 | 7 | 7 | |
| Sex | | | | | 9 | | | |
| Ethnic group | | | 4 | | | 4 | 4 | |
| Black | | | 4 | | | 4 | 4 | |
| Environment | | | 20 | 27 | 25 | 25 | 19 | |
| Classroom composition | | | 10 | 14 | 14 | 14 | 11 | |
| Peer sociodemographic characteristics | | | | | | | | |
| Percentage Anglo | | | 6 | 8 | 5a | 6 | 6 | |
| Percentage Spanish-surnamed | | | | 4- | | | | |
| Rural location | | | | 2- | | 2- | 2- | |
| Peer attitude toward school | | | | | 6 | | | |

| | | | |
|---|---|---|---|
| Teacher ability, training, and experience | 3 | | 5 |
| Verbal facility | 2– | | |
| Hours of special education in-service training | | | 4– |
| Educational status | 2 | | |
| Teacher sociodemographic characteristics | | | |
| Anglo | 4– | 2– | |
| Teacher educational attitudes | | 3 | |
| Importance of a structured, controlled environment | | 2– | |
| Instructional conditions | | 11 | |
| Class cognitive discourse | | 4 | |
| Very low index | | 2 | |
| Moderately low index | | 2– | |

Note. All figures are squared correlation coefficients and are statistically significant ($p < .05$). Bivariate correlations were performed with individual predictor variables and multiple correlations were performed with sets of predictor variables. For learner background, statistically significant variables are presented only if the contribution of learner background is significant in the total equation. Similarly, for the environmental domains (participant composition, socioemotional climate, and instructional conditions), statistically significant subdomains are presented only if the contribution of the domain is significant in the total equation, and significant variables are presented only if the contribution of the subdomain is significant. A minus sign follows the number if the correlation was negative.

a   No individual variable had an R2 above 1.

Within the background domain, sex was the only significant variable, with females expressing more positive attitudes toward school than males (Table 9-9).

Among the environment domains, classroom composition accounted for 14% of the variance, and instructional conditions accounted for 11%; socioemotional climate domain made no significant contribution. Only three subsets within the classroom composition domain were significant: peer attitudes, teacher educational attitudes, and peer sociodemographic characteristics. Nonhandicapped learners had more positive attitudes toward school when more of their peers enjoyed school and the teacher placed less value on maintaining a structured, controlled environment. No single variable within the peer sociodemographic characteristics subdomain accounted for more than 1% of the variance.

Within the instructional conditions domain, only classroom cognitive discourse was significant, with learners expressing more positive attitudes toward school when the level of discourse was very low.

## Regular Setting — Mainstreamed EMR Learners

### Academic Self-Concept
Background and environment together failed to explain a significant amount of the variance in academic self-concept.

### Attitude Toward School
Background and environment did account for significant amounts of the variance in attitude toward school, explaining 28% of the variance.

Learner background explained 7% of the variance, 3% uniquely and 4% jointly with environment. Within the background domain, ethnicity was the only significant variable, with Black mainstreamed EMR learners expressing more positive attitudes toward school than students of other ethnic groups.

## Resource Setting — Mainstreamed EMR Learners

### Academic Self-Concept
Learner background and environment accounted for 21% of the variance in the academic self-concept criterion.[4] Background accounted for 5% of the variance, but 4% was shared with environment. The environment accounted for 20% of the variance, 16% uniquely.

Within the background domain, ethnicity accounted for a significant amount of the variance, with Black learners having the most positive academic self-concepts.

Classroom composition was the only significant environment domain, accounting for 10% of the variance. Within this domain, the peer sociodemographic characteristics and teacher ability, training, and experience subdomains were significant. Teacher verbal facility was negatively related and teacher educational status positively related to the mainstreamed EMR learners' academic self-concept.

### Attitude Toward School

For attitudes toward school, background and environment together accounted for 23% of the variance. Background accounted for 7% of the variance, 4% uniquely and 3% shared with the environment. Environment explained 19% of the variance.

Again, ethnicity was the only significant variable within learner background, with Black students feeling most positive about school.

Only classroom composition explained a significant amount of variance among the environment domains. Peer sociodemographic characteristics again accounted for a significant amount of variance, with learners in classrooms with a high percentage of Spanish-surnamed students holding more negative feelings about school.

## Self-Contained Setting — Nonmainstreamed EMR Learners

### Academic Self-Concept

Background and environment explained 30% of the variance in academic self-concept. Background variables accounted for a nonsignificant amount of variance unique, and shared only 1% with environment. The environmental variables accounted for a total of 27% of the variance, 26% uniquely.

Among the environment domains, only classroom composition accounted for a significant amount of variance, explaining 14%. Both the peer sociodemographic and teacher sociodemographic subdomains were significant. The nonmainstreamed EMR learners in classrooms with lower percentages of Anglo classmates, in less rural settings, and with non-Anglo teachers tended to have more positive academic self-concepts.

### Attitude Toward School

For the nonmainstreamed EMR learners, background and classroom environment together did not account for a significant amount of variance in attitude toward school.

## Discussion

Perhaps the most salient feature of this set of results is the failure to account for significant amounts of variance in three of the eight academic-attitude models examined. In addition, most of the significant relationships found between attitudes and the variable subdomains and individual variables were quite low, accounting for less than 5% of the variance. When one considers the probability that the $R^2$s of the subdomains and individual variables were inflated by joint variances with other variables in the equation, it seems clear this set of predictors did not do a particularly good job of accounting for the variance in academic attitudes. Perhaps other environmental measures not included in these analyses are more predictive of academic attitudes. However, the predictor sets did include almost all variables which have to date been considered in the literature to be important to attitudes.

The expected significant relationships between the socioemotional climate variables and academic attitudes were not found. This is contrary to much recent writing in education which has suggested that warm, supportive, nondirective environments with cohesive peer groups are important determinants of the learners' academic attitudes. The findings of Project PRIME, being mixed, were consistent with other research using similar variables.

Sex, which in past research has consistently been found to be related to attitudes toward school, accounted for a significant amount of the variance in the attitudes toward school of the nonhandicapped learners, with females feeling more positively toward school than males. Age, which has been consistently found to be related to school attitudes, was not significantly related in this study, perhaps due to the narrow age range in this study.

Among the mainstreamed EMR learners, Black ethnicity was associated with positive attitudes toward school. This differs from past research with nonhandicapped students, which found no difference among students from different ethnic groups. One impetus to the mainstreaming movement was the realization that minority group students were disproportionately represented in self-contained EMR classrooms. Such students, it was argued, were only considered EMR learners during the six hours a day spent in school (President's Committee on Mental Retardation, 1969) and, except for academic skills, did not function differently from their peers in regular classrooms. Applying this argument to these data, it is possible that the Black mainstreamed students were similar in many ways to the students already in the regular classrooms, and thus had a more positive mainstreaming experience. However, if this is true, it is unclear why the Spanish-surnamed mainstreamed EMR learners were not similarly affected. The low English proficiency of these students may be a factor.

Among the environment domains, classroom composition was most often related to academic attitudes. Within this domain, peer sociodemographic characteristics were significantly related to the academic self-concepts of the EMR learners in the resource classrooms and to the attitudes toward school of the EMR learners in both the regular and the resource classrooms. The ethnicity of the peer group, in particular, was related to academic attitudes, although the relationships tended to be low. Among the nonhandicapped students, peer attitude toward school was found to be significantly related to individual learner attitudes toward school. This finding is similar to those of Anderson and Walberg (1968).

One interesting result was the significant, though low, relationship found among nonhandicapped students between the very low level of cognitive discourse and positive school attitudes. Chapter 6 showed that many of the regular classrooms in the Project PRIME sample had a majority of students who were one or more years behind in reading. If many of the nonhandicapped learners in the Project PRIME study were actually low-achieving learners, they might have preferred and been happiest in classrooms where the teacher's questions were relatively simple, requiring less demanding responses which they could respond to with success. This relationship may not be valid for groups of higher-achieving nonhandicapped learners.

The learner attitude results seem to have few implications for those wishing to develop educational programs to maximize the academic attitudes of EMR students. Few relationships were found between background or classroom environment facets and the attitude measures, and those relationships reaching significance tended to be low. Furthermore, the few significant relationships found generally did not involve easily manipulated variables. Learner ethnicity is a given, and in many situations the sociodemographic characteristics of the classroom or teacher are virtually givens as well. Thus, unless further research demonstrates more significant relationships, there seems little to guide those wishing to affect the attitudes toward school or academic self-concepts of EMR students.

## Summary and Implications

In this chapter, we have investigated the relationships between academic competence and the four domains: learner background, classroom composition, socioemotional climate, and instructional conditions within each of the three alternative educational settings. The findings in this chapter provide significant support for the contention that schools do make a difference, especially for EMR learners. The three environment domains as defined and measured in Project PRIME were shown to significantly contribute to explaining variations in learner academic competence, particulary for EMR learners. The significance of the classroom environment in explaining variations within and between learners in alternative classroom environments was consistently evidenced, though not always with similar strength or patterns.

While the classroom environment domains did explain variations in nonhandicapped learners' academic competence, these domains were particularly important for EMR children. Peer characteristics, whether ethnicity, socioeconomic status, or attitudes, make the major contribution to explaining the achievement status and academic behaviors of nonhandicapped learners. By contrast, teacher characteristics, socioemotional climate, and instructional operations contributed most heavily to explaining variations in EMR academic status and behaviors. The findings in this chapter support the adage that EMR children must be taught to learn.

Beyond this broad generalization of the significance of classroom environments and, more specifically, the importance of teachers in the education of EMR children, this chapter also identified specific as well as clusters of classroom variables likely to be associated with promoting the academic competence of EMR learners. The findings strongly suggest that regardless of whether an EMR child is in a regular, resource, or self-contained classroom environment, a similar profile of classroom composition, socioemotional climate, and instructional conditions was associated with improved academic competence. Instructional engagement occurs as a result of teacher activity with the student: teacher querying and student response, supervision, monitoring, feedback. Learning is optimized within a classroom when nonhandicapped and EMR peers cooperate in learning. The harmony seems to enhance peer exchanges as well as positive teacher-pupil interaction, increasing attention to task, and the acceptance and assimilation of the EMR learner into the regular classroom. The individualization required by the particular learner must be implemented by the teacher in a manner which does not isolate the learner in individual activities but groups him with other learners with similar needs, allowing for cooperative group learning opportunities. The profile of the classroom included:

- A classroom environment characterized by teacher directed and supervised instructional activities calculated to actively involve the learner.

- Instructional engagement which occurred as a result of teacher activity with the student: teacher querying and student response, supervision, monitoring, feedback.
- Harmony within the classroom, which seemed to enhance peer exchanges, positive teacher-pupil interaction, increased attention to task, and the acceptance and assimilation of the EMR learner into the regular classroom. Learning was optimized when nonhandicapped and EMR peers cooperated.
- The teacher's ability to create such a classroom environment was shown to be associated with their training and experience.

The data indicate that EMR learners work more effectively in groupings, and that these groupings maintain greater attention to task, allow them to learn from each other, and, most particularly, from the teacher's direction and continuing support. Individually assigned activities detracted from the EMR learner's attention to task and from his achievement status. It is critical, then, to make the distinction between instructional differentiation which describes strategies to individualize or adapt the curriculum to the particular student, and individualized instruction which seems to suggest that each EMR learner should work individually. EMR learner achievement status was enhanced when the curriculum was adapted to their needs, but also when the learning occurred in groups that worked harmoniously, with focus, structure, and teacher direction and feedback.

To the extent that other outcomes such as higher-order cognitive processing might be desired, it is unknown whether these classroom environment conditions will be similarly enhancing. In short, EMR learners seem to prosper when they know what is expected and they can gain support and direction from peers and teachers. To encourage more open-ended goals, it is probable that the student may still require direction, with teacher support encouraging more open-ended responses — not "failure proof" closed-end responding — but challenges that may allow "wrong" responses and frustration. The goal of teaching these students is to take them from this highly-defined and structured learning to comfort and good performance in more open-ended, generative learning situations. It is likely this higher-order cognitive processing could best be achieved when the classroom structure and focus remain clearly defined but encourage participation requiring open-ended responses and discussion among the students.

The reader should remember that the research findings which provide the evidence for the effectiveness of teacher-directed classroom environments were obtained from third, fourth, and fifth grade elementary classrooms. Further, that these classrooms were often characterized by below-grade level reading achievement among the nonhandicapped students. Finally, that the dependent measure used in Project PRIME was a normative achievement test.

The creation of classroom learning environments which incorporate higher-order cognitive processing will clearly challenge and test the limits of teacher leadership in the classroom regardless of setting. The critical finding is that the individualization required by particular learners must be implemented by the teachers in a manner which does not isolate these learners in tutorial types of activities but groups them with other learners with similar educational needs. Teachers will need added planning time in order to provide the opportunities for higher-order cognitive processing and consider the grouping strategies appropriate for individually differentiating instruction. For the mainstreamed EMR learners, this requires that the regular and resource teachers coordinate their instructional planning. Creating these conditions will clearly be facilitated by the provision of administrative support at the building level, teacher and student support services, in-service training, and more carefully considered assignment of students to groupings for learning.

The findings presented in this chapter provide guidance not only to classroom teachers but also to school administrators who must understand the implications for grouping strategies and support services. These findings indicate the need for building-level support services for teachers, instructional planning time, and careful attention to how students are assigned to classroom groupings. Equally important are suggestions for how administrators might more effectively use resource rooms. Special education service delivery needs to be carefully coordinated with regular education. Empirical findings were presented which indicated that this is especially true for the students at highest educational risk, e.g., the low-SES mainstreamed EMR learners. The effects of the resource program for these students were evidenced in the diminished strength of the Project PRIME model to explain variance in the normative academic status in contrast to high-SES mainstreamed EMR learners. The model for high-SES mainstreamed EMR learners explained significantly more variance in normative academic status. Thus, low-SES mainstreamed EMR learners probably require much closer coordination between regular and resource class teachers in order for this service delivery approach to be effective.

Mainstreaming is a viable option if administrators can develop the building-level strategies necessary to achieve an integrated educational program delivered in two different classroom environments rather than what appears to characterize many of the buildings studied: the additive combination of two separate educational programs. The challenge to administrators beyond providing support services to the individual teachers and their students is to create the administrative climate which facilitates communication and shared planning between regular and special education resource teachers. This coordinated planning is an administrative overhead that must be provided for in addition to classroom instructional planning time. Without this administrative support, the pull-out strategy may serve to weaken rather than strengthen the academic competence of mainstreamed EMR learners.

This chapter, then, provides empirical evidence which supports the importance of schools and teachers in contributing to the academic performance of nonhandicapped and EMR learners. In addition, a specific classroom environment profile has been identified which, regardless of setting, was found to be associated with higher normative academic status and desired academic behaviors. The school buildings and classrooms described in this study were based on naturally occurring, not experimentally manipulated environments or events. The degree of variability in desired building administrative support and classroom conditions suggests not only the magnitude of potential opportunity for improvement but the continued need for vigilance and attention that is required in the placement of mildly handicapped learners into mainstreamed or self-contained classrooms.

## Technical Notes

1. The reader should be cautioned that the figures in these tables are derived from square bivariate or multiple correlations of that variable or set of variables with each academic status measure. The figures are not additive; they are to some unknown extent inflated by variance that is shared among two or more variables.

2. Prediction of normative academic status using learner background and the restricted rather than complete definition of the regular classroom environment resulted in an $R^2$ of 0.31, a reduction of 0.04 in the variance accounted for by the regular classroom environment. Using the restricted resource environment definition reduces the variance predicted by the learner background and the resource environment from 0.27 to 0.21. Thus, the restricted environment definition reduces the predictive power of the combined environments by at most 0.10.

3. It is interesting to note that even though peer interest and attention were not related to learner attention to task in any setting, there are certain similarities in the instructional conditions that predict each one. Within the regular classrooms, both nonhandicapped learner and peer attention were related to the physical quality of the classroom. However, peer interest and attention were also related to the instructional activity (higher in classrooms with proportionately more self-directed large-group instruction and proportionately less self-directed individual instruction), while

learner attention was not. In the resource classrooms, both individual learner attention and peer interest and attention were higher with greater use of teacher-directed small-group instruction and teacher introducing or motivating and less use of student-directed small-group instruction and teacher supervising. In special self-contained classrooms, although the peer instructional activity was a significant predictor of both learner and peer attention, the particular activities associated with attention were different. Peer attention was associated with greater use of teacher-directed small-group instruction; learner attention was associated with greater use of student-directed individual instruction.

Comparing learner cognitive interactions with peer verbalization, we note first that peer verbalization is an important predictor of learner cognitive interaction in the two special classroom settings but not in the regular classroom. Second, although the instructional operations of the regular classroom made a significant contribution to the prediction of the nonhandicapped and the EMR learners' cognitive interaction, the prediction of peer verbalization from instructional operations in the regular classroom was significant. In the special classrooms, learner cognitive interaction and peer verbalization were both affected by the instructional operations. In the resource classroom, greater use of student-directed small- or large-group instruction was negatively related to both peer verbalization and learner cognitive interaction. However, more peer verbalization occurred when there was greater use of teacher-directed small-group instruction, while more learner cognitive interaction occurred when there was greater use of teacher-directed individual instruction. This would appear to reflect a greater opportunity for an individual pupil to respond when working alone with the teacher, as would be expected. High rates of both peer and learner verbal interactions were associated with greater use of teacher questioning rather than supervising, and to the frequency of classroom cognitive discourse and positive and information feedback.

In self-contained classrooms, learner cognitive interaction and peer verbalization were associated with greater use of teacher-directed individual and small-group instruction and with greater teacher questioning. Very low cognitive discourse and frequent discourse were related to both learner and peer verbal interactions, as were frequent feedback and positive feedback.

4.  Although learner background and the regular classroom environment also accounted for 21% of the variance, the regular classroom model was not significant because the regular classroom environment contained more variables. The number of variables in a regression equation affects the calculation of the F test of significance — given the same number of subjects, the more variables in the equation, the higher the $R^2$ must be to be significant.

# 10

# Social Competence

This chapter is concerned with the relationship of the dimensions of learner background and classroom environment with social competence. The social competence of EMR learners has been of interest to educators since the turn of the century when special classrooms were created in this country. Social deficiencies were thought to be more debilitating to these students in the long run than academic deficiencies (Goldstein, 1964). Special classrooms have had a strong concern for developing the social competence of EMR learners through curricula focussed on social and personal skills. The findings of research that compared the effects of special and regular classroom placement on the social adjustment of EMR learners were, however, equivocal. Though the body of this research showed EMR learners in special classrooms to be "better adjusted," there were serious sampling and measurement problems which raised questions as to the validity of the results (Kirk, 1964).

The recent trend toward mainstreaming represents a shift from formal emphasis on EMR learner social competence. It is probably safe to assume that mainstreamed EMR learners will not be taught social skills in regular classroom time. A premise of mainstreamed placement is that the increased contact of EMR learners with nonhandicapped peers will result in improved social skills; if need be, the resource room time can be partially allocated to social skills training. The major question addressed in this chapter is:

Which dimensions of the three classroom settings promote or inhibit social competence among EMR learners?

A parallel question:

What are the relationships between the regular classroom environment and the social competence of nonhandicapped students?

This latter question is asked to determine whether the relationships found for EMR learners were similar to those for nonhandicapped students. If EMR learners are affected by the regular classroom environment in the same way as nonhandicapped students, the findings would suggest that EMR learners can be accommodated in regular classrooms without having to make substantial alterations in the regular classroom environment.

Project PRIME assumed that the nature of the environment, rather than any characteristic inherent in the learner, is the predominant influence on learner social competence. If the socioemotional climate of classrooms is an important contributor, it is expected to be important in both special and regular classrooms. Conversely, if it is not an important contributor, it is expected to be unimportant in both settings.

Social competence was conceptualized as comprising social status, social behavior, and social attitudes (Figure 10-1). The following sections examine the three components of social competence, reviewing relevant research and theory related to each, suggesting why each may be affected by variations in dimensions of the classroom environment and learner backgrounds, and presenting the results found in this study.

# Social Status

Since the publication of Moreno's classic volume *Who Shall Survive?* in 1934, the study of a person's social acceptance by his peer group has been of growing concern to researchers in the fields of social science and education. The underlying assumption of sociometric research is that the more an individual is liked by peers and the less he is disliked, the better it is for his psychological well-being. Indeed, a number of researchers have reported significant positive correlations between social status and indices of mental health (e.g., Northway, 1944).

Most of the research employing sociometric techniques has focused on organismic or personological correlates of student social status. Pupils' sex (Lindzey & Bryne, 1968), intelligence (Dentler & Mackler, 1962), physical

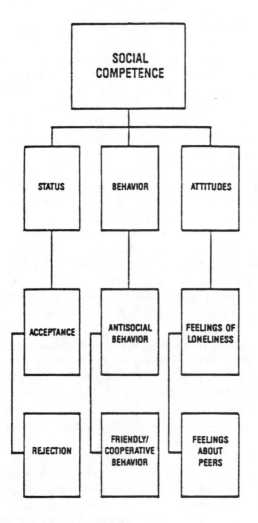

Figure 10-1
Social Competence
(Project PRIME Taxonomic Model)

appearance (Cavior & Dokecki, 1973), social behavior (Lippitt & Gold, 1959), and general mental health (Schmuck & Schmuck, 1975) have all been shown to be related to sociometric status. The underlying premise of this research approach is that the characteristics of the person being rated are primarily responsible for the peer group's perceptions. Characteristics external to the person, such as those of the raters or the situational context, were seldom investigated. It is reasonable to expect that the inclusion of additional variables descriptive of the learner's classroom environment will improve predictions of social status.

It can logically be asked which aspects of the environment can be expected to affect student social status? It might be expected that, in addition to influencing students' academic attainments, the teacher may also influence a student's social position in the peer group hierarchy. Flanders and Havumaki (1960) found that students who were praised by the teacher enjoyed a more favored social status than students who were not praised.

Similarly, peer cohesiveness may affect the social status of individual students. Cohesive classrooms are those in which acceptance is dispersed among students in the classroom — that is, classrooms in which students tend to like a number of other students (Schmuck & Schmuck, 1975). It could be hypothesize that students labelled EMR, who usually occupy an inferior social position in their peer group, are more likely to be accepted in highly cohesive classrooms. Other aspects of the classroom environment may influence social status, e.g., its composition. For example, lower ability nonhandicapped peers may be more likely than higher ability peers to befriend EMR learners.

The instructional conditions imposed by the teacher may indirectly affect student social status. If social status is in part dependent upon the appropriateness of the behavior students display in front of their peers (Gottlieb, 1976), then situations that encourage public displays of behavior inappropriate for the formal or informal standards of the group may affect a student's social status adversely. To illustrate, if the teacher's instructional strategy requires a heavy emphasis on higher-level, oral cognitive responses, a student's social status may be seriously threatened if, when called upon, he performs poorly. By contrast, the teacher who supervises students working individually at their desks or who relies on class choral response to questions minimizes the likelihood that any one student's inadequate performance will be exposed to the group.

## Results

The results of the commonality analyses which employed the two measures of social status, acceptance and rejection, as criteria for each of the three learner samples are presented in Tables 10-1 and 10-2. Table 10-1 presents all the total and unique percentages of variance explained in these measures by domains; Table 10-2 presents the significant total (but not unique) percentage of variance explained by subdomains and variables as well as by domains.

## Nonhandicapped Learners

For the nonhandicapped learners, learner background and classroom environment together explained significant portions of variance in both acceptance (26%) and rejection (32%) by their peers. Classroom environment accounted uniquely for this contribution. Learner background was not significant.

Inspection of the effects of the three classroom environment domains revealed that the socioemotional climate was the most important domain; classroom composition and instructional conditions did not significantly explain variation in either social status measure. Nonhandicapped learners enjoyed greater acceptance in classrooms in which the level of dislike among peers was low and experienced greater rejection if dislike among peers was high. The other predictors in this domain did not significantly relate to the nonhandicapped learner's social status.

## Mainstreamed EMR Learners

Background and environment separately and together explained significant portions of variance in the social acceptance (31%) and rejection (42%) of mainstreamed EMR learners. The joint contribution of background and environment was low in both equations.

The background characteristics significantly related to social status were sex, ethnic group, age, and family intactness. Males were significantly better accepted than females, and Anglo learners were less well accepted than Black and Spanish-surnamed learners. Other bivariate correlation coefficients indicated that younger learners and learners from nonintact families experienced greater social rejection than older learners and learners from intact families.

The total and unique contributions of both the classroom composition and socioemotional climate environment domains were significantly related to the social acceptance of mainstreamed EMR learners. Significant portions of variance in rejection were explained by the total and unique contributions of socioemotional climate and the total (but not unique) contribution of instructional conditions. Joint contributions among environment domains were low.

In the classroom composition domain, the mainstreamed EMR learners' acceptance was associated with teachers' general educational attitudes, peers' attitudes toward school, percentage of peers with reading deficiencies, and the sociodemographic composition of the classroom. Specific teacher attitude

### Table 10-1
### Total and Unique Percentage of Variance Explained in Social Status by Domain

| | Acceptance | | | Rejection | | |
|---|---|---|---|---|---|---|
| | Regular Class | | Special Self-Contained Class | Regular Class | | Special Self-Contained Class |
| Predictor | Nonhandi-capped Learners | Mainstreamed EMR Learners | Nonmainstreamed EMR Learners | Nonhandi-capped Learners | Mainstreamed EMR Learners | Nonmainstreamed EMR Learners |
| Full model (M1 or M2) | | | | | | |
| Total $R^2$ | 26 | 31 | 40 | 32 | 42 | 40 |
| Learner background | | | | | | |
| Total $R^2$ | 3(ns) | 6 | 3(ns) | 1(ns) | 6 | 2(ns) |
| Unique $R^2$ | 2(ns) | 5 | 1(ns) | 2(ns) | 4 | 1(ns) |
| Environment | | | | | | |
| Total $R^2$ | 24 | 26 | 39 | 30 | 38 | 39 |
| Unique $R^2$ | 23 | 25 | 37 | 31 | 36 | 38 |
| Classroom composition | | | | | | |
| Total $R^2$ | 10(ns) | 15 | 12(ns) | 8(ns) | 9(ns) | 10(ns) |
| Unique $R^2$ | 6(ns) | 9 | 5(ns) | 6(ns) | 6(ns) | 3(ns) |

| Socioemotional climate | | | | | | |
|---|---|---|---|---|---|---|
| Total R2 | 8 | 8 | 23 | 21 | 22 | 31 |
| UniqueR2 | 5 | 5 | 10 | 13 | 16 | 14 |
| Instructional conditions | | | | | | |
| Total R2 | 10(ns) | 9(ns) | 19 | 9(ns) | 14 | 16 |
| Unique R2 | 7(ns) | 7(ns) | 7(ns) | 5(ns) | 8(ns) | 5(ns) |

Note. Two commonality models were employed. In Model 1 (M1), two sets of variables—one representing learner background and another representing all the environment domains—were used to explain variance in learner competence. Model 2(M2), a four-set model, used the identical variables as Model 1 but divided the environment variables into three sets, representing the three environment domains—classroom composition, socioemotional climate, and instructional conditions.

measures were not significantly related to acceptance. The sociodemographic characteristics associated with acceptance were geographic location and ethnic composition of the peer group: Mainstreamed EMR learners enjoyed greater acceptance in urban schools and in classrooms with a small percentage of Anglo peers or a high percentage of Spanish-surnamed peers.

In the socioemotional climate domain, acceptance of the mainstreamed EMR learners was significantly affected by the cohesiveness of classroom peers, tending to be lower if dislike among peers was high. Rejection of the mainstreamed EMR learners was greater in classrooms with a high level of dislike among peers. Greater rejection of mainstreamed EMR learners was significantly associated with peer perception of deemphasized cognitive academic tasks in the instructional conditions domain. Certain peer instructional activities were also related to rejection. Rejection was greater when the classroom spent greater proportions of time working in student, self-directed small groups but was lower when the classroom spent more time in one large group taught directly by the teacher. In addition, EMR learners were more frequently rejected in an instructional context in which teacher-made materials were extensively used.

## Nonmainstreamed EMR Learners

Background and classroom environment together explained a significant percentage of the variance in both the acceptance (40%) and rejection (40%) of the nonmainstreamed EMR learners. Significant portions of variance in acceptance and rejection were uniquely accounted for by classroom environment, but not by background. Joint variance of background and environment was low in both equations.

The total contributions of socioemotional climate and instructional conditions to both acceptance and rejection were significant, and a significant portion of variance in both social status measures was uniquely explained by socioemotional climate. The joint contribution of socioemotional climate and instructional conditions accounted for 9% of the variance in acceptance and 7% of the variance in rejection; that is, that aspect of socioemotional climate which covaries with instructional conditions contributed to the social status of nonmainstreamed EMR learners.

Nonmainstreamed EMR learners were more likely to be accepted in classrooms with a directive teacher and/or cohesive peers as reflected by a low level of peer dislike or a high level of classroom harmony. Acceptance was negatively associated with the proportion of time spent in large-group, teacher-directed instruction and with the time the teacher spent in explaining or testing.

Nonmainstreamed EMR learners were more likely to experience rejection in classrooms where the teacher was nondirective or the peers noncohesive (as

Table 10-2

Total Percentage of Variance Explained in Social Status
by Domain, Subdomain, and Variable

| | Acceptance | | | Rejection | | |
|---|---|---|---|---|---|---|
| | Regular Class | | Special Self-Contained Class | Regular Class | | Special Self-Contained Class |
| Predictor | Nonhandi-capped Learners | Mainstreamed EMR Learners | Nonmainstreamed EMR Learners | Nonhandi-capped Learners | Mainstreamed EMR Learners | Nonmainstreamed EMR Learners |
| Full model | 26 | 31 | 40 | 32 | 42 | 40 |
| Learner background | | 6 | | | 6 | |
| Sex | | 3- | | | | |
| Age | | | | | 3- | |
| Ethnic group | | | | | | |
| Anglo | | 2 | | | | |
| Socioeconomic status | | 2- | | | 2 | |
| Family intactness | | | | | 2- | |
| Environment | 24 | 26 | 39 | 30 | 37 | 39 |
| Classroom composition | | 15 | | | | |
| Peer reading deficiency | | 2 | | | | |
| Peer sociodemographic characteristics | | 6 | | | | |
| Percentage Anglo | | 4- | | | | |
| Percentage Spanish-surnamed | | 2 | | | | |

| | | | | | | |
|---|---|---|---|---|---|---|
| Suburban location | 2- | | | | | |
| Urban location | 2 | | | | | |
| Peer attitude toward school | 4 | | | | | |
| Teacher educational attitudes | 3 | | | | | |
| Socioemotional climate | 8 | 8 | 23 | 21 | 22 | 31 |
| Teacher directiveness | | | 4 | | | 5 |
| Teacher control | | | 2 | | | 3- |
| Peer cohesiveness | 6 | 5 | 21 | 18 | 21 | 28 |
| Peer harmony | | | 4 | | | 5- |
| Peer dislike | 6- | 4- | 20- | 18 | 20 | 27 |
| Instructional conditions | | | 19 | | 14 | 16 |
| Instructional context | | | | | 3 | |
| Teacher-made materials | | | | | 3 | |
| Teacher strategies | | | | | 3 | |
| Peer perception of cognitive emphasis | | | | | 3- | |
| Peer instructional activity | | | 6 | | 4 | 5 |
| Teacher-directed, large group | | | 2- | | 2- | |
| Student-directed, small group | | | | | 2 | |

(Continued on next page.)

Table 10-2 (continued)

| Predictor | Acceptance | | | | Rejection | | | |
| | Regular Class | | Special Self-Contained Class | | Regular Class | | Special Self-Contained Class | |
| | Nonhandi-capped Learners | Mainstreamed EMR Learners | Nonmainstreamed EMR Learners | | Nonhandi-capped Learners | Mainstreamed EMR Learners | Nonmainstreamed EMR Learners | |
| Teacher instructional task | | | | | | | | |
| Explaining | | | 8 | | | | 6 | |
| Testing | | | 3- | | | | 2 | |
| | | | 3- | | | | | |

Note. All figures are squared correlation coefficients and are statistically significant ($p<.05$). Bivariate correlations were performed with individual predictor variables and multiple correlations were performed with sets of predictor variables. For learner background, statistically significant variables are presented only if the contribution of learner background is significant in the total equation. Similarly, for the environmental domains (classroom composition, socioemotional climate, and instructional conditions), statistically significant subdomains are presented only if the contribution of the domain is significant in the total equation, and significant variables are presented only if the contribution of the subdomain is significant. A minus sign follows the number if the correlation was negative.

evidenced by a high degree of dislike among peers and little classroom harmony). Peer instructional activities were also significantly associated with greater rejection of these learners although no specific activity significantly predicted rejection. One teacher instructional task — explaining — was positively related to rejection of nonmainstreamed learners as well.

## Discussion

The findings suggest that classroom environmental factors had a rather strong impact on learner social status. The classroom environment accounted for a unique proportion of variance (ranging from 23-38%) in both acceptance and rejection of all three groups of learners, particularly socioemotional climate. In classrooms with a low incidence of peer dislike, the learner, nonhandicapped or EMR, was better accepted and less rejected than in classrooms in which peer dislike was high. A word of caution is in order with regard to these findings. The peer dislike construct was comprised of several scores obtained from the sociometric instrument *How I Feel Toward Others* (HIFTO), from which each learner's acceptance and rejection were also derived. The relatively high relationships between peer dislike and social acceptance or rejection could possibly have resulted from an artifact of the measurement properties common to both sets of constructs.

Several features of the classroom environment controlled by the teacher were related to the acceptance and rejection of EMR learners. In the regular classrooms, mainstreamed EMR learners were less rejected if the teacher used large-group instruction rather than small, student-directed groups. The large-group activity may allow the cognitive deficiencies of the EMR learner to be minimized, whereas close interaction with peers on a group project may highlight them.

Nonmainstreamed EMR learners received more acceptance and less rejection from their peers in the special self-contained classrooms when the teacher was directive. It may be that the higher degree of teacher control structures the interactions among students in the classroom, making them more positive in nature.

Among the background characteristics of the mainstreamed EMR learners related to social status, the results indicated that males were significantly better accepted than females, and Black and Spanish-surnamed learners were better accepted than Anglo learners. Inspection of mean achievement scores in subsequent analyses indicated that although the normative academic status of the mainstreamed male EMR learners was similar to that of the mainstreamed female EMR learners, the discrepancy between achievement scores of these female EMR learners and the nonhandicapped females was greater than that between the mainstreamed male EMR learners and the nonhandicapped males. Similarly, although the mainstreamed male EMR learners on the average misbehaved more than did the mainstreamed female EMR learners, there was a greater discrepancy between the frequency of misbehavior of the two groups of females (mainstreamed and nonhandicapped) than the two groups of males. Differences between mean achievement scores of Anglo mainstreamed and nonhandicapped learners were also greater than those between non-Anglo mainstreamed and nonhandicapped learners, and a similar finding was obtained with regard to misbehavior. Thus, in relation to the nonhandicapped learners, the mainstreamed female and Anglo learners may have appeared less competent to their reference group of female and Anglo learners, respectively, than the differences between their male or non-Anglo counterparts, resulting in less acceptance by their nonhandicapped peers.

## Social Behavior

The acceptance of mainstreaming largely stems from the belief that the behavior of EMR learners will improve in the regular classroom (Dunn, 1968). Proponents of mainstreaming argue that regular classroom placement will provide EMR learners with more appropriate role models than those available in special classrooms and that their behavior will resemble that of their nonhandicapped peers. Empirical support for this assertion is provided by observational studies conducted with elementary and preschool children (Gampel, Gottlieb, & Harrison, 1974; Forman et al., 1980).

At present, little is known about variations in regular classroom environments that affect children's positive and negative behavior. The need to identify environmental variations associated with positive behavior is critical since many regular classroom teachers, believing that EMR learners are likely to exhibit inappropriate behavior that will upset the classroom routine, are reluctant to have them in their classrooms. If we can identify the classroom characteristics associated with a low incidence of negative behavior, we may improve our ability to place EMR learners in classrooms that minimize the frequency of their misbehavior.

A number of background and classroom environmental factors may affect the social behavior in school of nonhandicapped and EMR learners. First, characteristics of the learners may influence the type of behavior they exhibit. For example, males are expected to display more aggressive behavior than females — behavior often interpreted negatively by classroom teachers.

Second, environmental characteristics such as the socioemotional climate may affect social behavior. For example, classrooms marked by harmony and little dislike among peers may provide a climate conducive to appropriate social behavior, particularly if those behaviors represent the norm of the peer group. Teachers who exhibit warm behavior and provide a structured classroom environment are expected to foster better behavior among EMR learners than teachers who seldom exhibit warm behavior and/or allow a great deal of pupil freedom (Kirk & Johnson, 1950; Kolburne, 1965). Teachers who prefer loosely-run classrooms may create inappropriate environments for students who require structure, resulting in more behavior problems. Teachers who are more highly trained or have been teaching for a number of years may have developed more effective strategies for managing student behaviors.

Finally, the instructional conditions of classrooms can affect student social behavior. Classrooms with a heavy cognitive emphasis can be expected to create situations that frustrate EMR learners, thereby exposing their academic limitations to peers which may affect their social behavior adversely.

## Results

The results of the commonality analyses which employed the two measures of social behavior as criteria for each of the three learner groups are presented in Tables 10-3 and 10-4. Table 10-3 presents the total and unique percentages of variance explained in these measures by domains. Table 10-4 presents the significant total (but not unique) percentages of variance explained by subdomains and variables as well as by domains.

### Nonhandicapped Learners

Background and classroom environment together predicted identical portions of variance in the nonhandicapped learner's antisocial (29%) and friendly/cooperative (29%) behavior. A significant portion of variance in antisocial behavior was uniquely accounted for by learner background. The regular classroom environment explained a significant total but not unique portion of the variance in antisocial behavior. Classroom environment, but not background, uniquely accounted for a significant proportion of variance in friendly/cooperative behavior. The joint contribution of learner background and classroom environment was small in both equations.

Background characteristics of the nonhandicapped learners which were significantly correlated with antisocial behavior were sex and ethnic group. Males were apt to display more antisocial behavior than females, and Black learners exhibited more antisocial behavior than Anglo or Spanish-surnamed learners.

The total contributions of each of the environment domains — classroom composition, socioemotional climate, and instructional conditions — were significantly related to the nonhandicapped learner's antisocial behavior. None of the environment domains, however, uniquely accounted for significant portions of variance. Joint contributions among the three environment domains were low.

High levels of antisocial behavior of nonhandicapped learners were associated with several characteristics of their peer groups and the physical quality of the classroom. A high incidence of peers who were behind in reading, a low percentage of Anglo peers, low classroom harmony, and a low level of interest and attention among the peers were significantly related to antisocial behavior among nonhandicapped learners. Classrooms of poor physical quality were associated with high levels of antisocial behavior.

The total contributions of both the socioemotional climate and instructional condition domains were significantly related to the nonhandicapped learners' friendly/cooperative behavior. Moreover, significant portions of variance in friendly/cooperative behavior were uniquely accounted for by instructional conditions and marginally by socioemotional climate ($R = 0.03$, $p<.06$). Joint contributions among the three environment domains were low.

Friendly/cooperative behavior was exhibited more frequently by nonhandicapped learners whose teachers were warm, nondirective, used positive influence, and employed individual differentiation as a teaching strategy. The more extensive the teacher feedback to peers, the greater the likelihood the nonhandicapped learners would display friendly/cooperative behavior. More friendly/cooperative behavior was exhibited by nonhandicapped learners when more time was spent in student self-directed, small-group instruction and noninstructional activities.

## Mainstreamed EMR Learners

Background and environment together explained significant portions of variance in both the antisocial (33%) and friendly/cooperative (29%) behavior of the mainstreamed EMR learners. Significant portions of variance in antisocial behavior were uniquely accounted for by background and environment, whereas only environment uniquely accounted for a significant portion of the variance in friendly/cooperative behavior. The joint contribution of background and environment to the antisocial and friendly/cooperative behavior of the mainstreamed EMR learners was minimal.

The particular learner background characteristics which were found to affect the antisocial behavior of these learners were sex and ethnic group. Males exhibited more antisocial behavior than females, and Anglo learners displayed less antisocial behavior than Black or Spanish-surnamed learners. These relationships are similar to those found for nonhandicapped learners.

Table 10-3

Total and Unique Percentage of Variance Explained
in Social Behavior by Domain

| Predictor | Antisocial Behavior | | | Friendly/Cooperative Behavior | | |
| --- | --- | --- | --- | --- | --- | --- |
| | Regular Class | | Special Self-Contained Class | Regular Class | | Special Self-Contained Class |
| | Nonhandi-capped Learners | Mainstreamed EMR Learners | Nonmainstreamed EMR Learners | Nonhandi-capped Learners | Mainstreamed EMR Learners | Nonmainstreamed EMR Learners |
| Full model (M1 or M2) | | | | | | |
| Total R2 | 29 | 33 | 43 | 29 | 29 | 44 |
| Learner background | | | | | | |
| Total R2 | 11 | 5 | 8 | 1(ns) | 3(ns) | 4(ns) |
| Unique R2 | 8 | 5 | 6 | 1(ns) | 1(ns) | 1(ns) |
| Environment | | | | | | |
| Total R2 | 21 | 28 | 37 | 28 | 28 | 43 |
| Unique R2 | 18(ns) | 28 | 35 | 28 | 26 | 40 |

| | | | | | | |
|---|---|---|---|---|---|---|
| **Classroom composition** | | | | | | |
| Total R2 | 10 | 12 | 21 | 9(ns) | 12 | 18 |
| Unique R2 | 5(ns) | 8(ns) | 10 | 6(ns) | 6(ns) | 5(ns) |
| **Socioemotional climate** | | | | | | |
| Total R2 | 8 | 13 | 16 | 8 | 11 | 22 |
| UniqueR2 | 3(ns) | 9 | 6 | 3(ns) | 4 | 7 |
| **Instructional conditions** | | | | | | |
| Total R2 | 12 | 9(ns) | 19 | 16 | 14 | 27 |
| Unique R2 | 5(ns) | 8(ns) | 7(ns) | 13 | 10(ns) | 14 |

Note. Two commonality models were employed. In Model 1 (M1), two sets of variables—one representing learner background and another representing all the environment domains—were used to explain variance in learner competence. Model 2 (M2), a four-set model, used the identical variables as Model 1 but divided the environment variables into three sets, representing the three environment domains—classroom composition, socioemotional climate, and instructional conditions.

# Table 10-4
## Total Percentage of Variance Explained in Social Behavior by Domain, Subdomain, and Variable

| Predictor | Antisocial Behavior — Regular Class — Nonhandicapped Learners | Antisocial Behavior — Regular Class — Mainstreamed EMR Learners | Antisocial Behavior — Special Self-Contained Class — Nonmainstreamed EMR Learners | Friendly/Cooperative Behavior — Regular Class — Nonhandicapped Learners | Friendly/Cooperative Behavior — Regular Class — Mainstreamed EMR Learners | Friendly/Cooperative Behavior — Special Self-Contained Class — Nonmainstreamed EMR Learners |
|---|---|---|---|---|---|---|
| Full model | 29 | 33 | 43 | 29 | 29 | 44 |
| Learner background | 11 | 5 | 8 | | | |
| Sex | 7– | 2– | 5– | | | |
| Age | | | 2– | | | |
| Ethnic group | 3 | 3 | | | | |
| Anglo | | 2– | | | | |
| Black | 3 | 2 | | | | |
| Environment | 21 | 28 | 37 | 28 | 28 | 43 |
| Classroom composition | 10 | 12 | 21 | | 12 | 18 |
| Peer reading deficiency | 2 | | | | | |
| Peer sociodemographic characteristics | 3 | | | | 5 | 9 |
| Percentage Anglo | 2– | | | | 3– | |
| Percentage Black | | | | | | 5– |
| Percentage Spanish-surnamed | | | | | 2 | 4 |
| Percentage lower class | | | | | | 5 |
| Suburban location | | | | | | 2 |

| | | | | |
|---|---|---|---|---|
| Peer attitude toward school | | | | 4 |
| Teacher ability, training, and experience | | | | |
| Verbal facility | | 8 | 4 | 4 |
| Years of teaching experience | | 4 | 3- | 2- |
| Educational status | | 5- | | 3- |
| Teacher socio-demographic characteristics | | 2- | | 5 |
| Anglo | | 10 | | 4- |
| Black | | 9 | | 2 |
| Spanish-surnamed | | 6- | | |
| Teacher educational attitudes | 3 | | | 7 |
| Importance of open, warm environment | | | | 2 |
| Importance of structured, controlled environment | 3 | | | 2- |
| Belief in traditional authority | | | | 5- |
| Teacher attitudes toward mainstreaming | | 6 | | |
| Attitude toward integration of students with social problems | | 5 | | |
| Teacher report of adequacy of special support services | | 5- | | |

(Continued on next page.)

Table 10-4   (continued)

| Predictor | Antisocial Behavior | | | Friendly/Cooperative Behavior | | |
| --- | --- | --- | --- | --- | --- | --- |
| | Regular Class | | Special Self-Contained Class | Regular Class | | Special Self-Contained Class |
| | Nonhandicapped Learners | Mainstreamed EMR Learners | Nonmainstreamed EMR Learners | Nonhandicapped Learners | Mainstreamed EMR Learners | Nonmainstreamed EMR Learners |
| Socioemotional climate | | | | | | |
| Teacher warmth | 8 | 13 | 16 | 8 | 11 | 22 |
| Teacher directiveness | | | | 2 | | 8 |
| Peer freedom | | | 3 | 5 | 6 | 16 |
| Teacher control | | | | 3 | 5 | 14 |
| Teacher influence | | | 2– | 3– | 3 | 4– |
| Positive | | | | 3 | 3 | 9 |
| Coercive-legitimate | | | | 3 | | 2 |
| Peer cohesiveness | 6 | 12 | 11 | | | 7– |
| Peer harmony | 5– | 11– | 11– | | 3 | |
| Peer dislike | | | 2 | | 2– | |
| Instructional conditions | | | | | | |
| Instructional context | 12 | | 19 | 16 | 14 | 27 |
| Physical quality | 4 | | 3 | | 2 | 4 |
| Teacher-made materials | 3– | | 3– | | 2– | |
| Instructional engagment | 5 | | | | 3 | 3 |
| Peer interest and attention | 4– | | | | | 3 |
| Teacher strategies | | | | 4 | | 10 |
| Individual differentiation | | | | 3 | | 7 |
| Peer instructional activity | | | | 4 | | 5 |

| | | | |
|---|---|---|---|
| Teacher-directed, large group | | | 3 |
| Student self-directed, individual | | | 3– |
| Student-directed, small group | 2 | | 8 |
| | | | 5 |
| Teacher instructional task | 8 | | |
| Introducing or motivating | 2– | | |
| Summarizing or reviewing | 6– | | |
| Testing | | | |
| Class cognitive discourse | | 5 | |
| Moderately low index | | 3– | |
| Very high index | | 2– | |
| Teacher instructional feedback to peers | 2 | 4 | 5 |
| Positive index | | 4– | |
| Negative index | | | 4– |
| Frequency of feedback | | 3– | |

Note. All figures are squared correlation coefficients and are statistically significant ($p < .05$). Bivariate correlations were performed with individual predictor variables and multiple correlations were performed with sets of predictor variables. For learner background, statistically significant variables are presented only if the contribution of learner background is significant in the total equation. Similarly, for the environmental domains (classroom composition, socioemotional climate, and instructional conditions), statistically significant subdomains are presented only if the contribution of the domain is significant in the total equation, and significant variables are presented only if the contribution of the subdomain is significant. A minus sign follows the number if the correlation was negative.

Classroom composition and socioemotional climate were significant predictors of antisocial behavior while all three environment domains were significant predictors of friendly/cooperative behavior. However, significant portions of variance in both antisocial and friendly/cooperative behavior were uniquely accounted for only by socioemotional climate. Joint contributions among the three environment domains were low in both equations.

The mainstreamed EMR learners tended to exhibit more antisocial behavior if their teachers held certain educational attitudes such as favoring a structured, controlled environment. Antisocial behavior among these learners was also found to be more frequent in classrooms with little peer harmony.

The friendly/cooperative behavior of the mainstreamed EMR learners was modestly associated with a lack of harmony among the classroom peers and with the sociodemographic characteristics of the peers. The smaller the percentage of Anglo peers or the greater the percentage of Spanish-surnamed peers, the more likely the mainstreamed EMR learners were to display friendly/cooperative behavior. Mainstreamed EMR learners were also more likely to exhibit friendly/cooperative behavior if their teachers had few years of teaching experience, were nondirective, or used positive influence. Friendly/cooperative behavior occurred more frequently in certain instructional contexts (such as classrooms with poor physical quality), and in classrooms in which the level of cognitive discourse was generally neither moderately low nor very high. Surprisingly, the extent of teacher feedback to peers, particularly positive feedback, was inversely related to friendly/cooperative behavior.

## Nonmainstreamed EMR Learners

Together, learner background and classroom environment explained a significant percentage of the variance in the antisocial (43%) and friendly/cooperative (44%) behavior of nonmainstreamed EMR learners. While a significant portion of variance in antisocial behavior was uniquely accounted for by background, this relationship was not obtained with friendly/cooperative behavior. Significant portions of variance in both behavior measures were uniquely explained by environment. Joint variance between background and environment was small in both equations.

The total contributions of each of the three environment domains were significant to antisocial behavior and friendly/cooperative behavior. Significant portions of variance in antisocial behavior were uniquely accounted for by classroom composition and socioemotional climate; and in friendly/cooperative behavior by socioemotional climate and instructional conditions. The joint contribution of all three environment domains accounted for 6% of the variance in friendly/cooperative behavior. No other sizeable commonalities among environment domains were attained in either equation.

In the classroom composition domain, males and younger nonmainstreamed EMR learners displayed more antisocial behavior than did females and older learners. In addition, nonmainstreamed EMR learners exhibited more antisocial behavior in classrooms with Anglo teachers or teachers who had a high level of verbal facility, few years of teaching experience, low educational status, positive attitudes toward mainstreaming (particularly toward mainstreaming children with social problems), or who reported they received inadequate special support services.

In the socioemotional climate domain, nonmainstreamed learners displayed more antisocial behavior if their teachers were nondirective or their peers revealed a high level of dislike or a low level of harmony. With regard to instructional conditions, these learners exhibited more antisocial behavior in classrooms of poor physical quality. Antisocial behavior was more significantly associated with teacher instructional tasks that did not involve summarizing or testing.

Several variables in the classroom composition domain related to friendly/cooperative behavior of nonmainstreamed learners. Friendly/cooperative behavior was more frequent in suburban schools and among peers with certain sociodemographic characteristics, such as a low percentage of Black peers, a high percentage of Spanish-surnamed peers, or a high percentage of low-SES classroom peers. These behaviors were also more frequent in classrooms in which peer attitude toward school was positive. Teachers who had Spanish surnames; few years of teaching; low educational status; and valued a warm, open environment rather than a structured, controlled environment or traditional authority were more likely to have nonmainstreamed EMR learners who exhibited friendly/cooperative behavior.

In regard to socioemotional climate, friendly/cooperative behavior of nonmainstreamed learners was significantly associated with teacher warmth and nondirectiveness, as reflected in peer freedom, and with teachers' frequent use of positive influence and infrequent use of coercive-legitimate influence. In the instructional conditions domain, friendly/cooperative behavior was more frequent in classrooms in which peers were interested and paying attention or teachers used individual differentiation as an instructional strategy. Friendly/cooperative behavior of nonmainstreamed learners was also more likely to occur in instructional contexts characterized by extensive use of teacher-made materials. A high proportion of time spent in large-group instruction directed by the teacher or a low proportion of time spent in self-directed individual instruction was significantly associated with friendly/cooperative behavior. Also significantly associated was infrequent use of negative feedback to peers.

## Discussion

The background of all three groups of learners contributed significantly to the frequency of antisocial behavior. Males, regardless of grouping, exhibited more antisocial behavior than females, a reason often cited for their disproportionate enrollment in special education classes. It may be that regular classroom teachers are more likely to recommend these males for placement in special classrooms due to this behavior. It is interesting that the nonhandicapped males also exhibited antisocial behavior more often than their female counterparts.

The socioemotional climate of the classroom was generally related to antisocial behavior. Specifically, antisocial behavior of nonhandicapped and EMR learners occurred more frequently in classrooms characterized by little harmony among peers. Classrooms characterized by harmonious behavior may reduce the incidence of misbehavior by setting standards for appropriate behavior to which all students, including EMR learners, then conform.

Other than encouraging a harmonious climate, there is little suggested in these results that regular teachers can do to minimize the antisocial behavior of mainstreamed EMR learners. Nonmainstreamed EMR learner antisocial behavior, however, may be reduced by teachers who engage in frequent summarizing and testing and large-group organized and focussed activities that command student attention. Similarly, as expected, nonhandicapped students' behavior may be influenced by teachers who maintain the interest and attention of the students.

One should be aware that a causal interpretation of these findings is tenuous. It may be that a disruptive student, whether nonhandicapped or EMR, creates enough disturbance to reduce the level of harmony present among peers.

The finding that the warmth of special self-contained classroom teachers was associated with the friendly/cooperative behavior of nonmainstreamed EMR learners supports the traditional belief that EMR learners function better with warm teachers. Teacher warmth also contributed to the friendly/cooperative behavior of nonhandicapped learners. Interestingly, however, teacher warmth was not a significant determinant of mainstreamed EMR learner friendly/cooperative behavior. It is possible that mainstreamed EMR learners may be so overwhelmed by the teacher's academic demands and peer competence that the teacher's expressed warmth is insufficient to bring about friendly/cooperative behavior. Furthermore, the large number of students in the regular classroom may diffuse the warmth available to any one child. While the amount of warmth directed toward an individual child is sufficient for nonhandicapped students, EMR learners, given the higher levels of stress associated with the regular classroom setting, may require greater warmth and support in that setting.

A surprising finding was the significant relationship between teacher nondirectiveness and friendly/cooperative behavior of both mainstreamed and nonmainstreamed EMR learners. In special self-contained classrooms, a substantial amount of variance in the friendly/cooperative behavior of EMR learners was explained by teacher nondirectiveness (16%). This finding, contrary to conventional beliefs, suggests that EMR learners, like nonhandicapped students, exhibit more friendly/cooperative behavior in classrooms in which they have at least a moderate degree of freedom. An alternative explanation, of course, is that teachers of friendly, cooperative students can allow more pupil freedom. But EMR learners in special classrooms with nondirective teachers also exhibited more antisocial behavior as well. Freedom and reduced structure have both positive and negative effects: They encourage freer behaviors, some portion of which deteriorate into antisocial acts.

The results indicate nonhandicapped children engaged in more friendly/cooperative behaviors with teachers who were warm, nondirective, used positive influence, gave more individualized instruction, provided opportunities for student-directed small-group activities, or allowed time for noninstructional (peer-peer interaction) activities. EMR learners in both regular and special self-contained classrooms exhibited more friendly/cooperative behavior with teachers who were nondirective or used positive influence. The friendly/cooperative behavior of nonmainstreamed EMR learners was associated with teacher warmth and infrequent use of coercive-legitimate behavior. In sum, while EMR learners seem to need some controls over their behaviors to minimize negative outbursts, especially in special self-contained classrooms, they seem not to prosper behaviorally when the classrooms are too tightly structured, too stressful in their emphasis of academics, or too loosely structured so their problems in control over their behaviors result in negative outbursts.

## Social Attitudes

Student social attitudes are thought to be an integral part of their social competence, influencing behavior toward others as well as perceptions of others. Chapter 5 suggests that the legitimate goals of the school, particularly for EMR learners, are to reduce feelings of estrangement or loneliness and to enhance positive attitudes toward peers. Loneliness reflects a sense of exclusion, rejection, and inadequacy in social situations. Student attitudes toward agemates are indicated by the degree to which they accept their classmates. These social attitudes are thought to develop from experiences in social situations and influence behavior in and attraction to social situations (Gronlund, 1959; McCandless, 1973).

Relatively little research has been carried out to determine the relationships of variations in characteristics of student backgrounds or classroom environments to social attitudes. A few studies of self-concept have suggested that females have more positive self-concepts than males (Bledsoe, 1963) and lower-class students have more negative self-concepts than upper- or middle-class children (Rosenberg, 1963; Whiteman & Deutsch, 1968). It has been widely accepted that minority group membership is associated with a less positive self-concept (Johnson & Medinnus, 1967).

Despite the paucity of empirical research, theorists generally agree that the social environment of the classroom is highly related to the social attitudes of the individual student. Positive social attitudes are thought to be promoted by warm teachers who give frequent praise and encouragement and little scolding or punishment (Coopersmith, 1969; Schmuck & Schmuck, 1975). Democratic or nondirective regular classroom teachers whose students have frequent opportunities for interaction are thought to promote positive social attitudes (Gronlund, 1959), provided the peer interactions are positive (Bouchard, 1970; Joyce & Weil, 1972; Schmuck & Schmuck, 1975). Although "positive interaction" is often vaguely defined, it is usually considered in terms of warmth, support, and involvement or cohesiveness within the classroom group, with minimal levels of peer dislike, competitiveness, hostility, or alienation (Joyce & Weil, 1972; Schmuck & Schmuck, 1975).

These theories suggest that in cohesive regular classrooms with warm, nondirective teachers who use positive influence techniques, students will be less likely to feel lonely and more apt to have positive attitudes toward their peers. Individuals are more apt to like others who are similar to themselves in characteristics such as ability (Festinger, 1954), as well as those they perceive to like them (Jones, 1974). Mainstreamed EMR learners are lower in IQ and achievement than their peers and are not particularly liked by their nonhandicapped classmates (Goodman, Gottlieb, & Harrison, 1972; Johnson, 1950). It is therefore conceivable that, despite a warm teacher and cohesive regular classroom, EMR learners might perceive themselves as rejected by their peers and develop negative social attitudes. Thus, it is of interest to determine whether relationships between classroom environmental characteristics and social attitudes of nonhandicapped children pertain to mainstreamed EMR learners as well.

## Results

The results of the commonality analyses which employed the two measures of social attitude as criteria for each of the three learners groups are presented in Tables 10-5 and 10-6. Table 10-5 presents the total and unique percentages of variances explained in these measures by domains; Table 10-6 presents the significant total (but not unique) percentages of variance explained by subdomains and variables as well as by domains.

## Nonhandicapped Learners

Together the learner background and regular classroom environment of nonhandicapped learners failed to account for a significant portion of variance in their feelings of loneliness.

Nonhandicapped learners' feelings about peers, however, were significantly predicted by background and environment together, with nearly all the total variance uniquely accounted for by the environment domains. While the total contributions of both the socioemotional climate and instructional conditions were significantly related to feelings about peers, socioemotional climate uniquely accounted for the significant portion of variance. Joint contributions among classroom environment domains, and between environment and background, were low.

Within the socioemotional climate, teacher methods of influence were significantly related to nonhandicapped learners' feelings about peers, although no one specific influence was significant. Not surprisingly, learners had less positive feelings about their peers in classrooms where the dislike among classroom peers was high. Within the instructional conditions domain, only the subdomain of teacher instructional task significantly predicted nonhandicapped learners' feelings about peers; specific variables within this subdomain were not significantly related to these learners' feelings about peers, however.

## Mainstreamed EMR Learners

Together, background and environment explained significant portions of variance in mainstreamed EMR learners' feelings of loneliness (30%), with significant portions of variance uniquely accounted for by background and the environment domains.

Background characteristics found to be significantly related to feelings of loneliness were sex and ethnic group; more females and Anglo learners tended to express feelings of loneliness than males or Black and Spanish-surnamed learners.

The total and unique contributions of socioemotional climate to feelings of loneliness were significant, whereas neither the total nor unique contributions of the other two environment domains significantly affected this dependent measure. Commonalities among environment domains, and between background and environment, were low. Loneliness of mainstreamed EMR learners was found to be significantly related to teacher methods of influence. Learners who expressed feelings of loneliness tended to have teachers who used coercive-legitimate influence.

Table 10-3

Total and Unique Percentage of Variance Explained in Social Behavior by Domain

| | Feelings of Loneliness | | | Feelings About Peers | | |
| | Regular Class | | Special Self-Contained Class | Regular Class | | Special Self-Contained Class |
| Predictor | Nonhandicapped Learners | Mainstreamed EMR Learners | Nonmainstreamed EMR Learners | Nonhandicapped Learners | Mainstreamed EMR Learners | Nonmainstreamed EMR Learners |
|---|---|---|---|---|---|---|
| Full model (M1 or M2) | | | | | | |
| Total R2 | 18(ns) | 30 | 20(ns) | 25 | 24 | 37 |
| Learner background | | | | | | |
| Total R2 | 2(ns) | 7 | 2(ns) | 2(ns) | 2(ns) | 1(ns) |
| Unique R2 | 2(ns) | 7 | 2(ns) | 1(ns) | 2(ns) | 2(ns) |
| Environment | | | | | | |
| Total R2 | 16(ns) | 23 | 18(ns) | 24 | 22 | 35 |
| Unique R2 | 16(ns) | 23 | 18(ns) | 23 | 22 | 36 |
| Classroom composition | | | | | | |
| Total R2 | 10(ns) | 10(ns) | 9(ns) | 9(ns) | 9(ns) | 11(ns) |
| Unique R2 | 8(ns) | 8(ns) | 7(ns) | 4(ns) | 6(ns) | 7(ns) |

| | | | | | | |
|---|---|---|---|---|---|---|
| **Socioemotional climate** | | | | | | |
| Total R2 | 2(ns) | 5 | 3(ns) | 13 | 8 | 23 |
| UniqueR2 | 1(ns) | 6 | 1(ns) | 7 | 6 | 13 |
| **Instructional conditions** | | | | | | |
| Total R2 | 6(ns) | 9(ns) | 8(ns) | 11 | 6(ns) | 10(ns) |
| Unique R2 | 5(ns) | 9(ns) | 8(ns) | 5(ns) | 8(ns) | 8(ns) |

*Note.* Two commonality models were employed. In Model 1 (M1), two sets of variables—one representing learner background and another representing all the environment domains—were used to explain variance in learner competence. Model 2(M2), a four-set model, used the identical variables as Model 1 but divided the environment variables into three sets, representing the three environment domains—classroom composition, socioemotional climate, and instructional conditions.

## Table 10-6
## Total Percentage of Variance Explained in Social Attitudes
### by Domain, Subdomain, and Variable

| Predictor | Feelings of Loneliness | | | Feelings About Peers | | |
|---|---|---|---|---|---|---|
| | Regular Class | | Special Self-Contained Class | Regular Class | | Special Self-Contained Class |
| | Nonhandi-capped Learners | Mainstreamed EMR Learners | Nonmainstreamed EMR Learners | Nonhandi-capped Learners | Mainstreamed EMR Learners | Nonmainstreamed EMR Learners |
| Full model | 30 | | | 25 | 24 | 37 |
| Learner background | 7 | | | | | |
| Sex | 4 | | | | | |
| Ethnic group | 3 | | | | | |
| Anglo | 2 | | | | | |
| Socioeconomic status | 2 | | | | | |

| Environment | 23 | 24 | 22 | 35 |
|---|---|---|---|---|
| Socioemotional climate | 5 | 13 | 8 | 23 |
|   Teacher directiveness | | | | |
|   Teacher control | | | | 3 |
|   Teacher influence | 3 | 2 | | 2 |
|   Coercive-legitimate | 2 | | | |
| Peer cohesiveness | | 11 | 7 | 22 |
|   Peer dislike | | 11– | 7– | 22– |
| Instructional conditions | | 11 | | |
|   Teacher instructional task | | 4 | | |

Note. All figures are squared correlation coefficients and are statistically significant ($p < .05$). Bivariate correlations were performed with individual predictor variables and multiple correlations were performed with sets of predictor variables. For learner background, statistically significant variables are presented only if the contribution of learner background is significant in the total equation. Similarly, for the environmental domains (classroom composition, socioemotional climate, and instructional conditions), statistically significant subdomains are presented only if the contribution of the domain is significant in the total equation, and significant variables are presented only if the contribution of the subdomain is significant. A minus sign follows the number if the correlation was negative.

Background and environment together explained a significant portion of variance in mainstreamed EMR learners' feelings about peers (24%), with a significant portion of variance uniquely accounted for by environment but not by background. Joint variances between background and environment and among environment domains were low. The total and unique contribution of socioemotional climate to feelings about peers were significant. Specifically, positive feelings about peers were inversely related to peer dislike.

### Nonmainstreamed EMR Learners

Learner background and classroom environment together did not account for a significant portion of variance in nonmainstreamed EMR learners' feelings of loneliness.

A significant percentage of the variance in these learners' feelings about peers (37%) was predicted by background and environment together, with a significant portion of variance uniquely accounted for by environment but not background. The common variance of background and environment in this equation was minimal.

The total and unique contributions of socioemotional climate to feelings about peers were significant. Nonmainstreamed EMR learners tended to have positive feelings about peers if their teacher was directive or their classmates revealed a low level of peer dislike. Neither the total nor the unique contributions of classroom composition or instructional conditions reached significance, and commonalities among classroom environment domains were relatively small.

## Discussion

The socioemotional climate of classrooms was significantly related to feelings about peers among all three groups of learners. Peer dislike was negatively related to feelings about peers of each learner group, in keeping with social attraction theory and research, which suggests that individuals are attracted to and feel most positively about persons who like them (Homans, 1961; Thibaut & Kelley, 1959). In classrooms where many children express dislike for their classmates, the students are apt to feel rejected by others in the classroom and to express relatively negative attitudes toward their classmates. We must exercise caution in drawing this conclusion, however, because the two measures of peer dislike and feelings about peers were derived from the same sociometric instrument.

The nonmainstreamed EMR learners were found to have somewhat more positive feelings about peers in special classrooms where the teacher was directive than in classrooms where the teacher was nondirective. This finding is consistent with the traditional special education adage that many EMR learners function best in a structured environment. Although the specific dynamics which foster such a relationship are unclear, one possibility is that the structure imposed by the teacher minimizes the frequency of hostile, antagonistic incidents among peers which may eventually evolve into active dislike.

An interesting finding was the low but significant relationship between teacher use of coercive-legitimate influence and feelings of loneliness expressed by mainstreamed EMR learners. Though this relationship is implied in the general self-concept and influence literature, the precise nature of the link between teachers' influence style and individual learners' feelings of exclusion, rejection, and inadequacy is unclear. It may be that the EMR learners, lacking confidence in their ability or worth, internalize their teachers' negative or critical remarks whether or not they are specifically directed toward them. This notion is supported by research findings which have indicated that EMR learners perceive even neutral experiences as personal failure (MacMillan & Keogh, 1971). If EMR learners do internalize teachers' negative remarks, a generally lower sense of self-worth, feelings of being rejected by the teacher, and ultimately, perhaps, general feelings of loneliness and isolation may result.

Rather surprising were the low but significant findings that more female and Anglo mainstreamed EMR learners expressed feelings of loneliness than mainstreamed EMR learners who were male, Black, or Spanish-surnamed. Research on the self-concepts of nonhandicapped children has found females to have more positive self-concepts than males (Bledsoe, 1963) and negative self-concepts to be associated with minority group membership (Johnson & Medinnus, 1967). One possible explanation for this unexpected set of findings is found in the arguments of mainstreaming proponents who frequently contend that minority group children and males are disproportionately represented in the EMR population. Such students are more likely to be identified and labelled EMR learners and placed in a special classroom because of their acting-out behavior and/or the cultural biases of schools (Mercer, 1973).

This argument suggests that Anglo students and females who are actually labelled EMR learners may be less competent than similarly labelled male or minority group students because of the bias against labelling Anglo and female students. According to this logic, Anglo and female EMR learners who are mainstreamed into regular classrooms should deviate markedly from their nonhandicapped classmates with respect to behavior and/or ability, experience less acceptance by peers than other mainstreamed EMR learners, and, consequently, experience greater feelings of loneliness. Empirical support for this belief was presented earlier in this chapter: Mainstreamed EMR learners who were Anglo or female were found to be less accepted than their Black or Spanish-surnamed or male counterparts. But the regular classrooms and the special classrooms tended to be heavily Hispanic and the Anglo students who were less competent were "odd men out."

In general, these results suggest that the socioemotional climate of the classroom can influence the social attitudes of students, and these factors must be examined carefully in future research.

## Summary and Implications

In this chapter the relationships of social competence to learner background, the socioemotional climate, classroom composition, and instructional conditions of the classroom environments were explored. The results can be summarized as follows: The learners' background characteristics generally did not explain substantial portions of variance in the social competence of the nonhandicapped or EMR learners, regardless of whether the EMR learners were mainstreamed or not. Background characteristics were significantly related to the social status of the mainstreamed EMR learners but not to the status of the nonhandicapped learners or the EMR learners in special self-contained classrooms. Background characteristics explained significant amounts of variance in the antisocial behavior of the three groups of learners but failed to explain a significant amount of variance in the friendly/cooperative behavior of any of the three groups. Finally, learner background characteristics were not significantly related to feelings about peers in any of the three learner groups, although background was related to the feelings of loneliness expressed by the mainstreamed EMR learners.

On the whole, aspects of the classroom environment did explain substantial amounts of the variance in the social competence of the nonhandicapped and EMR learners. The socioemotional climate of the classroom explained considerably more variance in social competence for all learner groups than did learner background; in terms of social acceptance and rejection, friendly/cooperative and antisocial behavior, and feelings about peers. It was also significantly related to feelings of loneliness of the mainstreamed EMR learners.

The instructional conditions of the classroom were significantly related to the social acceptance and rejection of the nonmainstreamed EMR learners, as well as to the social rejection of the mainstreamed EMR learners, but did not significantly predict the social status of the nonhandicapped learners.

Instructional conditions were also significantly related to the expression of friendly/cooperative behavior among all groups of learners but only affected the antisocial behavior of the nonmainstreamed EMR and nonhandicapped learners. While nonhandicapped learners' feelings about peers were significantly related to instructional conditions, EMR learners' feelings about peers were not significantly related to instructional conditions. Also not significantly related to instructional conditions were EMR and nonhandicapped learners' feelings of loneliness.

Classroom composition influenced mainstreamed EMR learner social acceptance, but did not relate to the acceptance of the nonhandicapped learners or nonmainstreamed EMR learners nor to the social rejection of the three groups of learners. Classroom composition did relate to the friendly/cooperative and antisocial behavior of the mainstreamed and nonmainstreamed EMR learners. Only the antisocial behavior of the nonhandicapped learners was not significantly related to the social attitudes of any of the three groups of learners.

Degree of peer dislike was negatively related and peer harmony positively related to the social competence of the nonhandicapped and mainstreamed EMR learners. Other aspects of the environment were important for one group or the other, but there were no indications that aspects of the environment important to the social competence of one group would be deleterious to the other. Thus, there were no indications that an appropriate environment for the development of social competence of both EMR and nonhandicapped students could not be provided in the regular classroom.

What implications do the findings of this chapter have for educational practices with EMR children? Educators' efforts to improve EMR learner social competence reflect the judgment that social skills and social competence are important outcomes of schooling for EMR learners — that social competence deficits are more debilitating to these students in the long run than academic deficiencies. This argument refers to their ability to navigate socially as adults, whether in the community or at work.

The Project PRIME model identified three components of social competence: social status, social behaviors, and social attitude. Social status is enhanced by the same classroom conditions as enhance academic performance: a well-ordered, teacher-controlled classroom that also minimizes anti-social behaviors. Chapter 5 reported that variations in social acceptance and rejection were associated with a child's perceived classroom academic performance and misbehavior, respectively. Classroom academic performance and potential misbehavior of students can be more effectively managed in these teacher-controlled environments.

Friendly/cooperative social behaviors, by contrast, are enhanced by harmonious classrooms characterized by high levels of acceptance and low levels of rejection of classmates. A teacher-controlled classroom environment appears to provide little opportunity for children to develop friendly/cooperative social behaviors. A different teacher style seems desirable. As opposed to a teacher-controlled classroom environment, a teacher-managed classroom can be considered to be one where teachers have established explicit rules for behaving but which also provides for effective student self-management with teacher warmth, a less centralizing and controlling teaching style, and greater opportunity for small-group peer interactive activities. The findings lead us to the conclusion that teachers need to balance their instructional styles, classroom climate, and influence techniques with tasks and teaching content to promote the social status of the mainstreamed EMR learner while also working to enhance the development of social skills associated with friendly/cooperative behavior.

Having initially emphasized the importance of the teacher related to social competence, it is equally true that the peer social characteristics of the classroom into which EMR children are placed need to be considered. The socioemotional environment of the classroom was consistently the most significant predictor of individual learner social status, behavior, and attitudes. Those socioemotional characteristics positively associated with a learner's social competence were low levels of dislike and high levels of harmony among their classmates.

In summary, this chapter provides evidence which should assist educators in focussing attention on specific teacher and socioemotional characteristics of classroom environments in selecting appropriate placements for EMR children, and provides guidance for teachers concerned with the social competence of children in their classrooms.

# Part V

# 11

# Conclusions and Implications: Learners and Their Environment

Project PRIME (Programmed Re-Entry into Mainstreamed Education) was a descriptive correlational study designed to provide a conceptual, theoretical, and practical framework for examining naturally occurring variations in alternative classroom instructional settings. A basic premise underlying the study was that administratively defined educational settings such as regular, resource, and special self-contained education classrooms would probably vary as much within type of setting as across settings on a variety of classroom environmental features. These variations within setting should be considered as significant as those between settings when selecting the appropriate placement and programming for EMR learners.

To examine the effects of these variations, a taxonomic model was developed to classify and compare classroom environments. Since programming and placement decisions require information related to both learners and classroom environments, the model included variables related to the student, the teacher, and the environment. The taxonomic model was developed from theory, empirical evidence, and educational issues.

Competence was viewed as a function of learner performance within an environment defined by a specific setting. Mathematically, this model is depicted by the equation:

$$C=(L_r, E_s),$$

where:

$C$ = competence
$L$ = learner
$E$ = environment
$r$ = role
$s$ = setting

The learner was either an educable mentally retarded (EMR) or nonhandicapped child who functioned in the role of student in a specific environmental setting — regular, resource, or special self-contained classroom. In a larger context, the classroom is a subsystem of the school, school district, and community; and was considered the proximal unit of study. The individual child enters the classroom which provides an educational environment designed to promote certain learner competencies.

The research was organized around two broad questions:

- What are the environmental characteristics of the three settings — regular, resource, and special self-contained classrooms — which are available to EMR learners?
- What individual and classroom characteristics are important in explaining and predicting the academic and social competence of nonhandicapped and EMR learners in these alternative instructional settings?

A third question is implicit in the conceptual model:

- What are the background characteristics and competencies of nonhandicapped and EMR learners that must be considered when making educational placement and programming decisions?

The conceptual model posits learner academic and social competence as a function of learner background and classroom environment. Chapters 4-8 address the first question by presenting descriptive information for each variable domain of the model for the nonhandicapped, and mainstreamed and nonmainstreamed EMR learners.

Chapter 4 describes the learner's background: the individual, family, and school characteristics of the nonhandicapped, and mainstreamed and nonmainstreamed EMR learners who were drawn from third, fourth and fifth grade.

Chapter 5 describes the competence of these same learners in terms of their academic and social status, behaviors, and attitudes. Subsequent chapters describe the classroom environments: the characteristics of the peers and teachers composing each classroom setting (Chapter 6), the socioemotional climate (Chapter 7), and the prevailing instructional conditions (Chapter 8). The details of the constructs and variables composing each domain in the model are presented inside the front cover. In each case, relationships among the variables composing each domain are examined within each chapter.

Chapters 9 and 10 address the second question by examining the relationships between learner academic and social competencies, respectively, and the variable domains concerned with learner background and classroom environment. Each chapter also addresses specific associated issues related to placement and programming decisions which school personnel and parents either directly or implicitly consider when determining an appropriate setting and program for an EMR learner.

While Project PRIME recognized the significance of learner characteristics for making appropriate placement and programming decisions, it broadened the discussion to include the actual details of what happens in these three educational settings, and related both sets of variables to learner competence. The findings presented in this book are an initial effort to comprehensively relate learner characteristics to the variations in classroom environments — among peers, teachers, socioemotional climate, and instructional conditions characterizing these educational settings. The presentation and discussion of these findings seek to enrich and broaden the administrative, instructional, and parental consideration given to these variables when placement and programming decisions are being made. Further, the Project PRIME conceptual model provides an array of sophisticated measurement tools, which operationally define and provide instrumentation for use in analyzing classroom environments and learner competence. Examples of these instruments are presented in Appendix B.

Chapter 11 summarizes the conclusions and implications of Project PRIME. The first section presents the five major research findings and conclusions which emerged when the Project PRIME taxonomic model was considered in its entirety. These findings provide policy makers, administrators, and advocates with a basis for empirically reaffirming the significance and distinctiveness of special education and the challenge of educationally providing for and instructionally accommodating individual differences.

The second section summarizes the placement and programming issues examined in Chapters 4-10. These findings have direct application for school personnel in administering, organizing, and delivering regular and special education instruction and related services. The results also have immediate applicability in focussing and directing attention to the learner and classroom environmental characteristics to consider in developing and making placement and programming decisions.

The third section discusses the implications of the research conclusions and findings in terms of how school personnel can integrate the clinical, developmental, individual orientation of special education with the curricula and organizational structure of regular education. This discussion of integrating special and regular education presents assessment, administrative, and instructional suggestions for achieving this synchrony. The challenge is to integrate the developmental-clinical orientation, focussed around the unique needs of particular students, with the realities of how the school functions for regular education students — thus allowing EMR learners to utilize both educational systems for learning and socializing.

# The Major Conclusions of Project PRIME

This section presents five of the most significant findings and conclusions which emerged when the Project PRIME model was considered as a totality.

- Public schools and teachers significantly contribute to explaining the variations in nonhandicapped and EMR learner academic and social competence.
- The regular and special education services being provided in alternative settings are delivered in distinctively different ways.
- Variations in learner background and classroom environments were differentially associated with academic and social competence.
- The relationship between mainstreamed EMR learner academic achievement was markedly associated with the extent to which regular and special education services were coordinated.
- EMR learners, though homogeneous in relation to Federal/state eligibility criteria, present very heterogeneous educational profiles for purposes of placement and programming.

Each of these conclusions is discussed below.

## Schools and Teachers Make a Critical Difference in Learner Competence

The most striking finding in this study is the unequivocal evidence that schools and teachers make critical contributions to explaining the academic and social competence of EMR and nonhandicapped elementary grade children. The proportion of variation in learner academic achievement explained by learner background decreases as a function of the student's degree of educational risk, while the contribution of classroom environmental variables to academic performance remains significant for each group. While learner background variables accounted for 33% of the total variation in nonhandicapped learner normative academic achievement, these same variables accounted for only 13% of the variation in mainstreamed EMR learner academic achievement and 22% for nonmainstreamed EMR learners.

The classroom environment domains were found to be powerful predictors of EMR learner academic competence, accounting for 27% of the variance of the mainstreamed EMR learner academic status, 48% of the nonmainstreamed EMR learner variance, and 45% of the nonhandicapped learner variance; all significant proportions. The predictive strength of the model is even more dramatic when SES factors are controlled. In this instance, the full models explained 74% of the variation for low-SES nonhandicapped learners and 68% for high-SES EMR learners.

The variance in nonhandicapped learner academic normative achievement status was predominantly accounted for by the characteristics of their classroom peers. In contrast, the components which predicted the most variation in EMR learner normative achievement and behavior were teacher characteristics, socioemotional climate, and instructional operations. These findings reflect the importance of the characteristics of the classroom environment and provide powerful evidence that schools and teachers contribute to their students' academic status. They provide support for the adage that EMR children must be taught to learn.

## Regular and Special Education Services are Delivered in Distinctly Different Ways

The most distinguishing characteristics of special education settings, in contrast to regular classrooms, are the intensity and focus with which instruction can be planned and delivered. This is achieved as a result of small class size and scheduling practices, e.g., grouping students with similar problems in the resource room at the same time. The reduced class size and increased instructional homogeneity of children results in a classroom environment which permits significantly greater teacher-pupil interaction, is associated with increased learner attention, and facilitates differentiated instruction suited to the particular student's needs.

Instruction in the regular classroom environment is primarily dictated by the need for teachers to implement instruction while directing the learning of 2.5 to 4 times more pupils than the special education teacher has at any one time. The differences among the settings are detailed in Chapters 6-8. Salient features are briefly highlighted below.

In the regular classrooms, with a mean number of 29 students

- 75% of instruction was observed to be in whole-group, teacher- or student-directed activities;
- little or no individual differentiation was observed or reported by the students;
- there was a low incidence of verbal or cognitive interactions of the students with the teacher; and
- the teacher management strategies used were authoritarian in character, and based on coercive-legitimate demands.

The special self-contained classes enrolled less than half the number of students (mean of 12 students/class). In this educational setting, the teacher

- instructed the class as a whole only 44% of the class time, provided small-group instruction 30%, and individual instruction 20%;
- displayed more flexibility in the selection of strategies for managing and monitoring the students' instruction, maintaining student instructional engagement, and establishing peer harmony;
- had a higher observed frequency of individual differentiation strategies in student instructional activities which was supported by student statements about the flexibility of instruction in their classrooms; and
- sustained a higher rate of student verbal participation and cognitive demand.

The resource room served an average of 24 students per day, but only about 7 students at any one time. Resource room students were grouped administratively to maximize the homogeneity of the student needs addressed each period. Small class size and homogeneity of educational needs most directly determined the teaching characteristics of the resource room. The result was

- a high proportion of teacher-directed activities (65%); and
- a more intense rate of student-teacher interactions as evidenced by a higher rate of student verbal participation and teacher cognitive demands. (These were six times greater than the observed frequency in the regular classroom, and one-third greater than in the special self-contained classroom.)

## How Teachers Structure the Classroom Environment Influences Academic and Social Competence

Two types of teacher-directed classrooms can be described: 1) teacher-centered or controlled, and 2) teacher-managed.

In the teacher-centered classroom, the teacher exercises tight control over student transactions. The teacher tends to initiate, direct, and elicit student responses. The focus of control or the conduit for the events in the classroom is the teacher.

The "teacher as manager" model still posits the teacher as the focus of the class. However, the teacher can be viewed as a facilitator of the instructional process, and, as a corollary, as helping students manage their learning while also engaging other students in their learning efforts (when that is a suitable strategy).

The distinction is significant because, in the context of Project PRIME's findings, the two types of teacher-directed classrooms are associated with promoting somewhat different academic and social outcomes. In the more tightly controlled classroom, the teacher tends to rely on coercive-legitimate management strategies. This classroom seems to be associated with higher normative academic status, a concomitant higher social status, and few instances of antisocial behavior, but also a lower incidence of friendly/cooperative behaviors and more alienated students. Whereas, when the teacher operated as manager and facilitator of the learning process, more friendly cooperative behaviors were evident, with less student alienation.

In sum, the classroom environment most strongly associated with learner academic competence is teacher controlled, where explicit rules are established permitting teacher- and student-directed activities. Given the differences in class size and the degree of homogeneity of educational needs of the students in the regular, resource, and special self-contained classrooms, teachers must use different management strategies in order to achieve these instructional conditions associated with student academic and social performance, student instructional engagement, and peer harmony. Each of the three instructional settings has different typical classroom environments, requiring teachers to manage their classrooms differently in order to create and maintain such a classroom environment.

The challenge to school personnel and parents in developing and making placement and programming decisions is how to achieve a synchrony between individual learner characteristics/needs with the variations in classroom environments resulting from administrative scheduling, peer composition, behavior or cohesion, teacher characteristics, and instructional context. Creating classroom environments with these characteristics will clearly challenge and test the limits of teacher leadership in the classroom. In addition, it will also require support from special education and building-level administrators, as well as adequate pupil personnel support services and in-service training.

## The Coordination of Regular and Special Education Services Affects Learner Academic Achievement

The Project PRIME findings highlight the importance of coordinating the delivery of regular and special education services to mainstreamed EMR learners. The need for teachers and administrators to improve this coordination is supported by such findings as the differential access of regular and special education teachers to assessment and prescriptive information for designing individualized educational programs (IEPs), special education materials, teacher and student support services, and in-service training related to the education of EMR children.

The most compelling evidence supporting the significance of coordinating regular and special education services is gleaned from the differential power of the Project PRIME model to explain variations in the normative academic status of mainstreamed EMR learners. The analytic models for nonhandicapped students and EMR learners in special self-contained classrooms accounted for approximately 55% of the variance in normative academic achievement and only about 35% of the variation of mainstreamed EMR learners for regular and resource rooms settings. The full analytic model for the latter groups, which combined both educational settings, accounted for only 41% of the variance.

When mainstreamed and special self-contained EMR learners were stratified by socioeconomic status, the regular classroom environment accounted for 67% of the variation in high-SES mainstreamed EMR learner normative academic status whereas the same model explained only 33% of the variation among low-SES mainstreamed EMR learners. Low-SES mainstreamed EMR learners appear in greater jeopardy of failing to benefit from a regular/resource program when instruction is designed and delivered as independent uncoordinated program elements.

Thus, it is evident that if mainstreaming EMR learners is to enhance their education, administrators and teachers must effectively integrate regular and special education services. Given the different peer and teacher characteristics, socioemotional climate, and instructional conditions present in regular and resource classrooms, the best way to deliver special education services must be considered when EMR learners are mainstreamed. The choices basically include the type and amount of prescriptive and instructional services which can be provided in the regular classroom or in a special education resource room. Project PRIME, while providing an empirical description of the regular classroom environment, could not infer the characteristics of the EMR learner and classroom environment associated with developing academic or social competence because the incidence of special education services being provided in regular classrooms was insufficient.

The failure to administrate and instructionally coordinate the delivery of regular and special education resource room services can diminish rather than enhance the contribution schools make to the development of EMR learner academic achievement. Greater experience is needed to determine to what extent the discontinuities which often characterize the pull-out delivery of special education services in resource rooms can be remedied. Also needed is more experience in determining the realistic limits of regular classrooms as a setting for providing special education services when class size remains over 20.

## Eligibility Criteria are Prescriptively Inadequate for Placement and Programming Decisions

The EMR learners in this study were defined consistent with the Texas Education Agency definition for classification and eligibility to receive special education as an EMR student. These learners revealed a reduced rate of intellectual development and academic achievement, 2-3 standard deviation units below the mean of the general population (see Chapter 2), as evidenced by significant deficits in all essential learning processes. The Texas Education Agency definition presumes that students found eligible as EMR will present a homogeneous array of educational needs, characterized by a slower learning rate and markedly poor academic achievement.

The breadth and range of the Project PRIME variables included learner background (i.e., SES, IQ, prior educational experience) as well as academic and social status, behaviors, and attitudes. It also included observation of student performance in classrooms for a variety of learning-related and social behaviors, teacher reports of their learning and behavioral styles, and their responses to the learning tasks and opportunities in these naturalistic educational settings. Application of cluster analysis procedures to this broad array of variables revealed profiles of EMR learners that indicated educationally significant heterogeneity in their academic and social performance despite their presumed homogeneity for slowness to learn and academic deficiencies.

This diversity can be illustrated by listing the key phrases used to characterize the profile clusters. The nonhandicapped learners can serve as a comparison against which to view the profiles derived from the EMR learners in the mainstreamed and special self-contained settings. The reader should recall that all learners were in third, fourth, or fifth grade, or an equivalent nongraded special education classroom in a Texas public elementary school. Each profile is described more fully in Appendix D and compared with the profile descriptions in the other samples.

The characterizations of the eight profiles for the nonhandicapped learners included *reasonably successful and satisfied, social and academic leaders, serious academic and social deviants, academically weak but verbally active, active and gregarious but not seriously disruptive, shy and withdrawn, self-deprecating and unhappy*, and *competent and cooperative but a bit disdainful*. Each of the eight profile groups represented about the same proportion of students (10-19%) but were quite different in their pattern of competence.

Mainstreamed EMR learners fell into six profile clusters that bear a limited resemblance to those obtained for nonhandicapped learners. The characterizations of their profiles included such descriptions as *excessively and inappropriately socially active and academically inattentive, rejected and rejecting but did not admit to being lonely, friendly and socially accepted but academically weak and concerned about it, academically successful yet unsatisfied and unhappy, shy and withdrawn*, and *successful and satisfied*. The six mainstreamed EMR learner profiles represented about equal proportions of learners (14-19%).

The characterizations of the profiles of the nonmainstreamed EMR learners included *very slow academically, self-deprecating, and unhappy; quiet and reserved but happy; social deviants, rejected and rejecting; academically successful but personally unsatisfied; social leaders in their classrooms*; and *academic leaders in their classrooms*. The nonmainstreamed learners were roughly evenly distributed among the six profiles (10-21% in each profile).

What is evident is the heterogeneity within both EMR learner samples. This heterogeneity demonstrates yet again that even specific educationally descriptive eligibility criteria, such as those used by the Texas Education Agency, identify EMR learners who are very diverse in their academic and social status, behaviors, and attitudes. The message of this empirical analysis should be clear. Even with relatively restricted and specific criteria for identifying EMR learners, these students' characteristics are very different, and their responses to the school curriculum and to other students differ markedly.

Hence, given the variation within and between alternative settings as well as the marked variation within EMR learner groups, the implication is that individually determining the least restrictive environment for each child is of compelling importance. The reliance on test-based assessments for identifying EMR children using Federal and state eligibility criteria will in general discriminate EMR from nonhandicappped learners. However, the discrimination of learners for eligibility to receive special education as EMR learners will not result in an educationally homogeneous classification of children. The prescriptive information needed for placement and programming decisions needs to be obtained by increasing efforts to analyze classroom environments and assessing a broader array of learner performance characters. Only by relating this broader array of information about learner performance to alternative instructional interventions can appropriate placement and programming decisions be made.

The richness of the information generated by the Project PRIME taxonomic model provided a plethora of opportunities for selecting study findings. The significance of a finding is ultimately not determined by statistical probability but by its contribution to understanding the schooling process and the impetus it provides for improving current practice. The five major findings and conclusions presented in this section collectively highlight the significant contribution schools and teachers make toward developing the academic and social competence of all children. This contribution can be enhanced when schools recognize the variations which exist within and between instructional settings; the need operationally to integrate regular and special education services; and that children, regardless of how they are grouped by the usual diagnostic criteria (e.g., IQ scores and achievement discrepancies) present significantly different educational profiles which require individual consideration when determining an appropriate educational placement and program.

## Summary of Placement and Programming Issues

The previous section presents the major findings and conclusions when considering the Project PRIME conceptual model in its totality. Chapters 4-10 address placement and programming issues related to each major domain of the Project PRIME model. The following summarizes the findings associated with these placement and programming issues, outlined in Chapter 1, and directs the reader in locating the full presentation and discussion of these issues.

## With whom were the mainstreamed EMR children placed?

- Nonhandicapped learners were on the average one year younger in chronological age. *(Chapter 4)*

- Nonhandicapped learners were assessed as having average ability, evidenced by a mean intelligence quotient of 94.7. *(Chapter 4)*

- Nonhandicapped learners were significantly below grade level in reading. Teachers reported 41-76% of the children in their classes were one or more years below grade level. *(Chapter 6)*

## What were the integration patterns of the EMR learners?

- Mainstreamed EMR children were integrated into regular classrooms an average of 72.1% of the school day. *(Chapter 4)*

- EMR children placed in special self-contained classrooms were integrated into regular classrooms an average of 31.7% of the school day. *(Chapter 4)*

- Fifty-four percent and 60% of mainstreamed EMR children were integrated into regular classrooms for reading and mathematics respectively. Ninety-one percent of the mainstreamed EMR learners were integrated for science and social studies. *(Chapter 4)*

- Mainstreamed EMR children integrated for reading, mathematics, and language arts/spelling received 70-80% of their instruction in these subjects in regular classrooms. Mainstreamed EMR learners integrated for science and social studies received 97% of their total instruction in these subjects in the regular classroom. *(Chapter 4)*

## What were the characteristics of the EMR learners associated with the extent and nature of their integration into regular classrooms?

- There was no association between EMR learner background and competencies and the amount of time or subject matter in regular classrooms. Placement and programming decisions were interpreted as being predicated on factors other than individual characteristics. *(Chapter 4)*

## What were the academic and social competencies of the nonhandicapped, mainstreamed, and self-contained EMR learners?

- The normative academic status of the nonhandicapped learners was, on the average, in the lower third of the MAT norms. The mainstreamed and special self-contained EMR learners' MAT scores placed them, on the average, in the lowest percentile. *(Chapter 5)*

- On-task attention behavior of nonhandicapped learners was observed 83% of the time. The mainstreamed EMR learner in the regular classroom was observed to be on-task 72% of the time. In the resource classroom, on-task attention was observed 89% of the time. The EMR learner in a special self-contained classroom was observed to be on-task 80% of the time. *(Chapter 5)*

- The social status of the nonhandicapped learner was evidenced by 53% of his classmates indicating their acceptance and 18% indicating rejection. The mainstreamed EMR learner was accepted by 38% of his classmates and rejected by 27%. The EMR learner in a special self-contained classroom was accepted by 61% of his peers and rejected by 19%. *(Chapter 5)*

- Mainstreamed EMR learners had three or more classmates who liked them in 94% of the regular classrooms. Only 13% of the mainstreamed EMR learners were in classrooms where more than half the class rejected them. *(Chapter 5)*

- The positive, negative, or antisocial behavior of nonhandicapped, mainstreamed, and nonmainstreamed EMR children was basically the same as rated by teachers and recorded by observers. *(Chapter 5)*

## To what extent do the academic and social competencies of mainstreamed EMR and nonhandicapped learners overlap?

- The smallest overlap occurred on measures of academic status: 3% of the highest quartile and 94% of the lowest quartile consisted of EMR learners. However, the EMR learners made up 1/3 of the second highest quartile and 2/3 of the third quartile. Thus, in the interquartile range, significant overlap did occur. *(Chapter 5)*

- Mainstreamed EMR learners made up about 1/4 of the top quartile of social acceptance and about 3/4 of the bottom quartile. For social rejection, mainstreamed EMR learners constituted about 2/3 of the highest quartile and 1/3 of the lowest quartile. But the middle two quartiles of both social acceptance and rejection had a nearly equal representation of mainstreamed EMR and nonhandicapped learners. *(Chapter 5)*

- Mainstreamed EMR learners made up approximately 3/4 of the lowest quartile on cognitive interaction and attention-to-task behaviors, and 2/3 of the highest quartile on feelings of loneliness. However, the interquartile ranges, as with academic and social status, showed considerable overlap. *(Chapter 5)*

- Mainstreamed EMR children comprised 60% of the highest quartile of antisocial behavior, with 40% nonhandicapped learners. The mainstreamed EMR learners made up 45% of the highest quartile on friendly/cooperative behavior. Again, this distribution of observed and reported social behavior indicates extensive overlap between the mainstreamed EMR and nonhandicapped learners. *(Chapter 5)*

## Can regular class teachers be provided appropriate training and support materials and services which will enable them to instruct EMR learners effectively?

- Regular class teachers can be provided with appropriate training, support services, and materials. This did not occur because of administrative barriers which impeded the flow of materials and assignment of teacher aides. For example, the regular class teachers were responsible for 29 students, four of whom were reportedly handicapped; only 7% of these teachers had the support of an aide. *(Chapter 6)*

- Approximately 50% of the regular class teachers reported not having appropriate materials as a problem associated with having EMR children integrated into their classrooms. *(Chapter 6)*

## Do regular class peers provide more appropriate role models for EMR learners than do other EMR learners?

- The findings of Project PRIME suggest that the academic conditions associated with the tenets of role modelling theory are more evident in regular classrooms than in special self-contained classrooms. *(Chapter 6)*

- The regular class peers of EMR learners were one year younger and performed on the MAT similarly to the lowest third of those children upon whom the test was nationally normed. In contrast, EMR learners scored similarly to the lowest one percentile of students on whom the MAT was normed. However, there was sufficient overlap in achievement status, and the magnitude of discrepancy between the two samples is such that the placement strategy seems to optimize the conditions for role modelling to occur. *(Chapter 5)*

- Regular class peers reported one standard deviation greater cognitive emphasis in their classrooms than was reported by EMR learners in special self-contained classrooms. *(Chapter 8)*

- The academic attitudes and attention to task of nonhandicapped and special self-contained EMR learners did not significantly differ. *(Chapter 5)*

- EMR learners in special self-contained classrooms provided a cognitive discourse which was found to be one standard deviation lower in very/moderately low cognitive demands. Conversely, regular class peers experienced moderate/high cognitive demands one standard deviation greater than EMR learners in special self-contained classrooms. *(Chapter 8)*

## Do regular teachers have or develop negative attitudes toward the mainstreaming of EMR learners?

- In general, regular class teachers expressed moderately positive attitudes toward mainstreaming, indicating a greater confidence in being able to instruct children with cognitive rather than behavioral problems in their classrooms. Interestingly, regular class teachers expressed confidence in their ability to instruct handicapped children whom special education teachers felt were less likely to be successfully integrated. *(Chapter 6)*

- Approximately 50% of the regular class teachers reported having problems integrating EMR children into their classrooms due to the lack of time to work individually with students, the lack of appropriate materials, and the inability of EMR learners to participate in group projects. *(Chapter 6)*

## Do nonhandicapped students develop negative attitudes toward school when EMR learners are placed in their classrooms?

- The ratings provided by nonhandicapped students on *Your School Days* indicated they enjoyed school and found school rewarding. These children rated 17 of 21 items positively related to attitudes toward school. *(Chapter 6)*

## Are regular class teachers likely to provide the warm, supportive, structured environment that has been thought important for EMR learners?

- Observation data were consistent with teacher self-reported attitudes indicating that special education and regular class teachers differed little in the emphasis they placed on a warm, open environment and a structured setting. *(Chapter 6)*

- Regular and special self-contained class teachers were found to provide a similar amount of warmth. A highly structured, directive environment did not predominate in either setting. The exception was the resource classroom teacher, who displayed markedly greater warmth in the classroom. *(Chapter 7)*

### Do disruptiveness and friction occur in the regular classroom when EMR learners are mainstreamed?

- Observer and teacher ratings indicate that friction and disruptive behavior rarely occurred in classrooms in this study. In approximately 75% of classrooms, these behaviors were never observed. Thus, in about 1/4 of the classrooms, such behavior did occur. *(Chapter 7)*

- Regular class teachers (44%), when asked to indicate problems resulting from having EMR children in their classroom, stated that EMR learners disrupted classroom activity. However, observers did not record this level of disruptiveness. *(Chapter 6)*

### Does the regular class teacher need to devote excessive amounts of time to managing behavior when EMR learners are mainstreamed?

- Regular class teachers spent relatively little time managing off-task behavior in the classroom; 3/4 of the teachers spent an average of 1½ or less minutes per hour managing behavior. *(Chapter 7)*

- Teacher ratings of antisocial behavior indicated that such behavior rarely occurred either for nonhandicapped or mainstreamed EMR students. *(Chapter 5)*

- Negative social behavior, as observed using the FLACCS, indicated that nonhandicapped and EMR learners exhibited such behaviors 2-3 times per hour. *(Chapter 5)*

### Within the regular, resource, and special self-contained class-rooms, what are the instructional contexts and operations that result in the maximum instructional engagement?

- In the regular classroom, learner attention was maintained through the use of teacher-directed whole-class instruction. In the special education settings, small-group, teacher-managed activities were associated with instructional engagement. The size of the class was the significant factor in explaining the effects of instructional management decisions and peer instructional activities. The critical factor appeared to be the teacher's ability to monitor instruction and provide feedback. The techniques for achieving these instructional management objectives varied in relation to class size. *(Chapter 8)*

- In all three settings, peer interest and attention were related to the physical quality of the classroom. *(Chapter 8)*

**Within each of the three settings, what are the instructional contexts and operations which create an instructional atmosphere which provides for individual differentiation and an appropriate level of academic emphasis?**

- Instructional differentiation was not widely practiced in regular classrooms. Regular class teachers were the central focus of instruction about 2/3 of the time; they seldom provided students with instructional content or activity different from their peers. *(Chapter 8)*

- Instructional differentiation was reported and observed to be more prevalent in the special self-contained classroom. The resource classroom, though providing greater instructional differentiation than the regular classroom, was observed to have less than the special self-contained classroom. This difference between special self-contained classrooms and resource classrooms appears to be attributable to administrative scheduling which results in greater homogeneity of EMR learners in any given resource classroom period. This homogeneity of learner needs thus requires less instructional differentiation. *(Chapter 8)*

- Regular classrooms had a stronger academic focus than special self-contained classrooms. A larger portion of time was spent in regular classrooms on academic subject instruction, a higher level of cognitive processing was demanded, and a larger proportion of feedback remarks contained additional information. *(Chapter 8)*

- Creating instructional differentiation and an appropriate level of academic emphasis within a classroom is often juxtaposed with the objective of optimizing instructional engagement. Class size and administrative scheduling may be the most effective strategies for creating instructional differentiation, attaining the appropriate level of academic emphasis, and maintaining the optimum instructional engagement of the learner. *(Chapter 8)*

## What are the learner background and classroom environmental factors associated with the academic competence of the nonhandicapped and EMR learners in the three educational settings?

- The models predicting normative academic status were differentially powerful for the three learner groups. The full model explained about the same proportion of variance for the nonhandicapped (55%) and the nonmainstreamed EMR learners (54%). The model for the mainstreamed EMR learners, incorporating the regular and resource classroom environments, explained 41% of the variance. *(Chapter 9)*

- Learner background was a more important predictor of normative academic status for the nonhandicapped learners than for the EMR learners. Age, grade, ethnic group, and father's educational level each made important contributions to the prediction of normative academic status for the nonhandicapped learners; but only age was important for the EMR learners. For the nonhandicapped learners, learner background and classroom environment contributed equally to explaining variance in achievement. Whereas, for the EMR learners, classroom environmental variables were the significant predictors. *(Chapter 9)*

- The SES background of mainstreamed EMR learners significantly affected the predictive strength of the model. For high-SES mainstreamed EMR learners, the full model explained 67% of the variance in achievement scores. For low-SES mainstreamed EMR children, the model explained only 38% of the variance. Thus, the low-SES mainstreamed EMR learner appears to be significantly less affected by the educational program than the higher-SES mainstreamed EMR learner. *(Chapter 8)*

- The SES background of nonhandicapped learners was significantly related to the predictive strength of the model. In contrast, in this instance, the full model predicted 74% of the variance for low-SES and 52% of the variance for high-SES nonhandicapped learner achievement scores. The classroom environment domains contributed significantly more in explaining the low-SES nonhandicapped learner variance in achievement—66%, as compared to the high-SES nonhandicapped learner of 45%. *(Chapter 8)*

## Are the environmental factors associated with the academic competence of the nonhandicapped learners similar in magnitude and pattern to those associated with the academic competence of EMR learners?

- The significance of learner background and classroom environment in explaining variations within and between learners in alternative classroom environments was consistently evidenced, though not always with similar strength or pattern. Peer characteristics—whether ethnicity, SES, or attitudes—made the major contribution to explaining the achievement status and academic behaviors of nonhandicapped learners. By contrast, teacher characteristics, socioemotional climate, and instructional operations contributed most heavily to explaining variations in EMR learner academic status and behaviors. Schools and teachers clearly make a difference, and even more so for EMR learners. *(Chapter 9)*

## Are similar environmental factors associated with the development of the three different competency areas (academic status, behaviors, and attributes)?

- Regardless of whether an EMR child is in a regular, resource, or special self-contained classroom environment, a similar profile of classroom composition, socioemotional climate, and instructional conditions was associated with improved academic competence. The profile of the classroom included

  - teacher-directed and supervised instructional activities calculated to actively involve the learner;
  - instructional engagement as a result of teacher querying and student response, supervision, monitoring, and feedback; and
  - harmony and cooperation within the classroom which seemed to enhance peer exchanges, attention to task, and acceptance of EMR learners into the class.

  Teacher ability to create such a classroom environment was shown to be associated with teacher training and experience. *(Chapter 9)*

- Students worked most effectively in groupings, not individually or tutorially, and these groupings maintained attention to task, allowing students to learn from each other, and particularly from the teacher's direction and continuing support. *(Chapter 9)*

## Which dimensions of the three different classroom settings promote or inhibit social competence among EMR learners?

- Classroom environmental factors had a strong relationship with learner social status, accounting for a unique proportion of variance ranging from 23-38% in both acceptance and rejection of all three groups of learners. *(Chapter 10)*

- Social status and social behaviors of EMR learners were not predicted by similar classroom environmental variables. Social status was enhanced by the same classroom conditions as academic performance — a well-ordered, teacher-controlled classroom that minimizes antisocial behavior. Friendly, cooperative social behaviors, by contrast, were enhanced by harmonious classrooms. Creating such an environment requires, in contrast to a teacher-controlled environment, a teacher-managed classroom where explicit rules for behaving have been established which allow for effective student self-management. This learner responsibility is complemented by teacher warmth, a less centralizing and controlling teacher style, and greater opportunity for small-group peer-interactive activities. These findings lead to the conclusion that teachers will have to balance their instructional styles and influence techniques in order to promote the social status as well as behavior of EMR learners. *(Chapter 10)*

## What are the relationships between the regular classroom environment and the social competence of nonhandicapped students?

- Classroom environment significantly contributed to explaining the variations in nonhandicapped learner social competence. *(Chapter 10)*

- The regular classroom environment accounted for 23% and 31% of the unique variance in the social acceptance and rejection, respectively, of nonhandicapped learners. Thus, the contribution of the regular classroom environment on social status was similar for both nonhandicapped and mainstreamed EMR learners. *(Chapter 5)*

- Learner background and classroom environment together predicted identical portions of variance in the nonhandicapped learner's antisocial and friendly/cooperative behavior. Antisocial behavior was predominantly associated with peer group characteristics. Whereas, friendly/cooperative behavior was associated with teachers who exhibited warmth and nondirectiveness, used positive influence, and differentiated their instruction. *(Chapter 10)*

# Implications for
# Integrating Regular and Special Education

Increasingly, policy makers, administrators, regular and special educators, advocates, and the public at large are asking the question *What is different or special about special education?* This question is raised particularly with regard to the education of mildly handicapped learners. Professionally, politically, and practically, the need for special education services for these students must be clarified.

A range of factors are contributing to these requests for explanation, and the demands for accountability. They include:

- the failure of the "efficacy studies" to clearly indicate the superiority of special self-contained classes, which were historically considered to be the primary special education delivery model
- the significant growth in the numbers of mildly handicapped children receiving special education and related services in the past decade
- the large percentage of these children receiving the majority of their education in regular classes
- marked variations *among* the states in eligibility definitions and criteria for receiving special education and related services for mildly handicapping categories of exceptionality (Further, these variations in definition and criteria have resulted in significant differences in the percentage of handicapped children being similarly classified across states. These variations are interpreted by critics of special education as indicating there is not a clear understanding of who its clients are.)
- increased fiscal austerity at the Federal, state and local levels

The responses to this self examination and external scrutiny have often been most comfortably addressed by describing the children who need special education, not by describing the uniqueness or effectiveness of such services. Special educators and advocates frequently respond to the question defensively or with explanations that are met with skepticism. The major conclusions and findings with regard to the placement and programming issues, summarized above, provide empirical support for responding to the classical question *What is special about special education?*

Special education, in contrast to regular education, does not exist as a first-choice service delivery system except for students who arrive in school with visibly evident disabilities. Special education services are provided to learners who are failing to benefit from regular education and who meet the eligibility criteria. These services have evolved from professional concerns about the appropriate means to educate these students and, more recently, from judicial decisions and legislative actions. A continuum of services and settings has been developed to meet the individual educational needs of EMR children to the maximum extent possible within regular educational settings, maintaining their integration with nonhandicapped age-appropriate peers.

Special education settings and services, defined as those human, fiscal, and material resources and locations administratively and legislatively provided for EMR learners, need to be distinguished from special education as an instructional orientation. This special education instructional orientation is characterized by a clinical, developmental, individualized task orientation to teaching/learning. The administrative and organizational patterns and practices characterizing special education services reflect the circumstances thought necessary and feasible for delivering special education consistent with its instructional orientation. Thus, operationally, placement and programming decisions for EMR learners require a determination of the learning characteristics of the individual, the nature and extent of special education and related services needed, and the classroom setting and environment having the flexibility to provide these services consistent with the instructional orientation of special education.

The origins of this special education instructional orientation stem from initial treatment and research focussed on restoring functioning. This focus is most dramatically illustrated by Itard's efforts to train the "missing" human capabilities of the Wild Boy of Aveyron (Lane, 1976). When this effort failed, clinical and empirical inquiries focussed on charting the capabilities and educability of persons with different handicapping conditions at different chronological ages. This work moved into the laboratory and initially addressed concerns with intellectual capacity and performance on such simple functions as learning and motor tasks, and later, studies which examined the acquisition and retention characteristics of handicapped persons. This work described the parameters which characterize where the clinical, developmental, and individualized instructional orientation of special education can be integrated with delivery of the regular curricula.

The cumulative effect of this predominantly developmentally- and experimentally-based research has been the development of a knowledge base which convincingly demonstrates the educability of handicapped children. This research significantly advanced educators' understanding of how these children learn; their potential for new learning; and the conditions that facilitate or depress their acquisition, transfer, and generalization of new behaviors and knowledge.

The distinctive orientation and contribution of the special educator, whether direct service provider or researcher, is to focus attention on not only the learner and the task but also the classroom environment, the natural setting in which teaching and learning occurs in schools. Project PRIME's findings clearly demonstrate the significance of the classroom environment in understanding the instructional conditions which prevail in regular and special education settings. Further, these variations among settings and classrooms significantly contribute to explaining differences in the academic and social competencies of EMR learners. These findings have immediate practical implications for administrators and teachers concerned with improving the placement and programming of EMR learners.

Project PRIME studied three settings: the regular classroom, the special education resource room, and the special education self-contained classroom. These three settings differed from each other on such classroom environmental characteristics as curricula, goals, class size, grouping strategies, cognitive emphasis, use of individualization strategies, and intensity of teacher-pupil interactions. Though descriptive measures of central tendency distinguish these placement alternatives, the within-setting variation in classroom environments, as evidenced by the large standard deviations characterizing each variable mean, make this molar distinction of settings of limited value for individual placement and programming decisions.

The findings in this book build on prior efforts of the research community and provide direction for future inquiries that can achieve a greater degree of synchrony between the clinical, developmental, and individual orientation of special education and the organizational grouping, curricula demands, and scheduling practices which characterize regular education. The traditional reliance by psychologists and educators on test-based assessments, focussed on learner deficits, needs to be modified to include an analysis of classroom environments. Assessment of classroom environments should include evaluation of the effectiveness of instructional adaptations made to accommodate the individual differences of learners in making placement and programming decisions. This increased attention to classroom environment analysis and the prescriptive programming which should result, reflects the progression during the past two decades to modify assessment procedures. These assessment modifications represent the movement from a predominantly etiological/medical focus of determining eligibility for special education to one which also incorporates an educationally oriented diagnosis for purposes of determining programming placement and instructional prescription.

The Project PRIME model presented in this book and highlighted in this chapter provides a conceptual and measurement framework, as well as supporting evidence, for the characteristics which distinguish special education from regular education classroom environments. The model allows researchers and service practitioners to utilize an empirically derived and operationalized variable base for considering learner characteristics and classroom environments in determining the types and amount of special education and related services potentially required by an EMR learner. Clearly, the variable base will need revision and refinement. The challenge to service providers and researchers is to continue to expand our understanding of the relationships between learners and their classroom environments. Meeting this challenge will require the development of assessment procedures that permit specification of needed special education and related services necessary to adapt regular classroom environments as the standard by which to consider how to make special education resources/services available to an EMR learner.

The Project PRIME findings and variables provide a thread by which to more tightly weave the current interface between regular and special education. Special education resources and services have historically been implemented as additive elements which expanded the capacity of public schools to provide educational opportunities appropriate for handicapped children. The efforts to mainstream handicapped children require a more dynamic conception of delivering special education resources and services in synchrony with regular education. The mainstreaming of EMR learners will require regular and special educators to perceive that what on the surface may appear to be profound differences in their organizational and instructional approaches can be interwoven. This operational and attitudinal unity can result in providing a more dynamic continuum of regular and special education settings/services. In determining placement and programming decisions consistent with the concept of least restrictive environment, the challenge facing schools and parents is how and in what settings clinical, developmental and individualized special education services can be integrated within the regular education curricula and setting.

This vision of a tightly woven unity between regular and special classroom programs requires greater recognition of the classroom environment variations which exist within and among settings. Variations must be recognized if the special education instructional orientation and services are to be integrated into regular classroom instruction. The analysis of classroom environments and their consideration in making placement and programming decisions is not a pandering to personality differences of students or teachers. Rather, this analysis of classroom environments provides a more reasoned basis for considering not only learner deficits but instructional conditions in determining the least restrictive environment for providing special education and related services.

Administrative and instructional experience during the past decade and a half has highlighted the difficulties in achieving the desired synchrony between regular and special education. The findings from Project PRIME document and provide insights into some of the issues critical to integrating the clinical, developmental, individualized orientation of special education with the organization and curricula of regular education. The conclusions of Project PRIME convincingly illustrate the significance of classroom environments in explaining variations in the academic and social competence of EMR and nonhandicapped learners. The attention and vigilance needed to analyze and consider classroom environment variations in the placement and programming of EMR learners requires a commitment from both regular and special educators. Each will need to develop and maintain a sense of responsibility for creating the unity of regular and special education.

The basis upon which to build a unity of special and regular education exists in the current climate of accountability for schools and students characterizing educational reform activities. State and local education boards and agencies are increasing requiring handicapped learners to participate in minimum competency testing programs and meet performance objectives associated with the regular curricula in order to graduate. The burgeoning adoption of policies which stipulate the regular curricula as the cornerstone for educating so-called "mildly handicapped" students provides not only an opportunity but also a necessity for regular and special educators to communicate and coordinate their efforts to provide EMR learners with equal educational opportunities.

Determining the nature and amount of special education services needed by EMR learners requires consideration of learner strengths and deficits against the standard of the regular curricula. How and where to provide these special education resources and services requires analyzing the strengths and weaknesses of the classroom environments in regular and special education settings. The response to what is special about special education for the "mildly handicapped" is this precise diagnostic/prescriptive assessment which results in the delivery of special education and related services in a manner which maintains the unified goals developed with regular education. Operationally, this means determining, on an individual basis, the characteristics of the classroom environment in the least restrictive setting where the clinical, developmental, and individualized instructional orientation of special education can be integrated with delivery of the regular curricula.

Researchers and service providers have an ongoing responsibility to monitor the administrative, organizational, and instructional features of regular and special education settings, particularly as they relate to student outcomes or progress. In the immediate future experience, not theory, will provide school personnel and parents with the most reliable means to determine in which settings and classroom environments the special education instructional orientation can be unified with teaching the regular curricula. In the long run, researchers will continue to formulate and study potential alternatives and determine their respective effectiveness for achieving greater synergy and thus more synchrony between regular and special education.

# Appendix A
# Sampling Procedures

There were six stages to the sampling process, beginning with how school districts were chosen and extending through how individual EMR and nonhandicapped students were chosen in each educational setting. Plan A (Comprehensive Special Education for Exceptional Children in Texas) was designed to be implemented in stages. Of the 91 school districts that applied to the state agency for early implementation of Plan A, 20 were chosen for school year 1971-72 and an additional 36 for school year 1972-73. In choosing the participating school districts, the Texas Education Agency considered such factors as school board and community knowledge and support, support from the administrative staff, growth or decline in enrollment, the role of special education in providing educational services to children with language or cultural differences, the agreement on policies and philosophy among districts within a cooperative (districts that had joined together to secure a minimum planning base of 3,000 average daily attendance), the availability of space, and the expertise of current staff. An attempt was made to choose at least one district or cooperative in each of the state's 20 education service regions and select approximately one-third of the Plan A program applicants from special education cooperatives.

The districts selected to implement Plan A in school year 1971-72 or 1972-73 formed the base from which the districts, schools, teachers, and students were selected for the Project PRIME study. Districts, schools, teachers, and students were not randomly selected: They were selected on the basis of a variety of methodological and logistical considerations.

## Selection of School Districts

Stage I of the sampling process was the selection of school districts. Of the 56 districts or cooperatives chosen by the Texas Education Agency to implement a Plan A program in 1971-72 or 1972-73, 43 were selected as the district sample for the present study. All 20 districts or cooperatives that had been chosen to implement a Plan A program during the 1971-72 school year and 23 of the districts chosen to implement a Plan A program in the 1972-73 school year were selected.

The first criterion of this sample was that the districts included represent as many of the Texas education service regions as possible. If a service region included several districts that had been designated to implement a Plan A program, districts were selected which

- indicated an intention to mainstream a substantial number of EMR children,
- contained a large population, or
- contained a variety of ethnic or socioeconomic groups.

As indicated by the responses of district superintendents to a questionnaire in the spring of 1972, the 43 school districts or cooperatives were widely divergent in their ethnic characteristics. The mean percentage of the student population in each ethnic group was 63.71% Anglo ($SD = 25.76$), 12.97% Black ($SD = 12.04$), and 22.75% Spanish-surnamed ($SD = 25.71$). The ranges within districts for the three ethnic distributions were 4-98% Anglo, 0-40% Black, and 0-92% Spanish-surnamed. The wide disparity and large standard deviations attest to the fact that many districts comprised predominantly Anglo or Spanish-surnamed students while none were predominantly Black. Thirty-three district superintendents provided financial estimates of the average 1971-72 expenditure for each elementary-aged school child in special education: This average was $918, with a range of $400-2,050. The corresponding expenditure for each regular elementary-aged school child averaged $563, ranging from $333-720. Twenty-four of the 43 school district superintendents indicated the available tax base necessary to support these expenditures was increasing; the remaining 19 superintendents stated their district tax base was either stable or decreasing. Of those districts that had implemented Plan A at the time of data collection, about half indicated few problems with it; the remaining district superintendents indicated some problems in identifying and locating all handicapped children.

# Selection of Schools

Stage II of the sampling process involved the selection of school buildings. Schools were selected from each district on the basis of information provided by the district's special education director. Each specified the socioeconomic status (lower, middle, or upper) of the majority of students in each school building in the district, the location of each building (rural, suburban, or urban), and the number of eligible special education students enrolled in each building. To be eligible for inclusion in the study, a student had to be of appropriate chronological age for grades 3-5; designated the previous year as eligible for special education services; and identified as either educable mentally retarded (EMR), language and/or learning disabled (LLD), or minimally brain injured (MBI). Eligibility and diagnostic identification were based on state regulations and had been determined by each school district's placement committee prior to this investigation.[1]

Within each school, the names of these students; their ethnic group membership; the names of all the teachers with whom each student came in contact; and the grade level, subject matter, and number of hours the teacher taught the student were recorded. The number of hours each student was instructed by regular teachers and by special education teachers was calculated from this information. An EMR learner spending 50% or more of the day in the regular education program was considered mainstreamed and one spending more than 50% of the day in special education classrooms was considered nonmainstreamed.

The total number of mainstreamed and nonmainstreamed EMR students was calculated for each school and these totals were included in the criteria used to select the school buildings. Within each of the location/SES combinations, all the school buildings with at least one mainstreamed EMR learner were selected. A school was selected from those without at least one mainstreamed EMR learner if it had

- two or more special self-contained classrooms that each contained at least one nonmainstreamed EMR student, or

- four or more regular classrooms that each contained at least one mainstreamed student diagnosed as language or learning disabled or minimally brain injured, or
- four or more regular or special classrooms that each contained at least one EMR student.

If a school district had no schools in a particular location/SES combination that met the above criteria, the school that served the maximum number of eligible handicapped students, regardless of type of program, was selected.

Using the above criteria, 156 elementary schools were selected for inclusion in the study. Of these, 141 schools contained EMR students and thus remained as the school building sample from which the findings presented in this book are derived.

No attempt was made to select an equal proportion of the available school buildings within each district. Ten districts had five or more schools selected, whereas 24 districts had only one or two schools included in the study sample. The school buildings selected were not necessarily representative of the districts from which they were sampled. The sampling procedure assured that all eligible mainstreamed EMR learners were sampled and that the schools selected represented a range of socioeconomic characteristics and instructional practices.

## Selection of Teachers

Stage III involved the selection of teachers. One teacher was selected for each EMR learner in the grades 3-5 age range. A regular education teacher was designated for students placed in regular education classrooms for 50% of the day or more. This designated teacher was

- the teacher seen by the student for the longest period of time, or
- the one who taught reading or language arts if two or more teachers instructed the student for about the same length of time, or
- a teacher who taught another academic area and who had not been assigned to another student.

Students who were not mainstreamed were assigned the special education teacher with whom they spent the majority of the day. In addition, for each mainstreamed student, the principal resource teacher identified was the special education teacher who provided the mainstreamed student with the greatest amount (measured in time) of supplemental instruction.

It was possible for a mainstreamed student to receive special supplemental instruction from a teacher of a special self-contained classroom. It was also possible for a nonmainstreamed student to spend most of the day with a resource teacher. In such instances, the teacher designation was determined by the role the teacher performed with the student. All special teachers of nonmainstreamed students (those who spent more than 50% of the day in special classrooms) were designated as special self-contained classroom teachers, even those who were primarily resource teachers. Similarly, all special teachers of mainstreamed students were designated as resource teachers, even those who were primarily special self-contained classroom teachers.

The findings presented in this book are based upon 262 regular teachers, 132 resource teachers, and 127 self-contained teachers.

## Selection of Students

Since the districts and school buildings were selected in large part on the basis of the number of mainstreamed EMR learners, the sampling procedures resulted in the inclusion of almost all mainstreamed grade 3-5 EMR students in the Plan A 1971-72 and 1972-73 districts. Consequently, the EMR learners represent a population rather than a sample from a population. Since many of these students were assigned to the same selected teacher, they do not represent unique learner/classroom environment dyads.

The nonmainstreamed EMR learners, the nonhandicapped contrast students, and the classroom peers were selected in Stages IV, V, and VI, respectively. The nonmainstreamed learners were selected using a stratified random procedure. Specifically, the nonmainstreamed students assigned to each selected special education teacher were classified by ethnic membership. Then one student was randomly selected from each ethnic group taught by that teacher. If a teacher taught only one ethnic group, two students from that ethnic group were selected at random to allow for possible attrition.

The nonhandicapped contrast students were selected from the same classrooms as the target mainstreamed students. A random-numbers procedure was employed, with one nonhandicapped contrast student chosen for each mainstreamed student included in the study. In addition, one additional nonhandicapped student was selected per classroom to allow for attrition among the nonhandicapped students during the year. Since they were randomly selected, the nonhandicapped students can be considered a typical student representation of the regular classroom population.

The sample of nonhandicapped students was subsequently reduced to match numerically the number of mainstreamed EMR students in the classroom. The reduction of the nonhandicapped student sample was conducted post hoc. For each nonhandicapped student, the percentage of available (not missing) background and competency data was calculated. The nonhandicapped students within each classroom were ranked according to the percentage of available data and an appropriate number were selected to match the number of EMR students in that classroom. For example, in classrooms with two EMR and three nonhandicapped students, the two nonhandicapped students with the highest percentage of available data were selected.

The sample of students or learners upon which the findings in this book are based contains 356 mainstreamed EMR, 273 nonmainstreamed, and 356 nonhandicapped contrast students. Although no attempt was made to stratify the nonhandicapped and mainstreamed EMR learner sample by grade, the three grades are roughly evenly represented. For each learner sample, there were 107 third-grade nonhandicapped and mainstreamed EMR learners, 129 fourth-grade and 120 fifth-grade nonhandicapped and mainstreamed EMR learners. These learners were selected from 7598 peers in regular classrooms, 1525 peers in special self-contained classrooms, and 950 peers in resource classrooms.

For certain descriptive purposes, including sociometric ratings of selected students and descriptions of classroom behavior patterns, all students in the selected teacher's class who were present when the selected student was present were designated as the sample of peers.

Certain definitional considerations related to the EMR learner sample should be understood. First, the EMR learners in this study were designated using the appraisal and placement procedures of the school district guided by Texas Education Agency regulations. The regulations define EMR children as those who

> reveal a reduced rate of intellectual development and level of academic achievement below that of their peer age group as evidenced by significant deficits in all essential learning processes (p. 4).

Evidence for classification as an EMR child must include

> Written comprehensive intellectual assessment revealing deficit in all essential learning processes between two and three standard deviation units below the mean of general population; such deficit not attributable to lack of opportunity to learn or differences in linguistic patterns (p. 9).

The Project PRIME study made no attempt to verify though reassessment or other procedures the correctness of the diagnostic label of the students in the EMR learner sample.

Second, although all EMR learners had been diagnosed and determined eligible for special education the year prior to the Project PRIME study, their placement during that year varied. This was not the first year of mainstreaming for many of the mainstreamed learners.

Third, although for purposes of the research design, each EMR learner was designated either mainstreamed or nonmainstreamed based on the amount of time integrated with nonhandicapped students, this should not imply uniform temporal integration of each student. Mainstreamed learners ranged from 50-100% integrated. Most nonmainstreamed learners also spent some part of their day with nonhandicapped students and many even received some academic instruction in the regular classroom; thus, most nonmainstreamed learners were not segregated in the traditional sense of the term.

# Cautions Related to Interpretation of Results

The sampling procedures discussed above have certain implications that should be considered when interpreting the findings presented in this book.

## Research Site

Project PRIME was conducted during 1972, the second year of implementation of Comprehensive Special Education for Exceptional Children (Plan A) in the State of Texas. The newness of the plan, the lack of clarity which characterizes the implementation of any program, and the positive and negative expectations and attitudes that accompany organizational change had different implications for different school districts and different schools within each district. Certain school districts had already mainstreamed EMR learners and provided resource room services while others were just initiating or planning such services.

## School District

The school districts were not randomly chosen: They most often represented communities committed to providing a comprehensive continuum of special education services. The selected districts possessed a high level of administrative initiative, community support, and program capability in the area of special education. They were not representative of all school districts in the State of Texas; instead, these districts are probably representative of school systems which are open to innovation and improvement.

## School Building

Since the schools that were selected had to contain either a special education resource or self-contained classroom, they may not have been representative of the districts from which they were chosen. To the extent that special education classrooms for EMR learners are systematically located according to such factors as the principal's attitude, school enrollment, transportation, or homogeneous grouping, the schools in Project PRIME may not be representative of all elementary school buildings. However, they are likely to be representative of school buildings which do provide space for special education classrooms for EMR students.

A second caution concerns schools having resource and/or self-contained classes. A building may contain one or both of these alternative special education classroom settings. To the extent that the availability of resource and self-contained classes is systematically related to school factors such as neighborhood SES (e.g., schools in low-SES neighborhoods may be more likely to be designated to house special self-contained classes), comparisons between the two classroom settings should be made with caution.

## Teachers

Several potential biases in the teacher sample should be considered. First, directors of special education and school building principals indicated on administrative questionnaires that they thought regular classroom teachers should be selected to instruct EMR learners on the basis of their ability to individualize instruction and use remedial techniques as well as manage behavior with firmness, tolerance, and understanding (Agard, 1974). Other reasons for systematically assigning EMR students to specific teachers may be teacher preference or years of teaching experience. Regardless, the regular classroom teachers in the study may not be representative of all regular classroom teachers, instead being representative of the regular classroom teachers typically selected to instruct EMR children.

A second caution concerns how representative the resource classroom teachers were. As this study was conducted during the second year of implementation of Plan A, many districts were either expanding or initiating new resource classrooms. The sample of resource teachers includes (a) teachers who had previously been special self-contained classroom teachers, (b) teachers who were new graduates of university special education programs, and (c) teachers who had been regular classroom teachers and had obtained provisional special education certification. This latter group of teachers was comprised of superior regular classroom teachers who were offered a special education assignment contingent on their enrollment in a special education training program. To the extent classroom instruction is affected by teacher experience, the findings from this study may not be applicable to well-established resource classrooms. This concern is particularly relevant if one assumes that only over time will teachers in new assignments accrue materials, internalize a curriculum sequence, and develop effective instructional strategies.

## Learners

Nonhandicapped learners were selected from the regular classrooms in which the EMR learner was placed. If EMR learners are placed with certain types of nonhandicapped peers, then the nonhandicapped learner sample may have certain characteristics that allow this mix. For example, if EMR learners are placed with low-achieving peers, the randomly selected nonhandicapped learner, though representative of the classroom, will not be representative of all nonhandicapped students. Since the nonhandicapped learners were selected from the same regular classrooms as the mainstreamed EMR learners, they represent an interesting and appropriate comparison sample. Readers should be aware, as noted earlier, that the nonhandicapped and mainstreamed EMR learners are not comparable in sociodemographic background and this incomparability may affect other comparisons between these two learner groups.

Certain cautions regarding the comparability of the two EMR learner samples must also be explicitly considered. Particularly, we need to ascertain the extent to which the samples of learners placed in either a mainstreamed or nonmainstreamed program are comparable or reflect systematic biases in learner assignments resulting from administrative- and student-level placement decisions. At the student level, one might expect that the students who are mainstreamed have higher IQs or academic achievement and/or display more appropriate social behavior than the nonmainstreamed learners. However, such systematic differences were not evident. One reason for this lack of difference may be that real placement choices between alternative programs were not available. Many EMR learners were assigned to buildings that offered either resource or self-contained programs, but not both. Among the Project PRIME school buildings, only 26 (18%) contained both resource and self-contained programs for EMR learners. EMR learners in a building were assigned to the available special education service delivery mode, with exceptions made only for extremely divergent students. For example, in schools where only mainstreaming was available, the few EMR students unable to cope with the regular classroom may have remained in the resource room all day, while the other EMR students were integrated into regular classrooms.

Even if the assignment of EMR learners to alternative placement situations was not based on their individual characteristics, there may have been systematic differences in the schools or districts that elected to implement either a resource or self-contained classroom as the principal method for the delivery of special education services. These school or district differences may be systematically related to learner characteristics, such as ethnicity, which may indirectly bias the results. For example, building placement committees may have felt that Spanish-speaking EMR students needed the language stimulation provided in regular classrooms, and therefore selected a special education resource classroom to meet Spanish-speaking EMR students' needs. If this occurred often,the sample of mainstreamed EMR learners would be over-represented by Spanish-speaking students based on building policy. Consideration of such factors demands some caution in interpreting comparisons of the two EMR learner samples.

# Technical Notes

1.   The final sample of this study includes only the EMR learner portion of the original sample. However, since some school buildings were included in the study which might not have been included if the original sample had contained only EMR learners, the procedure for selecting the buildings for the larger sample is described here.

# Appendix B
# Samples of Instruments Used in Project PRIME

Material related to the following instruments appears in this Appendix.

About You and Your Friends (AYYF)
Classroom Integration Questionnaire (CIQ)
Children's Questionnaire (CQ)
Florida Climate and Control Questionnaire (FLACCS)
Guess Who (GW)
How Do You Feel - Part I (HDYF-I)
How Do You Feel - Part II (HYDF—II)
How I Feel Toward Others (HIFTO)
Indiana Behavior Management System (IBMS)
Indiana Cognitive Demand Schedule (ICDS)
Indiana Pupil Participation Schedule (IPPS)
Selected Children's Background Questionnaire (SCBQ)
Teacher Climate Control Questionnaire (TCCQ)
Teacher Educational Attitude Questionnaire (TEAQ)
Teacher Rating Scale (TRS)
Your School Days (YSD)

**ABOUT YOU AND YOUR FRIENDS**
Factors and Items

Factor I:  Loneliness and Rejection

Do you find it easy to get along with your classmates?
Do you wish children at this school were friendlier to you?
Do you wish you had extra help with your school work?
Do you get worried when you have tests in school?
Do you get nervous when the teacher calls on you?
Is the school work so hard that you are afraid you will fail?
Are you afraid to try new things?
Are you afraid you'll do something wrong at school?
Do you have trouble making up your mind?
Is it hard to talk with your classmates?
Do your classmates make fun of you?
Do you have only a few friends?
Are you one of the last to be chosen for games?
Is it hard for you to make friends?
Do you think you need more friends?
Would you rather play with children younger than you?
Do other children pick on you?
Do you wish you could be a leader more often?
Do you feel left out of things in your class?

Factor II:  Enjoys School

Do you want to learn to do your school work better?
Do you like to start work on new activities?
Are you happy in school?
Do you like to be called on in class?
Do you get along well with your teachers?
Do you have fun at school?
Is school interesting to you?
Are you doing the best work that you can?
Do you like school?
Would you stay home from school a lot if it were all right?
Do you like arithmetic?
Do you ever study things on your own?
Do you work well with the other children on projects?
Do you like reading?
Do you like to talk in the class discussions?
Do you like science?
Do you wish you were smarter in school?
Do you like to be with other children?
Do you wish you were better at games?
Do you try to be friends with children who don't like you?
Do you like gym?
Do you like music?
Do children usually ask you to play with them?
Do most of your classmates like you?
Do your friends want to help you?
Do you like to eat lunch by yourself?
Do you like to help other children?
Do you take an active part in class projects?
Do you like art?
Do you talk to new children at school?

**ABOUT YOU AND YOUR FRIENDS,** continued

Factor III:  Does Well in School

Are you doing well in your school work?
Do you forget what you learn?
Do you do your work quickly?
Are you a hard worker in school?
Are you slow in finishing your school work?
Can you figure out problems for yourself?
Are you smart?
Do you think you are one of the hardest workers?
Do you usually do well on tests?
Do most of your friends think you're smart?
Do you think you know as much as the other children in your classes?
Do you have good ideas?
Do you ever think up new ideas?
Can you give a good report in front of the class?
Are you a good reader?
Do you write good stories and reports?
Do people like you have much of a chance to be successful in life?
Would you be able to make the right decisions if you were president
   of your class?
Are you an important person in your class?
Are you one of the first to be chosen for a game?
Are you good at math?

Factor IV:  Misbehavior

Do you get into trouble in school?
Is your work sometimes so hard that you stop trying?
Do you get a lot of scolding at school?
Do you often disagree with what the teacher says?
Are you well behaved in school?
Does your teacher have to tell you to do your work?
Do you fight too much?
Do you laugh when others make mistakes?
Are you mean to other children?
Are you a bully?
Do you fool around too much in class?
If a classmate calls you a bad name, do you fight?
Would you do something you think is wrong if your friends ask
   you to?

## CLASSROOM INTEGRATION QUESTIONNAIRE
Scale and Items

Directions:  Read each behavioral description and circle the corresponding
letter to the left of each item as follows:

A.  In regular classroom

B.  In regular classroom all day with supplemental
materials and advice

C.  In regular classroom part of the day with supplemental
materials and advice

D.  In special class all day

E.  Not for public education

(Circle only one letter per item)

1.  Although Eric seems very bright doing science experiments and other
activities involving manuipulation of materials, he still does poorly
in his reading and arithmetic assignments.

2.  Richard is overly dependent on the teacher. He seeks out excessive
adult attention. He has no sense of self-direction. He never does
anything without being pushed or prodded.

3.  Chuck doesn't seem able to catch on to things as quickly as most, and
needs to have things explained over and over again; eventually, though,
he appears to learn everything the others do, even though it has taken
longer.

4.  Florence is immature and oversensitive, likely to burst into tears at
the slightest provocation. She pouts or sulks if she can't do what she
wants to do.

5.  Alfred is defiant and stubborn, likely to argue with the teacher, be
willfully disobedient and otherwise interfere with the normal classroom
discipline.

6.  John frequently misinterprets simple statements and directions given
to the group; he does better if he can repeat the directions to the
teacher.

7.  Doris is absent-minded and a daydreamer; she seems unusually quiet
and withdrawn, avoids others and is inhibited and restrained in her
behavior.

8.  Timmy is overly aggressive. He seems to pick fights, tease and
bully other children. He is a poor sport and argues about rules and
decisions.

**CLASSROOM INTEGRATION QUESTIONNAIRE,** continued

9.  Jerry does reasonably good work as long as he is left alone; he becomes extremely tense and anxious, however, whenever an adult speaks to him. He becomes very upset when he makes a mistake and just freezes up when called on in class.

10. Dotty is eight; she has difficulty following the class activities, and doesn't seem able to learn to read at all.

11. Richard is a likeable boy; he makes friends easily and is very sensitive of how others see him. He is two years behind his peers in math skills and four years behind in reading.

12. Stella can read orally but doesn't comprehend the meaning of what she reads. She can identify all the words in a sentence but cannot paraphrase the sentence or tell what it means.

13. Martha is a hyperactive child. She is always jumping out of her seat, running around the room; she can't seem to sit still for any length of time. While she's running around, she annoys and disrupts other children.

14. Betty works very rapidly and usually is the first one finished in her section. However, most of her responses are incorrect.

15. Chester is deceitful, tells lies and cheats in school and at play; he has been involved in several thefts and is a persistent truant.

16. Sammy, in second grade, can't correctly repeat oral directions or correctly repeat a 7-10 word statement. He omits and/or transposes words, can't recite days of the week, the alphabet or numbers in order.

17. Judy eventually mutilates or destroys everything that gets into her hands; her books are marked and torn, her desk is inkstained and scarred, and she has even managed to crack a blackboard panel.

18. Carla is a persistent walker, whisperer and notepasser.

19. Beth is not able to achieve in any area of academics on a level with the other children. All areas of academics must be done on an individual basis.

20. Milly is slow to comprehend instructions that involve directionality. She is confused about left-right, up-down and confuses prepositions (over, under) in her oral expression.

21. Earl is eight and wears cowboy boots to class because he hasn't learned to tie his own shoelaces; he is generally cheerful and well-behaved, but talks very little in class and is incapable of doing anything but the most simple work assignments.

22. Susan frequently reads words and numbers reversed and confuses similar words and letters when reading, but does alright with oral spelling.

**CLASSROOM INTEGRATION QUESTIONNAIRE,** continued

23. Brenda seems very unhappy and depressed in school. She sometimes appears to have been crying and never seems to smile even when she's playing with the other children.

24. Billy tends to skip words while reading and needs to use a moving finger, pencil or other artifact to avoid omissions.

25. Alan seems to have very few friends. He stays by himself most of the time watching the other children. He is never chosen for games and never interacts with other children about his school work.

## CHILDREN'S QUESTIONNAIRE
Administrator's Question Sheet

1.  How many people live in your home? Count your father, mother, brothers, sisters, aunts, uncles, grandparents and any others who live with you. Count yourself but don't count your pets.

2.  How many children are in your family? (It may help the child to ask, "How many brothers do you have? How many sisters do you have?" Then add the responses. Be sure to include the child himself.) (Children refers to children under 18.)

3.  Does your family have a telephone?

4.  Does your family have a record player, hi-fi or stereo?

5.  Does your family have a refrigerator? (If the child says "ice box" probe to find out if it is an electric "ice box" or one that takes ice.)

6.  Does your family have a dictionary? (A big book with lots of words and what they mean.)

7.  Does your family have an encyclopedia? (A set of books with lots of pictures and words that tell about different things.)

8.  Does your family have an automobile?

9.  Does your family have an air conditioner?

10. Does your family get a newspaper every day?

11. Does your family get any magazines regularly at home?

12a. Do you have any books to read at home?

12b. (If yes) How many do you have?

13a. Before you started school, did anyone at home read to you when you were small?

13b. (If yes) How often did they read to you?

14a. Do you read to yourself at home?

14b. (If yes) How often do you read to yourself?

15a. Does your mother or father or someone in your family read to you?

15b. (If yes) How often does someone read to you?

16a. Do you have any games to play with such as card games, checkers, Monopoly, Chutes and Ladders, Sand Land, Spirograph and any others?

**CHILDREN'S QUESTIONNAIRE,** continued

16b. (If yes)  How many games do you have?

17a. Do you play with these games with your friends or brothers and sisters?

17b. (If yes)  How often do you play with these games?

18.  Does your mother or father or some grownup in your family play these
     games with you?

18b. (If yes)  How often do grownups play these games with you?

19.  Do you go on trips to playgrounds, parks or other places for picnics,
     swimming or fishing with your family?

19b. (If yes)  How often do you go on trips?

20.  Do your mother and father help you learn to do important jobs around
     your home like cooking or fixing the car?

20b. (If yes)  How often do they help you learn your job?

21.  Does your family have a television set?

22.  On school days, how much time do you watch TV at home?  (You may have
     to ask, "How many programs do you watch?"  Then compute the time from
     the number of programs.)

23.  Does your mother or father usually watch TV with you?

24a. Do you have work to do at home for school?

24b. (If yes)  About how much time do you spend each day on homework?

25a. Do you and your parents talk about your school work?

25b. (If yes)  How often do you talk about your school work?

26.  Did you go to kindergarten?

27.  Did you go to nursery school before you went to kindergarten?

28.  How do you usually come to school in the morning?

29.  Do you want to stop going to school as soon as you can?  (At age 16)

30.  Do you want to finish high school?

31.  Do you want to go to college?

32.  When you finish school, what sort of job do you think you will have?
     (Record the child's response on the questionnaire booklet.)

33.  Do you like school better this year than you did last year?

**CHILDREN'S QUESTIONNAIRE,** continued

34. Do you like your teacher better this year than you did last year?

35. Do you have more friends this year than you did last year?

36. Do you like the children in your class this year better than the children in your class last year?

37. Do you like doing work in reading better this year than last year?

38. Do you like doing work in arithmetic (math) better this year than last year?

# FLORIDA CLIMATE AND CONTROL QUESTIONNAIRE

**16.**
**TIME STARTED**

| Hour | | Minute | |
|---|---|---|---|
| ⑧⑨⑩⑪⑫ ①②③④⑤ | ⓪①② ③④⑤ | ⓪①②③④ ⑤⑥⑦⑧⑨ | |

### TEACHER

(E)(C)(K) Teacher Central
(E)(C)(K) Leads singing, games, storytime
(E)(C)(K) Moves freely among pupils
(E)(C)(K) Withdraws from class
(E)(C)(K) Uses blackboard, A–V equip.
(E)(C)(K) Ignores, refuses to attend pupil
(E)(C)(K) Attends pupil briefly
(E)(C)(K) Attends pupil closely
(E)(C)(K) Attends pupils in succession
(E)(C)(K) Attends simultaneous activities

### VERBAL CONTROL

(E)(C)(K) Praises
(E)(C)(K) Asks for status
(E)(C)(K) Suggests, guides
(E)(C)(K) Feedback, cites reason
(E)(C)(K) Questions for reflective thought
(E)(C)(K) Correct w/o criticism (SM)
(E)(C)(K) Questions for control
(E)(C)(K) Questions states behavior rule
(E)(C)(K) Directs with reason
(E)(C)(K) Directs w/o reason
(E)(C)(K) Uses time pressure
(E)(C)(K) Calls child by name
(E)(C)(K) Interrupts pupil, cuts off
(E)(C)(K) Warns
(E)(C)(K) Supv. pupil closely, imblizes.
(E)(C)(K) Criticizes
(E)(C)(K) Orders, commands
(E)(C)(K) Scolds, punishes
(E)(C)(K) Uses firm tone
(E)(C)(K) Uses sharp tone

### NONVERBAL CONTROL

(E)(C)(K) Tolerates deviant behavior
(E)(C)(K) Positive redirection
(E)(C)(K) Nods, smiles for control
(E)(C)(K) Positive facial feedback
(E)(C)(K) Uses "body English"
(E)(C)(K) Gestures
(E)(C)(K) Gives tangible reward
(E)(C)(K) Touches, pats (gentle)
(E)(C)(K) Holds, pushes, spanks (firm)
(E)(C)(K) Takes equipment, book
(E)(C)(K) Signals, raps
(E)(C)(K) Shhh! Shakes head
(E)(C)(K) Glares, frowns

### PUPIL

(E)(C)(K) Pupil Central
(E)(C)(K) Pupil -- no choice
(E)(C)(K) Pupil -- limited choice
(E)(C)(K) Pupil -- free choice

(E)(C)(K) (Seat work w/o teacher
(E)(C)(K) (Seat work with teacher

(E)(C)(K) (Works, plays with much supervision
(E)(C)(K) (Works, plays with little supervision

(E)(C)(K) (Resists, disobeys directions
(E)(C)(K) (Obeys directions
(E)(C)(K) Asks permission
(E)(C)(K) Follows routine w/o reminder
(E)(C)(K) Reports rule to another
(E)(C)(K) Tattles
(E)(C)(K) Gives information
(E)(C)(K) Gives direction
(E)(C)(K) Gives reason
(E)(C)(K) Speaks aloud w/o permission

(Continued next column)

### PUPIL (Continued)

(E)(C)(K) Engages in out-of-bounds behavior
(E)(C)(K) Parallel work or play
(E)(C)(K) Work with socialization
(E)(C)(K) Collaborative work or play
(E)(C)(K) Works, plays competitively
(E)(C)(K) Task related movement
(E)(C)(K) Aimless wandering
(E)(C)(K) Fantasy
(E)(C)(K) Uses play object as itself
(E)(C)(K) Seeks reassurance, support
(E)(C)(K) Shows pride
(E)(C)(K) Shows fear, shame, humiliation
(E)(C)(K) Shows apathy

### SOCIALIZATION

(E)(C)(K) Almost never
(E)(C)(K) Occasionally
(E)(C)(K) Frequently

### MATERIALS

(E)(C)(K) Structure Teacher behavior
(E)(C)(K) Structure Pupil behavior

### PUPIL INTEREST ATTENTION
(Rank 1 low to 5 high)

| 1 | 2 | 3 | 4 | 5 |
|---|---|---|---|---|
| ○ | ○ | ○ | ○ | ○ |

**17.**
### ACTIVITY

(E)(C)(K) Reading    (E)(C)(K) Music
(E)(C)(K) Spelling    (E)(C)(K) Foreign lang.
(E)(C)(K) Language arts   (E)(C)(K) Perceptual
(E)(C)(K) Mathematics      training
(E)(C)(K) Science/health   (E)(C)(K) Transitional
(E)(C)(K) Social studies      activity
(E)(C)(K) Art    (E)(C)(K) Other

**18.** Position of E, C, T and O

FRONT OF CLASS

| (E)(C) (T)(O) | (E)(C) (T)(O) | (E)(C) (T)(O) |
|---|---|---|
| (E)(C) (T)(O) | (E)(C) (T)(O) | (E)(C) (T)(O) |
| (E)(C) (T)(O) | (E)(C) (T)(O) | (E)(C) (T)(O) |

**19.**
### STRUCTURE FOR CLASSROOM ACTIVITIES

(E)(C)(K) One large group
(E)(C)(K) Small group with teacher
(E)(C)(K) Small group(s) without teacher
(E)(C)(K) Individually with teacher
(E)(C)(K) Individually without teacher
(E)(C)(K) Free groups
(E)(C)(K) No apparent structure

## FLORIDA CLIMATE AND CONTROL QUESTIONNAIRE, continued

### NEGATIVE AFFECT

**TEACHER VERBAL**
(E)(C)(K) Says "Stop it," etc.
(E)(C)(K) Uses threatening tone
(E)(C)(K) Rejects child
(E)(C)(K) Criticizes, blames
(E)(C)(K) Warns
(E)(C)(K) Yells
(E)(C)(K) Scolds, humiliates
(E)(C)(K) Other
(0)(1)(2)(3) Code Involvement

**PUPIL VERBAL**
(E)(C)(K) Says "No," "I won't," etc.
(E)(C)(K) Teases
(E)(C)(K) Laughs
(E)(C)(K) Tattles
(E)(C)(K) Commands or demands
(E)(C)(K) Makes disparaging remark
(E)(C)(K) Demands attention
(E)(C)(K) Makes someone "feel small"
(E)(C)(K) Finds fault
(E)(C)(K) Threatens
(E)(C)(K) Other
(0)(1)(2)(3) Code Involvement

**TEACHER NONVERBAL**
(E)(C)(K) Waits for child
(E)(C)(K) Frowns
(E)(C)(K) Points, shakes finger
(E)(C)(K) Pushes or pulls, holds
(E)(C)(K) Shows disgust
(E)(C)(K) Takes material
(E)(C)(K) Refuses to respond to child
(E)(C)(K) Other

**PUPIL NONVERBAL**
(E)(C)(K) Makes faces, frowns
(E)(C)(K) Pouts, withdraws
(E)(C)(K) Uncooperative, resistant
(E)(C)(K) Stamps, throws, slams
(E)(C)(K) Interferes, threatens
(E)(C)(K) Takes, damages property
(E)(C)(K) Picks at child
(E)(C)(K) Pushes or pulls, holds
(E)(C)(K) Hits, hurts
(E)(C)(K) Is left out
(E)(C)(K) Other

### POSITIVE AFFECT

**TEACHER VERBAL**
(E)(C)(K) Says "Thank you," etc.
(E)(C)(K) Agrees with child
(E)(C)(K) Supports child
(E)(C)(K) Gives individual attention
(E)(C)(K) Warm, congenial
(E)(C)(K) Praises child
(E)(C)(K) Develops "we feeling"
(E)(C)(K) Is enthusiastic
(E)(C)(K) Other
(0)(1)(2)(3) Code Involvement

**PUPIL VERBAL**
(E)(C)(K) Says "Thank you," etc.
(E)(C)(K) Sounds friendly
(E)(C)(K) Agrees with another
(E)(C)(K) Initiates contact
(E)(C)(K) Offers to share, cooperate
(E)(C)(K) Supports another
(E)(C)(K) Is enthusiastic
(E)(C)(K) Praises another
(E)(C)(K) Helps another
(E)(C)(K) Other
(0)(1)(2)(3) Code Involvement

**TEACHER NONVERBAL**
(E)(C)(K) Accepts favor for self
(E)(C)(K) Waits for child
(E)(C)(K) Gives individual attention
(E)(C)(K) Warm, congenial
(E)(C)(K) Listens carefully to child
(E)(C)(K) Smiles, laughs, nods
(E)(C)(K) Pats, hugs, etc.
(E)(C)(K) Sympathetic
(E)(C)(K) Other

**PUPIL NONVERBAL**
(E)(C)(K) Helpful, shares
(E)(C)(K) Leans close to another
(E)(C)(K) Chooses another
(E)(C)(K) Smiles, laughs with another
(E)(C)(K) Pats, hugs another
(E)(C)(K) Agreeable, cooperative
(E)(C)(K) Enthusiastic
(E)(C)(K) Horseplay
(E)(C)(K) Other

**CODE INVOLVEMENT:** 0 = None involved  1 = Few involved  2 = Up to ½ the class  3 = More than half

**20. TEACHER TASK**
O Drilling          O Directing
O Introducing       O Testing
O Motivating        O Supervising
O Questioning       O Summarizing
O Demonstrating     O Reviewing
O Lecturing         O Other
O Explaining

**21. PUPIL TASK**
(E)(C)(K) Listening to teacher
(E)(C)(K) Interacting with teacher
(E)(C)(K) Interacting with other pupil(s)
(E)(C)(K) Interacting with aide
(E)(C)(K) Working with print material(s)
(E)(C)(K) Working with non-print material(s)

**22. SEATING ARRANGEMENT**
(E)(C)(K) Rows x columns   (E)(C)(K) Horse shoe
(E)(C)(K) Small groups     (E)(C)(K) Individual
(E)(C)(K) Circle           (E)(C)(K) Other

**23. TIME STOPPED**

| Hour | Minute | S |
|---|---|---|
| (8)(9)(10)(11)(12)  (0)(1)(2) | (0)(1)(2)(3)(4) | T |
| (1)(2)(3)(4)(5)  (3)(4)(5) | (5)(6)(7)(8)(9) | O P |

**FLORIDA CLIMATE AND CONTROL QUESTIONNAIRE,** continued

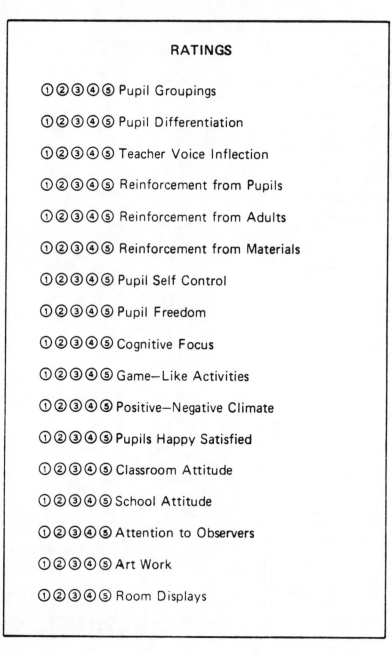

### RATINGS

① ② ③ ④ ⑤ Pupil Groupings

① ② ③ ④ ⑤ Pupil Differentiation

① ② ③ ④ ⑤ Teacher Voice Inflection

① ② ③ ④ ⑤ Reinforcement from Pupils

① ② ③ ④ ⑤ Reinforcement from Adults

① ② ③ ④ ⑤ Reinforcement from Materials

① ② ③ ④ ⑤ Pupil Self Control

① ② ③ ④ ⑤ Pupil Freedom

① ② ③ ④ ⑤ Cognitive Focus

① ② ③ ④ ⑤ Game—Like Activities

① ② ③ ④ ⑤ Positive—Negative Climate

① ② ③ ④ ⑤ Pupils Happy Satisfied

① ② ③ ④ ⑤ Classroom Attitude

① ② ③ ④ ⑤ School Attitude

① ② ③ ④ ⑤ Attention to Observers

① ② ③ ④ ⑤ Art Work

① ② ③ ④ ⑤ Room Displays

**GUESS WHO**
Scales and Items

Scale I:  Brightness

Is the smartest in the class
Always knows the answer
Is the best in math
Always gets school work done on time
Is the best in reading

Scale II:  Dullness

Is the worst in math
Never knows the answers in class
Is the worst in reading
Learns new things very slowly
Never gets school work done on time

Scale III: Disruptive Behavior

Is scolded by the teacher all the time
Is always bothering other children
Makes too much noise in class
Breaks the rules
Bothers the teacher all the time
Makes fun of other children
Always wants his/her own way
Gets into lots of fights
Likes to boss others around
Does not work well with others

Scale IV: Quiet/Good Behavior

Does not talk much to other children
Is the best behaved
Never talks in class discussions
Never gets mad at other children
Is friendly to everyone

# PROJECT PRIME
# HOW DO YOU FEEL
# (ADMINISTRATOR'S QUESTION SHEET)

1. Someone gave you an ice cream cone. Would you be happy or unhappy?  **A**

2. Suppose you were running and you tripped over a rock and fell. What would your face look like, happy, plain or unhappy?

3. You are walking to school in the morning and see someone driving down the street. How would you feel about that?

4. You are visiting your aunt and uncle. They ask you if you like your school. Color in the face that looks like yours would look.

5. Some children are playing a game at recess. You are playing by yourself. How do you feel?

### NOW LET'S MOVE ON TO THE BOX LETTERED "B"

6. You came to school in the morning. There is a sign near the door. It says, "No school today." Show how you feel.  **B**

7. You are walking to school. You see some children from your class. What is your face like?

8. Your teacher is changing to teach a different class. You will have a new teacher. Which is your face?

9. You got a new game for your birthday. It is the first time you have tried to play it. How do you feel?

10. You are talking to your friends about school. What is your face like?

### NOW LET'S MOVE ON TO THE BOX LETTERED "C"

11. You came to school early and talked with your teacher. How do you feel?  **C**

12. You have some time to read before you go to sleep. You pick your favorite book to read. What does your face look like?

13. Your parents ask you if you like the children in your class. What is your face like?

14. The teacher gave the class a test. She is disappointed in your grade. How do you feel?

15. You are talking to your classmates about your teacher. What is your face like?

### NOW LET'S MOVE ON TO THE BOX LETTERED "D"

16. It is time to do a page of math (arithmetic) problems. Show how you feel.  **D**

17. The children are making teams for a game. You are the last one picked. How do you feel?

18. It is report card day. You must let your parents see your report card. Which is your face?

19. Some of the children in your class are moving to a different school. Show how you feel about that.

20. The teacher asked you an easy question and you did not know the answer. Which is your face?

### NOW LET'S MOVE ON TO THE BOX LETTERED "E"

21. It is free time. You take out a book you have never read before. You start to read. How do you feel?  **E**

22. It is time to write a story. Show how you feel.

23. You are thinking about how good you are in reading. Which is your face?

24. The teacher says only the children who work hard can go out and play. How do you feel?

25. You start to study something new in math (arithmetic). How do you feel?

**HOW DO YOU FEEL - I,** continued

NOW LET'S MOVE ON TO THE BOX LETTERED "F"

26. The teacher has given you an art project to do all by yourself.  How do you feel?

27. There is a lot of time left to do math (arithmetic).  How do you feel?

28. The teacher calls you to the desk to answer a question.  How do you feel?

29. You get a comic book to read.  You find that it is all pictures and no words.  How do you feel about that?

30. You have a chance to work on an extra school project.  How do you feel?

**F**

NOW LET'S TURN THE PAGE OVER TO THE BOX LETTERED "G"

31. There is a slow student in your class.  The teacher asks you to help him with the new classwork.  How do you feel?

32. You are sitting at home.  You take out your reading book from school.  How do you feel?

33. You are looking at your math (arithmetic) book.  It tells you how to play an arithmetic game.  How do you feel about that?

34. The children in your class are playing.  You are playing with them.  What is your face like?

35. The class is sitting down and working.  You are also doing your work.  What is your face like?

**G**

NOW LET'S MOVE ON TO THE BOX LETTERED "H"

36. It is your birthday.  Two of your birthday presents are books to read.  How do you feel about this?

37. Your mother came to school to talk with your teacher.  What face would you wear?

38. You get presents for your birthday.  One of the presents is a box of pencils, pens and paper for school work.  How do you feel about that?

39. Tomorrow the class will use more time for math (arithmetic).  Show how you feel.

40. The teacher comes over to help you with your work.  Show how you feel.

41. You are walking down the hall at school.  You see your teacher walking down the hall.  How do you feel?

**H**

# PROJECT PRIME
# HOW DO YOU FEEL
# PART II
# (ADMINISTRATOR'S QUESTION SHEET)

1. Someone gave you an ice cream cone. Would you be happy or unhappy? **A**

2. Suppose you were running and you tripped over a rock and fell. What would your face look like, happy, plain or unhappy?

3. You are walking to school in the morning and see someone driving down the street. How would you feel about that?

4. Do you remember coming to school last year? Color in the face that shows how you felt about school last year.

5. Think about how you did in reading last year. What does your face look like?

### NOW LET'S MOVE ON TO THE BOX LETTERED "B"

6. Do you remember what school was like last year? Were you happy or unhappy about going to school last year? **B**

7. Do you remember how you felt when you worked on your math problems last year? Show how you felt last year doing your math problems.

8. Remember your teacher last year? Show how you felt about your teacher last year.

9. Do you remember the friends you had last year? Color in the face that shows how you felt about your friends last year.

10. Do you remember talking with your teacher last year? Color the face that shows how you felt about your teacher last year.

### NOW LET'S MOVE ON TO THE BOX LETTERED "C"

11. Do you remember the reading books you used last year? Show how you felt about last year's reading books. **C**

12. Do you remember playing with the children in your room last year? Color in the face that tells how you felt about playing with your friends last year.

13. Think about how you did in math last year. How does your face look?

14. Do you remember coming to school in the fall at the beginning of the year? Color in the face that shows how you felt about coming to school last fall.

15. Think about how you did in reading when you started school in the fall. What does your face look like?

### NOW LET'S MOVE ON TO THE BOX LETTERED "D"

16. Do you remember what school was like last fall? Were you happy or unhappy about coming to school last fall? **D**

17. Do you remember how you felt when you were working on your math problems at the first of the year? Show how you felt back in the fall doing your math problems.

18. Remember when you first came to school in the fall and found out who your teacher would be for this year. Were you happy or unhappy about who your teacher was in the fall?

19. Do you remember the friends you had last fall? Color the face that shows how you felt at the beginning of the year about your friends.

20. Do you remember when you talked to your teacher back in the fall? Color in the face that shows how you felt talking with your teacher in the fall.

**HOW DO YOU FEEL - II,** continued

### NOW LET'S MOVE ON TO THE BOX LETTERED "E"

21. Do you remember the reading books you used at the beginning of the year? Show how you felt about the books you had for reading then. **E**

22. Do you remember playing with the children in your room at the beginning of this school year? Color the face that shows how you felt about playing with your friends last fall.

23. Think about how you did in math when you started school in the fall. What does your face look like?

24. You have been coming to school almost all year. Think about how you feel about school now. What is your face like?

25. Think about how you are doing in reading now. What does your face look like?

### NOW LET'S MOVE ON TO THE BOX LETTERED "F"

26. Think about what school is like now. Are you happy or unhappy about coming to school now? **F**

27. Show how you feel when you think about working math problems now.

28. Think about the teacher you have now. How do you feel about her being your teacher?

29. Think about the friends you have now. Color in the face that shows how you feel about your friends now.

30. You are talking with the teacher you have now. Color the face that shows how you feel talking with your teacher.

### NOW LET'S TURN THE PAGE OVER TO THE BOX LETTERED "G"

31. Think about the books you use for your reading now. Show how you feel about these reading books. **G**

32. During the year you have been playing with many children. Color in the face that tells how you feel about playing with your friends now.

33. Think about how you are doing in math now. How does your face look?

### HOW I FEEL TOWARD OTHERS

#### BEFORE YOU BEGIN

#### PREPARING THE ANSWER SHEET

Prior to administering the instrument, prepare an answer sheet for each
student as follows:

1.  LIST ALL STUDENTS' NAMES ON EACH ANSWER SHEET.

    WRITE each student's first name on the answer sheet.

    ADD the student's last name or initial if it is necessary to
    distinguish children with the same first name.

    USE the student's nickname if other students use it.

IMPORTANT:      DO NOT list the students' names according to sex or ability
                group.

                The order of names on each Student Answer Sheet must be
                EXACTLY the same. You can use carbon paper to prepare
                several answer sheets simultaneously. However, check to
                be sure that all names are legible.

2.  If you are using Code numbers, record them on the answer sheets at
    this time. Each line will have a different student's name on it.
    Write each student's unique code number in the ID space to the right
    of the circles on the line containing his or her name.

3.  If a class has more than 35 students, follow the procedures in the
    HIFTO User's Guide.

**HOW I FEEL TOWARD OTHERS,** continued

RECORDING IDENTIFICATION INFORMATION

---

IF CODE NUMBERS HAVE BEEN ASSIGNED TO ASSURE THE STUDENT'S PRIVACY . . . (See the HIFTO User's Guide for details.)

Both the student's name and code number will appear on the front page. CHECK the student's name against the unique number you have assigned as you PASS OUT the student's answer sheet.

ASK the students to check that they have received the answer sheet with the right name on it.

Have the students erase their names from the answer sheet.

---

OR

---

IF THE STUDENTS ARE TO COMPLETE THE ID BLOCK . . . (See the HIFTO User's Guide for details.)

PASS OUT the answer sheets.

LIST the following items on the chalkboard:    date
                                            teacher's name
                                            school name
                                            district name

ASK the students to complete as much of the ID information as they can. If a student is having difficulty with this section, have that student write his or her name in the ID Block and tell him or her that you will complete the remainder of the information later.

After the answer sheets have been collected, CHECK to see that all ID Blocks have been completed and FILL IN any missing information.

---

OR

---

IF THE ADMINISTRATOR COMPLETES THE ID BLOCK . . . (See the HIFTO User's Guide for details.)

PASS OUT the answer sheets.

ASK the students to check that they have received the answer sheet with the right name on it.

---

**HOW I FEEL TOWARD OTHERS,** continued

Just prior to administering HIFTO, print the animal names listed in examples
A-E on the chalkboard.  Follow each name with the four circles as follows:

| | | | | |
|---|---|---|---|---|
| Dog | ⊙? | ☺ | 😐 | ☹ |
| Tiger | ⊙? | ☺ | 😐 | ☹ |
| Cow | ⊙? | ☺ | 😐 | ☹ |
| Capybara | ⊙? | ☺ | 😐 | ☹ |
| Monkey | ⊙? | ☺ | 😐 | ☹ |

Now read the following instructions to the class:

We are going to fill out a special worksheet.

Open your worksheet.  Notice that each line has the name of a student in
this class.  Look for your name on the list.

Has everyone found his or her name?  If your name is not on the list, tell
me now so we can add it.  Is anybody's name not on the list?

If a student's name has been omitted, print it on the blackboard.
Then direct the students' attention to the new name and ask them
to copy it onto their worksheets on the first empty line.  Tell
them which line number that will be.  Walk around the room to check
that they have printed the name on the correct line.

Now let's read the names.  I will read each name and you will repeat it.

After the students have gone over the list of names twice, continue
by reading the following:

You will use this worksheet to show how you feel about each of your classmates
by filling in one of the circles next to his or her name.

REFER TO THE FACES OF PRACTICE ITEMS WHILE EXPLAINING THE MEANING
OF EACH OF THE FOUR CHOICES.

The circle with the question mark stands for classmates you don't know very
well.  Maybe you have not been with them enough to tell much about them.  When
you fill in the worksheet, you will fill in the circle with the question mark
after the names of those children whom you don't know very well.

**HOW I FEEL TOWARD OTHERS,** continued

The face with the <u>smile</u> stands for your classmates who are your friends. You will fill in the smiling face after the names of the children who are your friends.

The face with the <u>straight mouth</u> stands for your classmates that you know pretty well but whom you don't especially care about. You will fill in the face with the straight mouth after the names of these children.

The face with the <u>frown</u> stands for children you do not want to have as friends as long as they are like they are now. These children may be all right in some ways. They may be good friends with other children, but not with you. You will fill in the frowning face after the names of these children who are not your friends.

Now find example A on the front of your worksheet. We are going to do these examples to make sure you understand what the faces mean. Example A is "DOG." Now fill in the face which is most like how you feel about dogs. Remember to fill in only one circle and to fill it in completely.

REFER TO THE PRACTICE ITEMS ON THE BOARD TO ILLUSTRATE TO THE STUDENTS WHERE TO MARK THEIR ANSWER SHEETS FOR "DOG." SHOW THEM HOW TO FILL IN THE FACES COMPLETELY. BE SURE THEY UNDERSTAND WHERE TO RESPOND ON THE WORKSHEET AND GIVE THEM TIME TO MARK THEIR WORKSHEETS.

Let's try example B which is Tiger. Now, on your worksheet, fill in the face which is most like how you feel about Tigers.

Example C is Cow. On your worksheet, fill in the face which is most like how you feel about Cows.

Example D is Capybara (kăp'-ĭ-bä'-rə). On your worksheet, fill in the face which is most like how you feel about Capybaras.

IF A STUDENT HAS DIFFICULTY WITH CAPYBARA, YOU MAY REMIND HIM OR HER OF THE QUESTION MARK CIRCLE.

Example E, Monkey, is last. On your worksheet, fill in the face which is most like how you feel about Monkeys.

AFTER THE STUDENTS HAVE ANSWERED THE FIVE PRACTICE ITEMS, GO BACK OVER THEM USING THEIR RESPONSES TO ILLUSTRATE THAT THERE ARE NO RIGHT OR WRONG ANSWERS. ENCOURAGE DISCUSSION ON HOW THE STUDENTS FEEL ABOUT THE ANIMALS. EMPHASIZE THAT ALTHOUGH SOME STUDENTS MARKED AN UNHAPPY FACE FOR A GIVEN ANIMAL, OTHERS MARKED A HAPPY FACE FOR THE SAME ANIMAL.

NUMBER FOUR, CAPYBARA, IS INCLUDED TO MAKE SURE THE STUDENTS UNDERSTAND WHEN TO COLOR THE CIRCLE WITH THE QUESTION MARK. A CAPYBARA IS THE LARGEST LIVING RODENT. IT IS THREE OR FOUR FEET LONG, LIVES ALONG THE SOUTH AMERICAN RIVERS, IS SAND-COLORED AND TAILLESS.

**HOW I FEEL TOWARD OTHERS,** continued

---

Now does everyone understand? Good. Go ahead and mark your worksheet the
same way for each of your classmates. Remember, the first circle with the
question mark should be filled in for those classmates you don't know very
well. The face with the smile should be filled in for your friends. The
face with the straight mouth should be filled in for your classmates you
don't care about one way or the other. The face with the frown should be
filled in for your classmates who are not your friends.

Remember, fill in only one face for each classmate. Fill in the whole face
like you would color in a coloring book.

You do not have to fill in a face for yourself.

If you cannot read some of the names, please raise your hand and I'll help
you.

There are no right or wrong answers for this worksheet. None of your classmates will be allowed to see your paper. Everything you write will be kept
very secret. You may use blank paper to cover your answers.

You may begin.

---

IF THE STUDENTS ARE HAVING DIFFICULTY KEEPING ON THE CORRECT LINE,
GIVE THEM A BLANK SHEET OF PAPER AND DEMONSTRATE HOW THEY CAN USE
IT AS A GUIDE.

AS THE STUDENTS FILL IN THEIR WORKSHEETS, CIRCULATE AROUND THE
ROOM AND HELP ANY STUDENT HAVING DIFFICULTY READING NAMES. IF THE
STUDENTS INSIST THEY WANT TO COLOR IN A FACE FOR THEMSELVES, THEY
MAY DO SO. IF THE STUDENTS TRY TO LOOK AT EACH OTHER'S RESPONSES,
ENCOURAGE THEM TO USE THEIR COVER SHEETS.

AT THE END OF THE SESSION, COLLECT ALL OF THE ANSWER SHEETS. IF A
SECOND ANSWER SHEET WAS USED, PLACE THE SECOND ANSWER SHEET FOR
EACH STUDENT INSIDE HER OR HIS FIRST ANSWER SHEET.

**HOW I FEEL TOWARD OTHERS,** continued

| # | | ? | ☺ | 😐 | ☹ | |
|---|---|---|---|---|---|---|
| 26. | | ? | ☺ | 😐 | ☹ | ☐ |
| 27. | | ? | ☺ | 😐 | ☹ | ☐ |
| 28. | | ? | ☺ | 😐 | ☹ | ☐ |
| 29. | | ? | ☺ | 😐 | ☹ | ☐ |
| 30. | | ? | ☺ | 😐 | ☹ | ☐ |
| 31. | | ? | ☺ | 😐 | ☹ | ☐ |
| 32. | | ? | ☺ | 😐 | ☹ | ☐ |
| 33. | | ? | ☺ | 😐 | ☹ | ☐ |
| 34. | | ? | ☺ | 😐 | ☹ | ☐ |
| 35. | | ? | ☺ | 😐 | ☹ | ☐ |

HOW I FEEL TOWARD OTHERS
STUDENT'S ANSWER SHEET

DISTRICT NUMBER

SCHOOL NUMBER

ADMINISTRATION DATE

STUDENT'S DESIGNATED TEACHER NUMBER

STUDENT NUMBER

STUDENT'S PERSONAL IDENTIFICATION INFORMATION

NAME

| GRADE | AGE | DATE OF BIRTH | | |
|---|---|---|---|---|
| | | MONTH | DAY | YEAR |
| | | | | |

STUDENT'S DESIGNATED TEACHER

SCHOOL

DISTRICT

| | | ? | ☺ | 😐 | ☹ |
|---|---|---|---|---|---|
| A. | Dog | ? | ☺ | 😐 | ☹ |
| B. | Tiger | ? | ☺ | 😐 | ☹ |
| C. | Monkey | ? | ☺ | 😐 | ☹ |

**INDIANA BEHAVIOR MANAGEMENT SYSTEM**
Abridged Coder's Manual

PUPIL CATEGORIES

## Task Behavior

1. task (t)

   "I'm doing what I'm
   supposed to."

   Pupil's head and eyes are oriented towards persons or objects related to the lesson or lesson instructions. "Lesson" is defined by the teacher.

## Off-Task Behavior

1. self-involvement (si)

   "I'm minding my own
   business."

   Student is "alone" and quiet. No verbal or physical interaction with others, e.g., staring, daydreaming, playing with self or other objects, muttering to self, wandering around by himself, sleeping.

2. noise (n)

   "I'm making a disturbance
   by myself."

   Verbal and physical behavior which is non-communicative and disruptive, e.g., slamming a desk, tapping feet, whistling, clapping, singing, etc., when NOT an integral part of task.

3. verbal interaction (vi)

   "I'm talking to someone
   but I'm not angry."

   Talking when not supposed to; not aggressive, e.g., interrupting teacher or another student when inappropriate.

4. physical interaction (pi)

   "I'm playing with someone
   else but I'm not angry."

   Non-verbal interactions that are not aggressive: playing a game, passing notes, touching someone else.

   Rule: All physical interactions take precedence over verbal. That is, if pi occurs simultaneously with vi, code pi.

5. verbal aggression (va)

   "I'm angry and I'm telling
   you about it."

   Insulting, abusive, angry statements directed to peers and/or teacher.

   Rule: Code va over vi.

6. physical aggression (pa)

   "I'm angry and I'm showing
   you how angry I am."

   Physical attack: punching, hitting, spitting, throwing something at someone—directed to peers and/or teacher.

   Rule: Code pa over pi
         Code pa over va

**INDIANA BEHAVIOR MANAGEMENT SYSTEM**, continued

7.  verbal resistance (vr)

    "I won't."

Verbal refusal to CARRY OUT TEACHER DIRECTIONS—either to do a particular task or to stop misbehaving. This ONLY occurs during an interaction with the teacher.

Rule: Code <u>vr</u> over <u>va</u>

8.  physical resistance (pr)

    "I won't and I'm showing you."

Physical refusal to cooperate with teacher directions. May include verbal and aggressive responses, continues misbehavior, sits silently, refuses to follow directions, uses physical force to resist teacher. This ONLY occurs during an interaction with teacher.

Rule: Code <u>pr</u> when both <u>pr</u> and <u>vr</u> occur at the same time.

## TEACHER CATEGORIES

<u>Task Behavior</u>

1.  Task (T)

    "I'm marching to the beat of my own drum."
    　　　　-or-
    ("I'm doin' my own thing.")

Any teacher behavior related to lesson, whether social or academic. In general, this includes all teacher behavior which has <u>not</u> been initiated by a pupil off-task behavior.

Teacher Control Behavior is <u>always</u> initiated by a pupil's off-task behavior. The teacher responds in one of the following control categories:

1.  Demand (D)

    "I want you to _____"
    (stop doing what you're doing)

Direct verbal commands to "cease and desist" in firm, authoritative tone. No pupil response expected, e.g., "Be quiet!"

2.  Value Law (VL)

    "We must ...."

Teacher <u>explicitly</u> reminds pupil of the established rules of behavior in the classroom by describing or referring to a <u>norm</u> of behavior. e.g., "You know we raise our hands when we wish to speak."

**INDIANA BEHAVIOR MANAGEMENT SYSTEM,** continued

3.  Conditioned Stimulus (CS)          A "signal" for the pupil to stop
                                       misbehaving; short phrases and
                                       gestures like "O.K.," calling the
                                       pupil's name, "Sh," pauses, stares.
    "Hey you!"
                                       Rule: CS frequently accompanies
                                       another control behavior; code the
                                       other control behavior when that
                                       happens.

4.  Criticism-Demeaning (C-D)          Psychological degradation of pupil
                                       with verbal attack, criticism, or
    "You are a ...."                    sarcasm, e.g., "I suppose you think
                                       you're being clever?"

5.  Punishment (Pu)                    A direct, verbal or physical
                                       application of negative sanctions,
    "Because you were off-task,        including loss of privileges and
     this is happening to you."         restrictions on pupil freedoms.

6.  Empathy-Sympathetic (E-S)          Teacher expression of his under-
                                       standing of the pupil's feelings.

    "I understand ...."                 Rule: If the teacher appears to be
                                       empathic-sympathetic at the same
                                       time he is using another type of
                                       control behavior, code the other
                                       control behavior.

7.  Interpretive (I)                   Teacher statements which explain
                                       the reason for a pupil's misbehavior,
    "The reason you've been            e.g., "You're not paying attention
    misbehaving is _____."             because you don't get enough sleep
                                       at night."

8.  Humor (H)                          Teacher efforts to reduce tension
                                       and control pupil behavior by means
    "_____ is a diddledee."            of jokes, clowning, asides, etc.
                                       No intent to criticize pupil.

9.  Consequences (Q+)                  Verbal statements stating or
                 (Q-)                   implying consequences to behavior.
                                       Incentives, rewards, or promises
    "If you _____ (behave            are positive consequences (Q+);
    this way), then _____             threats are negative consequences
    (this will happen)."                (Q-).

**INDIANA BEHAVIOR MANAGEMENT SYSTEM,** continued

10. Redirection (R)

   "I'm moving you to a task."

   Teacher subtle use of "task" to control misbehavior; a positive refocus of attention without reference to the misbehavior. Verbal or physical, but not punitive, e.g., "Will you read the next paragraph, John?" "Will you and George change seats for today?"

11. Probing (Pr)

   "Why are you _____ (off task)?"

   Teacher questions to find out (or get the pupil to think about) the reason for his misbehavior. The teacher expects the pupil to answer.

GENERAL CODING RULES

1. If the teacher is silent during an interaction with a pupil, continue coding whatever behavior the teacher was previously engaged in.

2. Following a teacher Redirection (R), as soon as the pupil appropriately responds to the teacher's redirecting statement or question, then you code both the pupil and the teacher as on-task. (This is the only exception to Rule #1.)

## INDIANA COGNITIVE DEMAND SCHEDULE
### Definition of Categories

<u>SUMMARY OF TEACHER AND PUPIL CATEGORIES</u>:  Low level cognitive demands

Habitual Responding (HR) - "Repeat after me."

> An activity that requires a simple, habitual, almost automatic
> response.  This response requires little or no thinking or memory.

Observing-Discriminating (OD) - "Say what you see."

> The child is required to notice, identify, and/or describe
> things which are in front of him.  (No memory is involved.)
> The child just reports what he observes without having to
> transform the information in any way.

Stringing (St) - "Read the first paragraph."

> The child is required to make already-learned responses
> which form a natural sequence.  Each part of the response
> suggests the next one to come so that the child is able to
> string the response without much thought:  E.g., spelling,
> counting, reciting by rote, singing.

Remembering (Re) - "Remember what happened in the story."

> The child is required to remember and tell something he has
> experienced himself or through reading.  The response does
> not require any transformation or information--just direct
> recall.

Explaining (Ex) - "How?  Why?"

> The child is required to pull together information and rules
> and explain the cause of an event.  The rules used in the
> response are those which the child already knows and understands.
> He is not required to contruct rules or to interpret them.

Defining-Classifying (DC) - "What is a wambat?"

> The child is required to demonstrate his understanding of a
> concept by supplying the correct meaning of a term or by giving
> the correct label for a set of examples.  The response may
> involve grouping of various objects, matching examples with
> different labels, giving examples of different concepts, etc.

Applying-Comparing (AC) - "What's the difference?"

> The child is required to compare and/or contrast <u>concepts</u> and
> to formulate generalizations.  Note: When the teacher requires a
> comparison of specific, concrete objects that are in front of a
> child, it is an OD.

**INDIANA COGNITIVE DEMAND SCHEDULE,** continued

Inferring (In) - "Did the butler do it?"

> The child is required to arrive at his own conclusions, deductions, hypotheses, or interpretation from available information. The response should involve some new discovery by the child, rather than a relation of previously learned facts (Ex).

Making Believe (MB) - "Let's pretend."

> The child is required to freely elaborate on an idea without any constraints. The response should involve free associations and personal and original outcomes.

Value-Judging (VJ) - "Do you think that's a nice thing to do?"

> The child is required to judge the goodness (worth, suitability, etc.) of something or to express how he feels about something. The response involves making comparisons with an explicit standard or an implicit one, as in the case of giving an opinion. Requiring the child to justify his judgment also belongs to this category.

Problem Solving (PS) - "How would you fix that?"

> The child is confronted with a puzzling situation and is required to analyze the situation and come up with a solution.

ADDITIONAL COGNITIVE DEMANDS

Going Over (GO) - "What did you get for Number Three?"

> The child is required to present a completed assignment (or parts of it) to the class or to the teacher. This includes all tasks which the child has completed at some previous time. The original task may belong to any category of cognitive demand, but the report on the task is always coded as GO. When the student is asked to read his answer, it is coded as GO rather than St.

Clarification (Cl) - "I didn't catch that one?"

> Before a teacher can make a Cl demand, the child should have responded to a previous demand. The teacher then asks the child to repeat, rephrase, or revise his previous response. Note: Clarification should not be confused with subsequent questions which require the child to give additional information, or expand on or explain his response. If the question belongs to any other category of cognitive demands, it does not belong to Cl.

## INDIANA COGNITIVE DEMAND SCHEDULE, continued

TEACHER FEEDBACK

No Feedback (0): The teacher does not respond to the pupil response—
i.e., he goes on without any specific comment about the pupil's
response.

Positive Feedback (4): The teacher "accepts" the pupil response. She can
indicate that the response is correct (e.g., "Right," "Exactly,"
"Correct," "Yes"), or she may praise the child (e.g., "Good," "Fine,"
"Excellent," "Beautiful," "That was a brilliant answer") or she may
repeat the child's response (e.g., "So you think that  ...."').

Negative Feedback (-): The teacher does not "accept" the pupil response.
She may scold the pupil for not giving an acceptable response or she
may criticize the child's response (e.g., "That was a dumb answer,"
"You haven't been paying attention," "How could you know when you
aren't looking at the board?") or she may indicate that the response
is incorrect (e.g., "No," "Wrong," "That's not right," "Not really,"
etc.).

Informational Feedback (I): The teacher provides cues and additional
information to aid the child in responding. He may direct the
child's attention to some item of information, or hint at the correct
answer. Sometimes he may even give the correct answer. He may
explain why a response is correct or incorrect. He may add information to the response and clarify it or he may ask the child to
elaborate on his previous response.
E.g., "I am waiting for you to say '36.'"
"That's a good response because you used the noun form of
the word."
"It won't work because it will be top-heavy. Try again."
"But look again at the picture."
"O.K. That's an idea. Tell us what you based your idea on."
"Yes, and it was green too."


### General Rules of Coding

1. Non-cognitive demands: Do not code procedural demands (e.g.,
"Mary, did you bring your milk money today?") or classroom-
management demands (e.g., "Be quiet, Mark, and listen to me.").

2. Pupil chorus responses: Do not code cognitive demands which elicit
two or more pupil responses occurring simultaneously (chorus response).
Also do not code the pupil chorus response. Only when the teacher
cognitive demand elicits one pupil response (at a time) do you code
the teacher and the pupil.

3. Series of teacher questions or rhetorical questions: Code only when
the teacher pauses to give room for an individual pupil's response.
If the teacher asks a series of questions and then pauses to allow a
pupil to respond, code the last question only.

**INDIANA COGNITIVE DEMAND SCHEDULE,** continued

4. More-than-one-level demand: When two levels of cognitive demands are suggested by a given teacher question and you cannot eliminate one of them, then code the lower level demand only.

5. Coding mistakes: Do not try to change a previous coding once it is down on paper. Even if you decide that it should be a different category, leave your original code.

## CODING PUPIL RESPONSES

1. We are not interested in whether the pupil's response is correct or incorrect. Code the category of his response without worrying about its correctness.

2. If the pupil does not respond to a teacher cognitive demand, leave the pupil code space blank. (E.g., pupil remains silent, shrugs shoulders, says "I dunno.")

3. The pupil response space is also left blank if the response is completely "irrelevant" or "inappropriate" to the on-going lesson.

4. Sometimes a child may initiate a cognitive demand by asking the teacher a question or by volunteering some information during the lesson. If the pupil response is appropriate or relevant to the lesson and if the teacher recognizes it, then code the pupil response and the teacher's feedback, if any. Then go to the next interchange box on your coding sheet.

## TEACHER FEEDBACK

1. Never use more than one category at a time for coding the flashback.

2. Informational feedback (I) takes priority over other categories. If the feedback is both positive (or negative) and informational at the same time, code it I (for informational).

3. When the feedback is both positive and negative, code it as negative (-).

4. When no feedback is given, code it 0.

# INDIANA PUPIL PARTICIPATION
## SCHEDULE°

**16. TIME STARTED**

| Hour | Minute |
|---|---|
| ⑧ ⑨ ⑩ ⑪ ⑫ | ⓪ ① ② | ⓪ ① ② ③ ④ |
| ① ② ③ ④ ⑤ | ③ ④ ⑤ | ⑤ ⑥ ⑦ ⑧ ⑨ |

**1** Pupil raises hand.

E | ⓪①②③④⑤⑥⑦⑧⑨
C | ⓪①②③④⑤⑥⑦⑧⑨
K | ⓪①②③④⑤⑥⑦⑧⑨

**2** Pupil raises hand; called on by teacher.

E | ⓪①②③④⑤⑥⑦⑧⑨
C | ⓪①②③④⑤⑥⑦⑧⑨
K | ⓪①②③④⑤⑥⑦⑧⑨

**3** Pupil raises hand; called on by teacher; makes a response.

E | ⓪①②③④⑤⑥⑦⑧⑨
C | ⓪①②③④⑤⑥⑦⑧⑨
K | ⓪①②③④⑤⑥⑦⑧⑨

**17. ACTIVITY**

Ⓔ Ⓒ Ⓚ Reading        Ⓔ Ⓒ Ⓚ Music
Ⓔ Ⓒ Ⓚ Spelling       Ⓔ Ⓒ Ⓚ Foreign lang.
Ⓔ Ⓒ Ⓚ Language arts  Ⓔ Ⓒ Ⓚ Perceptual
Ⓔ Ⓒ Ⓚ Mathematics            training
Ⓔ Ⓒ Ⓚ Science/health Ⓔ Ⓒ Ⓚ Transitional
Ⓔ Ⓒ Ⓚ Social studies          activity
Ⓔ Ⓒ Ⓚ Art            Ⓔ Ⓒ Ⓚ Other

**18. Position of E, C, T and O**

FRONT OF CLASS

| ⒺⒸ ⓉⓄ | Ⓔ Ⓒ ⓉⓄ | Ⓔ Ⓒ ⓉⓄ |
| Ⓔⓒ ⓉⓄ | Ⓔ Ⓒ ⓉⓄ | Ⓔ Ⓒ ⓉⓄ |
| Ⓔⓒ ⓉⓄ | Ⓔ Ⓒ ⓉⓄ | Ⓔ Ⓒ ⓉⓄ |

**19. STRUCTURE FOR CLASSROOM ACTIVITIES**

Ⓔ Ⓒ Ⓚ One large group
Ⓔ Ⓒ Ⓚ Small group with teacher
Ⓔ Ⓒ Ⓚ Small group(s) without teacher
Ⓔ Ⓒ Ⓚ Individually with teacher
Ⓔ Ⓒ Ⓚ Individually without teacher
Ⓔ Ⓒ Ⓚ Free groups
Ⓔ Ⓒ Ⓚ No apparent structure

**INDIANA PUPIL PARTICIPATION SCHEDULE,** continued

| 4 | Pupil does <u>not</u> raise hand; called on by teacher. | E | | ⓪①②③④⑤⑥⑦⑧⑨ ⓪①②③④⑤⑥⑦⑧⑨ |
| | | C | | ⓪①②③④⑤⑥⑦⑧⑨ ⓪①②③④⑤⑥⑦⑧⑨ |
| | | K | | ⓪①②③④⑤⑥⑦⑧⑨ ⓪①②③④⑤⑥⑦⑧⑨ ⓪①②③④⑤⑥⑦⑧⑨ |

| 5 | Pupil does <u>not</u> raise hand; called on by teacher; makes a response. | E | | ⓪①②③④⑤⑥⑦⑧⑨ ⓪①②③④⑤⑥⑦⑧⑨ |
| | | C | | ⓪①②③④⑤⑥⑦⑧⑨ ⓪①②③④⑤⑥⑦⑧⑨ |
| | | K | | ⓪①②③④⑤⑥⑦⑧⑨ ⓪①②③④⑤⑥⑦⑧⑨ ⓪①②③④⑤⑥⑦⑧⑨ |

| 6 | <u>Not</u> called on by teacher; speaks to the teacher. | E | | ⓪①②③④⑤⑥⑦⑧⑨ ⓪①②③④⑤⑥⑦⑧⑨ |
| | | C | | ⓪①②③④⑤⑥⑦⑧⑨ ⓪①②③④⑤⑥⑦⑧⑨ |
| | | K | | ⓪①②③④⑤⑥⑦⑧⑨ ⓪①②③④⑤⑥⑦⑧⑨ ⓪①②③④⑤⑥⑦⑧⑨ |

| 7 | Pupil asks a question. | E | | ⓪①②③④⑤⑥⑦⑧⑨ ⓪①②③④⑤⑥⑦⑧⑨ |
| | | C | | ⓪①②③④⑤⑥⑦⑧⑨ ⓪①②③④⑤⑥⑦⑧⑨ |
| | | K | | ⓪①②③④⑤⑥⑦⑧⑨ ⓪①②③④⑤⑥⑦⑧⑨ ⓪①②③④⑤⑥⑦⑧⑨ |

**20. TEACHER TASK**

- ○ Drilling
- ○ Introducing
- ○ Motivating
- ○ Questioning
- ○ Demonstrating
- ○ Lecturing
- ○ Explaining
- ○ Directing
- ○ Testing
- ○ Supervising
- ○ Summarizing
- ○ Reviewing
- ○ Other

**21. PUPIL TASK**

- Ⓔ Ⓒ Ⓚ Listening to teacher
- Ⓔ Ⓒ Ⓚ Interacting with teacher
- Ⓔ Ⓒ Ⓚ Interacting with other pupil(s)
- Ⓔ Ⓒ Ⓚ Interacting with aide
- Ⓔ Ⓒ Ⓚ Working with print material(s)
- Ⓔ Ⓒ Ⓚ Working with non-print material(s)

**22. SEATING ARRANGEMENT**

- Ⓔ Ⓒ Ⓚ Rows x columns    Ⓔ Ⓒ Ⓚ Horse shoe
- Ⓔ Ⓒ Ⓚ Small groups      Ⓔ Ⓒ Ⓚ Individual
- Ⓔ Ⓒ Ⓚ Circle            Ⓔ Ⓒ Ⓚ Other

**23. TIME STOPPED**

| Hour | | Minute | | S T O P |
|---|---|---|---|---|
| ⑧⑨⑩⑪⑫ | ⓪①② | ⓪①②③④ | |
| ①②③④⑤ | ③④⑤ | ⑤⑥⑦⑧⑨ | |

# SELECTED CHILDREN'S BACKGROUND QUESTIONNAIRE

1. Date of Child's Birth: _____ / _____ / _____
     month     day     year

2. Sex:

   _____ Male

   _____ Female

3. Ethnic Group:

   _____ Negro

   _____ Indian

   _____ Oriental

   _____ Spanish-Surnamed

   _____ Causcasian (other than Spanish-Surnamed)

4. Father's Occupation: (This question refers to the father or father substitute living in the home) (Check only one)

   _____ Professional and semi-professional workers. This includes individuals who perform advisory, administrative or research work which is based upon the established principles of a profession or science and which requres professional, scientific or technical training equivalent to that represented by graduation from a college or university of recognized standing.

   _____ Farmers and farm managers. This includes individuals who work their own farm or individuals who manage and supervise the running of farms for the owner.

   _____ Proprietors, managers and officials, except farm. A prorpietor is an entrepreneur who owns and, alone or with assistance, operates his own business and is responsible for making and carrying out its policies. A manager is one who manages all or a part of the business of another person or agency; who has large responsibility in the making and carrying out of the policies of the business; and who through assistant, is charged with planning and supervising the work of others. An official has large responsibilities in the making and carrying out of the policies of the concern.

   _____ Clerical, sales and kindred workers. A clerical or kindred worker is one who, under supervision, performs one or more office activities, usually routine, such as preparing, transcribing and filing written communications and records.

   _____ Craftsmen, foremen and kindred workers. This includes individuals "engaged in a manual pursuit, usually not routine, for the pursuance of which a long period of training or an apprenticeship is usually necessary and which in its pursuance calls for a high degree of judgment or manual dexterity, and for ability to work with a minimum of supervision and to exercise responsibility for valuable production and equipment." These individuals may direct other workers under supervision.

   _____ Operatives and kindred workers. This includes individuals engaged in manual pursuit, usually routine, for the pursuance of which only a short period or no period of preliminary training is usually necessary and which in its pursuance usually calls for the exercise of only a moderate degree of judgment of manual dexterity. Such jobs require only a moderate degree of muscular force.

   _____ Domestic service workers include those individuals performing personal services in private homes.

   _____ Protective service workers. A protective service worker is one engaged in protecting life or property.

   _____ Service workers, except domestic and protective, are those engaged in cleaning and janitor services in buildings other than private homes, or performing services often of an individual character for other persons as a barber, cook, waitress or practical nurse.

   _____ Farm laborers and foremen. A farm laborer is a hired worker or unpaid member of a farm operator's family who works on a farm. A farm foreman is one who directs farm laborers under the supervision of a farmer or farm manager.

   _____ Laborers, except farm, are those engaged in a manual pursuit, usually routine, for the pursuance of which no special training, judgment or manual dexterity is usually necessary and in which the worker usually supplies mainly muscular strength for the performance of coarse, heavy work.

   _____ Other (describe fully) _____

   _____

   _____

## SELECTED CHILDREN'S BACKGROUND QUESTIONNAIRE, continued

_____ Don't know (give best estimate) __ _____

_____

_____

_____ No father or father substitute living in the home

5. Mother's Occupation (The question refers to the mother or mother substitute living in the home) (Check only one.)

_____ Professional and semi-professional workers. This includes individuals who perform advisory, administrative or research work which is based upon the established principles of a profession or science and which requires professional, scientific or technical training equivalent to that represented by graduation from a college or university of recognized standing.

_____ Farmers and farm managers. This includes individuals who work their own farm or individuals who manage and supervise the running of farms for the owner.

_____ Proprietors, managers and officials, except farm. A proprietor is an entrepreneur who owns and, alone or with assistance, operates his own business and is responsible for making and carrying out its policies. A manager is one who manages all or part of the business of another person or agency; who has large responsibility in the making and carrying out of the policies of the business; and who through assistants, is charged with planning and supervising the work of others. An official has large responsibilities in the making and carrying out of the policies of the concern.

_____ Clerical, sales and kindred workers. A clerical or kindred worker is one who, under supervision, performs one or more office activites, usually routine, such as preparing, transcribing and filing written communications and records.

_____ Craftsmen, foremen and kindred workers. This includes individuals "engaged in a manual pursuit, usually not routine, for the pursuance of which a long period of training or an apprenticeship is usually necessary and which in its pursuance calls for a high degree of judgment or manual dexterity, and for ability to work with a minimum of supervision and to exercise responsibility for valuable production and equipment." These individuals may direct other workers under supervision.

_____ Operatives and kindred workers. This includes individuals engaged in manual pursuit, usually routine, for the pursuance of which only a short period or no period of preliminary training is usually necessary and which in its pursuance usually calls for the exercise of only a moderate degree of judgment or of manual dexterity. Such jobs require only a moderate degree of muscular force.

_____ Domestic service workers include those individuals performing personal services in private homes.

_____ Protective service workers. A protective service worker is one engaged in protecting life or property.

_____ Service workers, except domestic and protective, are those engaged in cleaning and janitor services in buildings other than private homes, or perfoming services often of an individual character for other persons as a barber, cook, waitress or practical nurse.

_____ Farm laborers and foremen. A farm laborer is a hired worker or unpaid member of a farm operator's family who works on a farm. A farm foreman is one who directs farm laborers under the supervision of a farmer or farm manager.

_____ Laborers, except farm, are those engaged in a manual pursuit, usually routine, for the pursuance of which no special training, judgment of manual dexterity is usually necessary and in which the worker usually supplies mainly muscular strength for the performance of coarse, heavy work.

_____ Other (describe fully) _____

_____

_____ Don't know (give best estimate) _____

_____

_____ No mother or mother substitute living in the home

**SELECTED CHILDREN'S BACKGROUND QUESTIONNAIRE,** continued

6. Father's Education (The question refers to the father or father substitute living in the home.) (Check only one.)

    \_\_\_\_\_ None

    \_\_\_\_\_ Some grade school

    \_\_\_\_\_ Completed grade school (1st – 6th grade)

    \_\_\_\_\_ Some junior high (7th – 8th grade)

    \_\_\_\_\_ Completed junior high (7th – 8th grade)

    \_\_\_\_\_ Some high school but did not graduate (9th grade is included in high school)

    \_\_\_\_\_ High school graduate

    \_\_\_\_\_ Vocational or business school after high school

    \_\_\_\_\_ Some college – less than four years

    \_\_\_\_\_ College graduate

    \_\_\_\_\_ Attended graduate or professional school

    \_\_\_\_\_ Don't know (give best estimate _____)

    \_\_\_\_\_ No father or father substitute

7. Mother's Education (this question refers to the mother or mother substitute living in the home.) (Check only one.)

    \_\_\_\_\_ None

    \_\_\_\_\_ Some grade school

    \_\_\_\_\_ Completed grade school (1st – 6th grade)

    \_\_\_\_\_ Some junior high (7th – 8th grade)

    \_\_\_\_\_ Completed junior high (7th – 8th grade)

    \_\_\_\_\_ Some high school but did not graduate (9th grade is included in high school)

    \_\_\_\_\_ High school graduate

    \_\_\_\_\_ Vocational or business school after high school

    \_\_\_\_\_ Some college – less than four years

    \_\_\_\_\_ College graduate

    \_\_\_\_\_ Attended graduate or professional school

    \_\_\_\_\_ Don't know (give best estimate _____)

    \_\_\_\_\_ No mother or mother substitute living in the home

8. Socio-Economic Status: (Check only one.)

    \_\_\_\_\_ Upper class

    \_\_\_\_\_ Upper middle class

    \_\_\_\_\_ Middle class

    \_\_\_\_\_ Lower middle class

    \_\_\_\_\_ Lower class

**SELECTED CHILDREN'S BACKGROUND QUESTIONNAIRE,** continued

9. Is this child from a family in which the primary supporter of the family is receiving welfare?

_____ Yes

_____ No

10. Family Status: (Check only one.)

_____ Mother and father present in the home

_____ Mother only present – no other male figure

_____ Mother (real) and father-substitute (family friend, uncle, brother, grandfather) in the home

_____ Father only present – no other female figure present

_____ Father (real) and mother-substitute (family friend, aunt, sister, grandmother) in the home

_____ Other (lives with grandparent, foster parents, etc.)

11. How many days was this child absent?

_____ Days during the 1970-71 school year

_____ Days during the 1971-72 school year as of_____/_____72 (date)
month ⁄ day

12. Did this child participate in any of the following before entering first grade? (Check only one.)

_____ Headstart or preschool sponsored by public school

_____ Headstart or preschool sponsored by O.E.O. or other public (federal, state or local) agency (other than public school)

_____ Preschool or nursery sponsored by private agency (including churches)

_____ Headstart, preschool or nursery (sponsorship unknown)

_____ Kindergarten sponsored by public school

_____ Kindergarten sponsored by other public agency

_____ Kindergarten sponsored by private agency (including churches)

_____ Kindergarten (sponsorship unknown)

_____ Information unavailable

13. How many different elementary schools has this child attended?

_____ Schools in this district

_____ Schools in other districts

14. What is the predominant language spoken in this pupil's home? (Check only one.)

_____ English

_____ An American Indian Language

_____ An Oriental Language

_____ Spanish

_____ French

_____ Other

15. What is this child's most recent I.Q. score?

15a. Date of most recent test _____/_____
month ⁄ year

15b. Name of test

**SELECTED CHILDREN'S BACKGROUND QUESTIONNAIRE,** continued

15c. Verbal Scale IQ score _____

15d. Performance Scale IQ score _____

15e. Full Scale IQ score _____

16.  How are parents of this child involved in his educational program? (Check one or more.)

_____ On-going regularly scheduled conferences with regular teacher(s)

_____ On-going regularly scheduled conferences with special education teacher(s)

_____ Periodic conferences with regular teacher(s)

_____ Periodic conferences with special education teacher(s)

_____ Periodic conferences with principal

_____ Periodic conference with other school personnel (describe _____)

_____ Periodic written reports on child's progress

17.  Are the parents of this child involved in any formal program of parent involvement?

_____ Yes

_____ No

18.  Are the parents of this child responsible for the implementation of certain activities in the home setting?

_____ Yes

_____ No

QUESTIONS 19-27 REFER TO HANDICAPPED CHILDREN ONLY

19.  At what age was this child first referred for special education services?

_____ age

20.  In what grade was this child <u>first</u> referred for special education services? (Check only one.)

_____ Before coming to school, in very early childhood – pre-nursery school

_____ Before coming to school – during Headstart or nursery school

_____ Kindergarten

_____ First grade

_____ Second grade

_____ Third grade

_____ Fourth grade

_____ Fifth grade

_____ Sixth grade

21a. Did this child repeat a grade before he began receiving special education services?

_____ Yes

_____ No

21b. If yes, what grade(s) _____

_____

22.  At what age was this child placed in the special education program?

_____ age

**SELECTED CHILDREN'S BACKGROUND QUESTIONNAIRE,** continued

23. How many total months was this child in a self-contained special education program? (Do not count summer months)

    _____ months

24. What instructional arrangement was this child in last year? (Check only one.)

    _____ Assigned to special education class all day

    _____ Assigned to special education class and attends non-academic regular class

    _____ Assigned to special education class and attends some academic and non-academic regular classes

    _____ Assigned to regular classroom and attends special education classroom (i.e. resource room)

    _____ Assigned to regular classroom all day

25. How many hours during the week does this child spend in each of the following situations? (Total should equal number of school hours) (Estimate to nearest half-hour.)

| Subject Matter Areas | With Special Education Children Only | Integrated With Regular Children |
|---|---|---|
| A. Reading | _____ hrs. | _____ hrs. |
| B. Language Arts | _____ hrs. | _____ hrs. |
| C. Handwriting | _____ hrs. | _____ hrs. |
| D. Spelling | _____ hrs. | _____ hrs. |
| E. Arithmetic | _____ hrs. | _____ hrs. |
| F. Science | _____ hrs. | _____ hrs. |
| G. Social Studies | _____ hrs. | _____ hrs. |
| H. Spanish (or other foreign language) | _____ hrs. | _____ hrs. |
| I. Other academic subjects | _____ hrs. | _____ hrs. |
| J. Physical Education | _____ hrs. | _____ hrs. |
| K. Music | _____ hrs. | _____ hrs. |
| L. Art | _____ hrs. | _____ hrs. |
| M. Library | _____ hrs. | _____ hrs. |
| N. Recess | _____ hrs. | _____ hrs. |
| O. Lunch | _____ hrs. | _____ hrs. |
| P. Visual-Perceptual Training | _____ hrs. | _____ hrs. |
| Q. Language Development | _____ hrs. | _____ hrs. |
| R. Motor Training | _____ hrs. | _____ hrs. |
| S. Auditory-Listening Training | _____ hrs. | _____ hrs. |
| T. Other (explain) _____ | | |
| U. Total | _____ hrs. | _____ hrs. |

**SELECTED CHILDREN'S BACKGROUND QUESTIONNAIRE,** continued

26. Is this child in a regular ADA count of your school district?

    _____ Yes

    _____ No

27. If this child has been designated as having a language and/or learning disability, what were his special diagnosed disabilities? (Check one or more).

    _____ Behavior control problems

    _____ Visual Perception

    _____ Auditory Perception

    _____ Motor Deficiency

    _____ Verbal Communication

    _____ Organization Deficit (memory, sequencing)

    _____ Specific academic difficulties

    _____ Other (describe) _____

    _____ Not an LLD child

    _____ Special Education Director initial when Section I is complete.

**TEACHER CLIMATE CONTROL QUESTIONNAIRE**
Factors and Items

Factor I:  Cooperation/Diversification

In my class the children like to work together on assignments
and projects.
The children in my class help me make plans for the day.
In my class I use many library books and reference materials in
addition to textbooks.
Students are encouraged to explore new activities independently.
The children in my classroom have permission to move their seats
together into groups in order to work together.
Children try to help each other with their work.
Students are required to test their hypotheses with experiments.
The class actively participates in discussions.
The class learning materials include lots of materials I have developed.
My class program includes use of the neighborhood resources.
The class learning materials include materials developed or supplied
by the children.
We have a lot of fun in my class.
I occasionally allow the children in my class to manage themselves.
Children use "books" written by their classmates as part of their
reading and reference materials.
Most members of the class aren't interested in what the class does.
The children look at and discuss each other's work.
Children are permitted to use most materials in the class without
asking permission.
Most students cooperate rather than compete with one another.
Decisions affecting the class tend to be made democratically.

Factor II:  Friction

Some children in my room don't like the other children in the room.
Certain students impose their wishes on the whole class.
There is constant bickering and fighting among the children in my class.
There are some children who are not happy in my class.
The work of the class is frequently interrupted when some students have
nothing to do.
There are periods of confusion when the class changes from one activity
to another.
Most of the children in my room do not cooperate well with each other.
There are a few children with whom I seem to have more casual
communications.
Some class members feel rushed to finish their work.
Certain students work only with their close friends.
In my class I have a few favorite children who are granted special
privileges.
Certain children in my class get their own way.
The children enjoy the class activities.

**TEACHER CLIMATE AND CONTROL QUESTIONNAIRE,** continued

Factor III:  Rigidity/Control

I ask that the children not talk when they are supposed to be working.
Children are not supposed to move about the room without asking permission.
I make sure children use materials only as instructed.
I base my instructions on curriculum guides or the textbooks for the
    grade level I teach.
The children in my class ask permission before doing things like
    sharpening their pencils.
I plan and schedule all the children's activities through the day.
The instructional groups formed in the fall are seldom changed.
Only the good students are given extra projects.

Factor IV:  Individualization

I make classroom work assignments based on each individual child's needs.
I often spend extra time with children who have individual learning
    problems.
I spend lots of time each day working on academic subjects with
    individual children.
All children are expected to do the same assignments.
Many different projects and activities go on in my class simultaneously.
I require all the children to take the same tests over the material
    presented to the whole class.
I keep records on each child's day-to-day educational activities for use
    in evaluating his or her development.
Children work directly with manipulative materials.
The class activities are well organized and efficient.
When children finish their class assignments, they know what to do next.
The class has plenty of time to cover the assigned amount of work.
The children in my class have some free time during the day.
Within the classroom, there is a wide enough diversity of books to meet
    each child's needs and interests.

Factor V:  Difficulty

Most students in the class find the work hard to do.
The class has difficulty keeping up with the assigned curriculum.
Many children in the class do not understand what work assignments
    they should be doing.
When the children start a new assignment, they are often confused.
Most of the children can do their work without help.
All the students know how to do the work assigned in my class.
Most children are deeply involved in what they are doing throughout the day.

## TEACHER EDUCATIONAL ATTITUDE QUESTIONNAIRE
### Scales and Items

## Scale I: Traditional Authority

The small gains in learning which result from all the educational innovations aren't really worth all the trouble and expense of making the changes.

The public school is sacrificing too much of our cultural heritage in its preoccupation with life adjustment and group living.

I dislike having to change my class plan in the middle of an undertaking.

Subject matter and skills are difficult to teach, therefore, the content of the curriculum must take precedence over the children's experiences.

Public schools should become more involved in implementing innovative practices in education.

It is frequently necessary for a teacher to demonstrate her authority.

Schools of today are neglecting the basic academic subjects.

A child shouldn't tell a teacher that she's wrong even if she is.

I do not enjoy having to adapt myself to new and unusual situations that occur in the classroom.

One of the big difficulties with schools today is that discipline is often sacrificed for the sake of freedom.

A child who doesn't show respect for his teacher won't learn much from her.

The reason that most innovations are dropped is that when the newness wears off, the old ways are found to be the best after all.

It may be alright to have parents visit the class once in a while, but it interferes with the teacher's work just the same.

What is needed in the classroom is a revival of respect for the teacher.

Good relations with parents may be important, but discussing their children's work with them is generally ineffective.

Teachers should exercise more authority over their students than they do.

Educational authorities have been negligent in allowing new materials and methods to interfere with the success of traditional approaches.

## Scale II: Professional Satisfaction

As far as I know, the other teachers think I am a good teacher.

The stress and strain resulting from teaching makes teaching undesirable for me.

Teaching gives me a great deal of personal satisfaction.

I am at a disadvantage professionally because other teachers are better prepared to teach than I am.

Teaching enables me to make my greatest contribution to society.

I love to teach.

I feel successful in my present position as a teacher.

As a teacher, I think I am as competent as most other teachers.

**TEACHER EDUCATIONAL ATTITUDE QUESTIONNAIRE,** continued

Scale III:  Teacher Cohesiveness

Experienced faculty members are supportive and helpful toward new and
    younger members in my school.
The teachers at this school share educational ideas and techniques
    with each other.
The teachers at this school don't seem to be able to work well
    together.
The teachers in our school cooperate with each other to improve
    education instruction in the school.

## TEACHER RATING SCALE I AND II
### Scales and Items

Scale I:  Academic Effort/Success

Needs constant supervision to complete school work
Finishes work on time
Can concentrate on tasks for long periods
Has difficulty keeping mind on school work
Receives better than average grades on his/her work
Plans his/her time well
Works at difficult assignments until he/she gets them done
Needs help in doing class assignments
Maintains attention throughout a task
Does well on tests
Does assigned work without prompting
Is well-organized in work, projects, personal possessions
Finishes classroom and homework assignments
Careful and methodical in work he/she undertakes
Tries to figure things out himself/herself before asking for help
Seeks excessive help from teacher

Scale II:  Antisocial Behavior

Attempts to dominate or bully other children
Is well-behaved in school
Is boisterous, shows off
Resists class limits or rules
Gets into fights
Has to be scolded or disciplined
Gets along well with the teacher
Is aggressive in underhanded ways
Is courteous to other children
Has trouble controlling temper
Criticizes other children
Needs reminders about classroom regulations
Talks back to teacher after being disciplined
Has to be physically separated from other children when he/she causes
   a disturbance
Is cooperative with the teacher
Obeys requests and suggestions of teacher
Responds to discipline with inappropriate behavior (slamming desk,
   kicking chair)

Scale III:  Outgoing/Expressive Behavior

Contributes to class discussions
Enjoys speaking in front of class
Is outgoing and makes friends easily
Enjoys new, unfamiliar, and novel tasks
Shows uneasiness (fidgeting, hesitancy) when called on in class
Prefers to work alone
Volunteers readily for a special activity
Makes new friends easily
Is eager to participate in class activities

**TEACHER RATING SCALE,** continued

<u>Scale IV</u>: <u>Anxiousness</u>

Becomes upset when makes a mistake
Expresses feelings of inadequacy about self
Becomes discouraged with his/her performance
Seems anxious and fearful in class situations
Becomes passive and withdrawn after being scolded or criticized
Is overly sensitive to criticism
Cries, pouts, or sulks for little apparent reason
Seems tense or nervous when asked to respond in discussions
Seems unhappy and/or depressed in class

**YOUR SCHOOL DAYS**
Factors and Items

Factor I:  Harmony

Do the children enjoy their school work in your class?
Does your teacher reward you when you do good work?
Does your teacher say nice things to you when you are good?
Do most children say your class is fun?
Do you do lots of experiments to prove your ideas?
Are most of your teachers friendly and understanding?
Does your teacher promise you more free time if you get your work done?
Do you and your classmates help the teacher make plans for this class?
Does everyone in your class share in making class plans?
Are some children in your class treated worse than the rest?
Are some of your teachers unfriendly or mean?
In your class do you have plenty of time to do the work you are
    supposed to do?
Do you have lots of games, toys, and equipment to use while you learn?
Do you use books written by the other children as part of your reading?
Are some children able to force the rest of the class to do what they want?
Does your teacher ask you to do your own special projects?
Do you have all the books you need in your room?
Do most of the children in your class like each other?
Are your best friends in your class?
Does the teacher ever work alone with you?
Do the children in your class try to help each other?

Factor II:  Discordance

Are most of the children unhappy in your class?
Are the children in your class always fighting with each other?
Are many children sent to the principal for misbehaving?
Are only the smart children given special projects to work on?
Does the teacher give you special assignments if you finish your work
    before the others?
Is your class work hard to do?
Do the children in your class get the grades they deserve?
Must you ask the teacher for permission to sharpen your pencils?
Can you do your class work?
Do the children have to hurry to finish their work?
Do you like to work with the other children in your class?
Do you have some time during this class to do what you want?
Does your teacher ask you a lot of questions?

Factor III:  Cognitive Emphasis

When your teacher asks you a question, is it important to give reasons
    for your answers?
Does your teacher tell you reasons why you shouldn't do something?
Do most children in your class want to finish their work first?
Is it important to make good grades in your class?
Have you ever looked at different things to see how they are alike?
Is it important to memorize things for your class?
Do the children in your room often talk about their work with each other?
Are you often asked to tell what the book said in your own words?
Do some children always try to do their work better than the others?

**YOUR SCHOOL DAYS,** continued

Are you ever asked to find as many different answers as you can to a
   problem?
Do you take part in class discussions?
Does your teacher ask for more than one answer to a question?
Do you ever have to tell why an idea was good or bad?
Are children asked to sit by themselves when they bother others?
Does the teacher move children apart when they talk to each other a lot?
When you start a new activity, are you confused about how to start?
Is there a lot of competition in your class?

Factor IV:  Flexibility

Do different projects go on at the same time in your room?
Can you use the class games and learning equipment without the teacher
   watching you?
Is everyone in your class given the same assignment?
Does your teacher use a lot of movies, tapes, and records to help
   you learn?
Can children in your class move around the room without asking permission?
Can you work with anyone you want?
Does your teacher help you with your school work?
When you finish your class work do you know what to do next?

# Appendix C

## Methods Employed to Assure the Quality of the Data Collection Procedures

The quality of data collection procedures is dependent upon the competence of those administering the instruments and the consistency of those coding classroom behavior. Information on test administrator background and the consistency of observer coding is presented to indicate the quality control of the data collection procedures.

## Background of Test Administrators

Background information on all Project PRIME test administrators is summarized in Table C-1. The personnel who administered the October and May MATs were generally older, better educated, and had more teaching experience than administrators of the January questionnaires. This was due to the stipulation that, whenever possible, achievement test administrators be experienced in administering achievement or other standardized tests. In selecting testers to administer the January questionnaires, the emphasis shifted from a preference for experience in testing to a preference for testers who would be able to develop a rapport with the children in the testing situation. During the January socio-affective testing, Project PRIME employed test administrators

Table C-1

Project PRIME Test Administrator Characteristics

| Characteristic | October Test Administrators N | % | January Test Administrators N | % | May Test Administrators N | % | Total Administrators N | % |
|---|---|---|---|---|---|---|---|---|
| **Age** | | | | | | | | |
| Less than 25 | 18 | 13.7 | 50 | 38.2 | 6 | 8.5 | 74 | 22.3 |
| 25-35 | 38 | 29.0 | 46 | 35.1 | 32 | 45.7 | 116 | 34.9 |
| 36-45 | 43 | 32.8 | 21 | 16.0 | 18 | 25.7 | 82 | 24.7 |
| 46-55 | 22 | 16.8 | 10 | 7.6 | 7 | 10.0 | 39 | 11.8 |
| Over 55 | 10 | 7.6 | 4 | 3.1 | 7 | 10.0 | 21 | 0.3 |
| Total | 131 | | 131 | | 70 | | 332 | |
| **Sex** | | | | | | | | |
| Male | 11 | 8.4 | 11 | 8.5 | 4 | 5.7 | 26 | 7.9 |
| Female | 120 | 91.6 | 118 | 91.5 | 66 | 94.3 | 304 | 92.1 |
| Total | 131 | | 129 | | 70 | | 330 | |
| **Ethnic group** | | | | | | | | |
| Anglo | 118 | 92.2 | 80 | 61.5 | 65 | 92.9 | 263 | 80.2 |
| Black | 7 | 5.5 | 9 | 6.9 | 3 | 4.3 | 19 | 5.8 |
| Mexican-American | 2 | 1.6 | 38 | 29.2 | 2 | 2.9 | 42 | 12.8 |
| Oriental | 1 | 0.8 | 0 | 0 | 0 | 0 | 1 | 0.3 |
| Other (Spanish-American) | 0 | 0 | 3 | 2.3 | | | 3 | 0.9 |
| Total | 128 | | 130 | | 70 | | 328 | |

| Years of teaching experience | | | | | | | | |
|---|---|---|---|---|---|---|---|---|
| None | 19 | 14.5 | 52 | 40.0 | 10 | 14.5 | 81 | 24.5 |
| Aide | 1 | 0.8 | 6 | 4.6 | 2 | 2.9 | 9 | 2.7 |
| Substitute teaching only | 11 | 8.4 | 28 | 21.5 | 12 | 17.4 | 51 | 15.5 |
| Three years or less | 24 | 18.3 | 10 | 7.7 | 15 | 21.6 | 49 | 14.8 |
| Over three years | 76 | 58.0 | 34 | 26.2 | 30 | 43.5 | 140 | 42.4 |
| Total | 131 | | 130 | | 69 | | 330 | |

who were bilingual, particularly in districts with a large proportion of Spanish-speaking children. Almost 30% of the January test administrators were Spanish-surnamed.

Throughout the year, the experience level of the personnel used by local districts for administering Project PRIME instruments was remarkably high. About 75% of the test administrators had some teaching experience, and about 40% had more than three years of teaching experience. Only a little over 10% of the test administrators had no college training, whereas almost 75% were college graduates and more than 50% had at least one course in testing.

## Observer Agreement

Observer agreement is usually defined as consistency among observers when simultaneously coding the same classroom behaviors using the same coding system (Medley & Mitzel, 1963). Observer agreement, while not synonymous with the reliability of an observational measure, is a necessary prerequisite to it. Two procedures are frequently used to determine observer agreement: (a) determining the extent to which an observer's coding agrees with the criterion coding of experts (criterion-related agreement) and (b) determining the extent to which an observer's coding is consistent with his previous coding of the same classroom events (intracoder consistency).

Coder agreement should be ascertained at least twice during a study using observation systems: First, after training but before data collection to assure that only adequately trained observers were actually coding; and second, at or near the end of the observation period to determine if coding skills were maintained throughout the study. There are several formulae available for the calculation of coder agreement. The selection of a particular formula depends on the nature of the observation system, the number of categories or behaviors recorded, the unit of analysis, and the types of scales or other measures to be derived from the data. A description and mathematical derivation of the several formulae available for assessing coder agreement and a discussion of the advantages and disadvantages of each formula for particular types of observation systems is provided in Frick and Semmel (1975).

Investigations of both criterion-related agreement and intracoder consistency scores were conducted at two times. The first or initial check period occurred during the training workshop when observers were tested to determine if they knew the system well enough to code consistently in the classroom. A second or maintenance observer agreement check period was conducted at the end of the observation period (May, 1972) to determine the

Table C-2

Observation Coder Agreement Estimates

| Observation System | Initial Coding Check Period | | | | | | Maintenance Coding Check Period | | | | | |
| | Criterion Agreement | | | Intraobserver Consistency | | | Criterion Agreement | | | Intraobserver Consistency | | |
| | $\bar{X}$ | SD | N | $\bar{X}$ | SD | N | $\bar{X}$ | SD | N | $\bar{X}$ | SD | N |
|---|---|---|---|---|---|---|---|---|---|---|---|---|
| IPPS | .62 | .17 | 441 | .72 | .17 | 441 | .77 | .11 | 171 | .87 | .10 | 170 |
| ICDS | .64 | .14 | 152 | .88 | .07 | 151 | .76 | .11 | 46 | .86 | .07 | 46 |
| IBMS | .62 | .20 | 153 | .86 | .10 | 149 | .85 | .17 | 46 | .87 | .05 | 46 |
| FLACCS | --------Not available-------- | | | | | | .67 | .01 | 65 | .83 | .05 | 65 |

**Note.** All intraobserver consistency measures are based on Flanders' (1967) proportional agreement of marginals formula. Criterion agreement scores for IPPS, IBMS, and ICDS are based on Garrett's (1972) average marginal agreement formula. FLACCS criterion agreement scores use Cohen's (1960) coefficient agreement formula.

degree to which observers had maintained their coding skills during the observation period. For the second coder agreement check, a sample (about one third) of the observers who had coded in the Project PRIME study during February, March, and April were tested.

For each coder agreement test, observers coded videotapes of simulated classroom activities containing unambiguous examples of the behavioral categories used in the observation system they coded. Each videotape was coded twice to obtain both criterion agreement and intraobserver consistency.

During the maintenance coder agreement check period, other tests in addition to the videotape test were also used on an experimental basis. These included:

- coding audiotapes played over the telephone;
- coding written scripts; and
- coding television programs.

A complete description of the coder agreement test materials and procedures is provided in Frick and Semmel (1975).

Coder agreement scores for each observation system were calculated for criterion-related agreement and intraobserver consistency for both the initial and maintenance coding check periods. Several formulae were used and, when appropriate, the scores were corrected for chance agreement. Coder agreement scores were computed for each individual behavior category and for the observation system as a whole. In addition to scores on the videotape tests, scores were also computed for the audio, written script, and TV coding tests.

The coding agreement coefficients for each observation system for the initial and maintenance coding agreement check periods are presented in Table C-2. The criteria developed by Frick and Semmel (1975) were used to select the most appropriate coefficient for the particular observation system under consideration; only these coefficients are presented. However, the various formulae seldom provided coefficients that were more than ±.10 different from the coefficients presented.

Although coder agreement coefficients were calculated for the individual behavioral categories, the scores in Table C-2 are based on all categories combined. Most of the observation measures reported in this book are broad composites of individual behavioral categories, therefore the individual category coder agreement coefficients would grossly underestimate the reliability of these composites. On the other hand, the coefficients based on all categories combined are probably a slight overestimate of the true reliability of the composite. Individual category coefficients were seldom lower than 0.50 and were usually in the 0.50-0.65 range. Individual category agreement coefficients and analyses of coder error patterns were considered in the development of composite observation measures. The coder errors suggested that low coder-agreement coefficients primarily represented confusion of the behavior categories; thus, collapsing across categories should increase the reliability of the resulting composite. Scores for the individual categories are available in Frick and Semmel (1975).

As can be seen in Table C-2, initial coder criterion agreement scores were in the low 0.60s, and initial intraobserver consistency scores were in the 0.70-0.90 range. Observers appeared to improve with coding experience, as evidenced by the fact that maintenance criterion agreement and intraobserver consistency scores were higher than initial training scores.

In general, the evidence provided on the background characteristics of the test administrators and the coding agreement scores of the observers suggests there was quality staffing of local data collection personnel.

# Appendix D

## Descriptions of the Profiles Derived from Each Sample

All learners were in third, fourth, or fifth grade or an equivalent nongraded special education classroom in a Texas public elementary school. The description of the profile clusters for the nonhandicapped sample are included to serve as a comparison for the profile clusters derived for the mainstreamed and nonmainstreamed samples.

### Nonhandicapped Learners

Nonhandicapped learners were, on average, about 9 years old, slightly more than half were male, and their IQ scores were in the average range ($\overline{X} = 94.7$). Ethnic distribution was about 40% Anglo, 40% Spanish surnamed, and 20% Black. They tended to be from lower-SES backgrounds — about 2 out of 5 learners' fathers had not attended high school and 1 out of 5 came from nonintact families. They were low academic achievers.

The nonhandicapped learners can be characterized by eight different learner profiles.

497

**Profile 1** consisted of well-behaved learners with a low rate of rejection who enjoyed school and their peers. Although not social or academic leaders, these students were *reasonably successful and satisfied*. This group was predominately female (three-fourths) but not disproportionately representative of any one ethnic group or SES class.

**Profile 2** was composed of learners with high academic status and positive self-concepts who were well accepted by their peers. These learners represented *social and academic leaders*, and included a relatively greater proportion of Anglo students and students from middle-SES backgrounds.

**Profile 3** consisted of learners with poor academic status who misbehaved, were inattentive, and were rejected by their peers. They were *serious academic and social deviants* and were disproportionately Black, male, from lower-SES levels, and from relatively lower-grade levels.

**Profile 4** consisted of learners with high verbal participation rates but low academic status. These students could be characterized as *academically weak but verbally active* in the classroom. They included relatively more Spanish-surnamed learners.

**Profile 5** was composed of students who said they liked both school and their peers, exhibited both positive and negative social behavior, were somewhat inattentive, and were disproportionately Black and from single parent families but not from low-SES levels. These learners were *active and gregarious but not seriously disruptive*.

**Profile 6** consisted of learners who have low social status, demonstrated little positive social behavior, were very attentive, and felt lonely. They were *shy and withdrawn*. These learners were not characterized by any specific demographic characteristics.

**Profile 7** contained learners with poor academic self-concepts and attitudes toward school, who disliked their peers and seldom participated verbally in the classroom. They can be characterized as *self-deprecating and unhappy*. Learners in this profile were disproportionately Spanish-surnamed and from low socioeconomic status families.

**Profile 8** consisted of learners with high academic status but low verbal participation rates. They disliked their peers but displayed positive social behavior; were *competent and cooperative but a bit disdainful*. This group was composed of proportionately more middle class and Spanish-surnamed students.

Each of the eight profile groups represented about the same proportion of students (0-19%) but were quite different in their pattern of competence. Among the eight *nonhandicapped learner* competency profiles, only one, Profile 3, would appear to present serious problems to teachers. Learners in Profiles 1, 2, and, to a lesser extent, 8 would appear to be a joy to teach. Profile

5 learners would appear to be a mild challenge and may well add a sparkle to the class. Learners in Profiles 5 and 7 potentially may go unnoticed but should cause teachers some concern.

## Mainstreamed EMR Learners

Mainstreamed EMR learners fell into six profile clusters which bear a limited resemblance to those obtained for nonhandicapped learners.

**Profile 1** included learners with extremely high positive and negative social behaviors and very low classroom academic status. They were inattentive and often rejected. These learners were *excessively and inappropriately socially active and academically inattentive.* They were similar to Profile 3 nonhandicapped learners except that their social activity pattern was more extreme and less academically appropriate. Their moderate rather than high social rejection and high positive social behavior suggested these learners were not extreme social deviants but instead lacked social judgment and self-control. Learners in this profile were disproportionately male and represented, disproportionately, students from non-Anglo and single-parent families.

**Profile 2** learners displayed poor social status but did not misbehave. They disliked their peers and school but did not feel lonely or rejected. They were *rejected and rejecting but did not admit to being lonely.* They resembled the Profile 7 nonhandicapped learners, although the nonhandicapped learners in this group were not rejected by their peers. Learners in this profile were not disproportionately representative of any background characteristics.

**Profile 3** learners had high social status relative to the other EMR students and were sociable and liked their peers. However, they had poor academic skills, academic self-concept, and attitudes toward school. They were *friendly and socially accepted but academically weak and concerned about it.* They resembled Profile 2 nonhandicapped learners except their success was social, not academic. They were broadly representative of the mainstreamed EMR learners' background characteristics.

**Profile 4** learners had high academic status relative to other mainstreamed EMR learners, were attentive, participated in classroom discussions, and did not misbehave. They also had poor self-concepts and attitudes toward school and were disproportionately Anglo. These students were *academically successful yet unsatisfied and unhappy* and had no counterpart among the nonhandicapped profiles. They were not the academic and social leaders found in nonhandicapped learner Profile 2. Their self-concepts were too poor for them to be self-satisfied, distinguishing them from the Profile 1 nonhandicapped learners and the Profile 6 mainstreamed EMR learners. Learners in Profile 4 tended to be older and in higher grades, which may partially explain their higher normative academic scores.

**Profile 5** was composed of learners who felt lonely and rejected and demonstrated little interactive behavior either socially or academically. They were *shy and withdrawn*, resembled Profile 6 nonhandicapped learners, and were disproportionately female.

**Profile 6** consisted of learners with high academic status who were attentive and participated in class, were accepted by and enjoyed their peers, had positive self-concepts and attitudes toward school, and were integrated for the greatest proportion of time. These learners were *successful and satisfied*. They were somewhat older, and disproportionately middle-SES and Black, and resembled Profile 1 nonhandicapped learners.

The six *mainstreamed EMR learner* profiles represented about equal proportions of learners (14-19%). Only one of these profiles, Profile 1, would appear to present teachers with behavior management problems. Profiles 2 and 5 represented learners whose integration was primarily temporal — they were not or did not feel a part of the classroom social milieu. Learners in Profiles 3 and 4 appeared to be doing satisfactorily in the mainstream, although their self-concepts and attitudes toward school were lower than one might hope. The only really successfully mainstreamed learners were those represented by Profile 6.

# Nonmainstreamed EMR Learners

The profiles of the nonmainstreamed EMR learners were somewhat parallel to those of the nonhandicapped and mainstreamed EMR learners.

**Profile 1** was composed of learners with very low academic status, poor self-concept, negative feelings about school, and low social status. They were *very slow academically, self-deprecating, and unhappy*, and resembled Profile 7 nonhandicapped learners except that the nonhandicapped learners were not academically slow. Learners in this profile were disproportionately Anglo and from single-parent families.

**Profile 2** consisted of learners who demonstrated little positive or negative social behavior, but liked their peers and school. They were *quiet and reserved but happy* and resembled Profile 6 nonhandicapped learners and Profile 5 mainstreamed EMR learners except that these nonmainstreamed learners did not feel lonely. Hence, *quiet and reserved* seems a more appropriate description than *shy and withdrawn*. Learners in this profile did not appear to be different from other nonmainstreamed EMR learners in their background characteristics.

**Profile 3** learners were inattentive, misbehaving, and socially rejected. They disliked their peers but participated actively in verbal discussions. These learners could be characterized as *social deviants, rejected and rejecting*, much like the Profile 3 nonhandicapped learners except that the nonmainstreamed learners were not academically different than the rest of their group and had no distinctive background characteristics.

**Profile 4** was composed of learners with high academic status within this group who also expressed some feelings of academic inadequacy and dislike of school. They were *academically successful but personally unsatisfied* and represented a combination not found among nonhandicapped learners although they were similar to Profile 4 mainstreamed learners. This profile group had the highest amount of academic integration and was disproportionately from Anglo, middle-SES, and intact family backgrounds.

**Profile 5** learners were those with high social status who were attentive and sociable but very quiet in discussions. They were the *social leaders* in their classrooms and were similar to the social leader dimension of Profile 2 nonhandicapped learners. The academic leaders of the nonmainstreamed EMR learners were those in Profile 6. Profile 5 learners spent little time in the regular classroom but were not otherwise different from other nonmainstreamed learners.

**Profile 6** consisted of learners who had high academic status, positive self-concepts, and positive attitudes toward school. They were the *academic leaders* in their classrooms, and resembled Profile 2 nonhandicapped learners and Profile 6 mainstreamed learners. These learners spent a high percentage of time in the regular classroom, and were disproportionately older, male, and from Black, middle-SES, and single-parent families.

The *nonmainstreamed EMR learners* were roughly evenly distributed among the profiles (10-21% in each profile). Profile 6 had the fewest nonmainstreamed learners (one-tenth) while the largest profiles — 2, 3, and 4 — each contained about one-fifth of the nonmainstreamed learners. Among the nonmainstreamed learners, Profile 3 learners were most likely to present teachers with behavior management problems. Profile 1 and 4 learners were unhappy, although only Profile 1 learners had serious academic problems. Profile 5 and 6 learners had achieved leadership status and success within the self-contained special classroom setting. Profile 2 learners, while not leaders, appeared to be content.

# References

Adams, R.S., & Biddle, B.J. *Realities of teaching: Explorations with video tape.* New York: Holt, Rinehart & Winston, 1970.

Ainsworth, S.A. *An exploratory study of educational, social and emotional factors in the education of mentally retarded children in Georgia public schools* (U.S. Office of Education, Cooperative Research Program, Project No. 171). Athens: University of Georgia, 1959.

Allport, G.W. What unit shall we employ? In G. Lindzey (Ed.), *The assessment of human motives.* New York: Holt, Rinehart & Winston, 1958. (Reprinted in G. Lindzey & G.S. Hall (Eds.), *Theories of personality: Primary sources and research.* New York: John Wiley & Sons, 1965.)

Anderson, G., & Walberg, H. Classroom climate and group learning. *International Journal of the Educational Sciences,* 2:178-180, 1968.

Anderson, R. Learning in discussions: A resume of authoritarian-democratic studies. *Harvard Educational Review,* 29:201-215, 1959.

Argyle, M. *Social interaction.* London: Metheun, 1969.

Argyle, M., & Little, B.R. Do personality traits apply to social behavior? *Journal of Theory of Social Behavior,* 2:1-35, 1972.

Armor, D. School and family effects on black and white achievement: A re-examination of the USOE data. In F. Mosteller & D. Moynihan (Eds.), *On equality of educational opportunity.* New York: Random House, 1972.

Arnold, D.S., Atwood, R.K., & Rogers, V.M. An investigation of relationships among question level, response level, and lapse time. *School Science and Mathematics,* 591-594, 1973.

Ausubel, D.P. *Learning theory and classroom practice* (Bulletin No. 1). Toronto: The Ontario Institute for Studies in Education, 1967.

Averch, H.A., Carroll, S.J., Donaldson, T.S., Kiesling, H.S., & Pincus, J. *How effective is schooling? A critical review and synthesis of research findings* (A report prepared for the President's Commission on School Finance under Contract OEC-0-71-0908, Rand Corporation Report No. R-956-PCSF/RC), March 1972.

Baarstad, D.L. A resource room for the educationally handicapped pupil. *California Education,* 3(4):14, 1965.

Bacher, J.H. The effect of special class placement on the self-concept, social adjustment, and reading growth of slow learners (Doctoral dissertation, New York University, 1964). *Dissertation Abstracts,* 25:7071, 1965. (University Microfilms No. 65-6570)

Baldwin, W. The social position of the educable mentally retarded child in the regular grades in the public school. *Exceptional Children,* 25:106-108, 1958.

Bales, R.S. Task roles and social roles in problem solving groups. In E. Maccoby, T. Newcomb, & E. Hartley (Eds.), *Readings in social psychology.* New York: Holt, Rinehart & Winston, 1958.

Bales, R.S., & Slater, P.E. Role differentiation in small decision making groups. In T. Parsons & R. Bales (Eds.), *Family socialization and interaction processes*. New York: Free Press, 1955.

Bandura, A. *Principles of behavior modification*. New York: Holt, Rinehart & Winston, 1969.

Bandura, A. Analysis of modeling processes. In A. Bandura (Ed.), *Psychological modeling: Conflicting theories*. New York: Atherton Press, 1971.

Bandura, A., Blanchard, E., & Ritter, B. *The relative efficacy of desensitization and modeling therapeutic approaches for inducing behavioral, affective and attitudinal changes*. Palo Alto, CA: Stanford University, 1968.

Bandura, A., Grusec, J., & Menlove, F. Observational learning as a function of symbolization and incentive set. *Child Development*, *37*:499-506, 1967.

Bandura, A., & Walters, R. *Social learning and personality development*. New York: Holt, Rinehart & Winston, 1963.

Bane, R.K. Relationships between measures of experimental cognitive and affective teaching behavior and selected teacher characteristics (Doctoral dissertation, University of Florida, 1969). *Dissertation Abstracts International* (University Microfilms No. 70-12, 225)

Bargen, M., & Walberg, H. School performance. In H. Walberg (Ed.), *Evaluating educational performance*. Berkeley, CA: McCutchan, 1974.

Barker, R.G. *Introduction to ecological psychology: Methods and concepts for an eco-behavioral science*. Palo Alto, CA: Stanford University Press, 1968.

Barksdale, M.W., & Atkinson, A.P. A resource room approach to instruction for the educable mentally retarded. *Focus on Exceptional Children*, *3*(4):12-15, 1971.

Beery, K.E. *Models for mainstreaming*. San Rafael, CA: Dimensions, 1972.

Bellack, A.A., Hyman, R.T., Smith, F.L., Jr., & Kliebard, H.M. *The language of the classroom* (Final report, U.S. Office of Education, Cooperative Research Program, Project No. 2033). New York: Teachers College Press, 1966.

Berk, L., Rose, M., & Stewart, D. Attitudes of English and American children toward their school experience. *Journal of Educational Psychology*, *61*:33-40, 1970.

Berrio, M. *Bases of influence in the kindergarten*. Unpublished masters thesis, Tufts University, 1972.

Bienvenu, M. *Effects of school integration on the self-concept and anxiety of lower class Negro adolescent males*. Unpublished doctoral dissertation, Florida State University, 1968.

Birch, J.W. *Mainstreaming: Educable mentally retarded children in regular classes*. Minneapolis: Leadership Training Institute/Special Education, University of Minnesota, 1974.

Blair, G., Jones, R., & Simpson, R. *Educational psychology*. New York: MacMillan, 1968.

Blatt, B. The physical, personality and academic status of children who are mentally retarded attending special classes as compared with children who are mentally retarded attending regular classes. *American Journal of Mental Deficiency*, *62*:810-818, 1958.

Bledsoe, J. *The self-concepts of elementary school children in relation to their academic achievement, intelligence, interest, and manifest anxiety.* Paper presented at the American Psychological Association Annual Meeting, August 1963.

Bloom, B.S., Engelhart, M.D., Furst, E.J., Hill, W.H., & Krathwohl, P.R. (Eds.), *Taxonomy of educational objectives: The classification of educational goals, Handbook I: Cognitive domain.* New York: David McKay, 1956.

Bonney, M. A sociometric study of the relationship of some factors to mutual friendships on the elementary, secondary, and college levels. *Sociometry, 9*:21-47, 1946.

Bonney, M. A study of friendship choices in college in relation to church affiliation, in-church preferences, family size, and length of enrollment in college. *Journal of Social Psychology, 29*:153-166, 1949.

Bosco, J. Individualization: Teachers' views. *Elementary School Journal, 72*:125-131, 1971.

Bouchard, R. An experiment in student self-concept change (Doctoral dissertation, St. Louis University, 1970). *Dissertation Abstracts International,* 1970. (University Microfilms No. 71-21, 371)

Bovard, E. The experimental production of interpersonal affect. *Journal of Abnormal and Social Psychology, 46*:521-528, 1951.

Bovard, E. Grouping error and interpersonal affect: A correction. *Journal of Abnormal and Social Psychology, 52*:283-284, 1956a.

Bovard, E. Interaction and attraction to the group. *Human Relations, 9*:481-489, 1956b.

Bowles, S., & Levin, H.M. The determinants of scholastic achievement: An appraisal of some recent evidence. *Journal of Human Resources, 3*(1):2-24, 1968.

Brodie, T. Attitude toward school and academic accomplishment. *Personnel and Guidance Journal, 43*:375-378, 1964.

Brookover, W., Paterson, A., & Thomas, S. *The relationship of self-images to achievement in junior high school subjects* (U.S. Office of Education, Cooperative Research Program, Project No. 845). East Lansing, MI: Michigan State University, College of Education, Bureau of Educational Research Services, 1962.

Brophy, J.E. *The student as the unit of analysis* (Report No. 75-12). Austin: University of Texas, Research Development Center for Teacher Education, 1975.

Brophy, J.E., & Evertson, C.M. *Process-product correlations in the Texas teacher effectiveness study* (Final report, Research Report No. 74-4). Austin: University of Texas, Research Development Center for Teacher Education, June 1974.

Brophy, J.E., & Evertson, C.M. *Teacher behavior and student learning in second and third grades* (Report No. 75-4). Austin: University of Texas, 1975.

Brophy, J.E., & Good, T.L. *Teacher-student relationships: Causes and consequences.* New York: Holt, Rinehart & Winston, 1974.

Brown, R. *Social Psychology.* New York: Free Press, 1965.

Bruininks, R.H., & Rynders, J.E. Alternatives to special class placement for educable mentally retarded children. *Focus on Exceptional Children, 3*(4):1-12, 1971.

Bruner, J.S. *Toward a theory of instruction.* New York: W.W. Norton, 1966.

Bryan, T.H. *Social relationships of learning disabled children.* Paper presented at the meeting of the Council for Exceptional Children, New York, April 1974.

Budoff, M. Comments on providing special education without special classes. *Journal of School Psychology*, *10*:199-205, 1972. [ED 058- 707]

Budoff, M., & Gottlieb, J. Special class EMR children mainstreamed: A study of an aptitude (learning potential) X treatment interaction. *American Journal of Mental Deficiency*, *81*:1-11, 1976.

Burgdorf, R.L., Jr. *The doctrine of the least restrictive alternative.* Unpublished manuscript, Council for Handicapped People, Columbia, South Carolina, 1975.

Byrne, D., Clore, G., & Worchel, P. The effect of economic similarity-dissimilarity on interpersonal attraction. *Journal of Personality and Social Psychology*, *4*:220-224, 1966.

Caplin, M. The relationships between self-concept and academic achievement. *Journal of Experimental Education*, *37*:13-16, 1969.

Carroll, J.B. A model for school learning. *Teachers College Record*, *64*:723-733, 1963.

Carroll, W.W. The effects of segregated and partially integrated school programs on self-concept and academic achievement of educable mentally retarded. *Exceptional Children*, *34*:93-96, 1967.

Cartwright, D., & Zander, A. *Group dynamics: Research and theory* (3rd ed.). New York: Harper & Row, 1968.

Cassidy, V., & Stanton, J. *An investigation of factors in the educational placement of mentally retarded children: A study of differences between children in special and regular classes in Ohio* (U.S. Office of Education, Cooperative Research Program, Project No. 043). Columbus, OH: Ohio State University, 1959.

Cavior, N., & Dokecki, P.R. Physical attractiveness, perceived attitude similarity, and academic achievement as contributors to interpersonal attraction among adolescents. *Developmental Psychology*, *9*:44-54, 1973.

Clark, K. *Dark ghetto.* New York: Harper Torchbooks, 1965.

Clark, K.B., & Clark, M.K. The development of consciousness of self and the emergence of racial identification in Negro preschool children. *Journal of Social Psychology*, *10*:591-599, 1939.

Cobb, J.A. Relationship of discrete classroom behaviors to fourth-grade academic achievement. *Journal of Educational Psychology*, *63*:74-80, 1972.

Coleman, J.S., Campbell, E.Z., Hobson, C.J., McPartland, J., Mood, A.M., Weinfeld, F.D., & York, R.L. *Equality of educational opportunity.* Washington, DC: U.S. Government Printing Office, 1966.

Combs, R., & Harper, J. Effects of labels on attitudes of educators toward handicapped children. *Exceptional Children*, *33*:399-403, 1967.

Connor, F., & Talbot, M. *An experimental curriculum for young mentally retarded children.* New York: Teachers College Press, 1970.

Cooley, W.W., & Lohnes, P. *Evaluation research in education.* New York: Irvington, 1976.

Coopersmith, S. How to enhance pupil self-esteem. *Today's Education*, *58*:28-29, 1969.

Cronbach, L.J. How can instruction be adapted to individual differences? In R.M. Gagne (Ed.), *Learning and individual differences.* Columbus, OH: Charles E. Merrill, 1967.

Cronbach, L.J. Test validation. In R.L. Thorndike (Ed.), *Educational measurement* (2nd ed.). Washington, DC: American Council on Education, 1971.

Dagenais, F., & Marascuillo, J.A. The effect of factor scores, Guttman scores, and simple sum scores on the size of the F-ratios in an analysis of variance design. *Multivariate Behavioral Research*, 491-502, 1973.

Davies, S.P., & Ecob, K.G. *The mentally retarded in society*. New York: Columbia University Press, 1959.

Davis, O.L., Jr., Morse, K.R., Rogers, V.M., & Tinsley, D.C. Studying the cognitive emphasis of teachers' classroom questions. *Educational Leadership*, 26:711-719, 1969.

Dennell, D. *Dimensions of self-concept of later elementary children in relationship to reading performance, sex role, and socioeconomic status*. Unpublished doctoral dissertation, University of Michigan, 1971.

Dennis, W., & Dennis, M.G. The effect of restricted practice upon the reaching, sitting and standing of two infants. *Journal of Genetic Psychology*, 47:21-29, 1935.

Dennis, W., & Najarian, P. Infant development under environmental handicap. *Psychological Monographs, 71* (7, Whole No. 436), 1957.

Denny, M.R. Research in learning and performance. In H.A. Stevens & R. Heber (Eds.), *Mental retardation: A review of research*. Chicago: University of Chicago Press, 1964.

Deno, E. *Instructional alternatives for exceptional children*. Reston, VA: Council for Exceptional Children, 1973.

Dentler, R.A., & Mackler, B. Ability and sociometric status among normal and retarded children: A review of the literature. *Psychological Bulletin*, 59:273-283, 1962.

Dewey, J. *Experience and nature*. Chicago: Open Court, 1925.

Diggs, E.A. A study of change in the social status of rejected mentally retarded children in regular classrooms (Doctoral dissertation, Colorado State College, 1963). *Dissertation Abstracts*, 25:220-221, 1964. (University Microfilms No. 64-4180)

Dobson, R., Goldenberg, R., & Elsom, B. Pupil control ideology and teacher influence in the classroom. *Journal of Educational Research*, 66:77-80, 1972.

Dreeben, R. The school as workplace. In R.M. Travers (Ed.), *Second handbook of research on teaching*. Chicago: Rand-McNally, 1973.

Drotar, D. Outerdirectedness and the puzzle performance of nonretarded and retarded children. *American Journal of Mental Deficiency*, 77:230-236, 1972.

Dugdale, R.L. *The Jukes: A study of crime, pauperism, disease, and heredity*. New York: Putnam, 1877.Dunkin, M.J., & Biddle, B.J. *The study of teaching*. New York: Holt, Rinehart & Winston, 1974.

Dunn, L.M. Special education for the mildly retarded: Is much of it justifiable? *Exceptional Children*, 35:5-22, 1968.

Dunn, L.M. Children with mild learning disabilities. In L.M. Dunn (Ed.), *Exceptional children in the schools: Special education in transition* (2nd ed.). New York: Holt, Rinehart & Winston, 1973.

Durost, W.N., Bixler, H.H., Wrightsone, J.W., Prescott, G.A., & Balow, I.H. *Metropolitan Achievement Test (MAT)*. New York: Harcourt, Brace, & Jovanovich, 1971.

Dusewicz, R. *Student attitude factors affecting achievement in the urban school.* Unpublished doctoral dissertation, University of Delaware, 1972.

Ebert, D.W., Dain, R.N., & Phillips, B.N. An attempt at implementing diagnosis-intervention class model. *Journal of School Psychology, 8*:191-197, 1970.

Ehrlich, V. *The dimensions of attitude toward school of elementary school children in grades 3 to 6.* Unpublished doctoral dissertation, Columbia University, 1968.

Ellis, N. (Ed.) *Handbook of mental deficiency.* New York: McGraw-Hill, 1963.

Erdman, R.L., & Olson, J.L. Relationships between educational programs for the mentally retarded and the culturally deprived. *Mental Retardation Abstracts, 3*:311-318, 1966. In J.H. Rothstein (Ed.), *Mental retardation: Readings and resources* (2nd ed.). New York: Holt, Rinehart & Winston, 1971.

Fagot, B., & Patterson, G. An in vivo analysis of reinforcing contingencies for sex role behaviors in the preschool child. *Developmental Psychology, 1*:563-568, 1969.

Feshbach, N. Student teacher preferences for elementary school pupils varying in personality characteristics. *Journal of Educational Psychology, 60*:126-132, 1969.

Festinger, L. A theory of social comparison processes. *Human Relations, 7*:117-140, 1954.

Festinger, L., Schacter, S., & Back, K. *Social pressures in informal groups.* New York: Harper & Row, 1950.

Fink, A.H., & Semmel, M.I. *Indiana behavior management system II.* Bloomington, IN: Center for Innovation in Teaching the Handicapped, Indiana University, 1971.

Flanders, N.A., & Havumaki, S. The effect of teacher-pupil contacts involving praise on the sociometric choices of students. *Journal of Educational Psychology, 51*:65-68, 1960.

Flavell, J.H. *The developmental psychology of Jean Piaget.* Princeton, NJ: D. VanNostrand, 1963.

Forman, E.A., Budoff, M., & White, B.N. *Final report. The development of concepts of deviance in children, Vol. II. A study of the classroom behaviors of handicapped children in mainstreamed preschools.* (U.S. Office of Education, Grant No. G007602459) 1980.

Forness, S.R., & Esveldt, K.C. Classroom observation of children with learning and behavior problems. *Journal of Learning Disabilities, 8*:382-385, 1975.

French, J., & Raven, B. The bases of social power. In D. Cartwright (Ed.), *Studies in social power.* Ann Arbor: University of Michigan, 1959.

Frick, T., & Semmel, M.I. *Project PRIME observer quality control* (Project PRIME working paper). Bloomington, IN: University of Indiana, Center for Innovation in Teaching the Handicapped, May 1975.

Frick, T., & Semmel, M.I. Observers' agreement and reliabilities of classroom observational measures. *Reviews of Educational Research, 48*(1):157-184, 1978.

Gagne, R.M. Contributions of learning to human development. *Psychological Review, 75*:177-191, 1968.

Gallagher, J.J. Expressive thought by gifted children in the classroom. *Elementary English, 42*:559-568, 1965.

Gampel, D.H., Gottlieb, J., & Harrison, R.H. A comparison of the classroom behaviors of special class EMR, integrated EMR, low IQ, and nonretarded children. *American Journal of Mental Deficiency*, 79:16-21, 1974.

Garber, H. Intervention in infancy: A developmental approach. In M.J. Begab & S.A. Richardson (Eds.), *The mentally retarded and society: A social science perspective*. Baltimore: University Park Press, 1974.

Gardner, O.S. The birth and infancy of the resource center at Hauula. *Exceptional Children*, 38:53-58, 1971.

Gardner, W.I. Social and emotional adjustment of mildly retarded children and adolescents: Critical review. *Exceptional Children*, 33:97-105, 1966.

Gickling, E., & Theobald, J. Mainstreaming: Affect or effect? *Journal of Special Education*, 9:317-328, 1975.

Glass, E.V. *The experimental unit and the unit of statistical analysis: Comparative experiments with intact groups*. Paper presented at the meeting of American Education Research Association, New York, March 1967.

Glass, E.V. *The growth of evaluation methodology* (Report No. 27). Boulder: University of Colorado, Laboratory of Educational Research, March 1969.

Goddard, H. *The Kallikak family*. New York: MacMillan, 1912.

Goddard, H.H. Four hundred feeble-minded children classified by the Binet method. *Journal of Psychoaesthenics*, 15:17-30, 1910. In M. Rosen, G.R. Clark, & M.S. Kivitz (Eds.), *The history of mental retardation: Collected papers* (Vol. 1). Baltimore: University Park Press, 1976.

Goldberg, L.R. Parameters of personality inventory construction and utilization: A comparison of prediction and tactics. *Multivariate Behavioral Research Monographs*, 72(2):1-59, 1972.

Goldenberg, R.E. *Pupil control ideology and teacher influence in the classroom*. Paper presented at the meeting of the American Educational Research Association, New York, 1971.

Goldstein, H. Social and occupational adjustment. In H.A. Stevens & R. Heber (Eds.), *Mental retardation*. Chicago: University Park Press, 1964.

Goldstein, H., Moss, J.W., & Jordan, L.J. *The efficacy of special class training on the development of mentally retarded children* (U.S. Office of Education, Cooperative Research Program, Project No. 619). Urbana, IL: University of Illinois, Institute for Research on Exceptional Children, 1965.

Goldstein, H., & Seigle, D. *The Illinois plan for special education of exceptional children: A curriculum guide for teachers of the educable mentally handicapped* (Circular Series B-3, No. 12). Springfield: Illinois Department of Public Instruction, 1958.

Good, T., & Brophy, J. Behavioral expressions of teacher attitudes. *Journal of Educational Psychology*, 63:617-624, 1972.

Goodlad, J.I., & Klein, M.F. *Behind the classroom door*. Worthington, OH: Charles A. Jones, 1970.

Goodman, H., Gottlieb, J., & Harrison, R.H. Social acceptance of EMRs integrated into a nongraded elementary school. *American Journal of Mental Deficiency*, 76:412-417, 1972.

Gorton, R.A. Comments on research: Do teachers equate good discipline with good teaching? *NASSP Bulletin*, *55*:29-36, 1971.

Gottlieb, J. Attitudes toward retarded children: Effects of labeling and behavioral aggressiveness. *Journal of Educational Psychology*, *67*:581-585, 1975a.

Gottlieb, J. *Predictors of social status among mainstreamed mentally retarded pupils.* Paper presented at the meeting of the American Association on Mental Deficiency, Portland, Oregon, June 1975b.

Gottlieb, J. *Observing social adaptation in schools.* Paper presented at the University of Washington and George Peabody College Conference, Application of Observational-ethnological Methods to the Study of Mental Retardation, Lake Wilderness, Washington, June 1976.

Gottlieb, J., Gampel, D.H., & Budoff, M. Classroom behavior of retarded children before and after reintegration into regular classes. *Journal of Special Education*, *9*:307-315, 1975.

Gronlund, N.E. Relationships between sociometric status of pupils and teacher's preference for or against having them in class. *Sociometry*, *16*:142-150, 1953.

Gronlund, N.E. *Sociometry in the classroom.* New York: Harper & Bros., 1959.

Guilford, J.P. *The nature of human intelligence.* New York: McGraw-Hill, 1967.

Gump, P.V. *The classroom behavior setting: Its nature and relation to student behavior* (Final Report, HEW Contract No. OE-4-10-107). Lawrence, KS: University of Kansas, 1967. (ERIC Document Reproduction No. ED 015 515)

Gump, P.V. What's happening in the elementary classroom? In I. Westbury & A.A. Bellack (Eds.), *Research in classroom processes.* New York: Teachers' College Press, 1971.

Guskin, S.L., & Spicker, H.H. Educational research in mental retardation. In N.R. Ellis (Ed.), *Internatonal review of research in mental retardation.* New York: Academic Press, 1968.

Guttman, L. Image theory for the structure of quantitative variates. *Psychometrika*, *10*:277-296, 1953.

Hall, A.D. Some fundamental concepts of systems engineering. In S.L. Optner (Ed.), *Systems analysis.* Baltimore: Penguin Books, 1973.

Hammill, D.D., & Weiderholt, J.L. *The resource room: Rationale and implementation.* Philadelphia: Buttonwood Farms, 1972.

Hanushek, E. Teacher characteristics and gains in student achievement: Estimation using microdata. *American Economic Review*, *61*:280-288, 1971.

Harootunian, B. *Self-other relationships of segregated and desegregated ninth graders.* Paper presented at the annual meeting of the American Educational Research Association, Chicago, February 1968. (ERIC Document Reproduction Service No. ED 023765)

Harrison, A., & Scriven, E. Can you be liberal and teach too? *Peabody Journal of Education*, *40*:355-359, 1970.

Hartman, R.K., & Rockhold, A.E. Case studies in the resource room approach. *Journal for Special Educators of the Mentally Retarded*, *9*:109-115, 1973.

Hartup, W., & Coates, B. Imitation as a function of reinforcement from the peer group and rewardingness of the model. *Child Development*, *38*:1003-1016, 1967.

Heath, R.W., & Nielson, M.A. The research basis for performance-based teacher education. *Review of Educational Research, 44*:463-484, 1974.

Herndon, J. *The way its spozed to be.* New York: Simon & Schuster, 1968.

*Hobson v. Hansen,* 269, F. Supp. 401, 513 (D.D.C. 1967).

Hoffman, L.W., & Lippitt, R. The measurement of family life variables. In P.H. Mussen (Ed.), *Handbook of research methods in child development.* New York: Wiley, 1960.

Holtzman, W.H. The changing world of mental measurement and its social significance. *American Psychologist, 26*:546-553, 1971.

Homans, G. *Social behavior: Its elementary forms.* New York: Harcourt, Brace, 1961.

Hoy, W., & Blankenship, J. A comparison of the ideological orientations and personality characteristics of teacher "acceptors" and "rejectors" of BSCS biology. *Science Education, 56*:71-77, 1972.

Hughes, M. What is teaching? One viewpoint. In R.T. Hyman (Ed.), *Teaching: Vantage points for study.* Philadelphia: J.B. Lippincott, 1968.

Hungerford, R., DeProspo, C., & Rosenzweig, L. *Philosophy of occupational education.* New York: The Association for the New York City Teachers of Special Education, 1948.

Hunt, D.E., & Sullivan, E.V. *Between psychology and education.* Hinsdale, IL: Dryden Press, 1974.

Iano, R. Shall we disband special classes? *Journal of Special Education, 6*:167-177, 1972.

Immegart, G.L., & Pilecki, F.J. *An introduction to systems for the educational administrator.* Reading, MA: Addison-Wesley, 1973.

Jackson, P.W. *Life in classrooms.* New York: Holt, Rinehart & Winston, 1968.

Jackson, P.W., & Belford, E. Educational objectives and the joys of teaching. *The School Review, 73*:267-291, 1965.

Jackson, P.W., & Lahaderne, H. Scholastic success and attitude toward school in population of sixth graders. *Journal of Educational Psychology, 58*:15-18, 1967.

Jensen, A.R. Another look at culture fair testing. In J. Hellmuth (Ed.), *Disadvantaged child* (Vol. 3). New York: Brunner/Mazel, 1970.

Johnson, G.O. A study of the social position of mentally handicapped children in regular grades. *American Journal of Mental Deficiency, 55*:60-89, 1950.

Johnson, G.O. Special education for the handicapped—a paradox. *Exceptional Children, 29*:62-69, 1962.

Johnson, G.O., & Kirk, S.A. Are mentally handicapped children segregated in regular grades? *Exceptional Children, 17*:65-68, 1959.

Johnson, R., & Medinnus, G. *Child psychology: Behavior and development.* New York: John Wiley & Sons, 1967.

Jones, S. The psychology of interpersonal attraction. In C. Nemeth (Ed.), *Social psychology: Classic and contemporary integrations.* Chicago: Rand McNally, 1974.

Jörger, J. Die familie zero. *Archiv fur Rassen-und Gesellschafts-Biologie, Einschiesslich Rassen-und Gesellschafts-Hygiene, 2*:495-559, 1905.

Joyce, B., & Weil, M. *Models of teaching.* Englewood Cliffs, NJ: Prentice-Hall, 1972.

Kaiser, H.F. Image analysis. In C.W. Harris (Ed.), *Problems in measuring change.* Madison: University of Wisconsin Press, 1963.

Kanner, L. *A history of the care and study of the mentally retarded.* Springfield, IL: Charles C. Thomas, 1964.

Katz, D., & Kahn, R.L. *The social psychology of organizations.* New York: John Wiley & Sons, 1966.

Kaufman, M.J., Agard, J.A., & Vlasak, J.W. *Current issues in appraisal.* Paper presented at the Annual National Convention of the Council for Exceptional Children, Dallas, April 1973a.

Kaufman, M.J., Agard, J.A., & Vlasak, J.W. *Comprehensive Special Education in Texas: An evaluative report—Part II The objective of comprehensiveness.* Austin: Texas Education Agency, June 1973b.

Kaufman, M.J., Gottlieb, J., Agard, J.A., & Kukic, M.B. Mainstreaming: Toward an explication of the construct. *Focus on Exceptional Children,* 7(3):1-12, 1975. [Reprinted in E.L. Meyen, G.A. Vergason, & R.J. Whelan (Eds.), *Alternatives for teaching exceptional children.* Denver: Love, 1975.]

Kaufman, M.J., Semmel, M.I., & Agard, J.A. *Project PRIME: Interim Report 1971-1972—Purposes and procedures.* Washington, DC: U.S. Office of Education, Bureau of Education for the Handicapped, 1973.

Kelly, J. *Organizational behavior.* Homewood, IL: Richard D. Irwin, 1974.

Kerlinger, F.N. The first and second order factor structure of attitudes toward education. *American Educational Research Journal,* 4:191-205, 1967.

Kerlinger, F.N., & Pedhazur, E.J. *Multiple regression in behavioral research.* New York: Holt, Rinehart & Winston, 1973.

Kern, W.H., & Pfaeffle, H.A. A comparison of social adjustment of mentally retarded children in various educational settings. *American Journal of Mental Deficiency,* 67:407-413, 1962.

Kirk, S.A. *Early education of the mentally retarded.* Urbana, IL: University of Illinois Press, 1958.

Kirk, S.A. Research in education. In H.A. Stevens & R. Herber (Eds.), *Mental retardation: A review of research.* Chicago: University of Chicago Press, 1964.

Kirk, S.A. *Educating exceptional children.* Boston: Houghton-Mifflin, 1972.

Kirk, S.A., & Johnson, G. *Educating the retarded child.* Cambridge, MA: Riverside Press, 1950.

Klein, S.P. The uses and limitations of standardized tests in meeting the demands for accountability. *UCLA Evaluation Comment* (Center for the Study of Evaluation), 2(4), 1971.

Kolburne, L. *Effective education for the mentally retarded child.* New York: Vantage Press, 1965.

Kolstoe, O.P. *Teaching educable mentally retarded children.* New York: Holt, Rinehart & Winston, 1970.

Kounin, J.S. *Discipline and group management in classrooms.* New York: Holt, Rinehart & Winston, 1970.

Kowatrakul, S. Some behaviors of elementary school children related to classroom activities and subject areas. *Journal of Educational Psychology,* 50:121-128, 1959.

Kozol, J. *Death at an early age.* Boston: Houghton-Mifflin, 1968.

Kreinberg, N., & Chow, S.H. (Eds.). *Configurations of change: The integration of mildly handicapped children into the regular classroom.* San Francisco: The Far West Laboratory for Educational Research and Development, 1973.

LaBelle, T. Differential perceptions of elementary school children representing distinct socio-cultural backgrounds. *Journal of Cross-Cultural Psychology,* 2:145-156, 1971.

Ladas, H., & Osti, L. Asking questions: A strategy for teachers. *High School Journal,* 56:174-189, 1973.

Lahaderne, H.M. Attitudinal and intellectual correlates of attention: A study of four sixth-grade classrooms. *Journal of Educational Psychology,* 59:320-324, 1968.

Lane, H. *Wild boy of Aveyron.* Cambridge, MA: Harvard University Press, 1976.

Lapp. E.R. A study of the social adjustment of slow-learning children who were assigned part-time to regular classes. *American Journal of Mental Deficiency,* 62:254-262, 1957.

*Larry P.* v. *Riles,* 343 F. Supp. 1306 (N.D. CA, 1972).

Lawrence, E., & Winschel, J. Self-concept and the retarded: Research and issues. *Exceptional Children, 39:*310-321, 1973.

Lazerson, M. *Educational institutions and mental subnormality: Notes on writing a history.* Paper presented at a meeting of the National Institute of Child Health and Human Development and the Rose F. Kennedy Center for Research in Mental Retardation, Albert Einstein College of Medicine, New York, April 1974.

Lewin, K., Lippitt, R., & White, R. Patterns of aggressive behavior in experimentally created "social climates." *Journal of Social Psychology,* 10:271-299, 1939.

Lewis, W.W., Newell, J.M., & Withall, J. An analysis of classroom patterns of communication. In R.T. Hyman (Ed.), *Teaching: Vantage points for study.* New York: J.B. Lippincott, 1968.

Lindzey, G., & Byrne, D. Measurement of social choice and interpersonal attractiveness. In G. Lindzey & E. Aronson (Eds.), *The handbook of social psychology* (Vol. 2, 2nd ed.). Reading, MA: Addison-Wesley, 1968.

Lippitt, R., & Gold, M. Classroom social structure as a mental health problem. *Journal of Social Issues, 15:*40-58, 1959.

Lipton, A. Relationship of teacher rigidity to progress of retarded readers. *International Reading Association Conference Proceedings 13:*757-763, 1968.

Lortie, D.C. *School teacher: A sociological study.* Chicago: University of Chicago Press, 1975.

Lott, A.J., & Lott, B.E. Group cohesiveness as interpersonal attraction. *Psychological Bulletin, 64:*259-309, 1965.

Lundgren, U.P. *Frame factors and the teaching process: A contribution to curriculum theory and theory on teaching.* Stockholm: Almquist & Wiksell, 1972.

Lynch, W.W., & Ames, C. *Individual cognitive demand schedule.* Bloomington, IN: Center for Innovation in Teaching the Handicapped, Indiana University, 1971.

MacMillan, D.L. The problems of motivation in the education of the retarded. *Exceptional Children, 37:*579-585, 1971.

MacMillan, D.L. *Mental retardation in school and society.* Boston: Little Brown, 1977.

MacMillan, D.L., Jones, R.L., & Aloia, G.F. The mentally retarded label: A theoretical analysis and review of research. *American Journal of Mental Deficiency, 79*:241-261, 1974.

MacMillan, D.L., & Keogh, B. Normal and retarded children's expectancy for failure. *Developmental Psychology, 4*:343-348, 1971.

MacMillan, D.L., & Semmel, M.I. Evaluation of mainstreaming programs. *Focus on Exceptional Children, 9*(4):1-16, 1977.

Mayer, L. The relationships of early special class placement and the self-concepts of mentally handicapped children. *Exceptional Children, 33*:77-80, 1966.

Mayeske, G.W., Okada, T., & Beaton, A.E., Jr. *A study of the attitude toward life of our nation's students* (DHEW publication No. (OE) 73-01700). Washington, DC: U.S. Government Printing Office, 1973.

Mayeske, G.W., Okada, T., Cohen, W.M., Beaton, A.E., Jr., & Wisler, C.E. *A study of the achievement of our nation's students* (DHEW Publication No. OE 72-131). Washington, DC: U.S. Office of Education, 1973.

Mayeske, G.W., Weinfield, F.D., Beaton, A.E., Jr., Davis, W., Fetters, W., & Hixson, E. *A study of our nation's students*. Washington, DC: U.S. Government Printing Office, 1972.

McCandless, B. *Children and youth: Behavior and development*. New York: Dryden Press, 1973.

McDonald, F.J., Elias, P., Stone, M., Wheeler; P., Lambert, N., Calfee, R., Sandoval, J., Ekstrom, R., & Lockheed, M. *Final report on the Phase II beginning teacher evaluation study* (Prepared for the California Commission on Teacher Preparation and Licensing, Sacramento, California). Princeton, NJ: Educational Testing Service, 1975.

McGord, J., McCard, W., & Thurber, E. Some effects of paternal absence on male children. *Journal of Abnormal and Social Psychology, 64*:361-369, 1962.

McKinney, J.D., Mason, J., Perkerson, K., & Clifford, M. Relationships between class-room behavior and academic achievement. *Journal of Educational Psychology, 67*:198-203, 1975.

Mead, G.H. *Mind, self, and society*. Chicago: University of Chicago Press, 1934.

Medley, D.M., & Mitzel, H.E. Measuring classroom behavior by systematic observation. In N.L. Gage (Ed.), *Handbook of research on teaching*. Chicago: Rand McNally, 1963.

Mercer, J.R. *Labeling the mentally retarded*. Berkeley: University of California Press, 1973.

Mercer, J.R. A policy statement on assessment procedures and the rights of children. *Harvard Educational Review, 44*:125-141, 1974.

Meyerowitz, J.H. Self-derogations in young retardates and special class placement. *Child Development, 33*:443-451, 1962.

Meyers, C.E., MacMillan, D.L., & Yoshida, R.K. *Correlates of success in transition of MR to regular class* (Final Report OEG-0-73-5263). Riverside, CA: The Psychiatric Institute, Pacific State Hospital Research Group, November 1975. (ERIC Document Reproduction No. ED 081 038)

Michelson, S. The association of teacher resourcefulness with children's characteristics. In *Do teachers make a difference?* (OE No. 58042). Washington, DC: U.S. Government Printing Office, 1970.

Miller, G.A., Galanter, E., & Pribram, K.L. Images and plans. In J. DeCecco (Ed.), *The psychology of language, thought and instruction.* New York: Holt, Rinehart & Winston, 1967.

Millet, J. *Social power analysis of the dyad in the classroom setting.* Unpublished doctoral dissertation, University of California, Los Angeles, 1973.

Minskoff, E.H. Verbal interactions of teachers and mentally retarded pupils. (Doctoral dissertation, Yeshiva University, 1967). *Dissertation Abstracts International, 28*:546-7A. (University Microfilms No. 67-9669)

Mischel, W. *Personality and assessment.* New York: John Wiley & Sons, 1968.

Mischio, G.S. Inductive reasoning techniques for the mentally retarded. In E.L. Meyen, G.A. Vergason, & R.J. Whelan (Eds.), *Alternatives for teaching exceptional children.* Denver: Love, 1975.

Moody, W., Bauswell, R, & Jenkins, J. The effect of class size on the learning of mathematics: A parametric study with fourth grade students. *Journal for Research in Mathematics Education, 4*:170-176, 1973.

Moos, R.H. Conceptualization of human environments. *American Psychologist, 8*:652-665, 1973.

Moreno, J.L. *Who shall survive?* Washington, DC: Nervous and Mental Disease Publishing Co., 1934.

Morine, G. *Training for teacher planning and decision making.* Paper presented at the meeting of the American Educational Association, Washington, D.C., March 1975.

Mosteller, F., & Moynihan, D.P. (Eds.) *On equality of educational opportunity.* New York: Vintage Books, 1972.

Mueller, D.E. Teacher questioning practices in reading. *Reading World, 12*:136-145, 1972.

Musgrove, W. A follow-up study of black and white kindergarten children on academic achievement and social adjustment. *Academic Therapy, 7*:123-129, 1971-72.

Neale, D., & Proshek, J. School-related attitudes of culturally disadvantaged elementary school children. *Journal of Educational Psychology, 58*:238-244, 1967.

Northway, M.L. Outsiders: A study of the personality patterns of children least acceptable to their age mates. *Sociometry, 7*:10-25, 1944.

Nunnally, J. *Tests and measurements: Assessment and prediction.* New York: McGraw Hill, 1959.

Nunnally, J. *Psychometric theory.* New York: McGraw-Hill, 1967.

Nussel, E., & Johnson, M. Who obstructs innovation? *Journal of Secondary Education, 44*:3-11, 1969.

Nuthall, G.A. A review of some selected studies of classroom interaction and teaching behavior. *New Zealand Journal of Educational Studies, 3*(2):125-147, 1968.

Office of the Governor. *Summary: Selected demographic characteristics from census data—fourth count.* Austin: Texas Office of Information Services, 1972.

Parsons, T., & Bales, R. *Family socialization and interaction processes.* New York: Free Press, 1955.

*Pennsylvania Association for Retarded Children* v. *Commonwealth of Pennsylvania,* 344 F. Supp. 12571 (E.D. Pa., 1971).

Perkins, H.V. A procedure for assessing the classroom behavior of students and teachers. *American Educational Research Journal, 1:*249-260, 1964.

Perkins, H.V. Classroom behavior and underachievement. *American Educational Research Journal, 2:*1-12, 1965.19

President's Committee on Mental Retardation. *The six-hour retarded child.* Washington, DC: U.S. Government Printing Office, 1969.

President's Committee on Mental Retardation. *Report to the President: Mental Retardation: Century of decision.* Washington, DC: U.S. Government Printing Office, 1976.

Prouty, R.W., & Prillaman, D. Diagnostic teaching: A modest proposal. *Elementary School Journal, 70:*265-270, 1970.

Raven, B. *Developmental processes and social power.* Unpublished report, University of Los Angeles, 1973.

Reger, R. What is a resource-room program? *Journal of Learning Disabilities, 6:*609-613, 1973.

Rexford, G., Willower, D., & Lynch, P. Teacher's pupil control ideology and classroom verbal behavior. *Journal of Experimental Education, 40:*79-82, 1972.

Robinson, N., & Robinson, H. *The mentally retarded child* (2nd ed.). New York: McGraw Hill, 1976.

Rosen, B. The achievement syndrome: A psychocultural dimension of social stratification. *American Sociological Review, 21:*203-211, 1956.

Rosen, B. Race, ethnicity, and the achievement syndrome. *American Sociological Review, 24:*47-60, 1959.

Rosenberg, M. Parental interest and children's self-conceptions. *Sociometry, 26:*35-49, 1963.

Rosenkrantz, M. Imitation in children as a function of perceived similarity to a social model and vicarious reinforcement. *Journal of Personality and Social Psychology, 7:*307-315, 1967.

Rosenshine, B. *Primary grades instruction and student achievement gain.* Paper presented at the annual meeting of the American Educational Research Association, New York, April 1977.

Rosenshine, B., & Furst, N. Research on teacher performance criteria. In B.O. Smith (Ed.), *Research in teacher education: A symposium.* Englewood Cliffs, NJ: Prentice-Hall, 1971.

Ruckhaber, C. *Differences and patterns of performance of low achieving and high achieving intellectually able fourth-grade boys.* Unpublished doctoral dissertation, University of Michigan, 1966.

Ryans, D.C. *Characteristics of teachers.* Washington, DC: American Council on Education, 1960.

Ryans, D.C. Teacher behavior theory and research: Implications for teacher behavior. In R.T. Hyman (Ed.), *Teaching: Vantage points for study.* New York: J.B. Lippincott, 1968.

Rynders, J.E., & Horrobin, J.M. Project EDGE: The University of Minnesota's communication stimulation program for Down's syndrome infants. In B.Z. Friedland et al. (Eds.), *Exceptional infant 3: Assessment and intervention.* New York: Brunner/Mazel, 1975.

Samuels, S.J., & Turnure, J.E. Attention and reading achievement in first-grade boys and girls. *Journal of Educational Psychology, 66:*29-32, 1974.

Sanders, N.M. *Classroom questions: What kinds?* New York: Harper & Row, 1966.

Sax, G. The use of standardized tests in evaluation. In W.J. Popham (Ed.), *Evaluation in education.* Berkeley, CA: McCutchan, 1974.

Schmuck, R.A., & Schmuck, P.A. *Group processes in the classroom* (2nd ed.). Dubuque, IA: Wm. C. Brown, 1975.

Schurr, K. *The effect of special class placement on the self-concept of ability of the educable mentally retarded child: Part II.* Unpublished doctoral dissertation, Michigan State University, 1967.

Semmel, M.I., & Hasselbring, T. *Classroom status data.* Bloomington, IN: Indiana University, Center for Innovation in Teaching the Handicapped, 1971.

Semmel, M.I., & Meyers, K. *Indiana pupil participation schedule.* Bloomington, IN: Indiana University, Center for Innovation in Teaching the Handicapped, 1971.

Sewell, W. Social class and childhood personality. *Sociometry, 24:*340-356, 1961.

Sewell, W., Haller, A., & Strauss, M. Social status and educational and occupational aspiration. *American Sociological Review, 22:*67-73, 1957.

Shaw, M., & Wright, J. *Scales for the measurement of attitudes.* New York: McGraw-Hill, 1967.

Shim, C. A study of the cumulative effect of four teacher characteristics on the achievement of elementary school pupils. *Journal of Educational Research, 59:*33-34, 1965.

Shotel, J., Iano, R., & McGettigan, J. Teacher attitudes associated with the integration of handicapped children. *Exceptional Children, 38:*677-683, 1972.

Silberman, C.E. *Crisis in the classroom: The remaking of American education.* New York: Random House, 1970.

Sister Josephina. Study of attitudes in the elementary school. *Journal of Educational Sociology, 33:*56-60, 1959.

Smith, B.O., & Meux, M.O. *A study of the logic of teaching.* Urbana, IL: University of Illinois Press, 1962.

Smith, M.S. Equality of educational opportunity: The basic findings reconsidered. In F. Mosteller & D.P. Moynihan (Eds.), *On equality of educational opportunity.* New York: Vintage Books, 1972.

Snyder, R.T. Personality adjustment, self-attitudes, and anxiety differences in retarded adolescents. *American Journal of Mental Deficiency, 71:*33-41, 1966.

Soar, R.S. Teacher-pupil interaction. In J.R. Squire (Ed.), *A new look at progressive education.* Washington, DC: Association for Supervision & Curriculum Development, 1972.

Soar, R.S. An integration of findings from four studies of teacher effectiveness. In G.D. Borich (Ed.), *The appraisal of teaching: Concepts and process.* Reading, MA: Addison-Wesley, 1977.

Soar, R., Soar, R., & Ragosta, M. *Florida climate and control system.* Gainesville, FL: Institute for Development of Human Resources, University of Florida, 1971.

Solomon, D., & Rosenberg, L. Teacher-student feedback and classroom social structure. *Journal of Social Psychology, 62*:197-210, 1964.

Stallings, J.A. Implementation and child effects of teaching practices in Follow-Through classrooms. *Monographs of the Society for Research in Child Development, 40*:7-8 (Serial No. 763), 1975.

Stallings, J.A., & Kaskowitz, D.H. *Follow-through classroom observation evaluation 1972-1973.* Menlo Park, CA: Stanford Research Institute, 1974.

Stevens, G.D. An analysis of the objectives for the education of children with retarded mental development. In J.H. Rothstein (Ed.), *Mental retardation: Readings and resources* (2nd ed.). New York: Holt, Rinehart & Winston, 1971.

Sullivan, H.S. *The interpersonal theory of psychiatry.* New York: Norton, 1953.

Susskind, E.C. Questioning and curiosity in the elementary school classroom (Doctoral dissertation, Yale University, 1969). *Dissertation Abstracts International* (University Microfilms No. 70-2814)

Taba, H. *Teaching strategies and cognitive functioning in elementary school children* (U.S. Office of Education, Cooperative Research Program Project No. 2404). San Francisco: San Francisco State College, 1966.

Tenenbaum, S. Uncontrolled expressions of children's attitudes toward school. *Elementary School Journal, 40*:670-678, 1940.

Tenenbaum, S. Attitudes of elementary school children to school, teachers and classmates. *Journal of Applied Psychology, 28*:134-141, 1944.

Tenenbaum, S. The teacher, the middle class, the lower class. In R. Shinn (Ed.), *Culture and school.* Scranton, OH: Intext, 1972.

Texas Education Agency. *Administrative guide and handbook for special education* (Plan A, Bulletin 711). Austin, TX: Texas Education Agency, 1971.

Thibaut, J., & Kelley, H. *The social psychology of groups.* New York: John Wiley & Sons, 1959.

Thurstone, T.G. *An evaluation of educating mentally handicapped children in special classes and in regular classes* (U.S. Office of Education, Cooperative Research Program, Project No. OE-SAE-6542). Chapel Hill, NC: University of North Carolina, 1960.

Torrance, E.P. Group size and question performance of preprimary children. *The Journal of Psychology, 74*:71-75, 1970.

Towne, R., & Joiner, L. *The effect of special class placement in the self-concept of ability of the educable mentally retarded child* (USOE Grant No. 32-32-0410-6001). Washington, DC: U.S. Government Printing Office, 1966.

Trent, R.D. The relationship of anxiety to popularity among institutionalized delinquent boys. *Child Development, 28*:379-384, 1957.

Turnure, J., & Ziegler, E. Outerdirectedness in the problem solving of normal and retarded children. *Journal of Abnormal and Social Psychology, 69*:427-436, 1964.

Veldman, D.J. *Fortran programming for the behavioral sciences*. New York: Holt, Rinehart & Winston, 1967.

Veldman, D.J. Simple structure and the number of factors problem. *Multivariate Behavioral Research, 9*:191-200, 1974.

Veldman, D.J., & Parker, G.V. Adjective rating scales for self-description. *Multivariate Behavioral Research, 5*, 295-302, 1970.

vonBracken, H. *Attitudes concerning mentally retarded children*. Paper presented at meeting of the First Congress of the International Association for the Scientific Study of Mental Deficiency, Montpelier, France, September 1967.

Walberg, H. Predicting class learning: An approach to the class as a social system. *American Educational Research Journal, 6*:529-542, 1969.

Walberg, H. A model for research on instruction. *School Review, 78*:185-200, 1970.

Walberg, H., & Anderson, G.J. Classroom climate and individual learning. *Journal of Educational Psychology, 59*:414-419, 1968.

Walker, V. *The efficacy of the resource room for educating mentally retarded children*. Unpublished doctoral dissertation, Temple University, 1972.

Westbury, I. Conventional classrooms, open classrooms and the technology of teaching. *Journal of Curriculum Studies, 5*(2):91-121, 1973.

Whiteman, M., & Deutsch, M. Social disadvantage as related to intellective and language development. In M. Deutsch, I. Katz, & A. Jensen (Eds.) *Social class, race, and psychological development*. New York: Holt, Rinehart & Winston, 1968.

Wiley, D.E. *Another hour, another day. Quantity of schooling, a potent path for policy* (Studies of Educative Processes, Report No. 3). Chicago: University of Chicago Press, 1973.

Wiley, D.E., & Harnischfeger, A. *Explosion of a myth: Quantity of schooling and exposure to instruction, major educational vehicles* (Studies of Educative Processes, Report No. 8). Chicago: University of Chicago Press, 1974.

Wiley, D.E., & Harnischfeger, A. *Distinct pupils, distinctive schooling: Individual differences in exposure to instructional activities*. Paper presented at the annual meeting of the American Educational Research Association, Washington, D.C., March 1975.

Williams, R., & Byars, H. Negro self-esteem in a transitional society: Tennessee self-concept scale. *Personnel and Guidance Journal, 47*:120-125, 1968.

Wilson, I.A. Changes in mean levels of thinking in grades 1-8 through use of an interaction analysis system based on Bloom's taxonomy. *Journal of Educational Research, 66*:423-429, 1973.

Wolfson, B.J. Pupil and teacher roles in individualized instruction. *Elementary School Journal 68*:357-366, 1968.

Wright, C.J., & Nuthall, G. Relationships between teacher behaviors and pupil achievement in three experimental elementary science lessons. *American Educational Research Journal, 7*:477-491, 1970.

Wrightstone, J.W., Forlano, G., Lepkowski, J.R., Sontag, M., & Edelstein, J.D. Some philosophies of education for the mentally retarded. In J.H. Rothstein (Ed.), *Mental retardation: Readings and resources* (2nd ed.). New York: Holt, Rinehart & Winston, 1971.

Wynter, A. *The borderlands of insanity.* London: Piccadilly, 1875.

Zahorik, J.A. Pupils' perception of teacher's verbal feedback. *The Elementary School Journal,* 7:105-114, 1970.

Zander, A., & Curtis, T. Effects of social power on aspiration setting and striving. *Journal of Abnormal and Social Psychology, 64:*63-74, 1962.

Zeaman, D., & House, B.J. The role of attention in retardate discrimination learning. In N.R. Ellis (Ed.), *Handbook of mental deficiency.* New York: McGraw-Hill, 1963.

Zerkel, P. Self-concept and the "disadvantage" of ethnic group membership mixture. *Review of Educational Research, 41:*211-225, 1971.

Zigler, E. Mental retardation: Current issues and approaches. In L.W. Hoffman (Eds.) *Review of child development research,* vol. 2. New York: Russell Sage Foundation, 1966.

# Subject Index

521

# Author Index

527